Anthology of
TANG AND
SONG TALES

The *Tang Song chuanqi ji*
of Lu Xun

Related Titles

Tang Dynasty Tales: A Guided Reader
ISBN: 978-981-4287-28-9

Tang Dynasty Tales: A Guided Reader
Volume 2
ISBN: 978-981-4719-52-0

Song Dynasty Tales: A Guided Reader
ISBN: 978-981-3143-27-2

Anthology of
TANG AND
SONG TALES

The *Tang Song chuanqi ji* of Lu Xun

Edited by

Victor Mair
University of Pennsylviania, USA

Zhenjun Zhang
St. Lawrence University, USA

NEW JERSEY · LONDON · SINGAPORE · BEIJING · SHANGHAI · HONG KONG · TAIPEI · CHENNAI · TOKYO

Published by

World Scientific Publishing Co. Pte. Ltd.

5 Toh Tuck Link, Singapore 596224

USA office: 27 Warren Street, Suite 401-402, Hackensack, NJ 07601

UK office: 57 Shelton Street, Covent Garden, London WC2H 9HE

Library of Congress Cataloging-in-Publication Data

Names: Lu, Xun, 1881–1936, editor. | Mair, Victor H., 1943–   editor. |
      Zhang, Zhenjun, editor.
Title: Anthology of Tang and Song tales : the Tang Song chuanqi ji of Lu Xun /
      editors, Victor Mair, Zhenjun Zhang.
Other titles: Tang Song chuan qi ji. English.
Description: New Jersey : World Scientific, [2020] | Includes bibliography and index.
Identifiers: LCCN 2019057971 | ISBN 9789811216503 (hardcover)
Subjects: LCSH: Chinese fiction--Tang dynasty, 618–907--Translations into English. |
      Chinese fiction--Song dynasty, 960–1279--Translations into English.
Classification: LCC PL2641 .T35813 2020 | DDC 895.13/3--dc23
LC record available at https://lccn.loc.gov/2019057971

British Library Cataloguing-in-Publication Data
A catalogue record for this book is available from the British Library.

ISBN 978-981-121-650-3

For any available supplementary material, please visit
https://www.worldscientific.com/worldscibooks/10.1142/11720#t=suppl

For

James R. Hightower

(1915–2006)

Contents

Acknowledgments

It has been a long-held wish of both editors to make Lu Xun's *Tang Song chuanqi ji* available to Western readers. Now, after around two years' hard work of our dynamic group, we are pleased to see that this wish is finally fulfilled.

We are indebted to all the translators for their precious time spent on this project and their profound knowledge, intelligence, and diligence shown in their excellent renditions, no matter whether they are newly finished or revised from an earlier version. A special debt of gratitude is due to the following people who have been very supportive to this project in different ways: William H. Nienhauser, Kenneth DeWoskin, Wilt L. Idema, Beata Grant, Richard J. Lynn, Paul W. Kroll, Robert J. Cutter, Alister Inglis, Jing Wang, and Xin Zou. We are also indebted to the two deceased contributors, James R. Hightower and Glen Dudbridge, who passed away in 2006 and 2017 respectively.

We are deeply grateful to Ms. Yu Shan Tay of the World Scientific Publishing Co., for her highly professional and extremely helpful work in the process of editing this book, and Ms. Lixi Dong, for her enthusiastic support in publishing this volume.

Two of the translations, "The Story of Yingying" and "Tale of the Transcendent Marriage of Dongting Lake," have already appeared in Victor Mair's edited volume, *The Columbia Anthology of Traditional Chinese Literature.* Several other pieces are revised from an earlier version that appeared elsewhere — in books or journals. We wish to register here our particular gratitude to their publishers and editors for granting permission to reprint or publish a revised version in this anthology.

Victor H. Mair
Zhenjun Zhang
January 30, 2020

Note to the Reader

We have aimed to provide here an authoritative, enjoyable, and useful anthology of Tang and Song dynasty tales for recreational readers, as well as a valuable reference for scholars, educators, and college students in the fields of Chinese literature, history, religion, and culture.

We have done our best to render the stories both literally and fluently, though it is always challenging to harmonize these two goals of translation.

The text on which we based our *Tales* is Lu Xun's *Tang Song chuanqi ji*, published numerous times since 1927. Our version also benefited from previous studies of Tang and Song tales, anthologies, and translations in both Chinese and English, as listed in the bibliography.

The Chinese text included in this volume is basically Lu Xun's edition. Sometimes we made corrections but, following Lu Xun's approach, did not list the variants in different versions.

Below are frequently used terms for weights and measures:

Dou 斗, a decaliter
Hu 斛, bushel, 10 *dou* before the Tang dynasty; 5 *dou* since the Song dynasty
Sheng 升, pint, 1/10 of *dou*
Jin 斤, catty, half a kilogram

Liang 兩, 1/10 of *jin*

Dan 石, bushel, 10 *dou*

Yi 鎰, 24 *liang*

Chi 尺, foot

Cun 寸, inch, 1/10 *chi*

Duan 端, 20 *chi*

Fen 分, 1/3 centimeter

Li 里, half a kilometer, or approximately one-third of a mile

Zhang 丈, pole, 10 *chi*, approximately 3 1/3 meters

Pi 匹, bolt [of silk cloth], 40 feet and 4 *zhang*

Introduction

Alongside the much-esteemed Tang poetry, *chuanqi* 傳 奇 (transmission of marvels), or "tale," is one of the two famous "wonders" of the Tang 唐 dynasty (618–907). Tang tales are a substantial achievement in early fiction in classical Chinese, and they represent a much more advanced genre compared with their predecessors, the Six Dynasty (220–589) *zhiguai* 志怪 (accounts of anomalies). The *chuanqi* thrived in the Tang, impressing readers with their much more elaborate plots, polished language, and, significantly, their "conscious creation" by their authors — that is, they were deliberately creating fiction.

Regarding the differences between these two genres, Lu Xun 魯迅 (1881–1936) remarks:

> Fiction, like poetry, underwent radical changes in the Tang dynasty. Though tales were still written about marvels and strange phenomena, the plots became more elaborate and the language more polished. Compared with the tales of the Six Dynasties, which give the bare outlines of stories, there was a marked advance. Another and more significant fact is that by this time writers were consciously writing fiction.[1]

---

[1] 小說亦如詩，至唐代而一變，雖尚不離於搜奇記逸，然敘述婉轉，文辭華豔，與六朝之粗陳梗概者較，演進之跡甚明，而尤顯者乃在是時則始有意為小說。Lu Xun, *Zhongguo xiaoshuo shilue* 中國小說史略 (Beijing: Renmin wenxue chubanshe, 1973), 54; Yang Hsien-Yi and Gladys Yang,

As to the artistic achievements of *chuanqi*, Song dynasty scholar Hong Mai 洪邁 (1123–1202) says:

> The Tang tale is indeed something that one must be familiar with: even minor love affairs in it can be depicted so as to cause an inconsolable melancholy. Truly there is something one can encounter with his/her spirit but not be aware of consciously. Together with the regulated poetry, it can be called the wonder of the dynasty.[2]

After reaching its first peak during the Tang, the *chuanqi* continued its development in the Song (960–1279), as well as in later times.

The *Tang Song chuanqi ji* 唐宋傳奇集 (Anthology of Tang and Song Tales), a monumental work masterfully selected and carefully edited by Lu Xun (1881–1936), is beyond doubt the most distinctive, authoritative, and influential *chuanqi* collection thus far. It includes not only the best tales of Tang and Song, but also the important ones in the history of Chinese fiction. Since its first publication in 1927, it has been republished numerous times by different publishers in the Chinese-speaking world, and several modern Chinese renditions of the book have also appeared in recent years. The collection has not only become a must-read for students and scholars of Chinese literature and culture, but also spread widely among millions of general readers, passing from generation to generation. In the West, however, only some individual tales from this collection have been translated into English and published (and those published in journals are not easy to find). Many important, marvelous pieces in this collection are still unknown to English

---

trans., *A Brief History of Chinese Fiction* (Peking: Foreign Language Press, 1964), 85.

[2]唐人小說，不可不熟，小小情事，淒婉欲絕. 洵有神遇而不自知者，與詩律可稱一代之奇。(Quoted in "Preface" of *Tangren shuohui* 唐人説薈).

readers, probably due to the difficulties of translation and lack of awareness of their importance and significance.

This volume is the first complete English rendition of all forty-five of the famous tales from Lu Xun's anthology, here translated by more than twenty scholars, including leading sinologists such as James Hightower, Glen Dudbridge, Wilt Idema, William Nienhauser, and Paul Kroll, etc. One third of all the tales are being rendered into English for the first time, and another third are new translations as well. We believe that the publication of this anthology will not only make an important contribution to the field of Chinese studies in the West, but also provide an enjoyable tale collection for general English readers.

The *Anthology of Tang and Song Tales* was finished by Lu Xun in October 1927 in Guangzhou, during a period of unemployment. According to his "Preface and Selection Rules," Lu Xun sought to provide a reliable version of the Tang and Song tales because of his following observation: "In order to make the books look splendid and bewilder the passerby, booksellers often altered the titles and changed the authors. Thus, almost all fiction written from Jin to Tang was ruined." This collection was first published in 1927 by Beixin shuju, then republished by Shanghai Lianhua Press (1934) and Wenxue guji kanxingshe (1956), and many other editions followed. Almost a century has passed, but Lu Xun's anthology is still the most popular collection of Tang and Song tales to date.

In regard to the development of Tang tales, Lu Xun states that early Tang tales, such as Wang Du's 王度 "Records of an Old Mirror," "still kept the style of Six Dynasties *zhiguai*, but with greatly increased magnificence." By the Mid-Tang, Tang tales had fully developed and were thriving:

> It was only from the Dali reign (766–779) to the middle of the
> Dazhong reign period (847–860), that authors appeared together
> as rising clouds, flourishing in the literary realm. Shen Jiji
> 沈既濟 and Xu Yaozuo 許堯佐 rose with talent at the beginning,

and Jiang Fang 蔣防 and Yuan Zhen 元稹 showed up with elegance in the end. However, the authors such as Li Gongzuo 李公佐, Bai Xingjian 白行簡, Chen Hong 陳鴻, and Shen Yazhi 沈亞之 were indeed the outstanding ones. (See the "Preface and Selection Rules" below in this book.)

Because of this, almost all the Tang tales Lu Xun selected are from the Mid-Tang. The only exceptions are "Records of an Old Mirror" and "A Record of the Detached Soul" from the early Tang and "The Tale of the Curly-Bearded Guest" and "The Tale of Feiyan" from the late Tang.

The Tang tales in Lu Xun's anthology are not only of the best quality but also feature the most popular topics that closely related to the time — the Mid-Tang. For example, the stories of love between scholar and courtesan — such as Jiang Fang's "The Tale of Huo Xiaoyu" and Bai Xingjian's "The Courtesan Li Wa," reflect beyond doubt the keynote of the time — "the rise of the culture of romance, with the representation of individually chosen and socially unauthorized relationships between men and women."[3] Similarly, those tales featuring Buddhist themes — such as Shen Jiji's "The World Inside a Pillow" and Li Gongzuo's "An Account of the Governor of the Southern Branch," indicate the popularity of Buddhism during the Tang, especially the Mid-Tang and Late Tang.

In addition, many of the tales are important in view of the history of Chinese fiction. For example, Li Gongzuo's "The Ancient Classic of Peaks and Waterways" is good evidence that the monkey king in the *Journey to the West* has a Chinese origin, Li Jingliang's "Li Zhangwu" and Shen Jiji's "Miss Ren" are the forerunners of the fascinating stories of ghost girls and fox girls in Pu Songling's *Strange Tales from Liaozhai,* and Niu Sengru's "My Journey to the Zhou and Qin" and Shen Yazhi's "A Record of a Dream of Qin" are

---

[3] Stephen Owen, *The End of the Chinese "Middle Ages"* (Stanford: Stanford University Press, 1996), 131.

testimonies to Lu Xun's argument that Tang tales were consciously written. Some scholars have argued recently that conscious writing might have occurred before the Tang, but they have not provided evidence, as Lu Xun did.

Commenting on Song tales, Lu Xun notes, "Song writers loved admonition and moral teachings, they collected materials in real life and stuck to them, so the charm of flying thought cannot be expected. Consequently, the life of the *chuanqi* was terminated at that time." Because of this, Lu Xun selected only thirteen Song tales for chapters 6, 7, and 8 in his collection while including thirty-two Tang tales in chapters 1 to 5.

The preference for Tang tales over Song tales originated in the Ming dynasty. Scholars from the Ming dynasty believed that "Song dynasty tales are not as good as Tang tales 宋人小說不及唐人."[4] The following commentary on Tang and Song tales by Hu Yinglin 胡應麟 (1551–1602) is very famous and influential:

Tang and earlier fiction mostly narrate fictional matters, and their writings are elegant and polished, but fiction since the Song mostly focuses on real events and especially lacks literary elegance.[5]

Similarly to Hu Yinglin, Lu Xun also undervalues Song tales:

The tales of the supernatural by Song dynasty scholars were flat and insipid, while their longer prose romances usually avoided

---

[4]Volume 71 "Xiaoshuo" 小說 in Yang Shen 杨慎 (1488–1559), *Sheng'an quanji* 昇庵全集. Cited from Li Jianguo, "Preface" in his *Songdai zhiguai chuanqi xulu*, 1.

[5]小說，唐人以前記述多虛，而藻繪可觀；宋人以後論次多實，而采艷殊乏。 Hu Yinglin 胡應麟, *Shaoshi shanfang bicong* 少室山房筆叢 (Taibei: Shijie shuju, 1963), 29: 377.

contemporary topics and dealt with the past; they were neither
good imitations of earlier works nor yet original tales.[6]

As a whole, it is true that Song dynasty tales are inferior to
Tang dynasty tales in quality and, coinciding with the spread of
Neo-Confucianism, contain many moral teachings. However,
viewing all Song tales as identical and attaching the same label to
them all is not helpful to the study of ancient Chinese fiction and is
also contrary to fact. Just as Li Shiren 李時人 has recently pointed
out, "The studies of Song dynasty tales have all along neglected the
dynamic of their development, their setups, their styles, as well as
the creative aspects within them."[7]

Over the past three decades, the study of Song dynasty tales
has drawn much attention in academic circles in mainland China.[8]
Many studies, such as Wu Zhida's 吳誌達 *Zhongguo wenyan
xiaoshuo shi* 中國文言小說史 (Jinan: Qi Lu shushe, 1994),
Xiao Xiangkai's 蕭相愷 *Song Yuan xiaoshuo shi* 宋元小說史
(Hangzhou: Zhejiang guji chubanshe, 1997), and Zhenjun Zhang
and Jing Wang's *Song Dynasty Tales: A Guided Reader* (Singapore:
World Scientific, 2017), also draw more attention to Song dynasty

---

[6]宋一代文人之為志怪，既平實而乏文采，其傳奇，又多托往事而避
近聞，擬古且遠不逮，更無獨創之可言矣。Lu Xun, *Zhongguo xiaoshuo
shilue,* 71; Yang Hsien-Yi and Gladys Yang, trans., *A Brief History of Chinese
Fiction,* 139.

[7]Li Shiren, "Song Dai lishi wenhua yu wenyan duanpian xiaoshuo de
liubian" 宋代歷史文化與文言短篇小說的流變, in *Qiushi xuekan* 求是學刊 2
(2011): 125–32.

[8]Important contributions include the publication of Cheng Yizhong's
程毅中 *Guti xiaoshuo chao: Song Yuan juan* 古體小說鈔：宋元卷 (Beijing:
Zhonghua shuju, 1995) and *Song Yuan xiaoshuo yanjiu* 宋元小說研究
(Jiangsu guji chubanshe, 1999), Li Jianguo's *Songdai zhiguai chuanqi xulu*
宋代志怪傳奇敘錄 (Tianjin: Nankai daxue chubanshe, 1997), and his
Songdai chuanqi ji 宋代傳奇集 [Beijing: Zhonghua shuju, 2001].

tales and try to explore their characteristics. In his "Preface to *Songdai chuanqi ji*" 宋代傳奇集, Cheng Yizhong 程毅中 remarks:

> The Song Tale is a combination of multiple genres; its style is not a single one; and there are also elegant and polished writings such as those collected in the *Yunzhai guanglu*. Moreover, Song tales value "realistic recording" and are closer to real life, like the Jin (265–420) saying that "the strings of a musical instrument are not as good as bamboo, but bamboo is not as good as flesh (human voice)" — because it is closer and closer to nature. Modern fiction originated from storytelling in the tile-roofed rooms, and there is no doubt the stories describe the minds of ordinary townsfolk. But in the *chuanqi* and *zhiguai*, there are also many pieces in collections like the *Zhiqing zashuo* that vividly depict the ways of the world, narrating events as if the author has witnessed them and recording words as if spoken by the author. Besides recording marvels, some Song tales depict the minds of beauties and the courage of warriors while some record the words of coachmen and peddlers, vividly depicting their voices, styles, and appearances, so that these can all be roughly seen a thousand years later.[9]

This is indeed a valuable comment on the Song dynasty tales.

Regarding the authorship and dates of five Song tales in this anthology, there has been dispute in recent years. Those tales include the "Leftover Record of the Sui Dynasty," "Records of Seas

---

[9]然而宋人小說文備眾體，本非一格，亦有藻繪可觀如《雲齋廣錄》所收者。且宋人小說崇尚實錄，漸近人生，如晉人所云"絲不如竹，竹不如肉，"以其漸近自然也。近體小說源出瓦舍說話，其為市井小民寫心，固無論矣；而傳奇志怪，亦多人情世態，聲色具繪，敘事則如經目睹，記言則若從口出，此可於《攬青雜說》等書覘之。宋之傳奇，於搜神志異而外，或摹壯士佳人之心膽，或述引車賣漿之言語，聲氣風貌，神情畢肖，千載而下，猶可髣髴。Li Jianguo, *Songdai chuanqi ji* 宋代傳奇集 [Beijing: Zhonghua shuju, 2001], 1.

and Mountains of Emperor Yang of Sui," "The Mansion of Enchantment," "Records of Constructing the Grand Canal," and "The Concubine Plum," there have been different opinions in recent years. By questioning Lu Xun's opinion, Li Jianguo 李劍國 argues that these five tales were written during the late Tang, instead of the Song.[10] Regarding the "Leftover Record of the Sui Dynasty," Li shares the idea with Lu Xun that this tale was not written by Yan Shigu, to whom it was originally attributed, but by the author of the postscript. Based on the sentence at the end, "Nowadays the spirit of King Yao has returned, and the virtuous cart is going on the right way" 德車斯駕, Li Jianguo argues that the tale was written during late Tang. But Zhang Peiheng 章培恒 disagrees with him, arguing that the "virtuous cart is going on the right way" does not have to have occurred in the late Tang but also possibly in the Song, and the tale never avoids using words that were forbidden during the Tang, such as "yuan" 淵, "zhi" 治, "世", "min" 民. And this is true in "The Mansion of Enchantment" and "Records of Constructing the Grand Canal."[11] In addition, based on the mention of *Zhongmenshi* 中門使 in "Records of Constructing the Grand Canal," it seems the tale might have been written during or after the Five Dynasties, instead of before those dynasties, because *Zhongmenshi* was a unique official title that appeared only in the Five Dynasties.

"The Concubine Plum" is originally from volume 38 of Tao Zongyi's *Shuo fu* 說郛. A shorter variant is found in Gu Yuanqing's 顧元慶 *Gushi Wenfang xiaoshuo* 顧氏文房小說. Neither edition is attributed to an author. However, Zhang Zongxiang's edition of *Shuo fu* and Qing dynasty Chen Liantang's 陳蓮塘 *Tangren shuohui*

---

[10] Li Jianguo, *Tang Wudai zhiguai chuanqi xulu* 唐五代志怪傳奇敘錄 (Beijing: Zhonghua shuju, 2017), vol. 3.

[11] Zhang Peiheng, "'Daye shiyiji,' 'Meifei zhuan,' deng wupian chuanqi de xiezuo shidai" 大業拾異記、梅妃傳等五篇傳奇的寫作時代, in *Shenzhen daxue xuebao* 深圳大學學報 1 (2008): 106–10.

唐人說薈 both attribute the tale to Cao Ye 曹鄴 of the Tang. In his "Baibian xiaozhui," 稗邊小綴 Lu Xun considers this attribution false. As for the tale's anonymously-written epilogue, which claims that "The Tale of Concubine Plum" was copied in the second year of the Dazhong reign period of the Tang and was later obtained from the home of Zhu Zundu, Lu Xun questions its authenticity (Ye Shaoyun was about two hundred years younger than Zhu) and believes the tale was written during the Song dynasty.

While most modern scholars concur with Lu Xun's argument regarding the authorship and dates of this tale, [12] Li Jianguo attributes it to the Tang author Cao Ye in his *Tang Wudai zhiguai chuanqi xulu* and a later article. [13] His evidence consists of the following key points: the tale in the Zhang Zongxiang edition of *Shuo fu* is credited to Cao Ye, and other collections, such as *Tangren shuohui*, also credit it to Cao Ye; this tale was recorded only in the Song bibliography, You Wu's 尤袤 *Suichutang shumu* 遂書堂書目, and was listed among the books of the Tang; the epilogue of the tale is logical and believable, and "obtained from the home of Zhu Zundu" should not be understood as "obtained from Zhu Zundu himself." [14] Thus in his later works, *Songdai zhiguai chuanqi xulu* and *Songdai chuanqi ji*, this tale is excluded. However, Cheng Yizhong 程毅中 believes that the two Ming handwritten versions of *Shuo fu* that Lu Xun used (now in the Beijing National Library) differ from the Zhang Zongxiang edition, which credits this tale to Cao Ye. Since there is no earlier evidence, it is problematic to attribute the

---

[12]The most recent effort in support of Lu Xun's argument is seen in Zhang Peiheng, "'Daye shiyiji,' 'Meifei zhuan,' deng wupian chuanqi de xiezuo shidai," in *Shenzhen daxue xuebao* 1 (2008): 106–10.

[13]"'Daye shiyiji' deng wupian chuanqi xuezuo shidai de zai taolun" 《大業拾遺記》 等五篇傳奇寫作時代的再討論, *Wenxue yichan* 文學遺產 1 (2009): 21–28.

[14]*Tang Wudai zhiguai chuanqi xulu* (Tianjin: Nankai daxue chubanshe, 1998), 547–51.

tale to Cao Ye. Furthermore, the tale's epilogue clearly states that the current version of the tale is a revised Song version, not the original Tang version. Thus, Cheng Yizhong considers "The Concubine Plum" a Song tale in his *Guti xiaoshuo chao: Song Yuan juan* 古體小說鈔：宋元卷 and *Song Yuan xiaoshuo yanjiu*.[15] Internal evidence from the tale itself is also indicative of its date. For example, the custom of appreciating plums, the practice of the tea contest, and Concubine Plum's calling Lady Yang "fat maiden" 肥婢, are all traits of Song dynasty culture.[16]

Based on the reasons stated above, we still consider Lu Xun's dates and attribution of these five tales to be reliable.

---

[15]*Guti xiaoshuo chao: Song Yuan juan* (Beijing: Zhonghua shuju, 1995), 344-47; and *Song Yuan xiaoshuo yanjiu* (Jiangsu guji chubanshe, 1999), 17–23.

[16]Cf. Takemura Noriyuki 竹村則行, *Yōkihi bungakushi kenkyu* 楊貴妃文學史研究 (Tōkyō: Kenbunshuppan 研文出版社, 2003), 208–15.

Preface and Selection Rules

By Lu Xun
Translated by Zhenjun Zhang and Victor H. Mair

Hu Yinglin of the Ming, a native of Dongyuan who was well versed in the Four Branches of literature, once said:

> Tales of miracles and the other world were popular during the Six Dynasties, but these were not entirely imaginary: most of them were based on hearsay and false reports. The Tang dynasty scholars, on the other hand, deliberately invented strange adventures and wrote them as fiction.[1] Tales such as the "Biography of Fur Point" and "An Account of the Governor of the Southern Branch" are acceptable and meaningful; as for the figures Cheng Zixu 成自虛 (Self-faked) in "Nocturnal Spirits near Dongyang" and the Yuan Wuyou 元無有 (Originally Nothing) in *Records of the Mysterious and Strange,* both can be brushed aside with a laugh, and the spirit of writing in these works was also lowly, not worth mentioning. Tales of the Song scholars are mostly close to real events and lack literary elegance.[2]

These words are roughly close to the fact.

---

[1]Above translation is from Yang Hsien-yi and Gladys Yang, trans., *A Brief History of Chinese Fiction*, 85.

[2]Hu Yinglin, *Shaoshi shanfang bicong*, 29: 377.

Satiated with poetry and rhapsodies, scholars started seeking for new ways to apply their overflowing fine inspiration in writing, and thus fiction thrived. But the worthies of later times, holding the orthodox view, belittled these as "dirt and seeds." Merely relying on the collectanea such as *Extensive Recordings from the Taiping Reign Period,* etc., one-tenth of the fiction were able to be seen today. Furthermore, running after profit, the booksellers collected and block-printed these as anthologies. Examples include *The Sea of Tales, Lost History Old and New, The Five Dynasties Fiction, Secret Books of Dragon Force, Collected Talks of the Tang,* and *Gathered Essence from the Art Gallery.* In order to make the books look splendid and bewilder the passerby, booksellers often altered the titles and changed the authors. Thus, almost all fiction written from Jin to Tang was ruined.

A little ant loves its nose just as much as a fragrant elephant does its, and this being the case, how could the ugly woman Momu 嫫母 act inferior to the beauty Mao Qiang 毛嬙 in protecting her face?[3] Although fiction has been considered lowly, not worth being listed among the nine schools, it is still a terrible disaster when its head is changed and its legs are cut off. I was annoyed by this in the past and thus intended to correct it. First, I gathered the tales from Han to Sui and put them together as the five volumes *Collected Lost Old Stories;* then I collected the tales of Tang and Song, intending to put them in one volume and hoping it will be more reliable, relatively at least, than the current ones. However, because of frequent moves, I had no time to put them in order. I just stuffed them in my traveling boxes, letting them, each on its own, fill the bellies of roaches and bookworms.

This summer, I was unemployed and living secludedly in Nanzhong (Guangzhou). By chance, I saw the *Anthology of Chinese Short Stories* edited by Mr. Zheng Zhenduo 鄭振鐸 (1898–1958), which sweeps the dust, gets rid of the faked and traces back the

---

[3]Both Momu and Mao Qiang are legendary figures.

stories to the original; my melancholy and despondence, which had accumulated for years, suddenly disappeared. The only problem was that "A Record of Nocturnal Spirits" was still attributed to Wang Zhu 王洙 and, as for "The Tale of Lingying", the attribution to the fake author, Yu Ti 于逖, was still not removed. Probably Mr. Zheng was still sentimentally attached to the old books. Then I read *A Textual Research on the Record of Those Who Ascended the [Selection] Subject* by Xu Song 徐松 of Daxing, which makes use of accumulated small stuffs to shed light on important issues and searches for the lost secrets of the past. To verify that Li Zhi 李徵 reached the ranks, however, Xu quoted Li Jingliang's 李景亮 "The Tale of a Man Who Becomes a Tiger" as evidence. Such an attribution by people of the Ming dynasty is groundless, and this tale was not written by Li Jingliang. I sighed further that even the short chit-chat of the alleyways, once being interpolated and distorted, will certainly bring harm to the commentaries of literature and also bring disaster to the textual study of history.

Suddenly I thought of my old manuscripts, and I opened the boxes to look carefully at them, which had become much darker, but the paper was still not worn out and the ink not yet blurred. I looked them over, sorting them according to a rough sequence of their period. And, indeed, I found that Wang Du's 王度 "Records of an Old Mirror" still kept the style of Six Dynasties *zhiguai* (accounts of anomalies), but with greatly increased magnificence. Fang Qianli's 房千里 "Courtesan Yang" and Liu Cheng's 柳珵 "Maiden Shangqing" became extremely lowly and weak, sharing the fate of poetry. Song writers loved admonition and moral teachings, they collected materials in real life and stuck to them, so the charm of thought flying and moving cannot be expected. Consequently, the life of the *chuanqi* was terminated at that time.

It was only from the Dali reign (766–779) to the middle of Dazhong reign period (847–860), that authors appeared together as rising clouds, flourishing in the literary realm. Shen Jiji 沈既濟 and

Xu Yaozuo 許堯佐 rose with talent at the beginning, and Jiang Fang 蔣防 and Yuan Zhen 元積 showed up with elegance in the end. However, the authors such as Li Gongzuo 李公佐, Bai Xingjian 白行簡, Chen Hong 陳鴻, and Shen Yazhi 沈亞之 were indeed the outstanding ones. "A Record of Nocturnal Spirits" has obviously fabricated everything, and now it has become banal; but in the Tang it was in fact innovative. Mr. Hu belittled it to such an extent that I myself do not agree with him.

Examining what I have gathered, even though no secret writings came to light, I myself still cherished them, because I had dedicated myself to collecting them. Furthermore, thinking that in recent years those who were able to earnestly work on the tales of the Tang and Song should be rare, filling the deep pool of stories with my water drops and offering them to my colleagues, just as the offering of humble celery, will perhaps reduce their toil in textual research and allow them to enjoy the pleasure of reading and pondering. Thus I closed my door, spread out my books, and collated them again. A month later the work was finished. It was totally eight volumes and was ready for printing. I was fortunate to be able to fulfill my wish, but as soon as I felt delighted, I sighed. Looking back toward my hometown, I knew I could not return there; instead, I consumed the flying time in my limited lifespan. Alas! How could this be something that betters my life?! But it is what I have to do.

I still have the various rules I employed for my selection, and now I will attach them below:

The sources of this anthology include the Ming edition of *Wenyuan yinghua* 文苑英華; Huang Sheng's 黃晟 Qing edition *Taiping guangji*, which was collated with Xu Zichang's 許自昌 Ming edition; the Song edition *Zizhi tongjian kaoyi*, photocopied by Hanfen lou 涵芬樓; Shili ju 士禮居 edition of *Qingsuo gaoyi*

青瑣高議, block-printed by Dong Kang 董康, and collated with the Zhang Mengxi 張夢錫 edition of the Ming and the old hand-copied edition; the Song edition *Baichuan xuehai* 百川學海, printed in the Ming; the original Ming hand-copy edition *Shuo fu* 說郛; Gu Yuanqing's 顧元慶 Ming edition *Wenfang xiaoshuo* 文房小說; Qing dynasty Hu Ting's 胡珽 printed edition in the *Linlang mishi* 琳琅祕室 book series, etc.

This anthology selects only independently circulated single pieces. If it is a piece from a book, even if the plot is well known or the book is lost, it will still not be selected. Examples include the "Red Threads" in Yuan Jiao's 袁郊 *Gan ze yao* 甘澤謠, "Du Zichun" 杜子春 in Li Fuyan's 李復言 *Xu Xuanguai lu* 續玄怪錄, the "Kunlun Slave" and "Nieyin niang" 聶隱孃 in Pei Xing's 裴鉶 *Chuanqi*. Huangfu Mei's 皇甫枚 "The Tale of Bu Feiyan" is a lost piece of *Sanshui xiaodu* 三水小牘, but the quotation of it in the *Taiping guangji* does not mention its source. It appears that it had been circulated independently, and for this reason it was included.

Of the tales included in this anthology, those from the Tang are chosen loosely; as for the Song tales, they were selected much more strictly. Of the collections by the people of Ming and Qing, those faked pieces have been examined, I dared not put them in print; I dismissed them as I sought reliability. "The Wandering with Goddesses in the Grotto" from Japan, written by Zhang Wencheng 張文成, should be put under the "Biography of the White Ape." Since Mr. Zhang Maochen's 章矛塵 edited version is about to be published, it is not included in this anthology.

Of the tales in this anthology, where they appeared in different books or different editions and thus could be collated against each other, I did so. As for the variants (words or sentences), I followed only the correct ones. To avoid trouble, I did not list the variants in different versions. If a reader wants to know more about it, the volume and pages of the source book are given at the end of each tale. One can check the original book for the details.

I have always read various kinds of books. Whenever I found ones related to Tang and Song tales that were worth being used as references, I wrote them down from time to time to avoid forgetting them. Because of moving, much of these have been lost. It is hard to get books as a traveler, and there is nothing that can be done about that. Now I have merely gathered these scattered items, added what I found recently, and combined them together as one volume, thereby to keep the old anecdotes.

Tales of the Tang have been used for their texts by playwrights since the Jin and Yuan dynasties. I list those that I have heard. But I have never dedicated myself to reading lyrics and plays, and it must be that the old books purchased from booksellers have many errors and omissions; these await fine examination and broad textual research by specialists.

The tales in this anthology are not many, but such a collection was still not easy to put together. At the beginning, Xu Guangping 許廣平 selected tales for it, mostly from the *Taiping guangji*. But what she based her selection on was only the Huang Sheng edition, and I was extremely worried about errors and mistakes in that. Last year, Wei Jiangong 魏建功 collated them against/with the edition of Xu Zichang 許自昌, a native of Changzhou of the Ming, which was housed in Peking University Library. Then I felt relieved. When I intended to collect the various notes to attach them to the end of the book, the old manuscript was illegible and thus there were many frustrations and doubts. Mr. Jiang Jingsan 蔣徑三 found me more than ten books, allowing me to check the text easily; consequently everything is in order. As for the book cover painted by Tao

Yuanqing 陶元慶, he sent me that more than a year ago. With the extensive efforts of many people, this anthology is finished. Relying merely on empty verbiage, I engrave this lofty friendship in my mind, and that is all.

Notes after collation by Lu Xun, September 10, the sixteenth year of the Republic of China [1927]; it was deep at night, the bright moon shining, gluttonous mosquitoes sighing in distance, and I am in Guangzhou.

序例

魯迅

東越胡應麟在明代，博涉四部，嘗云："凡變異之談，盛於六朝，然多是傳錄舛訛，未必盡幻設語。至唐人，乃作意好奇，假小說以寄筆端。如《毛穎》、《南柯》之類尚可，若《東陽夜怪》稱成自虛，《玄怪錄》元無有，皆但可付之一笑，其文氣亦卑下亡足論。宋人所記，乃多有近實者，而文彩無足觀。"其言蓋幾是也。

屬於詩賦，旁求新途，藻思橫流，小說斯燦。而後賢秉正，視同土沙，僅賴《太平廣記》等之所包容，得存什一。顧復緣賈人貿利，撮拾彫鐫，如《說海》，如《古今逸史》，如《五朝小說》，如《龍威秘書》，如《唐人說薈》，如《藝苑捃華》，為欲總目爛然，見者眩惑，往往妄製篇目，改題撰人，晉唐稗傳，黥劓幾盡。

夫蟻子惜鼻，固猶香象，嫫母護面，詎遜毛嬙，則彼雖小說，夙稱卑卑不足廁九流之列者乎？而換頭削足，仍亦駭心之厄也。昔嘗病之，發意匡正。先輯自漢至隋小說，為《鉤沈》五部訖；漸復錄唐宋傳奇之作，將欲匯為一編，較之通行本子，稍足憑信。而屢更顛沛，不遑理董，委諸行篋，分飽蟫蠹而已。

今夏失業，幽居南中，偶見鄭振鐸君所編《中國短篇小說集》，埽盪煙埃，斥偽返本，積年堙鬱，一旦霍然。惜《夜怪錄》尚題王洙，《靈應傳》未刪于逖，蓋於故舊，猶存眷戀。繼復讀大興徐松《登科記考》，積微成昭，鉤稽淵密，而於李徵及第，乃引李景亮《人虎傳》作證。此明人妄署，非景亮文。彌歎雖短書俚說，一遭篡亂，固貽害於談文，亦飛災於考史也。

頓憶舊稿，發篋諦觀，黯澹有加，渝敝則未。乃略依時代次第，循覽一周，諒哉，王度《古鏡》，猶有六朝志怪餘風，而大增華艷。千里《楊倡》，柳珵《上清》，遂極庳弱，與詩運同。宋好勸懲，摭實而泥，飛動之致，眇不可期，傳奇命脈，至斯以絕。惟自大歷以至大中中，作者雲蒸，蔚術文苑：沈既濟、許堯佐擢秀於前，蔣防、元稹振彩於後；而李公佐、白行簡、陳鴻、沈亞之輩，則其卓異也。特《夜怪》一錄，顯託空無，逮今允成陳言，在唐實猶新意，胡君顧貶之至此，竊未能同耳。

　　自審所錄，雖無秘文，而曩曾用心，仍自珍惜。復念近數年中，能懇懇顧及唐宋傳奇者，當不多有。持此涓滴，注彼說淵，獻我同流，比之芹子，或亦將稍減其考索之勞，而得翫繹之樂耶。於是杜門攤書，重加勘定，匝月始就，凡八卷，可校印。結願知幸，方欣已歘：顧舊鄉而不行，弄飛光於有盡，嗟夫，此亦豈所以善吾生，然而不得已也。

　　猶有雜例，並綴左方：

　　一、本集所取資者，為明刊本《文苑英華》；清黃晟刊本《太平廣記》，校以明許自昌刻本；涵芬樓影印宋本《資治通鑑考異》；董康刻士禮居本《青瑣高議》，校以明張夢錫刊本及舊鈔本；明翻宋本《百川學海》；明鈔本原本《說郛》；明顧元慶刊本《文房小說》；清胡珽排印本《琳琅秘室叢書》等。

　　一、本集所取，專在單篇。若一書中之一篇，則雖事極煊赫，或本書已亡，亦不收采。如袁郊《甘澤謠》之《紅線》，李復言《續玄怪錄》之《杜子春》，裴鉶《傳奇》之《崑崙奴》、《聶隱娘》等是也。皇甫枚《飛煙傳》，雖亦是《三水小牘》逸文，然《太平廣記》引則不云出於何書，似曾單行，故仍入錄。

　　一、本集所取，唐文從寬，宋制則頗加決擇。凡明清人所輯叢刊，有妄作者，輒加審正，黜其偽欺，非敢刊落，以求信也。日本有《遊仙窟》，為唐張文成作，本當置《白猿傳》之次，以章矛塵君方圖版行，故不編入。

　　一、本集所取文章，有複見於不同之書，或不同之本，得以互校者，則互校之。字句有異，惟從其是。亦不歷舉某字某本作某，以省紛煩。倘讀者更欲詳知，則卷末具記某篇出於何書何卷，自可覆檢原書，得其究竟。

　　一、向來涉獵雜書，遇有關於唐宋傳奇，足資參證者，時亦寫取，以備遺忘。比因奔馳，頗復散失。客中又不易得書，殊無可作。今但會集叢殘，稍益以近來所見，並為一卷，綴之末簡，聊存舊聞。

　一、唐人傳奇，大為金元以來曲家所取資，耳目所及，亦舉一二。第於詞曲之事，素未用心，轉販故書，諒多訛略，精研博考，以俟專家。

　一、本集篇卷無多，而成就頗亦匪易。先經許廣平君為之選錄，最多者《太平廣記》中文。惟所據僅黃晟本，甚慮訛誤。去年由魏建功君校以北京大學圖書館所藏明長洲許自昌刊本，乃始釋然。逮今綴緝雜札，擬置卷末，而舊稿潦草，復多沮疑，蔣徑三君為致書籍十餘種，俾得檢尋，遂以就緒。至陶元慶君所作書衣，則已貽我於年餘之前者矣。廣賴眾力，才成此編，謹藉空言，普銘高誼云爾。

　中華民國十有六年九月十日，魯迅校畢題記。時大夜彌天，璧月澄照，饗蚊遙歎，余在廣州。

Chapter 1

Tale 1.1

The Record of the Ancient Mirror

By Wang Du
Translated by Kelsey Seymour

The Sui dynasty scholar Hou from Fenyin was an extraordinary man.[1] Wang Du often served him as if Hou were his teacher. When Hou was about to die, he gave an ancient mirror to Du and said: "If you take this, then the hundred demonic influences will flee from you." Du accepted the mirror and treasured it. The mirror had a diameter of eight *cun* and on its central nob was the image of a crouching *qilin*.[2] Around the nob were four quadrants; a tortoise, dragon, phoenix, and tiger were arrayed in each quadrant. Outside of the four quadrants, the eight trigrams were arrayed, and outside of the trigrams were the twelve earthly branches and the animals that corresponded to them.[3] Outside of the animals, there were also

---

[1]Fenyin 汾陰 county, modern Wanrong 萬榮 of Shanxi 山西.

[2]The *qilin* 麒麟 is a fantastical creature that supposedly appears as an auspicious omen for future events. For example, a *qilin* allegedly appeared before the birth of Confucius.

[3]Rat with *zi* 子; ox with *chou* 丑; tiger with *yin* 寅; rabbit with *mao* 卯; dragon with *chen* 辰; snake with *si* 巳; horse with *wu* 午; goat with *wei* 未; monkey with *shen* 申; rooster with *you* 酉; dog with *xu* 戌; pig with *hai* 亥. *Wei*, *wu*, and *si* correspond with south, the phoenix; *chou*, *zi*, and *hai* correspond with north, the tortoise; *xu*, *you*, and *shen* correspond with west, the tiger; *chen*, *mao*, and *yin* correspond with east, the dragon. The

2

twenty-four characters along the border of the mirror. The style of the writing resembled clerical script, and there were no missing strokes, but they were not characters that could be found in dictionaries. Scholar Hou said: "These are the representations of the twenty-four *qi*."[4]

When reflected in the sun, the writing and images on the back were projected in the shadow, and every fine detail was visible. When one lifted it up and tapped on it, a pure tone was gently drawn out, sounding for a whole day before vanishing. Ah, this was certainly not an ordinary mirror; it should be appreciated by a lofty worthy and considered a numinous object. Scholar Hou always said: "In the past I heard that the Yellow Emperor cast fifteen mirrors. The first one had a diameter of one *chi* and five *cun*,[5] modeled on the numbers of days to reach the full moon. Each [of the following ones] had a comparative difference of one *cun*. This is the eighth mirror." Although it was ancient, and there was no record, it still seemed that what this lofty person had explained could not be doubted.

In the past Mister Yang received the rings,[6] and for several generations this was extensively celebrated. Mister Zhang lost a

---

trigram correspond to the directions as follows: *kan* 坎 ☵ with north; *gen* 艮 ☶ with northeast; *zhen* 震 ☳ with east; *xun* 巽 ☴ with southeast; *li* 離 ☲ with south; *kun* 坤 ☷ with southwest; *dui* 兌 ☱ with west; *qian* 乾 ☰ with northwest.

[4] That is, the Twenty-Four Solar Terms (二十四節氣), a way of dividing the year into twenty-four sections according to the Sun's ecliptic.

[5] There are 10 *cun* 寸 in a *chi* 尺, so this makes 15 *cun* total. The full moon occurs on the 15th day of each month.

[6] This refers to the account of Yang Bao 楊寶 in the twentieth *juan* of the *Soushen ji*: "During the Han, when Yang Bao of Hongnong was nine years old, he went to the north of Huayin Mountain and saw a yellow sparrow get attacked by an owl. It fell below the tree and it was then surrounded by mole crickets and ants. When Bao saw this, he pitied it. He

sword and his life was also lost.[7] Now, Du has been met with troubled times and is often discontent. The dynasty is in a state of decline, so where can he have a life and career? And furthermore, the precious mirror has also disappeared! What a pity! So now I will narrate its fantastic tale, to lay it out for posterity. If, after thousands of years, someone manages to obtain it, then they will know where it came from.

---

took it home and placed it in a towel box, feeding it cauliflower. After more than a hundred days, its feathers grew back, and it went out in the morning and returned at night. One night, during the third watch (11 pm– 1 am), Bao was reading and had not yet gone to bed, when there appeared a boy dressed in yellow. He bowed to Bao twice and said: 'I am the emissary of the Queen Mother of the West. I was sent to Penglai, but I was not careful, so I was attacked by that owl. Your compassion is what saved me, and I am truly moved by your extensive virtue.' So he gave Bao four white rings and said: '[This is] to make your descendants honest and pure, and they will ascend to the three highest positions, just like these rings.'" See Gan Bao 干寶, *Soushen ji*, Wang Shaoying 汪紹楹, ed. (Beijing: Zhonghua shuju, 1980), p. 238.

[7]This seems to refer to Zhang Hua 張華 (232–300) whose biography is in the *History of Jin* 晉. He loses two different magical swords: (1) Once the imperial armory caught fire, and instead of immediately putting out the blaze, Zhang Hua and his army held their defense. When they tried to put out the blaze after, it was too late. They lost shoes that had once belonged to Confucius, Wang Mang's head, and a legendary sword from the Han period which pierced through the wall and flew away. (2) Hua's friend Lei Huan uncovered a pair of legendary swords and sent one to Hua. After Hua died, his sword was lost. And after Huan died, Hua's son took his sword. When he was crossing a river, the sword suddenly leapt from his waist and over the side of the boat, into the water. When they sent a diver to find it, all he saw was a pair of coiling dragons, and when he came up from the water, there was a bright light and waves. The two swords had been reunited and reverted to their true form as dragons. See Fang Xuanling 房玄齡, et al., eds., "Zhang Hua," in *Jin shu* 晉書 (Beijing: Zhonghua shuju, 1974), pp. 1068–1077.

In the fifth month of the seventh year of the Daye reign (611), Du retired from his post as Imperial Censor and returned to Hedong.[8] Scholar Hou passed away then, and he obtained this mirror. In the sixth month of the same year, Du returned to Chang'an. At Changle Hill[9] he lodged overnight at the home of Cheng Xiong. Xiong had newly received a maid who was quite beautiful, named Parrot. Since Du had finished his holiday, he was putting away his hat and shoes, and he pulled out the mirror to look at his own reflection. Parrot saw it from a distance, and immediately kowtowed repeatedly, to the point of shedding blood. She exclaimed, "I don't dare dwell here!" So Du called the host and inquired about the reason for this. Xiong said: "Two months ago, a guest brought this maid along from the east. When the maid became very sick, the guest then left her here, saying: 'I'll fetch her when I return.' [But] he hasn't come back. I don't know this maid's origin." Du suspected she was a spirit, so he drew out the mirror and approached her. She then said: "I beg [mercy] for my life! I will change my form immediately!" Du then covered the mirror and said: "First explain yourself, and transform afterwards. Then I will spare your life." The maid bowed twice and explained herself: "I am the thousand-year-old fox from under the tall pine in front of the tutelary shrine at Mt. Hua.[10] I often transformed to trick [people], and my sins were punishable by death. Therefore I was pursued by the tutelary deity, and I fled to [the region] between the He and Wei rivers. I became the adopted daughter of Chen Sigong in Xiagui,[11] received extensive care, and was betrothed to a man called Chai Hua from the same village. But Hua and I were not satisfied with each other, so I fled to the east and got out of

---

[8]A commandery covering modern Shanxi 山西 during the Tang.
[9]To the east of Chang'an.
[10]In Shanxi province, east of Chang'an.
[11]Also in Shanxi.

Hancheng County.[12] But I was caught by the traveler Li Wu'ao. Wu'ao was a cruel and violent man, and he made me travel with him for several years. Then yesterday[13] we arrived here, and he suddenly left me alone here. I didn't expect to encounter a heavenly mirror; I had no way to hide myself." Du again said: "You were originally an old fox, and you changed your form into a human being. How could this not harm people?" The maid said: "I changed my form to serve people; it was not harmful. But when I fled and hid [my form] this tricked people. The spirits hate this, and so I should die for it." Du again asked: "Is it possible that you will be forgiven?" Parrot said: "I am indebted to your kindness; how could I ever forget your virtue? But I have already been reflected in the heavenly mirror, and I cannot escape. It's just that I've been in a human form for so long, so I am ashamed to return to my old form. I hope that you might enclose [the mirror] in a box, and allow me to become completely intoxicated with wine before I die." Du asked: "If I seal the mirror in a box, you won't flee, will you?" Parrot smiled and said: "Sir you have just graciously stated that you would still consent to spare my life. If I were to flee after you sealed away the mirror, would this not betray your kindness? It's just that after one glance at that heavenly mirror, I have nowhere to hide. I only hope that in these last few moments of my life that I could expend a whole lifetime's worth of happiness." Du immediately put away the mirror and also sent for some wine. He called together the Xiong family and their neighbors to feast and make merry together. After a little while the maid became remarkably drunk. She swished her sleeves and began to dance and sing: "Precious mirror, precious mirror! Alas, how tragic my fate is! How many surnames [of the royal house] have gone by since I left my original form? Although life could be joyful, death will certainly be painless.

---

[12]Also in Shanxi.

[13]There appears to be a timeline issue here: Parrot says she arrived yesterday, but a few lines earlier, Xiong says she arrived two months ago.

For what reason should I still be sentimentally attached to my life and keep staying in such a place?" When the song ended, she bowed again, then she changed into an old fox and died. The entire audience was awestruck.

On the first day of the fourth month of the eighth year of the Daye reign (612), there was a solar eclipse.[14] At that time Du was reclining in his office chambers. He felt that the sun was slowly becoming dimmer, and all the officials announced to Du that the sun was immensely eclipsed. Then he adjusted his clothes and pulled out the mirror. He noticed that the mirror had also become darker and was no longer lustrous. Du thought that when this precious mirror was made, it must have been in correspondence with the wonder of light and shadow. Otherwise, why would the mirror also lose its luster in accordance with the sun losing its brightness? While he sighed in wonder, it suddenly began to become lustrous again as the sun also gradually became brighter. When the sun had completely returned, the mirror was also as intensively bright as before. From then on, when the sun was eclipsed, or the moon waned, the mirror also became darker.

On the fifteenth day of the eighth month of that same year (612), Du's friend Xue Xia acquired a copper sword that was four *chi* in length. Attached to the sword was its hilt, and around the hilt coiled the forms of a dragon and phoenix. On the left was a flame-like pattern, and on the right was a wave-like pattern. It shone radiantly; it was not an ordinary object. Xia took it to Du and said: "I have continuously tested this sword. On the fifteenth day of each month,

---

[14]Two solar eclipses happened in this year, but not on the date given. They were on Feb. 7 and Aug. 2. According to NASA, neither one would have been visible in East Asia. There was, however, an eclipse on May 21, 616, that would have been visible. See Fred Espenak, "Five Millennium Catalog of Solar Eclipses: 0601 to 0700 (601 CE to 700 CE)," Eclipse Predictions by Fred Espenak (NASA's GSFC), Accessed Dec. 26, 2018, <https://eclipse.gsfc.nasa.gov/SEcat5/SE0601-0700.html>.

when Heaven and Earth are clear, I place it in a dark room and it produces light of its own accord, shining several *zhang* in each direction. I have possessed it for a while. You, sir, are fond of strange and ancient things, to the point of being as if you have a hunger or thirst for them. I sincerely wish that I can test it with you tonight." Du was very pleased. That night (15ᵗʰ day of the 8ᵗʰ month), it indeed happened that Heaven and Earth were clear. He sealed the two of them in a room together without any cracks [to allow in light] and stayed overnight with Xia. Du also took out the precious mirror and placed it to the side of seat. Suddenly, the surface of the mirror burst forth with light, illuminating the whole room. They could see each other as if it were daytime. The sword lay on its side, not emitting any light. Xia was surprised and said: "Please put the mirror back in the box." Du obeyed, and only after did the sword burst forth with light. But it was no more than one or two *chi*. Xia stroked the sword and sighed: "Even the amazing objects under heaven also have the principle of overcoming each other." After this, each time there was a full moon, [Du] would take out the mirror in a dark room, and the light would then shine several *zhang*. If moonlight entered the room, then the mirror would not shine. Isn't it [because] the radiance of the sun and the moon is unrivaled?

In the winter of that same year (612), Du received the concurrent appointment of Editorial Director of the Palace Library. He was summoned to compile a dynastic history[15] and he wanted to include a biography for Su Chuo.[16] Du's household had a servant called Baosheng who was seventy years old and originally was a bondservant for the Su family. He was quite knowledgeable about history and knew a bit of literary writing. He looked over the draft of Du's biography of Su Chuo and was thus overcome with sorrow.

---

[15]Since this story is taking place in the Sui 隋 dynasty, the history is probably that of the previous dynasty, the Northern Zhou 北周.

[16]Su Chuo was a military official during the Western Wei 西魏 who played a role in helping to establish the Northern Zhou.

Du asked why, and Baosheng replied: "I always received kind treatment from Mister Su; now that I see the effectiveness of his words, I am sad because of this. As for this precious mirror that you possess, it was bequeathed to Mister Su by his friend Miao Jizi from Henan. Mister Su greatly treasured it. In the year that Mister Su was approaching death, he became melancholy and unhappy. He summoned Mister Miao and said: 'I suppose that my death is not far off. I don't know whose hands this mirror will fall into. Now I would like to perform a yarrow stalk divination. Sir you may observe it.' Then he turned to me [Baosheng] to fetch the yarrow, and he portioned the stalks to produce a trigram. When the trigram was complete, Mister Su said: 'More than ten years after my death, my family will lose this mirror. I do know where it will go. But as for all the divine objects in the world, there are signs of their movement and stillness. Now, between the He and Fen rivers, there is a precious qi that corresponds to the sign of this trigram. It seems the mirror will end up there.' [Miao] Jizi said: 'And will it be obtained by anyone?' Mister Su further elaborated on the trigram and said: 'First it will enter the Hou household, and then it will belong to the Wang household. After this, no one knows where it will go.'" Baosheng wept when he finished speaking. Du asked the [descendants of the] Su household, and they indeed said they had owned this mirror in the past. After Mister Su's death, they had also lost it, just as Baosheng said. Therefore Du composed a biography of Mister Su, and also completely narrated this story in the last section. He also discussed Mister Su's outstanding talent at divining by yarrow stalks, which he alone practiced and did not transmit.

On the first day of the first month of the ninth year of the Daye reign (613), there was a foreign monk who came to beg for alms at Du's household. Du's younger brother Ji went out to see him and thought his aura seemed unusual. So he invited him inside, provided some food for him, and sat speaking with him for a long while. The foreign monk said to Ji: "Your household seems to possess a precious mirror. Would I be able to see it?" Ji said: "Venerable, how did you know this?" The monk said: "I have acquired the secret art of the Bright Record, and I can perceive precious *qi*. Every day there has been a jade-colored light emitting from your residence linking it to the sun, and a purple-red *qi* connected to the moon. These are the *qi* of the precious mirror. I have observed this for two years. Now I have selected an auspicious day and thus I wish to take a look." Ji brought it out, and the monk knelt, clasping it with joy. He then said to Ji: "This mirror has many kinds of numinous phenomena which you perhaps have not seen. You only need to apply a gold paste to it, wipe it with pearl powder, and hold it up to reflect in the sunlight, and its image will certainly shine through onto the wall." The monk sighed and said further: "If you test it further, you should be able to shine it to see one's internal organs [through the skin]. I just regret that I do not have the ingredients for it. You only need to fumigate it with alchemical smoke, rinse it with jade water, and then use the method of [applying] gold paste and wiping it with pearl powder. Then bury it in the mud, and it will never become dark." Thereupon he left the recipes for the alchemical smoke and jade water. Ji practiced them, and they always had an effect. But the foreign monk was never seen again.

In the autumn of that same year (613), Du left [the capital] for an additional appointment as the Magistrate of Ruicheng.[17] In the courtyard of the magistrate's office, there was a jujube tree. Its trunk was several tens of *zhang* in circumference. No one knew how many hundreds of years old it was. All the previous magistrates, up to now, all gave offerings to this tree. Otherwise, they would immediately receive calamities. Du thought that a demon was flourishing because of these people, and that the excessive sacrifices needed to stop. But the district functionaries all kowtowed and

---

[17]In present-day Shanxi 山西 province.

pleaded with Du, so he had no choice but to make a sacrifice to it. But he secretly thought that this tree probably had a demon inhabiting it. People could not eliminate it, so it had been cultivating its power. So Du secretly suspended his mirror between the branches. That night around the second watch (9–11 pm) he heard a continuous, thunder-like sound coming from the front courtyard. So he got up to inspect it, and he saw dark wind and rain encircling the tree. Lightning was flashing, jumping between above and below. The next morning, there was a great snake. It had purple scales, a red tail, a green head, and white horns. On its forehead was the character "Wang 王." Its body was covered in wounds, and it was dead by the tree. Du then took down the mirror and ordered the functionaries to remove the snake and burn it outside of the gate of the county seat. Then they dug into the tree, and in its center there was a cavity that gradually became larger as it went into the earth, and it had the vestiges of the coils of an enormous snake. They then filled the hole and the demon then vanished.

In the winter of that same year (613), Du was appointed Imperial Censor in addition to Magistrate of Ruicheng. He was sent to Hebei Administrative District and opened a granary to provide grain to Shandong for relief. At that time there was a great famine everywhere, and there were epidemics among the common people. Between the Pu and Shan regions, the plagues were particularly severe. There was a man from Hebei called Zhang Longju who served as a subordinate functionary under Du. Several tens of people in his household, his family members and servants, all had been struck with disease. Du took pity on them, and so he sent the mirror to his home and instructed Longju to take the mirror and reflect it during the night. When all the sick people saw the mirror, they all got up and gave a jolt of surprise: "We saw Longju come in holding a moon to shine on us. Wherever the moonlight reached, it was as if ice came into contact with our bodies. The cold penetrated into our organs." Their fever had disappeared right then, and by the [next] evening, they had all been healed. They thought that no harm had been done to the mirror, but it had saved everyone. So they made him secretly take the mirror and circulate among the common people. That night, the mirror began to make a ringing sound of its own accord from inside the box. The sound was very far-reaching, and it continued on for a long time before stopping. Du thought this was unusual. The next morning, Longju came to Du and said: "Last night I suddenly dreamed of a man with a dragon head and a snake body. He had a vermillion cap and purple clothing. He said to me: 'I am the spirit of the mirror. My name is Purple Treasure. I have always been virtuous towards your family. Therefore I have come to ask for your help in asking Mister Wang's pardon for me. The common people have committed transgressions, so Heaven has given them this illness. Why would you make me oppose Heaven to save things? Besides, this illness will last until next month, and then it will gradually disappear. Do not cause me more suffering.'" Du thought this was numinous and strange, and because of this, he recorded it. By the next month, the illness had indeed disappeared, just as the spirit said.

In the tenth year of the Daye reign (614), Du's brother Ji returned after resigning from his official position of Aide in Liuhe.[18] He also wanted to make excursions to scenic spots and planned to become a hermit. Du stopped him and said: "Now the world is facing disorder and it is full of thieves. Don't you want to pacify it? What's more, you and I are brothers and we have never been separated by long distance. As for this journey of yours, it seems that you will be leaving for good. In the past, Shang Ziping roamed the Five Sacred Peaks, and no one knows where he went. If you are trying to follow in the footsteps of previous worthies, I will not be able to bear it." Then he wept to Ji. Ji said: "My mind is made up, and I certainly cannot stay [here]. Elder brother, you are a considerate person now, and there is nothing that you cannot

---

[18]In present-day Jiangsu province.

apprehend. Confucius said: 'Even the will of a common man cannot be wrested from him.' A human life only lasts about a hundred years; it is as short as [a white horse] passing a crevice. Our happiness comes from attaining our passions, and sadness comes from losing our will. Following one's desires is what the sage intended." Du had no choice but to part with him. Ji said: "As for this parting, I also have one favor to ask. The precious mirror that you possess is not a mundane object. I have the lofty ambition to trek cloudy paths and [follow] hidden tracks through the mists. I hope that you would grant me this mirror." Du said: "How could I begrudge you of it?" So [Du] gave it to him. Ji took the mirror and then set out on his journey without saying where he would go.

In the sixth month of the thirteenth year of the Daye reign period (617), during the summer, Ji finally returned to Chang'an and returned the mirror. He said to Du: "This mirror is truly a treasure. After I took leave from you, I first traveled to Shaoshi Temple on Mount Song.[19] I descended down a stone bridge and sat at a jade altar. At sunset I came across a cavern with a stone hall that could hold three to five people. I stopped to rest there. At the second watch of this moonlit night, two people appeared. One appeared to be a foreigner whose beard and eyebrows were white and wispy. He said he was the Mountain Duke. The other had a broad face, with a white beard and long eyebrows. He was swarthy and short, and called himself Mister Hairy. They said to me: 'Who is residing here?' I said: 'Just someone who seeks the hidden, explores caverns, and investigates the marvelous.' The two people sat down and chatted with me for a long while, and strange ideas frequently appeared in their words. I suspected they were spirits, so I reached my hand behind me and opened the box to take out the mirror. The light of the mirror shone forth, and the two men cried out and fell prostrate on the ground. The short one turned into a turtle, and the foreign one turned into an ape. I hung up the

---

[19]In present-day Henan province.

mirror until dawn, and the two figures had completely perished. The body of the turtle had green fur, and the body of the ape had white fur.

Next I went to Mount Ji.[20] I crossed the Ying river, passed through Taihe county, and paid a visit to the Jade Well. Near the well was a pond with water that was a limpid green color. I asked a woodcutter [about this place] and he said: 'This is a numinous marsh. During the eight principle solar terms[21] sacrifices are made to it at the village gates in order to pray for good fortune and blessings. If a sacrifice is lacking, then black clouds and great hail will emerge from the pond water and immerse the levees and break the barriers.' I took out the mirror and shone it. The water began to bubble, and there was quaking thunder. Suddenly the water soared up out of the pond, not leaving even a tiny trickle. When it had risen over two hundred paces up, the water fell back to the ground. There was a fish that was more than a *zhang* in length, thicker than a person's arm. It had a red head with a white patch on its forehead, and its body was patched with green and yellow. It was slimy, with no scales, and shaped like a dragon with snake horns. Its mouth was pointy and sturgeon-shaped, and it glistened as it moved. It was trapped in the muddy water and could not flee. I thought it was a shark, and with the loss of the water it had no way to live. So I cut it up and roasted it; it was very oily and tasty, and could satisfy mouths and bellies for several days.

---

[20]In present-day Henan province.

[21] The eight most important of the Twenty-Four Solar terms (mentioned in note 3). They are the 1st, 4th, 7th, 10th, 13th, 16th, 19th, and 22nd terms, which are, respectively, the start of spring (lichun 立春), the spring equinox (*chunfen* 春分), the beginning of summer (*lixia* 立夏), the summer solstice (*xiazhi* 夏至), the beginning of fall (*liqiu* 立秋), the fall equinox (*qiufen* 秋分), the beginning of winter (*lidong* 立冬), and the winter solstice (*dongzhi* 冬至).

Next I emerged into the Song region city of Bian[zhou]. My host in Bian, Zhang Ke, had a woman in his household who was suffering from illness. At nightfall, she moaned in pain; it was truly unbearable. I asked the reason, and I was told that she had already suffered the illness for a year. During the day it was peaceful, but at night it was always like this. When I stayed there overnight, I heard the woman's wails, so I opened up the mirror and shined it. The aching woman said: 'The gentleman with the hat has been killed.' Under this sick woman's bed there was a large rooster; it was dead. It was the host's old rooster of seven or eight years.

Then I traveled to the area south of the Yangzi River. When I was about to cross the river in Guangling, suddenly dark clouds covered the water, and a sinister wind caused waves to surge. The boatman lost his calm and was anxious that the boat would capsize. I got onto the boat with the mirror, and it shined several paces into the water. As the light penetrated it, the wind and clouds from the four directions calmed, and the waves subsided. In a flash, we were able to cross the natural barrier. I went up to Wine Fragrance Peak on Mount She.[22] Whether climbing the highest summits, or entering deep caverns, whenever I came across flocks of birds that would surround me and squawk, or bears crouching on the road, I would brandish the mirror at them, and the bears and birds would rush away in panic.

At this time I was smoothly sailing on the Zhe River when I encountered a tide coming from the sea. The sound of the waves shook and roared, and it could be heard from several hundreds of *li* away. The captain of the boat said: 'The waves are approaching so we cannot cross to the south. If I don't turn this boat around, we will certainly perish in the bellies of fish.' I took out the mirror and shined it, and the waves in the river did not come any closer. They were stacked as tall as clouds. The river water opened up more than 50 paces on each side. The water gradually became clearer and

---

[22]In Jiangsu province.

shallower, and turtles and alligators scattered. We raised the sail, it fluttered, and we directly made it to the south shore. After that, when I looked back, I saw that the waves had gushed forth [again] several tens of *zhang* tall, and had hit the place where we had just been crossing.

Next I ascended Mount Tiantai[23] and completely viewed all the caverns and gullies. During the travels at night, I hung this mirror on me as I went through mountain valleys, and the light penetrated on all sides for a distance of a hundred paces, so that even the most minute [details] could all be seen. It startled the birds roosting in the forest and they flew off in panic.

Then I returned to Guiji [24] and met the eccentric Zhang Shiluan. He taught me the *Zhou Gnomon [Divination Classic] in Nine Sections*[25] and the [divination] method of the Bright Hall and the Six *Jia*.[26] Then I returned together with Chen Yong.

I further traveled to Yuzhang [27] and met the Daoist priest Xu Zangmi. He said he was the seventh generation descendent of Xu Jingyang,[28] and he had an incantation for a technique to walk on knives and tread over flames. Next we talked about demons, and he mentioned that Li Jingshen, the Granary Supervisor in

---

[23]In Zhejiang province.

[24]In the present-day Hangzhou 杭州 area.

[25] This is probably the *Zhou bi suan jing* 周髀算經, a text on mathematics from early China, used to calculate astronomical events. It contains a version of the Pythagorean theorem.

[26] *Liujia* 六甲 is a divination method that uses the compounds containing *jia* 甲 from the sexagenary cycle created by the heavenly stems (*tiangan* 天干) and earthly branches (*dizhi* 地支) in order to calculate auspicious times.

[27]In present-day Jiangxi province.

[28]A place name in present-day Sichuan province. This is probably an implication that he is related to the famous Daoist master Xu Xun 許遜, who held an official appointment in Jingyang 旌陽, and who was originally from Nanchang 南昌, another name for Yuzhang 豫章 in Jiangxi.

Fengcheng county, had three daughters in his household who had been stricken with demonic illness. No one knew what the illness was. Zangmi had treated them, but it was ineffective. An old friend of mine told me that Zhao Dan was talented and magnanimous and [at the time] was appointed as Commandant in Fengcheng county. Therefore I went to visit him. Dan ordered his attendant to go to the place where I was staying. I said to him: 'I would like permission to go to the residence of the Granary Supervisor Li Jingshen's family.' Dan immediately ordered Jing[shen] to host me. Then I asked about the cause [of his daughters' illness]. Jing[shen] said: 'My three daughters live together in the side room inside the hall. Each day at dusk, they apply makeup and dress in splendid clothing. After sunset, they return to their room and extinguish the lamps. When I listen to them, it sounds like they are secretly talking and laughing with someone. By daybreak they are fast asleep, and they won't awaken without rousing. Every day they gradually become thinner because they are unable to eat. When I tried to restrain them and not allow them to get so gussied up, they tried to hang themselves or throw themselves into the well. There is nothing I can do.' I said to him: 'Take me to this side room.' To the east of the room there was a window, and I feared that its door would be closed too firmly to open. So during the day I first cut out four parts of the window latticework and used something to prop them up, so they looked the same as before. At sunset, Jing[shen] reported to me: 'They've gotten all dolled up and gone into the room.' At the first watch (7–9 pm) I heard them talking and laughing spontaneously. I pulled out the window lattice work, held up the mirror, entered the room, and shined it. The three women called out: 'You have killed our husbands!' At first I didn't see anything, so I hung the mirror until dawn. [It turned out that] there was a weasel. From head to tail it was about one *chi* and three to four *cun* long, and it was completely hairless and toothless. There was also an old rat that was likewise hairless and toothless, and it was fat, probably weighing about five *jin*. And there was also a gecko, about as big as a person's hand. It was covered in scales that glittered in the five colors. It had two horns on its head, about half a *cun* long, and its tail was more than five *cun* long. One *cun* from the tip of the tail was completely white. [The three creatures were] all lying dead in front of a hole in the wall. After this, the illness was cured.

After this, I went in search of the Perfected on Mount Lu.[29] I lingered here for several months, sometimes resting in lofty groves, sometimes sleeping out in the open in meadows. Tigers, leopards, jackals, and wolves continually appeared. I would just raise this mirror and shine it on them, and not a single one did not flee and hide. The hermit of Mount Lu, Su Bin, was a scholar of extraordinary knowledge. He thoroughly understood the Way of the *Changes*, and he could both recall the past and predict the future. He said to me: 'The divine objects of the world never stay long among people. Now the universe is in a [period of] disaster and chaos, and foreign places are not necessarily worth dwelling in. As for this mirror still being here guarding you, it would be best for you to quickly return to your hometown.' I followed his advice and immediately returned to the north, and then traveled to Hebei. During the night, I dreamed that mirror said to me: 'I have received your elder brother's generosity. Now I must renounce the human world and depart to a far-off place. I first wish to bid your brother farewell, so I request that you return to Chang'an as soon as possible.' I agreed to this in my dream, but in the morning I thought about it by myself and felt bewildered and nervous. I immediately set out westwards on the road to Qin. Now I have seen you, and I no longer bear this promise. But in the end, I fear that this numinous object will no longer be possessed by you either."

After several months, Ji returned to Hedong. On the fifteenth day of the seventh month of the thirteenth year of the Daye reign

---

[29]In Jiangxi province.

(617), there was a mournful cry from within the box. At first the sound was delicate and remote, but before long it gradually became greater, like the roaring of a dragon or tiger. It was a long while before it quieted. [Du] opened the box to inspect it, and the mirror was missing.

古鏡記

王度

　　隋汾陰侯生，天下奇士也。王度常以師禮事之。臨終，贈度以古鏡曰："持此，則百邪遠人。"度受而寶之。鏡橫徑八寸，鼻作麒麟蹲伏之象。遶鼻列四方，龜龍鳳虎，依方陳布。四方外又設八卦，卦外置十二辰位，而具畜焉。辰畜之外，又置二十四字，周遶輪廓，文體似隸，點畫無缺，而非字書所有也。侯生云："二十四氣之象形。"

　　承日照之，則背上文畫，墨入影內，纖毫無失。舉而扣之，清音徐引，竟日方絕。嗟乎，此則非凡鏡之所同也。宜其見賞高賢，自稱靈物。侯生常云："昔者吾聞黃帝鑄十五鏡，其第一橫徑一尺五寸，法滿月之數也。以其相差，各校一寸，此第八鏡也。"雖歲祀攸遠，圖書寂寞，而高人所述，不可誣矣。昔楊氏納環，累代延慶；張公喪劍，其身亦終。今度遭世擾攘，居常鬱怏。王室如燬，生涯何地。寶鏡復去，哀哉！今具其異跡，列之於後。數千載之下，倘有得者，知其所由耳。

　　大業七年五月，度自御史罷歸河東，適遇侯生卒，而得此鏡。至其年六月，度歸長安，至長樂坡，宿於主人程雄家。雄新受寄一婢，頗甚端麗，名曰鸚鵡。度既稅駕，將整冠履，引鏡自照。鸚鵡遙見，即便叩首流血，云："不敢住。"度因召主人問其故，雄云："兩月前，有一客攜此婢從東來。時婢病甚，客便寄留，云：'還日當取。'比不復來，不知其婢之由也。"度疑精魅，引鏡逼之。便云："乞命，即變形。"度即掩鏡，曰："汝先自叙，然後變形，當捨汝命。"婢再拜自陳云："某是華山府君廟前長松下千歲老狸，大行變惑，罪合至死。遂為府君捕逐，逃於河渭之間，為下邽陳思恭義女，蒙養甚厚。嫁鸚鵡與同鄉人柴華。鸚鵡與華意不相愜，逃

20

而東；出韓城縣。為行人李无傲所執。无傲麤暴丈夫也，遂將鸚鵡遊行數歲。昨隨至此，忽爾見留。不意遭逢天鏡，隱形無路。”度又謂曰：“汝本老狐，變形為人，豈不害人也？”婢曰：“變形事人，非有害也。但逃匿幻惑，神道所惡，自當至死耳。”度又謂曰：“欲捨汝，可乎？”鸚鵡曰：“辱公厚賜，豈敢忘德。然天鏡一照，不可逃形。但久為人形。羞復故體。願緘於匣，許盡醉而終。”度又謂曰：“緘鏡於匣，汝不逃乎？”鸚鵡笑曰：“公適有美言，尚許相捨。緘鏡而走，豈不終恩？但天鏡一臨，鼠跡無路，惟希數刻之命，以盡一生之歡耳。”度登時為匣鏡；又為致酒，悉召雄家鄰里，與宴謔。婢頃大醉，奮衣起舞而歌曰：“寶鏡寶鏡，哀哉予命。自我離形，于今幾姓？生雖可樂，死必不傷。何為眷戀，守此一方！”歌訖，再拜，化為老狸而死。一座驚歎。

大業八年四月一日，太陽虧。度時在臺直，晝臥廳閣，覺日漸昏。諸吏告度以日蝕甚。整衣時，引鏡出，自覺鏡亦昏昧，無復光色。度以寶鏡之作，合於陰陽光景之妙。不然，豈合以太陽失曜而寶鏡亦無光乎？歎怪未已，俄而光彩出，日亦漸明。比及日復，鏡亦精朗如故。自此之後，每日月薄蝕，鏡亦昏昧。

其年八月十五日，友人薛俠者，獲一銅劍，長四尺。劍連於靶；靶盤龍鳳之狀，左文如火焰，右文如水波，光彩灼爍，非常物也。俠持過度，曰：“此劍俠常試之，每月十五日，天地清朗，置之暗室，自然有光，傍照數丈。俠持之有日月矣。明公好奇愛古，如飢如渴，願與君今夕一試。”度喜甚。其夜，果遇天地清霽。密閉一室，無復脫隙，與俠同宿。度亦出寶鏡，置于座側。俄而鏡上吐光，明照一室，相視如晝。劍橫其側，無復光彩。俠大驚，曰：“請內鏡於匣。”度從其言，然後劍乃吐光，不過一二尺耳。俠撫劍歎曰：“天下神物，亦有相伏之理也。”是後每至月望，則出鏡於暗室，光嘗照數丈。若月影入室，則無光也。豈太陽太陰之耀，不可敵也乎？

其年冬，兼著作郎。奉詔撰國史，欲為蘇綽立傳。度家有奴曰豹生，年七十矣。本蘇氏部曲，頗涉史傳，略解屬文。見度傳草，因悲不自勝。度問其故。謂度曰：“豹生常受蘇公厚遇，今見蘇公言驗，是以悲耳。郎君所有寶鏡，是蘇公友人河南苗季子所遺蘇公者。蘇公愛之甚。蘇公臨亡之歲，戚戚不樂，常召苗生謂曰：‘自度死日不久，不知此鏡當入誰手？今欲以著筮一卦，先生幸觀之也。’便顧豹生取著，蘇公自撰布卦。卦訖，蘇公曰：‘我死十餘

年，我家當失此鏡，不知所在。然天地神物，動靜有徵。今河汾之
間，往往有寶氣，與卦兆相合，鏡其往彼乎。’季子曰：‘亦為人
所得乎？’蘇公又詳其卦，云：‘先入侯家，復歸王氏。過此以往，
莫知所之也。’”豹生言訖涕泣。度問蘇氏，果云舊有此鏡，蘇公
薨後，亦失所在，如豹生之言。故度為蘇公傳，亦具言其事於末篇，
論蘇公著筮絕倫，默而獨用，謂此也。

大業九年正月朔旦，有一胡僧，行乞而至度家。弟勣出見之。
覺其神彩不俗，更邀入室，而為具食，坐語良久。胡僧謂勣
曰：“檀越家似有絕世寶鏡也。可得見耶？”勣曰：“法師何以得知
之？”僧曰：“貧道受明錄祕術，頗識寶氣。檀越宅上每日常有碧
光連日，絳氣屬月，此寶鏡氣也。貧道見之兩年矣。今擇良日，故
欲一觀。”勣出之。僧跪捧欣躍，又謂勣曰：“此鏡有數種靈相，
皆當未見。但以金膏塗之，珠粉拭之，舉以照日，必影徹牆壁。”
僧又歎息曰：“更作法試，應照見腑臟。所恨卒無藥耳。但以金烟
薰之，玉水洗之，復以金膏珠粉如法拭之，藏之泥中，亦不晦矣。”
遂留金烟玉水等法，行之無不獲驗。而胡僧遂不復見。

其年秋，度出兼芮城令。令廳前有一棗樹，圍可數丈，不知幾
百年矣。前後令至，皆祠謁此樹，否則殃禍立及也。度以為妖由人
興，淫祀宜絕。縣吏皆叩頭請度。度不得已，為之以祀。然陰念此
樹當有精魅所託，人不能除，養成其勢。乃密懸此鏡於樹之間。其
夜二鼓許，聞其廳前磊落有聲，若雷霆者。遂起視之，則風雨晦暝，
纏繞此樹。電光晃耀，忽上忽下。至明，有一大蛇，紫鱗赤尾，綠
頭白角，額上有王字。身被數創，死於樹。度便下收鏡。命吏出蛇，
焚於縣門外。仍掘樹，樹心有一穴，於地漸大，有巨蛇蟠泊之跡。
既而坎之，妖怪遂絕。

其年冬，度以御史帶芮城令，持節河北道，開倉糧賑給陝東。
時天下大飢，百姓疾病，蒲陝之間，癘疫尤甚。有河北人張龍駒，
為度下小吏，其家良賤數十口，一時遇疾。度憫之，齎此入其家，
使龍駒持鏡夜照。諸病者見鏡，皆驚起，云：“見龍駒持一月來相
照。光陰所及，如冰著體，冷徹腑臟。”即時熱定，至晚並愈。以
為無害於鏡，而所濟於眾，令密持此鏡，遍巡百姓。其夜，鏡於匣
中泠然自鳴，聲甚徹遠，良久乃止。度心獨怪。明早，龍駒來謂度
曰：“龍駒昨忽夢一人，龍頭蛇身，朱冠紫服。謂龍駒：‘我即鏡精
也，名曰紫珍。常有德於君家，故來相託。為我謝王公，百姓有罪，

天與之疾，奈何使我反天救物！且病至後月，當漸愈，無為我苦。”度感其靈怪，因此誌之。至後月，病果漸愈，如其言也。

大業十年，度弟勣自六合丞棄官歸，又將遍遊山水，以為長往之策。度止之曰：“今天下向亂，盜賊充斥，欲安之乎？且吾與汝同氣，未嘗遠別。此行也，似將高蹈。昔尚子平遊五嶽，不知所之。汝若追蹤前賢，吾所不堪也。”便涕泣對勣。勣曰：“意已決矣，必不可留。兄今之達人，當無所不體。孔子曰：‘匹夫不奪其志矣。’人生百年，忽同過隙，得情則樂，失志則悲，安遂其欲，聖人之義也。”度不得已，與之決別。勣曰：“此別也，亦有所求。兄所寶鏡，非塵俗物也。勣將抗志雲路，棲蹤煙霞，欲兄以此為贈。”度曰：“吾何惜於汝也。”即以與之。勣得鏡，遂行，不言所適。

至大業十三年夏六月，始歸長安，以鏡歸，謂度曰：“此鏡真寶物也！辭兄之後，先遊嵩山少室，降石梁，坐玉壇。屬日暮，遇一嵌巖，有一石堂，可容三五人，勣棲息止焉。月夜二更後，有兩人：一貌胡，鬚眉皓而瘦，稱山公；一面闊，白鬚，眉長，黑而矮，稱毛生。謂勣曰：‘何人斯居也？’勣曰：‘尋幽探穴訪奇者。’二人坐與勣談久，往往有異義出於言外。勣疑其精怪，引手潛後，開匣取鏡。鏡光出而二人失聲俯伏。矮者化為龜，胡者化為猿。懸鏡至曉，二身俱殞。龜身帶綠毛；猿身帶白毛。

即入箕山，渡穎水，歷太和，視玉井。井傍有池，水湛然綠色。問樵夫。曰：‘此靈湫耳，村閭每八節祭之，以祈福祐。若一祭有闕，即池水出黑雲，大雹浸堤壞阜。’勣引鏡照之，池水沸湧，有雷如震。忽爾池水騰出池中，不遺涓滴。可行二百餘步。水落於地。有一魚，可長丈餘，麤細大於臂，首紅額白，身作青黃間色，無鱗有涎，龍形蛇角，嘴尖，狀如鱘魚，動而有光，在于泥水，困而不能遠去。勣謂鮫也，失水而無能為耳。刃而為炙，甚膏，有味，以充數朝口腹。

遂出於宋汴。汴主人張珂家有女子患，入夜，哀痛之聲，實不堪忍。勣問其故。病來已經年歲，白日即安，夜常如此。勣停一宿，及聞女子聲，遂開鏡照之。病者曰：‘戴冠郎被殺！’其病者牀下，有大雄雞，死矣，乃是主人七八歲老雞也。

遊江南。將渡廣陵揚子江，忽暗雲覆水，黑風波湧，舟子失容，慮有覆沒。勣攜鏡上舟，照江中數步，明朗徹底，風雲四歛，波濤遂息，須臾之間，達濟天塹。躋攝山麟芳嶺，或攀絕頂，或入深洞，逢其羣鳥環人而噪，數熊當路而蹲，以鏡揮之，熊鳥奔駭。

是時利涉浙江，遇潮出海。濤聲振吼，數百里而聞。舟人曰：『濤既近，未可渡南。若不迴舟，吾輩必葬魚腹。』勣出鏡照，江波不進，屹如雲立。四面江水豁開五十餘步，水漸清淺，黿鼉散走。舉帆翩翩，直入南浦。然後却視，濤波洪湧，高數十丈。而至所渡之所也。

遂登天台，周覽洞壑。夜行佩之山谷，去身百步，四面光徹，纖微皆見，林間宿鳥，驚而亂飛。

還履會稽，逢異人張始鸞，授勣周髀九章及明堂六甲之事。與陳永同歸。

更遊豫章，見道士許藏祕，云是旌陽七代孫，有呪登刀履火之術。說妖怪之次，更言豐城縣倉督李敬慎家有三女，遭魅病，人莫能識。藏祕療之無効。勣故人曰趙丹有才器，任豐城縣尉。勣因過之。丹命祇承人指勣停處。勣謂曰：『欲得倉督李敬慎家居止。』丹遽命敬為主，禮勣。因問其故。敬曰：『三女同居堂內閣子，每至日晚，即靚粧銜服。黃昏後，即歸所居閣子，滅燈燭。聽之，竊與人言笑聲。及至曉眠，非喚不覺。日日漸瘦，不能下食。制之不令粧梳，即欲自縊投井。無奈之何。』勣謂敬曰：『引示閣子之處。』其閣東有窗。恐其門閉固而難啟，遂晝日先刻斷窗櫺四條，却以物支柱之，如舊。至日暮，敬報勣曰：『粧梳入閣矣。』至一更，聽之，言笑自然。勣拔窗櫺子，持鏡入閣，照之。三女叫云：『殺我壻也！』初不見一物。縣鏡至明，有一鼠狼，首尾長一尺三四寸，身無毛齒；有一老鼠，亦無毛齒，其肥大可重五斤；又有守宮，大如人手，身披鱗甲，煥爛五色，頭上有兩角，長可半寸，尾長五寸已上，尾頭一寸色白，並於壁孔前死矣。從此疾愈。

其後尋真至廬山，婆娑數月，或棲息長林，或露宿草莽，虎豹接尾，豺狼連跡，舉鏡視之，莫不竄伏。廬山處士蘇賓，奇識之士也，洞明易道，藏往知來，謂勣曰：『天下神物，必不久居人間。今宇宙喪亂，他鄉未必可止，吾子此鏡尚在，足下衛，幸速歸家鄉也。』勣然其言，即時北歸。便遊河北。夜夢鏡謂勣曰：『我蒙卿兄厚禮，今當捨人間遠去，欲得一別，卿請早歸長安也。』勣夢中許之。及曉，獨居思之，恍恍發悸，即時西首秦路。今既見兄，勣不負諾矣。終恐此靈物亦非兄所有。』

數月，勣還河東。大業十三年七月十五日，匣中悲鳴，其聲纖遠，俄而漸大，若龍咆虎吼；良久乃定。開匣視之，即失鏡矣。

A Supplement to Jiang Zong's[1] "Biography of the White Ape"

Anonymous
Translated by Weiguo Cao

At the end of the Datong reign period (535–546) of the Liang Dynasty, Lin Qin, the General Pacifying the South, was sent to launch a punitive expedition in the south.[2] When he reached Guilin, he crushed the troops of Li Shigu and Chen Che.[3] His deputy general Ouyang He (538–570)[4] overran territories, reached Changle

---

[1] Jiang Zong 江總 (519–594) was a famous literatus during the Southern Chen 陳 Dynasty. He served as the prime minister for the last emperor of the Chen dynasty.

[2] It has been pointed out that Lin Qin 藺欽 was not a historical figure and that the character Lin 藺 might have been a mistake for the character Lan 蘭, since these two characters look similar. Lan Qin was a general of Liang dynasty who once led troops to attack the minority peoples in southern China.

[3] The accounts here again deviate from the historical records. Chen Che 陳徹 might be a mistake for Chen Wenche 陳文徹. Lan Qin crushed Chen Wenche's troop not in Guilin, but in another campaign in Guangzhou.

[4] Ouyang He 歐陽紇 served as a general during the Chen dynasty and led the campaign against minority peoples in the Guangzhou area. However, at the end of Datong reign period of Liang dynasty he was only

and wiped out all the rebels residing in various caves.[5] He went deep into dangerous terrain in haste.

His wife was extremely beautiful, with slender waist and white skin. One of his subordinates told him, "Why do you, the general, bring a beautiful woman into this place? There is a divine being here who is good at stealing young girls. Those beautiful ones find it especially difficult to escape his clutches. You should carefully protect her." He was extremely apprehensive. At night he instructed his soldiers to guard his dwelling all around, and hid his wife in a secret room, carefully locking everything tight. He further made a dozen of maidservants attend and guard her.

On that night, it was gloomy with sinister wind. When it reached the fifth watch (3–5 o'clock in the morning), it was silent and no sound could be heard. The guards felt tired and fell into sleep. Suddenly it seemed a creature arrived. Feeling startled, the guards woke up. By that time, they had already lost the general's wife. Everything was still locked as before. No one knew how the creature came in and went out. They went outside the gate. The mountains stood dangerously steep. It was murky even in short distance. Thus they were unable to pursue and search for the missing wife. When it reached daybreak, not a single trace could be found.

Ouyang He was in great anger and grief. He vowed he would never return home without finding his wife. Accordingly he pleaded illness and stationed his troops there. Every day he went

---

a boy less than eight years old. Thus it is impossible for him to have served as a deputy general at that time.

[5]According to *Liang shu* 梁書 (*History of Liang*) 32.466, during Lan Qin's campaign against the southern minority peoples, "the rebels residing in various caves in Changle 長樂 were at that time all wiped out." However, this campaign took place near modern Hengyang city in Hunan, not in Guilin. Changle was probably located in the Dayunshan (Big Cloud Mountain) near Hengyang.

long distances all around. He trudged through deep valleys and climbed dangerous peaks in search of his wife. One month later, he suddenly found one of his wife's embroidered shoes in a bamboo grove about 100 *li* away.[6] Although the shoe was soaked by the rain, he could still tell it was hers. He felt especially mournful. His determination to seek his wife grew even stronger. He selected thirty brave and strong men. Carrying their own weapons and grain ration, they camped in the mountain rocks and ate in the wilderness.

After another ten days or so, in a place about 200 *li* away from their original dwelling site, they found a mountain in the distance to the south, which appeared towering and verdant. When they reached the foot of the mountain, they found a deep stream surrounding it. So they built a wooden raft to cross the stream. Among the precipitous cliffs and emerald bamboos, from time to time they had a glimpse of red silk, and heard the sound of talking and laughing. Dragging themselves up with vines and thick ropes, they ascended the mountain. Subsequently they found a place where fine trees were planted in lines, intermingled with famous flowers. Underneath the trees and flowers there was green grass, soft and lush like a carpet. It was vastly clear and quiet, far removed from the hustle of life.[7] There was a stone gate, facing east. A dozen

---

[6]In Chinese culture "shoes" have significant symbolic meaning for love. The pronunciation of "shoes" *xie*, is the same as that of another character, 協, which means "harmony." It is interesting to note that a similar motif (search for one's lover through a shoe) also appeared in the Cinderella story in Western folk literature. In another Tang tale from Duan Chengshi's 段成式 (c. 803–863) *Youyang zazu* 酉陽雜俎, the heroine Ye Xian 葉限 lost one of her golden shoes at a festive party. Later the shoe was recovered by a king, who used the shoe to find her and eventually married her.

[7]As Jue Chen (pp. 156–157) points out, the depiction of the residence of the white ape suggests a typical "immortal's domain" or a "Taoist Mountain Utopia."

women gathered there, wearing bright-colored and shiny clothes. They frolicked happily in and out, singing and laughing. When they saw people approaching, they all stood still and looked at them in a scornful manner.[8] When the people arrived, they asked, "Why do you come here?" Ouyang He told them the story in detail. They looked at each other and sighed, saying, "Your worthy wife has been here for more than a month now. She is currently lying on a sickbed. We should send you there to see her." After he entered the gate, he found out the doors inside were made of wood. There were three large rooms as spacious as halls. Beds were set up around the walls, all covered with brocade padding. His wife was lying on a stone couch, with layers of blankets and mattresses. Many delicacies were placed in front of her. He came close to see her. She turned her eyes and took a look at him, then she waved her hands quickly asking him to leave. Those women said, "We and your wife came here one after another. Some of us have been here for as many as ten years. This is a place occupied by a divine creature,[9] who can use his great strength to kill human beings. Even one hundred soldiers carrying weapons will not be able to conquer him. Fortunately he has not returned, so you should quickly leave

---

[8]The original word is *man shi* 慢視. Jue Chen ("A Supplement to Jiang Zong's *Biography of a White Ape*," *Renditions* 1998, p. 81) translated it as "stared at them," and noted that the word implied that the women were surprised at the arrival of the outsiders. However, the word *man shi* means "to look down upon" or "to despise." Furthermore, in the passage below it was indicated that the white ape already gave warning to the women that someone would visit the place to kill him. So it is unlikely that the women felt surprised at the arrival of the outsiders. Instead, since the women knew the great power of the white ape, they felt disdainful of Ouyang He and his soldiers because they knew the white ape could easily kill them.

[9]The original word is *shen wu* 神物. Jue Chen (p. 82) mistakenly translated it as "murderous god." As noted below, the author may have chosen the term to deify the birth of Ouyang Xun.

to avoid him. You just need to prepare two *hu* (about thirty gallons) of fine wine, ten edible dogs, and a few dozen pounds of hemp, then we will make a plot with you to kill him. If you come, it must be after the noon time.[10] Be careful, do not come too early. Let's set our meeting time in ten days." Accordingly they urged him to leave. Ouyang He thereby withdrew immediately.

Subsequently, he managed to obtain vintage wine, hemp and dogs, and went there at the appointed time. The women said, "This creature is fond of wine, and frequently gets drunk. After he gets drunk, he will definitely show off his strength and ask us to tie his hands and feet to the bed with colored ribbons. As soon as he jumps up, all the ribbons are broken. Once we used three layers of ribbons, then his strength was exhausted and he was unable to break loose. Now we will hide the hemp among the silk ribbons to tie him. We expect that will make him unable to break. His entire body is as hard as iron. The only place he frequently tries to protect is the spot several inches below his navel. This must be the spot where it cannot withstand the attack of a weapon." They pointed to a cave[11] nearby and said, "This is his granary. You should hide yourself there. Keep quiet and await an opportunity. We will set up the wine under the flowers, and scatter the dogs in the grove. When our plan is successful, we will summon you, and you will come out right away." Ouyang He followed their words. Holding his breath, he waited inside the cave.

---

[10]This is in accord with the women's account of the usual habit of the white ape in the passage below: the white ape always left the place a little after noon and came back near evening.

[11]The original word is *yan* 巖. Jue Chen (p. 83) translated it as "cliff wall." The word *yan* can mean "cave." Besides, as indicated below, this cave served as the granary of the ape and hiding place for Ouyang He.

In the late afternoon, a creature in the shape of white silk[12] came down from another mountain. He cut through the grove as if flying, and then went directly into the cave. After a short while, a man with beautiful whiskers came out. He was about six feet tall, wearing white clothes and dragging a stick, holding various women. Upon seeing the dog, he felt surprised. Then he jumped up and captured the dog. He split and tore open the dog, sucked and chewed, until he was full. The women were vying with each other to present wine with jade cups, joking and teasing each other frivolously. After he drank several huge jars of wine, the women helped him out of the place. Furthermore, Ouyang He heard the sound of playing and laughing. After a long while, a woman came out to summon him. Thereupon he carried his weapon and entered the place. He saw a large white ape, its four feet tied into the bedhead. When he saw the human approaching, he frowned and twisted, trying to break the silk rope off, but was unable to do so. His eyes flashed like lightning. People vied each other to strike at him with their weapons, but it was as if they hit iron and stone. When he stabbed the spot below his navel, it cut through and blood shot out in torrents. Then the ape let out a deep sigh and shouted in anger, "This is an indication that Heaven kills me. How can you accomplish this through your own ability? Your wife is already pregnant. Do not kill her son. He will meet with a sagacious emperor in the future, and will surely make his clan great." Having said this, he died.

Ouyang He searched his storehouse, where abundant precious vessels and numerous delicacies filled the tables and desks. It included everything people treasured in the human world. There were also several bushels of famous incense and a pair of precious swords. There were more than thirty women, all of whom were exceedingly beautiful. Those who lived here a long time had

---

[12]The white ape was described as being in the shape of "white silk" to show he was moving at a stunning speed.

arrived ten years ago. They told him that those who lost their charms through the years would definitely be carried away by the ape. No one knew their whereabouts. Furthermore, the ape captured and collected [13] women just by himself, without any comrades. The ape washed his face and hands in the morning. Then he put on a hat, a white shirt, and then wrapped himself with silk clothes. He wore the same thing regardless hot or cold weather. All over his body grew white hair, several inches long. At the place he stayed, he often read inscribed wooden slips. The characters were like a Daoist talisman and were totally incomprehensible. Having finished reading, he would put the slips under the stone steps. Sometimes he would play with his pair of swords on a sunny day. The movements of swords were like lightning flying around his body, forming a bright circle just like a moon. He had no constant habit regrading eating and drinking. He was fond of eating fruits and chestnuts. He was especially addicted to eating dogs, chewing their meat and drinking their blood. He would quickly disappear once the time passed noon. In half a day he would travel back and forth for thousands of *li*. He would definitely return home by evening. This is his usual habit. He could quickly obtain whatever he needed. At night he went to bed to play with the women. In one night he could play around with all of the women.[14] He never went to sleep. His talk was broad, erudite and articulated, embellished with flowery language. However, his appearance was just like an

---

[13]The original word is *bu cai* 捕採. Jue Chen (p. 84) argued that it refers to the art of Taoist Yoga (*caibu* 採補), in which the practitioners made love with various women to collect their *yin* (feminine) energy and transform it into their *yang* (masculine) energy.

[14]Jue Chen (p. 161) points out that the fact that the white ape had sexual intercourse with thirty women in one night is an indication that he was practicing the Taoist secret inner chamber art (*fang zhong shu* 房中術).

ape.[15] This year, when the tree leaves started to fall, he suddenly felt mournful, saying,[16] "I was accused by the mountain god, and will be sentenced to death. I should seek protection from various deities. Hopefully I can escape from the disaster." Last month, on the day when the moonlight started to become dimmer,[17] a fire broke out at the stone steps and burned his books in wooden slips. He became despondent and said, "I have already lived for one thousand years. But I had no son. Now I have a son, my days are doomed." Accordingly he turned his head and looked at his various women. For a long time, tears poured down his cheeks.[18] Then he said, "In this mountain the path is complicated and extremely dangerous. No one has ever arrived at this place. When I go up and look into the distance, I can absolutely see no woodcutter. Below in the mountain there are many tigers, wolfs and monsters. Now if someone arrives, how is he able to do that without heaven's help?"

Ouyang He then took the precious jade and other treasures as well as various women to return home. Some women still knew

---

[15] It is interesting to note that the white ape, despite his ugly appearance, could speak in an elegant and erudite manner. This might be an allusion to Ouyang Xun, who looked like an ape but at the same time was a great scholar. See further discussion in the endnote below.

[16] The original wording is *hu chuang ran yue* 忽愴然曰. Jue Chen (p. 84) translated it as "suddenly said." However, the word *chuang ran* means "mournful."

[17] The original wording is *zai sheng po* 哉生魄. This refers to the sixteenth day of the month in the lunar calendar. On that day the moon started to wane so that its light became dimmer. Jue Chen (p. 84) mistakenly translated it as "when the moon is new."

[18] The original wording is *gu zhu nü wan lan* 顧諸女汍瀾. Jue Chen (p. 85) translated it as "gazed miserably at the women." However, the word *wan lan* means "tears pouring down."

where their homes were. His wife gave birth to a son after a whole year.[19] His appearance was just like the ape.

Later, Ouyang He was executed by Emperor Wu of Chen (r. 557–559).[20] He was always on good terms with Jiang Zong. The latter loved his son because he was extraordinarily intelligent. Jiang Zong had once kept him at his home and brought him up. Therefore he escaped from the disaster. After the child grew up, he indeed became a literary talent and was good at calligraphy. He was a renowned scholar of his time.

Note: It was generally believed in the past that this tale was written as a hidden attack against Ouyang Xun 歐陽詢 (557–641), a famous calligrapher but one whose appearance was that of an ape. (See Chen Jue, "Revisiting the Yingshe Mode of Representation in Supplement to Jiang Zong's 'Biography of a White Ape,'" *Oriens extremus* 44 [2003]: 156.) However, upon a close examination of the text of the tale, it seems this argument is fundamentally flawed. Firstly, Ouyang Xun's father Ouyang He 歐陽紇 (538–570), the protagonist of this tale, was portrayed as a hero, who courageously rescued his wife from the clutches of the white ape. Secondly, the white ape was not described in any way like a monster; rather, he was mentioned two times in this tale as *shen* 神 or *shen wu* 神物 (divine creature) who possessed great magic power and who could even predict his own death as well as the glorious future of his son, Ouyang Xun. The place he lived was portrayed almost as a fairyland. The author also described the death of the white ape in a sympathetic and sorrowful manner. In Chinese mythical tradition there were many tales of miraculous births in which a hero was born from a human mother and a divine creature. It is quite possible the author might have attempted to use the mythical motif of miraculous birth to deify the birth of Ouyang Xun in

---

[19]The fact that it took a longer time than normal for his wife to give birth might be an indication of the divine origin of the son.

[20]He was actually executed by Emperor Xuan of Chen (r. 568–582) because he started to rebel. The author omitted the reason for his execution, probably because it would ruin the image of Ouyang He as a hero he was trying to portray in this tale.

this tale. It is well known that Ouyang Xun was ridiculed in his life for his ape-like appearance. This tale might have been written in defense of him by attributing his ugly appearance to his divine father. It is also noteworthy that the white ape shares several important traits (such as running very fast, having a body hard as iron) with the famous Monkey King in the novel *Journey to the West*. Although in the novel the Monkey King never had sexual relationships with women, in the Yuan dynasty dramas he was actually depicted as having a strong liking for abducting beautiful women. Furthermore, just like the ape in the tale, the Monkey King in the novel also likes stealing. Instead of stealing women, he steals the immortal peach from heaven.

補江總白猿傳

缺名

梁大同末，遣平南將軍藺欽南征，至桂林，破李師古、陳徹。別將歐陽紇略地至長樂，悉平諸洞，罙入深阻。

紇妻纖白，甚美。其部人曰：“將軍何為挈麗人經此？地有神，善竊少女，而美者尤所難免。宜謹護之。”紇甚疑懼，夜勒兵環甚廬，匿婦密室中，謹閉甚固，而以女奴十餘伺守之。

爾夕，陰風晦黑，至五更，寂然無聞。守者怠而假寐，忽若有物驚悟者，即已失妻矣。關扃如故，莫知所出。出門山險，咫尺迷悶，不可尋逐。迫明，絕無其跡。

紇大憤痛，誓不徒還。因辭疾，駐其軍，日往四遅，即深陵險以索之。既逾月，忽於百里之外叢篠上，得其妻繡履一隻。雖浸雨濡，猶可辨識。紇尤悽悼，求之益堅。選壯士三十人，持兵負糧，巖棲野食。

又旬餘，遠所舍約二百里，南望一山，葱秀迴出，至其下，有深溪環之，乃編木以度。絕巖翠竹之間，時見紅綵，聞笑語音。捫蘿引絙，而陟其上，則嘉樹列植，間以名花，其下綠蕪，豐軟如毯。清迴岑寂，杳然殊境。東向石門，有婦人數十，帔服鮮澤，嬉遊歌笑，出入其中。見人皆慢視遲立，至則問曰：“何因來此？”紇具以對。相視歎曰：“賢妻至此月餘矣。今病在牀，宜遣視之。”入其門，以木為扉。中寬闊若堂者三。四壁設牀，悉施錦薦。其妻臥石榻上，重茵累席，珍食盈前。紇就視之。回眸一睇，即疾揮手令去。諸婦人曰：“我等與公之妻，比來久者十年。此神物所居，力能殺人，雖百夫操兵，不能制也。幸其未返，宜速避之。但求美酒兩斛，食犬十頭，麻數十斤，當相與謀殺之，其來必以正午後。慎勿太早，以十日為期。”因促之去。紇亦遽退。

遂求醇醪與麻犬，如期而往。婦人曰："彼好酒，往往致醉。醉必騁力，俾吾等以綵練縛手足於床，一踊皆斷。嘗紉三幅，則力盡不解，今麻隱帛中束之，度不能矣。遍體皆如鐵，唯臍下數寸，常護蔽之，此必不能禦兵刃。"指其旁一巖曰："此其食廩，當隱於是，靜而伺之。酒置花下，犬散林中，待吾計成，招之即出。"如其言，屏氣以俟。

日晡，有物如匹練，自他山下，透至若飛，徑入洞中。少選，有美髯丈夫長六尺餘，白衣曳杖，擁諸婦人而出。見犬驚視，騰身執之，被裂吭咀，食之致飽。婦人競以玉盃進酒，諧笑甚歡。既飲數斗，則扶之而去，又聞嬉笑之音。良久，婦人出招之，乃持兵而入。見大白猿，縛四足於牀頭，顧人蹙縮，求脫不得，目光如電。競兵之，如中鐵石。刺其臍下，即飲刃，血射如注。乃大歎咤曰："此天殺我，豈爾之能？然爾婦已孕，勿殺其子。將逢聖帝，必大其宗。"言絕乃死。

搜其藏，寶器豐積，珍羞盈品，羅列几案。凡人世所珍，靡不充備。名香數斛，寶劍一雙。婦人三十輩，皆絕其色。久者至十年。云：色衰必被提去，莫知所置。又捕採唯止其身，更無黨類。且盥洗，著帽，加白袷，被素羅衣，不知寒暑。遍身白毛，長數寸。所居常讀木簡，字若符篆，了不可識；已，則置石磴下。晴晝或舞雙劍，環身電飛，光圓若月。其飲食無常，喜啗果栗，尤嗜犬，咀而飲其血。日始逾午，即欻然而逝。半晝往返數千里，及晚必歸，此其常也。所須無不立得。夜就諸牀嬲戲，一夕皆周，未嘗寐。言語淹詳，華旨會利。然其狀，即猨玃類也。今歲木落之初，忽悽然曰："吾為山神所訴，將得死罪。亦求護之於眾靈，庶幾可免。"前月哉生魄，石磴生火，焚其簡書，悵然自失曰："吾已千歲，而無子。今有子，死期至矣。"因顧諸女，汍瀾者久，且曰："此山複絕，未嘗有人至。上高而望，絕不見樵者。下多虎狼怪獸。今能至者，非天假之，何耶？"

紇即取寶玉珍麗及諸婦人以歸，猶有知其家者。紇妻周歲生一子，厥狀肖焉。

後紇為陳武帝所誅。素與江總善，愛其子聰悟絕人，常留養之，故免於難。及長，果文學善書，知名于時。

Tale 1.3

An Account of the Detached Soul

By Chen Xuanyou
Translated by Kenneth DeWoskin

In the third year of the Tianshou period of the Tang Dynasty (692 AD), there was a man from Qinghe[1] named Zhang Yi. For his duties as an official, he was living in Hengzhou.[2]

By nature he lived a simple and quiet life, so he had very few friends. Zhang did not have a son, but he did have two daughters. The elder died at an early age. The younger, called Qianniang, was a reserved and beautiful woman. Zhang Yi also had a nephew, a native in Taiyuan Prefecture,[3] his sister's son, named Wang Zhou. Zhou was a bright and insightful young man and also quite handsome. Zhang Yi looked upon this nephew with great favor and always said to him, "At the appropriate time, I will have you take Qianniang as your wife."

Later, when Zhou and Qianniang were grown and no longer children, they both became obsessed with each other, thinking longingly day and night. Others in their families did not realize what was going on.

Subsequently, one of Zhang Yi's staff was selected for an official position in the civil ministry and asked to marry Qianniang. Zhang Yi agreed to that. When Qianniang learned of this, she fell

---

[1]Present day Qinghe County, Hebei.

[2]A remote and newly established region around modern Hengyang in Hunan.

[3]Its seat located in modern Taiyuan City in Shanxi.

into deep depression. When Zhou learned of it, he was angry and resentful, and using the excuse that he had to make some changes for his career, he asked the Zhang family to allow him to leave for the capital. Zhang Yi was powerless to stop him. Zhou was accorded a lavish farewell event, and, swallowing his anger and resentment, he climbed into a boat and was off.

When the curtain of night fell, the boat had made its way through several miles of mountain passages. It was the middle of the night, and Zhou was not asleep, when he suddenly heard someone walking on the embankment where his boat was docked. He could hear how very fast the footsteps were, and in a blink's time, the person was at the boat. As soon as Zhou heard her, he understood of course it was Qianniang, who had come on her own two feet to the boat. Greatly startled and delighted, Zhou took her hand and asked how it was she had come. Through her tears, Qianniang said, "Your feelings were so intensely strong, I could not stop thinking of you day and night. Now my father has offered my hand in marriage to someone else, forcefully redirected my will. And I knew that your feelings would never change, so I feared you might take your life in response. That is why I threw all caution to the wind and didn't consider my own life, just fled here." This was so far beyond anything Zhou had hoped for that his happiness and joy were profound. He hid Qianniang in the boat and proceeded on his journey, traveling night after night.

They hastened along in their journey and in a few months arrived in the Shu region [of modern Sichuan]. Over the course of the next five years, they had two sons. They were no longer in correspondence with Zhang Yi. Qianniang now often thought about her mother and father. She tearfully told Zhou, "On that fateful day, I could not bear to ignore your commitment to me, so I tossed aside all propriety and absconded with you. Now five years have already passed. And though I am still on this earth, I am prevented from filial provision to my parents. What kind of face can I have?"

Zhou was deeply moved by her and said, "We will return and we will harbor no bitterness." And so together they returned to Hengzhou.

Upon arrival, Zhou first went to the Yi family home by himself. He began by apologizing for the entire affair, to which Zhang Yi replied, "Qianniang has been lying ill in her boudoir for several years. How come this lie from you?" Zhou said, "She is in the boat right now!" Zhang Yi was overjoyed to hear this and immediately sent someone to the boat to confirm. And indeed he found her in the boat, with her face vibrant and cheerful. She asked the servant, "Are my parents well?" He was of course astonished at this and hastily ran back to report to Yi.

At this point, the "woman" in the boudoir heard what was going on and happily rose from her bed. She groomed herself and changed clothes. She smiled but still said nothing. Then she came out to meet Qianniang, whereupon the two fused together into a single body, as did the clothing they were wearing.

The family thought this was so very abnormal that they kept it secret. Only relatives knew about it. After some forty years, both Zhou and Qianniang passed away. Their two sons, being filial and incorruptible and prevailing in the official examinations, rose to senior military positions.

When I was young, I often heard this story, sometimes exactly the same, sometimes with small variations, and sometimes people said it was all false. At the end of Dali reign period,[4] I encountered the County Magistrate of Laiwu,[5] Zhang Zhonggui. Zhang Yi was his great uncle, and Zhang told me the whole story from beginning to end in great detail. And that is why I record it here.

---

[4]766–779 under Emperor Daizong.

[5]Present-day Laiwu city in Shandong.

"Lihun ji" 離魂記

陳玄祐

天授三年，清河張鎰，因官家于衡州。

性簡靜，寡知友。無子，有女二人。其長早亡；幼女倩娘，端妍絕倫。鎰外甥太原王宙，幼聰悟，美容範。鎰常器重，每曰："他時當以倩娘妻之。"

后各長成。宙與倩娘常私感想於寤寐，家人莫知其狀。

後有賓寮之選者求之，鎰許焉。女聞而鬱抑；宙亦深恚恨。托以當調，請赴京，止之不可，遂厚遣之。宙陰恨悲慟，決別上船。

日暮，至山郭數里。夜方半，宙不寐，忽聞岸上有一人，行聲甚速，須臾至船。問之，乃倩娘徒行跣足而至。宙驚喜發狂，執手問其從來。泣曰："君厚意如此，寢夢相感。今將奪我此志，又知君深情不易，思將殺身奉報，是以亡命來奔。"宙非意所望，欣躍特甚。遂匿倩娘於船，連夜遁去。

倍道兼行，數月至蜀。凡五年，生兩子，與鎰絕信。其妻常思父母，涕泣言曰："吾曩日不能相負，棄大義而來奔君。向今五年，恩慈間阻。覆載之下，胡顏獨存也？"

宙哀之，曰："將歸，無苦。"遂俱歸衡州。

既至，宙獨身先鎰家，首謝其事。鎰曰："倩娘病在閨中數年，何其詭說也！"宙曰："見在舟中！"鎰大驚，促使人驗之。果見倩娘在船中，顏色怡暢，訊使者曰："大人安否？"家人異之，疾走報鎰。

室中女聞，喜而起，飾妝更衣，笑而不語，出與相迎，翕然而合為一體，其衣裳皆重。

其家以事不正，秘之。惟親戚間有潛知之者。后四十年間，夫妻皆喪。二男並孝廉擢第，至丞、尉。

41

　　玄祐少常聞此說，而多異同，或謂其虛。大曆末，遇萊蕪縣令
張仲規，因備述其本末。鎰則仲規堂叔［祖］，而說極備悉，故記之。

Tale 1.4

The World Inside a Pillow

By Shen Jiji
Translated by William H. Nienhauser, Jr.

In the seventh year of the Kaiyuan reign period (719) there was a certain old Taoist priest surnamed Lü who had acquired the arts of the divine immortals. While traveling on the road to Handan,[1] he rested at an inn. Taking off his cap and loosening his belt, he sat down and leaned up against his pack. Suddenly he saw a young traveler, one Mr. Lu. He was wearing a short robe[2] and riding a black colt, and he had also stopped at the inn on his way to the fields. He sat down on the same mat as the old man and they chatted and laughed amicably.

After a while Lu, looking at the shabbiness of his own dress, sighed deeply and said, "A great man born out of his time; such is my distress!"

---

[1]Handan was the capital of the Zhao 趙 in the Warring States period. During the Tang it was only the seat of a county government, and it was at the site of modern Handan city in Hebei province. See Liu Xu 劉昫 (877–946), *Jiu Tang shu* 舊唐書, 39. 1498, and Tan Qixiang 譚其驤, *Zhongguo lishi dituji* 中国歷史地圖集, 5. 49.

[2]Such apparel indicated the status of a commoner; officials wore long robes.

"To look at you, you don't seem to be suffering or ill," the old man said. "Just now we were chatting away happily; why do you suddenly moan about your distress?"

"But mine is such an insignificant life! How can you speak of being happy?"

"If yours can't be called a happy life, then what is a happy life?"

"A man is born to do great deeds and build a name for himself, to be a general outside the court and a minister in it, to arrange lavish caldrons to eat from, to select music to listen to, to bring prosperity to his clan and richness to his family. Only after this can one speak of happiness! I've 'set my heart upon learning' and have been enriched by engaging in the arts.[3] All these years I've considered that the green and purple official robes were mine for the taking. Now I'm already at my prime and still I toil in the fields and ditches. If this is not distress, what is it?" Having finished this speech the young man's eyes grew blurry and he felt sleepy.

At that time the innkeeper was steaming millet. The old man reached into his pack, took out a pillow, and gave it to Lu, saying, "Rest your head on this pillow. It'll surely allow you to experience a kind of success as full of splendor as that which you set your heart upon." The pillow was made of green porcelain, and there was an opening at each end. The young man nodded his head and lay down on it; then he noticed that the apertures were becoming large and bright. He stood up, entered the pillow, and found himself getting back to his own home.

Several months later he married a girl of the Cui family from Qinghe.[4] The girl was extremely beautiful, and the young man became wealthier and wealthier. He was greatly pleased. His

---

[3]Paraphrasing maxims of Confucius in the *Analects*.

[4]This clan from Qinghe (Qinghe; in modern Hebei) was one of the "Seven great surnames" of the Tang. Marriage to a girl of one of these families was considered a most important first step to making one's career and fortune.

clothes and equipage grew daily more bright and splendid. The following year he participated in the *jinshi* examination, ascended the rank, and put on the robe of collator in the Department of the Imperial Library. By taking a special imperial examination he was then transferred to be the magistrate of Weinan County (in modern Shanxi Province). Soon he was promoted to investigating censor, and then moved to be a diarist of imperial activity and repose and the director of decrees. Three years thereafter he was sent out to take charge of the prefecture of Tongzhou (in modern Shanxi), then transferred to become the prefect of Shan [prefecture] (in modern Henan). He had a natural proclivity for construction work and built a canal from Shan to a point eighty *li* west to bypass some impassable spots in the river. The people of the area so profited thereby they erected a stone tablet to record his accomplishments. He was given charge of the prefecture of Bianzhou (modern Kaifeng in Henan), then received the position of the investigating commissioner of the Henan Circuit, and was later summoned to be the mayor of the capital.

That year the Spiritual and Martial Emperor was about to engage the western and northern barbarians and thereby increase his lands, when the Tibetan generals Stagra [Konlog] (Ximoluo [Konglu]) and Cogro Manpoci (Zhulong Manbuzhi) attacked and seized the prefectures of Guazhou and Shazhou.[5] The regional commander, Wang Junchuo, had just recently been killed,[6] and the entire area between the Yellow River and the Huang River was in turmoil. The emperor, longing for a capable commander, appointed Lu as vice-president of the Censorate and regional commander of

---

[5]Both of these places are in present Gansu Province, with Shazhou much better known under its later name, Dunhuang 敦煌. Given the high degree of actuality in the historical data used in this story, "Guasha" may be the corruption of "Guazhou," as historically only Guazhou was attacked by the Tibetans in 727.

[6]Historically, Wang was indeed killed in 727.

the Hexi Circuit.[7] Lu crushed the barbarian rabble, cutting off seven thousand heads and opening up nine hundred *li* of land. Then he had three great fortifications built to protect the strategic positions. The people living along the frontier set up a tablet at the Juyen Mountain (In modern Gansu) to praise him. When he returned to court, his merits were recorded by the official historians, and the favor and courtesy he received were extremely splendid. He was transferred to be the second minister of the ministry of Personnel, and was later made concurrently the head of the Ministry of Finance and the president of the Censorate. His contemporaries viewed him as pure and dignified; the people loved him almost unanimously.

His success, however, was envied by the prime minister, who attacked him with unfounded slander; and thus he was demoted to prefect of Duanzhou.[8] After three years he was summoned to become a counselor to the emperor, and before long became the prime minister. Together with Xiao Song, the president of the Department of the Secretariat, and Pei Guangting, the president of the Department of the Chancellery,[9] he controlled major policy for the next dozen years. He saw the emperor three times a day with excellent plans and secret orders, and by presenting what needed to be renewed or replaced and enlightening the emperor, he became recognized as a capable prime minister.

Then his colleagues cast aspersions on him, accusing him of being in league with border commanders and plotting rebellion. An edict ordered that he be imprisoned; officers of the capital led their followers to his door and quickly restrained him. He was extremely

---

[7]Referring to the area to the west of the Yellow River, covering parts of modern Shanxi, Gansu, and Inner Mongolia.

[8]In modern Guangdong Province — a very remote area in Tang times.

[9]Historically, Xiao Song was appointed the president of the Department of the Secretory in mid-729, and Pei Guangting was made the president of the Department of the Chancellery in early 730.

frightened at this sudden turn of events and said to his wife, "At my home in Shandong I have about five hundred *mu* of fine land, enough to protect us from hunger and cold. What affliction could have caused me to seek an official's salary? Now that things have come to this, even if I long to put on that short coarse robe again and ride that black colt back down the road to Han-tan, it's impossible." Then he drew his knife and was about to slit his throat, but his wife stopped him in time. All others implicated died, but he alone was protected by the eunuchs so that his death sentence was commuted. He was then banished to the prefecture of Huanzhou.[10] After a few years the emperor learned that he was wronged and again sought him out to be the president of the Department of the Secretariat, enfeoffed him as duke of Yen, and favored him exceedingly.

He had five sons — Jian, Chuan, Wei, Ti, and Yi — all capable and talented. Jian passed the *jinshi* examination and became an auxiliary secretary in the Bureau of Scrutiny in the Ministry of Personnel. Chuan became a censor in the Bureau of General Affairs of the Censorate. Wei was made an assistant in the Office of Imperial Sacrifices, and Ti the magistrate of Wannian County.[11] Yi was the most virtuous, becoming a vice-president of the Department of State Affairs at the age of twenty-eight. Lu's in-laws were all of the most respected families in the empire, and he had over a dozen grandsons.

Twice banished to the barren frontiers, Lu returned both times as a pillar of the state. Serving out of and in the central court, roundabout the various offices and ministries, for over fifty years Lu's life was mighty and grand. Lu was naturally inclined to extravagance and luxury, fond of indulgence and pleasure. The sounds and sights of his harem were all of the uppermost beauty. Those fine lands, excellent mansions, beautiful women, and

---

[10]In modern Vietnam.

[11]In the present Shanxi Province.

celebrated steeds presented to him through the years were too numerous to tally.

In his later years he gradually became debilitated and often asked to be relieved of his posts, but this was not allowed. When he was ill, envoys from court would come to ask after him so frequently that they trod in one another's footsteps. Every famous physician and exalted medicine made its way to him. On the point of dying, he submitted the following memorandum:

> Your servant was originally a student from Shandong, with fields and gardens as his pleasures. By chance he encountered sagely fate and has obtained a series of official posts respectively. Receiving too much exceptional reward, particular bounty, and extensive favor, he was thronged by banners of an imperial representative as he went out from the capital and was elevated to be the prime minister on returning. In handling business both in and out of the central court, he has passed through many years. Ashamed of the imperial favor he has enjoyed, he has been of no aid to the morally efficacious emanations of Your Majesty. A base fellow playing a gentleman's role, he has bequeathed only plunder; treading as if on thin ice, he has increased his misgivings, so that, as each day he dreads the next, old age has arrived unawares. This year he will pass eighty but still holding the highest possible government post among the Three Dukes. His time has already run out; muscle and bone have already grown infirm. He senses that there will be no recovery; his health is failing fast, his time of service nearing its end. He considers that there is no deed which can repay the sagely approbation of Your Majesty. In vain has he carried the deep imperial favor. Now he takes leave forever of the saintly reign. Although his feeling of attachment is unbounded, he respectfully offers this memorandum to express his gratitude.

The reply read:

> With your eminent virtue you have served as our chief support. Outside the central court, you have screened us like a hedge, upheld us like a buttress. In the central court, you have assisted us in bringing about harmony and prosperity. The tranquility and peace of the last two dozen years have truly been in your trust. When you contracted this illness, we daily expressed our hope of your recovery. Not expecting this grave infirmity, we are truly taken with sympathy. Now we have ordered the Grand General of Cavalry, Gao Lishi,[12] to go to your house, ask after you. May we press you to take extra care of yourself for our sake. We still hope for nothing rash, and await your recovery.

That evening he died.

With a yawn Lu stretched and awoke to find himself lying in the inn. He found the oldster was sitting beside him and the millet which the host had been steaming was not yet ready. Everything was as before. Startled, the scholar got up, saying, "Could it all have been a dream?"

"The happinesses of human life are all like that," the old man replied.

Lu sat lost in thought for a long time, and then thanked the old man: "Of the ways of favor and disgrace, the vagaries of distress and prosperity, the pattern of accomplishment and failure, the emotions of life and death, I have thoroughly been made aware. In this way, sir, you have checked my desires. How could I dare fail to profit from this lesson?"

Then he kowtowed twice to the old man, and left.

Note: This translation is revised from my 1986 version in Y. W. Ma and Joseph S. M. Lau, ed., *Traditional Chinese Stories: Themes and Variations* (New York: Columbia University Press, 1978), pp. 435–38.

---

[12]The most trusted eunuch of Emperor Xuanzong 玄宗 (r. 712–756). He was given this lavish title in 748.

"Zhenzhong Ji" 枕中記

沈既濟

　　開元六年，道士有呂翁者，得神仙術，行邯鄲道中，息邸舍，攝帽弛帶，隱囊而坐。俄見旅中少年，乃盧生也。衣短褐，乘青駒，將適于田，亦止於邸中，與翁共席而坐，言笑殊暢。

　　久之，盧生顧其衣裝敝褻，乃長嘆息曰："大丈夫生世不諧，困如是也。"翁曰："觀子形體，無苦無恙，談諧方適，而談其困者，何也？"生曰："吾此苟生耳，何適之謂？"翁曰："此不謂適而何謂適？"答曰："士之生世，當建功樹名，出將人相，列鼎而食，選聲而聽，使族益昌而家益肥，然後可以言適乎。吾嘗志於學，富於遊藝，自惟當年，青紫可拾。今已適壯，猶勤畎畝，非困而何？"言訖，而目昏思寐。

　　時主人方蒸黍，翁乃探囊中枕以授之，曰："子枕吾枕，當令子榮適如志。"其枕青瓷，而竅其兩端。生俯首就之，見其竅漸大，明朗，乃舉身而入，遂至其家。

　　數月，娶清河崔氏女。女容甚麗，生資愈厚。生大悅，由是衣裝服馭，日益鮮盛。明年，舉進士，登第；釋褐秘校；應制，轉渭南尉，俄遷監察御史，轉起居舍人，知制誥。三載，出典同州，遷陝牧。生姓好土功，自陝西鑿河八十里，以濟不通。邦人利之，刻石紀德。移節汴州，領河南道採訪使，征為京兆尹。是歲，神武皇帝方事戎狄，恢宏土宇。會吐蕃悉抹邏及燭龍莽布支攻陷瓜沙，而節度使王君㚟新被殺，河湟震動。帝思將帥之才，遂除生御史中丞，河西道節度。大破戎虜，斬首七千級，開地九百里，築三大城以遮要害。邊人立石於居延山以頌之。歸朝冊勛，恩禮極盛。轉吏部侍郎，遷戶部尚書兼御史大夫。時望清重，群情翕習。大為時宰所忌，以飛語中之，貶為端州刺史。三年，征為常侍。未幾，同中書門下

50

平章事。與蕭中令嵩、裴侍中光庭同執大政十餘年，嘉謨密令，一日三接，獻替啟沃，號為賢相。同列害之，復誣與邊將交接，所圖不軌。下制獄。府吏引從至其門而急收之。生惶駭不測，謂妻子曰：

　　"吾家山東，有良田五頃，足以禦寒餒。何苦求祿？而今及此，思衣短褐、乘青駒，行邯鄲道中，不可得也。"引刃自刎。其妻救之，獲免。其罹者皆死，獨生為中官保之，減罪死，投驩州。數年，帝知冤，復追為中書令，封燕國公，恩旨殊異。生五子，曰儉、曰傳、曰位、曰倜、曰倚，皆有才器。儉進士登第，為考功員外；傳為侍御史；位為太常丞；倜為萬年尉；倚最賢，年二十八，為左襄。其姻媾皆天下望族。有孫十餘人。兩竄荒徼，再登台鉉，出入中外，徊翔台閣，五十餘年，崇盛赫奕。性頗奢盪，甚好佚樂。後庭聲色，皆第一綺麗。前後賜良田、甲第、佳人、名馬，不可勝數。後年漸衰邁，屢乞骸骨，不許。病，中人候問，相踵於道，名醫上藥，無不至焉。將歿，上疏曰："臣本山東諸生，以田圃為娛。偶逢聖運，得列官敘。過蒙殊獎，特秩鴻私。出擁節旌，入升台輔。周旋中外，綿歷歲時。有忝天恩，無裨聖化。負乘貽寇，履薄增憂。日俱一日，不知老至。今年逾八十，位極三事，鐘漏並歇，筋骸俱耄。彌留沈頓，待時益盡。顧無成效，上答休明，空負深恩，永辭聖代。無任感戀之至，謹奉表陳謝。"

　　詔曰："卿以俊德，作朕元輔。出擁藩翰，入贊雍熙，昇平二紀，實卿所賴。比嬰疾疹，日謂痊平。豈斯沉痼，良用憫惻。今令驃騎大將軍高力士就第候省。其勉加針石，為予自愛。猶冀無妄，期於有瘳。"是夕，薨。

　　盧生欠伸而悟，見其身方偃於邸舍，呂翁坐其傍，主人蒸黍未熟，觸類如故。生蹶然而興，曰："豈其夢寐也？"翁謂生曰："人生之適，亦如是矣。"生憮然良久，謝曰："夫寵辱之道，窮達之運，得喪之理，死生之情，盡知之矣。此先生所以窒吾欲也。敢不受教。"稽首再拜而去。

Tale 1.5

The Tale of Miss Ren

By Shen Jiji
Translated by William H. Nienhauser, Jr.

Miss Ren was a fox-fairy.

There was a certain prefect, named Wei Yin, who was the ninth son in his family and an external grandson of Li Wei, the prince of Xin'an. Since his youth, he had been uncontrolled and fond of drinking. His cousin's husband, Zheng the Sixth, whose given name was forgotten, had previously been a practitioner of martial arts and was also fond of wine and women. Zheng was poor and had no family left, so he threw his lot in with the clansmen of his wife. He became friends with Wei Yin and they always caroused together.

In the sixth month of the ninth year of the Tianbao reign period [750], in the middle of summer, Wei Yin and Zheng the Sixth had been riding together through the streets of Chang'an and were going to drink at the New Prosperity Quarter. When they reached a point south of the Peace Prevailing Quarter [immediately to the west of New Prosperity], Zheng requested to leave temporarily with an excuse, and he promised to go to the tavern later on. Wei then rode his white horse on to the east, while Zheng turned south on his donkey into the northern gate of the Peace Prevailing Quarter.

There Zheng happened upon three women walking in the

street. Among them was one dressed in white and of an enchanting beauty. When Zhang saw her he was delightfully surprised and whipped his donkey up alongside them, staying a bit behind or in front, wanting to dally with her but not daring to.

The one in white kept on making eyes at him as if she were interested in him. Zheng jested with her: "Why does such a beautiful girl as you travel on foot?."

"When someone has a mount but won't let me use it, what else can I do?" the girl replied, smiling.

"Though my nag's not good enough to carry you, I'd like to offer it to you at once, and I'll be content by following along on foot."

They looked at each other and laughed, and with the two maids taking turns leading him on, they were soon on quite intimate terms. Thus Zheng the Sixth followed them on their way eastwards. By the time they arrived at the Pleasure Gardens, night had fallen. He saw a mansion and, through a carriage gate in the earthen wall, the dignified arrangement of the household. As the girl in white was about to enter, she turned and told him, "Please wait for a moment," and then she went in. One of the maids who had accompanied her stayed in the gateway and asked his name and age. Zheng told her and asked similar questions about the lady in white.

"Her surname's Ren and she's the twentieth child in her family," the maid replied.

After a little while he was invited in. He hitched his donkey at the gate and placed his hat on the saddle, before noticing that a woman in her early thirties was bidding him welcome. This was Miss Ren's elder sister. Candles had been lit and a feast was laid out. By the time Zheng had drunk several goblets of wine, Ren appeared, freshly made up. They drank heartily to their heart's content. Far into the night they went to bed. Her lovely appearance and beautiful body, each song or smile, her manners and movements, all were captivating, almost otherworldly!

Just before dawn Ren said, "You must go! My sister and I are associated with the imperial music bureaus and serve in the Southern Tribunal.[1] We have to go out at dawn, so you can't tarry." So they arranged another rendezvous and he left.

He walked along until he reached the gate that led out of the quarter, but it was still barred. To one side there was a Tartar bakery. The proprietor had just lit a lamp and was preparing to start a fire in his stove. Zheng sat down to rest under the eaves of his shop to wait for the morning drums,[2] and he spoke with the bakery owner.

"If you go east from here, you'll come to a gate in the wall," Zheng said, pointing to the place where he had spent the night. "Whose residence is that?"

"There's only some broken-down walls, and grounds which have been let go — no house."

"But I just stopped there. How can you say it's not there?"

He argued obstinately with the man until the latter suddenly understood. "Ah, ha! I see! There's a fox spirit around there who often beguiles men into spending the night with her. She's been seen three times already. You met her, too?"

Zheng blushed, but to conceal it from him said simply, "No."

After it had become light, he went again to examine the place and found the earthen wall and the carriage gate as before. When he peered in, however, there were only overgrown fields and abandoned gardens.

When he had returned and saw Wei Yin, the latter upbraided him for failing to keep their appointment. Zheng did not reveal his

---

[1] In T'ang times, the Southern Tribunal referred collectively to the offices of the prime ministers because the departments of the Chancellery, the Secretariat, and State Affairs were all located at the southern portion of the imperial palace complex. Two imperial music bureaus were also located there.

[2] The morning drums signaled the opening of the gates.

secret but replied that he had been engaged in some other matter. But longing for the girl's bewitching beauty, he had never given up the desire of seeing her again.

After a fortnight or so, Zheng was out for a stroll, and as he went into a clothing stall in the Western Market, he caught a glimpse of her. She was attended by the same maids as before. Zheng hurriedly called to her, but she turned around and spun into the crowd to hide. Zheng continued to call her and pressed after her. It was only then she turned her back to him and, speaking from behind her fan, said, "You know all about me. Why do you get close to me again?"

"Although I know it," he answered. "What does that matter?"

"This whole affair is shameful. I find it difficult to face you."

"The way I long for you with all my heart, how can you bear to leave me again?"

"How could I dare? I'm just afraid you'll find me repugnant."

Zheng vowed his love in words even more sincere. Ren then glanced around at him and lowered her fan, revealing a ravishing beauty as brilliant as before. "I'm not the only one of us in the world of men," she said. "It's just that you can't recognize the others. Don't feel that I alone am strange."

Zheng demanded another rendezvous.

"People dread us because of the harm we do," she responded. "But I'm not like that. If you won't despise me, I'll wait on you hand and foot forever."

Zheng promised to find a place for her to stay. "East of here," she said, "there is a huge tree growing out of the ridgepole of a house on a quiet, secluded lane. We can rent it and live there. Last time we met someone riding off eastward from the south side of Peace Prevailing on a white horse. That was your wife's cousin, wasn't it? His house had a lot of superfluous furniture. We can borrow some of it."

At that time Wei Yin's uncles were all at posts in every corner of the country and three households of goods had been stored away there. Zheng made inquiries about the house as she had instructed him and went to Wei Yin to borrow the furnishings. His cousin wanted to know what he planned to use them for. Zheng replied, "I've recently acquired a beauty, and have already rented a place. I want to borrow these things to keep in service."

Wei Yin smiled. "With your looks, you must have got hold of some hag! How could she be that beautiful?" Then he loaned him everything — curtains, draperies, bedding, and mats — and had a clever young servant boy tag along to get a peek at the girl. Before long the boy came running back to report, out of breath and covered with sweat. Wei greeted him with a question, "Was she there?" And he asked further, "What'd she look like?"

"Uncanny! Like nothing in the world you've ever seen!"

Now there were a good many relatives in Wei Yin's clan, and he had of old followed such indulgent ways that he knew many beauties. So he asked, "Is she as beautiful as so-and-so?"

"She can't be compared to her!"

Wei reeled off the names of four or five beautiful women for comparison, but the reply was always: "Can't be compared to her!"

At that time Wei Yin's sister-in-law, the sixth daughter of the prince of Wu, was as captivating as a fairy. Among the girls in the clan of Wei and his cousins as well, she was always considered the most beautiful. Wei Yin asked, "How would she stack up against Prince Wu's sixth daughter?"

Again the answer was: "Can't be compared to her!"

Wei Yin clapped his hands in astonishment. "How on earth could there be such a beauty?" He hurriedly ordered water, washed his [face and] neck, put on a new turban, daubed some color to his lips, and set off for Zheng's.

He arrived as Zheng had just left. Upon entering he saw a young manservant with a broom in his hands sweeping up, and a maid standing near the door. No one else was to be seen. He questioned the lad, who smiled and replied that no one was at home. Wei looked around and saw a red skirt protruding from under a door. He stepped forward to take a closer look and saw Ren crouched in hiding behind the leaf of the door. He pulled her out into the light to get a better look — she was even more beautiful than she had been reported to be. Wei nearly went out of his mind with passion. He took her into his arms, intending to ravage her, but she would not submit. He restrained her physically, and when he had nearly forced her, she said, "I'll give in, but please let go of me for a moment!" As soon as he acquiesced, she struggled as hard as in the beginning. It went on like this several times. Then Wei held her tight with all his strength. Ren was exhausted, and she was sweating as if drenched in rain. Since she knew there was no way to avoid him, she relaxed and resisted no longer, but her expression suddenly became very sorrowful.

"What are you so unhappy about?" Wei Yin asked.

She sighed deeply and then replied, "What a pitiful man Zheng the Sixth is!"

"What do you mean by that?"

"Though Zheng is a full six feet tall, he can't even protect a woman. He's no real man! You've been living an unbridled and extravagant life since youth, and have taken numerous beauties, many of whom must have been similar to or even better than I. But Zheng is poor and I am all that he can call his contentment. How can you, in seeking to indulge yourself even further, take from someone who has never had enough? I take pity on him, because he's poor and hungry and can't support himself, because he wears your clothes, eats your food, and is completely controlled by you. If he could earn his own living, he would never come down to such a situation."

When Wei Yin, who was a chivalrous and righteous man, heard this speech, immediately let her go. He tidied his dress and sleeves and apologized, "I dare not to be impolite like this anymore." Soon Zheng returned and they met one another joyously.

From this time on, Wei Yin provided Ren with all her daily necessities such as firewood, rice, and meat. She often stopped by Wei's home on her way in or out, whether by carriage, on horseback, in a sedan chair, or on foot — she did not make a practice of staying at home. Wei took part in her daily excursions, and they enjoyed each other's company very much. Even though they became intimate to the extent that there was no taboo between them, they never went beyond the bounds of propriety. Thus Wei loved and respected her, and never grudged anything she needed. Even when eating or drinking, he never forgot her. Since Ren understood his love for her, she professed her thanks to him. "It shames me to be so loved by you, but I see myself too rude and unrefined to requite your magnanimity. Moreover, since I can't forsake Zheng, I can't act according to your wishes. I come from Qin, born and raised here in the capital — from a line of entertainers. Among my sisters and cousins there are many mistresses and concubines. Thus I know the gay quarters of Chang'an very well. If there is an attractive young lady you've admired, but have not yet been able to meet, I could carry her off for you. I would like to do this to repay your kindness."

"That would be perfect!" Wei Yin exclaimed. In the market there was a girl who sold clothes named Zhang the Fifteenth. She looked fair and pure. Wei had long admired her and therefore asked Ren if she knew her.

"She's one of my cousins. It will be easy to arrange."

And, indeed, in less than two weeks it was set up. After several months he grew tired of her and ended the affair.

"Market girls are easy enough to procure," Ren professed. "They don't serve to demonstrate my efficiency. If you know of some girl who is secluded and difficult to get at, please let me know. I would like to try my very best."

Wei Yin said, "The other day during the Cold Food Festival,[3] as a couple of friends and I were strolling by the Temple of a Thousand Blessings, we saw General Diao Mian's women giving a musical performance in the hall. There was one who was skilled at the flute, about sixteen years old, with braided hair hanging down about her ears. She was exquisitely beautiful. Do you know her by any chance?"

"She is [the general's favorite mistress] called Chongnu. Her mother is my elder sister. I can get her for you."

Wei Yin bowed down to her, and she again promised him help. Then she began to frequent the Diao residence, and this continued for more than a month. When Wei pressed her to learn of her plans, Ren requested two rolls of fine silk to be used as a bribe. He supplied them to her as ordered. Two days later, just as they had sat down to a meal, one of the general's servants leading a black steed came to pick up Ren. At the news of the invitation, she smiled and said to Wei, "Things are falling into place!" Ren had previously tainted Chongnu with an infection which neither acupuncture nor medicine could alleviate. Both the girl's mother and the general had become so worried that they were about to resort to the help of a number of shamanesses. One of them had been secretly bribed by Ren to indicate the area in which Ren lived as an auspicious place to move the patient. As soon as she had examined the girl, the shamaness said, "It is not good for her to stay here. She should be moved to a certain place to the southeast, so that she can regain the vital forces necessary for life."

The general and the girl's mother paid a visit to the area and realized that Ren lived there. General Diao then asked if his mistress might live there. Ren began to exaggerate the cramped nature of her quarters, but after the general had repeatedly entreated her, she finally consented. Then, in a carriage together

---

[3]The day before the spring festival Qingming, when no fire is lit and only cold food is served.

with her clothing and other playthings, and accompanied by her mother, the lady was carried to Ren's. On her arrival there she recovered. Before a few days had passed, Ren had secreted Wei in the house and brought them together. After a month the girl became pregnant. Her mother took fright and immediately brought her back to General Diao. Thus the affair was broken off.

One day Ren said to Zheng, "Can you get hold of five or six thousand in cash? I could help you make a good profit."

"Sure," Zheng replied. Then he got a loan of six thousand from someone.

"There's a horse trader in the market who has a horse with a blemish on one haunch," she explained. "Buy it and keep it home."

Zheng went to the market and there, indeed, he saw a man leading a horse with a dark blemish on its left haunch, which he was trying to sell. Zheng bought it and returned. His brothers-in-law all jeered at him. "That's a no-good beast! What did you buy it for?"

After a little while Ren told him that the horse could now be sold and that he should get thirty thousand for it. Zheng then took it out to sell. Someone offered him twenty thousand, but he refused. The entire marketplace buzzed with talk like "Why is he offering so much?" and "Why won't the other sell?" Zheng mounted and went home. The buyer followed him to the door, repeatedly raising his offers, until he had reached twenty-five thousand. Still not giving in, Zheng told him, "I won't sell for less than thirty." His brothers-in-law all railed at him. Zheng could not stand any more and, in the end, he sold it for under thirty thousand.

Later Zheng went on the sly to question the buyer and find out his true motives. He learned that an imperial horse with a blemish on its haunch kept at the Zhaoying County[4] had died three years ago. This man who had been the functionary in charge was about to leave the post, and the government would charge him sixty

---

[4]In modern Shanxi Province.

thousand for the horse. He had reckoned that if he could buy a substitute for half the price, his savings would be considerable. And, with this horse he could claim provisions for the horse for the past three years, making his losses quite minimal. For these reasons he had to buy it.

Since Ren's clothes were old and shabby, she asked Wei Yin for new ones. Wei was about to buy a roll of silk for her, but she did not want it: "I'd rather have ready-made clothes." Wei summoned a salesman, Zhang the Eldest, to buy for her, and sent him to learn what she had in mind. After Zhang had seen her, he told Wei in a state of bewilderment. "She must be a fairy or someone from the royal household whom you've stolen away. Furthermore, she can't belong to this mundane world! You should send her back right away; don't get yourself in trouble." Such was the effect that her beauty had on men. But what her reasons were for buying ready-made clothes rather than sewing them herself actually were, Wei had no way to find out.

More than a year later Zheng received his reassignment to become Courageous and Intrepid Deputy Commander of the Huaili Militia[5] in Jincheng County.[6] At that time Zheng had taken a lawful wife and, although he was free to go wherever he pleased during the day, at night he had to sleep at home. He often regretted that he could not devote his nights completely to Ren. As he was about to go to his new post, he entreated Ren to come along. She did not want to go: "We'll be on the road for half a month or so. That won't make for any fun. I beg you to leave me what you think I'll need for food and expenses, and I'll wait here for your return."

Though Zheng earnestly beseeched her, she only became more insistent. Zheng then went to Wei Yin for help. Wei exhorted her once more and pressed her for her reasons. After some time she

---

[5]Huaili Militia is a fictitious invention of the author.

[6]Near the present Gaolan County in Gansu Province.

replied, "A shamaness told me it would be unlucky for me to travel west this year. So I don't want to go."

Though Zheng was greatly puzzled, he did not press for further explanations. Together with Wei, he laughed at Ren: "How can anyone be as intelligent as you are and yet so bewildered by such groundless words?" Then he entreated her more firmly.

"If the prophecy comes true," she reasoned, "I'll die in vain for you. What good will that be?"

The two men merely replied, "That's ridiculous," and they begged her as earnestly as before. Since she could see no way out, Ren finally agreed to go. Wei lent her a horse and saw them as far as Lingao,[7] where they drank some wine in farewell and parted.

After a couple of days they came to Mawei Slope.[8] Ren rode in front, with Zheng close behind on his donkey. The maids on other horses trailed along after them. At that time some of the grooms of the imperial West Gate Stables were training dogs to hunt at Luochuan.[9] They had been at it for more than ten days. It so happened that just as they ran into one another on the road, a black dog sprang out from the grass. Zheng saw Ren suddenly drop to the ground, change back into her original shape, and race away to the south. The black dog followed. Zheng ran along after shouting, trying to stop them, but he could not. After a little more than a *li*, she was caught by the dog.

Fighting back tears Zheng took money from his pack to redeem

---

[7]A courier station to the west of the Tang capital.

[8]Mawei was a courier station well known in Chinese history as the location at which the celebrated Tang beauty Yang Guifei was put to death. See the preamble in "Hang Wuniang Sells Her Charms at the New Bridge Market" in this anthology for a summary of the event.

[9]Luochuan, probably a corruption of Luoshui (Luo River), joins with the Wei and Yellow Rivers, east of Chang'an. It would not be likely that Zheng's route would take them near this river, and there seems to be a geographical inconsistency here.

her body for burial, and cut some wood to make a marker. When he turned and looked at her horse, it was grazing alongside the road. Her clothes lay in a heap on the saddle and her shoes and stockings still hung from the stirrups, like the empty shell of a cicada. Only her jewelry had fallen to the ground. No other traces were to be seen. Her maids were also gone.

About ten days later Zheng returned to the capital. Wei Yin was delighted to see him back and asked him, "Is Ren well?"

With tears in his eyes Zheng replied, "She's dead."

When Wei heard this he was greatly saddened. Inside the house they gave in completely to their grief. Slowly Wei began to ask about the cause of her death. Zheng answered, "She had been killed by a dog."

"Even if the dog was fierce, how could it kill a human?" Wei queried.

"She wasn't human." Zheng answered.

"Wasn't human! What then?" Wei was startled.

Zheng then told him the whole story, from beginning to end. Astonished, Wei could not help sighing deeply and repeatedly. On the following day he ordered his carriage made ready and went with Zheng to Mawei Slope. He had the grave opened to look at her, mourned her for a long time, and then returned. When they recalled the events of the recent past, they realized that only in her not having clothes tailored was she much different from mortals.

Thereafter Zheng became a superintendent of imperial grounds. His household became very wealthy; he kept a stable of a dozen or so horses, and lived to the age of sixty-five and then died.

During the Dali reign period [766–779],[10] I, Shen Jiji, lived in Zhongling.[11] I often went out with Wei Yin, and since he frequently told me Ren's story, I am most familiar with all the details. Later on

---

[10] Dali is the title of the third reign period of the Tang emperor Daizong (r. 763–779).

[11] In modern Jiangsu Province.

Wei Yin became a censor in the Bureau of State Affairs of the Censorate and concurrently prefect of Longzhou.[12] He died there in office.

Ah, the principles of man can be found in the emotions of supernatural beings! To be accosted and not lose her chasity, to follow one man until death — even among the women of today there are those who could not measure up to her. Unfortunately, Zheng was not a very sensitive man. He only enjoyed Ren's beauty, and never fathomed her character. Had he been a man of truly deep understanding, he might have grasped the principle of changes, found out the limits between spirits and humans, and written it all up beautifully to transmit his more abstruse feelings, rather than just surfeiting himself with her manners and appearance. What a pity!

During the second year of the Jianzhong reign period [781], General Pei Ji of the palace guards, Deputy Mayor Sun Cheng of the capital, Secretary Cui Xu of the Ministry of Finance, Censor Lu Chun of the Department of the Secretariat, and I, at that time a censor in the Department of the Chancellery, were all banished to the southeast. On our way from Qin to Wu,[13] we traveled over land and water together. Zhu Fang, a former censor, purposely arranged a trip so that he could go along with us. As we floated down the Ying River and crossed the Huai River, we lashed our boats together and flowed with the current, feasting by day and talking all the night, each one summoning forth some bizarre tale. When the group had heard the events surrounding Ren, they all sighed and were astonished. Therefore, they asked me to write them up as a record of the unusual. Thus I came to write this account.

Note: This rendition is revised from my 1986 version in Ma and Lau, ed., *Traditional Chinese Stories*, pp. 339–45.

---

[12]In modern Shanxi.
[13]Approximates the present Jiangsu Province.

任氏傳

沈既濟

任氏，女妖也。

有韋使君者，名崟，第九，信安王褘之外孫。少落拓，好飲酒。其從父妹婿曰鄭六，不記其名。早習武藝，亦好酒色，貧無家，託身於妻族；與崟相得，遊處不間。

天寶九年夏六月，崟與鄭子偕行於長安陌中，將會飲於新昌里。至宣平之南，鄭子辭有故，請間去，繼至飲所。崟乘白馬而東。鄭子乘驢而南，入昇平之北門。

偶值三婦人行於道中，中有白衣者，容色姝麗。鄭子見之驚悅，策其驢，忽先之，忽後之，將挑而未敢。

白衣時時盼睞，意有所受。鄭子戲之曰："美豔若此，而徒行，何也？"

白衣笑曰："有乘不解相假，不徒行何爲？"

鄭子曰："劣乘不足以代佳人之步，今輒以相奉。某得步從，足矣。"

相視大笑。同行者更相眩誘，稍已狎暱。鄭子隨之東，至樂遊園，已昏黑矣。見一宅，土垣車門，室宇甚嚴。白衣將入，顧曰："願少踟躕。"而入。女奴從者一人，留於門屏間，問其姓第，鄭子既告，亦問之。

對曰："姓任氏，第二十。"

少頃，延入。鄭繫驢於門，置帽於鞍。始見婦人年三十餘，與之承迎，即任氏姊也。列燭置膳，舉酒數觴。任氏更妝而出，酣飲極歡。夜久而寢，其嬌姿美質，歌笑態度，舉措皆豔，殆非人世所有。

將曉，任氏曰：“可去矣。某兄弟名系教坊，職屬南衙，晨興將出，不可淹留。”乃約後期而去。

既行，及里門，門扃未發。門旁有胡人鬻餅之舍，方張燈熾爐。鄭子憩其簾下，坐以候鼓，因與主人言。鄭子指宿所以問之曰：“自此東轉，有門者，誰氏之宅？”

主人曰：“此隤墉棄地，無第宅也。”

鄭子曰：“適過之，曷以云無？”

與之固爭。主人適悟，乃曰：“吁！我知之矣。此中有一狐，多誘男子偶宿，嘗三見矣，今子亦遇乎？”

鄭子赧而隱曰：“無。”

質明，複視其所，見土垣車門如故。窺其中，皆蓁荒及廢圃耳。

既歸，見崟。崟責以失期。鄭子不泄，以他事對。然想其豔冶，願復一見之，心嘗存之不忘。

經十許日，鄭子游，入西市衣肆，瞥然見之，曩女奴從。鄭子遽呼之。任氏側身周旋於稠人中以避焉。鄭子連呼前迫，方背立，以扇障其後，曰：“公知之，何相近焉？”

鄭子曰：“雖知之，何患？”

對曰：“事可愧恥。難施面目。”

鄭子曰：“勤想如是，忍相棄乎？”

對曰：“安敢棄也，懼公之見惡耳。”

鄭子發誓，詞旨益切。任氏乃回眸去扇，光彩豔麗如初，謂鄭子曰：“人間如某之比者非一，公自不識耳，無獨怪也。”

鄭子請之與敘歡。

對曰：“凡某之流，爲人惡忌者，非他，爲其傷人耳。某則不然。若公未見惡，願終己以奉巾櫛。”

鄭子許與謀棲止。任氏曰：“從此而東，大樹出於棟間者，門巷幽靜，可稅以居。前時自宣平之南，乘白馬而東者，非君妻之昆弟乎？其家多什器，可以假用。”

是時崟伯叔從役於四方，三院什器，皆貯藏之。鄭子如言訪其舍，而詣崟假什器。問其所用。鄭子曰：“新獲一麗人，已稅得其舍，假具以備用。”

崟笑曰：“觀子之貌，必獲詭陋。何麗之絕也。”崟乃悉假帷帳榻席之具，使家僮之惠黠者，隨以覘之。俄而奔走返命，氣吁汗洽。崟迎問之：“有乎？”又問：“容若何？”

曰：“奇怪也！天下未嘗見之矣。”

崟姻族廣茂，且夙從逸遊，多識美麗。乃問曰："孰若某美？"

僮曰："非其倫也！"

崟遍比其佳者四五人，皆曰："非其倫。"

是時吳王之女有第六者，則崟之內妹，穠豔如神仙，中表素推第一。崟問曰："孰與吳王家第六女美？"又曰："非其倫也。"

崟撫手大駭曰："天下豈有斯人乎？"遽命汲水澡頸，巾首膏脣而往。

既至，鄭子適出。崟入門，見小僮擁篲方掃，有一女奴在其門，他無所見。徵於小僮。小僮笑曰："無之。"崟周視室內，見紅裳出於戶下。迫而察焉，見任氏戢身匿於扇間。崟引出就明而觀之，殆過於所傳矣。崟愛之發狂，乃擁而凌之，不服。崟以力制之，方急，則曰："服矣。請少迴旋。"既從，則捍禦如初，如是者數四。崟乃悉力急持之。任氏力竭，汗若濡雨。自度不免，乃縱體不復拒抗，而神色慘變。

崟問曰："何色之不悅？"

任氏長嘆息曰："鄭六之可哀也！"

崟曰："何謂？"

對曰："鄭生有六尺之軀，而不能庇一婦人，豈丈夫哉！且公少豪侈，多獲佳麗，遇某之比者眾矣。而鄭生，窮賤耳。所稱愜者，唯某而已。忍以有餘之心，而奪人之不足乎？哀其窮餒，不能自立，衣公之衣，食公之食，故為公所繫耳。若糠糗可給，不當至是。"

崟豪俊有義烈，聞其言，遽置之，斂衽而謝曰："不敢。"俄而鄭子至，與崟相視咍樂。

自是，凡任氏之薪粒牲餼，皆崟給焉。任氏時有經過，出入或車馬輿步，不常所止。崟日與之遊，甚歡。每相狎暱，無所不至，唯不及亂而已。是以崟愛之重之，無所恡惜，一食一飲，未嘗忘焉。任氏知其愛己，言以謝曰："愧公之見愛甚矣。顧以陋質，不足以答厚意。且不能負鄭生，故不得遂公歡。某，秦人也，生長秦城；家本伶倫，中表姻族，多為人寵媵，以是長安狹斜，悉與之通。或有姝麗，悅而不得者，為公致之可矣。願持此以報德。"

崟曰："幸甚！"廛中有鬻衣之婦曰張十五娘者，肌體凝結，崟常悅之。因問任氏識之乎。

對曰："是某表娣妹，致之易耳。"

旬餘，果致之，數月厭罷。

任氏曰："市人易致，不足以展效。或有幽絕之難謀者，試言之，願得盡智力焉。"

崟曰："昨者寒食，與二三子游於千福寺。見刁將軍緬張樂於殿堂。有善吹笙者，年二八，雙鬟垂耳，嬌姿豔絕。當識之乎？"

任氏曰："此寵奴也。其母，即妾之內姊也。求之可也。"

崟拜於席下。任氏許之。乃出入刁家。月餘，崟促問其計。任氏願得雙縑以爲賂。崟依給焉。後二日，任氏與崟方食，而緬使蒼頭控青驪以迓任氏。任氏聞召，笑謂崟曰："諧矣。"初，任氏加寵奴以病，針餌莫減。其母與緬憂之方甚，將徵諸巫。任氏密賂巫者，指其所居，使言從就爲吉。及視疾，巫曰："不利在家，宜出居東南某所，以取生氣。"

緬與其母詳其地，則任氏之第在焉。緬遂請居。任氏謬辭以逼狹，勤請而後許。乃輦服玩，並其母偕送於任氏。至，則疾愈，未數日，任氏密引崟以通之，經月乃孕。其母懼，遽歸以就緬，由是遂絕。

他日，任氏謂鄭子曰："公能致錢五六千乎？將爲謀利。"鄭子曰："可。"遂假求於人，獲錢六千。

任氏曰："鬻馬於市者，馬之股有疵，可買入居之。"

鄭子如市，果見一人牽馬求售者，眚在左股。鄭子買歸。其妻昆弟皆嗤之，曰："是棄物也。買將何爲？"

無何，任氏曰："馬可鬻矣，當獲三萬。"鄭子乃賣之。有酬二萬，鄭子不與。一市盡曰："彼何苦而貴賣，此何愛而不鬻？"鄭子乘之以歸；買者隨至其門，累增其估，至二萬五千也。不與，曰："非三萬不鬻。"其妻昆弟聚而詬之。鄭子不獲已，遂賣，卒不登三萬。

既而密伺買者，徵其由，乃昭應縣之御馬疵股者，死三歲矣，斯吏不時除籍。官徵其估，計錢六萬。設其以半買之，所獲尚多矣。若有馬以備數，則三年芻粟之估，皆吏得之。且所償蓋寡，是以買耳。

任氏又以衣服故弊，乞衣於崟。崟將買全綵與之。任氏不欲，曰："願得成制者。"崟召市人張大爲買之，使見任氏，問所欲。張大見之，驚謂崟曰："此必天人貴戚，爲郎所竊。且非人間所宜有者，願速歸之，無及於禍。"其容色之動人也如此。竟買衣之成者而不自紉縫也，不曉其意。

後歲餘，鄭子武調，授槐里府果毅尉，在金城縣。時鄭子方有妻室，雖晝遊於外，而夜寢於內，多恨不得專其夕。將之官，邀與任氏俱去。任氏不欲往，曰：「旬月同行，不足以爲歡。請計給糧餼，端居以遲歸。」

鄭子懇請，任氏愈不可。鄭子乃求崟資助。崟與更勸勉，且詰其故。任氏良久，曰：「有巫者言某是歲不利西行，故不欲耳。」鄭子甚惑也，不思其他，與崟大笑曰：「明智若此，而爲妖惑，何哉！」固請之。

任氏曰：「倘巫者言可徵，徒爲公死，何益？」

二子曰：「豈有斯理乎？」懇請如初。任氏不得已，遂行。崟以馬借之，出祖於臨皋，揮袂別去。

信宿，至馬嵬。任氏乘馬居其前，鄭子乘驢居其後；女奴別乘，又在其後。是時西門圉人教獵狗於洛川，已旬日矣。適值於道，蒼犬騰出於草間。鄭子見任氏欻然墜於地，複本形而南馳。蒼犬逐之。鄭子隨走叫呼，不能止。里餘，爲犬所獲。

鄭子銜涕出囊中錢，贖以瘞之，削木爲記。回睹其馬，齧草於路隅，衣服悉委於鞍上，履襪猶懸於鐙間，若蟬蛻然。唯首飾墜地，餘無所見。女奴亦逝矣。

旬餘，鄭子還城。崟見之喜，迎問曰：「任子無恙乎？」

鄭子泫然對曰：「歿矣。」

崟聞之亦慟，相持於室，盡哀。徐問疾故。答曰：「爲犬所害。」崟曰：「犬雖猛，安能害人？」

答曰：「非人。」

崟駭曰：「非人，何者？」

鄭子方述本末。崟驚訝嘆息不能已。明日，命駕與鄭子俱適馬嵬，發瘞視之，長慟而歸。追思前事，唯衣不自制，與人頗異焉。

其後鄭子爲總監使，家甚富，有櫪馬十餘匹。年六十五，卒。

大曆中，沈既濟居鍾陵，嘗與崟遊，屢言其事，故最詳悉。後崟爲殿中侍御史，兼隴州刺史，送歿而不返。

嗟乎，異物之情也有人焉！遇暴不失節，徇人以至死，雖今婦人，有不如者矣。惜鄭生非精人，徒悅其色而不徵其情性。向使淵識之士，必能揉變化之理，察神人之際，著文章之美，傳要妙之情，不止於賞玩風態而已。惜哉！

建中二年，既濟自左拾遺於金吳。將軍裴冀，京兆少尹孫成，戶部郎中崔需，右拾遺陸淳皆適居東南，自秦徂吳，水陸同道。時

前拾遺朱放因旅遊而隨焉。浮穎涉淮，方舟沿流，晝宴夜話，各徵
其異說。眾君子聞任氏之事，共深嘆駭，因請既濟傳之，以誌異云。
沈既濟撰。

Chapter 2

Tale 2.6

Zheng Qinyue Deciphers an Ancient Inscription of the Datong Reign Period

By Li Jifu
Translated by Alister Inglis

During the Tianbao reign period (742–755), there was a recluse from Shangluo[1] named Ren Shengzhi. He once sent a letter to Zheng Qinyue, Rectifier of Omissions for the Right.[2] The letter read:

> From Ren Shengzhi
> In recent years I retired to Shangluo and, for quite some time, have failed to send you news. Having lost contact with both friends and relations, I live a solitary life surrounded by the mountains and forests. I have it in mind to visit you someday as there is something I would ask you about. My ancestor from five generations back served the Liang dynasty as a chamberlain for ceremonials. While initially serving under the Prince of Nanyang, he obtained an ancient inscription from inside a collapsed grave located beneath a cliff at Bell Mountain. No

---

[1] Modern Shangluo, Shanxi.

[2] "Rectifier of omissions" was a bureaucratic title for officials whose duty was to remonstrate against the emperor's personal faults. Two bureaucrats usually served concurrently, distinguished by the terms "left" and "right."

name was given. The inscription, in seal-script, read: "The tortoise speaks of earth while alpine yarrow speaks of water. The princes' zone and the yellow bell open the numinous plot. Buried at three, above, the *geng* day, fallen on seven, middle, the *si* day. Six thousand, three hundred and a duodecad of transitions; two, nine, double three, four hundred to collapse." Although the writing was worn, it was still discernable. The grave subsided after heavy rain which enabled my ancestor to retrieve the inscription. This was in the fourth year of Emperor Wu of Liang's Datong reign period (538). Some days later happened to coincide with the festival of Ullambana.[3] My ancestor, therefore, accompanied the emperor's carriage to the Temple of Universal Peace. There he showed a copy of the inscription to the official historiographer, Yao Zi, and several other academicians. They discussed it for several months, but none knew what it meant. I still have the original in my scroll basket. Your erudition, sir, is nothing less than Heaven-sent while your understanding requires no overt calculation. This is something that past worthies could not attain; something unheard of in either the past or the present. I would have you ascertain and record the inscription's essential meaning so as to fulfill my ancestor's intention. This is my cherished wish.

Ren Shengzhi of Le'an

Several days elapsed and Zheng sent a reply, which read as follows:

I have received your letter. I must apologize for troubling you to write, nonetheless I have been much edified by your words. Your condescending to visit me shows that you have not forgotten our long-standing, mutual regard. You have, furthermore, shown me an ancient inscription from the Datong

---

[3]Ullambana is a Buddhist ceremony intended to deliver tormented souls from Hell. It partly gave rise to the Ghost Festival (*Zhongyuan jie*), during which time ancestral spirits are propitiated.

period. It shames me to say that I possess no far-reaching knowledge. How dare I speak lightly about something beyond the penetration of previous worthies? Yet as I am currently on the road, I have no reference matter to consult. Pondering the matter while in the saddle has yielded some insights.

While I do not know who dug the tomb, I do know that he who divined its location was the greatest sage of his era. For to have interred one in the past yet know the future like the back of one's hand, and to inscribe the end so as to address the beginning without the slightest inaccuracy is no less a feat than Kui Zhao's having predicted the arrival of Commissioner Gong;[4] nothing can surpass it. This may be inferred from the way in which he did not speak of the interment date, but rather recorded the day and hour the grave would collapse, by which he sought the initial omen [indicating an auspicious day for entombment]. The official historian Yao was a luminary of his day. Moreover, he pondered the question with other scholars and had more than enough time to do so. Yet he could not fathom the essentials. How could his erudition be limited to this? The original diviner's having concealed his meaning in subtle language indicates that he was waiting for me to act as Commissioner Gong. Why otherwise would you have approached me? By consulting all available calendars and almanacs, and attempting to throw light on abstruse terminology, I will attempt an explanation that might just elucidate the essentials.

---

[4]Kui Zhao 隗炤 had a deep understanding of the *Classic of Changes*. Before he died, he left his wife with strict, written instructions never to sell their house and charged her to produce them should anyone insist. Sometime after his death, a Commissioner Gong wished to buy the house. The wife refused and showed him her husband's instructions. Gong marveled at Kui's powers of prognostication.

The fourth year of Emperor Wu of Liang's Datong reign period was a *wuwu* year.[5] The reference to "the princes' zone" signifies five hundred whereas "yellow bell" denotes eleven.[6] Together these predict that the grave would collapse after five hundred and eleven years. If we count back five hundred and eleven years from the fourth year of Datong, we arrive at the fourth year of Jianwu (28 CE) in the reign of Emperor Guangwu of the Han dynasty, which was a *wuzi* year.

"Three, above, the *geng* day" refers to the *geng* day of the first cycle of ten days in the third (lunar) month. The new moon of the third month that year was a *xinsi* day. As the tenth day was a *gengyin* day, we may infer that it was early in the third month when the body was interred at Bell Mountain. "Seven, middle, the *si* day" is none other than the *wuwu* day of the seventh month on a day of the new moon. The twelfth was a *jisi* day. This was the day when the grave first collapsed and we know that it was a *jisi* day. "Duodecad" means twelve. From the third month of the fourth year of the Jianwu period to the seventh month of the fourth year of Datong, there are altogether six thousand, three hundred and twelve months. In view of the transition between each month, the inscription reads, "six thousand, three hundred and a duodecad of transitions." Two nines are eighteen while "double three" makes six. The conclusion mentions "four hundred." We

---

[5] This term evokes the ten heavenly stems and twelve earthly branches, a traditional astrologically-based numbering system used to denote years and days.

[6] The "princes' zone" (*dianfu* 甸服) referred to a provincial area beginning five hundred Chinese miles from the imperial capital according to an ancient system that geographically quantified regions according to their distance from the politico-cultural center. "Yellow Bell" (*huangzhong* 黄鐘) refers to the first note among twelve according to the traditional musical scale. Since it corresponded to the eleventh lunar month according to a system of correlative thinking pioneered in early China, the story's protagonist derives the idea of "eleven."

therefore know that six pertains to thousands and that eighteen pertains to tens of thousands. From the tenth *gengyin* day of the third month in the fourth year of the Jianwu period, when the body was initially interred, until the twelfth day of *jisi* in the seventh month of the fourth year of the Datong period when the grave subsided, there were one hundred and eighty-six thousand, four hundred days. The inscription, therefore, reads: "two, nine, double three, four hundred will collapse." What it refers to is merely the number of years, months and days. In regard to years, there are five hundred and eleven as signified by the terms "princes' zone" and "yellow bell"; as for months, there are six thousand, three hundred and twelve which corresponds to "six thousand, three hundred and a duodecad of transitions"; in terms of days, there are one hundred and eighty-six thousand, four hundred which correlates with "two, nine, double three, four hundred will collapse." Using calendars to calculate the period between "three, above, the *geng* day" and "seven, middle, *si* day" there is not a single error. Were there to have been the slightest mistake in regard to the years, months or days, they would not mutually tally. It is likely that the original diviner's meaning has been waiting for me to interpret. Your having approached me, my dear fellow, has made it so.

Nonetheless, I have spent a long time in the bureaucracy and, consequently, my skill has gone to seed. Furthermore, penetrating the meaning of the ancients is difficult. You would do well to make inquiries with someone possessing an understanding of these matters and inform me as to the result. Once the messenger returns, do not apprise them with what I have said.

                                                        Zheng Qinyue

During the Zhenyuan reign period (785–804), [I], Li Jifu, was attached to the Department for State Affairs in the capacity of a supernumerary in the Bureau of State Farms and concurrently an erudite for the Chamberlain of Ceremonials. At the time I had a kinsman, Xun, who was Director of the Ministry of Revenue. During our leisure time in the Department, our conversation touched on Confucian scholars of recent times. Xun told me that, "As for his having made a minute study of predestiny and for his penetrating understanding of the abstruse, the late Rectifier of Omissions for the Right in the Academy of Scholarly Worthies and Auxiliary Academician, Zheng Qinyue, surpassed even that of the monk, Yixing. Since he died at a young age, his name was not well known during his own lifetime. Do you know of him?" I replied, "How did you come to learn of him, brother?" He told me, "During the Tianbao reign period, a recluse of Shangluo, Ren Shengzhi, told me himself that his fifth-generation ancestor served the Liang as a chamberlain for ceremonials. In the fourth year of the Datong period, his ancestor found an ancient inscription at the foot of Bell Mountain. Its meaning was cryptic and so he extensively sought help from Confucian scholars of the day, yet none could fathom its import. He therefore sealed the inscription and charged his sons, 'Future generations of my offspring should take this inscription to those with an understanding of such matters. Should there be someone who apprehends its meaning, I will have no regret.' When it came to Shengzhi, he was learnèd and of good character with a strong love of the Confucian way. Having been apprised of Zheng's reputation, he acquainted him with his ancestor's wish. Zheng told him, 'Once it has been recorded, please show me and I will ponder the matter.' Shengzhi copied the inscription and sent it to him. At the time, Zheng happened to be on state business and had arrived at the Changle official hostel. Once he received the inscription, he began to tease out its mysteries. When he arrived at the River Zi some twenty *li* later, he had already solved the riddle. His letter, therefore, reads, 'Pondering the matter while in the saddle has yielded some insights.' Is this not extraordinary?"

In the *xinwei* year (791), I was transferred to the Ministry of War as a supernumerary. Zheng's son, Kejun, had been transferred from the position of record keeper in the Metropolitan Governor's Office to that of supernumerary in the Transit Authority Bureau. I verified Xun's account with him on several occasions. Although he confirmed the story, he confessed to having lost the written draft. Whenever I contemplated its profound subtlety, I could not help but regret not having perused it myself.

In the *renshen* year (792), I was banished to Ming Prefecture as an administrator. Among the islands thereabout was a recluse named Zhang Xuanyang. As the prefectural commandant highly valued his explication of the *Classic of Changes*, he was housed within the administrative compound. Since he was lecturing on prognostication in regard to the *Classic*, he showed me a manuscript copy of Zheng Qinyue's letter. My elation at receiving the letter could not have been greater had I been handed a treasure. I thereupon collated it and appended the following commentary.

A pile of earth has no sentience. Should it collapse in a rainstorm, it is no more than by chance. Yet one thoroughly conversant with the manifestations of fate had predicted this one hundred and eighty-six thousand, four hundred days in advance. How much less is the inexorable course of peace and disorder, the predestined nature of individual fortune, sages unable to realize their potential, and the [seemingly] serendipitous coming together of a sovereign and his ministers. Events such as Jiang Ya's receiving the title of chieftain after fishing from Semi-Circular Jade Rock, or Confucius' becoming an itinerant counsellor after having fallen from grace,[7] the dream of Fu Yue realized at Yanye,[8] or

---

[7]According to the Weizi section of the *Analects*, Jieyu 接輿, the Madman of Chu, sang a ditty to Confucius pointing to the perils of political office.

Zhang Liang's having received a divine gift while crossing a bridge;[9] these are all tokens of destiny's inevitability. Why was it necessary that Confucius had not sufficient time to sit on a mat for it to warm, or why was Mozi unable to wait for his chimney to grow black?[10] Or was Mengzi sentimental when he neglected to wash rice having departed the State of Qi,[11] or Jia Yi when he composed his elegy after arriving at the banks of the Xiang?[12] Does this mean that the great sages and worthies are themselves still mired in the workings of fate? Or did they resign themselves to destiny's defilement so as to demonstrate its inevitability vis-à-vis mankind? I have no way to know definitively.

---

[8]King Wuding 武丁 of the Shang dynasty dreamed of finding a wise councilor. After a thorough search, Fu Yue 傅説 (alternatively Fuyan) was located at Fuyan 傅岩.

[9]This refers to the story of Zhang Liang 張良 (250?–189 BCE) whom the founding emperor of the Han dynasty, Liu Bang 劉邦 (256–195 BCE), enfeoffed as Marquis of Liu. Before he came to prominence, he was said to have met a god disguised as an old man who gave him a book on military strategy. Zhang used the knowledge therein to support Liu Bang's struggle for supremacy.

[10]This refers to how the itinerant Warring States period (475–221 BCE) thinker, Mozi, did not remain long enough in one location for his chimney to blacken before travelling elsewhere. The allusion to Confucius refers to how he, too, was destined to travel from place to place.

[11]Mengzi 孟子 (c. 372–289 BCE) was a revered Confucian thinker of the Warring States period. After leaving the State of Qi, his haste to return to his beloved homeland was such that he did not bother to wash rice.

[12]Jia Yi 賈誼 (200–168 BCE) was a famous poet and man-of-letters. When he arrived in the Xiang river region of (modern) Hunan, he was reminded of the deceased Warring States period poet and folk-hero, Qu Yuan 屈原 (c. 340–278 BCE), who committed suicide after having been slandered. Jia therefore composed an elegy in his honor.

When Zheng Qinyue, as a Rectifier of Omissions for the Right, later became a Palace Censor, he incurred the enmity of the Grand Councilor, Li Linfu. He was consequently banished to the periphery and was unable to make himself known. Therefore, I have narrated what I heard and appended the two documents so as to illustrate the divine marvels of prognostication, the powerful understanding of a gifted, analytical mind, and the predestined nature of remarkable yet seemingly random occurrences. I offer it to interested parties for their edification and enjoyment.

The twenty-eighth day of the eleventh [lunar] month of the ninth year of Zhenyuan (793).

Recorded by Li Jifu of Zhao Commandery.

編次鄭欽悅辨大同古銘論

李吉甫

天寶中，有商洛隱者任昇之，嘗貽右補闕鄭欽悅書，曰："昇之白。頃退居商洛，久闕披陳，山林獨住，交親兩絕。意有所問，別日垂訪。昇之五代祖仕樑爲太常。初任南陽王帳下，於鐘山懸岸圮壞之中得古銘，不言姓氏。小篆文云：'鼁言土，菁言水，甸服黃鐘啓靈址。瘞在三上庚，墮遇七中巳，六千三百浹辰交，二九重三四百圮。'文雖剝落，仍且分明。大雨之後，纔墮而獲。即梁武大同四年。數日，遇盂蘭大會，從駕同泰寺。錄示史官姚詧並諸學官，詳議數月，無能知者。筐笥之內，遺文尚在。足下學乃天生而知，計舍運籌而會，前賢所不及，近古所未聞。願採其旨要，會其歸趣，著之遺簡，以成先祖之志，深所望焉。樂安任昇之白。"

數日，欽悅即復書曰："使至，忽辱簡翰，用浣襟懷。不遺舊情，俯見推訪。又示以大同古銘。前賢未達，僕非遠識，安敢輕言，良增懷愧也。屬在途路，無所披求，據鞍運思，頗有所得。發壙者未知誰氏之子，卜宅者實爲絕代之賢，藏往知來，有若指掌，契終論始，不差錙銖，隗炤之預識龔使，無以過也。不說葬者之歲月，先識圮時之日辰，以圮之日，卻求初兆，事可知矣。姚史官亦爲當世達識，復與諸儒詳之，沉吟月餘，竟不知其指趣，豈止於是哉。原卜者之意，隱其事，微其言，當待僕爲龔使耳。不然，何忽見顧訪也？謹稽諸歷術，測以微詞，試一探言，庶會微旨。當梁武帝大同四年，歲次戊午。言'甸服'者，五百也；'黃鐘'者，十一也。五百一十一年而圮。從大同四年，上求五百一十一年，得漢光武帝建武四年戊子歲也。'三上庚'，三月上旬之庚也。其年三月辛巳朔，十日得庚寅，是三月初葬於鐘山也。'七中巳'，乃七月戊午朔，十二日得己巳，是初圮墮之日，是日己巳可知矣。'浹辰'，

81

十二也。從建武四年三月至大同四年七月，總六千三百一十二月，
每月一交，故云‘六千三百浹辰交’也。‘二九’爲十八，‘重三’
爲六。末言‘四百’，則六爲千，十八爲萬可知。從建武四年三月
十日庚寅初葬，至大同四年七月十二日己巳初圮，計一十八萬六千
四百日，故云‘二九重三四百圮’也。其所言者，但說年月日數耳。
據年，則五百一十一，會於甸服黃鐘；言月，則六千三百一十二，
會於六千三百浹辰交；論日，則一十八萬六千四百，會於二九重三
四百圮。從三上庚至於七中巳，據歷計之，無所差也。所言年則月
日，但差一數，則不相照會矣。原卜者之意，當待僕言之。吾子之
問，契使然也。從吏已久，藝業荒蕪，古人之意，復難遠測。足下
更詢能者，時報焉。使還，不代。鄭欽悅白記。”

　　貞元中，李吉甫任尚書屯田員外郎，兼太常博士。時宗人巽爲
戶部郎中，於南宮暇日，語及近代儒術之士，謂吉甫曰：“故右補
闕集賢殿直學士鄭欽悅，於術數研精，思通玄奧，蓋僧一行所不逮。
以其夭閼，當世名不甚聞。子知之乎？”吉甫對曰：“兄何以覼
諸。”巽曰：“天寶中，商洛隱者任昇之自言五代祖仕梁爲太常。
大同四年，於鐘山下獲古銘。其文隱祕，博求時儒，莫曉其旨。因
緘其銘，誡諸子曰：‘我代代子孫，以此銘訪於通人。倘有知者，
吾無所恨。’至昇之，頗耽道博雅。聞欽悅之名，即告以先祖之意。
欽悅曰：“子當錄以示我。我試思之。’升之書遺其銘。會欽悅適
奉朝使，方授駕於長樂驛。得銘而繹之，行及滋水，凡二十里，則
釋然悟矣。故其書曰：‘據鞍運思，頗有所得。’不亦異乎？”

　　辛未歲，吉甫轉駕部員外郎，欽悅子克鈞自京兆府司錄授司門
員外郎，吉甫數以巽之說質焉。雖且符其言，然克鈞自云亡其草。
每想其微言至賾，而不獲見，吉甫甚惜之。壬申歲，吉甫貶明州長
史。海島之中，有隱者姓張氏，名玄陽，以明《易經》爲州將所重，
召置閣下。因講《周易》卜筮之事，即以欽悅之書示吉甫。吉甫喜
得其書，抃逾獲寶，即編次之。仍爲著論，曰：

　　“夫一邱之土，無情也。遇雨而圮，偶然也。窮象數者，已懸定
　　於十八萬六千四百日之前。矧於理亂之運，窮達之命，聖賢不逢，
　　君臣偶合。則姜牙得璜而尚父，仲尼無鳳而旅人，傅說夢達於巖
　　野，子房神授於圮上，亦必定之符也。然而孔不暇暖其席，墨不
　　俟黔其突，何經營如彼？孟去齊而接淅，賈造湘而投弔，又眷戀
　　如此。豈大聖大賢，猶惑於性命之理歟？將浼身存教，示人道之
　　不可廢歟？余不可得而知也。”

　　欽悅尋自右補闕歷殿中侍御史，爲時宰李林甫所惡，斥擯於外，不顯其身。故余敘其所聞，繫於二篇之後，以著蓍筮之神明，聰哲之懸解，奇偶之有數，貽諸好事，爲後學之奇玩焉。

　　時貞元九年十一月二十八日，趙郡李吉甫記。

Tale 2.7

The Tale of Miss Liu

By Xu Yaozuo
Translated by Richard J. Lynn

During the Tianbao era [742–756], Han Yi of Changli,[1] well-known as a poet and a rather bold and free personality, found himself hard up in extreme poverty. A certain scholar Li, a close friend of Yi whose family enjoyed great wealth, was rashly prone to appreciate talent to an unconventional degree. His favorite concubine, named Miss Liu, a gorgeous beauty of the day, loved to chat and jest and was an excellent singer and chanter of verse. Scholar Li had her stay in a separate place of her own, where, while having her sing, he wined and dined with Yi. He actually lodged Yi right next door.

Since Yi had been well-known for some time, those who came to call on him were all distinguished men of ability, so when Miss Liu had a chance to steal a look at him through his gate, she said to a maidservant, "How could Master Han possibly remain someone poor and humble for long!" She then decided that he

---

[1] Changli 昌黎 commandery; its seat was in modern Yi 義 County, Liaoning. Because the Han clan was influential in that commandery during the Northern dynasties period (386–534), many people surnamed Han in later times called themselves Changli Han. Han Yi 韓翊 was a famous poet of the Tang and a native of Nanyang, Henan.

was just the man for her. Scholar Li had up till then highly regarded Yi and begrudged him no expense. So as soon as he learned what Miss Liu had in mind, he had a banquet meal prepared, which he invited Yi to share. Once they were tipsy with wine Scholar Li said to him, "Lady Liu is extraordinarily good-looking, and you, Outstanding Talent Han, are an exceptionally fine writer. If I were to offer her for your pillow, would you accept?"

Yi, overcome with shock and surprise, respectfully left his seat to say, "I have long been so blessed by your kindness that you even took the clothes off your back for me and starved yourself to feed me, so how right now would it be to snatch away the woman you love!" But Scholar Li implored him to do it, and Miss Liu, knowing he was sincere, bowed twice, gathered up her robes and sat down next to him, where Li had seated Han in the position of honor. Pouring out full cups of wine they were as delighted as can be, Scholar Li then went on to present Han with three hundred thousand cash to defray his expenses. Since Yi adored Mis Liu's beauty and Miss Liu admired Yi's talent, the two both so hit it off emotionally that one could imagine how happy they were.

The following year, Ministry of Rites Vice-Director Yang Du recommended Yi as a likely first-class candidate for the civil recruitment examinations, for which he would have to prepare for a year in seclusion. This prompted Miss Liu to say, "An honored reputation extends to one's relations, something that people of the past held in high regard. So how right would it be now for this lowly washerwoman to obstruct you from being chosen the best of orchids! Furthermore, my living expenses would be sufficiently covered while I waited for you to return." Thereupon, Yi went off to visit and stay with his family in Qingchi.[2] However, after more than a year went by, she was running out of food so had to sell her

---

[2] Northeast to modern Cang County, Hebei.

toilet articles to support herself. Then came the end of the Tianbao era, when rebels sacked the two imperial capitals, from which all men and women were fleeing. Miss Liu, fearing that her beauty would make her so obvious that she would not escape, shaved her head, ruined her appearance, and took refuge in the Faling Temple.

It was at that time that Hou Xiyi moved from Pinglu to become Military Commissioner of Ziqing,[3] and, relying on what he had heard of Yi's reputation, invited him to become his secretary. Then, after Emperor Xuan set things right thanks to his divine martial prowess,[4] Yi dispatched a private agent to find Miss Liu, filling a white silken bag with gold dust on which he inscribed:

> Zhang Terrace Willow,
> Zhang Terrace Willow,
> Yesteryear so green and fresh,
>   do you now still live or no?
> Even if bough after bough seem
> to trail down as of old,
> Some surely were pulled down
>   and plucked by other hands.

Then Miss Liu held the gold with her both hands, sobbing piteously. Those around her were filled with sympathetic grief. She chanted in response:

> What willow branches
> In their fragrant season

---

[3] Hou Xiyi 候希逸, a native of Yingzhou 營州 (in modern Liaoning), was the military commissioner of Pinglu 平盧.

[4] Emperor Huan 宣帝, posthumous title of Suzong 肅宗, Li Heng 李亨 (r. 756–762).

Year after year hate:
    being given to those who part.
Though just one leaf has followed the wind
    in response to autumn,
Even if my lord should come,
    how should I be worth plucking!

Soon afterwards the foreign military general Shazhali, who had just made a name for himself, having surreptitiously learned of Miss Liu's beauty, stole her away to his personal residence, where he doted on her exclusively. And when Hou Xiyi was appointed Imperial Secretariat Vice-Director and attended court, Yi obtained a position on his staff, but by the time he arrived at the capital all trace of Miss Liu's whereabouts was lost, which left him constantly sighing over memories of her. However, at Dragonhead Hill by chance he saw a servant driving a curtained carriage pulled by a mottled ox and followed by two maidservants. As he happened to be following along behind it, a voice from inside the carriage said, "Aren't you Supernumerary Han? For I am Miss Liu." She then sent a maid to tell him clandestinely that she had lost her virtue to Shazhali and that since she was now hampered by her fellow carriage passengers would he be kind enough to wait for her the next morning at the gate to Daozheng Ward. When the time came, he went there, where from inside her carriage she gave him a jade box tied up in light white silk cloth, saying, "We must part forever right away — I hope you will keep me sincerely in your thoughts." She then had the carriage turned around, and waving her hand to him, her light sleeves fluttering as the splendidly decorated carriage rattled away, straining his eyes and his thoughts all a muddle, he lost sight of her in the carriage's dust. Thenceforth Yi was completely unable to master his feelings.

It was just then that high-ranking military officers of Ziqing garrison commandery were gathering at a wine shop to have a good time feasting and drinking, so they dispatched a messenger to invite Yi to join them. Yi forced himself to accept but was utterly dispirited, his voice forlorn and plaintive with sobs. Present was a Palace Police Officer named Xu Jun, who full of self-confidence because of his great strength and talent, grasped his sword and said, "There's certainly something behind this — let me be of service to you!" So Yi could not help but tell him all about it. Xu Jun then said, "You just provide me with a brief note and I'll bring her right to you!" He then donned his military uniform complete with helmet, hung a pair of quivers on his shoulders, and ordering a cavalryman to accompany him charged off straight to Shazhali's personal residence. There he waited outside until Shazhali had left home and gone well off a third of a mile or so. Then, in his foreign border region uniform and gripping the reins of his horse, he charged in at the gate and burst through it, galloping around furiously and shouting out, "The general has had a sudden accident and has sent me to summon his lady to him!" As the staff and servants recoiled in fright and none dared look up at him, he ascended the hall, took out the note that Yi had written and showed it to Miss Liu. Then, tucking her under one arm, he vaulted into his saddle and, beating leather, escaped in a cloud of dust to speed his way back. Pulling his jacket front tight to him he went up to Yi and announced, "I had the good fortune not to fail my mission!" The whole company, shocked and astonished as Miss Liu and Yi held hands and burst into tears, gave up all thought to continue the banquet.

However, since Shazhali then enjoyed the utmost favor of the emperor, Han Yi and Xu Jun feared the worst, so they went to Hou Xiyi for help. Amazed, Xiyi said, "I have done such exploits my whole life, and now Xu Jun has actually managed to pull this one off!" He immediately wrote an account to the emperor:

> Han Yi, Acting Inspector in the Secretariat now Supernumerary
> and Censor at the Treasury Bureau, has long been one of my

assistants and has repeatedly demonstrated meritorious achievements. Not long ago, while taking part in the imperial examinations, a concubine of his, Miss Liu, was cut off from him by murderous rebels and so took refuge with an eminent nun. But now that civilization is again the temper of the times and those near and far comply with Your instructions, it happened that General Shazhali, his willful viciousness bending the law and relying on minor meritorious service to get away with it, forced his will on a woman of high moral integrity — in violation of Your effortlessly perfect governance. Your official, Troop Commander and Palace Aide to the Censor-in-chief, Xu Jun, whose family is originally from the Youzhou and Jizhou border region, a man of lofty aspiration, resolute and brave, snatched Miss Liu away and restored her to Han Yi. Xu Jun is at heart endowed with a keen sense of justice. Although he showed utter sincerity in this act of moral outrage, since I failed to inquire into the situation before it occurred, I surely was remiss in carrying out orders as I have been instructed.

Not long afterwards the emperor issued an edict to the effect that Miss Liu should be restored to Han Yi without fail and that Shazhali should be granted two million cash in compensation.

After Miss Liu was restored to Yi, continually promoted, he eventually attained the office of Head Secretary in the Secretariat. Thus it was: Miss Liu was determined to defend and protect herself, but she failed to do so; although Xu Jun was stirred to moral outrage, this really had no positive outcome. If Miss Liu because of her beauty had been selected an imperial consort, she could have become a worthy successor to the one who fended off a bear and the one who acted in all sincerity to decline a palanquin seat.[5] If Xu Jun because of his abilities had been promoted to high

---

[5] References to Lady Feng Jieyu 馮婕妤 who fended off a bear and saved emperor Yuan of the Han 漢元帝 (r. 48–33 BCE) and Lady Ban Jieyu 班婕妤 who acted in all sincerity to decline a palanquin seat and

office, he could have accomplished such meritorious deeds as done by Cao [Mo] at Ke and [by Lin] at Mianchi.[6] Exploits depend on implementation before they come to light, and meritorious achievements depend on the exploits involved before they attain prominence. It is a pity that these two were blocked from having their chance and that their sense of justice and bravery, stirred in vain, for both did not lead to what was right. But how was this ever a perversion of what was right! It was actually all due to the circumstances that befell their lot.

---

saved emperor Cheng of the Han 漢成帝 (r. 32–7 BCE) from licentious scandal.

[6] References to Cao Mo 曹沫 at Ke 柯 to force Duke Huan of Qi 齊桓公 (?–643 BCE) at knife point to return all captured lands of Lu 魯 back to Lu and Lin Xiangru 藺相如 at Mianchi 澠池, where he forced the King of Qin 秦 at knife point to beat on an earthenware pot and saved the reputation of the King of Zhao 趙.

柳氏傳

許堯佐

　　天寶中，昌黎韓翊有詩名，性頗落托，羈滯貧甚。有李生者，與翊友善，家累千金，負氣愛才。其幸姬曰柳氏，豔豔一時，喜談謔，善謳詠，李生居之別第，與翊為宴歌之地。而館翊于其側。

　　翊素知名，其所問候，皆當時之彥。柳氏自門窺之，謂其侍者曰："韓夫子豈長貧賤者乎！"遂屬意焉。李生素重翊，無所吝惜。後知其意，乃具膳請翊飲。酒酣，李生曰："柳夫人容色非常，韓秀才文章特異。欲以柳薦枕于韓君，可乎？"

　　翊驚栗，避席曰："蒙君之恩，解衣綴食久之，豈宜奪所愛乎？"李堅請之。柳氏知其意誠，乃再拜，引衣接席。李坐翊于客位，引滿極歡。李生又以資三十萬，佐翊之費。翊仰柳氏之色，柳氏慕翊之才，兩情皆獲，喜可知也。

　　明年，禮部侍郎楊度擢翊上第，屏居間歲。柳氏謂翊曰："榮名及親，昔人所尚。豈宜以濯浣之賤，稽采蘭之美乎？且用器資物，足以待君之來也。"翊于是省家于清池。歲餘，乏食，鬻妝具以自給。天寶末，盜覆二京，士女奔駭。柳氏以豔獨異，且懼不免，乃剪髮毀形，寄迹法靈寺。

　　是時侯希逸自平盧節度淄青，素藉翊名，請為書記。洎宣皇帝以神武反正，翊乃譴使間行求柳氏，以練囊盛麩金，題之曰：

　　　"章台柳，章台柳！昔日青青今在否？
　　　縱使條條似舊垂，亦應攀折他人手。"

91

柳氏捧金嗚咽，左右悽憫，答之曰：

"楊柳枝，芳菲節，所恨年年贈離別。
一葉隨風忽報秋，縱使君來豈堪折！"

　　無何，有蕃將沙吒利者，初立功，竊知柳氏之色，劫以歸第，寵之專房。及希逸除左僕射，入覲，翊得從行。至京師，已失柳氏之所，歎想不已。偶于龍首岡見蒼頭以駁牛駕輜軿，從兩女奴。翊偶隨之，自車中問曰："得非韓員外乎？某乃柳氏也。"使女駐竊言失身沙吒利，阻同車者，請詰旦幸相待于道政里門。及期而往，以輕素結玉合，實以香膏，自車中授之，曰："當速永訣，願實誠念。"乃回車，以手揮之，輕袖搖搖，香車轔轔，目斷意迷，失于驚塵。翊大不勝情。
　　會淄青諸將合樂酒樓，使人請翊。翊強應之，然意色皆喪，音韻悽咽。有虞候許俊者，以材力自負，撫劍言曰："必有故。願一效用。"翊不得已，具以告之。俊曰："請足下數字，當立致之。"乃衣縵胡，佩雙鞬，從一騎，徑造沙吒利之第。候其出行里餘，乃被衽執轡，犯關排闥，急趨而呼曰："將軍中惡，使召夫人！"僕侍辟易，無敢仰視。遂升堂，出翊札示柳氏，挾之跨鞍馬，逸塵斷鞅，倏急乃至。引裾而前曰："幸不辱命。"四座驚歎。柳氏與翊執手涕泣，相與罷酒。
　　是時沙吒利恩寵殊等，翊俊懼禍，乃詣希逸。希逸大驚曰："吾平生所為事，俊乃能爾乎？"遂獻狀曰：

"檢校尚書、金部員外郎兼御史韓翊，久列參佐，累彰勳效，頃從鄉賦。有妾柳氏，阻絕凶寇，依止名尼。今文明撫運，遐邇率化。將軍沙吒利凶恣撓法，憑恃微功，驅有志之妾，干無為之政。臣部將兼御使中丞許俊，族本幽薊，雄心勇決，卻奪柳氏，歸于韓翊。義切中抱，雖昭感激之誠，事不先聞，故乏訓齊之令。"

　　尋有詔，柳氏宜還韓翊，沙吒利賜錢二百萬。
　　柳氏歸翊，翊後累遷至中書舍人。然即柳氏，志防閑而不克者；許俊，慕感激而不達者也。向使柳氏以色選，則當熊、辭輦之誠可繼；許俊以才舉，則曹柯、澠池之功可建。夫事由迹彰，功待事立。惜郁堙不偶，義勇徒激，皆不入于正。斯豈變之正乎？蓋所遇然也。

Tale 2.8

Tale of the Transcendent Marriage of Dongting Lake

By Li Chaowei
Translated by Glen Dudbridge

In the Yifeng period (676–678 C.E.), a young scholar named Liu Yi was presented as a provincial candidate but failed to be classed in the examination. As he prepared to go home to the banks of the Xiang[1] he recalled that a man from his part of the country was staying in Jingyang[2] and went over to bid him farewell. But six or seven tricents along the way a bird flew up, and his horse took fright. It left the road and bolted, covering six or seven more tricents before coming to a stop.

Liu now caught sight of a woman tending sheep by the wayside, and finding this strange he took a closer look. She was remarkably pretty, yet her delicate brows were knit, her clothes badly weathered. She stood listening intently, poised there as though expecting someone.

---

[1] The Xiang 湘 River flows north through the heart of modern Hunan province to empty into Dongting Lake.

[2] Jingyang 涇陽 was and is a few miles northwest from the site of the Tang western capital, Chang'an, situated on the southern bank of the Jing River.

Liu Yi asked her: "Why do you demean yourself so with this hard work?"

At first, in her distress, she refused to speak, but finally made a tearful reply: "Poor, unfortunate maid that I am, today I receive a gentleman's kind attention! But I am so full of bitterness that I cannot hold modestly back — I hope I may put my case to you! I am the youngest daughter of the Dragon Lord of Lake Dongting. My parents married me to the second son of the River Ching, but my husband is a playboy, infatuated with servant girls, and each day has brought new contempt and neglect from him. So I complained to my husband's parents, but they were too fond of their son to be able to control him. And as I complained more often and more urgently, they became displeased, put blame on me, and cast me out into this plight!"

With these words she sobbed and the tears flowed in uncontrolled grief. Then she went on: "Who knows how far this place is from Dongting? Over that vast tract of space no letter can get through. And with those closest to my heart so utterly cut off from me, they have no way to know my woes. But I hear that you are going back to Wu,[3] sir, and will pass close by Dongting. If perhaps I entrusted a letter to your care, I wonder if you might be willing to consent?"

Liu Yi said: "I am a man of chivalry, and hearing your tale has so stirred my system and roused my blood that I curse the lack of wings that stops me flying straight there. How can I possibly say no? However, Lake Dongting is deep water, and I live on dry land. So how could I deliver your message? My one fear is that, since no communication links this bright world with

---

[3]This is puzzling. If Liu Yi's home is on the banks of the Xiang River, in central southern China, it cannot be associated with Wu, a region far away on the east coast. But the actual site of his home is never stated, and he moves to other parts of China later in the story.

that dark one, I should fail your deeply felt request and frustrate my own strong desire. What magic do you have that could take me there?"

Weeping bitterly she thanked him and said: "The burden you are taking on is of such value that I shall say no more than this: if I receive a message in reply I'll repay you even though it costs my life! I would not have ventured to speak if you had not said yes, but since you have agreed and put the question — there is no difference worth mentioning between Dongting and the capital city."

Liu Yi asked to hear more.

She said: "On Dongting's southern shore is a large orange tree, known to the local people as the Orange Tree Soil God.⁴ You must take off this belt you are wearing and strap on something else. Next, knock three times on the tree, and someone will come in response. You then go with him, and nothing will stand in your way. I hope, sir, that apart from what is set out in the letter, you will convey all the heartfelt things I have said. On no account break your trust!"

Liu Yi said: "I am humbly at your service."

She then took out a letter from inside her jacket and handed it to him, bowing repeatedly. And as she gazed eastward she wept tears of sadness that she seemed unable to control. Liu Yi felt deeply distressed for her.

He now put the letter in his bag and asked another question: "I don't know what purpose you are tending sheep for — surely the gods do not slaughter them?"

She said: "These are not sheep, but rain-makers."

"And what are rain-makers?"

---

⁴There is a clear link in popular Taoist lore between trees (especially the orange or tangerine), the soil god, prayers for rain, and the dragon who controls rainfall.

"The same kind of things as peals of thunder."

When Liu Yi looked around at them they glanced with pride and trod with vigor, seeming most remarkable as they browsed and drank, although in their size, their coat, and horns there was nothing to distinguish them from other sheep.

Liu Yi spoke again: "If I act as your messenger I hope you will not avoid my presence when one day you go back to Dongting!"

She answered: "Not only shall I not avoid you — I shall treat you as a very kinsman!"

With these words they made their farewells, and he set off to the east. When he glanced back after a few dozen steps the woman and her sheep were all lost to sight.

That night he came to the county town and took leave of his friend. And after a month or more he reached his own district and went back home.

He now made a search of Lake Dongting, and sure enough there was the Orange Tree Soil God on its southern shore. On coming to it, he changed his belt, faced the tree, and struck it just three times. Presently a warrior emerged from the waves, bowed twice, and invited him in, asking: "Where have you come from, noble guest?"

But Liu Yi would not divulge the truth. He said: "I have just come to have audience with the king."

The warrior parted the water and, pointing the way, led Liu Yi forward with the instruction: "Close your eyes and count your breaths,[5] and you will be able to get through."

---

[5] Counting breaths was part of Zen Buddhist meditation practice. But Ge Hong's 葛洪 (280–340) *Master Who Embraces Simplicity (Baopuzi)* refers to a technique of one Lord Zheng: "If you simply practice holding your breath for as long as a thousand inhalations, then in the long run you will be able to stay underwater for a day or more." The passage goes on to describe the use of rhinoceros horn to enable humans to function underwater, in one case to "breathe underwater."

Liu Yi did as he said, and they arrived at the palace. Only now did he see terraces and towers in facing ranks, gateways in their countless thousands, every single known kind of rare herb and precious tree. The warrior made Liu Yi stop in the corner of a great chamber, saying: "Our guest must wait for him here."

Liu Yi asked: "What place is this?"

He answered: "The Hall of Transcendent Void."

On close inspection, every precious substance known to man proved to be there: the pillars were of white jade, the steps of green jade; the couches were of coral, the blinds of rock crystal. Carved colored glass studded the nephrite eaves, decorative amber adorned the rainbow ridge-beam. Words could do no justice to this scene of dim splendor.

Time went by, yet the king did not come. Liu Yi asked the warrior: "Where is the lord of Dongting?"

He said: "My Lord has graced with his presence the Tower of the Dark Pearl, where he is debating *The Book of Fire* with the Taoist Master of the Sun Principle. He will finish in a moment.

Liu Yi asked: "What is *The Book of Fire*?"

The warrior replied: "My Lord is a dragon, and dragons use water as their divine element. By wielding a single drop they are able to engulf valleys and hills. The Taoist master is a human, the race that uses fire as its sacred element. A man could burn down the Epang Palace,[6] by putting a single lamp to it. Yet, with those distinct transcendent functions they have different occult processes. The Taoist Master of the Sun Principle is expert in the ways of man, and my Lord has invited him here to hear him speak."

As they finished talking the palace gates opened and they saw, thronged about with a great concourse of followers, a man

---

[6]The royal palace at the Qin capital Xianyang, built in 212 B.C.E. and burned down in 206 by the usurper Xiang Yu 項羽 (232–202 BCE).

robed in purple and bearing a green jade tablet.[7] Leaping up, the warrior said: "This is my Lord!" and went forward to announce Liu Yi.

The Lord surveyed him, then asked: "You must surely come from the world of men?"

Liu Yi replied: "That is so," and proceeded to bow repeatedly. The Lord bowed too, and bade him sit at the lower end of the Hall of Transcendent Void.

He said: "In the deep obscurity of my watery realm I lack the blessings of enlightenment. But you, sir, have 'seen fit to travel a thousand tricents': do you 'have some purpose'?"[8]

Liu Yi said: "I am a fellow countryman of yours, Great King. I grew up in Chu, and my studies took me to Qin. But lately, when I failed to gain a class, I made a passing visit to the right bank of the Jing, where I saw your daughter tending sheep in the country. It was unbearable to watch her lovely hair being tossed in the wind and rain. So I questioned her, and she told me she was mistreated by her husband, ignored by her parents-in-law, and thus reduced to this plight. Her tears of woe streaming down truly cut to the heart. She then entrusted a letter to me, I gave her my promise, and now here I am with it."

He took out the letter and offered it up. When the Lord of Dongting had read it he covered his face with his sleeve and wept. "It was her father's fault," He said. "I failed to pay close attention, idly turned a blind eye and a deaf ear, causing a frail child from my ladies' chambers to come to violent harm far from her home! Yet you, sir, a mere passerby, were able to recognize her distress.

---

[7] The jade tablet (*gui*) was an ancient emblem of imperial sovereignty. The green jade tablet was identified specifically in the *Zhou Rituals (Zhou li)* with worship pf the East.

[8] A simple allusion to the *Mengzi*, IA. l, in which King Hui of Liang greets Mencius in these terms.

As long as I am blessed with health and strength I shall never dare forget your goodness."

Uttering these words he broke into long lament, and all around him shed tears. The Lord now handed the letter to a eunuch in close attendance on him, with instructions to take it into the inner palace. Moments later the inner palace filled with anguished weeping. In alarm the Lord told his attendants: "Quickly tell them to be silent in the palace, in case Qiantang finds out!"

Liu Yi asked: "Who is Qiantang?"

"He is my dear younger brother, once master of the Qiantang River, but now in retirement."

Liu Yi asked: "Why must he not be allowed to find out?"

"Simply because his valor surpasses other men's. When, long ago, Yao suffered nine years of flooding, that was a single outburst from this young man! And when he quarreled recently with a general in heaven, the Five Peaks all quaked. The Monarch on High was lenient with my brother's crime because I had performed various small services over the years. But he is still tethered up here, and for that reason the people of Qiantang await him day by day."[9]

He was still speaking when a mighty roar broke out, the sky split apart, the earth burst open, the palace halls heaved turbulently about, while clouds and mist seethed and boiled. Before long a crimson dragon appeared, over a thousand feet long, with flashing eyes and gory tongue, ruddy scales and fiery whiskers. It trailed a golden chain from its neck, and dangling from the chain was a pillar of jade. Thunderbolts in their

---

[9]A reference to the great tidal bore which sweeps up the Qiantang River from its estuary in Hangzhou Bay at certain times of the year, often causing serious flooding.

thousands whirled about its body; sleet, snow, rain, and hail all came down at once. It flew off, ripping the blue sky asunder.

In his terror Liu Yi stumbled and collapsed on the ground. The Lord rose personally to help him up, saying: "Don't be afraid! You will come to no harm, certainly!"

It was some time before Liu Yi settled himself a little and was able to regain his self-control. He then took leave, saying: "I want to go home alive, so as not to be here when he returns."

The Lord said: "He'll certainly not come like that! Though he set off in this style, he will not come back the same way. Now I hope we can do the honors for you as best we may." And he ordered drink to be served. They toasted one another in hospitable fellowship.

Presently, as a happy breeze and a cloud of bliss blew mild and warm, as banners and staffs of ceremony displayed their delicate crafting, and as music created by Emperor Shun moved along the company, a huge throng of thousands of lovely girls crowded in with gay chatter and bright laughter. In their midst was one whose gossamer brows were in repose, who wore shining jewels all over, whose gown of crepe silk rippled out around her. A close look revealed that this was she who had earlier sent the message. Both joy and grief showed through as her tears flowed in streams. And moments later, with one side veiled in red mist and the other wrapped in purple haze, circled about by scented airs, she moved into the inner palace. The Lord said smiling to Liu Yi: "The Prisoner from the River Jing is back!" And he took leave to go into the palace. A moment more brought sounds of bitter grief which lasted on and on.

Sometime later the Lord came out again and joined Liu Yi in eating and drinking. Another man — robed in purple and bearing the green jade, with buoyant looks and bursting pride — now took his place beside the Lord, who said to Liu Yi: "This is Qiantang!"

Liu Yi rose and made haste to bow to him. Qiantang likewise received him with all due courtesy. He said: "My niece had the ill luck to be shamefully used by a young lout. She owes it to you, a gentleman of shining chivalry and good faith, that the news of her distant sufferings came through to us. If not, she would now be dust in a grave by the River Jing. Words cannot express how grateful and indebted we feel for your goodness and favor!"

Modestly Liu Yi drew back and declined all this with courteous bows and polite murmurs. Then the man turned to report to his brother:

"Just now I set out from Transcendent Void at morning prime and came to Jingyang by midmorning; I fought there at noon, and was back here by midafternoon. Between times I sped up to the highest heaven to report the affair to the Monarch on High. And he, learning of our grievance, pardoned my crime. In this way I have been let off my earlier sentence. But in that violent surge of dauntless spirit I had not time to spare for due leavetaking. I have alarmed and disturbed the inner palace, and what is more I have insulted our guest. In fear and shame, I cannot imagine what offense I have given!"

He drew back and bowed repeatedly.

The Lord asked: "How many were killed?"

"Six hundred thousand."

"Crops damaged?"

"Eight hundred tricents."

"And where is that unfeeling husband?"

"I have eaten him."

In dismay the Lord said: "True, the young lout's attitude was not to be endured. But you were still too hasty. The Monarch on High has displayed his sage wisdom in understanding our profound grievance. If he had not, what case could I have made? But from now on, do not behave like that again!"

Qiantang bowed some more.

That night Liu Yi was lodged in the Hall of Unwavering Light. And the next day they feasted him anew in the Palace of Blue Cloud. Friends and kin were invited in, grand ballets were staged, sweet wines were served, and good food and fine tableware were set before him.

First, to the sound of reed pipes and military drums, wielding banners and pennons, swords and halberds, ten thousand men danced out on the right. One of their number stepped forward to say: "This is the ballet *Qiantang Breaks the Ranks.*"[10] The banners and weapons showed such superior style, and the wheeling and charging struck such terror, that the guests' hair bristled up as they watched.

Then, to music of the bells and chimes, of strings and wind, costumed in gauze and patterned silk, in pearls and jade, a thousand girls danced out on the left. One of their number stepped forward to say: "This is the ballet A *Princess Returns to the Palace.*" The pure notes curved in such sweet cadence, spoke with such yearning, that the seated guests found themselves shedding tears as they listened.

At the end of these two ballets the Dragon Lord in great delight bestowed gifts of fine silks to distribute among the dancers. And then they all drew their seats together in a close line to enjoy the full pleasure of hearty drinking. Once they were warmed up with drink, the Lord of Tung-t'ing sang this song, beating time on his mat:

The vast sky is deep blue/the great earth stretches broad.
Each man has his aim/but how can this be gauged?

---

[10]This made-up title mimics the standard court ballet *The Prince of Qin Breaks the Ranks,* which originally celebrated the military exploits of the future Taizong and served Tang China as a kind of national anthem in dance.

> Fox sprites and rat saints/may cling to Soil Altars, hug close to
>   walls,
> But when the thunderbolt shoots forth/which of them dares
>   hold its own?
> Thanks to this good man/so strong in chivalry and troth,
> Our flesh and blood/can return to her home.
> With one voice we speak our gratitude:/never shall we forget!

When the Lord of Dongting finished his song, the Lord of
Qiantang bowed twice and sang:

> High heaven matched them together, /but life and death go
>   separate ways.
> Hers was not to be his wife, /nor his to be her husband.
> Our dear hearth suffered hard times/beside the stream of
>   Ching:
> Frost and wind all over her hair, /rain and snow on her jacket.
> But thanks to you, noble sir, /who brought over her letter,
> Our flesh and blood was enabled/to come back to her old home.
> Forever shall we voice our high esteem, /and never fall silent!

As Qiantang's song came to its close the Lord of Dongting rose
together with him, and they offered a tankard to Liu Yi. With due
deference he accepted it, drank it up, then offered two more to the
lords. And he sang:

> As the pale blue clouds drifted by/and the River Ching flowed
>   east,
> I grieved for the lovely girl/with pouring tears and blossoming
>   sorrow.
> But her letter brought from far away/has served to clear my
>   Lord's distress:
> The woeful grudge now duly purged, /she comes back to dwell
>   in repose.
> I am obliged for this cordial and refined entertainment, /I thank
>   you for the excellent food.

But my rustic home is deserted:/I cannot stay longer.
As I prepare to take my leave/sadness blinds me about.

At the end of his song they all cheered.

The Lord of Dongting now produced a box of blue jade containing rhinoceros horn[11] that could part the waters, and in turn the Lord of Qiantang produced a tray of red amber containing a luminescent jewel. They both rose to present these to Liu Yi. Politely declining at first, he accepted them. Then the ladies of the inner palace all cast silk festoons, pearls, and jade disks down at Liu Yi's side. Theses piled up in dazzling heaps, and moments later he had vanished in the midst of them. Liu Yi looked all around, exclaiming and laughing, and scarcely had time to make his bows of gratitude.

When they had drunk their fill, Liu Yi rose and lodged once more in the Hall of Unwavering Light.

The next day they feasted him again in the Tower of Pure Light. Qiantang, flushed with wine, unceremoniously squatted down and said to Liu Yi: "You must have heard the saying 'a tough rock may be split but not bent, a chivalrous knight may be killed but not shamed'? Now I have a thought that I wish to put to you, sir. If you approve, then we shall soar together to the highest heaven; if not, we shall all be groveling in the muck. What do you say?"

Liu Yi asked to hear more.

Qiantang said: "The wife from Jingyang is the Lord of Dongting's beloved daughter, and her sweet nature and fine disposition are prized by all her kin. She had the ill luck to suffer shame from a scoundrel. But now that is all finished, and we are

---

[11]The horn of the rhinoceros was reputed to have this property: "If a horn is obtained at least three inches [*variant* one foot] long, carved in the form of a fish and placed in the mouth as the water is entered, the water will often be opened up to man." Compare with note 6 above.

hoping to entrust her to a man of lofty principle, to be kin of ours for generations to come so that she who received your kindness will know the man she is joining, and we who hold her dear will know the man we are giving her to. That surely is the way for a true gentleman to see through his work to the end!"

Liu Yi gravely rose to his feet and gave a sharp laugh: "Truly I never knew that the Lord of Qiantang was as wretched as this! When I first heard of your bestriding the Nine Provinces and enfolding the Five Peaks as you gave vent to your fury, and when later I saw you snap the golden chain and drag along the jade pillar as you rushed to an emergency, I thought that your firm resolution and clear integrity could have no rivals. For to face up to death when another affronts you, to risk your very life when your affections are stirred — this must show a true man's sense of purpose! But what now! — while flutes and pipes are serenading a peaceful gathering of relatives and guests, you spurn all principles to impose your might on another man! Not what I would once have expected! If I had met you among mighty waves or amid gloomy mountains, flourishing whiskers and scales and robed in clouds and rain as you pressed me to the point of death, then I would have regarded you as a mere beast and would have no grounds for complaint! But now you are clothed in cap and gown, you sit talking of ritual decorum and moral right, you have a commitment to the Five Relationships,[12] a command of the nuances of conduct that would surpass some of the best in the world of men, let alone the deities of the rivers! Yet with hulking body and violent temper, fortified by strong drink, you want to put pressure on another man. Is that anything like honest behavior? Now my substance is scarcely big enough to conceal

---

[12] The five Confucian social relations, those between prince and minister, father and son, older and younger brothers, husband and wife, and friends.

inside one of your scales. Yet even so, with unyielding spirit I dare defy your unprincipled passion! Pray consider that, Prince!"

Qiantang falteringly made apology: "Born and bred in palace chambers, we never received correct instruction. The words said just now were wild and reckless: they have rudely offended a man of wisdom and insight. When I step back to examine myself, my fault brooks no excuse. I hope, respected sir, that you will not let this come between us!"

That night they held another convivial banquet, enjoying the same pleasure as before, and Liu Yi and Qiantang now became the closest of friends.

Next day Liu Yi took leave to go home. The Lady of Dongting held a separate feast for him in the Hall of Hidden Vista. All the children, servants, and concubines came out to join in the party. The Lady said, weeping, to Liu Yi: "My flesh and blood, who received such great kindness from you, good sir, only wishes she could demonstrate her gratitude — yet now you have come to the moment of parting and separation." And she made that one-time woman of Jingyang bow before Liu Yi, there at the banquet, in token of thanks.

The Lady went on: "Now that you two are parting, will the day ever come when you meet again?"

Although in the first place he had rejected Qiantang's proposal, on the occasion of this feast Liu Yi bore a look of deep regret. And when at the end he bade farewell, the whole palace grieved. The treasure presented to him was wondrous beyond description.

He now followed the route back, and as he emerged upon the riverbank he saw some dozen attendants escorting him with sacks on their shoulders. They came as far as his home, then took leave and departed.

Liu Yi went to the jewelers' shops in Guangling[13] to sell what he had gained, and before a hundredth part of it was gone his wealth amounted to millions. The richest families of the region felt that he outstripped them all.

He now married a Zhang, who died.[14] Again he married a Han, who also died within few months. He moved house to Jinling where, saddened by his single state, he took some steps to find a new mate.

A marriage-broker reported: "There is a woman of the Lu family from Fan-yang, whose father is named Hao and was once magistrate of Qingliu.[15] In the evening of life he devoted himself to the Way and went roaming the wilderness alone. By now there is no news of his whereabouts. The girl's mother, called Zheng, married her a year ago to Zhang of Qinghe,[16] but unfortunately

---

[13]An ancient name for Yangzhou that was revived in 742. This canal port at the center of an important salt-producing area saw a great concentration of merchant wealth following migrations caused by the An Lushan 安禄山 (703–757) Rebellion and was a major center of international trade. It is clear why Liu Yi should choose to market his jewelry here.

[14]This family was one of the recognized clans in the Tang middle aristocracy, but its choice here must again reflect a play on the place Qinghe ("Clear River") and the river home of the dragon who was actually the girl's last husband.

[15]The name Hao suggests the vastness of a body of water — here by implication the Dongting Lake. The administration of Qingliu ("Clear Stream") district perhaps has a similar allusive intention, although the place (now Chu district) does actually lie only a few miles northwest of Jinling (now Nanjing), where Liu Yi is residing. The Lu of Fanyang were among the leading clans of the Tang aristocracy.

[16]This family was one of the recognized clans in the Tang middle aristocracy, but its choice here must again reflect a play on the place Qinghe ("Clear River") and the river home of the dragon who was actually the girl's last husband.

Zhang died early. The mother is now seeking a new husband to match her with, for she pities the girl's youth and sees her intelligence and beauty as precious assets. I wonder what you think?"

So Liu Yi fixed a day and went through the ceremony. Since both bride and groom were from great families, the ritual goods and gifts were of the utmost splendor. The whole of Jinling society was much impressed.

One evening a month or so later Liu Yi came home and, as he looked at his wife, had the strong sense that she resembled the dragon woman, though appearing even more lovely, buxom, and bonny. So he spoke to her of those past events.

She said to him: "Surely nothing like that could happen in the world of men! But you and I are expecting a child!"

Liu Yi showed her more affection than ever. Once the child was born and the first month seen out, she changed her clothes and adorned herself richly to invite in all their kin.[17] In the course of that reunion she said smiling to Liu Yi: "Don't you remember me from the past?"

He said: "I once delivered a letter for the Lord of Dongting's daughter, and she stays in my memory to this day!"

His wife said: "I am the daughter of Lord Dongting. Through you, sir, I was able to declare the wrongs I bore by the river Jing. I felt such gratitude for your kindness that I vowed in my heart to find a way to repay you. But when my uncle Qiantang proposed a marriage, you refused, and we then moved apart to far ends of the earth. Unable to keep in touch, I made myself ill with pining and fretting. My parents wanted to wed me to the youngest son of Zhuojin,[18] but I closed my door and cut off my hair to show how

---

[17] The reference is to the family celebration at the end of the traditional one-month ritual seclusion for the mother and newborn child.

[18] Name of a river flowing through Sichuan.

unwilling I was. The point was this: my private vow could not be set aside, yet neither could my parents' bidding be defied; I had been rejected by you, sir, without hope of reunion; yet, although able to report that first grievance to my parents, I had failed to see through my vow to repay you. Then, just when I hoped to come and declare myself before you, you were marrying one woman after another. You married Zhang, and when that was over you married Han. Once those ladies had each died in turn you made your home here, and my parents were pleased that I had the chance to carry out my aim of repaying you. Today I am able to serve as your wife, and we can spend the rest of our days in happiness together. I shall die without regrets!"

She sobbed, and the tears flowed down. Then she faced him and said: "I would not speak out at first because I knew you were not disposed to be swayed by woman's beauty. I speak now because I know you are minded to love your son. As a woman I am of small consequence, not able to create lifelong commitment through bonds of affection. So I entrust my humble self into your hands on the strength of your love for our son. I wonder what view you will take? Fear and sadness both possess my mind, and I'm not able to dispel them. That day when you accepted the letter you laughed and said to me: 'Be sure not to avoid my presence when one day you go back to Dongting!' Truly I wonder whether at that point you could have had today's situation in mind? And later, when Uncle put the proposal to you and you firmly refused, were you genuinely saying no, or was it just a fit of anger? Please tell me, sir!"

Liu Yi said: "It all seems fated. When I saw you first by the side of the Jing, crushed by your wrongs and stricken by your sufferings, I was moved by a true sense of injustice. Yet I kept my own feelings in check, because nothing was a concern of mine but bearing the news of your complaint. What I said at first about not avoiding my presence was no more than a chance remark —

certainly not a considered one! And when Qiantang put pressure on me there was something in the principle of the thing that could not be put straight —that alone provoked me to anger. You see, my intention from the start had been to act with chivalry —so how could I possibly get a husband put to death and then accept his wife in marriage? That was one thing wrong with it. And I have always given highest priority to maintaining my integrity. How could I compromise myself to surrender to my heart? That was the second thing wrong with it. What is more, with my blunt, frank nature in the thick of drinks plied to and fro, plain speaking was my only thought. I had none to spare for avoiding harm. Yet, on the day I was going to depart, I saw you look so longingly that I felt deep regret at heart. And in the end, tied up with worldly affairs, I had no way to respond with thanks. Ah!—now you are one of the Lu family and married into human society—so my early feelings were no mere daydream! From now on I shall always love you. Not the slightest trace of care shall trouble our hearts."

Deeply moved, his wife wept sweetly. It took her some time to recover; then after a pause she said to him: "Don't think that being another kind of creature deprives me of right feelings: I shall most certainly repay you. Dragons, you know, live ten thousand years. I will share this with you now, and you can go anywhere on water or land. Don't think I am being fanciful!"

Liu Yi was impressed. He said: "I never realized that this matchless beauty would also be a prescription for eternal life!"

They now went together to pay their respects to Dongting, and the lavish ceremonies of hospitality there were beyond description.

Afterward they moved their home to Nanhai.[19] Within a mere forty years Liu Yi's residences, carriages, horses, treasures, equipment, and adornment were such that no household of marquis or earl could have bettered them. Liu Yi's entire lineage shared in his bounty. And, to the amazement of all Nanhai, his looks showed no decline with the mounting years.

When the Kaiyuan period[20] came the emperor fixed his mind on matters of transcendence and immortality and diligently sought out Taoist techniques. Liu Yi had no peace, and so retired in company with his wife to Dongting. No one saw a trace of him for more than ten years.

Then, at the end of the Kaiyuan period, a maternal cousin of his called Xue Gu,[21] serving as a magistrate in the Western Metropolitan province, was demoted to a post in the southeast. As he sailed over Lake Dongting one clear day he gazed into the distance and presently saw a blue hill emerge far out among the waves. The sailors crowded to the side, saying: "There was no hill there before — surely it can only be a monster of the waters!"

In a brief moment the hill had come up close to the vessel, and a festooned boat sped over to welcome Xue Gu. A man on board hailed him: "Master Liu is here to wait upon you!" In a flash Xue Gu remembered him, and he hastened over to the foot of the hill, hitched up his gown, and climbed quickly upward.

---

[19] An old name for the administrative area around modern Guangdong, now Guangzhou.

[20] Second reign period (713–741) of the emperor Xuanzong 玄宗 (712–756).

[21] This known individual, who is credited with the transmission of the story in the author's comment below, may be its one firm point of historical reference. The official appointment noted for him in the genealogical tables of the *New Tang History* is consistent with that given here.

At the top of the hill was a palace just like one in the human world. He saw Liu Yi standing in a chamber of the palace with an orchestra of wind and strings formed up in front of him, and a company of bejeweled girls behind. The ornamental objects were many times more splendid than those in the human world. Liu Yi's discourse was more esoteric than ever, and his complexion more youthful.

He welcomed Xue Gu at the palace steps, seizing his hand with the words: "It is no time since we last met, yet your hair is already going gray!"

Xue Gu laughed: "Cousin, you are a divine being, I am dry bones. Such is fate!"

Liu Yi now produced fifty medicinal pills and gave them to Xue Gu, saying: "Each one of these pills can add just one year to your life. When those years are up, come back here. Don't make trouble for yourself by lingering on in the world of men."

After a merry feast Xue Gu took leave and went on his way. From that moment on there was neither sight nor sound of Liu Yi again. Xue Gu often told this story to others, but after some forty or fifty years he too vanished from sight.

Li Chaowei of the Longxi clan, who has written this account, offers an admiring comment: "Here we can see how, among creatures of the five breeds,[22] preeminence always comes from spiritual power. Man is the naked breed, but he can communicate his good faith to the scaly breed. Dongting's forbearance and uprightness, Qiantang's impetuosity and frank openness — these should be handed down. Xue Gu, whose poems on the subject were never recorded, was the only man able to come near that

---

[22]Five classes of living creatures, distinguished as feathered, hairy, shelled, scaly, and naked — the human race belonging to and being preeminent in the last, just as the dragon belonged to and was preeminent in the fourth class.

other region. I have written this piece because I see true chivalry in it."

Note: This translation is from Victor H. Mair, ed., *The Columbia Anthology of Traditional Chinese Literature* (New York: Columbia University Press, 1994), pp. 838–51. In order to be consistent with other renditions, the Wade-Giles transliteration has been converted to pinyin.

柳毅傳

李朝威

儀鳳中，有儒生柳毅者，應舉下第，將還湘濱。念鄉人有客於涇陽者，遂往告別。至六七里，鳥起馬驚，疾逸道左。又六七里，乃止。見有婦人，牧羊於道畔。毅怪視之，乃殊色也。然而蛾臉不舒，巾袖無光，凝聽翔立，若有所伺。毅詰之曰："子何苦而自辱如是？"

婦始楚而謝，終泣而對曰："賤妾不幸，今日見辱問於長者。然而恨貫肌骨，亦何能愧避？幸一聞焉。妾，洞庭龍君小女也。父母配嫁涇川次子，而夫婿樂逸，爲婢僕所惑，日以厭薄。既而將訴於舅姑，舅姑愛其子，不能御。迨訴頻切，又得罪舅姑。舅姑毀黜以至此。"言訖，歔欷流涕，悲不自勝。又曰："洞庭於茲，相遠不知其幾多也？長天茫茫，信耗莫通。心目斷盡，無所知哀。聞君將還吳，密通洞庭。或以尺書，寄託侍者，未卜將以爲可乎？"

毅曰："吾義夫也。聞子之說，氣血俱動，恨無毛羽，不能奮飛，是何可否之謂乎！然而洞庭，深水也。吾行塵間，寧可致意耶？惟恐道途顯晦，不相通達，致負誠託，又乖懇願。子有何術可導我邪？"

女悲泣且謝，曰："負載珍重，不復言矣。脫獲回耗，雖死必謝。君不許，何敢言。既許而問，則洞庭之與京邑，不足爲異也。"毅請聞之。女曰："洞庭之陰，有大橘樹焉，鄉人謂之'社橘'。君當解去茲帶，束以他物。然後叩樹三發，當有應者。因而隨之，無有礙矣。幸君子書敘之外，悉以心誠之話倚託，千萬無渝！"毅曰："敬聞命矣。"女遂於襦間解書，再拜以進。東望愁泣，若不自勝。

114

　　毅深爲之戚，乃致書囊中，因復謂曰：“吾不知子之牧羊，何所用哉？神祇豈宰殺乎？”女曰：“非羊也，雨工也。”“何爲雨工？”曰：“雷霆之類也。”毅顧視之，則皆矯顧怒步，飮齕甚異，而大小毛角，則無別羊焉。毅又曰：“吾爲使者，他日歸洞庭，幸勿相避。”女曰：“寧止不避，當如親戚耳。”語竟，引別東去。不數十步，回望女與羊，俱亡所見矣。

　　其夕，至邑而別其友。月餘到鄉，還家，乃訪友于洞庭。洞庭之陰，果有社橘。遂易帶向樹，三擊而止。俄有武夫出於波間，再拜請曰：“貴客將自何所至也？”毅不告其實，曰：“走謁大王耳。”武夫揭水止路，引毅以進。謂毅曰：“當閉目，數息可達矣。”毅如其言，遂至其宮。始見臺閣相向，門戶千萬，奇草珍木，無所不有。夫乃止毅，停於大室之隅，曰：“客當居此以俟焉。”毅曰：“此何所也？”夫曰：“此靈虛殿也。”諦視之，則人間珍寶，畢盡於此。柱以白璧，砌以青玉，牀以珊瑚，簾以水精，雕琉璃於翠楣，飾琥珀於虹棟。奇秀深杳，不可殫言。然而王久不至。毅謂夫曰：“洞庭君安在哉？”曰：“吾君方幸玄珠閣，與太陽道士講《火經》，少選當畢。”毅曰：“何謂《火經》？”夫曰：“吾君，龍也。龍以水爲神，舉一滴可包陵谷。道士，乃人也。人以火爲神聖，發一燈可燎阿房。然而靈用不同，玄化各異。太陽道士精於人理，吾君邀以聽焉。”

　　語畢而宮門闢，景從雲合，而見一人，披紫衣，執青玉。夫躍曰：“此吾君也！”乃至前以告之。君望毅而問曰：“豈非人間之人乎？”對曰：“然。”毅而設拜，君亦拜，命坐於靈虛之下。謂毅曰：“水府幽深，寡人暗昧，夫子不遠千里，將有爲乎？”毅曰：“毅，大王之鄉人也。長於楚，遊學於秦。昨下第，閒驅涇水右涘，見大王愛女牧羊於野，風鬟雨鬢，所不忍視。毅因詰之，謂毅曰：‘爲夫婿所薄，舅姑不念，以至於此’。悲泗淋漓，誠怛人心。遂託書於毅。毅許之，今以至此。”因取書進之。

　　洞庭君覽畢，以袖掩面而泣曰：“老父之罪，不珍堅聽，坐貽聾瞽，使閨牕孺弱，遠罹搆害。公，乃陌上人也，而能急之。幸被齒髮，何敢負德！”詞畢，又哀吒良久。左右皆流涕。時有宦人密視君者，君以書授之，令達宮中。須臾，宮中皆慟哭。君驚謂左右曰：“疾告宮中，無使有聲，恐錢塘所知。”毅曰：“錢塘，何人也？”曰：“寡人之愛弟，昔爲錢塘長，今則致政矣。”毅曰：“何故不使知？”曰：“以其勇過人耳。昔堯遭洪水九年者，乃此子一怒也。近與天將失意，塞其五山。上帝以寡人有薄德於古今，遂寬其同氣之罪。然猶縻繫於此，故錢塘之人，日日候焉。"

語未畢，而大聲忽發，天拆地裂。宮殿擺簸，雲煙沸涌。俄有赤龍長千餘尺，電目血舌，朱鱗火鬣，項掣金鎖，鎖牽玉柱，千雷萬霆，激繞其身，霰雪雨雹，一時皆下。乃擘青天而飛去。毅恐蹶仆地。君親起持之曰："無懼，固無害。"毅良久稍安，乃獲自定。因告辭曰："願得生歸，以避復來。"君曰："必不如此。其去則然，其來則不然，幸為少盡繾綣。"因命酌互舉，以款人事。

俄而祥風慶雲，融融怡怡，幢節玲瓏，簫韶以隨。紅妝千萬，笑語熙熙，後有一人，自然蛾眉，明璫滿身，綃縠參差。迫而視之，乃前寄辭者。然若喜若悲，零淚如絲。須臾，紅煙蔽其左，紫氣舒其右，香氣環旋，入於宮中。君笑謂毅曰："涇水之囚人至矣。"君乃辭歸宮中。須臾，又聞怨苦，久而不已。有頃，君復出，與毅飲食。又有一人，披紫裳，執青玉，貌聳神溢，立於君左。君謂毅曰："此錢塘也。"毅起，趨拜之。錢塘亦盡禮相接，謂毅曰："女侄不幸，為頑童所辱。賴明君子信義昭彰，致達遠冤。不然者，是為涇陵之土矣。饗德懷恩，詞不悉心。"毅撝退辭謝，俯仰唯唯。然後回告兄曰："暴者辰發靈虛，巳至涇陽，午戰於彼，未還於此。中間馳至九天，以告上帝。帝知其冤，而宥其失。前所譴責，因而獲免。然而剛腸激發，不遑辭候。驚擾宮中，復忤賓客。愧惕慚懼，不知所失。"因退而再拜。君曰："所殺幾何？"曰："六十萬。""傷稼乎？"曰："八百里。""無情郎安在？"曰："食之矣。"君憮然曰："頑童之為是心也，誠不可忍，然汝亦太草草。賴上帝顯聖，諒其至冤。不然者，吾何辭焉？從此以去，勿復如是。"錢塘君復再拜。是夕，遂宿毅於凝光殿。

明日，又宴毅於凝碧宮。會友戚，張廣樂，具以醪醴，羅以甘潔。初，笳角鼙鼓，旌旗劍戟，舞萬夫於其右。中有一夫前曰："此《錢塘破陣樂》。"旌釒坒傑氣，顧驟悍慄。座客視之，毛髮皆豎。復有金石絲竹，羅綺珠翠，舞千女於其左。中有一女前進曰："此《貴主還宮樂》。"清音宛轉，如訴如慕，坐客聽之，不覺淚下。二舞既畢，龍君大悅。錫以紈綺，頒於舞人，然後密席貫坐，縱酒極娛。酒酣，洞庭君乃擊席而歌曰：

"大天蒼蒼兮，大地茫茫。人各有志兮，何可思量。
狐神鼠聖兮，薄社依牆。雷霆一發兮，其孰敢當？

荷貞人兮信義長，令骨肉兮還故鄉。齊言慚愧兮何時忘！"

洞庭君歌罷，錢塘君再拜而歌曰：

"上天配合兮，生死有途。此不當婦兮，彼不當夫。
腹心辛苦兮，涇水之隅。風霜滿鬢兮，雨雪羅襦。
賴明公兮引素書，令骨肉兮家如初。永言珍重兮無時無。"

錢塘君歌闋，洞庭君俱起，奉觴於毅。毅踧踖而受爵，飲訖，復以二觴奉二君，乃歌曰：

"碧雲悠悠兮，涇水東流。傷美人兮，雨泣花愁。
尺書遠達兮，以解君憂。哀冤果雪兮，還處其休。
荷和雅兮感甘羞。山家寂寞兮難久留。欲將辭去兮悲綢繆。"

歌罷，皆呼萬歲。洞庭君因出碧玉箱，貯以開水犀；錢塘君復出紅珀盤，貯以照夜璣，皆起進毅，毅辭謝而受。然後宮中之人，咸以綃彩珠璧，投於毅側。重疊煥赫，須臾埋沒前後。毅笑語四顧，愧揖不暇。洎酒闌歡極，毅辭起，復宿於凝光殿。
翌日，又宴毅於清光閣。錢塘因酒作色，踞謂毅曰："不聞猛石可裂不可卷，義士可殺不可羞邪？愚有衷曲，欲一陳於公。如可，則俱在雲霄；如不可，則皆夷糞壤。足下以爲何如哉？"毅曰："請聞之。"錢塘曰："涇陽之妻，則洞庭君之愛女也。淑性茂質，爲九姻所重。不幸見辱於匪人。今則絕矣。將欲求託高義，世爲親戚，使受恩者知其所歸，懷愛者知其所付，豈不爲君子始終之道者？"毅蕭然而作，欻然而笑曰："誠不知錢塘君屚困如是！毅始聞跨九州，懷五岳，泄其憤怒；復見斷金鎖，掣玉柱，赴其急難。毅以爲剛決明直，無如君者。蓋犯之者不避其死，感之者不愛其生，此真丈夫之志。奈何蕭管方洽，親賓正和，不顧其道，以威加人？豈仆之素望哉！若遇公于洪波之中，玄山之間，鼓以鱗須，被以雲雨，將迫毅以死，毅則以禽獸視之，亦何恨哉！今體被衣冠，坐談禮義，盡五常之志性，負百行之微旨，雖人世賢傑，有不如者，況江河靈類乎？而欲以蠢然之軀，悍然之性，乘酒假氣，將迫于人，豈近直哉！且毅之質，不足以藏王一甲之間。然而敢以不伏之心，勝王不道之氣。惟王籌之！"錢塘乃逡巡致謝曰："寡人生長宮房，不聞正論。向者詞述疏狂，妄突高明。退自循顧，戾不容責。幸君子不為此乖問可也。”其夕，復飲宴，其樂如舊。毅與錢塘遂為知心友。

明日，毅辭歸。洞庭君夫人別宴毅于潛景殿，男女仆妾等，悉出預會。夫人泣謂毅曰：“骨肉受君子深恩，恨不得展愧戴，遂至睽別。”使前涇陽女當席拜毅以致謝。夫人又曰：“此別豈有復相遇之日乎？”毅其始雖不諾錢塘之請，然當此席，殊有嘆恨之色。宴罷，辭別，滿宮悽然。贈遺珍寶，怪不可述。毅於是復循途出江岸，見從者十餘人，擔囊以隨，至其家而辭去。毅因適廣陵寶肆，鬻其所得。百未發一，財已盈兆。故淮右富族，咸以為莫如。遂娶于張氏，亡。又娶韓氏。數月，韓氏又亡。徙家金陵。常以鰥曠多感，或謀新匹。有媒氏告之曰：“有盧氏女，范陽人也。父名曰浩，嘗為清流宰。晚歲好道，獨遊云泉，今則不知所在矣。母曰鄭氏。前年適清河張氏，不幸而張夫早亡。母憐其少，惜其慧美，欲擇德以配焉。不識何如？”毅乃卜日就禮。既而男女二姓，俱為豪族，法用禮物，盡其豐盛。金陵之士，莫不健仰。

居月餘，毅因晚入戶，視其妻，深覺類于龍女，而逸艷豐厚，則又過之。因與話昔事。妻謂毅曰：“人世豈有如是之理乎？然君與余有一子。”毅益重之。既產，逾月，乃穠飾換服，召親戚。相會之間，笑謂毅曰：“君不憶余之於昔也？”毅曰：“夙為洞庭君女傳書，至今為憶。”妻曰：“余即洞庭君之女也。涇川之冤，君使得白。銜君之恩，誓心求報。洎錢塘季父論親不從，遂至睽違。天各一方，不能相問。父母欲配嫁于濯錦小兒某。惟以心誓難移，親命難背，既為君子棄絕，分見無期。而當初之冤，雖得以告諸父母，而誓報不得其志，復欲馳白于君子。值君子累娶，當娶于張，已而又娶于韓。迨張韓繼卒，君卜居于茲，故余之父母乃喜余得遂報君之意。今日獲奉君子，咸善終世，死無恨矣。”因嗚咽，泣涕交下。對毅曰：“始不言者，知君無重色之心。今乃言者，知君有感余之意。婦人匪薄，不足以確厚永心，故因君愛子，以托相生。未知君意如何？愁懼兼心，不能自解。君附書之日，笑謂妾曰：‘他日歸洞庭，慎無相避。’誠不知當此之際，君豈有意于今日之事乎？其后季父請于君，君固不許。君乃誠將不可邪，抑忿然邪？君其話之。”

毅曰：“似有命者。仆始見君子，長涇之隅，枉抑憔悴，誠有不平之志。然自約其心者，達君之冤，余無及也。以言‘慎無相避’

者，偶然耳，豈有意哉。洎錢塘逼迫之際，唯理有不可直，乃激人
之怒耳。夫始以義行為之志，寧有殺其婿而納其妻者邪？一不可也。
善素以操真為志尚，寧有屈于己而伏于心者乎？二不可也。且以率
肆胸臆，酬酢紛綸，唯直是圖，不遑避害。然而將別之日，見君有
依然之容，心甚恨之。終以人事扼束，無由報謝。吁，今日，君，
盧氏也，又家于人間。則吾始心未為惑矣。從此以往，永奉歡好，
心無纖慮也。”妻因深感嬌泣，良久不已。有頃，謂毅曰：“勿以
他類，遂為無心，固當知報耳。夫龍壽萬歲，今與君同之。水陸無
往不適。君不以為妄也。”毅嘉之曰：“吾不知國客乃復為神仙之
餌！”。乃相與覲洞庭。既至，而賓主盛禮，不可具紀。

　　后居南海，僅四十年，其邸第輿馬珍鮮服玩，雖侯伯之室，無
以加也。毅之族咸遂濡澤。以其春秋積序，容狀不衰。南海之人，
靡不驚異。洎開元中，上方屬意于神仙之事，精索道術。毅不得安，
遂相與歸洞庭。凡十余歲，莫知其跡。

　　至開元末，毅之表弟薛嘏為京畿令，謫官東南。經洞庭，晴晝
長望，俄見碧山出于遠波。舟人皆側立，曰：“此本無山，恐水怪
耳。”指顧之際，山與舟相逼，乃有彩船自山馳來，迎問于嘏。其
中有一人呼之曰：“柳公來候耳。”嘏省然記之，乃促至山下，攝
衣疾上。山有宮闕如人世，見毅立于宮室之中，前列絲竹，后羅珠
翠，物玩之盛，殊倍人間。毅詞理益玄，容顏益少。初迎嘏于砌，
持嘏手曰：“別來瞬息，而發毛已黃。”嘏笑曰：“兄為神仙，弟
為枯骨，命也。”毅因出藥五十丸遺嘏，曰：“此藥一丸可增一歲
耳。歲滿復來，無久居人世，以自苦也。”歡宴畢，嘏乃辭行。自
是已后，遂絕影響。嘏常以是事告于人世。殆四紀，嘏亦不知所在。

　　隴西李朝威敘而嘆曰：“五蟲之長，必以靈者，別斯見矣。人，
裸也，移信鱗蟲。洞庭含納大直，錢塘迅疾磊落，宜有承焉。嘏詠
而不載，獨可鄰其境。愚義之，為斯文。”

Tale 2.9

The Story of Li Zhangwu

By Li Jingliang
Translated by Jing Hu

Li Zhangwu was styled Fei, and his ancestors were from Zhongshan prefecture.[1] He was born to be gifted, quick-witted, and erudite. He was insightful about everything he encountered. He excelled in literature and reached an extremely high level. Although he preached morality, had self-respect, and didn't fuss over his looks, his appearance was refined and his manner gentle. He became good friends with Cui Xin of Qinghe. Cui Xin was also an elegant man and collected a lot of antiques. Because Zhangwu was precise and quick-witted, he could thoroughly explain profound subtleties and explore their root causes in each discussion; people at that time compared him to Zhang Hua of the Jin Dynasty.[2]

In the third year (787 AD) of the Zhenyuan reign (785–804), Cui Xin took a position as a deputy prefect of Huazhou.[3] Li Zhangwu went to visit him from the capital of Chang'an. A few

---

[1]Its seat is modern day Dingzhou, Hebei Province.

[2]Zhang Hua (232–300) was a renowned poet and statesman. He compiled the *Bowuzhi* 博物志, a collection of reports of strange and supernatural phenomena.

[3]A prefecture in modern Henan and Shanxi Provinces, also named Huayin.

days later, when Zhangwu went out wandering, he saw a very beautiful woman in the North Street. So he lied to Cui Xin, "I have to visit my relatives and friends outside of Huazhou." Thereupon Li Zhangwu rented a room in the beautiful woman's house. The owner's surname was Wang. The beauty was his daughter-in-law. Zhangwu liked the woman and had an affair with her. After more than a month, Zhangwu had spent more than 30,000 cash on living expenses, and the money he lavished on the beauty was twice that. But their two hearts beat as one, and their feelings for each other became deeper and deeper.

Before long, Li Zhangwu had business he had to attend to, so he had to say goodbye to her and return to Chang'an. They affectionately bid each other farewell. Zhangwu left her a *duan* of fine silk with the pattern of love birds crossing their necks, and presented her with a poem, which read:

> The silk with the pattern of love birds,
> How many threads, oh threads of my thoughts, are woven into
>   it?
> Looking after parting at their necks crossing,
> We should be sorrowful for the time before our parting.

In return, the woman gave Zhangwu a white jade ring and also sent him a poem, which read:

> Holding the ring, we long for one another,
> Seeing the ring, you will recall our time together;
> I hope that you, sir, will always treasure it,
> So that your feelings will be as endless as the circle of the ring.

Zhangwu had a servant named Yang Guo. The woman gave him one thousand coins to reward him for serving diligently.

After they parted, Zhangwu settled down in Chang'an and was unable to communicate with Wang for eight or nine years.

In the eleventh year (795) of the Zhenyuan reign, Zhangwu set out from the capital to visit his friend Zhang Yuanzong, who lived in Xiagui County.[4] He suddenly thought of his former lover, so he turned his cart around and crossed the Wei River[5] to visit her.

As it got dark, he arrived in Huazhou, planning to stay at Wang's house. He came to the door, but found no trace of the people. There was only a guest bed outside. Zhangwu thought that her family had gone to the countryside, or left their old job to take up farming and were temporarily living outside the city, or perhaps they were invited to a party by relatives and friends and had not come back yet. So he stopped at her door to rest, planning to find another place to live. At this moment he saw a woman in the east neighbour's house, so he went up to inquire. The woman told him, "The elders of the Wang family left their jobs and went on a trip; as for their daughter-in-law, she died two years ago."

Zhangwu asked her for more details, and she said, "My surname is Yang, the sixth child in my family, and I am the wife of the east neighbour's household."

Yang then asked what Zhangwu's surname was, and he answered in some detail. The woman then asked, "Did you have a servant named Yang Guo?"

Zhangwu replied, "Yes."

So the woman cried and told him, "I've been married and living in this neighbourhood for five years and I was close to Wang. She once told me: 'My husband's house is like a hostel and we see a lot of people who stay here. Those who stayed and flirted with me all used up their wealth and properties, and made promises to me with sweet words — but none have ever touched my heart. A few

---

[4]A county in the prefecture of Huazhou.

[5]The river originated in Weiyuan 渭源 county, Gansu Province, and joined the Yellow River in Tongguan 潼關.

years ago, there was my beloved Li, the eighteenth son [of his parents][6] who once lived in my house. The first time I saw him, I fell for him before I knew it. Later, I slept with him and enjoyed his love.

"'I've been separated from him for several years now. Longing for him makes me unable to eat all day and sleepless all night.

"'My family is certainly unreliable. That husband of mine sent me from place to place.[7] So I have no chance to meet him again. If someone comes here, I hope you can find him according to his appearance and name. If you find him as expected, please be kind to him and tell him my deep feeling. As long as the person has a servant named Yang Guo, that's him.'

"Within two or three years, she was sick and bedridden. Before she died, she made this second plea: 'I have a humble background and was graced by this gentleman's deep affection. I've always longed for him. After a long time, I have fallen ill; I know that my illness cannot be cured. Please help me with the things I have entrusted to you. In case he comes here, I hope that you can convey my sadness from the grave and the endless sigh of my separation. I implore him to stay here, hoping that our souls will meet in an unknown world.'"

Zhangwu then asked the woman to let him in and told his servants to buy firewood, hay, and food. Just when he was about to prepare his bedding, a woman suddenly came into the room with a broom to sweep the floor. The woman next door didn't recognize her either. Zhangwu then asked his servants and they replied that she came from this house.

After pressing the woman, she slowly said, "The Wangs' dead daughter-in-law is grateful for your loving kindness to her

---

[6]Li Shiba 李十八.

[7]It seems that the husband prostituted her.

and will come to meet you; fearing that you would be afraid of her, she sent me to tell you." Zhangwu nodded and said, "This is why I came here. Although 'Light and Shade' travel different paths, and everyone is afraid to cross, I have neither doubt nor fear because our feelings of longing have reached this point."

After he said that, the woman with the broom gladly took her leave. Pausing at the doorway for a moment, she disappeared. Then he prepared a food offering and performed the ritual to beckon her spirit. After eating and drinking himself, he went to bed.

On the second of the five night watch periods (21:00–23:00) or so, the lamp placed on the southeast side of the bed suddenly flickered several times. Zhangwu realized that something was happening, and thus had the candles moved to the walls at the southeast corner of the room. Immediately he heard a rustle from the north end of the room, as if a person was slowly coming. After five or six steps, he could distinguish her appearance. Looking at her clothes, he knew she was the daughter-in-law, the same as before, except that when she moved she seemed floating and rushing, and her voice light and clear. Zhangwu got out of bed and rushed to embrace her, just like in the romantic encounters when she was alive. The woman herself said, "Since my name was entered on the registry of the netherworld, I have forgotten all my relatives, but the heart that misses you is still the same as in the past."

Zhangwu listened and became more affectionate with her and did not feel anything unusual. However, she sent servants to check for the Morning Star several times. When that star comes out, she must go back. She could not stay long. Each time when they were resting in between making love, she earnestly asked him to take good care of the neighbour madam Yang, saying, "Were it not for this person, who would have conveyed my lovesickness in the nether world?"

When it was the fifth watch (3:00–5:00 am), someone came to tell Madame Wang that it was time to go back. She got out of bed crying, and walked out of the door with Zhangwu arm in arm. She looked up at the Milky Way and sobbed bitterly. She then returned to the room, untied a brocade purse from her skirt band, from which she fished out an item for Zhangwu.

It was azure in color, hard and fine in texture, cool like jade, and shaped like a small leaf. Zhangwu did not recognize what it was. Wang said: "This is the so-called 'Mohe[8] treasure', which comes from the Wonderland in the Kunlun Mountain. It is not easy to get. Recently Madame Yujing[9] and I enjoyed ourselves at the West Sacred Mountain.[10] I saw this item on top of a pile of precious jade ornaments. I loved it and inquired about it. Madame Yujing gave it to me as a gift, telling me that, 'The immortals in the heavenly caves always take pride in having such a piece. Because you believe in Taoism with a profound understanding, I give it to you now, hoping you may cherish it forever. This is not something that can be found in the world of the mortal.'"

She then composed a poem for him, which read:

The Milky Way has tilted astray,
And my soul will fly away.
Would you turn to hold me again for the day?
From now on to meet there's no way!

---

[8]Mohe 靺鞨 is the name of an ethnic group in the northeast part in China in ancient times. The "Mo He treasure" is the treasure of the Mo He people.

[9]Madame Yujing 玉京夫人 is a female immortal in fairy tales.

[10]"Xiyue" 西嶽 refers to Hua Shan 華山.

Zhangwu took out a white jade hairpin to thank her and composed a poem in reply:

> Separated by darkness and light,
> How could we expect such a romantic day?
> There is no one to blame for our parting again,
> I sigh for not knowing where you will go.

The two stood hand in hand wiping tears for a long time. The woman presented him with another poem, which read:

> I expected reunion when we parted before,
> But today we have hope no more.
> The new sadness mixed with the old sorrow,
> Lock me up in the netherworld for thousands of years to follow.

Zhangwu responded with a poem:

> An appointment to meet again is hopeless,
> The regret in the past has started flooding my heart,
> There won't be any news from you on the path you depart on,
> How can I send you my longing for you?

After they bid each other emotional farewells, Wang returned to the northwest corner of the room. After taking a few steps, she looked back, wiping her tears, and said, "Darling, don't forget me, always think about this person in the netherworld."

She stood there sobbing again, but seeing that the sky was getting bright; she hurried to the corner and disappeared. The empty room looked mysterious and the dim candle sputtered. Zhangwu then packed up hurriedly and prepared to return to Wuding Castle in Chang'an from Xiagui County. The Xiagui Magistrate and Zhang Yuanzong brought wine to a farewell banquet. After they had a good drink, Zhangwu started to think about Wang again and improvised a poem, which read:

Water does not flow back to the west and the moon is only
   temporarily full,
Leaving me disconsolate at the edge of this ancient city.
What a depression the parting road will be tomorrow morning,
Who knows which year it will be when we meet again?

After finishing chanting, he said goodbye to the county magistrate. He travelled a few *li* alone and recited the poems by himself again. Suddenly he heard an exclamation of mournful admiration out of the air. Listening carefully again, he recognized that it was Wang, who said: "In the netherworld, each has her assigned area. We part here today and we can never meet again. Knowing that you missed me, I risked being punished by the Judge of the Netherworld and came all the way to see you off. You must take care of yourself!"

Zhangwu was even more deeply touched. After returning to Chang'an, he talked about this matter with Li Zhu of Longxi County, a Taoist friend, who was deeply moved by Wang's sincerity. He wrote a poem which read:

The stone sank in the vast expanse of the sea of Liao,
The sword dropped at the far end under the sky of Chu.
There will never be a day to reunite,
The sorrow of parting covers up the setting sun.

When Zhangwu worked in the Prime Minister's Office in Dongping, he had lots of free time, so he invited a jade worker to see the 'Mohe treasure' that Wang gave him; the jade worker also knew what it was, and dared not carve it. Later, he was ordered to go to Daliang.[11] He invited a jade worker there to see it too. The worker could roughly identify it, and he followed the original shape of the jade piece to carve a mistletoe leaf. When Zhangwu

---

[11]Daliang 大梁, modern day Kaifeng city, Henan Province.

went to the capital on official business, he always carried it against his breast.

Once he went to the east street of the city and came across a foreign monk who suddenly approached his horse, kowtowed and said, "You carry such a treasure above your heart; I beg to have a look." Zhangwu then led him to a secluded place and showed him. After appreciating it for a while, the monk said, "This is the best treasure in heaven, and is not of the human world."

After that, whenever Zhangwu travels to and from Huazhou, he always visits Lady Yang to present her with gifts. He has never stopped until today.

李章武傳

李景亮

李章武，字飛，其先中山人。生而敏博，遇事便了。工文學，皆得極至。雖弘道自高，惡爲潔飾，而容貌閑美，即之溫然。與清河崔信友善。信亦雅士，多聚古物，以章武精敏，每訪辨論，皆洞達玄微，研究原本，時人比晉之張華。

貞元三年，崔信任華州別駕，章武自長安詣之。數日，出行，於市北街見一婦人，甚美。因紿信云：「須州外與親故知聞。」遂賃舍於美人之家。主人姓王，此則其子婦也。乃悅而私焉。居月餘日，所計用直三萬餘，子婦所供費倍之。既而兩心克諧，情好彌切。

無何，章武系事，告歸長安，殷勤敘別。章武留交頸鴛鴦綺一端，仍贈詩曰：

「鴛鴦綺，知結幾千絲？
別後尋交頸，應傷未別時。」

子婦答白玉指環一，又贈詩曰：

「捻指環相思，見環重相憶。
願君永持玩，循環無終極。」

章武有僕楊果者，子婦齎錢一千以獎其敬事之勤。

既別，積八九年。章武家長安，亦無從與之相聞。

至貞元十一年，因友人張元宗寓居下邽縣，章武又自京師與元會。忽恩曩好，乃回車涉渭而訪之。

　　日暝，達華州，將舍於王氏之室。至其門，則闃無行跡，但外有賓榻而已。章武以爲下里或廢業即農，暫居郊野；或親賓邀聚，未始歸復。但休止其門，將別適他舍。見東鄰之婦，就而訪之。乃云：「王氏之長老，皆捨業而出遊，其子婦沒已再周矣。」

　　又詳與之談，即云：「某姓楊，第六，爲東鄰妻。」

　　復訪郎何姓。章武具語之。又云：「曩曾有傔姓楊名果乎？」

　　曰：「有之。」

　　因泣告曰：「某爲里中婦五年，與王氏相善。嘗云：『我夫室猶如傳舍，閱人多矣。其於往來見調者，皆殫財窮産，甘辭厚誓，未嘗動心。頃歲有李十八郎，曾舍於我家。我初見之，不覺自失。後遂私侍枕蓆，實蒙歡愛。今與之別累年矣。思慕之心，或竟日不食，終夜無寢。我家人故不可託，覆被彼夫東西，不時會遇。脫有至者，願以物色名氏求之。如不參差，相託祇奉，並語深意。但有僕夫楊果，即是。』

　　「不二三年，子婦寢疾。臨終，復見託曰：『我本寒微，曾辱君子厚顧，心常感念。久以成疾，自料不治。曩所奉託，萬一至此，願申九泉銜恨，千古睽離之嘆。仍乞留止此，冀神會於髣髴之中。』」

　　章武乃求鄰婦爲開門，命從者市薪蒭食物。方將具茵席，忽有一婦人，持帚，出房掃地。鄰婦亦不之識。章武因訪所從者，云：「是舍中人。」

　　又逼而詰之，即徐曰：「王家亡婦感郎恩情深，將見會。恐生怪怖，故使相聞。」章武許諾，云：「章武所由來者，正爲此也。雖顯晦殊途，人皆忌憚，而思念情至，實所不疑。」

　　言畢，執帚人欣然而去，逡巡映門，即不復見。乃具飲饌，呼祭。自食飲畢，安寢。

　　至二更許，燈在牀之東南，忽爾稍暗，如此再三。章武心知有變，因命移燭背牆，置室東南隅。旋聞室北角悉窣有聲；如有人形，冉冉而至。五六步，即可辨其狀。視衣服，乃主人子婦也。與昔見不異，但舉止浮急，音調輕清耳。章武下牀，迎擁攜手，款若平生之歡。自云：「在冥錄以來，都忘親戚。但思君子之心，如平昔耳。」

　　章武倍與狎暱，亦無他異。但數請令人視明星，若出，當須還，不可久住。每交歡之暇，即懇託在鄰婦楊氏，云：「非此人，誰達幽恨？」

至五更，有人告可還。子婦泣下沾襟，與章武連臂出門，仰望天漢，遂嗚咽悲怨，卻入室，自於裙帶上解錦囊，囊中取一物以贈之。其色紺碧，質又堅密，似玉而冷，狀如小葉。章武不之識也。子婦曰：「此所謂『靺鞨寶』，出崑崙玄圃中。彼亦不可得。妾近於西嶽與玉京夫人戲，見此物在衆寶璫上，愛而訪之。夫人遂假以相授，云：『洞天羣仙，每得此一寶，皆為光榮。』以郎奉玄道，有精識，故以投獻。常願寶之。此非人間之有。」

遂贈詩曰：

「河漢已傾斜，神魂欲超越。
願郎更回抱，終天從此訣。」

章武取白玉寶簪一以酬之，並答詩曰：

「分從幽顯隔，豈謂有佳期。
寧辭重重別，所嘆去何之。」

因相持泣，良久。子婦又贈詩曰：

「昔辭懷後會，今別便終天。
新悲與舊恨，千古閉窮泉。」

章武答曰：

「後期杳無約，前恨已相尋。
別路無行信，何因得寄心？」

款曲敍別訖，遂卻赴西北隅。行數步，猶回頭拭淚云：「李郎無舍，念此泉下人。」

復哽咽佇立，視天欲明，急趨至角，即不復見。但空室窅然，寒燈半滅而已。章武乃促裝，卻自下邽歸長安武定堡。下邽郡官與張元宗攜酒宴飲，既醑，章武懷念，因即事賦詩曰：

「水不西歸月暫圓，令人惆悵古城邊。
蕭條明早分歧路，知更相逢何歲年。」

吟畢，與郡官別。獨行數里，又自諷誦。忽聞空中有歎賞，音調悽惻。更審聽之，乃王氏子婦也。自云："冥中各有地分。今於此別，無日交會。知郎思眷，故冒陰司之責，遠來奉送，千萬自愛！"

章武愈感之。及至長安，與道友隴西李助話，亦感其誠而賦曰：

"石沉遼海闊，劍別楚天長。
會合知無日，離心滿夕陽。"

章武即事東平丞相府，因閒，召玉工視所得靺鞨寶，工亦知，不敢雕刻。後奉使大梁，又召玉工，粗能辨，乃因其形，雕作楞葉象。奉使上京，每以此物貯懷中。

至市東街，偶見一胡僧，忽近馬叩頭云："君有寶玉在懷，乞一見爾。"乃引於靜處開視，僧捧玩移時，云："此天上至物，非人間有也。"

章武后往來華州，訪遺楊六娘，至今不絕。

Tale 2.10

The Tale of Huo Xiaoyu

By Jiang Fang
Translated by Zhenjun Zhang

In the Dali period (766–779) of the Tang, there was a scholar from the area west of Long Mountain, named Li Yi,[1] who was picked out for the ranks by passing the imperial examination at the age of twenty. In the following year an examination for the preeminent scholar would be held,[2] so he waited for the test by the Ministry of Personnel. In the sixth month, in summer, he arrived at Chang'an and lodged in Xinchang Ward.

---

[1]Li Yi 李益 (748–827), styled Junyu 君虞, belonged to the clan of Li Kuei 李揆, who was the chief minister during the reign of Emperor Suzong 肅宗 (r. 756–762). He passed the *jinshi* examination in the fourth year of the Dali reign (769), and he was also a famous poet. He and Li He 李賀 (790–816) enjoyed equal fame at the end of the Zhenyuan 貞元 (785–805) period. Every time he finished a poem, the court musicians got it through bribery and took it as the lyrics of a song to sing for the emperor. However, he had a suspicious nature and was jealous of his wife and concubines, a tendency that was called "Li Yi's disease" during his time. He ended his official career as a Minister of the Board of Rites.

[2]One of the two imperial examinations for selecting officials beyond the normal selection in the Tang dynasty. People who passed either of the examinations would be offered an official position immediately.

The scholar was from a lofty clan, with a genius for writing even when he was young. His fine verses and excellent lines were noted as matchless at the time; the accomplished elders praised and admired him unanimously. He was often proud of his unrestrained spirit and gifts, and hoped to get a beautiful mate. He searched widely among the famous courtesans for a long time, but found no suitable candidate.

In Chang'an there was a matchmaker surnamed Bao, her name Shiyi niang, the eleventh daughter of her parents. Formerly, she had been a bondservant-maid in the family of Commandant-escort Xue, but more than ten years ago she tore up the indenture and followed a good man. Flattering by nature and with a ready tongue, she came and went through all the rich and powerful families and the residences of the royal relatives. As for having a hand in romantic affairs and arranging matches, she was esteemed as a great leader. When she received the scholar's sincere trust and generous gifts, she felt very much indebted to him.

After several months had passed, just as Li was sitting leisurely in the south pavilion of his lodgings between *shen* and *wei* in the afternoon,[3] he suddenly heard someone announcing that she was Bao, very urgently knocking at the door. Lifting up his robe, he hurried to greet her and asked: "What brings you here unexpectedly today, Bao?"

Bao replied with a smile, "Haven't you, the bookworm,[4] been having good dreams yet? There is a fairy who has been banished

---

[3]Around three o'clock in the afternoon. *Shen* 申 refers to the period from three to five o'clock, while *wei* 未 is from one to three o'clock in the afternoon.

[4]The meaning of *su guzi* 蘇姑子 is unknown. Wang Meng'ou says that it may be equivalent to *sao guzi* 騷姑子 (coquette). Another view is that it is a homophone of *shu guanzi* 書罐子 (bookworm), a kind of mocking name for the scholars. See Tan Fengliang 譚鳳梁, ed. *Lidai*

down to this lower realm, and she does not seek wealth or property, but only longs for the gifted and unconventional. With such a character and appearance, she is really a match for you."

On hearing this, the scholar leapt for joy, feeling his spirit soaring and his body lighter. Grasping Bao's hands, he said to her with respectful bows and thanks: "I will be your servant for the rest of my life — I would even give my life for you." He took the opportunity to ask about the girl's name and dwelling. Bao said, "She is the youngest daughter of the former Prince Huo, styled Xiaoyu. The prince was extremely fond of her. Her mother was named Jingchi, a favorite servant-girl of the prince. Immediately after the prince's death, all Xiaoyu's half-brothers refused to accept her as a true sister because she was given birth by a humble concubine mother; accordingly, they gave her some property and money, and sent her to live elsewhere. She changed her family name to Zheng, and few know that she is the prince's daughter. But her appearance and gestures are so beautiful and charming, such as I have never seen in my life, and her refined tastes and elegant grace are beyond compare. She is well-versed, too, in music and the classics. Yesterday, she asked me to find a good young man who would match her in nature and style. I told her all about you. She also knew the name of Li Shilang, the Tenth Gentlemen, and was filled with joy. She lives in Old Temple Lane in the Shengye Quarter,[5] at the southern end; specifically the yard with a gate for carriages on the left is her residence.[6] I have made

---

wenyen xiaoshuo jianshang cidian 歷代文言小說鑒賞詞典 (Nanjing: Jiangsu wenyi, 1991), p. 367.

[5]The Shengye 勝業 Quarter was located north of the Eastern Market and west of the Xingqing 興慶 Palace in the northeastern part of Chang'an. See the map of Chang'an (Wang Meng'ou, A, front matter).

[6]The phrase *fu shang che men zhai* 甫上車門宅 has puzzled many scholars. Uchiyama Chinari 內山知也 suspects *fu shang* 甫上 is *pu shang* 浦上 (*Tangdai xiaoshuo xuanzhu* 唐代小說選注, Tokyo, 1973); Dai

an appointment for you. Tomorrow at noon, just go to the entrance of the lane to look for a maid named Guizi, then you will find her."

Immediately after Bao's departure, the scholar began to prepare for the visit. He ordered the young servant, Qiuhong, to borrow a black charger with a gold bridle from his cousin Shang, who was adjutant-general of the capital. That evening, he washed his clothes, bathed, and shaved. The combination of joy and excitement kept him from falling asleep all night. At daybreak, he put on his kerchief, fetched a mirror and regarded his appearance in it, fearing only that he might fail. He paced back and forth until the noon hour. Then, ordering the charger harnessed, he galloped directly to the Shengye Quarter.

Having arrived at the appointed place, he saw a maid standing there, waiting as expected. She stepped forward and asked: "You are Li the Tenth, aren't you?" Li dismounted at once and ordered the maid to lead the horse to the rear of the house. She locked the door hurriedly. Li found, as expected, Bao coming out from inside. She smiled and quipped from a distance, "What kind of young fellow has broken into the house unannounced?" Bantering with him, she led the scholar through an inner gate. In the courtyard there were four cherry trees, and a parrot cage hung at the northwest corner. On seeing the scholar entering, the parrot cried: "Someone has come in, lower the curtains at once!"

Naturally bashful, Li still felt somewhat apprehensive. When he suddenly heard the words of the bird, he was stunned and dared not to enter. While he was hesitating, Bao led Jingchi down

---

Wangshu 戴望舒 suspects it is *jiao shang* 角上 (*Xiaoshuo xiqu lunji* 小說戲曲論集, Beijing: Zuojia chubanshe, 1958, p. 40); Wang Meng'ou considers it *pu shang* 铺上 (*Tangren xiaoshuo jiaoshi* [A], Taibei: Zhongzheng shuju, 1983, pp. 203–4). But all are obscure. Personally I think the *nan shang chemen zhai* 南上車門宅 in *Jiu Xiaoshuo* 舊小説 (2.117) is the best, because *nan* 南 makes much more sense than *fu* and *jiao*.

the steps to welcome him. They invited him inside and had him sit opposite them. Jingchi was a little more than forty, and she was graceful, charming and seductive as she talked and smiled. She said to the young man: "I heard all along that you are gifted and unconventional, now I see that you are handsome and elegant, too. Your fame is really deserved. I have a daughter who, though lacking in proper instructions, is at least not ugly. It should be suitable if she could make a match with you. I heard your intention from Bao many times, and today I would like to offer my daughter to serve you with dustpan and broom." The scholar replied gratefully, "Clumsy and mediocre as I am, it is unexpected for me to receive your favor. If I am really chosen as a match for her, I should take it as an honor for the rest of my life."

Then she ordered wine and dishes to be served, and asked Xiaoyu to come out from a chamber east of the hall. The scholar immediately welcomed her with bows, and felt as if the entire room was filled with a forest of gems and jade trees, which shone brilliantly over all sides. So bright were her eyes and so bewitching her glances! Xiaoyu sat down beside her mother, who said to her, "You once loved to recite the lines:

When the curtain was opened and the wind stirred the bamboo,
I suspect that my old friend is coming.

That is from a poem by Li the Tenth. You have been chanting his poem and thinking of him all day long, how is it compared with seeing him in person?"

Xiaoyu looked down with a smile and whispered, "Seeing him is not as good as hearing his fame, how could a gifted scholar not be handsome?"

The scholar got up several times and said while bowing, "The young lady [you] loves talent while this humble fellow adores beauty. The two set off each other, then we will have both talent and beauty."

The mother and the daughter glanced at each other and laughed. Then they raised cups to drink. After several rounds, the scholar stood up and asked Xiaoyu to sing a song. At first, she was not willing to, but her mother persistently insisted. Her voice was clear and resonant; the melody exquisite and wonderful.

When they had drunk their fill, it was dusk. Bao led the young man to the west courtyard to rest. It was a quiet courtyard with secluded rooms, and the curtains and screens were luxurious. Bao ordered the maids Guizi and Huansha to take off the scholar's boots and untie his belt. In a short while Xiaoyu came. She talked to him tenderly, the tone of her speech agreeable and charming. At the moment when her silk clothes were removed, her appearance and posture were exceedingly enchanting. They lowered the curtain and drew close to each other on the pillows, enjoying pleasure to their hearts' content. The scholar thought to himself that even [encountering the goddess] on Mount Wu or by the River Luo could not have surpassed what he experienced.[7]

In the middle of the night, Xiaoyu suddenly wept. She looked at the scholar and said, "I am merely a courtesan, and I myself know that I am not a match for you. Now, I am loved merely for my beauty, and [relying on beauty] I entrust myself to a benevolent and worthy man. But I worry that, when my beauty fades, your favor will shift and your love change likewise; this will make me like the vine that has nothing to cling to and the

---

[7]Wu shan 巫山 (Mount Wu) and Luo Pu 洛浦 (the bank of Luo River): a reference to King Xiang 襄 of Chu 楚 encountering the goddess of Mount Wu (see Song Yu 宋玉, "Gaotang fu" 高唐賦, in *Wenxuan* 文選 [Hong Kong: Shangwu yinshuguan, 1936, 19.393–97]) and Cao Zhi 曹植 encountering the goddess of 洛 River (see Cao's "Lo shen fu" 洛神賦, *Wenxuan*, 19.401–05).

autumn fan that is discarded.[8] Therefore at the zenith of my joy I cannot help grieving."

On hearing this, the scholar sighed with deep feeling. He then pillowed Xiaoyu's arm, and said to her gently, "My lifelong wish has been fulfilled today. I pledge not to leave you, though my bones be ground to powder and my body smashed to pieces. Why did you, my lady, say these words? Please let me get a piece of white silk and write my oath on it."

Xiaoyu stopped shedding tears, and ordered the maid, Yingtao, to lift the curtain up and hold the candle, while she gave the scholar a brush and inkstone. In her spare time from playing the pipes and plucking the strings, Xiaoyu was fond of poetry and calligraphy. Her book cases, brushes, and inkstone were all old ones from the royal household. She then brought out an embroidered bag, from which she took out three feet of white silk lined with black, which had been woven by the belles of the Yüe,[9] and handed it to him.

Being a literary genius, the scholar grasped the brush and finished his writing in no time. In this, he compared his love to the mountains and the rivers, and his fidelity to the sun and the moon. Every line was so sincere that anyone who might read it would be moved. After he finished, Xiaoyu ordered the maid to put it in her

---

[8]Nüluo 女萝, a kind of parasitic vine, can also be called *tusi* 菟絲. "Gushi" 古詩 (Old poems): 與君為新婚，菟絲附女萝 (I am newly married to you, just like the vine clings to the vine). See Shen Deqian 沈 德潜, ed., *Gu shiyuan* 古詩源 (Taibei: Taiwan shangwu yinshuguan, 1966), p. 54. The vine that has nothing to cling to is a metaphor for a woman who has lost the favor of a man she relies on. Qiushan jianjuan 秋扇見捐 (the autumn fan is thrown away) is another metaphor. See Ban Jieyu 班 婕妤, *Yuan ge xing* 怨歌行 (*Wenxuan*, 27. 598).

[9]*Yue* 越 is the name of a nationality. In ancient China, the area of Jiangxi, Zhejiang, Guangdong, and Fujian Province, occupied by the *Yue* people, was called *bai Yue* 百越 or *baiyue* 百粵 (Hundred *Yue*).

jewelry box. From then on, they loved each other in harmony, just like a pair of kingfishers flying freely in the clouds. They lived this way for two years, together day and night.

In the spring of the next year, the scholar ascended the [selection] subject by passing "the Preeminent" examination of written judgments, and was appointed Assistant Magistrate of Zheng County.[10] In the fourth month, he was about to leave for his post and, afterward, to visit his parents in East Luo.[11] Most of his relatives in Chang'an attended the farewell party for him. It was at the time in a year when the spring prospects still remained and the summer scene began to show its beauty. After the feast ended and the guests scattered, the sorrow of approaching separation occupied Xiaoyu's mind. She said to the scholar, "With your endowment, family and fame, you are admired by most people. Of course there will be many people who want to be related to you through marriage. Furthermore, you still have parents at home, but have no daughter-in-law yet in your family. Once you leave this time, you are certainly going to make a good match. The words in your pledge are but empty ones. However, I have a small wish that I want to tell you right now, and hope that you will keep it in mind forever. Would you still be willing to listen?"

The scholar was startled, pleading, "What fault have I committed, that you say these words unexpectedly? Please tell me what you want to say, I will certainly respectfully follow it."

Xiaoyu said, "I am just eighteen years old, you are merely twenty-two; there are still eight years before you reach the prime of your life. I hope to complete the joy and love of my life during this period. After that, it would still not be too late for you to select from a high-ranking family to harmonize the Qin and the

---

[10]Modern Hua County, Shanxi.
[11]Dong Lo 東洛 here refers to the Eastern Capital, Loyang 洛陽.

Jin.[12] I will then abandon the affairs of this world, cut off my hair, and put on black clothes.[13] That would be enough for the long-cherished wish of my life."

The scholar was regretful and moved, and he couldn't help but shed tears. He promised Xiaoyu, "I will fulfill the pledge I made by the bright sun, no matter whether I am alive or dead. Even if I live with you for the rest of my life, I would still fear that it is too short to satisfy my long-held wish. How dare I think otherwise? I wholeheartedly beg you not to doubt me. Just stay here calmly and wait until the eighth month, I will return to Huazhou and look for someone to welcome you.[14] The date of our reunion is not far." After another several days, the scholar bid farewell to Xiaoyu and left for the east.

About ten days after he arrived at his post, Li asked leave to visit his parents at the East Capital. Before his arrival home, his mother had discussed his marriage with his cousin, Ms. Lu, and the agreement had already been settled. His mother was always strict and firm. The scholar, though hesitant, dared not refuse. Thus he followed the confirmation rites, and then a close date was set for the wedding.[15] The Lu clan was also a magnificent one.

---

[12]Xie Qin Jin 諧秦晋 ("harmonize the Qin and the Jin") means to get married. This idiom originated from the generations-long intermarriage between the two states in the Spring and Autumn period.

[13]Pizi 披緇 (put on black clothes) means to renounce the family and become a nun. *Zi* is the gray-black colored clothes worn by nuns.

[14]Huazhou 華州, modern Hua County in Shanxi Province. Zheng County belonged to Huazhou in the Tang dynasty.

[15]Since the Spring and Autumn period, *Liu li* 六禮, six rites, became the fixed rites for marriage which lasted in China for two thousand years. They are: *nacai* 納彩, sending first gift, normally a chicken or a goose, to the girl's home to request discussing and processing the marriage; *wenming* 問名, asking the girl's family background and birth date; *naji* 納吉, divining in the boy's ancestral temple to consult his ancestors to see

When marrying a daughter to another clan, they must get a promise of a million cash for betrothal money. If the money offered was less than this amount, the marriage would, on principle, not be allowed to proceed. The scholar's family had always been poor, so for the marriage they had to ask for loans. He took false reasons as the pretext to look up his relatives and friends far away, crossing the Yangzi River and the Huai River, traveling from autumn till the next summer. Aware that he had reneged on his pledge and greatly exceeded the promised time, the scholar remained silent and hidden from others, with the intent to make Xiaoyu give up her hope. From afar, he also trusted his relatives and friends to not make a slip of the tongue.

Since the scholar exceeded the appointed time, Xiaoyu had inquired about his whereabouts many times. The false news and unreliable messages she received differed one from the other each day. Filled with sorrow and regret, she sought widely for the fortune tellers and consulted with diviners, and this went on for more than a year. Then, with emaciated body lying in the empty chamber, she fell into a severe and lingering illness. Even though the scholar's letters never came again, Xiaoyu's longing for him never altered. She sent gifts to her relatives and friends, hoping they would bring her news of him. Her inquiries were so urgent and sincere that her resources were exhausted time and again. She

---

if the marriage would be auspicious; *nazheng* 納徵, sending betrothal gifts to the girl's family: the marriage is formally effective if the girl's family accepts the gifts; *qingqi* 請期, setting the wedding date through consultation with the girl's parents; and *qinying* 親迎, when the bridegroom, acting on the order of his father, goes to the bride's home to welcome her. See Sun Xidan 孫希旦, "Hunyi" 婚儀 in *Liji jijie* 禮記集解 (Beijing: Zhunghua shuju, 1989), pp. 1416–23. Here Li Yi's mother had completed all the first three rites, and Li Yi himself just went to send the betrothal gifts to confirm the marriage. After that a close date for wedding was set.

frequently sent her maid out secretly to sell dresses and playthings from her suitcase, and most of them were entrusted to Hou Jingxian's commission shop in the West Market to sell.

Once, she sent the maid, Huansha, with a purple jade hairpin to sell at the residence of Jingxian. On the way, Huansha encountered an old jade craftsman who once served in the court. Seeing what Huansha was holding, he came up to identify it and said, "I crafted this hairpin. Many years ago, when the youngest daughter of Prince Huo was about to have her hair pinned up,[16] the prince ordered me to make this pin, and he gave me 10,000 cash as reward. I have never forgotten it. Where did you get it?" Huansha replied, "My mistress is precisely the daughter of Prince Huo. Her family was impoverished, and she lost her chastity to a man. Her husband went to the East Capital last year, but there has been no word from him. Languishing in sorrow, she fell ill. It has been nearly two years. She asked me to sell this to bribe someone and ask him to seek news of her husband."

The jade craftsman shed tears in sadness, lamenting, "How could the high born sons and daughters of noblemen be so out of luck and in dire straits like this! My remaining days are nearly at an end, but I cannot bear the sorrow of seeing this fluctuation of fortune." He then led Huansha to the mansion of the Princess of Yanxian,[17] and related to her the story in detail. The Princess also sighed in sadness for a long while, and she gave the maid 120,000 cash for the hairpin.

At this time the girl of the Lu family, to whom the scholar was engaged, was in Chang'an. Having finished raising the necessary sum for the betrothal gifts, the scholar went back to

---

[16]In ancient China, a girl had her hair pinned up with a hairpin at the age of fifteen.

[17]The Princess *Yanxian* should be *Yanguang*, the seventh daughter of Emperor Suzong.

Zheng County, and in the last month of the year, he again asked for leave to go to the capital for his wedding. He chose a secluded lodging in secret, and let no one know. There was a *mingjing* named Cui Yunming,[18] who was the scholar's cousin. He was extremely honest and kind in nature. In the years past, he had often enjoyed time together with the scholar in Miss Zheng's house. They laughed and chatted over food and drink, and there had been no distance between them (i.e., they had been on intimate terms). Every time he received news of the scholar, he would relay the news to Xiaoyu candidly. Xiaoyu frequently helped Cui with firewood, provisions, and clothes. For that, Cui was extremely grateful to her. After the scholar arrived [in Chang'an], Cui faithfully told Xiaoyu all what he knew. Xiaoyu sighed in indignation, saying, "How could this kind of thing happen in the world!" She then asked all her relatives and friends to make [Li Yi] meet her by any means.

The scholar was aware that he had exceeded the appointed time and broken his pledge, and he also knew that Xiaoyu's illness was serious and lingering. Ashamed of himself, he reluctantly cut off his relationship with her and refused to go. He would go out in the early morning and return only in the late evening, trying to avoid everyone. Xiaoyu wept day and night, and completely forgot to sleep and eat. She wished to meet Li Yi just once, but, unexpectedly, could not find the chance. While her resentment and indignation deepened, she was exhausted and was confined to her bed. From then on, this was gradually known by people in Chang'an. Men of sentiment were all moved by Xiaoyu's affection,

---

[18]*Mingjing* 明經 was a type of imperial examination in the Tang Dynasty. The exam consisted not of writing poems and rhapsodies, as required in the *jinshi* exam, but explaining the meaning of the classics. It was easier to pass the *mingjing* exam compared to taking the *jinshi* exam, but those who passed the *mingjing* exam were still commoners and couldn't get an official position.

while gallant men were all enraged at the scholar's frivolous conduct.

It was the third month of the year, and many people were going on spring outings. In the company of five or six of his friends, the scholar went to Chongjing Temple to enjoy the peonies in bloom. They strolled along the west corridor, taking turns composing verses [for the occasion]. A man of Jingzhao named Wei Xiaqing, who was a close friend of the scholar, was then also walking along with the party. He said to the scholar, "The scenery is so beautiful, and the grasses and trees are so luxuriant and glorious. What a pity that Miss Zheng should nurse a bitter sense of wrong in her empty chamber! You could really abandon her at last. You are indeed a hard-hearted man! But a real man's heart shouldn't be like this. You should think it over again."

As Wei was sighing and reproaching Li, there suddenly appeared a gallant wearing a yellow silk shirt and carrying a bow. He was handsome, full of vigor, splendidly dressed, and followed only by a boy of the northern tribe with short-cut hair. Following them secretly, he overheard what they were discussing. After a moment, he went forward and greeted the scholar with hands clasped, exclaiming, "Aren't you Li the Tenth? My family comes originally from Shandong, and we are related to the relatives of the emperor through marriage. Though I lack literary talent, I like to make friends with talented men. Having been admiring your splendid reputation, I have always longed to make your acquaintance. Today I am so lucky to meet you and have an opportunity to behold your exquisite appearance. My humble residence is not far from here, and there are also songs and music that are enough for entertainment. Besides, there are eight or nine bewitching girls and more than ten fine horses, all of which you can do with what you desire. I merely hope that you will come and have a visit."

The scholar's friends all carefully listened to these words, and each in turn sighed with admiration so that they rode along with the gallant. After winding through a few wards, they arrived at Shengye Ward. Because it was close to Xiaoyu's residence, the scholar did not want to go. He made an excuse and wanted to turn the head of his horse back, when the gallant said, "My humble residence is well within reach; how can you bear to discard me?" He took hold of the scholar's horse and pulled it along. Delaying in this way, they had reached the entrance of the lane where Miss Zheng lived. The scholar was distracted. Whipping his horse, he intended to turn back. The gallant hurriedly ordered a few servants to take hold of him and force him to go. Walking quickly, they pushed Li into the carriage gate; [the gallant] at once had it locked, and announced, "Li the Tenth has arrived!" The whole household called out in happy astonishment, which could be heard even outside.

The previous night, Xiaoyu had dreamed that a man wearing a yellow shirt brought the scholar to her; when he reached the mat, he asked her to take off her shoes. When she woke with a start, she related the dream to her mother and interpreted it herself, "The word *xie* (shoe), being homophonous with the word *xie* (in harmony), refers to the reunion of a husband and his wife; the word *tuo* (take off) means 'to divide'. Being divided immediately after the reunion also means to be separated forever. Judging from this, I am sure that Li Yi and I will meet soon, and after we see each other, I shall die."

In the early morning she asked her mother to comb her hair and put on her makeup for her. Considering that she might be somewhat distraught because of her lingering illness, her mother didn't really believe her. Reluctantly she tried to do her makeup for her. No sooner had she finished the makeup than the scholar indeed arrived. Xiaoyu had been ill so long that she needed other's assistance even turn over in bed. But when she suddenly heard that the scholar had arrived, she got up swiftly, changed her clothes and emerged, as if some divine force were assisting her. She met the scholar and stared at him in indignation, saying nothing. Her body was so slim and frail that it seemed as if she could hardly bear it. From time to time, she covered her face with her sleeve and looked back at scholar Li. Moved by the heart-rending past events and taking pity on the lady, all those present were sobbing.

In a little while, several dozen dishes of food and wine were brought in from outside. All present were surprised to see the feast. They asked immediately where the food had come from and found that all of it had been ordered by the young gallant. Thus they laid out the food and wine and sat down side by side.

Xiaoyu turned away [from Li], and turned her face back, staring sideways at the scholar for a long time. She raised her cup of wine and poured it on the ground, saying, "As a woman, I am so unfortunate. You, as a man, are so heartless. Pretty and young as I am, I will die with a grievance in my heart. My kind mother is still alive at home, but I cannot look after her; [as for] silk dresses, pipes and strings, from now on I have to leave them forever. In suffering, I shall go to the Yellow Spring,[19] and all of this is caused by you. Mr. Li, Mr. Li! Now we shall say farewell forever! After my death, however, I shall certainly become an avenging ghost and cause your wife and concubines to never have peace!" Then she grasped Li's arm with her left hand, and threw her cup to the ground. With several long and bitter cries, she passed away.

Her mother immediately lifted her body and placed it in the scholar's arms, asking him to call her. But she could not be revived. Attired in white mourning clothes for her, the scholar wept sorrowfully day and night.

---

[19]*Huang quan* 黄泉, Yellow Spring, refers to the netherworld.

The night before the burial, the scholar suddenly saw Xiaoyu within the funeral curtains, her appearance as beautiful as in life. She was wearing a pomegranate-red skirt, a purple tunic, and a red and green cape. Leaning against the curtain and holding the embroidered sash in hand, she looked back at the scholar and said, "I feel ashamed for your sending me [to the other world], and it seems that you still have some feelings for me. In the netherworld, how can I restrain my sighs!" As soon as she finished speaking, she disappeared. The next day, she was buried at the Yüsu Plain of Chang'an. The scholar went to the place of burial, expressed all his mourning [for the dead] by wailing, and then returned.

More than a month later, the scholar carried out the wedding ceremonies with Miss Lu. In grief and moved by the past events, he fell into melancholy.

In the fifth month of the year, during summer, Li went back to Cheng County together with Miss Lu. About ten days after they arrived, when the scholar was in bed with Miss Lu, he heard a whispering sound outside the bed curtain. The scholar was startled and looked out, and found that there was a man around twenty years old, with a handsome appearance and gentle gestures, concealing himself within the curtain and repeatedly beckoning to Miss Lu. With fear and panic, Li rose and chased him around the curtain a few times, but the man suddenly disappeared. From then on the scholar harbored suspicion and evil thoughts in his mind, doubt and distrust consuming him. Between husband and wife, there was no longer any peace. One of his relatives or friends persuaded and soothed him mildly and tactfully, and the scholar's suspicions were relieved a little.

Ten days later, the scholar returned from outside just as Miss Lu was playing the zither on the couch; suddenly, they saw an engraved rhinoceros-horn box was thrown in from the gate. It was over an inch in size, a ribbon of light silk in a knot of one heart tied to the middle. It was thrown exactly into Miss Lu's lap. The scholar opened it and looked inside, he found two love seeds, a kowtow beetle, a passion pill, and a modicum of aphrodisiac made from the mouth of a newborn donkey. At that point the young man roared in rage, his voice like a jackal or tiger. He grasped the zither and hit his wife with it, closely questioning and commanding her to tell the truth. But even Miss Lu could not clear herself. Thereafter, he often beat her fiercely, and treated her with all cruelties. At last he accused her in the court and sent her back [to her home].[20]

After he divorced Miss Lu, the scholar was always jealous and distrustful of the women, such as the maidens or concubines, with whom he had shared a pillow and mat. There was even one whom he killed just because of his jealousy.

Once, the scholar visited Guangling[21] and obtained a famous courtesan called Ying the Eleventh. Her appearance was sleek and charming. The scholar was very fond of her. Every time they sat face to face, he would tell her, "I once obtained such and such a concubine from such and such a place, she committed such and such a crime, and I killed her in such and such a way." He

---

[20]*Qianzhi* 遣之, discard her. We also can say *chu zhi* 出之 or *qu zhi* 去之. In ancient China a husband could abandon his wife using various unreasonable excuses. "Ben ming" 本命, *Da dai li* 大戴礼, "婦有七去：不順父母，去；无子，去；淫，去；妒，去；有惡疾，去；多言，去；盜竊，去。" (There are seven kinds of situations in which a woman should be discarded. If she does not obey her parents-in-law, she should be discarded; if she cannot give birth to a son, she should be discarded; if she is promiscuous, she should be discarded; if she is jealous of other women of her husband, she should be discarded; if she has a serious disease, she should be discarded; if she is gossipy, she should be discarded; if she steals things, she should be discarded). See Gao Ming 高明, *Da dai li jinzhu jinyi* 大戴禮今注今譯 (Taibei: Taiwan shangwu yinshuguan, 1975), p. 469.

[21]Modern Yangzhou in Jiangsu Province.

repeated it every day, intending to make her fear him, and through this to keep her boudoir clean.

When he went out, he covered Miss Ying on the bed with a wash tub, sealing it and making marks around it. After he returned, he checked it carefully and then opened it. Furthermore, he kept a dagger that was very sharp. He looked around at his maidens, warning, "This is [made of] Gexi steel from Xinzhou.[22] It will only be used to cut off the head of a woman who commits a crime!" All the women whom the scholar met always caused him to be jealous. He married three times, but each marriage ended up just like the first had.

Note: This is a revised version of my 2010 rendition in William Nienhauser, ed., *Tang Dynasty Tales: A Guided Reader* (Singapore: World Scientific, 2010, pp. 233–76), where more annotations and commentary are provided.

---

[22]Northwest of modern Shangrao in Jiangxi Province. The steel produced there is the best for making swords.

霍小玉傳

蔣防

大歷中，隴西李生名益，年二十，以進士擢第。其明年，拔萃，俟試於天官。夏六月，至長安，舍於新昌里。

生門族清華，少有才思，麗詞嘉句，時謂無雙。先達丈人，翕然推伏。每自矜風調，思得佳偶，博求名妓，久而未諧。

長安有媒鮑十一娘者，故薛駙馬家青衣也，折券從良，十餘年矣。性便辟，巧言語，豪家戚里，無不經過，追風挾策，推為渠帥。常受生誠託厚賂，意頗德之。

經數月，李方閑居舍之南亭。申未間，忽聞扣門甚急，云是鮑十一娘至。攝衣從之，迎問曰："鮑卿，今日何故忽然而來？"

鮑笑曰："蘇姑子作好夢也未？有一仙人，謫在下界，不邀財貨，但慕風流。如此色目，共十郎相當矣。"

生聞之驚躍，神飛體輕，引鮑手且拜且謝曰："一生作奴，死亦不憚。"因問其名居。鮑具說曰："故霍王小女，字小玉，王甚愛之。母曰淨持。淨持即王之寵婢也。王之初薨，諸弟兄以其出自賤庶，不甚收錄。因分與資財，遣居於外，易姓為鄭氏，人亦不知其王女。資質穠艷，一生未見，高情逸態，事事過人，音樂詩書，無不通解。昨遣某求一好兒郎，格調相稱者。某具說十郎。他亦知有李十郎名字，非常歡愜。住在勝業坊古寺曲，甫上車門宅是也。已與他作期約。明日午時，但至曲頭覓桂子，即得矣。"

鮑既去，生便備行計。遂令家僮秋鴻，於從兄京兆參軍尚公處假青驪駒，黃金勒。其夕，生澣衣沐浴，修飾容儀，喜躍交並，通夕不寐。遲明，巾幘，引鏡自照，惟懼不諧也。徘徊之間，至於亭午。遂命駕疾驅，直抵勝業。

至約之所，果見青衣立候，迎問曰："莫是李十郎否？"即下馬，令牽入屋底，急急鎖門。見鮑果從內出來，遙笑曰："何等兒郎，造次入此？"生調誚未畢，引入中門。庭間有四櫻桃樹；西北懸一鸚鵡籠，見生入來，即語曰："有人入來，急下簾者！"

生本性雅淡，心猶疑懼，忽見鳥語，愕然不敢進。逡巡，鮑引淨持下階相迎，延入對坐。年可四十餘，綽約多姿，談笑甚媚。因謂生曰："素聞十郎才調風流，今又見儀容雅秀，名下固無虛士。某有一女子，雖拙教訓，顏色不至醜陋，得配君子，頗為相宜。頻見鮑十一娘說意旨，今亦便令承奉箕帚。"生謝曰："鄙拙庸愚，不意顧盼，倘垂採錄，生死為榮。"

遂命酒饌，即令小玉自堂東閣子中而出。生即拜迎。但覺一室之中，若瓊林玉樹，互相照曜，轉盼精彩射人。既而遂坐母側。母謂曰："汝嘗愛念'開簾風動竹，疑是故人來。'即此十郎詩也。爾終日念想，何如一見？"

玉乃低鬟微笑，細語曰："見面不如聞名。才子豈能無貌？"

生遂連起拜曰："小娘子愛才，鄙夫重色。兩好相映，才貌相兼。"

母女相顧而笑，遂舉酒數巡。生起，請玉唱歌。初不肯，母固強之。發聲清亮，曲度精奇。酒闌，及暝，鮑引生就西院憩息。閒庭邃宇，簾幕甚華。鮑令侍兒桂子、浣沙與生脫靴解帶。須臾，玉至，言敘溫和，辭氣宛媚。解羅衣之際，態有餘妍，低幃昵枕，極其歡愛。生自以為巫山、洛浦不過也。

中宵之夜，玉忽流涕觀生曰："妾本倡家，自知非匹。今以色愛，托其仁賢。但慮一旦色衰，恩移情替，使女蘿無托，秋扇見捐。極歡之際，不覺悲至。"

生聞之，不勝感嘆，乃引臂替枕，徐謂玉曰："平生志願，今日獲從，粉骨碎身，誓不相捨。夫人何發此言？請以素縑，著之盟約。"

玉因收淚，命侍兒櫻桃褰幄執燭，受生筆研。玉管弦之暇，雅好詩書，筐箱筆研，皆王家之舊物。遂取繡囊，出越姬烏絲欄素縑三尺以授生。生素多才思，援筆成章，引諭山河，指誠日月，句句懇切，聞之動人。染畢，命藏於寶篋之內。自爾婉孌相得，若翡翠之在雲路也。如此二歲，日夜相從。

其后年春，生以書判拔萃登科，授鄭縣主簿。至四月，將之官，便拜慶於東洛。長安親戚，多就筵餞。時春物尚餘，夏景初麗，酒闌賓散，離思縈懷。玉謂生曰："以君才地名聲，人多景慕，願結婚媾，固亦眾矣。況堂有嚴親，室無冢婦，君之此去，必就佳姻。盟約之言，徒虛語耳。然妾有短願，欲輒指陳。永委君心，復能聽否？"

　　生驚怪曰："有何罪過，忽發此辭？試說所言，必當敬奉。"玉曰："妾年始十八，君纔二十有二，迨君壯室之秋，猶有八歲。一生歡愛，願畢此期。然后妙選高門，以諧秦晉，亦未為晚。妾便捨棄人事，剪髮披緇，夙昔之願，於此足矣。"生且愧且感，不覺涕流。因謂玉曰："皎日之誓，死生以之。與卿偕老，猶恐未愜素志，豈敢輒有二三。固請不疑，但端居相待。至八月，必當卻到華州，尋使奉迎，相見非遠。"更數日，生遂訣別東去。

　　到任旬日，求假往東都覲親。未至家日，太夫人已與商量表妹盧氏，言約已定。太夫人素嚴毅，生逡巡不敢辭讓，遂就禮謝，便有近期。盧亦甲族也，嫁女於他門，聘財必以百萬為約，不滿此數，義在不行。生家素貧，事須求貸，便托假故，遠投親知，涉歷江淮，自秋及夏。

　　生自以辜負盟約，大愆回期，寂不知聞，欲斷期望。遙託親故，不遺漏言。玉自生逾期，數訪音信。虛詞詭說，日日不同。博求師巫，便詢卜筮，懷憂抱恨，周歲有餘。羸臥空閨，遂成沉疾。雖生之書題竟絕，而玉之想望不移，略遺親知，使通消息。尋求既切，資用屢空，往往私令侍婢潛賣篋中服玩之物，多託於西市寄附鋪侯景先家貨賣。

　　曾令侍婢浣沙將紫玉釵一隻，詣景先家貨之。路逢內作老玉工，見浣沙所執，前來認之曰："此釵，吾所作也。昔歲霍王小女將欲上鬟，令我作此，酬我萬錢。我嘗不忘。汝是何人，從何而得？"浣沙曰："我小娘子，即霍王女也。家事破散，失身於人。夫婿昨向東都，更無消息。悒怏成疾，今欲二年。令我賣此，略遺於人，使求音信。"

　　玉工悽然下泣曰："貴人男女，失機落節，一至於此！我殘年向盡，見此盛衰，不勝傷感。"遂引至延先公主宅，具言前事。公主亦為之悲嘆良久，給錢十二萬焉。

　　時生所定盧氏女在長安，生即畢於聘財，還歸鄭縣。其年臘月，又請假入城就親。潛卜靜居，不令人知。有明經崔允明者，生之中表弟也。性甚長厚，昔歲常與生同歡於鄭氏之室，杯盤笑語，曾不相間。每得生信，必誠告於玉。玉常以薪芻衣服，資給於崔。崔頗感之。生既至，崔具以誠告玉。玉恨嘆曰：“天下豈有是事乎！”遍請親朋，多方召致。

生自以愆期負約，又知玉疾候沈綿，慚恥忍割，終不肯往。晨出暮歸，欲以回避。玉日夜涕泣，都忘寢食，期一相見，竟無因由。冤憤益深，委頓牀枕。自是長安中稍有知者。風流之士，共感玉之多情；豪俠之倫，皆怒生之薄行。

時已三月，人多春游。生與同輩五六人詣崇敬寺翫牡丹花，步於西廊，遞吟詩句。有京兆韋夏卿者，生之密友，時亦同行。謂生曰：“風光甚麗，草木榮華。傷哉鄭卿，銜冤空室！足下終能棄置，實是忍人。丈夫之心，不宜如此。足下宜為思之！”

嘆讓之際，忽有一豪士，衣輕黃紵衫，挾弓彈，風神儁美，衣服輕華，唯有一剪頭胡雛從后，潛行而聽之。俄而前揖生曰：“公非李十郎者乎？某族本山東，姻連外戚。雖乏文藻，心實樂賢。仰公聲華，常思觀止。今日幸會，得睹清揚。某之敝居，去此不遠，亦有聲樂，足以娛情。妖姬八九人，駿馬十數匹，唯公所欲。但願一過。”

生之儕輩，共聆斯語，更相嘆美。因與豪士策馬同行，疾轉數坊，遂至勝業。生以進鄭之所止，意不欲過，便托事故，欲回馬首。豪士曰：“敝居咫尺，忍相棄乎？”乃挽挾其馬，牽引而行。遷延之間，已及鄭曲。生神情恍惚，鞭馬欲回。豪士遽命奴僕數人，抱持而進。疾走推入車門，便令鎖卻，報云：“李十郎至也！”一家驚喜，聲聞於外。

先此一夕，玉夢黃衫丈夫抱生來，至席，使玉脫鞋。驚寤而告母。因自解曰：“鞋者，諧也。夫婦再合。脫者，解也。既合而解，亦當永訣。由此徵之，必遂相見，相見之後，當死矣。”凌晨，請母妝梳。母以其久病，心意惑亂，不甚信之。僶勉之間，強為妝梳。妝梳纔畢，而生果至。玉沈綿日久，轉側須人。忽聞生來，欻然自起，更衣而出，恍若有神。遂與生相見，含怒凝視，不復有言。羸質嬌姿，如不勝致，時負掩袂，返顧李生。感物傷人，坐皆欷歔。

頃之，有酒肴數十盤，自外而來。一坐驚視，遽問其故，悉是豪士之所致也。因遂陳設，相就而坐。

玉乃側身轉面，斜視生良久，遂舉杯酒，酬地曰：“我為女子，薄命如斯！君是丈夫，負心若此！韶顏稚齒，飲恨而終。慈母在堂，不能供養。綺羅弦管，從此永休。徵痛黃泉，皆君所致。李君李君，今當永訣！我死之后，必為厲鬼，使君妻妾，終日不安！”乃引左手握其臂，擲盃於地，長慟號哭數聲而絕。

母乃舉尸，實於生懷，令喚之，遂不復蘇矣。生為之縞素，旦夕哭泣甚哀。

將葬之夕。生忽見玉繐帷之中，容貌妍麗，宛若平生。著石榴裙，紫褡襠，紅綠帔子。斜身倚帷，手引繡帶，顧謂生曰：“愧君相送，尚有餘情。幽冥之中，能不感嘆。”言畢，遂不復見。明日，葬於長安御宿原。生至墓所，盡哀而返。

后月余，就禮於盧氏。傷情感物，鬱鬱不樂。

夏五月，與盧氏偕行，歸於鄭縣。至縣旬日，生方與盧氏寢，忽帳外叱叱作聲。生驚視之，則見一男子，年可二十餘，姿狀溫美，藏身映幔，連招盧氏。生惶遽走起，繞幔數匝，倐然不見。生自此心懷疑惡，猜忌萬端，夫妻之間，無聊生矣。或有親情，曲相勸喻。生意稍解。

后旬日，生復自外歸，盧氏方鼓琴於牀，忽見自門拋一斑犀鈿花合子，方圓一寸餘，中有輕絹，作同心結，墜於盧氏懷中。生開而視之，見相思子二，叩頭虫一，發殺觜一，驢駒媚少許。生當時憤怒叫吼，聲如豺虎，引琴撞擊其妻，詰令實告。盧氏亦終不自明。爾后往往暴加捶楚，備諸毒虐，竟訟於公庭而遣之。盧氏既出，生或侍婢媵妾之屬，蹔同枕席，便加妒忌。或有因而殺之者。

生嘗游廣陵，得名姬曰營十一娘者，容態潤媚，生甚悅之。每相對坐，嘗謂營曰：“我嘗於某處得某姬，犯某事，我以某法殺之。”日日陳說，欲令懼己，以肅清閨門。

出則以浴斛覆營於床，週迴封署，歸必詳視，然后乃開。又畜一短劍，甚利，顧謂侍婢曰：“此信州葛溪鐵，唯斷作罪過頭！”大凡生所見婦人，輒加猜忌，至於三娶，率皆如初焉。

Chapter 3

Tale 3.11

The Ancient Classic of Peaks and Waterways

By Li Gongzuo
Translated by Trever McKay

In the *dingchou* year (797) of the Zhenyuan period, Li Gongzuo from Longxi floated down the Xiao and Xiang rivers to Cangwu. On the way, he encountered Inspector for Southern Conquests Yang Heng from Hongnong. They moored their boats on an old levee and found lodging in the Buddhist temple there.

When evening came and the moon reflected on the empty river, the topic of conversation turned to strange and abnormal happenings. Yang related the following story to Gongzuo:

During the Yongtai period (765–766), when Li Tang was serving as the prefectural governor of Chu, a fisherman was fishing one night by Turtle Mountain.[1] His hook became snagged on something and would not come loose. The fisherman was a strong swimmer, so he dove into the water and was quickly fifty meters down,[2] where he found a large chain that circled the base

---

[1]Located in Xuchi County, Jiangsu.

[2]The original states "50 *zhang* 丈," which would be the equivalent of 166 meters. As a free dive this is impossible and even well beyond the depths reached by all but the most expert scuba divers. Thus, I have

157

of the mountain. He searched around but could not locate the end of it.

Later, he recounted the events to Tang, who instructed him and scores of other able swimmers to retrieve the chain. Their combined strength, however, was not enough to budge it. With the additional help of more than fifty oxen pulling, the chain started to move slowly to the shore. At first, the wind and water were calm. Then suddenly the waters started to churn, frightening the onlookers. At the end of the chain was a beast that resembled an ape with a white head and a long mane. Its snow-white teeth and golden claws were visible as it rushed on the shore. Fully erect it stood some five meters tall. The way it squatted was also very ape-like. Its two eyes could not open as if it were in a daze. Watery mucus flowed from its eyes and nose like a stream. Its drool was so putrid no one could get close to it.

After some time, it craned its neck and stretched. Both eyes suddenly opened, emitting a brilliance like lightning. It studied the humans as if it were about to fly into a fit of rage. Those who were there watching fled. The beast slowly dragged the chain and the oxen into the water. Once gone, it did not resurface. At the time, Tang and many distinguished men from Chu stared at each other dumbfounded, not knowing what just transpired. From then on, the fishermen knew where the chain was, but the beast was never seen again.[3]

---

switched (instead of converting) units of measurement throughout the story to increase readability and relatability.

[3]This last line follows the passage in *Taiping guangji*, which places the *shi* 時 after the *er* 爾 (3845).

In winter of the eighth year of Yuanhe [813], Gongzuo left Changzhou to see off Supervising Secretary Meng Jian.[4] He accompanied him to Zhufang, where the Investigation Commissioner Duke Xue Ping lodged them and treated them with great courtesy. At the time, Ma Zhi from Fufeng, Lu Jianneng from Fanyang, and Pei Qu from Hedong were also staying there. Sitting around the brazier, they talked throughout the night. Gongzuo recounted the event to them, just as Yang had told him.

Then, in the next spring [814], Gongzuo was visiting ancient Dongwu. He accompanied Commandery Governor Duke Yuan Xi down the river to Dongting, where he ascended up Bao Mountain and stayed with the Daoist hermit Zhou Jiaojun in his cottage. The two of them entered a spirit cave to look for books on immortality. In the cave was an ancient copy of the eighth fascicle of the *Classic of Peaks and Waterways*, written in strangely-shaped ancient characters.[5] The strings holding the strips together had been eaten away by grubs and, being out of order as the strips were, the text was nearly impossible to decipher. However, Gongzuo and Jiaojun were able to read the following passage:

> When Yu was trying to control the flood waters, he got as far as Tongbai Mountain three times. Each time, however, the wind howled, and thunder clapped all about him. The stones whined, and the woods whistled. The Five Earls stopped up

---

[4] Seeing off a friend during the Tang dynasty involved traveling with them for some distance, often to a body of water or a river, before finally parting ways.

[5] This book bears strong titular resemblance to the *Classics of Mountains and Seas*. In fact, *Tang guoshi bu* 唐國史補, a work written in the early 800s, quotes a passage from the *Classic of Mountains and Seas* not found in the received version. This passage is on Wu Zhiqi 無支祁 and, while much shorter, has all the same elements as the more detailed account found here in Li Gongzuo's story.

the river, and the Old One of Heaven advanced troops so that Yu's efforts could not come to fruition.⁶ Yu became angry and called together the hundred spirits. He commanded Kui the dragon to clear out the demonic obstructions. The thousand spirit lords of Tongbai kowtowed and pled for their lives. Yu did not heed their pleadings but imprisoned Hongmeng, Zhangshang, Doulu, and Lilou. Thus he was able to capture the water god of the Huai River and Guo River, called Wuzhiqi.⁷ Wuzhiqi could respond when spoken to and could tell the depths of the Yangtze and Huai Rivers and the proximity of highlands and lowlands. His shape resembled that of an ape or monkey, with a contracted nose and a protruding forehead. He had a blue body⁸ and a white head, with golden eyes and snow-white teeth. His neck could extend 100 feet, and his strength was more than nine elephants. His strikes and jumps were lightning fast, as he was light and quick; yet his attention span was very limited.⁹ Yu turned him over to Zhang Lü who could not control him. Wuzhiqi was

---

⁶Yuan Ke 袁珂 has *tubo* 土伯 or the Earl of the Earth (a lord under the God of the Earth *houtu* 后土, who guards the way of the Gate of Darkness) instead of *wubo* 五伯 or the Five Earls. Yuan also states that the Old One of Heaven is a minister under the Yellow Emperor. See Yuan Ke, *Gu shenhua xuanshi* 古神話選釋 (Beijing: Renmin wenxue, 1979), 305–6.

⁷Wuzhiqi 無支祁 is one of the most famous creatures in Chinese mythology and has an important connection to Sun Wukong. For Lu Xun's take on this connection, see Xianyi Yang and Gladys Yang, trans., *A Brief History of Chinese Fiction* (Beijing: Foreign Language Press, 2014), 78. For an in-depth look at the legend of Wuzhiqi, see Poul Andersen, *The Demon Chained under Turtle Mountain: The History and Mythology of the Chinese River Spirit Wuzhiqi* (Berlin: G + H Verlag, 2001).

⁸The color *qing* 青 refers to a variety of distinct colors: blue, green, cyan, or black. Since the original meaning is blue, it was used here.

⁹This last sentence could also be read as "one could not keep him in sight or earshot for very long." Details in the story give credence to both readings.

then given to Wu Muyou, who was equally unable. Finally, Geng Chen was able to subdue him. As Geng Chen came forward, the dragon spirits,[10] wood nymphs, water fairies, mountain goblins, and rock monsters charged with a howl to stop him. They tried countless tactics but Geng Chen managed to drive them back. Geng put a large chain around Wuzhiqi's neck and pierced his nose with a golden bell. Then he transported him to the base of Turtle Mountain in Huaiyin so that the Huai River could ever after flow peacefully into the ocean. After Geng Chen, all who traveled on the river carried an image of Wuzhiqi to avoid the difficulties of waves, wind, and rain on the Huai.

Thus we see that what Li Tang saw and what he told Yang Heng matches what is written in the *Classic of Peaks and Waterways*.

---

[10]The term *chipihuan* 鴟脾桓 is extremely enigmatic. Hu Yinglin changed it to *chipi* 鴟脾 and *huanhu* 桓胡, which is equally unclear (*Shaoshi shanfang bicong*, 32.414). Lu Xun follows this change in his *Zhongguo xiaoshuo shilüe* (in *Lu Xun quanji* 魯迅全集 [Taibei, Tangshan, 1989], vol. 3, 91). The present translation takes it to be something similar to *chiwen* 鴟吻 (or 螭吻), a mythical dragon-fish mix commonly found represented on rooftops as far back as the Han dynasty. Another alternative, following Cheng Xiaoming 程小銘, is *yaoying jing* 鷂鷹精, or sparrow hawk sprite (*Tang Song chuanqi ji quanyi* 唐宋傳奇集全譯 [Guiyang: Guizhou renmin chubanshe, 2009], 104). Cheng gives no explanation, however, of how he arrived at this translation.

古岳瀆經

李公佐

貞元丁丑歲，隴西李公佐泛瀟湘蒼梧。偶遇征南從事弘農楊衡，泊舟古岸，淹留佛寺。

江空月浮，征異話奇。楊告公佐云："永泰中，李湯任楚州刺史時，有漁人，夜釣於龜山之下。其釣因物所制，不復出。漁者健水，疾沉於下五十丈。見大鐵鎖，盤繞山足，尋不知極。

"遂告湯。湯命漁人及能水者數十，獲其鎖，力莫能制。加以牛五十餘頭，鎖乃振動，稍稍就岸。時無風濤，驚浪翻湧。觀者大駭。鎖之末見一獸，狀有如猿，白首長鬐，雪牙金爪，闖然上岸，高五丈許。蹲踞之狀若猿猴。但兩目不能開，兀若昏昧。目鼻水流如泉，涎沫腥穢，人不可近。

"久，乃引頸伸欠，雙目忽開，光彩若電。顧視人焉，欲發狂怒。觀者奔走。獸亦徐徐引鎖拽牛，入水去，竟不復出。時楚多知名士。與湯相顧愕慄，不知其由，爾乃漁者時知鎖所，其獸竟不復見。"

公佐至元和八年冬，自常州餞送給事中孟簡至朱方，廉使薛公蘋館待禮備。時扶風馬植，范陽盧簡能，河東裴蘧，皆同館之，環爐會語終夕焉。公佐復說前事，如楊所言。

至九年春，公佐訪古東吳，從太守元公錫泛洞庭，登包山，宿道者周焦君廬。入靈洞，探仙書。石穴間得古《岳瀆經》第八卷，文字古奇，編次蠹毀，不能解。公佐與焦君共詳讀之：

"禹理水，三至桐柏山，驚風走雷，石號木鳴，五伯擁川，天老蕭兵，不能興。禹怒，召集百靈，搜命夔龍。桐柏千君長稽首請命。禹因囚鴻蒙氏，章商氏，兜盧氏，犁婁氏。乃獲淮渦水神，名

162

無支祁，善應對言語，辨江淮之淺深，原隰之遠近。形若猿猴，縮鼻高額，青軀白首，金目雪牙。頸伸百尺，力逾九象，搏擊騰踔疾奔，輕利倏忽，聞視不可久。禹授之章律，不能制；授之鳥木由，不能制；授之庚辰，能制。鴟脾桓木魅水靈山祆石怪，奔號聚繞，以數千載。庚辰以戰逐去。頸鎖大索，鼻穿金鈴，徙淮陰之龜山之足下。俾淮水永安流注海也。庚辰之後，皆圖此形者，免淮濤風雨之難。〞

即李湯之見，與楊衡之說，與《岳瀆經》符矣。

Tale 3.12

An Account of the Governor of the Southern Branch[1]

By Li Gongzuo
Translated by William H. Nienhauser, Jr.

Chunyu Fen[2] of Dongping[3] was a knight-errant who wandered about the Wu and Chu [the lower Yangzi]. He was too fond of drinking and given to impulse, paying little attention to the finer

---

[1]Besides Lu Xun's *Tang Song chuanqi ji,* this translation consulted with Wang Meng'ou 王夢鷗, *Tangren xiaoshuo jiaoshi* 唐人小說校釋 (Taibei: Zhengzhong Shuju, 1985), 2:171–99 [hereafter "Wang Meng'ou"], Li Jianguo's text (*Tang Song chuanqi pindu cidian* 唐宋傳奇品讀辭典 [Beijing: Xin Shijie Chubanshe, 2007; hereafter "Li Jianguo"], and the *TPGJ* edition (475.3910–5).

[2]The surname of Chunyu 淳于, in addition to the ancestral home in Shandong, causes the reader to think of two earlier men from the same area: Chunyu Kun 淳于髡 and Chunyu Yi 淳于意, both of whom have biographies in the *Shiji* 史記 (chapters 126 and 105, respectively).

[3]This reference, as is common in Tang tales and other fictional narratives, is anachronistic, referring to the small State of Dongping in early Han times (located about 35 miles north of modern Jining City in Shandong; Tan Qixiang, 2:19). Similarly, Wu and Chu in the following phrase are names of states that ceased to exist after the Qin unification, but continued to be identified with the regions they once ruled.

points of convention. He had amassed a great deal of property and supported a retinue of gallants. Once, because of his military skills, he had been appointed a deputy general in the Huainan Army.[4] He drank too much, so that he gave rein to his passions and offended his commander. Thus he was dismissed and drifted about with nothing to do, spending all his time in unrestrained drinking.

His family lived a few miles east of the seat of Guangling Commandery.[5] To the south of the house in which they lived was a grand, old locust tree, its branches and trunk long and interwoven, its cool shade spreading for nearly an acre. Chunyu and his hearties would drink profusely beneath it every day.

In the ninth month of the seventh year of the Zhenyuan reign period (791 A.D.),[6] Chunyu drank so heavily that he became ill. The two friends who were seated with him at the time carried him into his house and laid him in the gallery to the east of the main hall.

---

[4]Huainan 淮南 (South of the Huai) was a Tang province, centered on Yangzhou, that stretched from the seacoast in the east about 240 miles westward, with the Han 漢 River as its western border, the Huai River as its northern limit, and the Yangzi 楊子 to its south (see Tan Qixiang, 5:54).

[5]A commandery established in 758 that approximated the eastern portion of Huainan province. Yangzhou was also its seat.

[6]Because the chronology in the text of the tale presents problems, Wang Meng'ou (n. 5, p. 179) says that *qi* 七 "seven" here is a scribal error for *shi* 十 "ten," making the date 794. The *TPGJ* (475.3910) reading of Tang 唐 before the date seems to have been an addition by the *TPGJ* editors and is not followed in either Wang Meng'ou or Li Jianguo.

"You should get some sleep," they said to him. "We'll feed the horses, wash our feet,[7] and wait for you to recover a bit before we go."

When Chunyu took off his headband and put his head on the pillow,[8] everything went dark and seemed to spin about, as if in a dream. He saw two envoys clad in purple,[9] kneeling before him, who said: "The King of the Huaian Guo (The State of Locust Tranquility) has sent us to deliver his message of invitation to you."

Chunyu got down off the couch unconsciously, straightened his clothing, and followed the two envoys toward the gate. There he saw a black-lacquered carriage driven by four steeds with seven or eight attendants to the left and right.[10] They helped him up into the carriage and departed, pointing after they went out the main gate to an opening under the old locust tree and immediately speeding into the opening. Chunyu found this most strange, but he didn't dare to ask any questions.

Suddenly he saw that the landscape, climate,[11] vegetation, and roadways were not at all[12] different from those of the world he

---

[7]Presumably they washed their feet so that they could lie down on a couch to wait for Chunyu to improve.

[8]Pillows were a means of entry into the dream world as can be seen in "The World Inside a Pillow" in this volume.

[9]Li Jianguo (p. 271, n. 15) points out that, although high-ranking officials wore purple in the Tang, the reference here is to those minor officials in charge of receiving and entertaining guests who dressed in a purple coarse-silk shirts, as the *Tang hui yao* 唐會要 (*juan* 31) notes.

[10]As Wang Meng'ou points out (p. 179, n. 6), according to Tang ritual, a black-lacquered carriage was intended for the crown prince. This foreshadows the announcement that Chunyu Fen is to marry the king's daughter.

[11]The translation follows a number of modern Chinese translations here in rendering *feng hou* 風候 as "landscape and climate" (cf., for example, Zhang Wenqian 張文潛 et al., *Tang Song chuanqi xuan zhuyi ben*

knew. After they had gone a dozen or so miles they came to the ramparts and parapets of a city wall. [There] vehicles and people both flowed along the road. To the left and right of him those who attended his carriage called out orders very sternly and passersby on either side strove to give way. Farther on they entered a great city wall with red gates and double gate-towers. On the gate-towers "The Great State of Locust Tranquility" was written in golden letters. The gate guards made haste to pay their respects and perform their attendant duties. After a short period of time a man on horseback called out, "Because the [future] royal son-in-law has traveled far, the king has ordered that you rest a while in the Eastern Flowery Lodge." Then he went ahead to lead the way. All of a sudden Chunyu saw a wide-open door. He descended from the carriage and went in. There were many-colored railings next to carved columns, flowering trees with rare fruits, row upon row beneath a dais. Benches and tables, cushions and mats, curtains and a feast were all arranged on the dais. In his heart he was most pleased.[13] Again someone called out, "The Chief Minister on the

---

唐宋傳奇選注譯本 [Fuzhou: Fujian Jiaoyu Chubanshe, 1983], n. 24, p. 103, and translation on p. 111).

[12]Reading *wu* 無 for *shen* 甚, following Wang Meng'ou (pp. 179–80, n. 7; Wang's revision is based on the Ming mss. of the *Taiping guangji* and Feng Menglong's 馮夢龍 [1574–1646] *Taiping guangji chao* 太平廣記鈔). Following Wang's suggestion, the text allows Chunyu Fen to believe that he is still in the "real world" until he wakes up back in his home in Guangling and discovers that he has been living in an ant colony in his dream.

[13] Chunyu Fen's inability to speak here recalls a like-named predecessor, Chunyu Kun 淳于髡. Kun was an advisor to both King Wei 魏 of Qi 齊 (r. 378–343 B.C.) and King Hui 惠 of Liang (r. 370–335 B.C.). Although Kun was known for his eloquence, he, like Fen, was silent the first two times King Hui first granted him audience (see the two biographical sketches on Sima Qian 司馬遷 (145–86? BCE) *Shiji*, 74.2347 and 126.3197). It may also be that in this early, transitionary phase from

Right[14] is about to arrive." Chunyu then descended the stairs to receive him respectfully. A man wearing a purple robe[15] and holding an ivory court-tablet came forward quickly, and they greeted each other according to all the rules of propriety of host and guest.

"My Liege has not considered our humble land too far out of the way to receive Milord," the Chief Minister on the Right began, "He is hoping to contract a formal marriage with you.

"With such a lowly, humble body, how could this humble person dare to hope for such a thing?" Chunyu replied.

The Chief Minister on the Right thereupon asked that Chunyu accompany him to where the king was. After they had gone about one hundred paces, they entered a red gate. With spears, lances, axes, and halberds arranged [in front of the gate] to the left, several hundred guards stepped back to let them pass.[16] Zhou Bian, a lifelong drinking companion of Chunyu, hastened to be among them. Chunyu was secretly pleased to see him, but did not dare to step forward and ask him [about things]. The Chief Minister on the Right led the way up into a spacious hall, heavily

---

the real world to the dream world Fen has not yet acquired the power to speak.

[14]In Tang officialdom, *You xiang* 右相 referred to the head of the Secretariat (*Neishi sheng* 內侍省) and the *Zuo xiang* 左相, Chief Minister of the Left, to the head of the Chancellery (Menxia sheng 門下省); cf. Robert des Rotours, *Le traité des examens* (Paris: Ernest Leroux, 1932), p. 266. Both held the second-degree rank.

[15]According to Tang rites, officials of the third-degree (of nine levels) and above were allowed to wear purple. Thus the reader understands both that this is a high official and that the worlds of Locust Tranquility and the Tang empire were strikingly similar (cf. Li Jianguo, n. 31 on p. 271).

[16]Spears, lances and other weapons were commonly arrayed before a gate of a rich or powerful home during the Tang.

guarded as if it were the king's. There he saw a man, large and imposing, sitting on the throne, dressed in a white silken gown and wearing a crimson-flowered crown. Chunyu Fen trembled and didn't dare to look up. The attendants to the left and right told him to bow down.

Then the king said, "Sometime before, I received your father's word that he wouldn't despise our small nation out of hand and he agreed to allow my second daughter, Yaofang (Jade Fragrance), to serve you respectfully as your wife."

Chunyu could only bow his head and prostrate himself on the ground, not daring to say anything.

The king went on, "For now go back to the guest lodge, we will carry out the ceremony later!" There was also a formal edict [to this effect]. In addition, the Chief Minister on the Right went back with him to the guest lodge.

Chunyu thought this over. As far as he knew, his father had commanded [troops] on the border and because of that had fallen captive to the enemy, so that it wasn't known whether he was dead or alive.

[Chunyu] for the time being suspected that his father, through the friendly intervention of the northern barbarians, had conducted this matter. [But] he was very confused and he didn't really know how it had come about.

That evening everything for the ceremony was in complete readiness: the gifts of lambs, geese, money, and silk[17] were awe-inspiring and grand, as were the female singers and musicians, wines and savory foods, lamps and candles, carriages and riding

---

[17]Traditional wedding gifts provided by the groom. Lambs were considered "humane" (ren 仁) and with good deportment; geese were supposed to keep a single mate for life. The gifts are typical of those given by upper class gentlemen in early China. The money was for various expenses connected to the ceremony (cf. Li Jianguo, p. 271, n. 45).

horses.[18] There was a group of women: one Miss Flowery Slope, another Miss Green Steam, another Lady Higher Transcendent, and yet another Lady Lower Transcendent).[19] There seemed to be a large number of them, each with several thousand attendants. They wore kingfisher and phoenix hats,[20] golden-cloud cloaks, gems of all colors, and golden jewelry, so that they overwhelmed the eye. Roaming about and enjoying themselves, they stopped by his door, striving to trifle with Master Chunyu. Their manner was very bewitching, their speech seductive, so that he did not know how to respond. One of the girls said to him, "Once on the third day of the third lunar month[21] I went along with Lingzhi

---

[18]The syntax here is notable. *Weirong yidu* 威容儀度 (here, "awe-inspiring and grandiose") is sometimes seen to modify the entire ceremony, as in the Yangs' rendition (*op. cit.*, p. 19): "That evening, amid pomp and splendour, betrothal gifts of lambs, swans and silk were displayed . . . ."

[19]Herbert Franke and Wolfgang Bauer argue that "the names [of these women] allude to the various groups inside the ant state, to the ants with and those without wings" (*Die Goldene Truhe*, p. 430, n. to p. 94; translation by Levenson, *The Golden Casket*, p. 117, n. 2). Cai Shouxiang 蔡守湘 (1934–1998) points out that Huayang Gu refers to the Goddess of the Southern Slope of Mount Hua (Huayang Shan Xiangu 華陽山仙姑娘; Mount Hua was a home to Daoists from at least as early as the Han dynasty), that Qingxi Gu is a variant of Qingxi Shennü 青溪神女, and that the other names seem to have been constructed by Li Gongzuo to suggest other goddesses [*Tangren xiaoshuo xuanzhu* 唐人小說選注 [3v., Taibei: Liren 里仁 Shuju, 2002], 1:278, n. 34]. See also the comments in André Lévy's comments in his apparatus (*Histoires extraordinaires*, p. 95, n. 14).

[20]Some modern Chinese translations believe these refer to feathered hats, others argue that phoenix and kingfisher indicate the headdresses were jade-green in color.

[21]This is the spring purification festival, Shang si jie 上巳節, one of the three major holidays of the Tang. People went out of the cities into

Furen (Madame Mithridate) to the Chanzhi Si (Wisdom of Zen Temple).[22] In the Tianzhu Yuan (Hindu Courtyard) we saw Shi Yan[23] dance the *Poluomen* (Brâhmana [Dance]).[24] I sat on the stone bench under the north window[25] with some of my companions. At that time you were still young, but just you dismounted and came to watch,[26] trying to force yourself on us, teasing and flirting. My little sister Qiongying 窮英 (Hortensia Flower) and I knotted a red scarf and put it on a bamboo branch.[27] How could you have just

---

nature, supposedly to rid themselves of miasmas of the winter by bathing. It was therefore one of those rare opportunities when men and women mixed in public. See also Derk Bodde, "The Lustration Festival," *Festivals in Classical China* (Princeton: Princeton University Press, 1975), pp. 273–88.

[22]A noted Chan (Zen) temple in Yangzhou.

[23]A famous dancer from Sogdiana (Shi guo 石國, approximating modern Uzbekistan) in Central Asia. As Li Jianguo (p. 271, n. 51) points out, the royal house was surnamed Shi, and many of those Sogdianians who came to Chang'an during the Tang had (or adopted) that surname. The natives of Sogdiana were famed for their dancing skills.

[24]*Tianzhu* was a transliteration of the Indian term Hinduka~hinkdukh employed at least as early as the *Hou Han shu* 後漢書 (cf. *Hanyu* da cidian, 2:1420). *Poluomen* is the transliteration of the Indian surname given to the Brahman (priest) clan or caste. The *Poluomen* dance was performed in the whirling style of Central Asian dance tradition (see Zhou Shaoliang, pp. 204–5).

Li Jianguo (p. 271, n. 52) cites Du You's 杜右 (735–812) claim that the *Poluomen* 婆羅門 dance was revised by Emperor Xuanzong's musicians to become the Nishang yuyi qu 霓裳羽衣曲 (Tune of the Feathered Rainbow Dance).

[25]Presumably the most secluded part of the temple (as the main doors would have been on the south side).

[26]The inference seems to be that Chunyu came to the temple with a group (friends, family?), but he alone took notice of the women.

[27]This is similar to dropping a handkerchief for a gentleman to pick up in Western society.

forgotten? Another time on the sixteenth of the seventh lunar month I was in the Xiaogan Si 孝感寺 (Temple of Filial Feelings) attending Shangzhen Zi (Lady Higher Purity) and listening to Monk Qi Xuan (Bound to Mystery)[28] lecture on the *Guanyin jing* (*Avalokiteśvara Sutra*). I left a pair of golden-phoenix hairpins as a donation beneath the podium and Lady Higher Purity left a box made of rhinoceros horn. At the time you were also on the lecture mat and you asked the monk for the hairpins and the box to examine them, sighing repeatedly with appreciation and uttering cries of admiration for some time. Turning to look at us you said, 'Both you and your things are not the sort we have in this world.' [Then] whether you asked about my family or where I lived, I would not respond. Your heart was filled with love and you were loath to take your eyes off us. How could you not remember?"

"In my heart it's set, how could I ever forget,"[29] Chunyu replied.

The women in one voice said, "Who would have imagined that today we would become your family dependents?"

Three men, very grand in their official hats and sashes, also came forward and bowed to the young man: "We have received a

---

[28]Li Jianguo (p. 271, n. 55) cites a poem by Lu Lun 盧綸 (738–798) written to Qi Xuan. Lévy notes (*Histoire extraordinaires*, p. 95, n. 21) that his 'sermons' were popular in the final quarter of the eighth century, but this seems to be simply an inference drawn based upon this tale and Lu Lun's poem. These sermons, known *su jiang* 俗講 (popular lectures), mixed reciting of Buddhist scriptures and storytelling and were particularly popular among women in the early ninth century (see Zhou Shaoliang, pp. 206–7).

[29]These are the last two lines of "Shi sang" 隰桑 (The Mulberry of the Lowland), Mao #228 in the *Shi jing* 詩經. Arthur Waley (*The Book of Songs* (New York: Grove Press, 1960 [1937]) classifies the poem as one of marriage and translates the lines as "To the core of my heart I treasure him, / Could not ever cease to love him" 中心藏之，何日忘之？

command to serve the royal son-in-law as best men." Among them was a man who was also an old friend of Chunyu Fen. Fen pointed to him and said, "Aren't you Tian Zihua of Pingyi?"[30]

"Yes, I am," T'ien replied.

Fen came forward, took his hands, and talked over old times for a long while. Then he asked, "How have you come to live here?"

"I was wandering about at large, when the Chief Minister on the Right, Mr. Duan 段, the Marquis of Wucheng (Martial Completion),[31] recognized my abilities, so I've become dependent on him."

"Zhou Bian is here. Did you know?" Fen went on to ask.

"Mr. Zhou," Zihua replied, "is an honored man. He is serving as Metropolitan Commandant,[32] and great are his power and influence. Several times I have benefited from his protection." And so they chatted and laughed very joyously.

In a short time a messenger called out, "The Royal Son-in-law may go in now!" The three men then outfitted him in a sword, a belt, a cap, and clothes.

"I never thought the day would come when I could personally witness such a marriage," said Zihua. "Don't forget me [once you're married]!"

Then several dozen of those transcendent beauties played the most extraordinary music for them, insinuating and subtle, bright and pure, but with a melancholy melody, such as never had been

---

[30]The seat of Tong 同 Prefecture during the Tang, some sixty miles east-northeast of Chang'an (modern Dali 大荔 in Shaanxi province, Tan Qixiang, 5:41).

[31]Wucheng 武成 is an honorific title, not a place name. This was the noble title of the Chief Minister of the Right whom Chunyu Fen met in the tale above (cf. Li Jianguo, p. 272, n. 66).

[32]*Sili* 司隸 was a Chou-dynasty official title (Wang Meng'ou, p. 182, n. 30).

heard in the human world.[33] There were also several dozen of them holding candles and leading the way for him. To the left and right appeared cloth partitions of various hues and lusters [screening the walkway], embroidered with kingfisher feathers and golden thread, which ran on for over a mile. Fen sat upright in the carriage, his mind swirling, unable to settle down. Tian Zihua several times offered a remark or joke to help dispel the tension. Those women he had previously [spoken with] each rode in phoenix-wing carriages and were also coming and going in the palace. They came to a gate which was called "Xiuyi Gong" (The Palace for Cultivating Proper Ceremony). Those transcendent women all gathered on either side of the gate, allowing him to get out of the royal cart and bowing to him. [Then] there was polite gesturing, deferring to one other, and ascending and descending according to etiquette — all just as it is in the world of men. When they removed the screen [from the other carriage that had arrived] and took away the fan [carried by her attendants to shield the princess from view],[34] he saw a young woman who was called Jinzhi Gonzhu (Princess of the Golden Branch).[35] She was about fourteen or fifteen and seemed just like an immortal. All the rites for this wedding night were indeed clearly on display.

---

[33] After the initial depiction of mountains, rivers, climate and customs that are the same as in the human world, this is the first of several descriptions which remind the reader, and perhaps should have alerted Chunyu Fen, to the fact that this is a preternatural state in which he is living.

[34] Each action was part of the marriage ritual. Wang Meng'ou (pp. 182–3, n. 31) cites several Tang-dynasty texts that detail this second ceremonial step of a Tang marriage.

[35] Perhaps a play on the expression *Jinzhi yuye* 金枝玉葉 (Jade Leaf/Leaves of the Golden Branch), which referred to descendants of a royal house (cf. Morohashi, 11:463, entry 49152.492).

From this time on, with each day Chunyu Fen's affection for her grew deeper as his fame and glory increased day by day. The carriages and vestments in which he went about, the guests and attendants with whom he went on excursions or to banquets, were always second only to those of the king. The king ordered Chunyu Fen and his fellow officials to ready the palace guard to go on a grand hunt at Linggui Shan (Efficacious Tortoise Mountain)[36] to the west of the capital. There were mountains and hills steep and lofty, streams and marshes far and wide, forests of trees in abundance and luxuriance, and of the birds that fly and the beasts that run, there were none which were not bred there. The soldiers had a huge catch, and only when the night was spent did they go home.[37]

One day, Chunyu Fen asked the king for instruction. "On that day not long ago when I got married, Your Majesty said he was following my father's orders. Not long after my father was caused to serve as an assistant frontier commander, he was defeated in battle and fell into Tartar hands. Since then I haven't had a letter from him in seventeen or eighteen years. As Your Majesty knows his whereabouts, I beg to be allowed to visit him."

"My daughter's father-in-law," the king quickly replied, "is serving guard over the northern lands. We haven't lost contact with him. You need only prepare a letter letting him know [of you]. There's no need to go to see him immediately!"

---

[36]This hunt, as were most royal hunts in traditional China, was intended as a test of the military capabilities of the State of Locust Tranquility. The place name Linggui Shan is aptly chosen, since the God of War, Xuan Wu 玄武, was supposed to have taken the form of a tortoise (or a hybrid snake-tortoise; see *Hanyu da cidian*, 2:3707b).

[37]There are a number of references to "nights" rather than days in this text, perhaps suggesting the way time was measured in this darker, dream world (see also n. 53 below).

He [the king] ordered his wife to prepare presents congratulating [Fen's father] on gaining a daughter-in-law to send with the letter to his father. After a few nights, a reply arrived. As Fen examined the basic ideas in this letter, he found that they all contained traces of those [ideas] his father had held all his life. In the letter his concerns and instructions were set in indirect expressions of affection, all as in the past. He also asked whether their relatives were still alive and about the prosperity of their village. And he said that the road between them was separated by some distance and blocked by winds and mists. The tone [of his letter] was sad and there was distress in his language. Further, he would not allow Fen to come to visit him, explaining, "In the *dingchou* year (797), I will meet you again." Fen clasped the letter and choked back a sob, overcome with emotion.

Some days later, Fen's wife said to him, "Why don't you ever think about serving in the government?"[38]

"I am a reckless sort who has no experience in governmental affairs," Fen replied.

"Just do it and I will support and assist you," she said. Then she reported [this conversation] to the king. After some time had passed, the king said to Fen, "In our Nanke 南柯 (Southern Branch) governmental affairs are not well managed. The governor has been dismissed and I'd like to rely on your talents. If you would condescend to take such a limited position, you could go there forthwith with our young daughter!"

Fen respectfully accepted these instructions. The king then ordered those in charge of such things to outfit the new governor for his journey. For this reason they arrayed gold and jade, brocades and silks, baskets and boxes, servants and maids,

---

[38] *Wei zheng* 為政 ("to serve in the government, exercise governmental affairs") is the title of the second section of the *Lun yu* 論語 (Confucian Analects).

carriages and horses along a broad thoroughfare as a way to bid a grand farewell to the princess on her journey.

As a youth, Fen had been a knight-errant and had never dared to have such hopes, so when he achieved this position he was greatly pleased. Accordingly, he submitted a memorial, saying:

> Your subject is the remaining descendant of generals, just an ordinary man with no cultural refinement or administrative craft. It would be improper for him to serve in such an important position and would certainly disrupt the regulations of the court. I would be saddened to ride in a carriage with a burden on my back or would easily overturn the pottage [in the cauldron].[39]

---

[39]Two allusions to the *Yi jing* 易經 (Book of Changes). The first, *fu cheng* 負乘, found in the commentary on the images (*xiang* 象) under hexagram 40 (Xie 解, "To Release") reads: "If one bears a burden on his back yet also rides in a carriage, it will attract robbers to him" 負且乘, 致寇至 (*Yi jing yin de* 易經引得 [A Concordance to the *Yi jing*; Rpt. Taibei: Chinese Materials and Research Aids Service Center, 1966], p. 25; translation by Richard John Lynn, *The Classic of Changes* [New York: Columbia University Press, 1994], p. 383). The *Xi ci* 繫辭 commentary expands on this: "The Master said, 'Do you think that the makers of the *Changes* did not understand what robbers were! The *Changes* says, "If one bears a burden on his back yet also rides in a carriage, it will attract robbers to him." Bearing burdens on the back, this is the business of a petty man; a carriage, this is the rig of a noble man. When one is a petty man, yet rides in the rig of a noble man, robbers think to take his things by force. When the one above [the sovereign] is careless and those below are harsh, enemies will indeed think to attack it [such a state]" (Lynn, pp. 59–60). The second allusion is *fu su* 覆餗 which refers to hexagram 50, Ding 鼎 "The Cauldron": "The cauldron breaks its legs and overturns all its pottage, so its form is drenched, which means misfortune." The *Xi ci* commentary explains: "This speaks of someone who is unequal to his responsibilities" 言不勝其任也 (*Yi jing yin de*, pp. 31 and 47; Lynn, pp. 455 and 484).

Now I want to search far and wide for the worthy and the sagacious to assist me in areas I am unable to manage. Your Subject has found that the Metropolitan Commandant, Zhou Bian from Yingchuan,[40] is loyal, upright, law-abiding, and has the talents to assist me. Tian Zihua from Pingyi, a gentleman still unemployed, is honest, prudent, and keeps in step freely with change. [41] He thoroughly comprehends the origins of governmental effectiveness. I have been friends with these two for ten years. I completely understand their talents and can rely on them in governmental matters. I'd like to request that Chou be appointed Minister of Justice of Southern Branch and Tian be appointed Minister of Agriculture. This would allow my administration to achieve merit and fame and our legal system to maintain order.

The king made the appointments completely in accordance with the memorial.

That night, the king and his wife gave them a farewell banquet in the southern part of the capital. The king said to Fen, "Southern Branch is a large commandery in our state, its land filled with rich soil, its people and goods abundant. Without your kindly administration, there will be no way to govern it. Moreover, there are your two assistants, Zhou and Tian — may you do your utmost to meet the nation's expectations!"

[Then] his wife admonished the princess, "Mr. Chunyu is by nature inflexible, intemperate with wine, and in addition he is young. The way to be a proper wife is to honor a yielding and

---

[40]A commandery and also the seat of Xuzhou 許州 (Xu Prefecture) near modern Xuchang in Henan (Li Jianguo, p. 272, n. 98).

[41]Another allusion, *tong bian* 通變, to the *Xi ci* 繫辭 commentary of the *Yi jing*: "The means to know the future through the mastery of numbers is referred to as 'prognostication,' and to keep in step freely with change is referred to as 'the way one should act'" 極數知來者謂占, 通變之謂事 (*Yi jing yin de*, p. 41; translation by Richard Lynn, p. 54).

compliant nature. If you can serve him well, I will not have any worries. Although the border to Southern Branch is not that far, mornings and nights we'll be separated.[42] [Thus] today as we part, how could I hold back my tears?"

Chunyu Fen and his wife paid their respects and left for the South, mounting their carriage and urging on their horses, all the while talking and laughing in great happiness. After a few nights they reached the commandery. At the commandery officials, clerks, Buddhist monks, Daoist priests, local elders, musicians, carriages, military guards, and horses with bells pressed forward to welcome and attend them. People clamored about them, bells and drums sounded, without stopping for about five miles. They could see city walls, parapets, towers, and lookouts. There was an abundance of good auras.

As they entered the grand city-gate, it also had a large plaque written in golden characters which read: "Nanke Jun Cheng" (The Seat of Southern Branch Commandery). The homes with red gates and ornamented halberds before their doors were imposing and set back [from the streets].

After Chunyu Fen "got out of his carriage,"[43] he examined the local customs, healed disease, and put an end to suffering. Political matters he entrusted to Zhou and Tian and throughout the commandery a grand order reigned. Twenty years after he took the position of governor, morals and teaching spread widely, and the people sang his praises, erecting a Meritorious Virtue Tablet and setting up a shrine for him.

---

[42]The queen was reminding her daughter that by traditional ritual children were expected to call on their parents every morning and evening.

[43]A figurative expression indicating an official arriving to take up a new post. One of the first duties of such officials was to look into "local customs" to determine whether the moral influence of the government was in force.

The king greatly valued him and bestowed upon him a fief town, conferred on him rank and position, and had him occupy the position of Prime Minister. Zhou and Tian both became famous because they governed well and were successively promoted to higher positions. Chunyu Fen had five sons and two daughters. The sons received official positions through the hereditary rank system and the daughters were all married to members of the royal clan. His fame and glory were radiant beyond that of all his contemporaries.

In that year the Tanluo Guo (State of Sandalwood Creepers) came to launch a military campaign against this commandery. The king ordered Chunyu Fen to train his commanders and exhort his armies so that they could overcome the invaders. Fen submitted a memorial asking that Zhou Bian be put in command of thirty thousand soldiers to defend against the bandit host at Jade Tower City. Zhou was bold but inflexible and underestimated the enemy, so his troops were defeated. Under the cover of night he returned alone on horseback, having cast off his armor to flee the enemy. The bandits also collected the provisions and armor his troops had abandoned and withdrew. Chunyu Fen for these reasons imprisoned Zhou Bian and asked that he be punished as well, but the king pardoned them both.

In the same month the Minister of Justice, Zhou Bian, got an ulcer on his back and died.

Chunyu Fen's wife, the princess, became ill and after ten days she also passed away. Chunyu Fen therefore asked to be relieved of his governorship to escort her body back to the capital; the king granted his request. Then [the king] entrusted the Minister of Agriculture, Tian Zihua, with the duties of Governor of Southern Branch. Moved by his sadness, Chunyu Fen set out, accompanying her hearse. As they moved in a dignified manner along the road men and women wailed, people set out offerings of food, and those who grasped the carriage shafts or blocked the road were too numerous to count. When they finally reached the capital city, the king and his wife, in white mourning clothes, were in the suburbs, weeping and awaiting the arrival of the hearse. The princess received the posthumous title of Shunyi Gongzhu (The Princess of Compliant Bearing). An honor-guard to carry a feathered canopy and beat drums had been prepared, and she was buried a few miles east of the capital city at Panlong Gang (Coiled Dragon Tumulus). The same month the son of the former Minister of Justice, Zhou Rongxin,[44] also escorted his father's remains back to the capital city.

Though Chunyu Fen guarded the outer marches for a long time, he had close friends in the capital city, and all the noble and prominent families were on good terms with him.[45] Since he had been dismissed from his position as governor and returned to the capital city, he came and went constantly, going out with friends and followed by retainers, so that his prestige and fortune increased daily. The king began to suspect and fear him. At that time someone from the capital city submitted a memorial, which read:

> In the mysterious heavenly signs blame appears; in the state there is great fear of a disaster. The capital will be moved, and the royal ancestral temple will collapse. The cause of this strife will come from another tribe of people, but the matter lies within Your Majesty's own officials.[46]

---

[44]Zhou Bian's 周弁 son.

[45]Readers of the early ninth century would have recognized that this kind of relationship between powerful provincial officials and groups in the capital was a contemporary problem (cf. Zhou Shaoliang, pp. 211–2).

[46]Literally "within the screen of increased reverence" (*xiao qiang* 蕭牆), i.e., the screen behind which the ruler sat. Officials were expected to become more reverential when they reached this screen. The term alludes to *Lunyu*, 16.1 in which Confucius warns against advisors

At the time deliberations at court [determined] that this was an omen corresponding to Fen's extravagance. In the end Fen's bodyguard was taken away, he was forbidden to see his band of friends, and he was placed under house arrest. Fen, certain that in his many years as governor of the commandery he had not failed in his policies and that rumors unjustly found fault with him, was melancholy and unhappy. The king understood this and said to Fen, "You have been related to us by marriage for more than twenty years. It was unfortunate that my daughter died early and wasn't able to accompany you in your old age. This must be exceedingly sorrowful!"

For this reason, his wife, the queen, kept her grandchildren in her charge to care for and to educate. [On another occasion] the king also said to Fen, "You have been separated from your family for a long time. You ought to go home to your village for a time and see your relatives. You can leave your children here. There is nothing you need to be concerned about. After three years[47] we shall welcome you back."

"This is my home," Fen replied. "Where should I return to?"

The king laughed and said, "You originally come from the world of men. Your home is not here!"

Suddenly Fen grew groggy with sleep[48] and with tears in his eyes his sight was blurred for a long while, until he became aware of his former life again. Then he wept and asked to go back. The

---

causing the downfall of a ruling family (cf. James Legge, *The Chinese Classics*, 1:309 and notes). *Xiao qiang* is used here metonymically for one of the king's own officials, i.e., Chunyu Fen.

[47]I.e., in the *dingchou* 丁丑 year, 797, as Chunyu Fen's father had predicted in the letter cited above.

[48]*Hun shui* 惛睡; in dream tales the dreamer is often depicted as being in a groggy state entering (as above) and leaving the dream.

king turned to his attendants indicating they should see him off.[49] Bowing twice, Fen left, and again saw the two purple-clad envoys from before following him.

Once he had gotten beyond the main palace gate, he was astonished to see that the carriage he was to ride in was dilapidated and there were no personal attendants or palace servants [as when he had come]. He got into the carriage and after they had gone a few miles they again emerged from the great city walls. It seemed to be the road along which he had in past years come [to the capital] from the east. The mountains, streams, plains, and fields were the same as of old. But his two attendants were not at all as awe-inspiring, leaving him even less pleased. He asked the envoys, "When will we arrive at Guangling Commandery?" The two went on singing and paid him little heed, until, after a long time, they answered, "Be there soon."

Suddenly they emerged from a hole and he saw the lane through his own village which had not changed from past days. Secretly moved, he could not hold back his tears. The two envoys helped Fen out of the carriage, into his gate, and up his stairs, where his own body was already lying in the gallery east of the main hall. Fen was shocked and fearful and did not dare to advance farther. The two envoys thereupon called out his name in a loud voice a few times and Fen then came back to his senses as before. He saw a young household servant sweeping the courtyard with a broom and one of his friends sitting on a bench washing his feet. The setting sun had not yet sunk behind the western wall of his compound and the wine left in their goblets was still clear and fresh by the eastern window. In the dream which flashed by him it was as if he had passed an entire lifetime.

---

[49]As Li Jianguo (p. 273, n. 159) points out, this shows that the king, and later his envoys, have begun to treat Fen with disrespect.

As Fen recalled [his dream], he was moved to sigh. Then he called his two friends to him and recounted what had happened. Amazed, they then went out with him to search for the hole beneath the locust tree. Fen pointed to it and said, "In my dream, this is the place where I entered." The two friends supposed [the place] must have been possessed by fox spirits or tree sprites.[50]

In the end they ordered servants to shoulder axes, cut through the knotted roots, break off the newly sprouted secondary branches, locate the mouth of the holes, and explore them to their ends. Nearby running north to south for about ten feet there was a hole which penetrated through to the other side and was well lit, large enough to have accommodated a couch. On the roots there was soil piled up in a form that one could take for city walls, escarpments, towers, and palaces. There were several bushels of ants hiding together among them. In their midst was a small, raised platform, its color a kind of crimson. Two large ants about three inches in length with white wings and red heads[51] were positioned upon it. Several dozen large ants assisted them there, and all the other ants dared not to approach them. This was their royal pair and none other than the capital city of Locust Tranquility.

Farther on they explored to the end another hole which ran straight up nearly forty feet into a southern branch. Twisting and turning, it reached the center, where there were earthen walls and small towers. A colony of ants was also there. This was none other than the Southern Branch Commandery which Fen had commanded.

---

[50]*Mu mei* 木媚 (alternately *mu mei* 木魅) were tree sprites which often did harm to humans. They were closely associated in early texts with *shan jing* 山精 (mountain spirits / ghouls / wraiths).

[51] Recalling the "crimson-flowered crown" of the king depicted above.

Farther on was another hole, going west for over twenty feet, broad and expansive with tightly packed walls and a deep pit of strange shape. In its midst was a rotting turtle-shell as big as a peck measure. It was immersed in rainwater that had gradually permeated it. Small plants growing thick and luxuriant weeds overshadowed the old shell. This was none other than the Efficacious Tortoise Mountain where Fen had hunted.

Farther on they explored to the end another hole which ran east for more than ten feet: old roots twisted about, shaped like dragons and snakes. In its midst there was a small earthen mound, a little over a foot tall. This was none other than the grave at Coiled Dragon Tumulus where Fen had buried his wife.

When he recalled those former affairs, he gave a heartfelt sigh. Those places they had opened up, examined, explored, and searched through all fit closely with those of which he had dreamed. Not wanting his two friends to destroy them, he quickly ordered them covered up and filled in as before.

That night a violent storm broke out. In the morning, when he looked into the holes, the colonies of ants had thus disappeared — no one knew where they had gone. Therefore, what had been said earlier — "In the state there is great fear of a disaster. The capital will be moved" — had its fulfillment in this.

Next Chunyu Fen remembered the events of the Sandalwood Creepers' campaign [against him] and again asked his two friends to look for traces of it outside. Not a mile to the east of his home was an old dried-up brook. On its bank was a huge sandalwood tree heavily entwined with vines and creepers so that looking up one couldn't see the sun. There was a small hole to the side of the trunk in which indeed was a colony of ants hiding together. Could the state of Sandalwood Creepers be anywhere else than here?!

Alas! If even the spiritual mysteries of ants is unfathomable, how much more are the transformations of those larger beings who hide in the mountains or conceal themselves in forests!

At the time, Fen's drinking companions Zhou Bian and Tian Zihua both lived in Liuhe County, but they had not come by to visit for ten days. Fen quickly sent his servant-boy to hurry and ask after them. Mr. Zhou had suddenly taken ill and passed away, and Mr. Tian was also bedridden with a disease. Feeling even more the transience of the Southern Branch and understanding man's life was only a sudden moment, Fen then settled his mind in the school of the Dao, giving up wine and women. Three years later, in the *dingchou* 丁丑 year, Fen indeed died in his home at the age of forty-seven, just fulfilling the time limit agreed upon formerly.[52]

In the fall of the eighth lunar month of the eighteenth year of the Zhenyuan reign (802), I, [Li] Gongzuo, having sailed from Wu[53] to Luo [yang] and moored my boat temporarily along the banks of the Huai 淮,[54] chanced to meet Master Chunyu face to face. I inquired about and visited what remained of these places, and we went over [the story] a number of times. As the events were all verifiable, I recorded and edited them at once, forming this account to provide material for those fond of such things. Although it is all searching after spirits and speaking of the strange rather than matters involving the classics, I hope it will be a warning to those young men who wish to steal their way into an official position. May later gentlemen take Southern Branch as an example of how chance works and not because of fame or position, act in a haughty manner in this world!

---

[52]As the king had predicted above.

[53]I.e., sailing up the Grand Canal from Suzhou (Wu) to Luoyang (see also the following note).

[54]Huaipu 淮浦 (along the banks of the Huai) refers to the terminus of that section of the Yunhe 運河 (Grand Canal) north of the Yangzi, known in Tang times as the Yancao Ju 沿漕渠, which extends to the Huai River (Li Jianguo, p. 274, n. 186).

The former Military Adviser of Huazhou,[55] Li Zhao,[56] composed a coda:

> Honor reaching a peak in emolument and position,
> Power to overthrow capital cities of lands —
> The wise man regards these things
> As nothing different from a colony of ants.

Note: This is a revised version of my 2016 rendition in my *Tang Dynasty Tales: A Guided Reader*, pp. 131–87; more detailed annotations are provided there.

---

[55]Near modern Hua County in Henan, equidistant (about thirty-five miles) from Anyang in the north and Kaifeng in the south (Tan Qixiang, 5:40).

[56]Li Zhao 李肇 (ca. 780–ca. 850) probably served as *Canjun shi* 參軍事 (Military Advisor) in Huazhou sometime between 812 and 819. During the 820s he held a number of court positions, including that of Hanlin Academician.

南柯太守傳

李公佐

　　東平淳于棼，吳楚遊俠之士。嗜酒使氣，不守細行。累巨產，養豪客。曾以武藝補淮南軍裨將，因使酒忤帥，斥逐落魄，縱誕飲酒爲事。

　　家住廣陵郡東十里。所居宅南有大古槐一株，枝幹修密，清陰數畝。淳于生日與羣豪，大飲其下。

　　貞元七年九月，因沈醉致疾。時二友人於座扶生歸家，臥於堂東廡之下。二友謂生曰："子其寢矣！余將秣馬濯足，俟子小愈而去。"

　　生解巾就枕，昏然忽忽，彷彿若夢。見二紫衣使者，跪拜生曰："槐安國王遣小臣致命奉邀。"生不覺下榻整衣，隨二使至門。見青油小車，駕以四牡，左右從者七八，扶生上車，出大戶，指古槐穴而去。使者即驅入穴中。生意頗甚異之，不敢致問。

　　忽見山川風候草木道路，與人世甚殊。前行數十里，有郛郭城堞。車輿人物，不絕於路。生左右傳車者傳呼甚嚴，行者亦爭闢於左右。又入大城，朱門重樓，樓上有金書，題曰"大槐安國"。執門者趨拜奔走。旋有一騎傳呼曰："王以駙馬遠降，令且息東華館。"因前導而去。

　　俄見一門洞開，生降車而入。彩檻雕楹；華木珍果，列植於庭下；几案茵褥，簾幃餚膳，陳設於庭上。生心甚自悅。復有呼曰："右相且至。"生降階祗奉。有一人紫衣象簡前趨，賓主之儀敬盡焉。

　　右相曰："寡君不以弊國遠僻，奉迎君子，託以姻親。"
　　生曰："某以賤劣之軀，豈敢是望。"

右相因請生同詣其所。行可百步，入朱門。矛戟斧鉞，佈列左右，軍吏數百，辟易道側。生有平生酒徒周弁者，亦趨其中。生私心悅之，不敢前問。右相引生升廣殿，御衛嚴肅，若至尊之所。見一人長大端嚴，居王位，衣素練服，簪朱華冠。生戰慄，不敢仰視。左右侍者令生拜。

王曰：“前奉賢尊命，不棄小國。許令次女瑤芳，奉事君子。”

生但俯伏而已，不敢致詞。王曰：“且就賓宇，續造儀式。”有旨，右相亦與生偕還館舍。

生思念之，意以爲父在邊將，因歿虜中，不知存亡。將謂父北蕃交遜，而致茲事。心甚迷惑，不知其由。

是夕，羔雁幣帛，威容儀度，妓樂絲竹，餚膳燈燭，車騎禮物之用，無不咸備。有羣女，或稱華陽姑，或稱青溪姑，或稱上仙子，或稱下仙子，若是者數輩。皆侍從數千，冠翠鳳冠，衣金霞帔，彩碧金鈿，目不可視。遨遊戲樂，往來其門，爭以淳于郎爲戲弄。風態妖麗，言詞巧艷，生莫能對。復有一女謂生曰：“昨上巳日，吾從靈芝夫人過禪智寺，於天竺院觀右延舞《婆羅門》。吾與諸女坐北牖石榻上，時君少年，亦解騎來看。君獨強來親洽，言調笑謔。吾與窮英妹結絳巾，掛於竹枝上，君獨不憶念之乎？又七月十六日，吾於孝感寺侍上真子，聽契玄法師講《觀音經》。吾於講下捨金鳳釵兩隻，上真子捨水犀合子一枚。時君亦講筵中於師處請釵合視之，賞嘆再三，嗟異良久。顧餘輩曰：‘人之與物，皆非世間所有。’或問吾氏，或訪吾里。吾亦不答。情意戀戀，矚盼不捨。君豈不思念之乎？”

生曰：“中心藏之，何日忘之。”

羣女曰：“不意今日與君爲眷屬。”

復有三人，冠帶甚偉，前拜生曰：“奉命爲駙馬相者。”中一人與生且故。生指曰：“子非馮翊田子華乎？”

田曰：“然。”

生前，執手敘舊久之。生謂曰：“子何以居此？”

子華曰：“吾放遊，獲受知於右相武成侯段公，因以栖託。”

生復問曰：“周弁在此，知之乎？”

子華曰：“周生，貴人也。職爲司隸，權勢甚盛。吾數蒙庇護。”言笑甚歡。

俄傳聲曰：“駙馬可進矣。”三子取劍佩冕服，更衣之。子華曰：“不意今日獲覿盛禮。無以相忘也。”

　　有仙姬數十，奏諸異樂，婉轉清亮，曲調悽悲，非人間之所聞
聽。有執燭引導者，亦數十。左右見金翠步障，彩碧玲瓏，不斷數
里。生端坐車中，心意恍惚，甚不自安。田子華數言笑以解之。向
者羣女姑娣，各乘鳳翼輦，亦往來其間。至一門，號「修儀宮」。
羣仙姑姊亦紛然在側，令生降車輦拜，揖讓升降，一如人間。徹障
去扇，見一女子，云號「金枝公主」。年可十四五，儼若神仙。交
歡之禮，頗亦明顯。

　　生自爾情義日洽，榮曜日盛。出入車服，遊宴賓御，次於王者。
王命生與羣寮備武衛，大獵於國西靈龜山。山阜峻秀，川澤廣遠，
林樹豐茂，飛禽走獸，無不蓄之。師徒大獲，竟夕而還。

　　生因他日啓王曰：「臣頃結好之日，大王云奉臣父之命。臣父
頃佐邊將，用兵失利，陷沒胡中。爾來絕書信十七八歲矣。王既知
所在，臣請一往拜覲。」

　　王遽謂曰：「親家翁職守北土，信問不絕。卿但具書狀知聞，
未用便去。」

　　遂命妻致饋賀之禮，一以遺之。數夕還答。生驗書本意，皆父
平生之跡。書中憶念教誨，情意委曲，皆如昔年。復問生親戚存亡，
閭里興廢。復言路道乖遠，風煙阻絕。詞意悲苦，言語哀傷。又不
令生來覲，云：「歲在丁丑，當與汝相見。」生捧書悲咽，情不自
堪。

　　他日，妻謂生曰：「子豈不思爲政乎？」

　　生曰：「我放蕩不習政事。」

　　妻曰：「卿但爲之，余當奉贊。」妻遂白於王。累日，謂生曰：
「吾南柯政事不理，太守黜廢。欲籍卿才，可曲屈之。便與小女同
行。」

　　生敦受教命。王遂敕有司備太守行李。因出金玉、錦繡、箱奩、
僕妾車馬，列於廣衢，以餞公主之行。

　　生少遊俠，曾不敢有望，至是甚悅。因上表曰：「臣將門餘子，
素無藝術，猥當大任，必敗朝章。自悲負乘，坐致覆餗。今欲廣求
賢哲，以贊不逮。伏見司隸潁川周弁，忠亮剛直，守法不回，有毗
佐之器。處士馮翊田子華，清慎通變，達政化之源。二人與臣有十
年之舊，備知才用，可託政事。周請署南柯司憲，田請署司農。庶
使臣政績有聞，憲章不紊也。」王並依表以遺之。

其夕，王與夫人餞於國南。王謂生曰：“南柯國之大郡，土地豐壤，人物豪盛，非惠政不能以治之。況有周田二贊。卿其勉之，以副國念。”

夫人戒公主曰：“淳于郎性剛好酒，加之少年。爲婦之道，貴乎柔順。爾善事之，吾無憂矣。南柯雖封境不遙，晨昏有間。今日曉別，寧不沾巾。”

生與妻拜首南去，登車擁騎，言笑甚歡。累夕達郡。郡有官吏、僧道、耆老、音樂、車輿、武衛、鑾鈴，爭來迎奉。人物闐咽，鐘鼓喧譁，不絕十數里。見雉堞臺觀，佳氣鬱鬱。

入大城門，門亦有大榜，題以金字，曰“南柯郡城”。見朱軒棨戶，森然深邃。

生下車省風俗，療病苦，政事委以周、田，郡中大理。自守郡二十載，風化廣被，百姓歌謠，建功德碑。立生祠字。

王甚重之，賜食邑，錫爵位，居臺輔。周、田皆以政治著聞，遞遷大位。生有五男二女。男以門蔭授官，女亦聘於王族。榮耀顯赫，一時之盛，代莫比之。

是歲，有檀蘿國者，來伐是郡。王命生練將訓師以征之。乃表周弁將兵三萬，以拒賊之衆於瑤臺城。弁剛勇輕敵，師徒敗績。弁單騎裸身潛遁，夜歸城。賊亦收輜重鎧甲而還。生因囚弁以請罪。王並捨之。

是月，司憲周弁疽發背，卒。生妻公主遘疾，旬日又薨。生因請罷郡，護喪赴國。王許之。便以司農田子華行南柯太守事。生哀慟發引，威儀在途，男女叫號，人吏奠饌，攀轅遮道者不可勝數。遂達於國。王與夫人素衣哭於郊，候靈輿之至。謚公主曰“順儀公主”。備儀仗羽葆鼓吹，葬於國東十里盤龍岡。是月，故司憲子榮信，亦護喪赴國。

生久鎮外藩，結好中國，貴門豪族，靡不是洽。自罷郡還國，出入無恆，交遊賓從，威福日盛。王意疑憚之。時有國人上表云：“玄象謫見，國有大恐。都邑遷徙，宗廟崩壞。釁起他族，事在蕭牆。”時議以生侈僭之應也。遂奪生侍衛，禁生遊從，處之私第。生自恃守郡多年，曾無敗政，流言怨悖，鬱鬱不樂。王亦知之，因命生曰：“姻親二十餘年，不幸小女夭枉，不得與君子偕老，良有痛傷。”

夫人因留孫自鞠育之。又謂生曰：“卿離家多時，可暫歸本里，一見親族。諸孫留此，無以爲念。後三年，當令迎卿。”

生曰："此乃家矣，何更歸焉？"

王笑曰："卿本人間，家非在此。"

生忽若惛睡，曶然久之，方乃發悟前事，遂流涕請還。王顧左右以送生。生再拜而去，復見前二紫衣使者從焉。

至大戶外，見所乘車甚劣，左右親使御僕，遂無一人，心甚嘆異。生上車，行可數里，復出大城。宛是昔年東來之途，山川原野，依然如舊。所送二使者，甚無威勢。生逾怏怏。生問使者曰："廣陵郡何時可到？"二使謳歌自若，久乃答曰："少頃即至。"

俄出一穴，見本里閭巷，不改往日，潸然自悲，不覺流涕。二使者引生下車，入其門，升其階，已身臥於堂東廡之下。生甚驚畏，不敢前近。二使因大呼生之姓名數聲，生遂發寤如初。見家之僮僕擁篲於庭，二客濯足於榻，斜日未隱於西垣，餘樽尚湛於東牖。夢中倏忽，若度一世矣。

生感念嗟嘆，遂呼二客而語之。驚駭，因與生出外，尋槐下穴。生指曰："此即夢中所驚入處。"二客將謂狐狸木媚之所爲祟。遂命僕伕荷斤斧，斷擁腫，折查枿，尋穴究源。旁可袤丈。有大穴，根洞然明朗，可容一榻。上有積土壤以爲城郭臺殿之狀。有蟻數斛，隱聚其中。中有小臺，其色若丹。二大蟻處之，素翼朱首，長可三寸。左右大蟻數十輔之，諸蟻不敢近。此其王矣。即槐安國都也。

又窮一穴，直上南枝可四丈，宛轉方中，亦有上城小樓，羣蟻亦處其中，即生所領南柯郡也。

又一穴：西去二丈，磅礴空圬，嵌窞異狀。中有一腐龜殼，大如斗。積雨浸潤，小草叢生，繁茂翳薈，掩映振殼，即生所獵靈龜山也。

又窮一穴：東去丈餘，古根盤屈，若龍虺之狀。中有小土壤，高尺餘，即生所葬妻盤龍岡之墓也。

追想前事，感嘆於懷，披閱窮跡，皆符所夢。不欲二客壞之，遽令掩塞如舊。

是夕，風雨暴發。旦視其穴，遂失羣蟻，莫知所去。故先言"國有大恐，都邑遷徙"，此其驗矣。

復念檀蘿征代之事，又請二客訪跡於外。宅東一里有古涸澗，側有大檀樹一株，藤蘿擁織，上不見日。旁有小穴，亦有羣蟻隱聚其間。檀蘿之國，豈非此耶？

嗟呼！蟻之靈異，猶不可窮，況山藏木伏之大者所變化乎？

　　時生酒徒周弁、田子華並居六合縣，不與生過從旬日矣。生遽遣家僮疾往候之。周生暴疾已逝，田子華亦寢疾於牀。生感南柯之浮虛，悟人世之倏忽，遂棲心道門，絕棄酒色。後三年，歲在丁丑，亦終於家。時年四十七，將符宿契之限矣。

　　公佐貞元十八年秋八月，自吳之洛，暫泊淮浦，偶覯淳于生棼，詢訪遺蹟，翻覆再三，事皆摭實，輒編錄成傳，以資好事。雖稽神語怪，事涉非經，而竊位著生，冀將爲戒。後之君子，幸以南柯爲偶然，無以名位驕於天壤間云。

　　前華州參軍李肇贊曰：

　　　貴極祿位，權傾國都，達人視此，蟻聚何殊！

Tale 3.13

The Story of Lady Feng of Lujiang

By Li Gongzuo
Translated by Jing Hu

Old Lady Feng, the wife of a farmer[1] of Lu Jiang,[2] was a poor widow without a son, who was looked down upon and ignored by her fellow villagers.

In the fourth year of the Yuanhe Reign (806–820), famine caused by a poor harvest struck the Huai-Chu region.[3] Feng passed by the Mudu Villa on her way to beg at Shu Prefecture.[4] It was windy and raining, so Feng rested under a mulberry tree. Suddenly she noticed a hut by the corner of the road, and the light was dim and glimmering. Going forward to ask for lodging, she saw a woman in her twenties, and both her appearance and dress were beautiful. She was carrying a three-year-old child, leaning on the doorframe, and weeping sadly. As she approached, she also saw an old man and an old woman sitting on the bed, whispering and looking upset, as if they were hounding someone for debts. Seeing Feng coming, the old man and the old woman left quietly.

[1]*Sefu* 嗇夫 means also minor official.

[2]A prefecture in modern Anhui Province.

[3]Huai-Chu 淮楚 region is roughly in modern Henan and Hubei provinces.

[4]Shu 舒 was a prefecture in the Tang dynasty in modern Anhui Province, southwest of Lu Jiang.

The woman cried for a long time before she stopped, entered the house to prepare food, make a bed, and invited Feng to eat and stay there.

Feng asked the woman what had happened. The woman started to weep again and said, "This child's father, my husband, will marry another woman tomorrow." Feng asked, "Who were those two old people I saw? What did they want from you? Why were they mad?" The woman said, "They are my parents-in-law. Now that their son is marrying another woman, they demand the baskets, scissors and rulers, and household ritual objects that I used before to give to the new bride. I don't have the heart to give them. That was what they were reproaching me for."

Feng asked, "Where is your husband?" The woman answered, "I am the daughter of Liang Qian, the county magistrate of Huaiyin. It has been seven years since I married Mr. Dong Jiang, and we have two sons and one daughter. Both sons are with their father, and the daughter is this child. Dong Jiang lives in the town down the road and is a deputy official of Cuo County.[5] His family has accumulated a huge amount of property." She kept crying as she talked.

Feng had no doubt about her story. She had been cold and hungry for a long time, and now, with a good meal and comfortable lodging, she did not talk any more. But the young woman cried till dawn.

Feng took her leave, travelled twenty *li*, and arrived at Tongcheng County.[6] East of the county, in a huge estate, screens and curtains were suspended and a dowry of lambs and geese prepared. Many people were busying themselves, saying that an official's wedding would take place. Feng inquired about the groom. It was none other than Dong Jiang!

---

[5]Cuo 鄌, modern Yongcheng County in Henan.

[6]This is the same as modern Tongcheng County in Anhui Province.

Feng said, "Dong has a wife. How can he remarry?"

"Dong's wife and daughter are dead," said the locals.

"Last night I was caught in rain," Feng explained. "I stayed in Dong's wife Liang's house. How can you say that she died?"

The locals inquired about the place; it turned out to be the graveyard of Dong's wife. They then asked about the looks of the two elders, which matched that of Dong Jiang's late parents. Dong Jiang was a native of Shu Prefecture, and the locals knew his family well.

Someone reported all this to Dong Jiang. Dong accused Feng of witchcraft and ordered his subordinates to kick the old woman Feng out quickly. Feng told her story to the town people, and they all gasped in amazement. Nonetheless Dong married that night.

During the fifth lunar month in the summer of the sixth year (811) of the Yuanhe Reign, Li Gongzuo, a retainer of the Jiang Huai area, travelled to the capital on government business. On his way back, he stopped at the southern bank of the Han River to meet with Gao Yue of Bohai,[7] Zhao Zan of Tianshui,[8] and Yu Wending of Henan at a hostel. They asked each other about unusual events throughout the night and everyone told all his stories. Gao Yue told the whole story above and Gongzuo put it in writing.

---

[7]This is roughly in the area of the Heilongjiang and Wusuli rivers.

[8]Tianshui 天水 was a prefecture in Tang dynasty of the modern Tianshui city in Gansu.

廬江馮媼傳

李公佐

馮媼者，廬江里中嗇夫之婦，窮寡無子，為鄉民賤棄。

元和四年，淮楚大歉。媼遂食於舒，途經牧犢墅。值風雨，止於桑下。忽見路隅一室，燈燭熒熒。媼因詣求宿。見一女子，年二十餘，容服美麗，攜三歲兒，倚門悲泣。前，又見老叟與媼，據牀而坐。神氣慘戚，言語呫囁，有若征索財物、追逐之狀。見馮媼至，叟媼默然捨去。

女久乃止泣，入戶備餴食，理牀榻，邀媼食息焉。

媼問其故。女復泣曰：“此兒父，我之夫也。明日別娶。”媼曰：“向者二老人，何人也？於汝何求，而發怒？”女曰：“我舅姑也。今嗣子別娶，征我筐筥刀尺祭祀舊物，以授新人。我不忍與，是有斯責。”

媼曰：“汝前夫何在？”女曰：“我淮陰令梁倩女，適董氏七年。有二男一女。男皆隨父，女即此也。今前邑中董江，即其人也。江官為鄝丞，家累巨產。”發言不勝嗚咽。

媼不之異；又久困寒餓，得美食甘寢，不復言。女泣至曉。

媼辭去，行二十里，至桐城縣。縣東有甲第，張簾帷，具羔雁，人物紛然，云今夕有官家禮事。媼問其郎，即董江也。

媼曰：“董有妻，何更娶焉？”

邑人曰：“董妻及女亡矣。”

媼曰：“昨宵我遇雨，寄宿董妻梁氏舍，何得言亡？”

邑人詢其處，即董妻墓也。詢其二老容貌，即董江之先父母也。董江本舒州人，里中之人皆得詳之。

有告董江者，董以妖妄罪之，令部者追逐媼去。媼言於邑人，邑人皆為感歎。是夕，董竟就婚焉。

　　元和六年夏五月，江淮從事李公佐使至京，回次漢南，與渤海高鉞，天水趙儹，河南字文鼎會於傳舍。宵話徵異，各盡見聞。鉞具道其事，公佐為之傳。

Tale 3.14

An Account of Xie Xiao'e

by Li Gongzuo
Translated by Xin Zou

Xiao'e, whose maiden name was Xie, was a native of Yuzhang and the daughter of a travelling merchant.[1] Eight years after she was born, she lost her mother. She was married to the knight-errant Duan Juzhen of Liyang County.[2] Juzhen was spirited, valued good conduct, and associated with a circle of gallants.[3] Xiao'e's father amassed great wealth but kept his reputation hidden among traders. He often shipped goods with his son-in-law Duan on the same boat, travelling back and forth on the lakes and rivers. When Xiao'e turned fourteen years old, just starting to wear the hairpin, her father and husband were both killed by bandits, who robbed

---

[1]Yuzhang, near modern Nanchang in Jiangxi Province, belonged to Jiangnan Xidao 江南西道 (Jiangnan Western Circuit) and was the seat of Hong Prefecture 洪州 in the Tang dynasty. See Tan Qixiang, *Zhongguo lishi ditu ji*, 5:57–58.

[2]Liyang County 歷陽縣, in modern Anhui, belonged to the Huannan Circuit 淮南道 and was the seat of He Prefecture 和州, see Tan Qixiang, 5:54.

[3]Wang Mengou (Wang, 2:35, n. 2) points out that Duan Juzhen's knight-like characteristics are not demonstrated in this story and hence he suggests that this description of Juzhen is only to foreshadow Xiao'e's heroic and resolute action.

them of all their supplies of gold and silks. Duan and Xie's brothers and nephews, together with several dozen servants, were all thrown into the river. Xiao'e also suffered a breast injury and broke her leg. She drifted along in the water until another boat found her. After a night, she revived. Afterward she wandered about begging from place to place, and came to Shangyuan County,[4] where she attached herself to a nun called Jingwu, from the Miaoguo (Marvelous Results) Temple.[5]

Earlier, her father having died, Xiao'e dreamed that her father said to her: "The one who killed me was *the monkey in a carriage, the grass east of the gate.*" A few days afterwards, she again dreamed that her husband said to her, "The one who killed me *walked through the grain; he was a man for one day.*" Xiao'e could not decipher these words by herself. She wrote these phrases down, and sought far and wide for wise men to explain them. Yet as years went by, she was still not able to find such a wise person.

It was the spring of the eighth year of the Yuanhe era (813). Having been relieved of my post as a Retainer in Jiangxi, I sailed eastward in a skiff and moored at Jianye, where I ascended the pagoda of the Waguan Temple.[6] There was a monk named Qiwu,

---

[4]Shangyuan 上元 County, in modern Nanjing, belonged to Run Prefecture 潤州 of the Eastern Jiangnan Circuit 江南東道 in the Tang dynasty (Tan Qixiang, 5:55–56). A few lines later, the same place is also called Jianye 建業.

[5]Li Jianguo, (*Cidian*, p. 289. n. 8) notes that the Miaoguo Temple was first established in the Three Kingdoms period and was once called Ruixiang Yuan 瑞相院.

[6]It is a 350-foot tall pagoda, which stands in the Waguan Temple. There were at least two narrative traditions on the naming of the Waguan Temple. In one tradition, the temple was known as the Waguan Temple 瓦官寺 (Potters' Temple) because it was located at the site where potters, or *waguan*, worked during the Jin dynasty (265–420). According to another tradition, however, the temple took the name

a man who respected the worthy, loved learning, and was on good terms with me. He told me, "There is a widow named Xiao'e, who often comes to this temple. She once showed me a twelve-character riddle, which I have not been able to solve." I asked Master Qi to write it down. Then, leaning over the railing and tracing the characters in the air with my fingers, I concentrated my attention and contemplated quietly. Before my companions could get bored, I fully comprehended the meaning of her text. I had a servant-boy [of the temple] bring Xiao'e forward immediately and asked her where the riddle came from. Xiao'e sobbed for quite a while and said, "My father and husband were both killed by bandits. Thereafter, I dreamed my father told me, 'The one who killed me was *the monkey in a carriage, the grass east of the gate.*' I also dreamed my husband told me, 'The one who killed me *walked through the grain; he was a man for one day.*' For years no one has been able to understand this." I said, "If that was the case, I think I have figured it all out now. The one who killed your father is Shen Lan, the one who killed your husband is Shen Chun. Take "*the monkey in the carriage*": the character for carriage (*ju* 車), when the top and bottom strokes are removed, becomes *Shen* (申). Moreover, *Shen* is associated with the monkey [in the system of twelve Earthly Branches].[7] That's why it was called "*the monkey in a carriage.*" If the character for gate (*men* 門) is placed under the grass radical (艸), inside of which there is the character east (*dong* 東), then it becomes the character *lan* (蘭). Furthermore, to *walk through the grain* is to penetrate through the field (*tian* 田), and this

---

Waguan 瓦棺 (Brick Coffin) in the seventh century because lotuses grew out of the brick coffin of a monk who was buried in the temple. Wang Meng'ou (2:36, no. 8) notes that the temple was established in the Liang 梁 dynasty (502–557) and was initially known as Shenyuan ge 昇元閣.

[7]*Shen* 申 is the ninth of the twelve Early Branches, the one of the monkeys. The twelve Early Branches are used in combination with the Heavenly Stems to designate years, months, days and hours.

also becomes the character *shen* (申). As for "*a man for one day,*" when one adds a stroke on top of man (*fu* 夫), and below that there is a sun, this becomes the character *chun* (春). It is sufficient to know that the one who killed your father is Shen Lan and the one who killed your husband is Shen Chun." Moved to tears, Xiao'e bowed to me repeatedly. She wrote down the four characters "Shen Lan, Shen Chun" and put them inside her coat. She vowed that she would seek out and kill the two bandits to set right the injustice. Xiao'e then inquired about my surname and official service, and left in tears.

From this time on, Xiao'e dressed as a man and hired herself out as a laborer on the lakes and rivers. More than a year later, she came to Xunyang Commandery[8] and saw a placard fixed on a bamboo gate, which read "Laborers wanted." Xiao'e then went to the gate in response to the placard and inquired about her future master: it was none other than Shen Lan! Lan led her in. Although Xiao'e's heart was filled with much hatred, she gave the appearance of being submissive and became most beloved among Shen's close attendants. All the gold and silks that came in and went out were entrusted to Xiao'e. For more than two years, Lan still did not know that Xiao'e was a woman. The gold, treasures, embroidered silks, clothing, and vessels previously seized from the Xie family were stored at Lan's house. Every time Xiao'e held her old belongings, she could not help weeping secretly for a long time. Lan and Chun were cousins. At that time, Chun's family lived in Dushu Pu (Lone-tree Bank) on the north shore of the Great River,[9] and they worked closely together. Chun

---

[8]Xunyang Commandery 潯陽郡 belonged to the Jiangnan Western Circuit 江南西道 in the Tang dynasty, with Xunyang County (modern Jiujiang) as its seat (Tan Qixiang, 5:57–58).

[9]Wang Meng'ou (2:37, n. 18) notes that *Dushu Pu* is on the northern bank of the Yangtze River. The place name also appears in Bai Juyi's poem "To Li the Sixth from Lone-tree Beach on a Rainy Night" 獨樹浦雨

and Lan would go off together for more than a month and often return with the money and silks they had seized. They would always leave Xiao'e, together with Lan's wife, Ms. Lan, to keep watch together over the household. Wine, meat and clothes were generously provided for Xiao'e.

One day, carrying some carp and wine, Chun came to visit Lan. Xiao'e sighed to herself and thought, "What Master Li understood with his ingenuity and judgment all fits the words in my dream. In this, Heaven simply must have inspired him. Now my goal is about to be achieved." That evening, Lan and Chun had a gathering, to which all of the bandits came, and they drank heavily. After the rest of the gang had left, Chun got completely drunk and slumped in the chamber; Lan had also fallen asleep exposed out in the courtyard. Stealthily locking Chun inside, Xiao'e drew her sword and first cut off Lan's head, and his screaming reached the neighbors. By the time other people arrived, Chun was captured within and Lan lay dead outside. The goods recovered from the loot they had seized were valued in the tens of millions. Lan had had more than several dozen accomplices, whose names Xiao'e had kept in mind. They were all captured and executed.

His Honor Zhang, Governor of Xunyang at the time, valued Xiao'e's aspirations and conduct, reporting them in detail, and requesting that an arch of honor[10] be erected for her. Only then was Xiao'e able to be exempted from the death penalty. The time was the summer of the twelfth year of the Yuanhe reign (817). After avenging the death of her father and husband, she returned to her native village to see her relatives. Local magnates competed

---

夜. Both notes seem to suggest that Li Gongzuo was very careful about the accuracy of historical details, which increases the degree of verisimilitude of his account.

[10]*Jingbiao* 旌表 were the ornate tablets on independent gates (*pailou* 牌樓) set up to honor filial sons and chaste widows.

to seek after her in marriage, but Xiao'e vowed in her heart that she would never marry again. In the end, she cut off her hair, donned sackcloth and sought the Way on Ox-head Mountain, where she served under Vinaya Master Jiang, the bodhisattva, as a novice.[11] Her determination was firm and her actions austere. In the frost, she pounded rice; in the rain, she cut wood, never sparing her muscles and strength. It was not until the fourth month of the thirteenth year (818) that she was fully ordained[12] at the Kaiyuan Temple in Sizhou.[13] She eventually used Xiao'e as her ordination name, not forgetting her origins.

In the summer of that year, I first returned to Chang'an, travelling along the banks of the Si River, and stopped at the Shanyi Si (Right Purpose Temple) to pay my respects to the fully-ordained Abbess Ling. There I saw several dozen newly consecrated nuns — their heads were cleanly shaved, and their robes were new. Poised, with a serious mien, they were arranged to the left and right of the abbess. One nun among them asked the

---

[11]According to Li Jianguo (*Cidian*, p. 289), the Ox-head Mountain, southwest of modern Nanjing, was an important Buddhist sacred mountain, where the Monk Farong 法融 (594–657) established the Ox-head School of Chan Buddhism. For more information, see John R. McRae (1947–2011), "The Ox-head School of Chinese Ch'an Buddhism: From Early Ch'an to Golden Age," in: *Studies in Ch'an and Hua-yen* edited by Robert M. Gimello, Peter N. Gregory (Honolulu: University of Hawaii Press, 1983), pp. 169–252.

[12]*Ju jie* 具戒, or *Ju zujie* 具足戒, means to receive the full set of precepts, which were normally 250 precepts for a *bhikṣu* 比丘 (Buddhist monk), and 348 for a *bhikkhuni* (Buddhist nun).

[13]In the Tang dynasty, Si Prefecture 泗州 belonged to Huainan Circuit 淮南道 with its seat at Linhuai 臨淮, southeast of modern Sihong County in Jiangsu (Tan Qixiang, 5:54). The Kaiyuan Temple in Si Prefecture was built during Empress Wu's reign (r. 684–705) and was originally called Dayun Temple 大雲寺. The name was changed to Kaiyuan Temple in the twenty-sixth year of the Kaiyuan reign (738).

abbess: "Isn't this official the Administrative Assistant Li of Hongzhou, the twenty-third of his generation?"[14] The abbess answered, "It is." The nun said, "It was this Administrative Assistant's kindness that enabled me to avenge my family, and wipe out my grievance and shame." Sorrowfully weeping, the nun turned to look at me. As I did not recognize her, I inquired into what she meant. Xiao'e replied: "My humble name is Xiao'e. Not long ago, I was a widow begging for food. Back then the Administrative Assistant helped to determine the names of the two bandits, Shen Chun and Shen Lan. Does he really not remember?" I said, "I did not recall you at first, now I remember." Xiao'e then wept and described in detail from her writing down the names of Shen Chun and Shen Lan to her fulfilling the promise of avenging the death of her father and husband. She recalled the bitter hardships she underwent from start to finish. Xiao'e then said to me, "The day will come when I shall repay the Administrative Assistant's kindness. This is not merely an empty promise."

Ah, I was able to determine the names of the two bandits, and Xiao'e was able to eventually avenge the death of her father and husband. It is now clear that the Way of the gods is not obscure. Xiao'e's appearance was sincere and her words profound; she was intelligent and quick-witted.[15] She burned her fingers and lamed her feet [in line with Buddhist practices], swearing to seek *Bhūta*

---

[14]Hongzhou 洪州 belonged to Western Jiangnan Circuit 江南西道 in the Tang dynasty (Tan Qixiang, 5:55–56). Its seat was Yuzhang 豫章, modern Nanchang in Jiangxi Province.

[15]It is very likely that the phrase *houmao shenci* 厚貌深辭 derives from *houmao shenqing* 厚貌深情 in *Zhuangzi* 莊子, in which the speaker argues that a man's mind is hard to know under his thickly veiled exterior, thus he offers nine tests to tell an inferior man apart from the superior.

tathatā.[16] Ever since she took the Way, she had never again worn silk or cotton, nor had she eaten with salt or spice. Except for [Buddhist] precepts, regulations, and Chan principles, she would not talk. A few days later, she told me that she would return to the Ox-head Mountain. In a small skiff, she sailed along the Huai River and roamed through the southern provinces. I have never met her since.

The gentleman says:[17] "To never give up one's resolve and ultimately to avenge the death of one's father and husband, this is integrity; to mingle with servants and menials and not to be recognized as a woman, this is chastity. As for the virtues of women, they are only keeping integrity and chastity from beginning to end. A woman like Xiao'e is sufficient to warn all those under Heaven who attempt to oppose the Way and disrupt norms, and to encourage all loyal men and filial daughters under Heaven to perform virtuous deeds. I knew all the details of the events above and was able to clarify the mysterious texts, which tacitly brought the dark world [of dreams] into accord with the minds of human beings. To know of a good thing and not to

---

[16]Li Jianguo (*Cidian*, p. 289, n. 46) notes that the term *lianzhi* 煉指 refers to the Buddhist practice of tying the finger and the incense to burn the finger. Wang Meng'ou (2:39, n. 32) notes that such actions as burning one's finger or breaking one's legs were common religious practices in the Tang dynasty. People at the time believed that through such suffering, they could see Buddha. For details on this self-immolation, see James A. Benn, *Burning for the Buddha: Self-immolation in Chinese Buddhism* (Honolulu: University of Hawai'i Press, 2007).

[17]This motif *junzi yue* 君子曰 (the gentleman says) is taken from the *Zuo zhuan*. In keeping with this back frame, the author clearly shows his adherence to the principles of the *Chunqiu* (Spring and Autumn Annals).

record it, this is not the intent of the *Spring and Autumn Annals*.[18] Thus I have composed this account to honor and praise her.

Note: This is a revised version of my 2016 rendition in William H. Nienhauser, ed., *Tang Dynasty Tales: A Guided Reader* v. 2 (Singapore: World Scientific, 2016, pp. 339–64), where more detailed annotations and commentary are provided.

---

[18]The editorship of the *Spring and Autumn Annals*, the earliest extant Chinese chronological history, was traditionally attributed to Confucius. It is generally believed that the work passes moral judgment on historical figures and events in subtle ways.

謝小娥傳

李公佐

　　小娥，姓謝氏，豫章人，估客女也。生八歲，喪母；嫁歷陽俠士段居貞。居貞負氣重義，交遊豪俊。小娥父畜巨產，隱名商賈間，常與段壻同舟貨，往來江湖。時小娥年十四，始及笄。父與夫俱為盜所殺，盡掠金帛。段之弟兄，謝之生姪，與僮僕輩數十，悉沉於江；小娥亦傷胸折足，漂流水中，為他船所獲，經夕而活。因流轉乞食至上元縣，依妙果寺尼淨悟之室。

　　初，父之死也。小娥夢父謂曰："殺我者：車中猴，門東草。"又數日，復夢其夫謂曰："殺我者：禾中走，一日夫。"小娥不自解悟，常書此語，廣求智者辨之。歷年不能得。

　　元和八年春，余罷江西從事，扁舟東下，淹泊建業，登瓦官寺閣。有僧齊物者，重賢好學，與余善。因告余曰："有孀婦名小娥者，每來寺中，示我十二字謎語，某不能辨。"余遂請齊公書於紙，乃憑檻書空，凝思默慮。坐客未倦，予悟其文。令侍童疾召小娥前至，詢訪其由。小娥嗚咽良久，乃曰："我父及夫，皆為賊所殺。邇後嘗夢父告曰：'殺我者，車中猴，門東草'。又夢夫告曰：'殺我者，禾中走，一日夫'。歲久無人悟之。"余曰："若然者，吾審詳矣。殺汝父是申蘭，殺汝夫是申春。且車中猴，車字去上下各一畫，是申字；又申屬猴，故曰車中猴。草下有門，門中有東，乃蘭字也。又，禾中走，是穿田過，亦是申字也。一日夫者，夫上更一畫，下有日，是春字也。殺汝父是申蘭，殺汝夫是申春，足可明矣。"小娥慟哭再拜，書申蘭申春四字於衣中，誓將訪殺二賊，以復其冤。娥因問余姓氏官族，垂涕而去。

　　爾後小娥便為男子服，傭保於江湖間。歲餘，至潯陽郡，見竹戶上有紙牓子，云"召傭者。"小娥乃應召詣門，問其主，乃申蘭

208

也。蘭引歸，娥心憤貌順，在蘭左右，甚見親愛。金帛出入之數，無不委娥。已二歲餘，竟不知娥之女人也。先是謝氏之金寶錦繡衣物器具，悉掠在蘭家，小娥每執舊物，未嘗不暗泣移時。蘭與春，宗昆弟也。時春一家住大江北獨樹浦，與蘭往來密洽。蘭與春同去經月，多獲財帛而歸。每留娥與蘭妻蘭氏同守家室，酒肉衣服，給娥甚豐。或一日，春攜文鯉兼酒詣蘭，娥私歎曰：「李君精悟玄鑒，皆符夢言。此乃天啟其心，志將就矣。」是夕，蘭與春會群賊，畢至醋飲。暨諸兇既去，春沉醉，臥於內室，蘭亦露寢於庭。小娥潛鎖春於內，抽佩刀先斷蘭首，呼號鄰人並至，春擒於內，蘭死於外，獲贓收貨，數至千萬。初，蘭、春有黨數十，暗記其名，悉擒就戮。

時潯陽太守張公，善其志行，為具其事上旌表，乃得免死。時元和十二年夏歲也。復父夫之讎畢，歸本里，見親屬。里中豪族爭求聘，娥誓心不嫁。遂剪髮披褐，訪道於牛頭山，師事大士尼將律師。娥志堅行苦，霜舂雨薪，不倦筋力。十三年四月，始受具戒於泗州開元寺，竟以小娥為法號，不忘本也。其年夏月，余始歸長安，途經泗濱，過善義寺謁大德尼令。操戒新見者數十，淨髮鮮帔，威儀雍容，列侍師之左右。中有一尼問師曰：「此官豈非洪州李判官二十三郎者乎？」師曰：「然。」曰：「使我獲報家仇，得雪冤恥，是判官恩德也。」顧余悲泣。余不之識，詢訪其由。娥對曰：「某名小娥，頃乞食孀婦也。判官時為辨申蘭、申春二賊名字，豈不憶念乎？」余曰：「初不相記，今即悟也。」娥因泣，具寫記申蘭申春，復父夫之仇，志願相畢，經營終始艱苦之狀。小娥又謂余曰：「報判官恩，當有日矣。豈徒然哉！」

嗟呼！余能辨二盜之姓名，小娥又能竟復父夫之讎冤。神道不昧，昭然可知。小娥厚貌深辭，聰敏端特，煉指跛足，誓求真如。爰自入道，衣無絮帛，齋無鹽酪，非律儀禪理，口無所言。後數日，告我歸牛頭山。扁舟汎淮，雲遊南國，不復再遇。

君子曰：誓志不捨，復父夫之讎，節也；傭保雜處，不知女人，貞也。女子之行，唯貞與節能終始全之而已。如小娥，足以儆天下逆道亂常之心，足以勸天下貞夫孝婦之節。余詳備前事，發明隱文，暗與冥會，符於人心。知善不錄，非春秋之義也。故作傳以旌美之。

Tale 3.15

The Courtesan Li Wa

By Bai Xinjian
Translated by Zhenjun Zhang

The Lady of Qian,[1] Li Wa, was originally a courtesan in Chang'an. Her character was noble, and her conduct particular, with points worthy of praise. Therefore Bai Xingjian (776–826), the investigating senior, wrote this biography about her.

During the Tianbao reign (742–756), the prefect of Changzhou (in Jiangsu), a gentleman of Xingyang whose real name is omitted here,[2] was highly renowned and had a household filled with numerous servants. At the age of fifty, he had a son who was only twenty years old. His son had delicate features as well as literary talent, was clearly distinct from ordinary people, and therefore was deeply esteemed and admired by his peers. His father loved him dearly, and regarded him highly, saying, "This is the winged steed of our family."

When the young man was recommended by the local prefecture to the Capital to participate in the imperial Civil Service

---

[1] Qian 汧 refers to Qianyang 汧陽 commandery, centered around modern Long County in Shanxi.

[2] Xingyang 滎陽 commandery, modern Xingyang County in Henan, was the hometown of the noted Zheng clan, one of the seven noble clans during the Tang dynasty.

Examination and was about to set out, his father prepared for him an ample supply of clothes, utensils, and a decorated horse-drawn carriage. The father had also calculated the living expenses his son would incur while living in the Capital, and he told him, "Based on my observation of your talent, you will place first on your first attempt. I have now prepared two years' worth of expenses for you, and it is an ample amount. This will help you realize your ambitions." The scholar was very conceited, and he regarded the effort it took to obtain a rank in the examinations to be as easy as counting his fingers. He set out from Piling, arriving in Chang'an a little over a month later. He took up residence at Buzheng Ward.

One day, he was returning from a ramble around the East Market and was entering through the Eastern Gate of Pingkang Ward to visit a friend in its southwest corner.[3] Having strolled to Mingke Lane, he noticed a residence with a courtyard. Its doorway was narrow, but the houses within were neat, deep and tranquil. One panel of the double doors was closed. A young girl stood there, leaning against her servant maid with double bun-type hairdos, that is, coiled hair knots. The young girl possessed a charming grace and exquisite countenance, truly not of this world. Beholding her without warning, the scholar, distracted, stopped his horse unawares for quite a while, lingering, reluctant to leave. He then pretended that his hand had slipped, dropping the horsewhip onto the ground, and he waited for his servant to come up to him and ordered the whip to be retrieved. Taking advantage of the interim, he stole many glances at the girl. The girl also turned her gaze towards him and observed him, expressing a look of great adoration for him. In the end, however, the scholar did not dare exchange one word with her, and he simply left.

After that, the scholar looked distracted. Then he located friends familiar with Chang'an in order to inquire about her

---

[3]Pingkang Ward 平康里 was famous as a residence of courtesans.

secretly. His friends informed him, "That is the house of a courtesan with the surname of Li."

He asked, "Is that girl available?"

His friends answered, "The Li family is very rich. Those who associated with her previously were all wealthy aristocrats, so she had made a lot of money. If your wealth does not exceed a million, don't expect to move her heart."

The scholar replied, "I only fear that I will not succeed — otherwise, even if I spend over a million, what is there to regret?"

A few days later, the scholar donned neat, immaculate clothes and brought along many guests to accompany him to the Li residence. After he knocked on the door, a servant girl came in no time to open it.

The scholar asked, "Whose esteemed residence is this?"

The servant girl did not answer, but rather raced back at lightning speed while loudly yelling, "The young gentleman who dropped his horsewhip last time has come!"

Li Wa was ecstatic, telling her maid, "Ask him to please wait a few moments. I must fix myself up anew, change my clothes, and then come out to meet him."

The scholar was privately pleased upon hearing this. The servant girl thus led him to a screen, where he saw a white-haired hunch-backed old granny, who was Li Wa's mother. The scholar went up to her to kowtow and pay his respects, inquiring, "I have heard that there is a vacant unoccupied yard here, and I wish to rent it to live in — if it is true."

The old granny replied, "I just fear that it is too shabby and cramped, not deserving to be lived by a nobleman — how could I dare ask for rent?" She then ushered him into the drawing room, which had extremely resplendent furnishings.

The old granny sat opposite the scholar, then mentioned, "I have a daughter, petite, and not skilled, but who really enjoys meeting guests. I hope you can make her acquaintance." Upon saying this, she called Li Wa out. Li Wa had clear bright eyes and flawless white wrists; her every move was delicate and charming, simply enchanting.

Amazed, the scholar immediately stood up, not daring to lift up his head to look. After bowing to her in greeting, he paid his respects and offered correct social formalities.

Each of her movements was seductive and arousing, unlike anything he had ever seen before. They retook their seats and steeped the tea and poured the wine. The cups, plates, and utensils were immaculately clean.

After quite a while, the sky darkened and the sound of the drum announcing evening could be heard. The old granny asked the scholar if his residence was far. The scholar lied to her with an answer, "It is many *li* beyond the Yanping Gate," hoping she would ask him to stay the night because of the distance.

The old granny cautioned him, "The evening drum has already sounded. You should hurry back to avoid violating the curfew."

The scholar said, "I was lucky enough to have made the acquaintance of you all, so that, between chatting and laughing, I did not notice that it had already turned dark. The road is very far... and having no relatives in the city — what am I to do?"

Li Wa offered, "Since you don't mind the remoteness and simplicity of this place, and furthermore, are going to rent a house here, what does it matter if you stay here for a night?"

The scholar repeatedly glanced at the old granny, who consented, "Yes, okay."

So the scholar called his servant boy over and presented two bolts of fine silk to the women, asking them to accept it as payment for the night's dinner expenses. Li Wa, smiling, stopped him and said, "It does not work like this according to the etiquette between guest and host. For tonight's expenses, please allow my poor humble family to serve you with some casually-prepared simple fare. If you insist on being the host, let's wait until some other time." The scholar repeatedly refused her offer, but in the end Li Wa still disagreed with him.

Soon, everyone moved to the west hall to sit. The splendor of the bed curtains, bamboo drapery, and wooden couch drew everyone's gaze. The vanity box, coverlets, and pillows were also all luxurious and resplendent. They lit the candles and laid out the banquet, a lavish assortment of dishes and wine spread out before them.

After the meal, the old granny rose and left. It was following this that the scholar and Li Wa's conversation started to become more intimate, joking and teasing without reserve.

The scholar admitted, "Last time, passing your doorstep by chance, I saw you at that moment standing before the screen. Ever since then, you have occupied my thoughts constantly — even when eating or sleeping, I could not leave off [thinking about you] for a moment."

Li Wa replied, "My heart was likewise."

The scholar further revealed, "I came here today not only because I wished to rent a house, but more in the hope of realizing my entire life's desire. It is only that I don't know what my fate is ... ?"

Before he could finish, the old granny walked in and asked them what they were discussing. The scholar told her everything.

Smiling, the old granny said, "It is natural that a desire for romance develops between a young man and woman. If they fall in love, there is no way to prevent it, even if their parents command it. It is just that my daughter's visage is ugly. How is she worthy to serve you!"

The scholar immediately walked down the steps, kowtowed to the old granny and expressed his gratitude. He vowed, "I willingly become your servant."

The old granny thus regarded him as her son-in-law. They drank wine to their heart's content before dispersing.

The next day, the scholar moved all of his belongings and thus took up residence at the Li house. From that point on, he went into hiding, vanishing without a trace, no longer contacting his relatives and friends. He spent every day with courtesans, performers, and the like, eating, drinking, and making merry. When he had spent all the money he carried, he just sold his fine horses, then his servant boy. Over a year later, his money, servants, and horses were all gone. As a result, the old granny's attitude towards him gradually cooled. Yet, Li Wa's affection for him deepened and became more sincere.

One day, Li Wa said to the scholar, "I have been together with you, in love, for a year now, but I still have not become pregnant. I frequently hear people speak of a Bamboo Forest God that is very effective. Let's prepare some food and wine to make a prayer, shall we?"

The scholar did not know that this was their ruse, so, thrilled, he went to the pawnshop and pawned his clothes. He took the money and spent it on preparing the Three Sacrifices and wine, then went together with Li Wa to pray in the temple. They stayed for two nights before returning, with the scholar riding on a donkey, following behind Li Wa's carriage.

Upon reaching the north gate of Pingkang Ward, Li Wa said to the scholar, "My aunt's home is in the lane that turns east from here. Let's go there to rest for a bit and, incidentally, pay her a visit, shall we?"

The scholar assented. After walking forward for less than one hundred steps, they indeed beheld a carriage gate. Peering in through the crack in the gate revealed a very spacious interior. The servant girl, from the back of the carriage, told him to stop, adding, "We're here."

The scholar dismounted from his donkey. Coincidently, a person walked out at that moment and asked, "Who is it?"

The scholar answered, "It's Li Wa."

The person withdrew inside to report this.

A short while later, an old lady approximately in her forties emerged. Facing the scholar, she walked towards him, asking, "So, has my niece come?"

Li Wa descended from the carriage. The old lady stepped up to welcome her and reproached her, "Why haven't you visited me in so long?"

They looked at each other and started laughing.

Li Wa led the scholar to greet her aunt, then they entered together a side courtyard by the side of the western gate. Inside, there were imitation mountains and pavilions, verdant bamboo and trees, and a remarkably tranquil pond and waterside terrace.

The scholar asked Li Wa, "Is this your aunt's own house?"

Li Wa smiled but did not answer, changing the subject by speaking of other matters. A little while later, tea and fruit were offered, all of which were quite precious and exotic.

The time it takes to eat a meal passed. Suddenly, a person riding a swift Dayuan horse appeared.[4] He ran over, drenched in sweat, reporting, "The old granny has suddenly taken ill with an acute illness, very serious, and can barely recognize anyone. You should go back quickly."

Li Wa said to her aunt, "I am so distracted. I will ride back first, let the horse return, then you and he can come together."

The scholar wanted to return with Li Wa, but saw her aunt whispering to the servant girl and waving the scholar over. Her aunt asked him to stop just outside the door and said, "I fear the

---

[4]Dayuan 大宛 was a state located west of the Pamir Range, covering the middle and lower course of the River Syr Darya and the Ferghana Basin. It is famous for its so-called "blood-sweating" horses.

old granny is dying. We should discuss how to manage the funeral affairs together to rescue Li Wa in her crisis — why are you in a hurry to go with her?"

The scholar had no choice but to remain behind to calculate the expenses for the funeral and memorial.

It was getting dark, but the horse still had not returned. Her aunt said, "There still hasn't been a word... I wonder why? Hurry over to see what's happening. I will be right behind you."

The scholar thus set off. When he reached his original residence, he only beheld tightly locked doors sealed with mud. The scholar was shocked, and so questioned a neighbor. The neighbor said, "The Li family had originally rented this house to live in. Now that the lease has reached its full term, the landlord has reclaimed the house. The granny moved away, two days ago now."

Upon asking "where did she move to," the reply was, "I don't know where."

The scholar wanted to rush to Xuanyang to question Li Wa's aunt, but it was already too late. Calculating the journey, he realized he could not possibly make it before the curfew. So, he could only take off his clothes as guaranty in exchange for a meal, and rent a bed to sleep in. The scholar was greatly irritated and furious, unable to close his eyes the entire night from dusk to dawn.

As soon as it was light, he went on his way astride his donkey. Upon reaching her aunt's house, he knocked on the door repeatedly, but a long time passed without anyone answering. The scholar shouted loudly many times before an official finally leisurely strolled out.

The scholar hastily asked him, "Is aunt here?"

The person replied, "There's no such person."

The scholar retorted, "She was still here last night at dusk. Why are you hiding her?" He then asked whose house it was.

The person answered, "This is Minister Cui's house. Yesterday, someone rented this courtyard supposedly to wait for some cousins who were traveling here from afar. The person left before it was dark."

Upon hearing this, the scholar was aghast and alarmed, frantic to the point of madness. He did not know what to do, and so could only return to the old house in Buzheng Ward. The landlord pitied him and gave him food. The scholar's resentment and anger made him unable to eat anything for three days. He became severely ill. After some ten days, his illness worsened. The landlord was afraid he would die, so he moved him to a funeral parlor. The scholar's illness was critical and dragged on for quite a while. Everyone in the funeral parlor bewailed and sympathized with what he had experienced, and so together took care of him.

As time went on, his illness improved slightly, and he could move about propped up on crutches. From then on, the funeral parlor employed him daily, letting him hold the screen in the funeral hall so that he could earn some money to support himself. He gradually recovered his health after a few months. Every time he heard the strains of a dirge, he would sigh that he was worse off than the dead, frequently weeping and shedding tears, unable to control himself. Immediately after returning, he would try to imitate what he had heard, learning to sing the dirges. The scholar was a clever person, and before long, he sang quite wonderfully and movingly. Within the entire city of Chang'an, there could not be found anyone who was his match.

Earlier, there had been two competing funeral parlors in the business of renting funeral supplies. The carriage supplies of the eastern shop were novel and magnificent, to which the other shop simply could not compare, though their dirge performances were somewhat inferior. The shopkeeper of the eastern shop knew that the scholar sang laments extraordinarily well, so he gathered together 20,000 coins to hire him. The elders in the group together seriously discussed this and, combining their various specialties, secretly taught the scholar to sing new tunes, as well as helping him with vocal accompaniment on the side. For dozens of days, no one else knew of this.

One day, the shopkeepers of the two funeral parlors consulted with each other, saying, "We will each display our rental funeral supplies on Heavenly Gate Street, and compete to determine whose are superior and whose inferior. The loser will be fined 50,000 cash, to be used for the cost of hosting a feast — how about it?" Both houses agreed.

So, they engaged a middleman, established a contract, signed it, and then held the exhibition.

When that day arrived, men and women all came to observe, resulting in a gathering of tens of thousands of people. As a result, the local officer reported the event to the head of the bureau of banditry, who in turn informed the governor of the capital. People from all directions went to participate. No shadow of a human figure was to be found even in the small lanes.

The exhibition began in the early morning; at noon, the two shops laid out the carriage and ritual items piece by piece to compare them. The western shop could not win any of these, and the foreman felt somewhat ashamed. Thus just at the street's southern corner he set up a double-layered couch, and a long-bearded man, large bell in hand, stepped forward, with a few guards beside him. Shaking his beard and raising his eyebrows, wringing his wrist in despair and nodding his head, he stepped onto the lofty bed and started singing the "White Horse Song." Relying on his continuous past success, he glanced left and right, and seemed to regard the spectators as if they weren't there. Everyone lauded him in unison. He thought himself unrivaled; for the moment, no one could surpass him.

After a while, the eastern parlor's shopkeeper placed a few couches side by side at the northern corner of the street. With five or six people beside him, there came a youth wearing a black headscarf and holding a large feather palm fan. He was none other than the scholar. Straightening his clothes, he acted leisurely and calmly. When he opened his throat to vocalize, it seemed that he could not bear it. He sang the song "Dew on the Scallions": the sound was clear and sonorous, and even shook the trees.[5] Long before he finished the dirge, the spectators had already covered their faces in order to weep.

Mocked by the crowd, the shopkeeper of the western parlor felt even more ashamed, and he quietly placed the money he lost before the couch, and then stealthily slipped away. People from all corners gazed in astonishment, not knowing exactly what had happened.

Just prior to this event, the emperor had issued an edict commanding all the officials from each prefecture throughout the country to go the Capital annually. This was called "Entry for Auditing." At this moment, it just so happened that the scholar's father was also at the Capital. He and his colleagues had changed into civilian clothes, and had secretly gone forth to observe.

An old servant — in fact the scholar's wet nurse's husband — marked that the singer's manner of movement and voice resembled that of the scholar's. The servant wanted to go up to identify him, yet did not dare; he was so distressed that tears began to flow. The scholar's father was startled and questioned him about why he was crying. The old servant then informed him, "This singer's appearance is strikingly similar to that of the deceased young master."

The gentleman of Xingyang replied, "My son was killed by robbers for his wealth because he possessed a lot of money. How

---

[5]"Xielu" 薤露, Dew on the Scallions, was a famous dirge since the Warring States period.

would he end up in this state?" Upon saying this, he also started to cry.

After they went back, the old servant took the opportunity to rush over again, asking the scholar's companions, "Who was the singer just a moment ago? He sang so wonderfully."

Everyone all answered, "He was so and so's son."

Inquiring again after his name, he found it had already been changed. The old servant was shocked, and slowly approached to carefully identify him.

On beholding the old servant, the scholar's face changed color; dodging and evading, he wanted to hide in the crowd.

The old servant grasped his sleeve with one hand, and asked, "But aren't you my young master?" The two held hands and wept loudly. They rode the carriage back together.

When they arrived in his father's room, his father rebuked him, "Your character and conduct have degenerated to this state, and you have disgraced our family's reputation! What face do you have to appear before me again?" He led the scholar to go out by foot to a place west to the Crooked River and east to the Apricot Garden, and then stripped him of his clothes. Using the horsewhip, he fiercely whipped his son a few hundred times. The scholar could not bear such a vicious beating and died. The father left him there and walked away.

At the same time, one of the scholar's teachers had ordered a close companion to secretly follow him. The man returned and informed his associates of what had occurred. Everyone sighed in dejection. They sent two people with a reed mat to retrieve his body and bury him. When the pair got there, they discovered that the scholar's chest still had some faint warmth remaining. So, they helped him up. After a long while, his breathing finally slightly eased. The two men carried him back together. They used a reed pipe to trickle soup to feed him. The night passed before he regained consciousness.

A little over a month later, the scholar still could not move his hands and feet. All the areas where he had been viciously beaten festered and oozed pus; it was quite foul. His companions also grew tired of it. One night, they discarded him by the side of the road. Passers-by all pitied him, frequently throwing him leftover scraps for him to eat. He relied on this to alleviate his hunger.

A hundred days passed before he was finally able to stand up by leaning on crutches. Draped over him was a cloth coat, mended a thousand times and patched a hundred, tattered beyond recognition. He held a broken bowl, begging for food along the streets to subsist. From autumn to winter, he would hide inside the caves for piling garbage at night, roving around the city streets begging by day.

One day, with the heavy snow swirling down, the scholar had to venture out in the snow, forced by hunger and cold. The sound of his begging was very wretched. There were none who heard him who did not feel sorrowful and pity him. At the time, the snow was just coming down fast and heavily, and the outer gates around people's houses were mostly closed. He walked to the eastern gate of Anyi Ward, and, following along the walls, he roamed over seven or eight houses northwards. Only one household had the left panel of a door open. That was Li Wa's residence. The scholar did not know this, and kept continuously shouting. Since he was so hungry and so cold, the forlorn and disconsolate voice was truly mournful and difficult to bear hearing.

Li Wa heard it in her room, and exclaimed to the servant girl, "That must be the scholar! I recognize his voice!"

Upon saying this, she hurriedly rushed out with quick steps. She saw the scholar: his muscles thin as kindling, scabies sores over his entire body, seemingly not human at all. Li Wa was deeply moved, so she asked him, "Aren't you the young gentleman?"

On seeing her, the scholar fainted onto the ground out of anger; rendered speechless, he only nodded his head. Li Wa went forward and embraced his neck, wrapping an embroidered coat around him and helping him back to the west wing. She cried bitterly, her voice cracking, "It is my fault that you have fallen to this state!" She sobbed her heart out.

The old granny, quite astonished, ran over to ask, "Who is this?"

Li Wa replied, "It is that young gentleman."

The old granny hastily ordered, "We must drive him out! How could you let him come here?"

Hearing this, Li Wa's face turned solemn. She turned to look at the old granny and asserted, "We can't do this. He is descended from a respectable family! At the outset, he drove a lofty carriage and fine steed, and carrying money, came to our house. Yet within one year, he had spent it all. We also designed a scheme together to get rid of him — that just simply was not a human act. We finally made him fall into depravity, scorned by others. The affection between a father and son is innate, but this matter caused his father to break his affection and sever their relationship, beating him to death and simultaneously abandoning him. Now, he has become impoverished to this state — everyone knows he is thus because of me. The majority of the scholar's relatives are officials in the imperial court — one day when those who have power figure out clearly the ins and outs of this matter, then disasters will befall us. Besides, even ghosts and gods will not protect those who deceive Heaven and wrong others. Don't create further trouble for yourself! I have been your daughter for twenty years now. The money I have made you exceeds a thousand *liang* of gold. Now, you are over sixty years of age; I wish to calculate and repay twenty years' worth of living costs to buy back my freedom. I will rent another place to live in with this young gentleman. The house I rent won't be very far, so I will still be able to come to pay my respects in the mornings and evenings. This way, my wish will be satisfied."

The old granny concluded that her determination was not to be altered, and so could only assent. After Li Wa paid the old granny to redeem herself, she had a hundred *liang* of gold remaining. So she rented an empty house in a place to the north, four or five houses over. She washed the scholar's hair, bathed him, and changed his clothes. She initially cooked porridge for him to ease his stomach into food, followed by cheese to moisturize his internal organs. After more than ten days, she finally gave him fish, meat, and the like to eat. For the scholar's scarf and hat, shoes and stockings, Li Wa picked the most luxurious and costly for him to wear. Within a few months, the scholar's body had filled out somewhat. After a year had passed, he had recovered to his original condition.

One day, Li Wa told him, "Your body has recovered and your energy is abundant. Think back carefully and calmly — can you still take up your former studies?"

The scholar thought about this, and admitted, "I only recall two or three tenths of it." So Li Wa ordered the carriage be harnessed to go out. The scholar followed on horseback.

When they reached a bookshop selling classics, by the southern side gate of the market tower, she asked the scholar to pick out the ones he needed, for which she spent one hundred teals of gold and had all of them transported back to their home. Then she told the scholar to cast aside all distracting thoughts and devote himself to studying whole-heartedly. Taking nights as days, he worked tirelessly. Li Wa frequently sat at his side to keep him company, retiring only when it was late into the night. Sometimes, when she saw that he was fatigued, she would tell him to compose poetry and rhapsodies.

Two years later, the scholar's knowledge had progressed profoundly. There were no books in the world he had not read.

The scholar announced to Li Wa, "Now I can register to take the examination." Li Wa cautioned, "Not yet. You must study until you are even more proficient and skilled, so that you can deal with all kinds of exam questions." Another year passed. Li Wa finally said, "You can take the tests."

Then the scholar became an advanced scholar by passing the Type-A examination. [6] His renown resounded throughout the imperial Board of Rites. Even among the senior scholars, there were none who were not filled with deep respect and admiration for him after reading his essays, desirous to become friends with him but afraid that it was beyond their reach. However, Li Wa warned, "It's not time to celebrate yet. Scholars today presume that, by passing one imperial examination, they can get a high position in the royal court and their fame will spread throughout the world. Your past moral conduct is stained, your behavior not honorable, and thus your character cannot be compared to that of an ordinary scholar. You must continue to assiduously delve into your studies and try to succeed once more in another imperial examination. Only in this way can you then associate and interact with the multitude of scholars, contending with the giants to vie for supremacy." From then on, the scholar became even more diligent and hard-working, his reputation also rising even higher and higher.

That year, it happened that the imperial court was holding the national examination. The emperor issued an edict recruiting talent from all four corners of the nation. The scholar registered for the exam on the subject "candid extreme admonishment," placed first, and was appointed the adjutant of Chengdu

---

[6]*Jiake* 甲科, Type A exam, was one of the imperial exams during the Tang dynasty; the other one was *Yike* 乙科, Type B exam, which was taken more frequently.

Prefecture. Everyone in the imperial court below the Three Dukes all became friends with him.

As he was about to take his post, Li Wa said to him, "Now that you have regained your former aspect, I no longer have anything to apologize to you for. I wish to use my remaining days to return to look after my old granny. You should marry a young lady from a noble family, for the convenience of managing your familial sacrifices. You must find one whose family is your equal in rank, and unite in a happy marriage. Never again abase yourself. I hope you take care. From here on, I will leave you!"

The scholar sobbed, "If you abandon me, I will slit my throat in front of you."

Li Wa resolutely refused to go along with him to take up his new office. The scholar pleaded bitterly, with an even more sincere attitude. In the end, Li Wa conceded, "I will see you off across the river, but when we reach Jianmen you must let me return." The scholar agreed.

A little over a month later, they arrived at Jianmen. However, before he had a chance to set off, the emperor's imperial decree appointing the new official arrived. The scholar's father had been summoned to the capital from Changzhou prefecture, and appointed the governor of Chengdu, as well as the investigation commissioner of Jiannan Ciucuit.[7] The scholar had no choice but to remain and wait.

Twelve days later, the scholar's father arrived. The scholar therefore went to the courier station to pay respects to his father, offering his name card. His father dared not claim to know him until he saw the scholar's paternal ancestors' official ranks and names, back to three generations. He was then stunned, and asked his son up the stone steps. Gently stroking his son's back, he wept

---

[7]Its seat was modern Chengdu, Sichuan.

in pain and sorrow for a long time, saying, "Let us restore our father-son relationship as it was originally."

Accordingly, he proceeded to inquire about the course of events, and his son related the matter to him from beginning to end. Amazed, he asked where Li Wa was.

The scholar answered, "After seeing me off here, I was preparing to let her go back."

His father replied, "This will not do." The next day, he ordered the carriage so that he and the scholar could go to Chengdu first, leaving Li Wa in Jianmen. He had a house built for her to live in. The very next day after they arrived in Chengdu, he sent a matchmaker to go ask for Li Wa's hand in marriage, and completed the entire six wedding formalities to welcome her. Thus, the scholar and Li Wa became husband and wife in the manner of a formal marriage.

After Li Wa became, through the full marriage rites, the daughter-in-law of the gentleman of Xingyang, every new year's day and holiday, she would carefully and attentively fulfill her responsibilities as a wife and daughter-in-law. She managed her household strictly, and was deeply beloved and respected by their relatives.

After a few years, the scholar's father and mother both died. She handled the funeral arrangements very considerately. A *ganoderma lucidum* started to grow beside the straw hut where she observed mourning, with one branch growing three ears. The local officials informed the emperor of these occurrences. Additionally, tens of white swallows built nests on the roof beams of her home. The emperor thought these incidents extraordinary, and consequently placed his particular confidence in the scholar and rewarded him especially. Following the period of mourning, the scholar thus repeatedly rose to hold important positions. Within ten years' time, he had been governor of several regions. Upon Li Wa was conferred the title "Lady of Qian." They had four sons, all of whom became high-ranking officials. Amongst these, even the lowest office held was the governor of Taiyuan. The brothers all married ladies of distinguished and prominent families. Inside and out, they had impressive power and influence. No one could compare to them.

Ah, a courtesan from a brothel, yet one whose integrity and conduct are like this — such that not even an ancient female martyr could surpass! How can I not sigh in admiration of her?

My granduncle had been prefect of Jinzhou, then was transferred to the Ministry of Revenue, and also once held the position of Water and Land Transport Commissioner. These three posts were all assumed to replace the scholar, so my granduncle was familiar with his story. During the Zhenyuan reign (785–805), I was discussing the noble character of women with Li Gongzuo (778–848),[8] a native of Longxi, and so spoke of Lady Qian's deeds. Having listened to it attentively while clapping his hands, Li Gongzuo asked me to write a biography. I grabbed a brush, dipped it in ink, and so recorded these matters in detail. It is now the eighth month in the autumn of the *yihai* year (795). The above is recorded by Bai Xingjian, a native of Taiyuan.

---

[8]Li Gongzuo, a famous tale writer of the Tang and the author of "Governor of the Southern Tributary Branch."

李娃傳

白行簡

　　汧國夫人李娃，長安之倡女也。節行瑰奇，有足稱者，故監察禦史白行簡為傳述。

　　天寶中，有常州刺史滎陽公者，略其名氏，不書。時望甚崇，家徒甚殷。知命之年，有一子，始弱冠矣，雋朗有詞藻，迥然不群，深為時輩推伏。其父愛而器之，曰：“此吾家千里駒也。”

　　應鄉賦秀才舉，將行，乃盛其服玩車馬之飾，計其京師薪儲之費。謂之曰：“吾觀爾之才，當一戰而霸。今備二載之用，且豐爾之給，將為其志也。”生亦自負，視上第如指掌。自毗陵發，月余抵長安，居于布政里。

　　嘗遊東市還，自平康東門入，將訪友于西南。至鳴珂曲，見一宅，門庭不甚廣，而室宇嚴邃。闔一扉，有娃方憑一雙鬟青衣立，妖姿要妙，絕代未有。生忽見之，不覺停驂久之，徘徊不能去。乃詐墜鞭于地，候其從者，敕取之。累眄于娃，娃回眸凝睇，情甚相慕。竟不敢措辭而去。

　　生自爾意若有失，乃密徵其友遊長安之熟者，以訊之。友曰：“此狹邪女李氏宅也。”曰：“娃可求乎？”對曰：“李氏頗贍。前與通之者多貴戚豪族，所得甚廣。非累百萬，不能動其志也。”生曰：“苟患其不諧，雖百萬，何惜！”

　　他日，乃潔其衣服，盛賓從，而往扣其門。俄有侍兒啓扃。生曰：“此誰之第耶？”侍兒不答，馳走大呼曰：“前時遺策郎也！”娃大悅曰：“爾姑止之。吾當整妝易服而出。”

　　生聞之私喜。乃引至蕭牆間，見一姥垂白上僂，即娃母也。生跪拜前致詞曰：“聞茲地有隙院，願稅以居，信乎？”姥曰：“懼

229

其淺陋湫隘，不足以辱長者所處，安敢言直耶？"延生于遲賓之館，館宇甚麗。

與生偶坐，因曰："某有女嬌小，技藝薄劣，欣見賓客，願將見之。"乃命娃出。明眸皓腕，舉步豔冶。生遂驚起，莫敢仰視。與之拜畢，敘寒燠，觸類妍媚，目所未覩。復坐，烹茶斟酒，器用甚潔。

久之，日暮，鼓聲四動。姥訪其居遠近。生紿之曰："在延平門外數里。"冀其遠而見留也。姥曰："鼓已發矣。當速歸，無犯禁。"生曰："幸接歡笑，不知日之云夕。道里遼闊，城內又無親戚，將若之何？"娃曰："不見責僻陋，方將居之，宿何害焉。"生數目姥，姥曰："唯唯。"

生乃召其家僮，持雙縑，請以備一宵之饌。娃笑而止之曰："賓主之儀，且不然也。今夕之費，願以貧窶之家，隨其粗糲以進之。其余以俟他辰。"固辭，終不許。

俄徙坐西堂，帷幌簾榻，煥然奪目；妝奩衾枕，亦皆侈麗。乃張燭進饌，品味甚盛。

徹饌，姥起。生娃談話方切，诙諧調笑，無所不至。

生曰："前偶過卿門，遇卿適在屏間。厥後心常勤念，雖寢與食，未嘗或捨。"

娃答曰："我心亦如之。"

生曰："今之來，非直求居而已，願償平生之志。但未知命也若何？"

言未終，姥至，詢其故，具以告。姥笑曰："男女之際，大欲存焉。情苟相得，雖父母之命，不能制也。女子固陋，曷足以薦君子之枕席！"生遂下階，拜而謝之曰："願以己為廝養。"姥遂目之為郎，飲酣而散。

及旦，盡徙其囊橐，因家于李之第。自是生屏迹戢身，不復與親知相聞，日會倡優儕類，狎戲遊宴。囊中盡空，乃鬻駿乘，及其家童。歲余，資財仆馬蕩然。迩來姥意漸怠，娃情彌篤。

他日，娃謂生曰："與郎相知一年，尚無孕嗣。常聞竹林神者，報應如響，將致薦酹求之，可乎？"

生不知其計，大喜。乃質衣于肆，以備牢醴，與娃同谒祠宇而禱祝焉，信宿而返。策驢而後，至里北門，娃謂生曰："此東轉小曲中，某之姨宅也。將憩而覲之，可乎？"生如其言，前行不踰百步，果見一車門。窺其際，甚弘敞。其青衣自車後止之曰：“至矣。”生下，適有一人出訪曰：“誰？”曰：“李娃也。”乃入告。

俄有一嫗至，年可四十餘，與生相迎曰：“吾甥來否？”娃下車，嫗逆訪之曰：“何久疎絕？”相視而笑。娃引生拜之。既見，遂偕入西戟門偏院中。有山亭，竹樹蔥蒨，池榭幽絕。生謂娃曰：“此姨之私第耶？”笑而不答，以他語對。俄獻茶果，甚珍奇。

食頃，有一人控大宛，汗流馳至，曰：“姥遇暴疾頗甚，殆不識人。宜速歸。”娃謂姨曰：“方寸亂矣。某騎而前去，當令返乘，便與郎偕來。”生擬隨之。其姨與侍兒偶語，以手揮之，令生止于戶外，曰：“姥且歿矣，當與某議喪事以濟其急，奈何遽相隨而去？”乃止，共計其凶儀齋祭之用。

日晚，乘不至。姨言曰：“無復命，何也？郎驟往覘之，某當繼至。”生遂往，至舊宅，門扃鑰甚密，以泥緘之。生大駭，詰其鄰人。鄰人曰：“李本稅此而居，約已周矣。第主自收，姥徙居，而且再宿矣。”徵徙何處，曰：“不詳其所。”生將馳赴宣陽，以詰其姨，日已晚矣，計程不能達。乃弛其裝服，質饌而食，賃榻而寢，生患怒方甚，自昏達旦，目不交睫。

質明，乃策蹇而去。既至，連扣其扉，食頃無人應。生大呼數四，有宦者徐出。生遽訪之：“姨氏在乎？”曰：“無之。”生曰：“昨暮在此，何故匿之？”訪其誰氏之第。曰：“此崔尚書宅。昨者有一人稅此院，云遲中表之遠至者，未暮去矣。”

生惶惑發狂，罔知所措，因返訪布政舊邸。邸主哀而進膳。生怨懣，絕食三日，遘疾甚篤，旬餘愈甚。邸主懼其不起，徙之于凶肆之中。綿綴移時，合肆之人共傷歎而互飼之。

後稍愈，杖而能起。由是凶肆日假之，令執繐帷，獲其直以自給。累月，漸復壯，每聽其哀歌，自歎不及逝者，輒嗚咽流涕，不能自止。歸則効之。生聰敏者也。無何，曲盡其妙，雖長安無有倫比。

初，二肆之傭凶器者，互爭勝負。其東肆車轝皆奇麗，殆不敵，唯哀挽劣焉。其東肆長知生妙絕，乃醵錢二萬索顧焉。其黨者舊，共較其所能者，陰教生新聲，而相讚和。累旬，人莫知之。其二肆長相謂曰：“我欲各閱所傭之器于天門街，以較優劣。不勝者罰直五萬，以備酒饌之用，可乎？”二肆許諾，乃邀立符契，署以保證，然後閱之。

　　士女大和會，聚至數萬。于是里胥告于賊曹，賊曹聞于京尹。四方之士，盡赴趨焉，巷無居人。

　　自旦閱之，及亭午，曆舉輦轝威儀之具，西肆皆不勝，師有慚色。乃置層榻于南隅，有長髯者擁鐸而進，翊衛數人，于是奮髯揚眉，扼腕頓顙而登，乃歌《白馬》之詞。恃其夙勝，顧眄左右，旁若無人。齊聲贊揚之，自以為獨步一時，不可得而屈也。

　　有頃，東肆長于北隅上設連榻，有烏巾少年，左右五六人，秉翣而至，即生也。整衣服，俯仰甚徐，申喉發調，容若不勝。乃歌《薤露》之章，舉聲清越，響振林木。曲度未終，聞者歔欷掩泣。

　　西肆長為衆所诮，益慚恥。密置所輸之直于前，乃潛遁焉。四座愕眙，莫之測也。

　　先是，天子方下詔，俾外方之牧，歲一至闕下，謂之入計。時也，適遇生之父在京師，與同列者易服章，竊往觀焉。

　　有小豎，即生乳母婿也，見生之舉措辭氣，將認之而未敢，乃泫然流涕。生父驚而詰之，因告曰：“歌者之貌，酷似郎之亡子。”

　　父曰：“吾子以多財為盜所害，奚至是耶？”言訖，亦泣。

　　及歸，豎間馳往，訪于同黨曰：“向歌者誰，若斯之妙歟？”皆曰：“某氏之子。”徵其名，且易之矣，豎凜然大驚；徐往，迫而察之。生見豎，色動，回翔將匿于衆中。豎遂持其袂曰：“豈非某乎？”相持而泣，遂載以歸。

　　至其室，父責曰：“志行若此，污辱吾門，何施面目，復相見也？”乃徒行出，至曲江西杏園東，去其衣服，以馬鞭鞭之數百。生不勝其苦而斃。父棄之而去。

　　其師命相狎暱者陰隨之，歸告同黨，共加傷歎。令二人齎葦席瘞焉。至則心下微溫。舉之，良久，氣稍通。因共荷而歸，以葦筒灌勺飲，經宿乃活。月餘，手足不能自舉，其楚撻之處皆潰爛，穢甚。同輩患之。一夕，棄于道周。行路咸傷之，往往投其餘食，得以充腸。

　　十旬，方杖策而起。被布裘，裘有百結，襤褸如懸鶉。持一破甌，巡于閭里，以乞食為事。自秋徂冬，夜入于糞壤窟室，晝則周遊廛肆。

　　一旦大雪，生為凍餒所驅，冒雪而出，乞食之聲甚苦。聞見者莫不悽惻。時雪方甚，人家外戶多不發。至安邑東門，循理垣北轉第七八，有一門獨啓左扉，即娃之第也。生不知之，遂連聲疾呼“饑凍之甚。”音響悽切，所不忍聽。

娃自閤中聞之，謂侍兒曰："此必生也，我辨其音矣。"連步而出。見生枯瘠疥厲，殆非人狀。娃意感焉，乃謂曰："豈非某郎也？"

生憤懣絕倒，口不能言，頷頤而已。娃前抱其頸，以繡襦擁而歸于西廂。失聲長慟曰："令子一朝及此，我之罪也！"絕而復蘇。

姥大駭，奔至，曰："何也？"娃曰："某郎。"姥遽曰："當逐之，奈何令至此？"

娃斂容卻睇曰："不然。此良家子也。當昔驅高車，持金裝，至某之室，不逾期而蕩盡。且互設詭計，捨而逐之，殆非人行。令其失志，不得齒于人倫。父子之道，天性也。使其情絕，殺而棄之。又困躓若此。天下之人，盡知為某。生親戚滿朝，一旦當權者熟察其本末，禍將及矣。況欺天負人，鬼神不祐，無自貽其殃也。某為姥子，迨今有二十歲矣。計其貲，不啻直千金。今姥年六十餘，願計二十年衣食之用以贖身，當與此子別卜所詣。所詣非遙，晨昏得以溫清，某願足矣。"

姥度其志不可奪，因許之。給姥之餘，有百金。北隅因五家，稅一隙院。乃與生沐浴，易其衣服；為湯粥，通其腸；次以酥乳潤其臟。旬餘，方薦水陸之饌。頭巾履襪，皆取珍異者衣之。未數月，肌膚稍腴。卒歲，平愈如初。

異時，娃謂生曰："體已康矣，志已壯矣。淵思寂慮，默想曩昔之藝業，可溫習乎？"生思之曰："十得二三耳。"娃命車出遊，生騎而從。至旗亭南偏門鬻墳典之肆，令生揀而市之，計費百金，盡載以歸。因令生斥棄百慮以志學，俾夜作晝，孜孜矻矻。娃常偶坐，宵分乃寐。伺其疲倦，即諭之綴詩賦。

二歲而業大就，海內文籍，莫不該覽。生謂娃曰："可策名試藝矣。"娃曰："未也，且令精熟，以俟百戰。"更一年，曰："可行矣。"

于是遂一上登甲科，聲振禮闈。雖前輩見其文，罔不斂衽敬羨，願友之而不可得。娃曰："未也。今秀士苟獲擢一科第，則自謂可以取中朝之顯職，擅天下之美名。子行穢跡鄙，不侔于他士。當礱淬利器，以求再捷。方可以連衡多士，爭霸群英。"生由是益自勤苦，聲價彌甚。

其年，遇大比，詔徵四方之雋。生應直言極諫科，名第一，授成都府參軍。三事以降，皆其友也。將之官，娃謂生曰："今之復

子本軀，某不相負也。願以殘年，歸養老姥。君當結媛鼎族，以奉
蒸嘗。中外婚媾，無自黷也。勉思自愛。某從此去矣。”

　　生泣曰：“子若棄我，當自剄以就死。”娃固辭不從，生勤請
彌懇。娃曰：“送子涉江，至于劍門，當令我回。”生許諾。

　　月餘，至劍門。未及發而除書至，生父由常州詔入，拜成都尹，
兼劍南采訪使。

　　浹辰，父到。生因投刺，谒于郵亭。父不敢認，見其祖父官諱，
方大驚，命登階，撫背慟哭移時。曰：“吾與爾父子如初。”

　　因詰其由，具陳其本末。大奇之，詰娃安在。曰：“送某至此，
當令復還。”父曰：“不可。”翌日，命駕與生先之成都，留娃于
劍門，築別館以處之。明日，命媒氏通二姓之好，備六禮以迎之，
遂如秦晉之偶。

　　娃既備禮，歲時伏臘，婦道甚修，治家嚴整，極為親所眷。

　　向後數歲，生父母偕歿，持孝甚至。有靈芝産于倚廬，一穗三
秀。本道上聞。又有白燕數十，巢其層甍。天子異之，寵錫加等。
終制，累遷清顯之任。十年間，至數郡。娃封汧國夫人。有四子，
皆為大官，其卑者猶為太原尹。弟兄姻媾皆甲門，內外隆盛，莫之
與京。

　　嗟乎，倡蕩之姬，節行如是，雖古先烈女，不能踰也。焉得不
為之歎息哉！

　　予伯祖嘗牧晉州，轉戶部，為水陸運使，三任皆與生為代，故
谙詳其事。

　　貞元中，予與隴西公佐話婦人操烈之品格，因遂述汧國之事。
公佐拊掌竦聽，命予為傳。乃握管濡翰，疏而存之。時乙亥歲秋八
月，太原白行簡云。

Tale 3.16

An Account of Three Dreams

Bai Xingjian
Translated by Zheng Wen

Among people's dreams, there are the ones that are different from the normal type: the cases in which one person dreamed of going to a place while another person met him/her there; the cases in which one person did something while another person dreamed of the person doing it; and the cases in which two people appeared in each other's dream.

Under the reign of the Heavenly Empress,[1] Liu Youqiu[2] served as an Assistant Magistrate of Chaoyi.[3] Once, he was sent out as an envoy and returned at night. Over ten *li* away from his home, there happened to be a temple courtyard by the side of the road, where singing and laughter in a happy and cordial atmosphere were heard. Since the walls of the temple were short and had missing sections, passersby could see everything inside of it. Liu leaned forward and peeked in. He saw over ten people, men and women, sitting together. The plates of food were laid out,

---

[1]Refers to Empress Wu Zetian 武則天 (624–705) who ruled China from 690 to 705 and was the only empress regnant in the history of China.

[2]Liu Youqiu 劉幽求 (655–715) served as an official during the reigns of Empress Wu and Emperors Zhongzong, Ruizong and Xuanzong.

[3]Present day's Dali County in Shanxi province.

and people were sitting around the food and eating together. His wife was talking and laughing among them.

Liu was stunned at first. For a long while, he could not figure out why his wife was there. He also did not think she could go there, but he could not just leave her there. Again, he carefully looked at her appearance, behavior, speaking and laughing — all had no difference from those of his wife. He intended to get closer to inspect her, but the door of the temple was closed and he could not get in. Liu threw a piece of tile at the people. It hit the basin for hand-washing. The basin was broken, the water splashed, and the people fled in all directions and suddenly disappeared. Liu climbed over the wall and went straight in. He and his entourage inspected the place together: there was nobody at the hall or in the rooms in the east and the west wings. But the door bolt was untouched. Liu was astonished even more. He then rushed home on his horse.

When he arrived at home, his wife had just gone to bed. Hearing Liu's arrival, she asked about his day-to-day life, and then smiled and said: "Just now in a dream, I visited a temple with dozens of people, all of whom I didn't know, and gathered to eat in the yard of the temple. Someone threw rubbles of tiles toward us from the outside. The dishes and cups were in a mess. As a result, I then woke up." Liu also told in detail what he saw. This probably was the so-called "one person dreamed of going to a place while another person met him there."

In the fourth year of the Yuanhe reign [806–820], Yuan Weizhi[4] from Henan served as an Investigating Censor and was sent to the south of Jiange (in Sichuan) as an envoy. After he had

---

[4]Yuan Zhen 元稹 (799–831), style name Weizhi 微之, was an official scholar and one of the two best known writers of the Mid Tang.

been gone for over ten days, my second brother Letian[5] and I, as well as Li Biaozhi from Longxi, toured Qujiang Pool together.[6] We went to the Ci'en Buddhist Temple and visited all sections of the temple, lingering for a long time. When it was late in the day, we went together to Biaozhi's residence at Xiuxing Ward. Biaozhi ordered people to bring out wine, and the three of us toasted each other and were quite elated.

My second brother stopped drinking for a long while and said: "Weizhi should have already arrived at Liangzhou (in Shanxi)." He wrote a poem about this on a wall of the room, which read:

> Spring arrived, I have no way to break away from the melancholy of the spring.
> Tipsily I picked flowery branches to make the chips for drinking games.
> Suddenly, I remembered that my old friend has gone to the edge of the world.
> I counted the miles; today he should arrive at Liangzhou.

That date was actually the twenty-first of the month.

Over ten days later, a messenger from Liangzhou arrived with a letter from Weizhi; attached at the back was a poem "Recording a Dream," which read:

> I dreamed that you and your brothers were at the bank of Qujiang.
> You also went inside the Ci'en temple to visit.
> I urged a clerk to summon servants to arrange the horses, and woke up to find that I was at the ancient Liangzhou.

---

[5]Bai Juyi 白居易 (772–846), style name Letian 樂天, was one of the best-known poets of Tang and the older brother of Bai Xingjian (776–826), the author of this tale.

[6]It is located in the south-east part of today's Xi'an.

The month and day of this poem was roughly the same as that of the poem by Letian about touring the temple. This probably was the so-called "one person did something while another person dreamed of the person doing it."

During the Zhenyuan reign (785–805), Dou Zhi from Fufeng[7] and Wei Xun from Jingzhao (Chang'an) went together to Qin from Bozhou (in Anhui) and stayed overnight at an inn at Tongguan pass.[8] Dou dreamed of going to Huayue Ancestral Temple and seeing a female shaman who was tall and had dark skin. Wearing a black skirt and a white top, she waited on the road, folding her hands and making deep bows, and asked to pray to the gods for him. Dou had no choice and thus, let her do it. He asked her name. She claimed Zhao as her last name. When Dou woke up, he told Wei the dream in detail.

The next day, when they came to the foot of the temple, they saw that there was a shaman welcoming guests. Her appearance and clothes were all like those in the dream. Dou looked at Wei and said: "My dream has been verified." He then asked his subordinate to take from his bag two coins to give to her. The shaman clapped her hands and laughed aloud, and said to her companions: "Just like what I have dreamed!" Wei asked her [about that] in surprise. She answered: "Yesterday I dreamed that two people came from the east. One bearded and short man offered wine to pray. I received two coins from him. In the morning, I told [the dream] to all my companions. The dream has now come true." Dou thus asked the shaman's surname. Her companions said: "Zhao." From the beginning to the end, the two dreams matched exactly. This probably was the so-called "two people appeared in each other's dream."

---

[7]A prefecture in today's Shanxi province.
[8]North of today's Tongguan County in Shanxi.

Xingjian's commentary: There are many writings about dreams in the *Spring and Autumn Annals*, and other historical and philosophical books, but none of them records these three dreams. Also, while people's dreams are numerous, none are like these three dreams. Is this coincidental? Or it is predetermined? I cannot know about this. Now I write down what happened in the dreams in detail to preserve them here.

三夢記

白行簡

　　人之夢，異於常者有之：或彼夢有所往而此遇之者，或此有所爲而彼夢之者，或兩相通夢者。

　　天后時，劉幽求爲朝邑丞。嘗奉使，夜歸。未及家十餘里，適有佛堂院，路出其側。聞寺中歌笑歡洽。寺垣短缺，盡得睹其中。劉俯身窺之，見十數人兒女雜坐，羅列盤饌，環繞之而共食。見其妻在坐中語笑。

　　劉初愕然，不測其故久之。且思其不當至此，復不能捨之。又熟視容止言笑，無異。將就察之，寺門閉不得入。劉擲瓦擊之，中其罍洗，破迸走散，因忽不見。劉逾垣直入，與從者同視，殿廡皆無人，寺扃如故。劉訝益甚，遂馳歸。

　　比至其家，妻方寢。聞劉至，乃敘寒暄訖，妻笑曰："向夢中與數十人遊一寺，皆不相識，會食於殿庭。有人自外以瓦礫投之，杯盤狼籍，因而遂覺。"劉亦具陳其見。蓋所謂彼夢有所往而此遇之也。

　　元和四年，河南元微之爲監察御史，奉使劍外。去逾旬，予與仲兄樂天，隴西李杓直同遊曲江。詣慈恩佛舍，遍歷僧院，淹留移時。日已晚，同詣杓直修行里第，命酒對酬，甚歡暢。

　　兄停杯久之，曰："微之當達樑矣。"命題一篇於屋壁。其詞曰：

"春來無計破春愁，醉折花枝作酒籌。
忽憶故人天際去，計程今日到梁州。"

　　實二十一日也。

十許日，會梁州使適至，獲微之書一函，後記《紀夢詩》一篇，其詞曰：

"夢君兄弟曲江頭，也入慈恩院里遊。
屬吏喚人排馬去，覺來身在古梁州。"

日月與遊寺題詩日月率同。蓋所謂此有所爲而彼夢之者矣。

貞元中，扶風竇質與京兆韋苟同自亳入秦，宿潼關逆旅。竇夢至華嶽祠，見一女巫，黑而長。青裙素襦，迎路拜揖，請爲之祝神。竇不獲已，遂聽之。問其姓，自稱趙氏。及覺，具告於韋。

明日，至祠下，有巫迎客，容質妝服，皆所夢也。顧謂韋曰："夢有徵也。"乃命從者視囊中，得錢二鐶，與之。巫撫掌大笑，謂同輩曰："如所夢矣！"韋驚問之。對曰："昨夢二人從東來，一髯而短者祝酹，獲錢二鐶焉。及旦，乃徧述於同輩。今則驗矣。"竇因問巫之姓。同輩曰："趙氏。"自始及末，若合符契。蓋所謂兩相通夢者矣。

行簡曰：《春秋》及子史，言夢者多，然未有載此三夢者也。世人之夢亦衆矣，亦未有此三夢。豈偶然也，抑亦必前定也？予不能知。今備記其事，以存錄焉。

Tale 3.17

The Account of the Song of Lasting Regret

By Chen Hong
Translated by Paul W. Kroll

During the Kaiyuan era (713–742) the ranks of the August Stepway were in proper order[1] and within the Four Seas were no untoward matters. For many years Xuanzong had been on the throne, but he had had enough of "supping late and dressing early." Governmental questions, whether great or small, he had now turned over to the Chancellor of the Right,[2] and he gradually receded more deeply into pleasure excursions and entertainments, indulging himself in sensuous sound and sight. Prior to this, Empress Yuanxian and Gracious Consort Wu had successively enjoyed his favor, each in her own time.[3] Although there were

---

[1] The August Stepway (Taijie 泰階), also called the Triple Platform (Santai 三台), is a constellation made up of three pairs of stars traditionally thought to symbolize three major classes of society: emperor and empress; higher levels of dignitaries and lower ministers; servicemen and commoners. Thus, as here, the astronomical term stands also for its symbolic reference.

[2] This was Li Linfu 李林甫, traditionally characterized as a virtual dictator, who had dominant control of the government from 736 to his death in early 752.

[3] The first of these favorites was a woman of the Yang 楊 clan and was mother of Xuanzong's third son, Li Heng 李亨, who later became the

now a thousand-some maidens of good families in the palace, none of them could please His Highness's eye; his heart was dull and depressed, unhappy.

In those days, in the tenth month of every year, the imperial equipage graced with its presence the Palace of Floriate Purity.[4] The women of titled status from the royal family or attached to courtly officials, dazzling and radiant, clustered close as form and shadow, and were granted the gift of bathing in the hot-spring pools alongside those that "laved the sun"[5] — it seemed an ethereal dew under spring-like waftings, irenic and unruffled there. It was then that His Highness's heart was smoothly taken upon what seemed a chance encounter,[6] and those he looked on to left and right, before or behind, were now but as dirt in their finest

---

emperor posthumously titled Suzong 肅宗 (r. 756–62). The title of Empress Yuanxian 元獻皇后 (Principal and Submissive) was bestowed on her posthumously after Li Heng became the emperor. She was one of Xuanzong's favorites from 710 to her death in 729. The second woman mentioned, Gracious Consort Wu, was daughter to Wu Youzhi 武攸之, a nephew of the redoubtable Empress Wu (r. 690–705), and was a favorite from 726 to 737, having entered the emperor's harem in 713. She was the mother of Prince Shou 壽王, into whose harem Yang Guifei 楊貴妃 was first entered in 734 (see below).

[4]The Palace of Floriate Purity (Huaqing gong) was the emperor's hot-springs compound on Mount Li 驪山, twenty-five miles east of Chang'an. It is not true that the emperor visited each year in the tenth month (beginning of winter by the lunar calendar); the visits more often were during the last two months of the year, and in some years no visits were made. This is one of several historical inaccuracies in Chen Hong's 陳鴻 (fl. 805–829) account, not all of which will be noted here.

[5]I.e., that bathed the emperor, a metaphorical sun-king.

[6]The reference is to the famous anecdote of the emperor seeing Lady Yang emerging from one of the Huaqing pools and being smitten by her beauty.

make-up. So he ordered Gao Lishi[7] quietly to search through the outer palaces, where he obtained from Prince Shou's mansion the daughter, who had now just come of age, of a certain Yang Xuanyan who hailed from Hongnong.[8]

Her lustrous black hair was arrayed in fine fashion, her figure was ideally measured between slender and statuesque, her movements were languidly alluring, like the famous Lady Li of the Han emperor Wu. By imperial order a separate bathing pool was given over to her gleaming pulchritude. When she emerged from its water, her body was weak and her strength listless, as though unable to support the sheerest gossamer; she gave off a glistening brilliance whose every movement seemed to shed light. His Highness was entranced. The day she was presented in audience, she performed the tune "Rainbow Skirt and Feathered Vestment" to seduce him.[9] The night he promised his love, he bestowed a two-pronged hairpin of gold and a filigreed cosmetic case to pledge her, conferring also a hair-ornament that quivered when she walked and earrings of gold that hung down.

---

[7] A eunuch and long-time confidant of the emperor.

[8] Prince Shou, Xuanzong's eighteenth son, was, like most of the emperor's many offspring, reared in an "outer palace," hence the phrasing here. The marriageable age of girls was traditionally their sixteenth year by Chinese count (fifteen by Western reckoning). In fact, Lady Yang had entered Prince Shou's harem in 734, when she was indeed just that age. But in 741, when she enthralled the emperor, she was twenty-two. Chen Hong makes it seem as though her intervening seven years in the prince's establishment had never happened. Hongnong, whence her father hailed, was in present-day Sichuan.

[9] Originally an exotic Indo-Iranian melody, this tune had been rescored and retitled by Xuanzong. Lady Yang is said to have danced in a costume resembling the fairy garments of moon maidens, as, according to one tradition, the emperor was said to have brought the melody back with him from a mystical voyage to the moon.

The next year she was invested as Precious Consort, accorded the treatment of a demi-empress. From then on, she made her appearance ravishing, made her words engaging, so invitingly alluring in every circumstance, that she perfectly satisfied His Highness's moods and he was ever more infatuated with her. At this time, when he "examined the customs" throughout the Nine Provinces and "sealed tablets with gold" on the Five Marchmounts,[10] whether on snowy nights at Mount Li or springtime mornings in the Shangyang Palace,[11] she rode in the same conveyance with His Highness, stayed in the same quarters, banqueted only on his mat, and lay down to sleep only in his chamber. Although he had three Grand Ladies, nine Concubines, twenty-seven Women of Hereditary Families, eighty-one Imperial Mates, as well as talented maidens of the Rear Court and female entertainers of the Music Bureau, they could not make the Son of Heaven turn to give them even a sidelong glance. Thereafter no one from the Six Mansions of palace ladies was ever again brought forward to receive his favor. Not only her exceptional allure and uncommon manner brought this about, but indeed her apt awareness and discerning intelligence, her superior shrewdness and skillful glibness, anticipating his whims and intuiting his desires, are not able to be accurately described.

Her father and uncle, her older and younger brothers, were all granted positions of honor in the mainstream bureaucracy and titled ranks in the highest nobility. Her older and younger sisters were enfeoffed as Ladies of principalities, with wealth tantamount to that of the royal house, their carriage trappings and stately

---

[10]Referring to various ritual activities of the emperor.

[11]The Shangyang Palace was in Luoyang, the empire's secondary capital, here made to balance grammatically the palace compound on Mount Li which was attached to the chief capital, Chang'an.

mansions being on a par with those of the emperor's princess-sisters, while their favors and allotments, their power and dominance, even exceeded the latter. Being permitted to enter and exit the forbidden gates unannounced, they could only be glanced at timidly by the senior officials of the capital precincts. Thus, there was at that time a popular quip, saying, "At the birth of a girl, one won't be sour and sad; at the birth of a boy, one won't be pleased and glad." Another quip said, "A boy won't now be granted a noble title but a girl can be a consort; you see a daughter instead, as a doorway's lintel, can be your house's support" — such then had become the hopes and wishes of people's minds.

Near the end of the Tianbao era (742–56), Yang Guozhong, Lady Yang's elder brother,[12] appropriated the position of Prime Minister and witlessly took over the helm of state. It came to pass that An Lushan led his troops toward the palace-towers, upon the pretext of chastising the Yangs. When the Tong Barrier was no longer defended,[13] the monarch's halcyon-fringed conveyance graced a southward course. Departing Xianyang, it stopped en route at the Mawei post-station.[14] There the imperial armies paused, vacillating, gripping their halberds but advancing no more. Bowing before His Highness's horse, the attending officials and gentleman functionaries requested that Chao Cuo be executed in order to make amends to the empire;[15] Guozhong submitted to

---

[12]Actually, he was a second cousin of Lady Yang.

[13]About seventy-five miles east of Chang'an, this strategic pass protected access to the capital from the Central Plains. When it fell to the rebel forces, their path to Chang'an lay open.

[14]This post-station was about thirty miles west of the capital and was reached by the emperor's entourage two days after the hurried departure from Chang'an (referred to in this sentence by its old name of Xianyang).

[15]In 154 BCE the Han-dynasty emperor Jing had his high minister Chao Cuo 晁錯 (c. 200–154 BCE) executed in order to appease the leaders

the censure and punishment due a malefactor and died by the bend of the road. But the sentiments of those close at hand were not appeased and those who dared speak up requested that the Precious Consort be made to expiate the complaints of the empire. His Highness realized it was unavoidable, but he could not bear to watch her die; covering his face with his sleeve, he had her taken away, and amid the flush and fluster of milling turmoil she breathed her last, strangled at the end of a foot-long cord. After this Xuanzong took the route to Chengdu, and Suzong would receive in Lingwu his abdication.[16]

The next year, the reign-era was changed and a great amnesty declared, and the imperial equipage returned to the capital. Xuanzong took the honorific of Most High Majesty and was maintained in retirement at the Southern Palace, later being removed to the Western Compound.[17] With the passing of time

---

of the "Revolt of the Seven Kings" who claimed Chao's aggressive policies toward them as the pretext for their rebellion. Here Chao Cuo metaphorically suggests Yang Guozhong 楊國忠 (d. 756); but Guozhong was actually killed without permission by Tang troops who thought he was plotting with a small group of Tibetan soldiers who were also accompanying Xuanzong on his flight from the capital.

[16]The day after the dramatic events at Mawei, the heir apparent (the future Suzong) led a portion of the troops away, going northwest to Lingwu in present-day Ningxia where he organized the royalist resistance to the rebels, while Xuanzong and his entourage proceeded on to safe refuge southwest in Sichuan. It would be a year and a half before Chang'an would be retaken by Tang forces.

[17] The Southern Palace refers to the Xingqing gong, "Palace of Ascendant Felicity," located northeast of Chang'an's Eastern Market (but south of the large residential and ceremonial complex of the Daming 大明 gong, "Palace of Great Light"); it had special meaning for Xuanzong, being where he had lived before assuming the throne and where, afterward, he had held celebrations and gatherings of a more personal

and changing of events, sadness came in place of joy. Whenever springtime days arrived or winter nights, and when lotuses in the pool opened in summer or sophora trees by the palace shed leaves in the autumn, as the Pear Garden entertainers played music on their jade pipes and he heard a snatch of "Rainbow Skirt and Feather Vestment," his sublime countenance turned despondent and those close at hand broke down in sobs.

With this single thought throughout three years, his memories of her never waned. He sought her by his soul in dreams but could not find her in the dark. It happened then there came from Shu a Daoist adept who knew that the retired monarch's memories of Consort Yang were like this, and he claimed to possess the arts of that long-ago wizard, Master Li.[18] Xuanzong was overjoyed and ordered him to bring her spirit thither. The adept then exerted his esoteric arts to search for her, but could not reach her; he was able to set his own spirit free, driving the ethers beyond the bounds of heaven and into the caverns of earth to seek her, but could not see her. He sought then throughout the fourfold emptiness, both above and below. In the uttermost east he came to the Great Sea and overstepped the paradise isles of Penglai and Fanghu, and there saw the most high mountain of the transcendents. Atop it were many loft-buildings and gate towers, and by a side-way was a grotto-door facing eastward whose portal was shut but inscribed with the words "Cloister of the Jade Consort, Greatest Perfection."[19] The adept

---

nature. The Western Compound refers to the Taiji gong, "Palace of the Grand Apogee," located southwest of the Daming gong complex.

[18]Who, according to legend, had once brought back for the grieving Emperor Wu of Han a postmortem visit of that ruler's deceased and much-loved consort.

[19]"Greatest Perfection" (Taizhen) was the religious name bestowed on Lady Yang when she had briefly taken orders as a Daoist priestess,

pulled out a hatpin and with it rapped on the door, and there came out in answer a young girl with her hair done up in twin tufts. Before the adept could perfunctorily say a word, she went back in. Shortly, there appeared a serving-maid in cyan-blue clothing who inquired from whence he came. Then the adept, identifying himself as the Son of Heaven's envoy, spoke of the order he had been given. Said the blue-garbed maid, "Just now the Jade Consort is at rest. I bid you wait a while." At that time a sea of clouds spread deep and thick though sunlight shone in the grotto-heaven; as the gemstone doors were doubly barred, all was still and soundless. The adept, with bated breath and unstirring feet, stood respectfully with clasped hands by the portal. A long while passed, and then the blue-garbed maid came to conduct him in, saying, "The Jade Consort is coming forth."

One saw then a person in a gold-lotus cap and purple raw-silk cloak, bedecked with rose-jade pendants and shod in phoenix-patterned slippers, accompanied by seven or eight servants to her right and left. Bowing to the adept, she asked whether the emperor was at ease or not and then asked of events that had happened since the fourteenth year of Tianbao.[20] When their words were finished, she was so moved at heart that she motioned for the blue-garbed maid to fetch the two-pronged hairpin of gold and the filigreed cosmetic case the emperor had once given her. She broke them in two and handed over half of each to the adept-envoy, saying, "Express for me gratitude to His Most High Majesty, to whom I proffer these objects in deference, in which he may discover our bygone love." The adept accepted the words and the tokens, but on the verge of leaving there

---

after being removed from Prince Shou's establishment and given a period of "purification" prior to becoming Xuanzong's consort.

[20]That is, 755, when An Lushan's rebellion began. She wishes to hear of what has happened to the country and the emperor, since she died the next year.

seemed something that still troubled him. When the Jade Consort pressed him about his feelings, he knelt before her and made this plaint, "I pray there be one matter from those times that others could not know of but which can only be attested by His Most High Majesty. Otherwise I fear that the hairpin and case will call down accusations of fraud, as were laid in the past on Xinyuan Ping."[21] The Jade Consort stepped back uncertainly, as though lost in thought, and then softly said, "Sometime ago, in the tenth year of Tianbao, I accompanied the imperial palanquin which, to escape the hot weather, had gone to the Mount Li compound. It was autumn, the seventh month, during that night when the Ox-puller and Weaving Maid stars meet one another.[22] According to customs from Qin times, on this night one spreads out brocade embroidery, sets out food and drink, presents gourds and flowering plants, and burns incense in the courtyard, in what is called the practice of 'invoking adroitness,' which was especially observed in the side apartments of the palace women's quarters. When the night was nearly half-done, the servants and guards

---

[21]Likewise an adept of esoteric arts, in the second century BCE Xinyuan Ping 新垣平 was for a while a favorite of Emperor Wen of the Han, but eventually he was charged with fabricating the physical items of "proof" associated with the prognostications he offered and was executed.

[22]That is, the seventh night of the seventh month, which in the tenth year of Tianbao would have been 2 August 751 by the Western calendar. But in fact, in that year there was no imperial visit to Mount Li until the tenth month. Indeed Xuanzong never went to Mount Li in the summer or the autumn months. But the date of 7/7 is significant because of the romantic legend of the two stars ("Ox-puller" = Altair, "Weaving Maid" = Vega) representing lovers who, on opposite sides of the Milky Way, can meet only once a year, on that night. The activities of the palace women, mentioned by Lady Yang in the next sentence, are various rituals that had traditionally become part of the night's celebrations.

were dismissed from the east and west wings, and I alone was at His Highness's side. He stood with his hands placed on my shoulders and, moved by the story embodied in the two stars, looked up to heaven and made a secret vow from his heart, swearing that we would be husband and wife from one lifetime to the next. When he finished speaking, we clasped hands and each of us sobbed with affection. This is something that only the sovereign ruler himself would know of." Then she said with great tenderness, "Because of this one memory, I will no longer be able to dwell here. I will descend once more to the lower world, where we shall make fast our predestined bond; for whether it be in heaven or among men, we are resolved to meet with each other again and our happy union will be as of old." Then finally she said, "For his part, His Most High Majesty shall not be much longer in the human realm, so let him take comfort in his fortune and not distress himself needlessly."

The envoy returned and reported this all to His Most High Majesty, whose heart was shaken with grief; and day after day he became more indisposed. In summer of that year, in the fourth month, he passed away in the Southern Palace.[23]

In the twelfth month, winter, of the first year of the Yuanhe era,[24] Bai Letian of Tianyuan was being transferred from his position as collator in the imperial library to constable of Zhouzhi. I and Wang Zhifu of Langye were housed in this town, and on a day of leisure we all went together to visit the Temple of Transcendent Journeying. Speaking of this matter [of Xuanzong and Lady Yang], we sighed feelingly. Zhifu raised a glass of wine to Letian and said, "With regard to singular incidents in the world, if they are not written of in glowing terms by someone of

---

[23]This was in 762 and in fact in the fourth month, on the day equivalent to 3 May.

[24]Equivalent to 13 January through 10 February, 807.

outstanding talent, they will melt away with the times and be heard of no more. Letian, you are proficient in verse and abundant of sentiment. What if you give a try at putting this into song?" Letian's thought was that one should not only be moved by the events but also should take warning from the "most blameworthy figure" of Lady Yang and thus foreclose the stepway to disorder, so as to be a lesson for those who come after. So when he completed the poem, he asked me to write a prose account of it. As to those matters not heard of in the world, I, not being a survivor of Kaiyuan times, am not able to know them. As to those that are known, there is extant *The Basic Annals of Xuanzong*.[25] Now I merely give the account more or less from "The Song of Lasting Regret,"[26] which goes as follows:

> Monarch of Han, [27] he doted on beauty, yearned for a
>   bewitching temptress,[28]
> Through the dominions of his sway, for many years he sought
>   but did not find her.
> There was in the family of Yang a maiden just then reaching
>   fullness,
> 4   Raised in the women's quarters protected, unacquainted yet
>   with others.

---

[25]This text was known to and used by Sima Guang 司馬光 (1019–1086) when writing his comprehensive history of pre-Song China, the *Zizhi tongjian* 資治通鑑; but it has not come down to the present day.

[26] There actually are several narrative discrepancies, as well as differences of omission and enhancement, between Bai Juyi's poem and Chen Hong's prose account.

[27]Bai Juyi here adopts the convention — often used by Tang poets when writing of contemporary political matters — that he is speaking of the first great Chinese imperium, the Han.

[28]"Bewitching temptress" is literally "state-toppler," i.e., a beauty for whom one would lose everything.

Heaven had given her a ravishing form, impossible for her to hide,

And one morning she was chosen for placement at the side of the sovereign king.

When she glanced behind with a single smile, a hundred seductions were quickened;

8   All the powdered and painted ones in the Six Palaces[29] now seemed without beauty of face.

In the coolness of springtime, she was permitted to bathe in the Huaqing pools,

Where the slickening waters of the hot springs washed over her firm flesh.

Supported as she rose by a waiting-maid, she was so delicate, listless:

12   This was the moment when first she acceded to His favor and beneficence.

Cloud-swept tresses, flowery features, quivering hair-pendants of gold,

And behind the warmth of lotus-bloom drapings, they passed the springtime nights —

Springtime nights so grievously brief, as the sun rose again high!

16   From this time onward the sovereign king no longer held early court.

Taken with pleasure, she attended on the feasts, continuing without let,

Springtime followed springtime outing, evening after evening she controlled.

Of the comely beauties of the rear palace,[30] there were three thousand persons,

---

[29]The dwellings of the imperial concubines.

20 And preferments and affection for all three thousand were
placed on her alone.
In her golden room, with makeup perfect, the Delicate One[31]
serves for the night;
In a tower of jade, with the feast concluded, drunkenness befits
love in spring.

Her sisters and brothers, older or younger, all were enfeoffed
with land;
24 The most enviable brilliance and glory quickened their
doorways and gates.
Then it came to pass, throughout the empire, that the hearts of
fathers and mothers
No longer valued the birth of a son but valued the birth of
daughters.

The high sites of Mount Li's palace reached into clouds in the
blue,
28 And transcendent music, wafted on the wind, was heard there
everywhere.

Measured songs, languorous dancing merged with sounds of
strings and bamboo,
As the sovereign king looked on all day long, never getting
enough . . .

---

[30]The women's quarters, whose numerous maidens are now wholly
neglected by the emperor, for whom Lady Yang is the only woman that
exists.

[31]The "Delicate One" (*jiao*) figures Lady Yang in the person of Ajiao,
beloved of Emperor Wu of Han in his youth and about whom he once
said, "If I could have Ajiao, I should have a room of gold made in which
to treasure her."

Until, out of Yuyang,[32] horse-borne war-drums came, shaking
the earth,

32   To dismay and smash the melody of "Rainbow Skirt and
Feathered Vestment."

By the nine-layered walls and watchtowers, dust and smoke
arose,

And a thousand chariots, ten thousand riders moved off to the
southwest.[33]

The halcyon-plumed banners jounced and joggled along,
moving and stopping again,

36   As they went forth westward from the metropolis' gates,
something more than a hundred *li*.

And then the Six Armies would go no farther — there was no
other recourse,

But the fluently curved moth-eyebrows[34] must die before the
horses.

Floriform filigrees were strewn on the ground, to be retrieved
by no one,

40   Halcyon tailfeathers, an aigrette of gold, and hairpins made of
jade.

The sovereign king covered his face — he could not save her;

When he looked back, it was with tears of blood that mingled
in their flow.

        *   *   *   *

Yellowish grit spreads and scatters, as the wind blows drear
and doleful;

44   Cloudy walkways turn and twist, climbing Saber Gallery's[35]
heights.

---

[32]An Lushan's headquarters, about seventy miles east of present-
day Beijing.

[33]The emperor and his personal retinue are fleeing the capital.

[34]Those of Lady Yang.

[35] The lofty pass that connects the territory of Qin (in which
Chang'an is located) with that of Shu (or Sichuan) where Yang

Below Mount Emei[36] there are very few men who pass by;
Lightless now are the pennons and flags in the sun's dimmer
    aura.

Waters of Shu's streams deepest blue, the mountains of Shu are
    green —
48 For the Paragon, the Ruler, dawn to dawn, night upon night,
    his feelings:
Seeing the moon from his transient palace — a sight that tears
    at his heart;
Hearing small bells in the evening rain — a sound that stabs
    his insides.[37]

         *   *   *   *

Heaven revolves, the days roll on, and the dragon carriage was
    turned around;
52 Having reached the spot, faltering he halted, unable to leave it
    again.
But amidst that muddy earth, below Mawei Slope,
Her jade countenance was not to be seen — just a place of
    empty death.

Sovereign and servants beheld each other, cloaks wet from
    weeping;
56 And, looking east, to the metropolis' gates, let their horses take
    them homeward.

Guozhong had a fortified sphere of influence, which was the safe haven
where the emperor and his entourage were headed.

[36] About one hundred miles southwest of Chengdu, this is the most
important mountain in Sichuan. It was officially ennobled in Tang times
for its supernatural potency. The emperor's route did not actually take
him past Mount Emei 峨眉.

[37] The sight of the moon pains him because he remembers other
nights when he and Lady Yang enjoyed it together, just as he recalls the
music he used to play as he hears the plaintive sound of little bells
tinkling in the rain under the eaves of a roof.

*   *   *   *

Returned home now, and the ponds, the pools, all were as
　　before —
The lotuses of Grand Ichor Pool, the willows by the Night-Is-
　　Young Palace.[38]

The lotus blossoms resemble her face, the willow branches her
　　eyebrows;
60　Confronted with this, would it be possible that his tears should
　　not fall?
From the day that peach and plum flowers open, in the
　　springtime breezes,
Until the leaves of the "we-together" tree[39] are shed in the
　　autumn rain. . . .

The West Palace and the Southern Interior[40] were rife with
　　autumn grasses,
64　And fallen leaves covered the steps, their red not swept away.
The artistes, once young, of the Pear Garden[41] have hair gone
　　newly white;

---

[38]Both were famous Han-time sites. The House of Tang had its own
pool of this name within the grounds of the emperor's Palace of Great
Light (Daming gong).

[39]The *wutong* tree (*Sterculia platanifolia*). Its name is homophonous
with the phrase "we together" (*wu tong*), and the falling of its leaves in
the autumn rain suggests to Xuanzong the extinction of the love he once
shared with Lady Yang.

[40]Referring respectively to the Sweet Springs Hall in the "palace city"
and the Palace of Ascendant Felicity near Chang'an's east-market ward.
Both were residences assigned by the new emperor Suzong to the retired
emperor who was not permitted to live in the grander compound of the
Palace of Great Light again.

[41]This garden had housed Xuanzong's group of private musicians in
the years of his glory and pleasure.

The Pepper Room[42] attendants and their budding nymphs are
     become aged now.
Fireflies flit through the hall-room at dusk, as he yearns in
     desolation;
68   When all the wick of his lone lamp is used, sleep still fails to
     come.
Ever later, more dilatory, sound watch-drum and bell in the
     lengthening nights;
Fitfully sparkling, the River of Stars[43] streams onward to the
     dawn-flushed sky.

The roof-tiles, paired as love-ducks, grow chilled, and flowers
     of frost grow thick;
72   The halcyon-plumed coverlet is cold — whom would he share
     it with?
Dim-distanced, far-faded, are the living from the dead, parted
     more than a year ago;
Neither her soul nor her spirit have ever yet come into his
     dreams.

             *   *   *   *

A Daoist adept from Linqiong,[44] a visitor to the Hongdu Gate,[45]
76   Could use the perfection of his essential being to contact souls
     and spirits.
Because of his broodings, the sovereign king, tossing and
     turning, still yearned;
So he set to task this adept of formulas, to search for her
     sedulously.

Cleaving the clouds, driving the ethers, fleeting as a lightning-
     flash,

---

[42]The dwelling of the chief consort.
[43]The Milky Way.
[44]In modern Sichuan.
[45]A Han-dynasty designation for one of the capital portals.

80   Ascending the heavens, entering into the earth, he sought her
        out everywhere.
     On high he traversed the sky's cyan drop-off,[46] and below to
        the Yellow Springs;[47]
     In both places, to the limits of vision, she was nowhere to be
        seen.

     Of a sudden he heard rumor then of a transcendent mountain
        in the sea,
84   A mountain resting in void and nullity, amidst the vaporous
        seemings.

     High buildings and galleries shimmer there brightly, and five-
        colored clouds mount up;
     In the midst of this, relaxed and unhurried, were hosts of
        tender sylphs.
     And in *their* midst was one, known as Greatest Perfection,
88   Whose snow-white skin and flower-like features appeared to
        resemble *hers*.

     In the western wing of the gatehouse of gold, he knocked at the
        jade bolting,
     In turn setting in motion Little Jade who made report to
        Doubly Completed.[48]

---

[46]The distant deep-blue reaches of the sky, and more specifically —
to Daoist initiates — the region bearing that name in the Heaven of
Nascent Azure.

[47]The traditional Chinese underworld destination of one's *po* or
carnal (earth-bound) souls.

[48]"Little Jade" (Xiaoyu) and "Doubly Completed" (Shuangcheng)
are Taizhen's maids. The latter was known in Daoist tradition as an
attendant of the goddess Xiwangmu ("Queen Mother of the West"); the
former was the beautiful daughter of King Fuchai 夫差 (r. 495–473 B.C.E.)
of the ancient state of Wu.

When word was told of the Son of Heaven's envoy, from the
House of Han,

92 Then, within the nine-flowered drapings, her dreaming spirit
startled.

She searched for her cloak, pushed pillow aside, arose, walked
forth distractedly;

Door-screens of pearl, partitions of silver, she opened out one
after another.

With her cloud-chignon half-mussed to one side, newly
awakened from sleep,

96 With flowered cap [49] set awry, down she came to the
ceremonial hall.

Her sylphine sleeves, puffed by a breeze, were lifted, flared
and fluttering,

Just the same as in the dance of "Rainbow Skirt and Feathered
Vestment."

But her jade countenance looked bleak, forlorn, crisscrossed
with tears —

100 A single branch of pear blossom, in springtime laden with rain.

Restraining her feelings, focusing her gaze, she asked her
sovereign king's indulgence:

"Once we were parted, both voice and face were lost to
limitless vagueness.

There, within Zhaoyang Basilica,[50] affection and favor were cut
short,

104 While here in Penglai's[51] palaces, the days and months have
lengthened.

"Turning my head and looking down to the sites of the mortal
sphere,

---

[49]That worn by Daoist priests and priestesses.

[50]The Zhaoyang 昭陽 ("Splendid Sunshine") Basilica was one of the
halls occupied by imperial consorts during the Han.

[51]Named after the Daoist isles of immortality in the eastern ocean.

I can no longer see Chang'an, what I see is dust and fog.

Let me take up these familiar old objects to attest to my deep love:

108 The filigree case, the two-pronged hairpin of gold, I entrust to you to take back.

"Of the hairpin but one leg remains, and one leaf-fold of the case;

The hairpin is broken in its yellow gold, and the case's filigree halved.

But if only his heart is as enduring as the filigree and the gold,

112 Above in heaven, or amidst men, we shall surely see each other."

As the envoy was to depart, she entrusted poignant words to him as well,

Words in which there was a vow that only two hearts would know:

"On the seventh day of the seventh month, in the Hall of Protracted Life,[52]

116 At the night's mid-point, when we spoke alone, with no one else around —

'In heaven, would that we might become birds of coupled wings!

On earth, would that we might be trees of intertwining limbs! . . .' "

Heaven is lasting, earth long-standing, but there is a season for their end,

120 *This* regret stretches on and farther, with no ending time.

---

[52]The Hall of Protracted Life (Changsheng dian 長生殿) was part of the Huaqing complex on Mount Li. Its name was used as the title of a famous early Qing drama about the ill-fated love affair between Xuanzong and Lady Yang, ten years and three drafts in the writing by Hong Sheng 洪昇 (1650?–1704).

長恨傳

陳鴻

開元中，泰階平，四海無事。玄宗在位歲久，勌於旰食宵衣，政無大小，始委於右丞相，稍深居遊宴，以聲色自娛。先是，元獻皇后、武淑妃皆有寵，相次即世。宮中雖良家子千數，無可悅目者。上心忽忽不樂。

時每歲十月，駕幸華清宮，內外命婦，熠耀景從，浴日餘波，賜以湯沐，春風靈液，澹蕩其間。上心油然，若有所遇，顧左右前後，粉色如土。詔高力士潛搜外宮，得弘農楊玄琰女於壽邸，既笄矣。

鬢髮膩理，纖穠中度，舉止閑冶，如漢武帝李夫人。別疏湯泉，詔賜澡瑩。既出水，體弱力微，若不任羅綺。光彩煥發，轉動照人。上甚悅。進見之日，奏《霓裳羽衣曲》以導之；定情之夕，授金釵鈿合以固之。又命戴步搖，垂金璫。

明年，冊爲貴妃，半后服用。繇是冶其容，敏其詞，婉變萬態，以中上意。上益嬖焉。時省風九州，泥金五嶽，驪山雪夜，上陽春朝，與上行同輦，居同室，宴專席，寢專房。雖有三夫人、九嬪、二十七世婦、八十一御妻、曁後宮才人、樂府妓女，使天子無顧盼意。自是六宮無復進幸者。非徒殊豔尤態致是，蓋才智明慧，善巧便佞，先意希旨，有不可形容者。

叔父昆弟皆列位清貴，爵爲通侯；姊妹封國夫人，富埒王宮，車服邸第，與大長公主侔矣。而恩澤勢力，則又過之，出入禁門不問，京師長吏爲之側目。故當時謠詠有云："生女勿悲酸，生男勿喜歡。"又曰："男不封侯女作妃，看女卻爲門上楣。"其人心羨慕如此。

　　天寶末，兄國忠盜丞相位，愚弄國柄。及安祿山引兵嚮闕，以
討楊氏爲詞。潼關不守，翠華南幸，出咸陽，道次馬嵬亭。六軍徘
徊，持戟不進。從官郎史伏上馬前，請誅晁錯以謝天下。國忠奉犛
纓盤水，死於道周。左右之意未快。上問之。當時敢言者，請以貴
妃塞天下怨。上知不免，而不忍見其死，反袂掩面，使牽之而去。
倉皇展轉，竟就死於尺組之下。既而玄宗狩成都，肅宗禪靈武。

　　明年，大赦改元，大駕還都，尊玄宗爲太上皇，就養南宮。自
南宮遷於西內。時移事去，樂盡悲來。每至春之日，冬之夜，池蓮
夏開，宮槐秋落，梨園弟子，玉琯發音，聞《霓裳羽衣》一聲，則
天顏不怡。左右歔欷。

　　三載一意，其念不衰。求之夢魂，杳不能得。適有道士自蜀來，
知上心念楊妃如是，自言有李少君之術。玄宗大喜，命致其神。方
士乃竭其術以索之，不至。又能遊神馭氣，出天界，沒地府以求之，
不見。又旁求四虛上下，東極天海，跨蓬壺。見最高仙山，上多樓
闕，西廂下有洞戶，東嚮，闔其門，署曰「玉妃太真院」。方士抽
簪扣扉，有雙鬟童女，出應其門。方士造次未及言，而雙鬟復入。
俄有碧衣侍女又至，詰其所從。方士因稱唐天子使者，且致其命。
碧衣云：「玉妃方寢，請少待之。」於時雲海沈沈，洞天日曉，瓊
戶重闔，悄然無聲。方士屏息斂足，拱手門下。久之，而碧衣延入，
且曰：「玉妃出。」

　　見一人冠金蓮，披紫綃，佩紅玉，曳鳳舄，左右侍者七八人，
揖方士問皇帝安否，次問天寶十四載已還事。言訖憫然，指碧衣女
取金釵鈿合，各折其半，授使者曰：「爲我謝太上皇，謹獻是物，
尋舊好也。」方士受辭與信，將行，色有不足。玉妃固徵其意，復
前跪致詞：「請當時一事，不為他人聞者，驗於太上皇。不然，恐
鈿合金釵，負新垣平之詐也。」玉妃茫然退立，若有所思，徐而言
曰：「昔天寶十載，侍輦避暑於驪山宮。秋七月，牽牛織女相見之
夕，秦人風俗，是夜張錦繡，陳飲食，樹瓜華，焚香於庭，號爲乞
巧。宮掖間尤尚之。時夜殆半，休侍衛於東西廂，獨侍上。上憑肩
而立，因仰天感牛女事，密相誓心，願世世爲夫婦。言畢，執手各
嗚咽。此獨君王知之耳。」因自悲曰：「由此一念，又不得居此。
復墮下界，且結後緣。或為天，或為人，決再相見，好合如舊。」
因言：「太上皇亦不久人間，幸唯自安，無自苦耳。」

　　使者還奏太上皇，皇心震悼，日日不豫。其年夏四月，南宮晏
駕。

元和元年冬十二月，太原白氏樂天自校書郎尉於盩厔。鴻與琅琊王質夫家於是邑，暇日相攜遊仙遊寺，話及此事，相與感歎。質夫舉酒於樂天前曰：“夫希代之事，非遇出世之才潤色之，則與時消沒，不聞於世。樂天，深於詩、多於情者也。試爲歌之，如何？”樂天因爲《長恨歌》。意者不但感其事，亦欲懲尤物，窒亂階，垂於將來者也。歌既成，使鴻傳焉。世所不聞者，予非開元遺民，不得知；世所知者，有《玄宗本紀》在。今但傳《長恨歌》云爾。

漢皇重色思傾國，　　御宇多年求不得。
楊家有女初長成，　　養在深閨人未識。
天生麗質難自棄，　　一朝選在君王側。
回眸一笑百媚生，　　六宮粉黛無顏色。
春寒賜浴華清池，　　溫泉水滑洗凝脂，
侍兒扶起嬌無力，　　始是新承恩澤時。
雲鬢花顏金步搖，　　芙蓉帳暖度春宵，
春宵苦短日高起，　　從此君王不早朝。
承歡侍宴無閒暇，　　春從春遊夜專夜。
漢宮佳麗三千人，　　三千寵愛在一身。
金屋妝成嬌侍夜，　　玉樓宴罷醉和春。
姊妹弟兄皆列土，　　可憐光彩生門戶。
遂令天下父母心，　　不重生男重生女。
驪宮高處入青雲，　　仙樂風飄處處聞。
緩歌慢舞凝絲竹，　　盡日君王看不足。
漁陽鞞鼓動地來，　　驚破霓裳羽衣曲。
九重城闕煙塵生，　　千乘萬騎西南行。
翠華搖搖行復止，　　西出都門百餘里。
六軍不發無奈何，　　宛轉蛾眉馬前死。
花鈿委地無人收，　　翠翹金雀玉搔頭。
君王掩面救不得，　　回看血淚相和流。
黃埃散漫風蕭索，　　雲棧縈迴登劍閣。
峨眉山下少行人，　　旌旗無光日色薄。
蜀江水碧蜀山青，　　聖主朝朝暮暮情，
行宮見月傷心色，　　夜雨聞鈴腸斷聲。
天旋日轉回龍馭，　　到此躊躇不能去。
馬嵬坡下塵土中，　　不見玉顏空死處。
君臣相顧盡沾衣，　　東望都門信馬歸。
歸來池苑皆依舊，　　太液芙蓉未央柳。
芙蓉如面柳如眉，　　對此如何不淚垂？

春風桃李花開日，秋雨梧桐葉落時。
西宮南苑多秋草，落葉滿階紅不掃。
梨園弟子白髮新，椒房阿監青娥老。
夕殿螢飛思悄然，孤燈挑盡未成眠。
遲遲鐘漏初長夜，耿耿星河欲曙天。
鴛鴦瓦冷霜華重，翡翠衾寒誰與共？
悠悠生死別經年，魂魄不曾來入夢。
臨邛道士鴻都客，能以精誠致魂魄。
爲感君王展轉思，遂令方士殷勤覓。
排空馭氣奔如電，昇天入地求之遍。
上窮碧落下黃泉，兩處茫茫皆不見。
忽聞海上有仙山，山在虛無縹緲間。
樓殿玲瓏五雲起，其中綽約多仙子。
中有一人名玉妃，雪膚花貌參差是。
金闕西廂叩玉扃，轉教小玉報雙成。
聞道漢家天子使，九華帳裏夢魂驚。
攬衣推枕起徘徊，珠箔銀鈎迤邐開。
雲髻半偏新睡覺，花冠不整下堂來。
風吹仙袂飄飄舉，猶似霓裳羽衣舞。
玉容寂寞淚闌干，梨花一枝春帶雨。
含情凝睇謝君王，一別音容兩渺茫。
昭陽殿里恩愛絕，蓬萊宮中日月長。
回頭下望人寰處，不見長安見塵霧。
空將舊物表深情，鈿合金釵寄將去。
釵留一股合一扇，釵擘黃金合分鈿。
但令心似金鈿堅，天上人間會相見。
臨別殷勤重寄詞，詞中有誓兩心知。
七月七日長生殿，夜半無人私語時，
在天願爲比翼鳥，在地願爲連理枝。
天長地久有時盡，此恨綿綿無絕期。

Tale 3.18

The Elder of the Eastern Wall

By Chen Hong[1]
Translated by Robert Joe Cutter

The elder was named Jia Chang, and he was a person of the Xuanyang Ward in Chang'an. He was born in the first year, *guichou*, of the Kaiyuan period, and in the *gengyin* year of the Yuanhe period, he was ninety-eight.[2] His vision and hearing were undiminished, his speech was very calm and relaxed, and his mental abilities were intact. When he talked about the events of the time of great peace, it was lucid and interesting.

His father Jia Zhong was nine feet tall and so strong he could drag an ox backwards. From infantryman, he became a yeoman of tents in the inner palace. In the fourth year of the Jingyuan reign period [710], carrying a tent pole, he entered the Daming Palace with Xuanzong. They killed Empress Wei and accompanied Ruizong [r. 684–690, 710–712] to receive in audience all of the

---

[1]This ninth-century tale is usually attributed to Chen Hong (fl. ca. 805–829). Although the narrator refers to himself once as Chen Hongzu 陳鴻祖 and three times by the given name Hongzu 鴻祖, this is possibly the result of an error in the text. Most anthologists, including Lu Xun, accept Chen Hong as the author.

[2]This means he was born between December 22, 713, and January 20, 714. The *gengyin* 庚寅 year, when he was ninety-eight, ran from February 8, 810, through January 27, 811.

numerous lords.³ Subsequently, he was a meritorious subject of the Jingyun period [710–712] and, with a long sword, filled the post of palace guard. He was instructed to move his household to the Eastern Yunlong Gate.

When Jia Chang was seven, his nimbleness and agility were exceptional. He could shinny up a pillar and climb onto a crossbeam. He was good at repartee and understood the sounds of bird speech.⁴ When Xuanzong was still living in a mansion as a prince, he enjoyed the sport of cockfighting among the people during the Qingming Festival, and once he ascended the throne, he established a Gamecock Academy between the two palace compounds. He sought Chang'an's roosters, and over a thousand with golden down, iron-like spurs, tall combs, and tails held high were raised in the Gamecock Academy. He selected five hundred lads from the six armies and had them tame, domesticate, train, and feed them. Since the emperor was fond of it, the popularity of this custom grew especially intense. All of the households of the royal hereditary houses, of the imperial relatives by marriage, of the noble princesses, and of the marquises emptied their coffers and went bankrupt dealing in chickens in order to come up with the price of a cock. The men and women of the capital took to dabbling in gamecocks as their preoccupation; the poor dabbled in faux gamecocks.

The emperor went on an outing and saw Jia Chang handling a wooden gamecock by the roadside at the Yunlong Gate. He drafted him into the palace and made him a lad of the Gamecock Academy, clothing and feeding him as a member of the Militant

---

³This refers to the removal of Empress Wei 韦后, who controlled the court, by Li Longji 李隆基 (the future Xuanzong) and others, and to the restoration of Ruizong 睿宗 to the throne.

⁴"Bird speech," or "bird language" has two meanings: the language of birds, and non-Chinese languages. In context, the former seems more likely here.

as Dragons Army of the Right. This three-foot boy went into the flock of gamecocks as though he were playing with a bunch of kids. The strong, the weak, the brave, the timid, the times for water and grain, the signs of illness and disease — he was able to recognize them all. He chose two gamecocks, and the gamecocks were so intimidated and docile that he ordered them about like people. Wang Cheng'en, the Palace Receptionist who oversaw the Gamecock Academy, told Xuanzong about it. Summoned for an interview in a palace courtyard, he was entirely to Xuanzong's liking, and that very day he was made chief of the five hundred lads. Moreover, because he was loyal and sincere, prudent and circumspect, the Son of Heaven greatly doted on him. Gifts of gold and silk arrived at his home daily.

In the thirteenth year of the Kaiyuan period [725], he caged up three hundred roosters and went along to the *feng* sacrifice at the Eastern Sacred Mountain [Mount Tai].[5] When his father Jia Zhong died at the foot of Mount Tai, the son was able, in accordance with ritual, to escort the deceased's remains back for burial in Yongzhou [Chang'an]. The county magistrate provided burial goods and a hearse, and Jia Chang rode post station carriages on the Luoyang road.

In the third month of the fourteenth year [of the Kaiyuan period], clad in his cockfighting garb, he had an audience with Xuanzong at Wenquan.[6] In those days, the whole world called him The Rooster Whiz. People of the time came up with a saying about him that went:

---

[5]On this pilgrimage to Mount Tai, see Denis Twitchett, ed., *The Cambridge History of China*, vol. 3, *Sui and T'ang China 589–906*, Part 1 (Cambridge: Cambridge University Press, 1979), 387–9.

[6]Wenquan 溫泉 (Warm Springs) Palace was the name given in 671 to the palace at Lishan 驪山 near Chang'an. It was restored by Xuanzong, who spent a good deal of time there. But he may not have been there at the time designated in the tale.

If a son is born, no need for him to be literate:
Cockfighting and horseracing beat reading books.
The Jia kid is just thirteen,
But in wealth and rank, glory and splendor, nobody matches
    him.
He can make metal spurs decide outcomes in advance,
And in embroidered singlet of silk gauze accompanies the
    imperial sedan-chair.
When his father died a thousand *li* from Chang'an,
Official runners led the way and pulled the hearse.

When Empress Zhaocheng was in the palace of the Prince of
Xiang, she gave birth to the emperor on the fifth day of the eighth
month.[7] After the restoration, he made this the Qianqiu Festival.[8]
He bestowed upon the people of the empire the enjoyment of beef
and wine for three days, designated it a Revelry, and made it a
recurring event. He would assemble musicians within the palace on
a grand scale, and over the years sometimes held a Revelry in
Luoyang. The New Year's Audience and Qingming Festival were
generally both at Lishan.[9] Whenever such a day arrived, ten
thousand musicians set out together, and the women of the palace
all went along. Jia Chang, wearing a gold ornamented cap with
eagle and kingfisher feathers, brocaded sleeves and embroidered
jacket and trousers, holding a bell and a whisk, would lead the
flock of gamecocks to stand in order in a broad arena. He would
turn his head and look around like a god, then gesture and signal

---

[7]Empress Zhaocheng is Lady Dou 竇, consort of Ruizong, who did
give birth to Li Longji on the date mentioned (September 8, 685). Prince
of Xiang refers to Ruizong.

[8]This was done in 729.

[9]Zhou Shaoliang 周紹良 shows that Xuanzong likely only spent the
New Year at Lishan in 750 and 754 and that he never spent Qingming
there; Zhou Shaoliang, "'Dong cheng laofu zhuan' jian zheng" 東城老父
傳箋證, *Wen shi* 文史 1983, no. 17: 171.

with flair. Their feathers stood erect and they flapped their wings; they sharpened their beaks and whetted their spurs, controlled their fury, and awaited victory. Their advances and retreats were well timed, and they moved up and down without fail to the gestures of his whip. When Jia Chang considered that the outcome had been decided, the stronger ones went to the fore and the weaker to the rear, and they followed Jia Chang in formation to return to the Gamecock Academy. The myriad wrestlers, the sword vaulters, pole climbers, kickballers, tightrope walkers, and those who danced atop poles, disheartened and dispirited, hesitated and did not dare enter. How could he be like those who would teach a gibbon [to climb trees] or tame a dragon [by bribing it with what it wanted to eat and drink]!

In the twenty-third year [735], Xuanzong obtained the daughter of the Pear Garden Apprentice Pan Datong as a wife for him. The jade worn on the belt of the groom and the embroidered jacket worn by the bride both came from the imperial stores. Jia Chang had two sons: Zhixin and Zhide. During the Tianbao period [742–756], his wife Pan was greatly favored by Precious Consort Yang for her singing and dancing.[10] Husband and wife enjoyed preferential treatment for forty years, and the bounties bestowed on them never changed. How could they not be attentive to their crafts and circumspect in their hearts?

The emperor was born in an *yiyou* year [685], a year of the cock, and his having people engage in cockfighting while wearing court dress foretold a disturbance in the great peace.[11] But the emperor's heart was unaware of this. In the fourteenth year [of the

---

[10]The ultimately tragic relationship between Precious Consort Yang (Yang *guifei*) and Xuanzong is one of the most famous in Chinese history and is the subject of Li Bai's 李白 (701–762?) "Song of Unending Sorrow" and Chen Hong's "Tale of Unending Sorrow."

[11]*You* is the tenth of the twelve earthly branches and is identified with the cock in correlative thinking.

Tianbao period (755)], the Hu-Jie [An Lushan] captured Luoyang, and Tong Pass was undefended.[12] The imperial carriage left for Chengdu.[13] Jia Chang raced off to guard the emperor, but going out the Bian Gate, his horse tripped in a pothole.[14] He injured his foot and could not go on, so using a staff he went into the southern hills. Whenever it got to be a day for roosters, he faced southwest and wept loudly.

In a previous year, An Lushan had gone to court at the capital and had become acquainted with Jia Chang outside the Heng Gate.[15] When he later threw the two capitals into chaos, he offered a reward of a thousand in gold for Jia Chang in the markets of Chang'an and Luoyang. Jia Chang changed his name and took refuge in a Buddhist monastery, where he swept the ground and struck the bell and devoted his energy to Buddhism. Once the Most High Sovereign returned to the Xingqing Palace, Suzong [r. 756–762] received the mandate in a separate hall.[16] Jia Chang

---

[12]Hu-Jie 胡羯 is a combination of the two ethnonyms Hu and Jie and is used here specifically to refer to An Lushan, whose father was Sogdian and whose mother is said to have been Turkish. See Edwin G. Pulleyblank, *The Background of the Rebellion of An Lu-shan* (London: Oxford University Press, 1955), 10–11. Luoyang fell in 756, and Tong Pass actually held out for quite some time but was lost due to an ill-advised attack on the rebels insisted on by the emperor. See Twitchett, *The Cambridge History of China*, 3.1: 455, 459–60, 477–8.

[13]This is a reference to Xuanzong's flight southwest from the capital to Chengdu. On this event, see Paul W. Kroll, "Po Chü-i's 'Song of Lasting Regret': A New Translation," *T'ang Studies* 8–9 (1990–91): 97–105.

[14]Bian 便 Gate refers to an informal auxiliary gate that was located in the southwest of the imperial park.

[15]The Heng 橫 Gate was in the northwest corner of the old Han wall.

[16]"Most High Sovereign," a title for a ruler who has abdicated, refers to Xuanzong. The heir apparent, known to posterity as Suzong, remained behind to fight the rebels and on August 12, 756, proclaimed himself emperor. Xuanzong returned to Chang'an from Chengdu on January 18,

returned to his old ward. The house in which he had lived had been plundered by soldiers, and nothing remained of his household. Clad in cotton clothes and looking thin and pallid, he could no longer enter the palace gates. The next day he was again going out a southern gate of Chang'an when on the way he saw his wife and sons in the Zhaoguo Ward looking malnourished and miserable. His sons were toting firewood, and his wife was carrying old cotton wadding on her back. Jia Chang joined them and cried, then they made their farewells by the road. Subsequently he withdrew for a long time to the Buddhist monasteries of Chang'an and studied the essentials of the dharma from eminent monks.

In the first year of the Dali period [766–780], he attached himself to Venerable Yunping of Zisheng Monastery and dwelled by the Pelagic Pond of the Eastern Market, where he erected a *dhāraṇī* pillar.[17] As for writing, he could only sign his name. But when it came to reciting Buddhist sutras, he was in that case able to understand fully their profound meanings and perfect truths and, by means of his good heart, to transform the people of the marketplace. He built a monk's quarters and planted beautiful vegetation and pleasant trees. By day he took soil and put it around the roots and drew water to irrigate his bamboos; at night he meditated in his meditation chamber.

758, and resided in the Xingqing Palace. The reference to Suzong's receiving the mandate in a detached palace refers to Xuanzong's having conferred the emperorship on Suzong on February 17, 758, in the Xuanzheng Hall of the Daming Palace.

[17]On Tang dynasty *dhāraṇī* spells, see Paul W. Kroll, *Dharma Bell and Dhāraṇī Pillar: Li Po's Buddhist Inscriptions* (Kyoto: Scuola Italiana di Studi sull'Asia Orientale, 2001), 39–75. The Zisheng Monastery was partially located in the northwest corner of Chang'an's Eastern Market. The Pelagic Pond was in the northeast corner of the market and was a place where one might release live fish.

In the third year of the Jianzhong period [782], the monk Yunping's allotted span ran out. Once he had finished complying with the rites, Jia Chang provided a *śarīra* stupa in the eastern part of the Zhenguo Monastery outside the eastern gate of Chang'an and planted with his own hands a hundred pines and cypresses.[18] He built a small hut and lived at the foot of the stupa. Morning and evening he burned incense and sprinkled and swept, serving his master as though he were still alive. Shunzong [r. February– September of 805] was still heir apparent, and he donated three hundred thousand cash for Jia Chang to erect for the Venerable a portrait hall and abstinence retreat. He also erected outbuildings to house the homeless and collect rent and offerings. Jia Chang accordingly ate just a single cup of porridge per day, drank a single *sheng* of water, slept on a straw mat, and dressed in cotton-padded clothes. Anything beyond this went to Buddha.

As for his wife Pan, he later lost track of her, too. During the Zhenyuan period [785–805], his elder son Zhixin, clad in the armor of Bingzhou, accompanied Grand Minister of Education Ma Sui to go to the capital for an audience and visited Jia Chang in the Changshou Ward.[19] Jia Chang rebuffed him and sent him away, as though he had never been born. His younger son Zhide came back. He sold silk fabrics in the market in Luoyang and came and went between there and Chang'an. Every year he offered gold and silk to Jia Chang, but he always refused them. In due course, they both went away and did not come again.

During the Yuanhe period [806–820], Chen Hongzu of Yingchuan, hand-in-hand with a friend, went out the Chunming

---

[18]A *śarīra* stupa was a reliquary.

[19]It is known that Ma Sui 馬燧 (726–795) went to the capital for an audience in 781 and did so again six years later, which fits the tale's account.

Gate.[20] He saw bamboos and cypresses growing thickly, and the incense smoke could be smelled from the road. He dismounted his horse and paid his respects to Jia Chang beneath the stupa. Listening to his words, he forgot that it was late in the day. Jia put Chen up in the abstinence retreat and talked about his service and retirement, all with systematic thoroughness. In due course, they came round to the royal administration. Chen Hong asked about order and disorder in the Kaiyuan period.

Jia Chang said, "When this old man was but a boy, he won favor with the emperor through cockfighting. The emperor kept him the way he did singers and musicians, and my home was in the palace outer grounds. How is that sufficient for understanding court affairs? But there are things that I will tell you about. I saw Vice Director of the Chancellery Du Xian [d. 740] go out as Military Commissioner of Qixi, concurrently Censor-in-Chief, and only then was a censor used to overawe distant peoples.[21] I saw

---

[20]It is at this point in the tale that the name Chen Hongzu appears. The sentence could be read as, "During the Yuanhe period, Chen Hongzu of Yingchuan, taking along a friend, went out the Chunming Gate." But Wang Meng'ou argues that the word *xie* 攜 ("to take along," "to hold hands") does not belong in the text. In that case, *zu* 祖 becomes not part of a name but a verb meaning "to hold a parting banquet," so that the sentence would read, "Chen Hong went out the Chunming Gate to hold a parting banquet for a friend." See Wang Meng'ou (1907–2002), *Tang ren xiaoshuo yanjiu*, 4 vols. (Taipei, 1978), 4:215, and Wang Meng'ou, *Tang ren xiaoshuo jiao shi*, 2 vols. (Taipei, 1983), 1:159–60.

[21]The Military Commissioner for Qixi had under his command the two large protectorates Anxi and Beiting in the deserts of the far west. Du Xian 杜暹 seems to have been appointed Military Commissioner in 724. It is possible that what is translated here as "and then make use of customs and laws to overawe distant peoples" could mean "and then as [a guardian of the] customs and laws overawe distant peoples." The account of Du Xian does not precisely adhere to what is known from official sources, but one should not expect it to.

that when Geshu Han defended Liangzhou, he captured Shibao Fortress, garrisoned Kokonor Enceinte, went out from Bailong, crossed the Congling Mountains, established the border at Tie[men] Pass, and was Commander-in-Chief for Hezuo Circuit.[22] Only after seven appointments, did he become concurrently Censor-in-Chief. I saw that when Zhang Yue [667–731] controlled Youzhou, every year carts with long thills and spoked wheels entered the pass carrying bolts of silk for the labor and household taxes of Hejian and Jizhou. Axle-cap to axle-cap and yoke-to-yoke they entered the gates of the pass *en masse*. Transported to the royal treasury: patterned silks and crepe-gauze from the region of the Yangzi and Huai Rivers, brocades and embroideries from Ba and Shu, merely amusements for the palace ladies. When Hezhou and Dunhuang Province harvested the crops of the military colonies and provided food on the frontier, surplus grains were hauled to Lingzhou, shipped down the Yellow River, and put in the Taiyuan granary in case of a famine year within the pass.

---

[22]Bailong 白龍 (White Dragon) is the name of a yardang located in the northeastern part of Lop Nor. It is named for its purported resemblance to a white dragon. The reference to Tiemen Pass is puzzling. There are two places with that name. Since the tale reports that Geshu Han crossed the Congling Mountains, the tale seems to be referring to the Tiemen Pass mentioned in Xuanzang's 玄奘 (602–664) *Da Tang xi yu ji* 大唐西域記 — a place about ninety miles south-southeast of Samarkand, located roughly on a line between that city and Kabul and part of the Anxi Protectorate in Tang times. But Geshu Han did not go that far west. Historical sources state that he set the frontier at Chiling, a range just east of Kokonor, so it is likely that Congling is a mistake for Chiling and that Tiemen Pass refers to the pass by that name located on the northern Silk Road route, just north of Korla and west of Karasahr in modern Xinjiang. Finally, there was no Hezuo Circuit. This could have been intentional — the sort of mistake an uneducated character like Jia Chang might make; or it could be an error in the text that occurred at some point in the transmission of the tale.

Within the pass cereals were stored by the common people. When the emperor visited the Five Marchmounts, the thousands of carriages and myriads of mounted accompanying officers did not eat off of the populace.

"During the seasons of the year, at the *fu* and *la* festivals, I got to go home and rest, and walking through the markets of the capital, I saw that there were sellers of white clothes and white cotton cloth. As I walked among the neighboring shops, there would be people exorcising illness. The prescribed method called for a bolt of black cloth, but even if one had the exorbitant price, one couldn't get it, so people wound up substituting the silk gauze of a black headwrap. Nowadays if I take my walking stick and go out the door, hunting through the streets and avenues and looking for them in all directions, I see scarcely a hundred people in white clothes. Can everyone in the world have become a soldier?[23]

"In the twelfth year of the Kaiyuan period [724], the emperor ordered that when there was a vacancy among the Vice Directors of the Three Departments, they should first seek someone who had been a Prefect; and when the post of Director was vacant, they should first seek someone who had been a District Magistrate. When I was forty, I saw that among the gentlemen and functionaries of the Three Departments who had a talent and reputation for administering justice, the greatest were assigned to lead commanderies, while the lesser governed districts. But ever since I have lived beside this main road, there have frequently

---

[23]Chen Yinke 陳寅恪 (1890–1969) points out that the author here contrasts the white clothing of civilians with the black uniforms of soldiers. He cites financial reports from the early 800s that show a significant increase in the numbers of soldiers since the Tianbao era (742–756); Chen Yinke, "Du 'Dongcheng laofu zhuan'" 讀東城老父傳, in *Chen Yinke xiansheng lun ji* 陳寅恪先生論集 (Taipei: Zhongyang yanjiuyuan Lishi yuyan yanjiusuo, 1971), 390–91.

been governors of commanderies resting their horses here, and they have all been upset and unhappy that the court had excluded them and was sending them to govern commanderies. When they selected officials back in the Kaiyuan period, those who were filial to their parents and deferential to their elder brothers governed the people, and that was that. You didn't hear of the presented scholar or grand composition or selection of the pre-eminent examinations being its way of choosing the right person.[24] Things were pretty much like this."

Then he wept. Again he spoke, "To the north our supreme emperor subjugated the yurt-dwellers, to the east he subjugated Silla, in the south he subjugated Dian Lake, and to the west he subjugated Kunyi. Once every three years they came for a court audience. He gave them an audience with ritual deportment, shone on them with kindness and favor, clothed them in brocades and cotton padding, provided them with wine and food, and had them settle their business and leave. There were no visitors from foreign countries who remained in the city. Currently aliens from the north live intermingled in the capital, taking wives and having children. The youths of Chang'an now have foreign values. Look, my dear sir, at the styles of headwear, boots, and clothing. They are not like those in former times. Are they not a strange

---

[24]The presented scholar (jinshi) examination had been in use since the beginning of the dynasty and gradually grew in importance, so that by the time of Xuanzong's reign, holders of this degree had already begun to constitute an elite. The selection of the pre-eminent (bacui) and erudite learning and grand composition (boxue hongci) examinations enabled a successful examinee to obtain an immediate posting. The former seems to have begun in 701 and the latter in 731. But there is some truth to Jia Chang's 賈昌 observation. There was an increase in the annual number of jinshi graduates in the ninth century, and special palace examinations increased in importance after 780.

phenomenon?" Chen Hongzu was silent and, not daring to speak, took his leave.

Note: "The Elder of the Eastern Wall" begins just a little before Li Longji, the famous Tang emperor known posthumously as Xuanzong (r. 712–756), became ruler. It continues through Xuanzong's extravagant reign to the devastating An Lushan rebellion, which caused Xuanzong to flee the capital Chang'an for Chengdu and reaches its denouement in 810 or 811. The rebellion was the dominant event in the collective memory of post-An Lushan writers, and its trauma is responsible for the bifurcated life of the protagonist Jia Chang in this tale. Jia Chang's experiences, first as a favored master cockfighter in Xuanzong's retinue and later as a devout Buddhist, both position him as an eye-witness capable of offering his perspective on the events of the time, and his lengthy monologue is replete with references to real people and events, places and spaces, institutions and policies, religion and religious practices, and cultural activities and trends. In the early part of the tale, Jia Chang personifies the more prodigal pursuits and extravagance associated with Xuanzong's reign. His later conversion to life as a committed Buddhist contrasts sharply with his former life and underscores the ephemeral nature of the voluptuary decades leading up to the rebellion. It is perhaps worth noting that the name Jian Chang may contain a pun and that the resultant translation would be something like "False Glory."

An important aspect of the tale is its concern with Tang relations with the western frontier and, in the end, with the decline of Tang power, marked by increased militarization, careerism among officials, and the adoption of aspects of frontier and foreign habits by the youth of the capital. Although Chen Hong had a historian's interest in the past, there are some slips in Jia Chang's account of Tang events — he is, after all, a character in a tale — but the overall story of Tang glory and Tang decline, also embodied in other works of poetry and prose, is clear and well told.

This new translation corrects errors in the 1986 version in my "History and 'The Old Man of the Eastern Wall'" (*Journal of the American Oriental Society* 106.3 [1986]: 503–528), but the analysis there is more detailed and the notes more complete.

東城老父傳

陳鴻

老父，姓賈名昌，長安宣陽里人。開元元年癸丑生。元和庚寅歲，九十八年矣。視聽不衰，言甚安徐，心力不耗，語太平事曆曆可聽。

父忠，長九尺，力能倒曳牛，以材宮為中宮幕士。景龍四年，持幕竿隨玄宗入大明宮，誅韋氏，奉睿宗朝群后，遂為景雲功臣。以長刀備親衛。诏徒家東雲龍門。

昌生七歲，蹻捷過人，能搏柱乘梁，善應對，解鳥語音。玄宗在藩邸時，樂民間清明節鬥雞戲。及即位，治雞坊于兩宮間。索長安雄雞，金毫鐵钜高冠昂尾千數，養于雞坊，選六軍小兒五百人，使馴擾教飼。上之好之，民風尤甚。諸王世家，外戚家，貴主家，侯家，傾幣破產市雞，以償雞直。都中男女，以弄雞為事，貧者弄假雞。

帝出遊，見昌弄木雞于雲龍門道旁，召入，為雞坊小兒，衣食右龍武軍。三尺童子，入雞群，如狎群小，壯者，弱者，勇者，怯者，水穀之時，疾病之候，悉能知之。舉二雞，雞畏而馴，使令如人。護雞坊中謁者王承恩言于玄宗，召試殿庭，皆中玄宗意。即日為五百小兒長。加之以忠厚謹密，天子甚愛幸之。金帛之賜，日至其家。

開元十三年，籠雞三百，從封東嶽。父忠死太山下，得子禮奉屍歸葬雍州。縣官為葬器喪車，乘傳洛陽道。

十四年三月，衣鬥雞服，會玄宗于溫泉。當時天下號為“神雞童”。時人為之語曰：“生兒不用識文字，鬥雞走馬勝讀書。賈家小兒年十三，富貴榮華代不如。能令金钜期勝負，白羅繡衫隨軟舉。父死長安千里外，差夫持道輓喪車。”

279

　　昭成皇后之在相王府，誕聖于八月五日。中興之後，制為千秋節。賜天下民牛酒樂三日，命之曰酺，以為常也。大合樂于宮中，歲或酺于洛。元會與清明節，率皆在驪山。每至是日，萬樂具舉，六宮畢從。昌冠雕翠金華冠，錦袖繡襦袴，執鐸拂道。群雞敘立于廣場，顧眄如神，指揮風生。樹毛振翼，砺吻磨距，抑怒待勝，進退有期，隨鞭指低昂不失。昌度勝負既決，強者前，弱者後，隨昌鴈行，歸于雞坊。角觝萬夫，跳劍尋橦，蹴球踏繩，舞于竿顛者，索氣沮色，逡巡不敢入。豈教猱擾龍之徒歟？

　　二十三年，玄宗為娶梨園弟子潘大同女，男服佩玉，女服繡襦，皆出御府。昌男至信、至德。天寶中，妻潘氏以歌舞重幸于楊貴妃。夫婦席寵四十年，恩澤不渝，豈不敏于伎，謹于心乎？

　　上生于乙酉雞辰，使人朝服鬥雞，兆亂于太平矣。上心不悟。十四載，胡羯陷洛，潼關不守。大駕幸成都，奔衛乘轝。夜出便門，馬踣道穿。傷足，不能進，杖入南山。每進雞之日，則向西南大哭。

　　祿山往年朝于京師，識昌于橫門外。及亂二京，以千金購昌長安、洛陽市。昌變姓名，依於佛舍，除地擊鍾，施力於佛。洎太上皇歸興慶宮，肅宗受命于別殿，昌還舊里。居室為兵掠，家無遺物。布衣鯢顇，不復得入禁門矣。明日，復出長安南門，道見妻兒于招國里，菜色黯焉。兒荷薪，妻負故絮。昌聚哭，訣于道。遂長逝息長安佛寺，學大師佛旨。

　　大曆元年，依資聖寺大德僧運平住東市海池，立陁羅尼石幢。書能紀姓名；讀釋氏經，亦能了其深義至道，以善心化市井人。建僧房佛舍，植美草甘木。畫把土擁根，汲水灌竹，夜正觀于禪室。

　　建中三年，僧運平人壽盡。服禮畢，奉舍利塔于長安東門外鎮國寺東偏，手植松柏百株。構小舍，居于塔下，朝夕焚香灑掃，事師如生。順宗在東宮，舍錢三十萬，為昌立大師影堂及齋舍。又立外屋，居遊民，取傭給。昌因日食粥一杯，漿水一升，臥草席，絮衣。過是，悉歸于佛。

　　妻潘氏後亦不知所往。貞元中，長子至信衣並州甲，隨大司徒燧入覲，省昌于長壽里。昌如己不生，絕之使去。次子至德歸，販繒洛陽市，來往長安間，歲以金帛奉昌，皆絕之。遂俱去，不復來。

　　元和中，潁川陳鴻祖攜友人出春明門，見竹柏森然，香煙聞于道，下馬覲昌于塔下。聽其言，忘日之暮。宿鴻祖于齋舍，話身之出處，皆有條貫。遂及王制，鴻祖問開元之理亂。

昌曰："老人少時，以鬥雞求媚于上。上倡優畜之，家于外宮，安足以知朝廷之事？然有以為吾子言者。老人見黃門侍郎杜暹出為磧西節度，攝御史大夫，始假風憲以威遠。見哥舒翰之鎮涼州也，下石堡戍青海城，出白龍，逾蔥嶺，界鐵關，總管河左道，七命始攝御史大夫。見張說之領幽州也，每歲入關，輒長轅挽輻車輦河間、薊州庸調繒布，駕轊連軏，坌入關門。輸于王府，江淮綺縠、巴蜀錦繡，後宮玩好而已。河州敦煌道歲屯田，實邊食，余粟轉輸靈州，漕下黃河，入太原倉，備關中凶年。關中粟米，藏于百姓。天子幸五嶽，從官千乘馬騎，不食于民。

"老人歲時伏臘得歸休，行都市間，見有賣白衫白疊布。行鄰比鄽間，有人禳病，法用皂布一匹，持重價不克致，竟以幞頭羅代之。近者，老人扶仗出門，閱街衢中，東西南北視之，見白衫者不滿百。豈天下之人皆執兵乎？

"開元十二年，詔三省侍郎有缺，先求曾任刺史者。郎官缺，先求曾任縣令者。及老人四十，見三省郎吏，有理刑才名，大者出刺郡，小者鎮縣。自老人居大道旁，往往有郡太守休馬於此，皆慘然，不樂朝廷沙汰使治郡。開元取士，孝弟理人而已。不聞進士宏詞拔萃之為其得人也。大略如此。"

因泣下。復言曰："上皇北臣穹廬，東臣雞林，南臣滇池，西臣昆夷，三歲一來會。朝覲之禮容，臨照之恩澤，衣之錦絮，飼之酒食，使展事而去，都中無留外國賓。今北胡與京師雜處，娶妻生子。長安中少年，有胡心矣。吾子視首飾靬服之制，不與向同，得非物妖呼？"鴻祖默不敢應而去。

Tale 3.19

The Origin of the
Peaceful Kaiyuan Reign Era

By Wu Jing
Translated by Josiah J. Stork

Yao Yuanchong was originally deemed guilty because he resisted Princess Taiping,[1] but the Emperor thought him to be rather virtuous.[2] After executing Princess Taiping, the emperor intended to appoint Yuanchong as a chief minister and thus first promoted him to the position of Prefect of Tongzhou.[3] Zhang Yue had always been in discord with Yuanchong,[4] so he ordered Zhao Yanzhao to forcefully bring accusations against him, but the emperor did not agree to it. Before Yao had been in his position long, the emperor

---

[1]Yao Yuanchong 姚元崇 (650–721) was an influential official of the Tang served under several emperors. Princess Taiping 太平公主 (ca. 665–713) was a powerful and treacherous princess of the Tang, daughter of Gaozong and Wu Zetian.

[2]Referring to Xuanzong (r. 712–756).

[3]Tongzhou 同州 is close to the capital city, near modern day Dali County. Although this was not a court position, it was not far from the Emperor.

[4]Zhang Yue 張說 (663–730), a native of Luoyang, was a famous minister of the Tang.

was about to go hunting on the banks of the Wei and secretly summoned Yuanchong to meet him at the hunting ground.

At first, Yuanchong heard the emperor was going to train the troops at Mt. Li;[5] and he said to those to whom he was close, "According to regulations, if the Emperor takes the carriage out, the Prefects within 300 *li* must assemble and pay their respects; but I will certainly be pushed aside by the powerful officials. What should I do?" The Administrator Li Jingchu came forward and said, "I have a concubine whose father is the head of the Music Office and often goes in and out of the palace. If my lord were to give him a heavy bribe and ask him to risk breaking the law to submit a letter, he could deliver it." Yao went along with this and it was immediately effective.

The Duke of Yan, Zhang Yue, sent Jiang Jiao [670–722] to enter the palace and say to the emperor, "Your Majesty has long been choosing the Commander in Chief for the area to the east of Shihe,[6] but finding this person has been burdensome and difficult. I have a solution, but with what reward shall I meet?"

The emperor said, "Who? If I am satisfied, you will have a reward of ten thousand gold pieces."

Jiang then said, "The Governor of Pingyi,[7] Yao Yuanchong; his talent in all matters, civil and martial, is complete. He is just the man."

The emperor said, "This is Zhang Yue's idea. A subject who deceives his emperor should be put to death." Jiao kowtowed and

---

[5]Mount Li 驪 was just outside of modern day Xi'an.

[6]Shihe is in modern day Bozhou 亳州. Not far to the east of it is Xuzhou 徐州, where Yao once served as prefect. Others have taken it that the Emperor is looking for a Commander in Chief of Hedong. While this does make sense, it is either ignoring the character *shi* 十 or using it as a grammatical complement. Some editions omit this character, but most reliable editions include it.

[7]To the northeast of Xi'an.

admitted his guilt, declaring himself to be worthy of ten thousand deaths.

The emperor immediately ordered a court eunuch to seek out Yuanchong and have him visit the hunting ground. Only then did the emperor go hunting on the banks of the Wei.

Yao arrived and bowed his head. The emperor stated, "Are you rather knowledgeable about hunting?"

Yuanchong said, "When I was young, I was an orphan and lived near the Guangchang Pool.[8] My eyes knew no books. I only cared for shooting and hunting. It wasn't until the age of 40 that I met Zhang Jingzang.[9] He said that I should study literature in order to prepare for the position of a general or prime minister and that I should not quit on myself. From then on, I changed my ways and devoted myself to reading. Now, although my position is beyond my capability, when it comes to riding and shooting, I am still able, even though I am old." Thus they called for the hawks and loosed the dogs, and their speed suited the Emperor's wishes. The Emperor was greatly pleased.

The Emperor said, "I have not seen you for a long time and have thoughts I would like to ask you. You may walk in the ranks with the Grand Councilors." He walked as before at the back. The Emperor released the reins and let the horse run for a long time. He looked back and said, "Why are you walking at the back?"

Yao replied, "My office is unimportant and lowly, I ought not join the ranks of the Grand Councilors."

The Emperor said, "You can have the position of Minister and Joint Manager of Affairs of the Ministry of War." Yao did not thankfully accept the order. The Emperor looked at him with astonishment.

---

[8]Part of the imperial hunting grounds outside the capital city.

[9]A character famous for physiognomy (telling fortunes by looking at people's faces).

When they arrived at their stopping place, the emperor ordered the ministers and officials to sit. Yuanchong knelt and addressed the emperor, "The reason that I did not thankfully accept the orders I just received to serve and provide assistance is that I wish to present ten items to the emperor. If there are any that cannot be implemented, I dare not accept the imperial command."

The Emperor said, "Enumerate them fully! We should first assess our abilities and then determine whether or not they are possible."

He said, "Since the Chuigong Reign Era (685–689), the court has brought order to all under heaven by law and punishment. I ask Your Sagacity to rule first through benevolence and righteousness. Is that acceptable?"

The Emperor said, "From the depths of my heart I have hope in you."

Yuanchong continued, "Since our army's loss at Qinghai,[10] this dynasty has not had the regret to lead it back [to proper conduct]. I request that in the next thirty years no accomplishments along the border will be sought. Is that acceptable?"

The Emperor said, "It is."

Yuanchong continued, "Since the Empress Dowager reigned from the throne, the responsibilities of a spokesperson have occasionally fallen to the shoulders[11] of the castrati. I ask that the eunuchs not participate in official matters. Is that acceptable?"

The Emperor said, "I have long harbored this thought."

---

[10] In 670 the Tibetan Empire captured a large swath of Western China. Emperor Gaozong attempted to reclaim this territory but lost.

[11] The Chinese literally reads *the responsibility has come out of the mouths of castrati.*

Yuanchong continued, "Since the relatives of the Wu clan inappropriately encroached upon the places of the respectable, influential, powerful, and important, and Lady Wei, Princess Anle, and Princess Taiping were in power afterwards, the classes and ranks have been confused and stirred up. I ask that the imperial relatives not take positions in the Three Departments.[12] Please also cease all unofficially granted offices, empty appointments, and sold positions. Is this acceptable?"

The Emperor said, "This is my long-held ambition."

Yuanchong continued, "Recently, whenever those who are close to Your Majesty and enjoy your favor have trespassed the statutes and principles, they have all been excused because of Your Majesty's indulgence. I ask that the law be applied to them. Is this acceptable?"

The Emperor said, "I have long [angrily] gnashed my teeth about this."

Yuanchong continued, "Of late, great families and imperial relatives have sent tribute to the emperor to seek his favor. This practice has extended to high-ranking and local officials. I ask that, except for commissions and taxes, all other tributes be blocked. Is that acceptable?"

The Emperor said, "I wish to implement this."

Yuanchong continued, "The Empress Dowager built the Fuxian Temple, Emperor Zhongzong built the Shengshan Temple, and the last Emperor built the Jinxian and Yuzhen Monasteries. Each cost several millions, and this is like an insect that eats into the people. All temples, monasteries, and palaces, I ask that you stop building them. Is this acceptable?"

The Emperor said, "Every time I see them, my heart is ill at ease. How could we possibly dare to continue this?"

---

[12] Department of State Affairs 尚書省, Secretariat 中書省, Chancellery 門下省.

Yuanchong continued, "The previous dynasty was inappropriately familiar with the officials and that sometimes did not sufficiently fulfill the respect between ruler and ministers. I ask your majesty to receive them with ritual. Is this acceptable?"

The Emperor said, "This is honestly only natural, what could be unacceptable (with that)?"

Yuanchong continued, "Since Yan Qinrong and Wei Yuejiang were deemed guilty because they submitted their honest opinions, from then on, the Remonstrators have looked dejected. I ask that all among the officials may touch the dragon's scales and break taboos.[13] Is this acceptable?"

The Emperor said, "I can not only tolerate them, but also implement their suggestions."

Yuanchong continued, "Chan and Lu of the Lü clan almost seized the Western Capital.[14] Ma, Deng, Yan, and Liang[15] also brought disorder to the Eastern Han. This has eternally terrified every dynasty since, especially our current dynasty. I ask Your Majesty to write this type of events in the annals that they may

---

[13]Namely, remonstrate with the Emperor.

[14]Before she died in 180 BCE, the Empress Dowager Lü 呂太后 left her two relatives, Lü Chan and Lü Lu, with powerful positions. This was seen as an attempt to overthrow the Han Dynasty in what is known as the Lü Clan Disturbance 呂氏之亂.

[15]Here he is referencing four powerful Empresses of the Han Dynasty who all plotted to gain power for their clans or offspring in ways similar to Empress Dowager Lü and Wu Zetian. They are Empress Ma 馬皇后 (whose personal name is unknown) (40–79 CE), wife of Emperor Ming 漢明帝 (28–75 CE, r. 58–75 CE); Deng Sui 鄧綏 (81–121 CE), wife of Emperor He 漢和帝 (19–106 CE, r. 88–105); Yan Ji 閻姬 (?–126 CE), wife of Emperor An 漢安帝 (94–125 CE, r. 106–125 CE); and Liang Na 梁妠 (116–150 CE), wife of Emperor Shun 漢順帝 (115–144 CE, r. 125–144 CE).

forever be a 'Yin's Mirror' [16] and be a modeled alarm for ten thousand generations. Is this acceptable?"

The Emperor sat tearfully for a good while and then said, "These events can really be cut into muscle and cut into bone [as a lasting reminder]."

Yao bowed twice and said, "This is truly the beginning of Your Majesty's path to benevolent governance. This is a day that officials only meet once in a thousand years. I am willing to take the place of a harmonious assistant. All under heaven is very fortunate! All under heaven is very fortunate!" He once again bowed and, dancing, shouted "Long live the Emperor" three times. The ten million following officials all wept.

The Emperor said, "Sit!" Yao sat under Duke Yan. Duke Yan yielded to him and dared not sit. The Emperor asked about this. He replied, "Yuanchong is an old minister from the previous dynasty. He should take the honored seat."

Yuanchong said, "Zhang Yue is the Envoy [17] from the Ziwei Palace,[18] now I am a guest Grand Councilor, I should not take the honored seat."

The Emperor said, "The Envoy from the Ziwei Palace may sit in the honored seat."

---

[16] A lesson for posterity.

[17] This was an alternate title for the Head of the Secretariat 中書令. For a brief 5-year period, the Secretariat was known as the Ziwei Bureau 紫微省.

[18] The imperial palace.

開元昇平源

吳兢

　　姚元崇初拒太平得罪，上頗德之。既誅太平，方任元崇以相，進拜同州刺史。張說素不叶，命趙彥昭驟彈之；不許。居無何，上將獵於渭濱，密召元崇會於行所。

　　初，元崇聞上講武於驪山，謂所親曰："準式，車駕行幸，三百里內刺史合朝覲。元崇必為權臣所擠，若何？"參軍李景初進曰："某有兒母者，其父即教坊長，入內。相公儻致厚賂，使其冒法進狀，可達。"公然之，輒效。

　　燕公說使姜皎入曰："階下久卜十河東總管，重難其人。臣有所得，何以見賞？"

　　上曰："誰邪？如愜，有萬金之賜。"

　　乃曰："馮翊太守姚元崇，文武全材，即其人也。"

　　上曰："此張說意也。卿罔上，當誅。"皎首服萬死。

　　即詔中官追赴行在。上方獵于渭濱。

　　公至，拜首。上言："卿頗知獵乎？"

　　元崇曰："臣少孤，居廣成澤，目不知書，唯以射獵為事。四十年方遇張憬藏，謂臣當以文學備位將相，無為自棄，爾來折節讀書。今雖官位過忝，至於馳射，老而猶能。"於是呼鷹放犬，遲速稱旨。上大悅。

　　上曰："朕久不見卿，思有顧問，卿可於宰相行中行！"公行猶後。上縱轡久之，顧曰："卿行何後？"

　　公曰："臣官疏賤，不合參宰相行。"

　　上曰："可兵部尚書、同平章事。"公不謝。上顧訝焉。

　　至頓，上命宰臣坐。公跪奏："臣適奉作弼之詔而不謝者，欲以十事上獻。有不可行，臣不敢奉詔。"

289

上曰："悉數之！朕當量力而行，然後定可否。"

公曰："自垂拱已來，朝廷以刑法理天下。臣請聖政先仁義，可乎？"

上曰："朕深心有望於公也。"

又曰："聖朝自喪師青海，未有牽復之悔。臣請三數十年不求邊功，可乎？"

上曰："可。"

又曰："自太后臨朝以來，喉舌之任，或出於閹人之口。臣請中官不預公事，可乎？"

上曰："懷之久矣。"

又曰："自武氏諸親猥侵清切權要之地，繼以韋庶人、安樂、太平用事，班序荒雜。臣請國親不任臺省官。凡有斜封、待闕、員外等管，悉請停罷，可乎？"

上曰："朕素志也。"

又曰："比來近密佞幸之徒，冒犯憲網者，怕皆以寵免。臣請行法，可乎？"

上曰："朕切齒久矣。"

又曰："比因豪家戚里，貢獻求媚，延及公卿方鎮，亦為之。臣請除租庸、賦稅之外，悉杜塞之，可乎？"

上曰："願行之。"

又曰："太后造福先寺，中宗造聖善寺，上皇造金仙玉真觀，皆費鉅百萬，耗盡生靈。凡寺觀宮殿，臣請上絕建造，可乎？"

上曰："朕每覿之，心即不安，而況敢為者哉！"

有曰："先朝褻狎大臣，或虧君臣之敬。臣請陛下接之以禮，可乎？"

上曰："事誠當然。有何不可？"

又曰："自燕欽融、韋月將獻直得罪，由是諫臣沮色。臣請凡在臣子，皆得觸龍鱗，犯忌諱，可乎？"

上曰："朕非唯能容之，亦能行之。"

又曰："呂氏產、祿幾危西京，馬、鄧、閻、梁亦亂東漢，萬古寒心，國朝為甚。臣請陛下書之史冊，永為殷鑒，作萬代法，可乎？"

上乃潸然良久曰："此事真可為刻肌刻骨者也。"

　　公再拜曰：“此誠陛下致仁政之初，是臣千年一遇之日，臣敢當弼諧之地。天下幸甚！天下幸甚！”又再拜、蹈舞稱萬歲者三。從官千萬皆出涕。

　　上曰：“坐！”公坐於燕公之下。燕公讓不敢坐。上問。對曰：“元崇是先朝舊臣，合首坐。”

　　公曰：“張說是紫微宮使，今臣是客宰相，不合首坐。”

　　上曰：“可紫微宮使居首座！”

Chapter 4

Tale 4.20

The Story of Yingying

By Yuan Zhen
Translated by James R. Hightower

During the Zhenyuan period[1] there lived a young man named Zhang. He was agreeable, refined, and good-looking, but firm and self-contained, and capable of no improper act. When his companions included him in one of their parties, the others could all be brawling as though they would never get enough, but Zhang would just watch tolerantly without ever taking part. In this way he had gotten to be twenty-three years old without ever having had relations with a woman. When asked by his friends, he explained, "Dengtu zi[2] was no lover, but a lecher. I am the true lover — I just never happened to meet the right girl. How do I know that? It's because things of outstanding beauty never fail to make a permanent impression on me. That shows I am not without feelings." His friends took note of what he said.

---

[1]Zhenyuan 貞元 (785–804) was the last of the three reign periods of Emperor Dezong of the Tang dynasty.

[2]Dengtu 登徒 was an archetypal lecher. This allusion originates from the character ridiculed in Song Yu's (fl. 3rd century B.C.E.) rhapsody, "The Lechery of Master Dengtu."

Not long afterward Zhang was traveling in Pu,[3] where he lodged some ten tricents east of the city in a monastery called the Temple of Universal Salvation. It happened that a widowed Mrs. Cui had also stopped there on her way back to Chang'an. She had been born a Zheng; Zhang's mother had been a Zheng, and when they worked out their common ancestry, this Mrs. Cui turned out to be a rather distant cousin once removed on his mother's side.

This year Hun Zhen[4] died in Pu, and the eunuch Ding Wenya proved unpopular with the troops, who took advantage of the mourning period to mutiny. They plundered the citizens of Pu, and Mrs. Cui, in a strange place with all her wealth and servants, was terrified, having no one to turn to. Before the mutiny Zhang had made friends with some of the officers in Pu, and now he requested a detachment of soldiers to protect the Cui family. As a result all escaped harm. In about ten days the imperial commissioner of inquiry, Du Que,[5] came with full power from the throne and restored order among the troops.

Out of gratitude to Zhang for the favor he had done them, Mrs. Cui invited him to a banquet in the central hall. She addressed him: "Your widowed aunt with her helpless children would never have been able to escape alive from these rioting soldiers. It is no ordinary favor you have done us; it is rather as though you had given my son and daughter their lives, and I want to introduce them to you as their elder brother so that they can

---

[3]Puzhou 蒲州, also known as Hezhong in Tang times, was under the jurisdiction of Jiangzhou. It is modern Yongji district in Shanxi province, located east-northeast of Chang'an.

[4]Hun Zhen, the regional commander of Jiangzhou, died in Puzhou in 799.

[5]Du Que 杜確, originally prefect of Tongzhou (in modern Shanxi), was appointed, after the death of Hun Zhen, the prefect of Hezhong as well as the imperial commissioner of inquiry of Jiangzhou.

express their thanks." She summoned her son Huanlang, a very attractive child of ten or so. Then she called her daughter, "Come out and pay your respects to your brother, who saved your life." There was a delay; then word was brought that she was indisposed and asked to be excused. Her mother exclaimed in anger, "Your brother Zhang saved your life. You would have been abducted if it were not for him — how can you give yourself airs?"

After a while she appeared, wearing an everyday dress and no make-up on her smooth face, expect for a remaining spot of rouge. Her hair coils straggled down to touch her eyebrows. Her beauty was extraordinary, so radiant it took the breath away. Startled, Zhang made her a deep bow as she sat down beside her mother. Because she had been forced to come out against her will, she looked angrily straight ahead as though unable to endure the company. Zhang asked her age. Mrs. Cui said, "From the seventh month of the fifth year of the reigning emperor to the present twenty-first year, it is just seventeen years."

Zhang tried to make conversation with her, but she would not respond, and he had to leave after the meal was over. From this time on Zhang was infatuated but had no way to make his feelings known to her. She had a maid named Hongniang with whom Zhang had managed to exchange greetings several times, and finally he took the occasion to tell her how he left. Not surprisingly, the maid was alarmed and fled in embarrassment. Zhang was sorry he had said anything, and when she returned the next day he made shame-faced apologies without repeating his request. The maid said, "Sir, what you said is something I would not dare repeat to my mistress or let anyone else know about. But you know very well who Miss Cui's relatives are; why don't you ask for her hand in marriage, as you are entitled to do because of the favor you did them?"

"From my earliest years I have never been one to make any improper connections," Zhang said. "Whenever I have found myself in the company of young women, I would not even look at them, and it never occurred to me that I would be trapped in any such way. But the other day at the dinner I was hardly able to control myself, and in the days since, I walk without knowing where I am going and eat without hunger — I am afraid I cannot last another day. If I were to go through a regular matchmaker, taking three months and more for the exchange of betrothal presents and names and birthdates[6] — you might just as well look for me among the dried fish in the shop.[7] Can't you tell me what to do?"

"Miss Cui is so very strict that not even her elders could suggest anything improper to her," the maid replied. "It would be hard for someone in my position to say such a thing. But I have noticed she writes a lot. She is always reciting poetry to herself and is moved by it for a long time after. You might see if you can seduce her with a love poem. That is the only way I can think of."

Zhang was delighted and on the spot composed two stanzas of spring verses which he handed over to her. That evening Hongniang came back with a note on colored paper for him, saying, "By Miss Cui's instructions."

The title of her poem was "Bright Moon on the Night of the Fifteenth":

> I await the moon in the western chamber
> Where the breeze comes through the half-opened door.
> Sweeping the wall the flower shadows move:
> I imagine it is my lover who comes.

---

[6]To determine an astrologically suitable date for a wedding.

[7]An allusion to the parable of help that comes too late in the "waiwu" 外物 chapter of the pre-Qin philosophical work *Zhuangzi* 莊子.

Zhang understood the message: that day was the fourteenth of the second month, and an apricot tree was next to the wall east of Cuis' courtyard. It would be possible to climb it.

On the night of the fifteenth Zhang used the tree as a ladder to get over the wall. When he came to the western chamber, the door was ajar. Inside, Hongniang was asleep on a bed. He awakened her, and she asked, frightened, "How did you get here?"

"Miss Cui's letter told me to come," he said, not quite accurately. "You go tell her I am here."

In a minute Hung-niang was back. "She's coming! She's coming!"

Zhang was both happy and nervous, convinced that success was his. Then Miss Cui appeared in formal dress, with a serious face, and began to upbraid him: "You did us a great kindness when you saved our lives, and that is why my mother entrusted my young brother and myself to you. Why then did you get my silly maid to bring me that filthy poem? You began by doing a good deed in preserving me from the hands of ravishers, and you end by seeking to ravish me. You substitute seduction for rape — is there any great difference? My first impulse was to keep quiet about it, but that would have been to condone your wrongdoing, and not right. If I told my mother, it would amount to ingratitude, and the consequences would be unfortunate. I thought of having a servant convey my disapproval, but feared she would not get it right. Then I thought of writing a short message to state my case, but was afraid it would only put you on your guard. So finally I composed those vulgar lines to make sure you would come here. It was an improper thing to do, and of course I feel ashamed. But I hope that you will keep within the bounds of decency and commit no outrage."

As she finished speaking, she turned on her heel and left him. For some time Zhang stood, dumbfounded. Then he went back over the wall to his quarters, all hope gone.

A few nights later Zhang was sleeping alone by the veranda when someone shook him awake. Startled, he rose up to see Hongniang standing there, a coverlet and pillow in her arms. She patted him and said: "She is coming! She is coming! Why are you sleeping?" And she spread the quilt and put the pillow beside his. As she left, Zhang sat up straight and rubbed his eyes. For some time it seemed as though he were still dreaming, but nonetheless he waited dutifully. Then there was Hongniang again, with Miss Cui leaning on her arm. She was shy and yielding, and appeared almost not to have the strength to move her limbs. The contrast with her stiff formality at their last encounter was complete.

This evening was the night of eighteenth, and the slanting rays of the moon cast a soft light over half the bed. Zhang felt a kind of floating lightness and wondered whether this was an immortal who visited him, not someone from the world of men. After a while the temple bell sounded. Daybreak was near. As Hongniang urged her to leave, she wept softly and clung to him. Hongniang helped her up, and they left. The whole time she had not spoken a single word. With the first light of dawn Zhang got up, wondering, was it a dream? But the perfume still lingered, and as it got lighter he could see on his arm traces of her makeup and the teardrops sparkling still on the mat.

For some ten days afterward there was no word from her. Zhang composed a poem of sixty lines on "An Encounter with an Immortal" which he had not yet completed when Hongniang happened by, and he gave it to her for her mistress. After that she let him see her again, and for nearly a month he would join her in what her poem called the "western chamber," slipping out at dawn and returning stealthily at night. Zhang once asked what her mother thought about the situation. She said, "She knows there is nothing she can do about it, and so she hopes you will regularize things."

Before long Zhang was about to go to Chang'an, and he let her know his intentions in a poem. Miss Cui made no objections at all, but the look of pain on her face was very touching. On the eve of his departure he was unable to see her again. Then Zhang went off to the west. A few months later he again made a trip to Pu and stayed several months with Miss Cui.

She was a very good calligrapher and wrote poetry, but for all that he kept begging to see her work, she would never show it. Zhang wrote poems for her, challenging her to match them, but she paid them little attention. The thing that made her unusual was that, while she excelled in the arts, she always acted as though she were ignorant, and although she was quick and clever in speaking, she would seldom indulge in repartee. She loved Zhang very much, but would never say so in words. At the time she was subject to moods of profound melancholy, but she never let that appear. She seldom showed on her face the emotions she felt. On one occasion she was playing her zither alone at night. She did not know Zhang was listening, and the music was full of sadness. As soon as he spoke, she stopped and would play no more. This made him all the more infatuated with her.

Some time later Zhang had to go west again for the scheduled examinations. It was the eve of his departure, and though he said nothing about what it involved, he sat sighing unhappily at her side. Miss Cui had guessed that he was going to leave for good. Her manner was respectful, but she spoke deliberately and in a low voice: "To seduce someone and then abandon her is perfectly natural, and it would be presumptuous of me to resent it. It would be an act of charity on your part if, having first seduced me, you were to go through with it and fulfill your oath of lifelong devotion. But in either case, what is there to be so upset about in this trip? However, I see you are not happy, and I have no way to cheer you up. You have praised my zither-playing, and in the past

I have been embarrassed to play for you. Now that you are going away, I shall do what you so often requested."

She had them prepare her zither and started to play the prelude to the "Rainbow Robe and Feather Skirt."[8] After a few notes, her playing grew wild with grief until the piece was no longer recognizable. Everyone was reduced to tears, and Miss Cui abruptly stopped playing, put down the zither, and ran back to her mother's room with tears streaming down her face. She did not come back.

The next morning Zhang went away. The following year he stayed on in the capital, having failed the examinations. He wrote a letter to Miss Cui to reassure her, and her reply read roughly as follows:

I have read your letter with its message of consolation, and it filled my childish heart with mingled grief and joy. In addition you sent me a box of ornaments to adorn my hair and a stick of pomade to make my lips smooth. It was most kind of you; but for whom am I to make myself attractive? As I look at these presents my breast is filled with sorrow.

Your letter said that you will stay on in the capital to pursue your studies, and of course you need quiet and the facilities there to make progress. Still, it is hard on the person left alone in this far-off place. But such is my fate, and I should not complain. Since last fall I have been listless and without hope. In company I can force myself to talk and smile, but come evening I always shed tears in the solitude of my own room. Even in my sleep I often sob, yearning for the absent one. Or I am in your arms for a moment as it used to be, but before

---

[8]After this Brahman music was introduced into China, it was dignified by the elegant name given to it by Emperor Xuanzong of the Tang dynasty and by the performance of his favorite consort, Yang Guifei.

the secret meeting is done I am awake and heartbroken. The bed seems still warm beside me, but the one I love is far away.

Since you said good-bye the new year has come. Chang'an is a city of pleasure with chances for love everywhere. I am truly fortunate that you have not forgotten me and that your affection is not worn out. Loving you as I do, I have no way of repaying you, except to be true to our vow of lifelong fidelity.

Our first meeting was at the banquet, as cousins. Then you persuaded my maid to inform me of your love; and I was unable to keep my childish heart firm. You made advances, like that other poet, Sima Xiangru.[9] I failed to repulse them as the girl did who threw her shuttle.[10] When I offered myself in your bed, you treated me with the greatest kindness, and I supposed, in my innocence, that I could always depend on you. How could I have foreseen that our encounter could not possibly lead to something definite, that having disgraced myself by coming to you, there was no further chance of serving you openly as a wife? To the end of my days this will be a lasting regret — I must hide my sighs and be silent. If you, out of kindness, would condescend to fulfill my selfish wish, though it came on my dying day it would seem to be a new lease on life. But if, as a man of the world, you curtail your feelings, sacrificing the lesser to the more important, and look on this connection as shameful, so that your solemn vow can be dispensed with, still my true love will not vanish though my bones decay and my frame dissolve; in wind and dew it will seek out the ground you walk on. My love in life and death is told in this. I weep as I write, for feelings I cannot express. Take care of yourself; a thousand times over, take care of your dear self.

---

[9]An allusion to the story of the Han poet, Sima Xiangru 司馬相如 (179–117 B.C.E.), who enticed the young widow Zhuo Wenjun 卓文君 to elope by his zither-playing.

[10]A neighboring girl, named Gao, repulsed Xie Kun's 謝鯤 (280–322) advances by throwing her shuttle in his face. He lost two teeth.

This bracelet of jade is something I wore as a child; I send it to serve as a gentleman's belt pendant. Like jade may you be invariably firm and tender; like a bracelet may there be no break between what came before and what is to follow. Here are also a skein of multicolored thread and a tea roller of mottled bamboo. These things have no intrinsic value, but they are to signify that I want you to be true as jade, and your love to endure unbroken as a bracelet. The spots on the bamboo are like the marks of my tears,[11] and my unhappy thoughts are as tangled as the thread: these objects are symbols of my feelings and tokens for all time of my love. Our hearts are close, though our bodies are far apart and there is no time I can expect to see you. But where the hidden desires are strong enough, there will be a meeting of spirits. Take care of yourself, a thousand times over. The springtime wind is often chill; eat well for your health's sake. Be circumspect and careful, and do not think too often of my unworthy person.

Zhang showed her letter to his friends, and in this way word of the affair got around. One of them, Yang Juyuan,[12] a skillful poet, wrote a quatrain on "Young Miss Cui":

For clear purity jade cannot equal his complexion;
On the iris in the inner court snow begins to melt.
A romantic young man filled with thoughts of love,
A letter from the Xiao girl,[13] brokenhearted.

---

[11]Alluding to the legend of the two wives of the sage ruler Shun, who stained the bamboo with their tears.

[12]The poet Yang Juyuan (fl. 800) was a contemporary of Yuan Zhen.

[13]In Tang times the term "Xiaoniang" referred to young women in general. Here it means Yingying.

Yuan Zhen [14] of Henan [15] wrote a continuation of Zhang's poem "Encounter with an Immortal," also in thirty couplets:

Faint moonbeams pierce the curtained window;
Fireflies glimmer across the blue sky.
The far horizon begins now to pale;
Dwarf trees gradually turn darker green.
A dragon song crosses the court bamboo;
A phoenix air brushes the well-side tree.
The silken robe trails through the thin mist;
The pendant circles tinkle in the light breeze.
The accredited envoy accompanies Xi Wangmu; [16]
From the clouds' center comes Jade Boy. [17]
Late at night everyone is quiet;
At daybreak the rain drizzles.
Pearl radiance shines on her decorated sandals;
Flower glow shows off the embroidered skirt.
Jasper hairpin: a walking colored phoenix;
Gauze shawl; embracing vermilion rainbow.
She says she comes from Jasper Flower Bank
And is going to pay court at Green Jade Palace.

---

[14]Yuan Zhen was a key literary figure in the middle of the Tang period.

[15]The Henan Circuit in Tang times covered the area to the south of the Yellow River in both the present provinces of Shandong and Henan, up to the north of the Huai River in modern Jiangsu and Anhui.

[16]Xi Wangmu, the Queen Mother of the West, is a mythological figure supposedly dwelling in the Kunlun Mountains in China's far west. In early accounts she is sometimes described as part human and part beast, but since early post-Han times she has usually been described as a beautiful immortal. Her huge palace is inhabited by other immortals. Within its precincts grow the magic peach trees which bear the fruits of immortality once every three thousand years. This might be an allusion to Yingying's mother.

[17]The Jade Boy might allude to Yingying's brother.

On an outing north of Luoyang's[18] wall,
By chance he came to the house east of Song Yu's.[19]
His dalliance she rejects a bit at first,
But her yielding love already is disclosed.
Lowered locks put in motion cicada shadows;[20]
Returning steps raise jade dust.
Her face turns to let flow flower snow
As she climbs into bed, silk covers in her arms.
Lover birds in a neck-entwining dance;
Kingfishers in a conjugal cage.
Eyebrows, out of shyness, contracted;
Lip rouge, from the warmth, melted.
Her breath is pure: fragrance of orchid buds;
Her skin is smooth: richness of jade flesh.
No strength, too limp to lift a wrist;
Many charms, she likes to draw herself together.
Sweat runs: pearls drop by drop;
Hair in disorder: black luxuriance.
Just as they rejoice in the meeting of a lifetime
They suddenly hear the night is over.
There is no time for lingering;
It is hard to give up the wish to embrace.
Her comely face shows the sorrow she feels;
With fragrant words they swear eternal love.
She gives him a bracelet to plight their troth;
He ties a lovers' knot as sign their hearts are one.
Tear-borne powder runs before the clear mirror;
Around the flickering lamp are nighttime insects.

---

[18]Possibly a reference to the goddess of the Luo River. This river, in modern Honan, is made famous by the rhapsody of Cao Zhi (192–232; see selection 26), "The Goddess of Luo."

[19]In "The Lechery of Master Dengtu" (see note 2 above), Song Yu tells about the beautiful girl next door to the east who climbed up on the wall to flirt with him.

[20]Referring to her hairdo in the cicada style.

Moonlight is still softly shining
As the rising sun gradually dawns.
Riding on a wild goose she returns to the Luo River,[21]
Blowing a flute he ascends Mount Song.[22]
His clothes are fragrant still with musk perfume;
The pillow is slippery yet with red traces.
Thick, thick, the grass grows on the dike;
Floating, floating, the tumbleweed yearns for the isle.
Her plain zither plays the "Resentful Crane Song";
In the clear Milky Way she looks for the returning wild goose.[23]
The sea is broad and truly hard to cross;
The sky is high and not easy to traverse.
The moving cloud is nowhere to be found —
Xiao Shi stays in his chamber.[24]

All of Zhang's friends who heard of the affair marveled at it, but Zhang had determined on his own course of action. Yuan Zhen was especially close to him and so was in a position to ask him for an explanation. Zhang said, "It is a general rule that those women endowed by Heaven with great beauty invariably either destroy themselves or destroy someone else. If this Cui woman were to meet someone with wealth and position, she would use the favor her charms gain her to be cloud and rain or dragon or monster — I can't imagine what she might turn into. Of old, King Xin of the Shang and King You of the Zhou[25] were brought low by women,

---

[21]Again the theme of the goddess of the Luo River.

[22]Also known as the Central Mountain, it is located to the north of Dengfeng county in Henan province. Here the one ascending the mountain may refer to Zhang.

[23]Which might be carrying a message.

[24]Xiao Shi 簫史 was a well-known flute-playing immortal of the Spring and Autumn period.

[25]Xin Zhou 辛紂 was the infamous last ruler of the Shang dynasty, whose misrule and fall are attributed to the influence of his favorite

in spite of the size of their kingdoms and the extent of their power; their armies were scattered, their persons butchered, and down to the present day their names are objects of ridicule. I have no inner strength to withstand this evil influence. That is why I have resolutely suppressed my love."

At this statement everyone present sighed deeply.

Over a year later Cui was married, and Zhang for his part had taken a wife. Happening to pass through the town where she was living, he asked permission of her husband to see her, as a cousin. The husband spoke to her, but Cui refused to appear. Zhang's feelings of hurt showed on his face, and she was told about it. She secretly sent him a poem:

> Emaciated, I have lost my looks,
> Tossing and turning, too weary to leave my bed.
> It's not because of others I am ashamed to rise;
> For you I am haggard and before you ashamed.

She never did appear. Some days later when Zhang was about to leave, she sent another poem of farewell:

> Cast off and abandoned, what can I say now,
> Whom you loved so briefly long ago?
> Any love you had then for me
> Will do for the one you have now.

After this he never heard any more about her. His contemporaries for the most part conceded that Zhang had done well to rectify his mistake. I have often mentioned this among

concubine, Daji 妲己. King You (reigned 781–771 B.C.E.), last ruler of the Western Zhou, was misled by his consort Baosi 褒姒. The behavior of both rulers is traditionally attributed to their infatuation with the women they loved.

friends so that, forewarned, they might avoid doing such a thing, or if they did, that they might not be led astray by it. In the ninth month of a year in the Zhenyuan period, when an official, Li Gongchui, [26] was passing the night in my house at the Pacification Quarter, the conversation touched on the subject. He found it most extraordinary and composed a "Song of Yingying" to commemorate the affair. Cui's child-name was Yingying, and Gongchui used it for his poem.

Note: "The Story of Yingying" (the name of the heroine means "Oriole") is perhaps the most celebrated of all classical-language short stories. It is also probably the best known of all Chinese love stories, regardless of genre or language. Extremely well crafted, this beautiful and moving story formed the basis for the medley entitled "Master Dong's Western Chamber Romance" and the splendid Yuan drama, *Record of the Western Chamber* (recently translated in full into English as *The West Wing*) by Wang Shifu (fl. 1234).

The writing of fiction, even in the classical language, was traditionally considered by Confucian purists to be a trivial pursuit, and literati would seldom publicly admit that they indulged in it (this was, of course, particularly the case with vernacular-language fiction). Nonetheless, there are good grounds for attributing the story of Yingying to the famous poet and statesman, Yuan Chen. Among these is the long, stuffy poem by him that appears near the end of the story. Yuan was descended from Tabgatch royalty (the non-Han rulers of the Northern Wei dynasty). At the age of fourteen, he was already well versed in the classics and had passed the first of several competitive examinations. In 822 he was appointed to one of the highest bureaucratic offices in the empire but was removed from it shortly thereafter due to factional infighting at court. Yuan was a close friend of the renowned poet-official Bai Juyi.

---

[26]Gongchui was the style name of the Tang poet Li Shen (780–846).

(This translation is from Victor H. Mair, ed., *The Columbia Anthology of Traditional Chinese Literature*, pp. 851–61.)

莺莺傳

元稹

　　貞元中，有張生者，性溫茂，美風容，內秉堅孤，非禮不可入。或朋從遊宴，擾雜其間，他人皆洶洶拳拳，若將不及；張生容順而已，終不能亂。以是年二十三，未嘗近女色。知者詰之。謝而言曰："登徒子非好色者，是有兇行。余真好色者，而適不我值。何以言之？大凡物之尤者，未嘗不留連于心，是知其非忘情者也。"詰者識之。

　　無幾何，張生遊于蒲，蒲之東十餘里，有僧舍曰普救寺，張生寓焉。適有崔氏孀婦，將歸長安，路出於蒲，亦止茲寺。崔氏婦，鄭女也。張出于鄭，緒其親，乃異派之從母。是歲，渾瑊薨于蒲。有中人丁文雅，不善于軍，軍人因喪而擾，大掠蒲人。崔氏之家，財産甚厚，多奴仆。旅寓惶駭，不知所托。

　　先是，張與蒲將之黨有善，請吏護之，遂不及于難。十餘日，廉使杜確將天子命以總戎節，令于軍，軍由是戢。鄭厚張之德甚，因飾饌以命張，中堂宴之。復謂張曰："姨之孤嫠未亡，提攜幼稚，不幸屬師徒大潰，實不保其身。弱子幼女，猶君之生，豈可比常恩哉？今俾以仁兄禮奉見，冀所以報恩也。"命其子，曰歡郎，可十餘歲，容甚溫美。次命女："出拜爾兄，爾兄活爾。"久之辭疾，鄭怒曰："張兄保爾之命。不然，爾且擄矣，能復遠嫌乎？"久之，乃至。常服晬容，不加新飾，垂鬟接黛，雙臉銷紅而已。顏色豔異，光輝動人。張驚，為之禮。因坐鄭旁，以鄭之抑而見也，凝睇怨絕，若不勝其體者。問其年紀。鄭曰："今天子甲子歲之七月，終今貞元庚辰，生年十七矣。"張生稍以詞導之，不對。終席而罷。

　　張自是惑之，願致其情，無由得也。崔之婢曰紅娘，生私為之禮者數四，乘間遂道其衷。婢果驚沮，腆然而奔。張生悔之。翼日，婢復至，張生乃羞而謝之，不復云所求矣。婢因謂張曰：“郎之言，所不敢言，亦不敢泄。然而崔之姻族，君所詳也，何不因其德而求娶焉？”張曰：“余始自孩提，性不苟合。或時紈綺間居，曾莫流盼。不為當年，終有所蔽。昨日一席間，幾不自持。數日來，行忘止，食忘飽，恐不能逾旦暮。若因媒氏而娶，納采問名，則三數月間，索我于枯魚之肆矣。爾其謂我何？”婢曰：“崔之貞慎自保，雖所尊不可以非語犯之。下人之謀，固難入矣。然而善屬文，往往沈吟章句，怨慕者久之。君試為喻情詩以亂之不然，則無由也。”張大喜，立綴春詞二首以授之。是夕，紅娘復至，持彩箋以授張，曰：“崔所命也。”題其篇曰《明月三五夜》。其詞曰：

“待月西廂下，迎風戶半開。拂牆花影動，疑是玉人來。”

張亦微喻其旨。是夕，歲二月旬有四日矣。崔之東有杏花一株，攀援可逾。既望之夕，張因梯其樹而踰焉。達于西廂，則戶半開矣。紅娘寢于床，生因驚之。紅娘駭曰：“郎何以至？”張因紿之曰：“崔氏之牋召我也，爾為我告之。”無幾，紅娘復來，連曰：“至矣！至矣！”張生且喜且駭，必謂獲濟。及崔至，則端服嚴容，大數張曰：“兄之恩，活我之家，厚矣。是以慈母以弱子幼女見託。奈何因不令之婢，致淫逸之詞，始以護人之亂為義，而終掠亂以求之。是以亂易亂，其去幾何？誠欲寢其詞，則保人之姦，不義。明之于母，則背人之惠，不祥。將寄與婢仆，又懼不得發其真誠。是用托短章，願自陳啓。猶懼兄之見難，是用鄙靡之詞，以求其必至。非禮之動，能不愧心。特願以禮自持，無及于亂！”言畢，翻然而逝。張自失者久之。復踰而出，于是絕望。

數夕，張生臨軒獨寢，忽有人覺之。驚駭而起，則紅娘斂衾攜枕而至。撫張曰：“至矣！至矣！睡何為哉？”並枕重衾而去。張生拭目危坐久之，猶疑夢寐。然而修謹以俟。俄而紅娘捧崔氏而至。至，則嬌羞融冶，力不能運支體，曩時端莊，不復同矣。是夕，旬有八日也，斜月晶瑩，幽輝半床。張生飄飄然，且疑神仙之徒，不謂從人間至矣。有頃，寺鍾鳴，天將曉。紅娘促去。崔氏嬌啼宛轉，紅娘又捧之而去，終夕無一言。張生辨色而興，自疑曰：“豈其夢邪？”及明，睹妝在臂，香其衣，淚光熒熒然，猶瑩于茵席而已。

是後又十餘日，杳不復知。張生賦《會真詩》三十韻，未畢，而紅娘適至。因授之，以貽崔氏。自是復容之，朝隱而出，暮隱而入，同安于曩所謂西廂者，幾一月矣。張生常詰鄭氏之情，則曰：
"我不可奈何矣。"因欲就成之。

無何，張生將之長安，先以情諭之。崔氏宛無難詞，然而愁怨
之容動人矣。將行之再夕，不可復見，而張生遂西下。

數月，復遊于蒲，會于崔氏者又累月。崔氏甚工刀札，善屬文。
求索再三，終不可見。往往張生自以文挑，亦不甚睹覽。大略崔之
出人者，藝必窮極，而貌若不知；言則敏辯，而寡于酬對。待張之
意甚厚，然未嘗以詞繼之。時愁豔幽邃，恆若不識，喜慍之容，亦
罕形見。異時獨夜操琴，愁弄悽惻，張竊聽之，求之，則終不復鼓
矣。以是愈惑之。

張生俄以文調及期，又當西去。當去之夕，不復自言其情，愁
歎于崔氏之側。崔已陰知將訣矣，恭貌怡聲，徐謂張曰："始亂之，
終棄之，固其宜矣，愚不敢恨。必也君亂之，君終之，君之惠也。
則歿身之誓，其有終矣，又何必深感于此行？然而君既不懌，無以
奉寧。君常謂我善鼓琴，向時羞顏，所不能及。今且往矣，既君此
誠。"因命拂琴，鼓《霓裳羽衣序》，不數聲，哀音怨亂，不復知
其是曲也。左右皆唏噓。張亦遽止之，投琴，泣下流連，趨歸鄭所，
遂不復至。明旦而張行。

明年，文戰不勝，張遂止於京。因貽書於崔，以廣其意。崔氏
緘報之詞，粗載于此，曰："捧覽來問，撫愛過深，兒女之情，悲
喜交集。兼惠花勝一合，口脂五寸，致耀首膏唇之飾。雖荷殊恩，
誰復為容？睹物增懷，但積悲歎耳。伏承便于京中就業，進修之道，
固在便安。但恨僻陋之人，永以遐棄。命也如此，知復何言？自去
秋已來，常忽忽如有所失。於喧嘩之下，或勉為語笑，閒宵自處，
無不淚零。乃至夢寢之間，亦多感咽。離憂之思，綢繆繾綣，暫若
尋常。幽會未終，驚魂已斷。雖半衾如暖，而思之甚遙。一昨拜辭，
倏逾舊歲。長安行樂之地，觸緒牽情。何幸不忘幽微，眷念無斁。
鄙薄之志，無以奉酬。至於終始之盟，則固不忒。鄙昔中表相因，
或同宴處。婢僕見誘，遂致私誠。兒女之心，不能自固。君子有援
琴之挑，鄙人無投梭之拒。及薦寢席，義盛意深，愚陋之情，永謂
終託。豈期既見君子，而不能定情。致有自獻之羞，不復明侍巾幘。
沒身永恨，含歎何言？倘仁人用心，俯遂幽眇，雖死之日，猶生之
年。如或達士略情，舍小從大，以先配為醜行，以要盟為可欺。則
當骨化形銷，丹誠不泯，因風委露，猶託清塵。存沒之誠，言盡于
此。臨紙嗚咽，情不能申。千萬珍重！珍重千萬！玉環一枚，是兒

嬰年所弄，寄充君子下體所佩。玉取其堅潤不渝，環取其終始不絕。
兼亂絲一絢，文竹茶碾子一枚。此數物不足見珍，意者欲君子如玉
之真，弊志如環不解。淚痕在竹，愁緒縈絲。因物達情，永以為好
耳。心迩身遐，拜會無期。幽憤所鍾，千里神合。千萬珍重！春風
多厲，強飯為嘉。慎言自保，無以鄙為深念。"張生發其書於所知，
由是時人多聞之。

　　所善楊巨源好屬詞，因為賦《崔娘詩》一絕云："清潤潘郎玉
不如，中庭蕙草雪銷初。風流才子多春思，腸斷蕭娘一紙書。"河
南元稹，亦續生《會真詩》三十韻，詩曰：

> 微月透簾櫳，螢光度碧空。遙天初縹緲，低樹漸蔥朧。
> 龍吹過庭竹，鸞歌拂井桐。羅綃垂薄霧，環佩響輕風。
> 絳節隨金母，雲心捧玉童。更深人悄悄，晨會雨濛濛。
> 珠瑩光文履，花明隱繡龍。瑤釵行彩鳳，羅帔掩丹虹。
> 言自瑤華浦，將朝碧玉宮。因遊洛城北，偶向宋家東。
> 戲調初微拒，柔情已暗通。低鬟蟬影動，回步玉塵蒙。
> 轉面流花雪，登床抱綺叢。鴛鴦交頸舞，翡翠合歡籠。
> 眉黛羞偏聚，唇朱暖更融。氣清蘭蕊馥，膚潤玉肌豐。
> 無力慵移腕，多嬌愛斂躬。汗流珠點點，髮亂綠蔥蔥。
> 方喜千年會，俄聞五夜窮。留連時有恨，繾綣意難終。
> 慢臉含愁態，芳詞誓素衷。贈環明運合，留結表心同。
> 啼粉流宵鏡，殘燈遠暗蟲。華光猶苒苒，旭日漸瞳瞳。
> 乘鶩還歸洛，吹簫亦上嵩。衣香猶染麝，枕膩尚殘紅。
> 冪冪臨塘草，飄飄思渚蓬。素琴鳴怨鶴，清漢望歸鴻。
> 海闊誠難渡，天高不易沖。行雲無處所，蕭史在樓中。

　　張之友聞之者，莫不聳異之，然而張志亦絕矣。稹特與張厚，
因徵其詞。張曰："大凡天之所命尤物也，不妖其身，必妖於人。
使崔氏子遇合富貴，乘寵嬌，不為雲，不為雨，為蛟為螭，吾不知
其所變化矣。昔殷之辛，周之幽，據百萬之國，其勢甚厚。然而一
女子敗之，潰其眾，屠其身，至今為天下僇笑。予之德不足以勝妖
孽，是用忍情。"於時坐者皆為深歎。

　　後歲餘，崔已委身於人，張亦有所娶。適經所居，乃因其夫言
於崔，求以外兄見。夫語之，而崔終不為出。張怨念之誠，動於顏
色。崔知之，潛賦一章詞曰：

"自從消瘦減容光，萬轉千回懶下床。不為旁人羞不起，為郎憔悴卻羞郎。"

竟不之見。後數日，張生將行，又賦一章以謝絕云：

"棄置今何道，當時且自親。還將舊時意，憐取眼前人。"

自是絕不復知矣。時人多許張為善補過者。予常於朋會之中，往往及此意者，夫使知者不為，為之者不惑。貞元歲九月，執事李公垂宿於予靖安里第，語及於是。公垂卓然稱異，遂為《鶯鶯歌》以傳之。崔氏小名鶯鶯，公垂以命篇。

Tale 4.21

A Chronicle of My Journey through Zhou and Qin

By Niu Sengru
Translated by Josiah J. Stork

During the Zhenyuan Reign Era (785–805 CE), I took the presented scholar examinations and failed. I returned back to Wan and Ye.[1] Once I had gotten to the road south of Yique beneath Mt. Minggao,[2] I was going to seek lodging in the house of a resident of Da'an.[3] The sun was setting, and I lost my way and had not yet arrived. I went a little over ten *li* further and came to an incredibly easy road. When night arrived and the moon started to come out, I suddenly smelled a strange fragrance and thus hastened to walk towards it, not knowing how far I walked. I saw the light of a fire and thought it might be a farmhouse. I once again spurred myself forward and came to a manor. Its door and courtyard were like those of a rich and powerful family. There was a doorkeeper in yellow who asked, "Master, where are you from?"

---

[1]Wan Ye 宛葉, these two neighboring areas constitute a relatively large area across central Henan province.

[2]Yique 伊闕 refers to modern-day Luoyang. Mt. Minggao 鳴皋山 is better known as Mt. Jiugao 九皋山 today.

[3]Also south of Luoyang.

I replied, "I am Sengru, my surname is Niu. I tried for the Presented Scholar but failed the test and am returning home. I was originally heading toward the house of a resident of Da'an, but I took the wrong road and came here. I only beg to be allowed to spend the night — I ask for nothing else."

A young serving girl with a little bun came out and reproached the man in yellow, saying, "Who is outside of the door?"

The man in yellow said, "There is a visitor." The man in yellow went in to inform [the owner of the house]. Shortly thereafter, he came out and said, "Master, please come in."

I asked which family's house this was, and the man in yellow said, "Just go in and there will be no need to ask."

I went through more than ten doors and came to a great hall, which was covered by a beaded curtain. There were around one hundred people clothed in red or purple standing on the steps of the dais. Those to my left and right said, "Bow to meet Her Majesty."

Someone spoke from within the curtain, saying, "I am the mother of Emperor Wen of Han (r. 180–157 BCE), Empress Dowager Bo. This is a temple, and you should not have come. How do you come here?"

I said, "My home is Wan, and I was about to return, but lost my way. I am afraid of being killed by jackal or tiger and venture to entrust you with my life and beg to stay a night. Empress Dowager, please understand and accept my request."

The Empress Dowager ordered that the curtains be wound up, left the seat, and said, "I am the mother of old Lord Wen of Han, you are a famous scholar of the Tang courts. Our relation is not that of minister and ruler. I hope that we may simplify courtesies.[4] Simply come up into the hall and meet with me."

---

[4]Do not be overly polite.

The Empress Dowager was wearing white silk clothes, and her stature and appearance were refined and grand, but she was not very ornamented. She comforted me, saying, "I hope your journey was not too wearying." She bade me sit, and in a meal's time, there was the sound of cooking in the hall. The Empress Dowager said, "The breeze and the moon tonight are so lovely. By chance there are two women who are seeking me out to accompany me. Moreover, I have chanced upon an esteemed guest, so how could I not call a gathering?"

She called to her attendants, "May I trouble the two ladies to come out and meet this refined scholar?"

After a good while, two women came out from inside followed by several hundred people. The one who stood in the front had a narrow waist, a long face, and thick hair; but she was unadorned. She was wearing green clothing and was only about twenty-something. The Empress Dowager said, "This is Gaozu's Lady Qi."[5]

I bowed down, and the lady also bowed. There was another person with a round forehead, a soft face, and a steady body. Her appearance was relaxed and her attitude leisurely. Radiance shone from her, extending near and far. She was fond of frequently knitting her eyebrows.[6] Much of her clothing was embroidered with flowers, and she was younger than Empress Bo. The Empress looked and pointed at her, saying, "This is Emperor

---

[5]Lady Qi 戚 (?–194 BCE) was a consort of Emperor Gaozu of Han 漢 高祖 (256–195 BCE), better known as Liu Bang 劉邦. She was viciously treated by Liu Bang's wife and empress, Empress Dowager Lü 呂太后 (241–180 BCE) after his death because Liu Bang favored Lady Qi's son as heir over Empress Dowager Lü's son.

[6]The verb here rendered as *knitting her eyebrows* is rare enough that it is not in most computer software. The only time I can see it being mentioned other than here is in a passage in the *Zhuangzi* where it is used to describe Xi Shi 西施, another famous beauty of China.

Yuan's Wang Qiang."[7] I bowed to her as I had done to Lady Qi. Wang Qiang also bowed. Each of us then took our seats.

After we were seated, the Empress Dowager ordered a nobleman from among those in purple clothes, saying, "Let us welcome Ms. Yang and Ms. Pan as they come."

After a long time, five-colored clouds appeared in the sky, descending. I heard the sound of laughter and talking approaching.[8] The Empress Dowager said, "Yang and Pan have arrived." Suddenly, the sound of carriages and the ringing of horse hooves mixed together. Gauze and silk shone and sparkled, and I could not take it all in.

There were two women who came down from the clouds. I stood up at the side. I saw the first, who had a slender waist, a delicate body, and a clear complexion. She was incredibly at ease, wore yellow clothing and a jade crown, and was thirty-something years old. The Empress Dowager looked and pointed at her, saying, "This is Consort Taizhen of the Tang Court."[9]

I then knelt down to greet her, solemnly bowing with the ritual of a minister [to his lord]. Taizhen said, "I offended a former

---

[7]Wang Qiang 王嬙 (c. 52 BCE–8 CE) is better known as Wang Zhaojun 王昭君. She is said to have entered Emperor Yuan of Han's 漢元帝 (r. 48–33 BCE) harem and was then gifted to a Xiongnu 匈奴 leader for political reasons. She is one of the four great beauties of Chinese history, and the legends about her are many.

[8]More literally, the verb here is to *lie down and draw closer*.

[9]719–756 CE. Better known as Yang Guifei (Prized Consort Yang). The epithet here used is the name given to her during the brief time she spent as a Daoist nun, which was done to alleviate potential criticism that Emperor Xuanzong (r. 713–756 CE) was taking her from his son, the Prince of Shou, Li Mao 李瑁.

emperor (the *former emperor* refers to Suzong),[10] and the imperial court did not install me in the ranks of imperial concubines. Is performing this ritual not empty? I dare not accept it." Nevertheless, she bowed in return.

Another woman came, with thick flesh and clever vision, a petite frame, as well as spotless white skin. She was extremely young and was clad in loose, thick clothing. The Empress Dowager looked and pointed at her, and said, "This is the Virtuous Consort Pan of Qi."[11] I bowed to her as I had with Wang Zhaojun. The imperial concubine bowed in return.

Soon after this, the Empress Dowager ordered that food be brought forward, and after a little while, the food came. It was fragrant and clean and in a great variety. I could not name any of the dishes. With my unrefined and avaricious appetite, I could not try them all.

When this was finished, wine was set out. The utensils that they used were all made of precious jade. The Empress Dowager said to Taizhen, "Why have you not come to see me for so long?"

Taizhen calmed her countenance and replied, "The third master (During the Tianbao Reign Era, most of the people in the

---

[10]This note appears in the text and is not my addition. Suzong 肅宗 (r. 756–762 CE) was the emperor immediately after Xuanzong and two emperors before the current ruler, Dezong.

[11]This seems to be conflating two consorts of Chinese history. The first, Pan Yuer 潘玉兒 or Pan Yunu 潘玉奴 (?–501 CE), was a consort of Xiao Baojuan 蕭寶卷 (r. 498–501 CE), a ruler of the Southern Qi Dynasty 南齊. She, however, was made a Prized Consort 貴妃, not a Virtuous Consort 淑妃. (Although both are among the four highest ranks of imperial concubines, their titles and status are somewhat different.) The second is the unnamed Virtuous Consort Pan (?–453) 潘淑妃, a concubine of Emperor Wen of the (Liu) Song Dynasty (劉)宋文帝 (r. 424–453 CE). While she is called by this title, she is clearly from the wrong dynasty.

palace called Xuanzong *third master*.) has visited the Huaqing Palace several times. I accompanied and waited on him, so I have had no time to come."

The Empress Dowager then spoke to Consort Pan, "You also don't come. Why is that?" Consort Pan was unable to hide her laughter and could not answer.

Taizhen then looked at Consort Pan and said to her, "Consort Pan told Yunu (Taizhen's name)[12] that she is vexed by the Marquis of Donghun's[13] unrestrained behavior. He stays out hunting all day long, and thus she does not have time to visit."

The Empress Dowager asked me, "Who is the current Son of Heaven?"

I replied, "The current emperor is named Kuo, he is the eldest son of Emperor Daizong."[14]

Taizhen laughed and said, "Old lady Shen's[15] son is the Son of Heaven? How strange!"

The Empress Dowager said, "What kind of Lord is he?"

I replied, "This lowly minister is insufficient to know the virtue of the Monarch."

---

[12] This note is incorrect. It is, in fact, Consort Pan whose name is Yunu. Yang Guifei's given name was Yuhuan 玉環. Clearly, however, this is to be understood as meaning that Yang Guifei is reporting what Consort Pan told her. In all likelihood, there was a copyist's error somewhere in this text's history by which Yuhuan became Yunu. This could be most clearly stated as *Consort Pan told me that*.

[13] The posthumous title of Xiao Baojuan 蕭寶卷, Consort Pan's master.

[14] Kuo 適 refers to Emperor Dezong (r. 779–805 CE).

[15] An unofficial and potentially disrespectful way of referring to Empress Ruizhen 睿真皇后, consort of Daizong. (It is known that her family name was Shen 沈. Other personal information, including given name, date of birth, and date of death are all unknown. She disappeared in 759 during the aftermath of the An Lushan Rebellion.)

The Empress Dowager said, "You need not be modest. Simply say it."

I said, "Among the people it is said that he is a wise sovereign."

The Empress Dowager nodded three or four times, and she ordered that alcohol be brought forward and music be added. All of the musicians were young women. After the alcohol had gone around several times, the music also subsequently stopped. The Empress Dowager asked Lady Qi to drum the zither. The Lady wore a jade ring, and it shone from her finger. (*Miscellaneous Notes on the Western Capital* says, "The gold ring, whose metal had been refined 100 times, and which Gaozu gave the lady, mirrored the bones of her finger.") She drew up the zither and drummed it, and its sound was extremely sorrowful.

The Empress Dowager said, "The Refined Scholar Niu came here by chance seeking lodging. All of you ladies also come to visit me by chance. Yet now we have nothing with which [to express] fully the joy of all our lives. The Refined Scholar Niu is indeed a talented man. Why don't we each compose a poem to express our feelings? Is this not also a good idea?" She then gave each a pen and paper; and in an instant, the poems were completed.

The Empress Dowager's poem read:

When the moon rested over the flowery palace, I was able to
   wait on the monarch
Till now I still blame Lady Guan.[16]

---

[16]Lady Guan was another of Liu Bang's concubines. According to the 49th *juan* of *The Grand Scribe's Records*, Empress Dowager Bo (then only a concubine), and Zhao Zi'er 趙子兒 made a pledge that if any of them gained favor, they would not forget the others. The other two found favor with Liu Bang before the Empress Dowager but did not attempt to share this blessing with her.

Of old, the House of Han was a place of music and song;
How many falls and springs have the misty grasses
   experienced?

Wang Qiang's poem read:

Amidst the snow, I cannot see the spring from this yurt.
Although the Han clothes are old, the tearstains on them are
   forever new.
Now I still despise Mao Yanshou,[17]
Who loved to misrepresent people in his painting.

Lady Qi's poem read:

Since leaving Han Palace, I have stopped dancing the dances of
   Chu.
Unable to adorn myself or wear makeup, I hate the king.
Without gold how can I welcome the Old Men of Shang
   Mountain?[18]
Did Ms. Lü ever fear the man of steel?[19]

Taizhen's poem read:

When my golden hairpin fell to ground, I said goodbye to the
   king.

---

[17]The story goes that he was a court painter who, because Wang
Zhaojun would not bribe him, intentionally made her portrait ugly.
Because of this, the Emperor never came to see her; and, when looking
for a woman to give to the Huns, gave her away.

[18]Four old Daoist practitioners that Liu Bang, Lady Qi's husband,
admired and asked to serve in his court.

[19]This Ms. Lü refers to Empress Lü. She wanted to kill Lady Qi's son,
but Liu Bang appointed Zhou Chang 周昌 to counsel his son in hopes
that he could save him. In the *History of Han* 漢書 Zhou Chang is called a
man of steel (literally something more like *wooden strength*).

Tears like pearls of blood fall to fill the imperial bed.
After the clouds and rain parted at Mawei[20]
Li Palace[21] never again heard "Rainbow Skirts."[22]

Consort Pan's poem read:

How many times have the autumn moon and spring zephyrs
    returned?
Rivers and mountains remain the same, yet the Palace of Ye is
    no more.
Long ago Donghun[23] made a Lotus Palace,[24]
And once vainly thought of wearing gold-embroidered clothes.

Over and over they urged me to write a poem. I could not
decline. I then responded by making a poem that read:

A fragrant wind led me to the highest heaven.[25]
I climb a staircase of clouds from the earth to the moon and
    bow to the cave immortals.
Together we talk about mournful events from the world of
    men.
I do not know what year tonight is.

────────────────────

[20]This is the location where guards mutinied and forced Xuanzong
to execute Yang Guifei. Also, the phrase *clouds and rain* is frequently a
symbol of sexual love.

[21]The location most associated with the love between Xuanzong and
Yang Guifei.

[22]This is part of the name of a song which Yang Guifei was famous
for dancing.

[23]The title to which Consort Pan's husband was demoted after his
death.

[24]Literally, a *lotus place*. This is apparently a reference to palaces or
even the houses of wealthy people who could afford to plant these
flowers.

[25]This actually specifies that it is Daluotian 大羅天, literally *the great
gauze heaven*, the highest of the heavenly realms in Daoism.

Additionally, there was a woman who was talented with a flute. Her hair was bound in a short bun and her shirt fastened with a Wu belt. Her appearance was incredibly lovely and she was very charming. She had come with Consort Pan. The Empress Dowager had her sit near to herself, occasionally ordered her to play the flute, and also frequently gave her wine. The Empress Dowager looked [at me] and said, "Do you know her? She is Green Pearl of the Shi Family. Consort Pan adopted her as a younger sister and thus she came together with Consort Pan." Consequently, the Empress Dowager said, "How can Green Pearl be without a poem?"

Green Pearl bowed in gratitude, and composed a poem that said:

> Today we are already not the people of olden days.
> The sound of my flute vainly blames Lun, King of Zhao,[26]
> The red (face) destroyed and the green (jewelry) shattered below a flowery tower.[27]
> The Golden Valley[28] will not see spring again for a thousand years.

When her poem had finished, the wine came around again. The Empress Dowager said, "The Refined Scholar Niu has come a long way. Who will accompany him tonight?"

---

[26]This king killed her lover, Shi Chong 石崇, in 300 CE. See p. 592 n2 for detailed information about Shi chong.

[27]As flowers tend to represent women and Green Pearl is said to have jumped from a tower, this should be understood as discussing her suicide.

[28]In Luoyang.

Lady Qi first got up and declined, saying, "My son, Ruyi 如意[29] is already grown, and thus I cannot and should not do this. Moreover, I truly cannot."

Consort Pan declined, saying, "Donghun believes that [I] Yu'er (the consort's name) have died and left the kingdom. I do not intend to turn my back on him."

Green Pearl declined, saying, "The Chamberlain for the Palace Garrison, Shi, is naturally severe and jealous. Now, even if I were to die, I could not reach this level of illicit behavior."

The Empress Dowager said, "Taizhen is the prized consort of a former emperor of this dynasty. There is nothing else to be said." She then looked at and spoke to Wang Qiang, saying, "Zhaojun originally married Chanyu Huhan[30] and was again married by Chanyu Zhuleiruodi.[31] You have certainly done as you wished. Moreover, what can the foreign devils from those bitterly cold places do? Zhaojun, please do not decline." Zhaojun did not respond but lowered her eyebrows in shame and regret.

Shortly thereafter, each returned to their own resting place, and I was sent into Zhaojun's courtyard by those on my left and right.

As dawn was about to break, the attendants told me that I must get up. Holding my hands, Zhaojun cried at saying goodbye. Suddenly, I heard an order from the Empress Dowager outside, and I then went out to see the Empress Dowager. The Empress Dowager said, "This is not a place where you, my master, can stay

---

[29]Liu Ruyi 劉如意, 208–194 BCE, King Yin of Zhao 趙隱王. He is the previously mentioned favorite of Liu Bang who caused enmity between Lady Qi and Empress Lü Zhi 呂雉.

[30]Chanyu is a title for rulers of the Xiongnu 匈奴 peoples during the Qin Dynasty. This particular chanyu is actually named Huhanye 呼韓邪 and ruled approximately from 58 BCE until his death in 31 BCE.

[31]This is the chanyu who succeeded Huhanye and is usually known as Fuzhuleiruodi 复株絫若鞮. His reign was from 31 BCE to 20 BCE.

for a long time. You should speedily return, so quickly make your goodbyes. Please do not forget your previous joys."

She once again asked for wine, and the wine went around again. Lady Qi, Consort Pan, and Green Pearl all cried and then said goodbye. The Empress Dowager ordered [a servant in] cinnabar clothes to send me toward Da'an. Once we arrived at the western path, the servant suddenly disappeared.

At that time, it was starting to brighten.

Once I reached Da'an, I asked the people of the village. The people of the village said, "More than ten *li* from here is Empress Bo's ancestral shrine."

I then went back and looked at the shrine. It was desolate and destroyed, and I could not go in. It was not what I had seen before. There was a fragrance on my clothes that after ten days still had not dispersed, and I never did know why.

周秦行纪

牛僧孺

　　余真元中舉進士落第，歸宛葉間。至伊闕南道鳴皋山下，將宿大安民舍。會暮，失道，不至。更十餘里，行一道，甚易。夜月始出，忽聞有異香氣，因趨進行，不知近遠。見火明，意謂莊家，更前驅，至一大宅，門庭若富豪家。有黃衣閽人曰："郎君何至？"

　　余答曰："僧孺，姓牛，應進士落第往家。本往大安民舍，誤道來此。直乞宿，無他。"

　　中有小鬟青衣出，責黃衣曰："門外誰何？"

　　黃衣曰："有客。"黃衣入告，少時出曰："請郎君入。"

　　余問誰氏宅。黃衣曰："第進，無須問。"

　　入十餘門，至大殿。殿蔽以珠簾，有朱衣紫衣人百數，立階陛間。左右曰："拜陛下。"

　　簾中語曰："妾漢文帝母薄太后，此是廟，郎不當來，何辱至？"

　　余曰："臣家宛下，將歸，失道，恐死豺虎，敢託命乞宿。太后幸聽受。"

　　太后遣軸簾，避席曰："妾故漢文君母，君唐朝名士，不相君臣，幸希簡敬，便上殿來見。"

　　太后着練衣，狀貌瑰偉，不甚粧飾。勞余曰："行役無苦乎？"召坐。食頃間，殿內庖廚聲。太后曰："今夜風月甚佳，偶有二女伴相尋。況又遇嘉賓，不可不成一會。"

　　呼左右"屈兩箇娘子出見秀才。"

　　良久，有女二人從中至，從者數百。前立者一人，狹腰長面，多髮不粧，衣青衣，僅可二十餘。太后曰："此高祖戚夫人。"

326

余下拜，夫人亦拜。更一人，圓額柔臉穩身，貌舒態逸，光彩射遠近，時時好矉，多服花繡，年低薄后。后顧指曰：“此元帝王嬙。”余拜如戚夫人，王嬙復拜。各就坐。

坐定，太后使紫衣中貴人曰：“迎楊家潘家來。”

久之，空中見五色雲下，聞笑語聲寢近。太后曰：“楊潘至矣。”忽車音馬跡相雜，羅綺煥耀，旁視不給。

有二女子從雲中下，余起立於側，見前一人，纖腰身修，睟容，甚閒暇，衣黃衣，冠玉冠，年三十以來。太后顧指曰：“此是唐朝太真妃子。”

予即伏謁，肅拜如臣禮。太真曰：“妾得罪先帝（先帝謂肅宗也），皇朝不置妾在后妃數中。設此禮，豈不虛乎？不敢受。”却答拜。

更一人，厚肌敏視，身小，材質潔白，齒極卑，被寬博衣。太后顧而指曰：“此齊潘淑妃。”余拜之如王昭君，妃復拜。

既而太后命進饌。少時饌至，芳潔萬端，皆不得名字。粗欲之腹，不能足食。

已，更具酒，其器盡寶玉。太后語太真曰：“何久不來相看？”

太真謹容對曰：“三郎（天寶中，宮人呼玄宗多曰三郎）數幸華清宮，扈從不暇至。”

太后又謂潘妃曰：“子亦不來，何也？”潘妃匿笑不禁，不成對。

太真乃視潘妃而對曰：“潘妃向玉奴（太真名也）說，懊惱東昏侯疎狂，終日出獵，故不得時謁耳。”

太后問余：“今天子爲誰？”

余對曰：“今皇帝名适，代宗皇帝長子。”

太真笑曰：“沈婆兒作天子也，大奇！”

太后曰：“何如主？”

余對曰：“小臣不足以知君德。”

太后曰：“然無謙，但言之。”

余曰：“民間傳英明聖武。”

太后首肯三四。太后命進酒加樂，樂妓皆年少女子。酒環行數周，樂亦隨輟。太后請戚夫人鼓琴，夫人約指以玉環，光照於手（《西京雜記》云：“高祖與夫人百鍊金環，照見指骨也”），引琴而鼓，聲甚怨。

太后曰："牛秀才邂逅逆旅到此，諸娘子又偶相訪，今無以盡平生歡。牛秀才固才士，盍各賦詩言志，不亦善乎？"遂各授與牋筆，逡巡詩成。

太后詩曰：

月寢花宮得奉君，至今猶愧管夫人。
漢家舊日笙歌地，煙草幾經秋又春。

王嬙詩曰：

雪裏穹廬不見春，漢衣雖舊淚長新。
如今猶恨毛延壽，愛把丹青錯畫人。

戚夫人詩曰：

自別漢宮休楚舞，不能粧粉恨君王。
無金豈得迎商叟，呂氏何曾畏木強。

太真詩曰：

金釵墮地別君王，紅淚流珠滿御牀。
雲雨馬嵬分散後，驪宮無復聽《霓裳》。

潘妃詩曰：

秋月春風幾度歸，江山猶是鄴宮非。
東昏舊作蓮花地，空想曾拖金縷衣。

再三趣余作詩，余不得辭，遂應教作詩曰：

香風引到大羅天，月地雲階拜洞仙。
共道人間惆悵事，不知今夕是何年。

別有善笛女子，短鬟，衫吳帶，貌甚美，多媚。潘妃偕來，太后以接座居之，時令吹笛，往往亦及酒。太后顧而謂曰："識此否？

石家綠珠也。潘妃養作妹，故潘妃與俱來。"太后因曰："綠珠豈能無詩乎？"

綠珠拜謝，作詩曰：

此地原非昔日人，笛聲空怨趙王倫。
紅殘綠碎花樓下，金谷千年更不春。

詩畢，酒既至。太后曰："牛秀才遠來，今夕誰人與伴？"

戚夫人先起辭曰："如意兒長成，固不可，且不宜如此。況實為非乎？"

潘妃辭曰："東昏以玉兒（妃名），身死國除，玉兒不擬負他。"

綠珠辭曰："石衛尉性嚴忌，今有死，不可及亂。"

太后曰："太真今朝先帝貴妃，不可言其他。"乃顧謂王嬙曰："昭君始嫁呼韓單于，復爲株纍若鞮單于婦，固自用。且苦寒地胡鬼何能爲？昭君幸無辭。"昭君不對，低眉羞恨。

俄各歸休，余爲左右送入昭君院。

會將旦，侍人告起得也。昭君泣以持別。忽聞外有太后命，余遂出見太后。太后曰："此非郎君久留地，宜亟還。便別矣。幸無忘向來歡。"

更索酒，酒再行，戚夫人、潘妃、綠珠皆泣下，竟辭去。太后使朱衣送往大安，抵西道，旋失使人所在。

時始明矣。

余就大安里，問其里人。里人云："去此十餘里，有薄后廟。"

余卻回，望廟宇，荒毀不可入，非向者所見矣。余衣上香經十餘日不歇，竟不知其何如。

Tale 4.22

Lament from the Xiang River:
A Prose with a Preface

By Shen Yazhi
Translated by Xin Zou

"Lament from the Xiang River" is a bewitchingly beautiful story, and no scholar has ever narrated it. Yet those who indulge in licentious affairs are often not awakened [to the danger of their behavior]. Now I wish briefly to outline this story, hoping simply to illustrate the sincere feeling in it. My friend Wei Ao is skillful in composing *yuefu* ballads, and thus I have drawn on Wei's work and elaborated on it, in response to his ballad on this story.

During the Chuigong reign period (685–688), His Majesty graced the Ascendant Vigor Palace in Luoyang with his presence.[1]

---

[1]The Chuigong era was the reign of Emperor Ruizong 睿宗 (662–716) but it was his mother, Empress Wu 武 (r. 690–705), who was actually the power behind the throne. Shangyang Palace was located west of the imperial palace in Luoyang, the Eastern Capital of the Tang. Readers will also see places names such as those of the Luo Bridge and the Tongluo Ward as the story progresses. These were all actual places that a visitor to Tang dynasty Luoyang would see. According to Nienhauser, the Luo Bridge (also known as Luoyang Bridge or the Tianjin Bridge) spans the Luo River which divides the northern and southern sections of Luoyang. Tongluo li was located northeast of the bridge. See Nienhauser, "Creativity and Storytelling," p. 51, footnote no. 78.

Scholar Zheng, a candidate recommended [for the presented-scholar examination] by the College of Ultimate Learning, set out early one morning from the Bronze Camel Ward. As he was about to cross the Luo Bridge under the dawn moon, he heard a sound of sobbing arising from under the bridge — it was a sound of great distress. The scholar dismounted and sought the source. Under the bridge, he found a dazzlingly beautiful young lady. Shyly covering up her face with her sleeve, she sighed and said to the scholar, "I am an orphan reared by my elder brother; my sister-in-law is fierce and often torments me. I've made up my mind to drown myself in this river and just wanted to lament my own fate for a moment before I go."

"Are you willing to follow me back home?" The scholar asked.

"I will serve as your maid and servant with no regrets." She answered.

The lady thus lived with the scholar and came to be called *Siren* (literally, the lady by the river). She could recite from memory works from the Chu state, such as the "Nine Songs," "Summoning the Soul," and the "Nine Disputations," and used these works as models for composing her own plaintive lines set to the tunes of this *Chuci* style. Her wording was so beautiful that she remained unrivalled at the time. In this style, she came to write "On a Warm Breeze," which read:[2]

---

[2]The term *guangfeng* 光風 appears in "Summoning the Soul," a classic of the Songs of Chu. After depicting the hostile outside world, the poet describes an ideal residence to summon the wandering soul back home: "O soul, come back! Return to your old abode. All the quarters of the world are full of the harm and evil. Hear while I describe for you your quiet and respectful home... A warm breeze bends the melilotus and sets the tall orchids swaying..." 魂兮歸來！反故居些。天地四方，多賊姦些。像設君室，靜閒安些…光風轉蕙，氾崇蘭些。For a complete English translation, see David Hawks, *The Songs of the South: An Anthology of Ancient Chinese Poems by Qu Yuan and Other Poets* (New York:

Blooming flowers illustrate the splendor of springtime.

Green plants have now returned as fragrant blossoms.

[I] wish to live in the house of sprouts and stay amidst calyxes,

To hide deep in this boudoir to adorn myself.

Seeing my elegant deportment in fullness, I feel bashful,

Let the long mist be my veil and cover me up.

Intoxicated in this steamy sunlight, endless and vast,

Enchanted in this expanse of waves and shore, stretching a
    thousand miles.

Dawn will find me content, at dusk I will rejoice.

I dance, like willow branches, tender and pliant,

Always gracefully, swiftly or slow.

Flushed with wine, I extol flora in my song,

Like fine silken gauze, like lightening, the ripples sparkle;

[and under the ripples] lichens swing and swirl.[3]

Penguin Books Ltd, 1985), p. 226. To some extent, Siren, the heroine in this tale, also suffered hardship like the wandering soul in "Summoning the Soul." It therefore makes sense that she would write in the style of *Chuci* to celebrate her own new life when she finally settled down. Moreover, as readers will soon find out as the story unfolds, the heroine is actually a dragon lady from Lake Dongting in the South. That may also explain why she was well versed in *Chuci*, or the Songs from the South.

[3]It is difficult to understand the last line of this poem. Indeed, multiple variants are found in different editions, suggesting that earlier readers and compilers might also have been unsure of its exact meaning. I tried to follow the logic of the poem itself while taking into consideration potential references to other *Chuci* style poems. For example, the last line seems to echo a line from the "Nine Disputations": The lovely girls are drunk with wine, their faces are flushed. With amorous glances and flirting looks, their eyes like wavelets sparkle 美人既醉，朱顏酡些。娭光眇視，目曾波些。See Hawks, The *Songs from the South*, p. 228.

The scholar was living in poverty. One day, Siren opened a basket, took out a bolt of delicate silk, and asked the scholar to sell it. He did and a Tartar paid him a thousand *liang of* gold. And so they lived for several years, until a time approached when the scholar was about to visit Chang'an. That evening, Siren said to him, "I used to be a concubine from the Dragon Palace in the Xiang River. After my banishment, I followed you around. My time with you has now come to an end, and there is no reason for me to stay with you any longer. Yet before I depart, I just wanted to bid you farewell." With these words, the scholar and Siren held each other's hands and wept. The scholar tried very hard to persuade her to stay but was unable to do so. In the end, she left.

More than ten years later, the scholar's elder brother became the Prefect of Yuezhou (in modern Hunan). One day, it was the "Lustration Festival".[4] The scholar went along with his family to climb the Yueyang Tower. At its top, they set out a feast and looked out towards the E zhu Islet.[5] While others were busy rapturously enjoying themselves, the scholar sorrowfully intoned these lines:

My sorrows are boundless, resembling the vast lake waters,
Gazing at the three rivers of the Xiang, my longing for those
good old days grew intense.

---

[4] The exact time and meaning of the *Shangsi jie* 上巳節 or the "Lustration Festive" changed throughout history. During the Tang, it was celebrated on the third day of the third lunar month and was then one of the three major holidays. It was a common practice to have a gathering by a local river or lake to enjoy the spring time. See note 87 in Nienhauser's work and Derk Bodde, *Festivals in Classical China* (Princeton: Princeton University Press, 1975), pp. 273–288.

[5] The tower is located in the city of Yueyang on the banks of the Yangzi River.

Before his song ended, through the waves of the lake came a patterned boat. In its center stood a decorated theater stage, over a hundred feet tall, with curtains and ornamented railings around it. As the curtains rose gradually, musicians emerged playing string and percussion instruments. The musicians, all transcendent beauties, were draped in fine silk garb as light as mists and as colorful as rainbow, with long and broad skirts and sleeves. From among them, one beauty stood up and started to dance, yet her knitted brows hinted that she was full of anguish and misery, and she resembled Siren. As she danced, she sang this song:

> Heading upstream through the blue mountains, I came to the
>   river's shore,
> Like a swaying green skirt, the waves of the Xiang River curl
>   up as they flow;
> The lotus leaves are yet to unfurl/unfold, [Resembling my
>   pent-up heart],
> Except for returning together, where else should I go?

When the dance ended, the beauty straightened her sleeves, and fixed her gaze peacefully [on the tower]. People in the tower were enjoying this performance just when suddenly the wind and waves rose furiously. As a result, they lost sight of the boat and did not know where it had gone.

In the thirteenth year of the Yuanhe reign period (818), I heard this story from friends. I took the opportunity to supplement this old story with further details and all the poems above, and titled it "Lament from the Xiang River," hoping to make it a companion piece to Nan Zhaosi's (fl. 828) "A Record [of the Lady] from the Mist."[6]

---

[6]The "Yanzhong zhizhi" 煙中之志 (A Record [of The Lady] from the Mist), or "Yanzhong yuan jie" 煙中怨解 (An Explication of the Lament

Note: This tale has at least three different titles. It is sometimes referred to as "Xiangzhong yuan ci" 湘中怨辭, as seen here in Lu Xun's edition, which suggests that Shen Yazhi intended to use this work to provide a prose version of the story, with more details and his poems to match Wei Ao's ballad on the same topic. It is also called "Xiangzhong yuan jie" 湘中怨解, or an "explication" of the *original event* 本事 behind Wei's ballad. Occasionally, it is simply titled "Xiangzhong yuan" 湘中怨. For further details, see Li Jianguo, *Tang Wudai zhiguai chuanqi xulu* 唐五代志怪傳奇敘錄 (Tianjin: Nankai Daxue Chubanshe, 1993), pp. 404–06.

While preparing this translation, I consulted the complete translations of this tale by William Nienhauser Jr. and Michael Broschat. I am greatly indebted to their careful and creative renditions. See William H. Nienhauser, Jr., "Creativity and Storytelling in the Ch'uan-ch'i: Shen Ya-chih's T'ang Tales," *Chinese Literature: Essays, Articles, Review* 20 (1998), pp. 50–53, and Michael Broschat, "Lament from the Hsiang River: A Prose Version," in *Classical Chinese Tales of the Supernatural and the Fantastic*, Karl S. Y. Kao ed., (Bloomington: Indiana University Press, 1985), pp. 205–208. Other translations of this work include E. D. Edwards, *Chinese Prose Literature of the T'ang Period* (London: Arthur Probsthain, 1937–38), vol. 1, pp. 167–169.

---

from the Mist) by Nan Zhaosi 南昭嗣, is no longer extant. According to Li Jianguo, an outline of the story can be found in the Southern Song collection *Lüchuang xinhua* 綠窗新話 (New Tales from within the Green Window), which tells of a romantic encounter between a student named Xie 謝 and a banished river goddess. Like this tale translated above, Nan Zhaosi's tale includes an exchange of poetry between the hero and heroine as does the tale translated above. It is likely that Shen Yazhi modeled his piece on Nan's work in terms of structure and incorporation of poetry. The coda of this tale along with its preface provides us with an interesting example of the writing, circulation and reading of what we now know as Tang tales. Here we can also get a sense of how the community of literati shaped Tang tales in those times.

湘中怨辭 并序

沈亞之

《湘中怨》者，事本怪媚，為學者未嘗有述。然而淫溺之人，往往不寤。今欲概其論，以著誠而已。從生韋敖，善撰樂府，故牽而廣之，以應其詠。

垂拱年中，駕幸上陽宮。大學進士鄭生，晨發銅駝里，乘曉月度洛橋。聞橋下有哭聲，甚哀。生下馬，循聲索之。見有艷女，縈然蒙袖曰："我孤，養於兄。嫂惡，常苦我。今欲赴水，故留哀須臾。"生曰："能遂我歸之乎？"女應曰："婢禦無悔！"

遂與居，號曰氾人。能誦楚人《九歌》、《招魂》、《九辯》之書，亦嘗擬其調，賦為怨句，其詞麗絕，世莫有屬者。因撰《光風詞》，曰：

> 隆佳秀兮昭盛時，播薰綠兮淑華歸。
> 願室荑與處萼兮，潛重房以飾姿。
> 見雅態之韶羞兮，蒙長靄以為幃。
> 醉融光兮渺瀰，迷千里兮涵洇湄，晨陶陶兮暮熙熙。
> 舞婑娜之穢條兮，娉盈盈以披遲。
> 酡遊顏兮倡蔓卉，縠流電兮石髮髓施。

生居貧，氾人嘗解篋，出輕綃一端，與賣，胡人酬之千金。居數歲，生遊長安。是夕，謂生曰："我湘中蛟宮之娣也，謫而從君。今歲滿，無以久留君所，欲為訣耳。"即相持啼泣。生留之，不能，竟去。

後十餘年，生之兄為岳州刺史。會上巳曰，與家徒登岳陽樓，望鄂渚，張宴。樂酣，生愁吟曰：

"情無垠兮蕩洋洋。懷佳期兮屬三湘。"

聲未終，有畫艫浮漾而來。中為綵樓，高百尺餘，其上施幃帳，欄籠畫飾。帷褰，有彈絃鼓吹者，皆神僊蛾眉，被服煙霓，裾袖皆廣長。其中一人起舞，含嚬淒怨，形類汜人。舞而歌曰：

溯青山兮江之隅，
拖湘波兮裛綠裾。
荷卷卷兮未舒。
匪同歸兮將焉如！

舞畢，斂袖，翔然凝望。樓中縱觀方怡。須臾，風濤崩怒，遂迷所往。

元和十三年，余聞之於朋中，因悉補其詞，題之曰《湘中怨》，蓋欲使南昭嗣《煙中之志》，為偶倡也。

Tale 4.23

Registering a Strange Dream

By Shen Yazhi
Translated by William H. Nienhauser, Jr.

During the tenth year of the Yuanhe reign period (815 A.D.), I followed the Duke of Longxi[1] as a record keeper to garrison Jingzhou.[2] Those worthy scholars in Chang'an all came to serve as his retainers.

On the eighteenth day of the fifth month (28 June 815) the Duke of Longxi arranged a time with his retainers to have a party at the guesthouse near the Eastern Pond. After everyone had been seated, the Duke of Longxi said, "When I was young I went about with Xing Feng and was able to record some of his unusual events. May I tell you them?"

The retainers said, "We would like to hear all about them."

"Feng," the Duke of Longxi said, "was the son of a military man and had no other abilities. Later, he lived in the southern part of the Pingkang Ward in Chang'an, where with more than a

---

[1]This title had first been given to Li Guangbi 李光弼 (708–764). He was of Khitan blood and not from Longxi, but was made an honorary member of Longxi clan, one of the most powerful families during the Tang, as a reward for his military service.

[2]Modern Jingchuan county in Gansu.

million in cash he was able to rent a former noble family's residence that features moon gates and secluded inner rooms."

When he was taking a nap in the bedroom, he dreamed that a beautiful woman appeared to him, walking through the columns to the western [wing]; she walked in a relaxed manner taking deliberate steps, holding a scroll and intoning [lines of a poem]. She was made up in the old-fashioned style, with her hair curled up high [in the palace style] and long eyebrows; she was wearing a square collar with a long embroidered belt and girdle, topped by a short jacket with broad sleeves.

Feng was greatly pleased and said, "Lovely lady, where have you come from to visit me?"

The beautiful woman smiled and said, "This is my house. You, sir, are a guest under my roof. Why do you ask where I come from?"

Feng said, "May I see what you have written?"

The beautiful woman said, "I am fond of poetry and often write poems myself."

Feng said, "Would the lovely lady tarry a bit so that I can take a look at them?"

At this, the beautiful woman handed him her poems and sat down on the western divan. Feng unrolled the scroll until he caught sight of the first poem. It was titled "Chunyang qu" (Song of Spring's Vigor) and contained only four lines. The other pieces after it ran several dozen lines in all. The beautiful woman said, "If you intend to pass these on to others, you can copy no more than one."

Feng immediately stood up and took some decorative letter-paper from the low table under the eastern veranda to copy "Song of Spring's Vigor." It read:

A young woman of Chang'an stepping to "Spring's Vigor,"
Where does "Spring's Vigor" not break hearts?
Dancing sleeves "bend the bow" and nearly forget

That thin silken clothes will change in vain for the frosts of
autumn.

When Feng was finished with the poem, he asked, "What
does 'bending the bow' mean?"

"In former years my father and mother taught me to perform
this dance."

The beautiful woman then got up, straightened her clothing
and shook out her sleeves. She danced through a few movements
to show Feng how to 'bend the bow.' When she finished, the
beautiful woman wept for a long time. Then she said her farewells.

Feng said, "I would like you to do me the honor of staying a
little longer."

Finally, she was gone. Feng then woke up, a little muddled,
and unable to remember things clearly. After a little while, Feng
changed his clothing and in the wide lapels and sleeves he found
her lyrics. He was shocked to see them and recall what he had
dreamed.

This event took place in the Zhenyuan era (785–805). Later
Feng told me the story like this.

On that day, the Army Supervising Commissioner, the Junior
Guest of Superior Prefectures and Commanderies, and the guests
at the party — Dugu Xuan of Longxi, Lu Jianci of Fanyang, Zhang
Youxin of Changshan, Su Di of Wugong — all sighed and said,
"This should be recorded." Therefore, I withdrew and wrote it
down.

The next day there were late arriving guests: Gao Yunzhong
(ca. 773–ca. 848) of Bohai, Wei Liang from the capital city, Tang
Yan from Jinchang, Li Yu from Guanghan, Yao He (fl. 815–840)
from Wuxing, and I again gathered at the Bright Jade Spring. I
thereupon showed them what I had written; at this Yao He said,

"Our friend Wang Yan (fl. 795–806),[3] early in the Yuanhe reign (806–820), dreamt one night that he traveled to Wu and served the King of Wu. After a long time, he heard men pulling the imperial carriage out of the palace to the sound of reed-pipes blowing and drums rolling. They said they were burying Xishi.[4] The king's sorrow found no bounds. He immediately issued a decree ordering the writer to compose a dirge. Yan then, as he had been instructed, wrote a poem which read:

> Westward I gaze towards the capital of the king of Wu:
> In cloudy characters a Phoenix-character pennant.
> From the continuous River arises a pearl curtain,
> A watery place picked to bury the golden hairpins.
> 'Red-hearted grasses' cover the ground,
> In three tiers, green-jade stairs.
> The spring wind has no place to go;
> Grief and regret overfill my heart.

When the text was presented, the king took great pleasure in it.

When Yan awoke, he was able to recollect these events. Yan was originally a man of Taiyuan.

Note: This new rendition corrects errors in the 1998 version in my "Creativity and Storytelling in Ch'uan-ch'i: Shen Ya-chih's Tang Tales," CLEAR 20 (1998): 31–70, though more detailed analysis is found there.

---

[3] Wang Yan 王炎 was one of the three brothers who together acquired a degree of fame in late Zhenyuan era (785–805) for passing the examinations in rapid succession. He died early while serving as *Taichang boshi* (Erudite of the Court of Imperial Sacrifices).

[4] Xishi 西施 was one of two beautiful women (the other was Zheng Dan 郑旦) who were sent by the King of Yue, Goujian 勾践 (r. 496–465 BCE), to the King of Wu, Fuchai (r. 495–473 BCE), to distract the latter from state affairs (see *Wu Yue chuanqiu* [Taipei: Shijie shuju, 1980], 9. 24ff.).

異夢錄

沈亞之

　　元和十年，亞之以記室從隴西公軍涇州，而長安中賢士，皆來客之。

　　五月十八日，隴西公與客期，宴於東池便館。既坐，隴西公曰："余少從邢鳳遊，得記其異，請語之。"

　　客曰："願備聽。"

　　隴西公曰："鳳帥家子，無他能。後寓居長安平康里南，以錢百萬質得故豪家洞門曲房之第。

　　"即其寢而晝偃，夢一美人自西楹來。環步從容，執卷且吟。爲古妝，而高鬟長眉，衣方領，繡帶俯紳，被廣袖之襦。

　　"鳳大說曰：'麗者何自而臨我哉？'

　　"美人笑曰：'此妾家也，而君客妾宇下，焉有自耶？'

　　"鳳曰：'願示其書之目。'美人曰：'妾好詩，而常綴此。'鳳曰：'麗人幸少留，得觀覽。'

　　"於是美人授詩，坐西牀。鳳發卷，示其首篇，題之曰《春陽曲》，纔四句。其後他篇，皆累數十句。美人曰：'君必欲傳之，無令過一篇。'

　　"鳳即起，從東廡下几上取彩箋，傳《春陽曲》。其詞曰：

　　　　'長安少女踏春陽，何處春陽不斷腸。
　　　　舞袖弓鸞渾忘卻，羅衣空換九秋霜。'

　　"鳳卒詩，請曰：'何謂弓彎？'

　　"曰：'昔年父母使妾敩此舞。'

　　"美人乃起，整衣張袖，舞數拍，爲弓彎以示鳳。既罷，美人泫然良久，即辭去。

　　"鳳曰：'願復少留。'

　　"須臾間，竟去。鳳亦覺，昏然忘有所記。及更衣，於襟袖得其詞，驚視，復省所夢。

　　"事在貞元中。後鳳爲余言如是。"

　　是日，監軍使與賓府郡佐，及宴客隴西獨孤鉉、范陽盧簡辭、常山張又新、武功蘇滌，皆嘆息曰："可記！"故亞之退而著錄。

　　明日，客有後至者，渤海高允中、京兆韋諒、晉昌唐炎、廣漢李瑀、吳興姚合，泊亞之，復集於明玉泉，因出所著以示之。於是姚合曰："吾友王炎者，元和初，夕夢遊吳，侍吳王久。聞宮中出輦，鳴笳簫擊鼓，言葬西施。王悼悲不止，立詔詞客作輓歌。炎遂應教，詩曰：'西望吳王國，雲書鳳字牌，連江起珠帳，擇水葬金釵。滿地紅心草，三層碧玉階。春風無處所，悽恨不勝懷。'詞進，王甚嘉之。

　　及寤，能記其事。"炎本太原人也。

Tale 4.24

A Record of Dream of Qin

By Shen Yazhi
Translated by William H. Nienhauser, Jr.

At the beginning of the Taihe era (827–835), Shen Yazhi was on his way to Bin.[1] Having left the city of Chang'an, he stayed in the guest-lodge at Tuo Springs.[2] It was springtime and he fell asleep while it was still daylight, dreaming of entering [the capital of] Qin and living in the household of Liao, the Scribe of the Capital.[3] Liao, the Scribe of the Capital, recommended Yazhi [for an official position].

---

[1]Bin 邠 was a Tang prefecture with its seat at Xinping 新平 (modern Bin County 彬縣 in Shanxi) about fifty miles northwest of modern Xi'an on the Jing River 涇水 (Tan Qixiang, 5:41).

[2]Tuo Springs 橐泉 was a palace built by Duke Xiao of Qin 秦孝公 (r. 361–338 B.C.) at the site of Duke Mu's 秦穆公 (r. 659–621 B.C.) mausoleum and was located southeast of modern Fengxiang 鳳翔 in Shanxi about eighty-five miles west of the capital. It was the site of a postal station and inn during the Tang.

[3]*Nei shi* Liao 內史廖. In the Warring States era the Scribe of the Capital was in charge of the administration of the city, essentially its mayor. Liao is a historical figure who in 626 B.C. was instrumental in guiding Duke Mu in 626 B.C. to take actions that weakened the power of the Rong 戎 tribe (cf. *Shiji*, 5.193 and *Grand Scribe's Records*, 1:100-1).

344

The Duke of Qin [4] summoned him to the [reception] hall, moved forward on the mat,[5] and said, "We want to strengthen the state and desire to know the method. How would you, sir, instruct Us?"[6]

Yazhi drew upon [the examples] of Kun[wu], Peng[zu] and [Duke] Huan of Qi in his response.[7] The duke was pleased and in the end appointed him to fill the vacancy of Palace Purifier and sent him to assist Xi Qi Shu[8] in the campaign in Hexi. Yazhi

---

[4]I.e. Duke Mu. Shen Yazhi here enters the realm of the dead through this gateway of Tuo Springs which was where Duke Mu had been buried, along with seventy-seven people, still alive, who were intended to accompany the duke in the afterlife (see *Shih chi*, 5.194).

[5]Literally "moved his knees forward on the mat" 膝前席. In early China one knelt, rather than sat, on mats. This is a conventional trope to indicate that the ruler is paying close attention.

[6]*Gua ren* 寡人, literally "this lonely one," is the conventional way Chinese rulers referred to themselves.

[7]These three men were what the Han-era considered to have been the first of the Five Hegemons 五霸 of antiquity: the Lord of Kunwu 昆吾 was supposedly a descendant of Emperor Zhuanxu 顓頊 and the eldest son of Lu Zhong 陸終. He (or his descendants in Kunwu) became known as the Hegemon of Xia 夏伯 and was killed when Tang of Shang 商湯 overthrew Jie of Xia 夏桀; Peng Zu 彭祖 was also one of Lu Zhong's sons and he (or his descendants) became Hegemon of Shang 商伯. Duke Huan 桓 (r. 685–642 B.C.) was the first hegemon under the Zhou. Since Kunwu was thought to have invented pottery, it is possible that Shen Yazhi was advocating that Duke Mu should promote handicraft and the arts; Pengzu is said to have lived hundreds of years from the Xia through the Shang. What precedents Shen Yazhi would have ascribed to him are unclear. Duke Huan became hegemon through the advice of his minister Guan Zhong 管仲; thus Shen's narratives in his regard would suggest that Duke Mu should make Shen a close advisor and he could thereby achieve the same domination of the other states that Duke Huan reached.

[8]Xi 西 was his surname, Shu 術 his given name, and Qi 乞 his style name (another theory argues that Xishu was his surname, possibly the

commanded the foot soldiers in the assaults and caused five cities to surrender.[9] When he returned to give his report, the duke was greatly pleased, stood up in recognition of his service, and said, "The gentleman has endured a great deal. Let him take his rest!"

After some time, Xiao Shi, the husband of the duke's youngest daughter, Nongyu, died early.[10] The duke said to Yazhi,

---

son of Qian Shu 蹇叔 of the state of Song 宋). He was one of the three generals sent to attack Zheng in 628 B.C. and, in what turned out to be a debacle, was captured by Jin 晉 (cf. *Shiji*, 5.190–1 and *Grand Scribe's Records*, 1:99–100; Xi Qi Shu was still active as an envoy from Qin to Lu in 615 B.C.). Duke Mu's campaign in Hexi (the lands just northwest of the confluence of the Wei and Yellow rivers in modern Shanxi that were in dispute between Qin and Jin [Tan Qixiang, 1:22]) directed against Jin took place seventeen years earlier in 645 B.C. (*Shiji*, 5.188–9 and *Grand Scribe's Records*, 1:97). In the *Shiji* account of this campaign (5.187), there were eight cities in play. However, the *Shiji* does not mention Xi Qi Shu's leading troops. It seems that Shen Yazhi is conflating the information from several texts here.

[9]This passage conflates several accounts of Qin-Jin relations under Duke Mu. In "Qin benji" 秦本紀 (*Shiji*, 5.187) we read that in 651 B.C., when Duke Hui of Jin 晉惠公 (r. 650–638 B.C.) took power he promised to cede eight cities in Hexi 河西, the lands in modern Shanxi just west of the Yellow River, to Qin. He reneged on this pledge and ceded the cities only in 643 B.C. only after Qin had attacked Jin (*Shiji*, 5.189). The number of five cities seems to have come from the account of these events as recorded in the *Zuo zhuan* 左傳 (Xigong 僖公, 15; Yang Bojun 楊伯峻, *Chunqiu Zuozhuan zhu* 春秋左傳注 [Beijing: Zhonghua, 1982], p. 352).

[10]According to legend, Xiao Shi 簫史 was a scribe (*shi* 史) who was also a skilled pan-pipes player (*xiao* 簫). Duke Mu married his daughter to him and he taught her to play. Their songs called for phoenixes which settled on their roof. Duke Mu built a Phoenix Tower for the couple and they remained in it, never descending. After a few years they flew away with the phoenixes (See *Lie xian zhuan* 列仙傳, *Linlang Mishi congshu* 琳瑯密室叢書, ed. (in *Baibu congshu jicheng* 百部叢書集成), 1.15a–b. Here Shen Yazhi is again modifying a traditional narrative by making Nongyu 弄玉

"If not for you, sir, we would not possess the five cities of Jin. We are greatly in your debt, sir. We have a beloved daughter and, as a mark of gratitude, would like to give her to you to attend to all wifely duties. Would this meet with your approval?"

Yazhi had depended on himself since he was young; he really did not want to become a favorite vassal of the duke and be maintained by him. He adamantly refused, but his refusal was not granted and he was appointed Grandee of the Tenth Order,[11] married to the princess, and presented two hundred catties of gold.[12] Among the people she was still called the Princess of the Xiao Family.[13] On the appointed day, a eunuch dressed in yellow[14] galloped up on a horse to escort Yazhi into the palace. Everything in the palace and at the gate-towers was extremely dignified. The princess was called forth — she had thick, black hair, wore a short, broad-sleeved jacket without too much adornment. Her fragrance and her beauty were more seductive that pen and ink can depict. Several hundred of her maids reverently divided themselves to stand to her left and right. The duke summoned

---

a widow. Nongyu's name could be read "to play with jade," thus having a sexual connotation. She is mentioned in this context in a letter from Xu Ling 徐陵 (507–583) to Zhou Hongrang 周弘讓 cited by van Gulik (op. cit., p. 151).

[11]*Zuo shu zhang* 左庶長, the eleventh highest of twenty titles of honorary nobility conferred on meritorious subjects (see Hucker, *Official Titles*, #6997, p. 525 and Liang Yulian, p. 404, n. 14).

[12]According to Liang Yulian (p. 404, n. 15) during Duke Mu's era *jin* 金 should refer to bronze (*tong* 銅). Here, however, it seems to have been intended to suggest the largesse allowed Shen Yazhi.

[13]Thus although he was nominally Nongyu's husband, his social status was much lower, perhaps intended to resemble those aristocrats who married imperial princes during the Tang.

[14] This again is an anachronistic reference to the clothing that eunuchs wore under the Tang (cf. *Hanyu dacidian*, 12:975a).

Yazhi to a guest lodge and had him reside there. Above the gate to Yazhi's palace was Cuiwei Gong (The Palace of Endless Greenery). Those in the palace called it the Shen Lang Yuan (Master Shen's Courtyard).

Although the rank he held was that of a lower grandee, because of the princess, he had an armed guard wherever he went.[15] The princess was fond of playing the phoenix pan-pipes. Whenever she played the pipes, she had to be in the tall tower in the Palace of Endless Greenery.[16] Her tunes spread into the distance and saddened people — everyone who heard them would lose themselves [in the music].

The princess had been born on the seventh day of the seventh lunar month,[17] but Yazhi at that time had nothing for her birthday. Liao, the Scribe of the Capital, had arranged to send female musicians to the Western Rong on behalf of Qin.[18] The leader of the Rong had given Liao a small box made of rhinoceros horn.[19] Yazhi obtained it from Liao and presented it to the princess. The princess received it joyfully and often wore it knotted on the belt of her skirt. Duke Mu treated Yazhi twice as politely as he did those of the same rank, with favors and gifts [sent] one after the other along the road.

---

[15]Another possible reading for 緣公主故，公入禁衛 is "because of the princess, he could come and go freely through the palace guards."

[16]It would seem that the princess retained her practice of remaining as much of the time as possible in the tall tower, a practice begun with her first husband.

[17]Suggesting that the princess was comparable to the legendary Weaving Girl who was separated from her lover, the Herder Boy — as Nongyu was from Xiao Shi — a pair who could only meet on the seventh day of the seventh month.

[18]On Liao's plan to undermine the King of the Rong by sending him female musicians, see *Shiji*, 5.193 and *Grand Scribe's Records*, 1:100-1).

[19]Which was considered a talisman against bad influences.

In the spring of the next year, when the Duke of Qin went to Shiping,[20] the princess suddenly died without having been ill. The duke was devastated by his mourning for her and could not get over it.[21] When they were about to bury her in the plains above Xianyang, the duke ordered Yazhi to compose a dirge; in response to the command he wrote:

Sobbing we bury a sprig of crimson,
In life together, with your death apart.
Her golden filigree falls into sweet-smelling grasses,
Her fragrant embroidery swells with the spring breeze.
In days of old, where one heard your pan-pipes
Now only the high tower in the light of the moon.
Pear blossoms [22] on the Cold Food Festival night,[23]

---

[20]Shiping 始平 was about fifteen miles northwest of Xianyang. The place name was not used until the Jin 晉 dynasty and was revived during the Tang. Thus the usage here is anachronistic (see also the following note).

Shen Xiaxian wenji, 21a, reads Qin Gongzhu 秦公主 (the Princess of Qin); Wang Meng'ou (*op. cit.*, p. 216, n. 18) points out that the *Quan Tang shi* 全唐詩 (Rpt. Taipei: Ming-lun, 1871, 12:9831) calls Nongyu the Shiping Princess and that this text should be read the same way: "The duke's Princess of Shiping died suddenly . . . ." However, since Shiping is not a place name in pre-Qin times, it would seem rather that the *Quan Tang shi* editors have misread this text.

[21]Here Shen Yazhi nods, since in Duke Mu's time the Qin capital was at Yong 雍 (modern Fengxiang 鳳翔), about eighty-five miles from Xianyang.

[22]One type of white powder used by Tang women on their faces was made from pear blossoms.

[23]Although the Hanshi Jie 寒食節 (Cold Food Festival) is originally associated with the legend of Jie Zhitui 介之推 (see Donald Holzman, "The Cold Food Festival in Early Medieval China," *HJAS* 46 [1986]: 51–79), here it seems to indicate its ancillary role as a holiday which precedes Qingming Jie 清明節 (Clear and Bright Festival) to honor the

But the Palace of Endless Greenery is shut tight.

He presented it to the duke and, when the duke had read the lyrics, he found it to be excellent.

At that time some of the palace attendants cried aloud as if they couldn't bear it; the duke sobbed along with them. He also had Yazhi write an inscription and poem for the grave tablet.[24] I only recall the poem that read:

> Through white willows[25] the winds weep,
>> on the walls around the grave, bristles of grass;
> All sorts of blossoms cover the ground
>> the spring scene blending with the mists.
> Pearls that cause grief, a powdered beauty wasted away,
>> no life in her summer silks.
> Deeply so deeply buried is this jade-like [corpse],[26]
>> how intense are our regrets!

Yazhi also accompanied the funerary procession to the plains above Xianyang; fourteen palace attendants were buried with

---

dead. The holiday is poignant here because of the princess' recent passing and the importance it enjoyed during the mid-Tang (cf. Lü Simian 呂思勉, *Sui Tang Wudai shi* 隋唐五代史 [Rpt. Hong Kong: Taiping Shuju, 1985], v. 2, p. 1014).

[24]The *Mu zhi ming* 墓志銘 consists of a *zhi* 志, a prose biographical sketch which is carved on a square stone and placed in the grave, and a *ming* 銘, a shorter rhymed piece which expressed the emotions of the mourners towards the deceased.

[25]*Bai yang* 白楊, "white willows," is a traditional yuefu tune title tied to funerals. It also appear in a dirge by Tao Qian 陶潛 (365–427) entitled "Ni wange ci, di san shou" 擬輓歌辭，第三首 (*Tao Yuanming ji* 陶淵明集, Lu Qinli 逯欽立, ed. [2nd printing; Beijing: Zhonghua, 1982], p. 142.

[26]*Yu* 玉 "jade" play on Nongyu's name which literally means "to handle or play with jade."

her.[27] Because Yazhi grievously mourned to excess, he fell ill. Thus he was placed in a special room outside the palace halls and could not enter the palace.

After more than a month, he had almost recovered. The duke said to him, "Originally I had the hope to entrust my little daughter to you for a long time. I did not expect that before she would be able to attend to your needs, sir, she would pass on. Our humble Qin is such a tiny state,[28] not worthy of disgracing you further. The fact is, whenever the lonely one sees you, he cannot help but grieve [for his daughter]. Would it not be better for you, sir, to depart for some greater state?"

Yazhi replied, "Your servant is a person of little account, yet you have treated me as a close relative.[29] I fear committing an offense occupying the [undeserved] office of Grandee of the Eleventh Order.[30] Though I am unable to follow the princess in death, Milord has absolved me of my offenses and allowed me to return my bones to my parents' state. Your servant will not forget Milord's kindness, [his gratitude will remain] as it is today."

---

[27]Note that seventy-seven attendants had been buried alive with Duke Mu's corpse (see text above and n. 5).

[28]Jia Yi in his "Guo Qin lun" 過秦論 (On the Faults of Qin; cited on *Shiji*, 6.282) describes Qin as a tiny state: "But Qin, with such a tiny territory and force of one thousand chariots, had been able to command the other eight lands and bring the lords of equal rank to its court for more than one hundred years" 然秦以區區之地，千乘之權，招八州而朝同列，百有餘年矣。 The duke is of course merely denigrating his state as a means to encourage Shen Yazhi to leave.

[29]*Feifu* 肺腑, literally "lungs and bowels," is also an allusion to the *Shiji* (107.2844 and 2853), where it means to be related to the imperial house by marriage, i.e. as close as lungs and bowels.

[30]*You shu zhang* 右庶長, see Hucker, *Official Titles*, #806, p. 586. Probably an error for *Zuo shu zhang*, the position that the duke originally gave to Yazhi.

When he was about to leave, the Duke sent him off with wine and a feast, the singing of Qin songs and the dancing of Qin dances. The dancers hit their shoulders, slapped their thighs, and cried out; the measured cadence of their voices was mingled with unhappiness and their voices were very melancholy.

The Duke held up his wine to Yazhi and said, "Long life! We consider these songs have a few good passages, but we hope that Master Shen would write a sequel in order to make our parting complete."

The duke then ordered brush and ink slab brought forward. Yazhi accepted the command and immediately wrote a song. Its lyrics ran:

> As the dancers beat their bodies,
> my regret fills both mist and sunlight, with nowhere it can be placed.
> Tears fall like rain,
> I intended to write a song, but cannot find the words.
> In former times in your golden phoenix robe laced with crimson thread,
> how many times did we watch dancing in the embroidered palace together?
> A spring day in this world is fit for merriment —
> as the sun sets, I return eastward, but where should I go?

When the song was finished, he gave it to the dancers, harmonized their voices and joined in with them; those who were seated around them all wept.

When the feast was completed, Yazhi bowed twice and said his farewells. The duke ordered him to go to the Palace of Endless Greenery and say good-bye to the princess's serving women. When he entered the palace hall again, he saw beneath the green staircase fragments of her bridal headdress, the gauze over the windows flecked with lip-rouge as before. The palace women wept when they faced Yazhi, and he was so moved he could not utter a word for some time. Accordingly, he wrote a poem on the palace gate which read:

> Milord, overwrought with sadness, has sent me to return to the
>   east,
> From this time on I'll never see the Qin palace,
> In the spring scene I'm sick at heart for the lost Qin princess,
> Flowers fall like rain, every tear a drop of her rouge.

Finally, he departed. The duke ordered the imperial chariot to escort him out of the Hangu Pass.[31]

When they emerged from the pass and came to a halt, the escorting officer said, "The duke has ordered us to stop here. We are about to leave." Yazhi was saying farewell to him, but before he finished what he had to say, he suddenly woke up, lying in the lodge.

The next day Yazhi told his friend Cui Jiuwan[32] everything [about the dream]. Jiuwan was a member of the Boling [Cui] Clan[33] and was versed in matters of antiquity. He said, "The Huanglan (For Imperial Reading)[34] says, 'Duke Mu of Qin was

---

[31]The pass through which traffic from the east gained access to the capital region; it was located about eighty miles east of the Qin capital and a few miles northeast of modern Lingbao 靈寶 (Henan), at that time marking the eastern border of Qin (Tan Qixiang, 1:41).

[32]This given name, literally "Ninety Thousand," suggests a fictional character.

[33]Boling 博陵 was the name of a Tang commandery with its seat at Dingzhou 定州 (near modern Ding County 定縣 in Hebei). The Cuis of Boling were one of the most powerful and respected clans during the Tang dynasty.

[34]An encyclopedic collection compiled by Liu Shao 劉邵 (ca. 170–ca. 245) and others at the command of Cao Pi 曹丕, Emperor Wen of the Wei 魏文帝 (r. 220–226).

buried beneath the Qinian Gong (Prayers for the Harvest Palace)[35] at Tuo Springs in Yong.' Could [your dream] be evidence that his soul exists?"

Yazhi sought out more local records from Qin times and what they said was as Jiuwan had argued. Alas! Nongyu had already become an immortal — how could she then die?

[Colophon:]

[This story] comes from the *Yiwen ji* [Collection of Strange Hearsay].

Note: This tale has been considered Shen Yazhi's representative work. The story is constructed drawing on four earlier texts: Shen's own earlier tale "Yi meng lu" (Records of Strange Dreams), the story of Nongyu and her husband Xiao Shi, Li Gongzuo's tale "Nanke Taishou zhuan" (An Account of the Governor of the Southern Branch, and the "Qin benji" (Basic Annals of Qin) in Sima Qian's (145–ca. 86 BCE) *Shiji*.

This is a revised version of my 2016 rendition in my *Tang Dynasty Tales: A Guided Reader vol. 2*, pp. 181–206, where more detailed annotations are provided.

---

[35]Also known as Qinian Guan 祈年觀, this palace was built by Duke Mu and located in the ancient Qin capital of Yong, near the location where Tuo Springs Palace was later constructed.

秦夢記

沈亞之

太和初，沈亞之將之邠，出長安城，客橐泉邸舍。春時，畫夢入秦，主內史廖家，內史廖舉亞之。

秦公召之殿，膝前席曰："寡人欲強國，願知其方。先生何以教寡人？"

亞之以昆彭、齊桓對，公悅，遂試補中涓（秦官名），使佐西乞伐河西（晋秦郊也）。亞之率將卒前，攻下五城。還報，公大悅。起勞曰："大夫良苦，休矣。"

居久之，公幼女弄玉婿蕭史先死。公謂亞之曰："微大夫，晉五城非寡人有，盛德大夫。寡人有愛女，而欲與大夫備灑掃，可乎？"

亞之少自立，雅不欲幸臣蓄之。固辭，不得請。拜左庶長，尚公主，賜金二百斤。民間猶謂蕭家公主。其日有黃衣中貴騎疾馬來，延亞之入，宮闕甚嚴。呼公主出，鬢發，著偏袖衣，裝不多飾。其芳殊明媚，筆不可模樣。侍女祇承，分立左右者數百人。召見亞之便館，居亞之于宮，題其門曰"翠微宮"。宮人呼為"沈郎院"。雖備位下大夫，由公主故，公入禁衛。公主喜鳳簫；每吹簫，必翠微宮高樓上。聲調遠逸，能悲人，聞者莫不自廢。

公主七月七日生，亞之嘗無貺壽。內史廖會為秦以女樂遺西戎，戎主與廖水犀小合。亞之從廖得以獻公主，主悅，嘗愛重，結裙帶之上。穆公遇亞之禮兼同列，恩賜相望于道。復一年春，秦公之始平，公主忽無疾卒，公追傷不已。將葬咸陽原，公命亞之作輓歌。應教而作曰：

355

泣葬一枝紅，生同死不同。金鈿墜芳草，香繡滿春風。
舊日聞簫處，高樓當月中。梨花寒食夜，深閉翠微宮。

進公，公讀詞，善之。時宮中有出聲若不忍者，公隨泣下。又
使亞之作墓誌銘，獨憶其銘，曰：

白楊風哭兮石鬣髯莎，雜英滿地兮春色煙和。
珠愁紛瘦兮不生綺羅，深深埋玉兮其恨如何！

亞之亦送葬咸陽原，宮中十四人殉之。
亞之以悼惆過戚，被病，臥在翠微宮。然處殿外室，不入宮中
矣。居月餘，病良已。公謂亞之曰：“本以小女相托久要，不謂不
得周奉君子，而先物故。弊秦區區小國，不足辱大夫。然寡人每見
子，即不能不悲悼。大夫盍適大國乎？”亞之對曰：“臣無狀，肺
腑公室，待罪右庶長，不能從死公主。君免罪戾，使得歸骨父母國。
臣不忘君恩，如今日。”
將去，公追酒高會，聲秦聲，舞秦舞。舞者擊髆附髀嗚嗚，而
音有不快，聲甚怨。
公執酒亞之前曰：“予顧此聲少善，願沈郎賣楊歌以塞別。”
公命遂進筆硯。亞之受命，立為歌，辭曰：

擊體舞，恨滿煙光無處所。
淚如雨，欲擬著詞不成語。
金鳳啣紅舊繡衣，幾度宮中同看舞。
人間春日正歡樂，日暮東歸何處去。

歌卒，授舞者，雜其聲而道之，四座皆泣。既，再拜辭去。
公覆命至翠微宮，與公主侍人別。重入殿內時，見珠翠遺碎青
階下，窗紗檀點依然。宮人泣對亞之，亞之感咽良久。因題宮門，
詩曰：

君王多感放東歸，從此秦宮不復期。
春景自傷秦喪主，落花如雨淚臙脂。

竟別去。公命車駕送出函谷關。出關已，送吏曰：“公命盡此。
且去。”亞之與別。語未卒，忽驚覺，臥邸舍。

　　明日，亞之與友人崔九萬具道。九萬，博陵人，諳古。謂余曰：
"《皇覽》云，'秦穆公葬雍橐泉祈年宮下'，非其神靈憑乎？"
亞之更求得秦時地志，說如九萬云。

　　嗚呼！弄玉既仙矣，惡又死乎？

Tale 4.25

The Tale of Wushuang the Peerless

By Xue Diao
Translated by Jing Wang

Wang Xianke (Immortal Guest) was nephew of Liu Zhen, a court official during the reign of Jianzhong (780–783).[1] Earlier, after Xianke's father had passed away, he and his mother went to live with his maternal uncle and his family. Zhen had a daughter of his own by the name of Wushuang who was several years younger than Xianke. Wushuang and Xianke were both young and innocent. They played together and shared a special intimacy, such that Zhen's wife often teased Xianke by calling him son-in-law from the Wang family. It was like this for several years. Zhen took especially good care of his widowed elder sister, taking it upon himself to see to the proper upbringing of Xianke.

One day, Zhen's sister, the widowed Mrs. Wang, fell ill and her condition started deteriorating. She summoned Zhen [to her deathbed] intending to make an agreement with him, saying, "I have only one son and you know that I care deeply about him. I regret not seeing him get married. Wushuang is beautiful and smart, and I deeply care about her too. Do not marry her into a different clan in the future. I entrust Xianke to you. If you truly

---

[1]This was the first of the three reign periods of Emperor Dezong (r. 780–805) of the Tang dynasty.

promise me [to see to their union], I will die without any regret." Zhen responded, "Sister, you should put your mind at ease and look after yourself. Do not trouble yourself over other matters." In the end, his sister did not recover.

Xianke escorted his mother's coffin back to the Xiang-Deng region[2] to bury her. When his three-year mourning period ended, he thought, "I am an orphan who has been left all on my own in quite a lonely situation. I should seek marriage in order to have decendants to continue my family line. Wushuang has grown up. How would my uncle abandon his old agreement with my mother because of his respectful and celebrated official position?" He then packed his belongings and went to the capital.

At the time, Zhen was a Minister and also served as Special Supply Commissioner.[3] His residence was grand and its front yard was filled with high-ranking visitors. After Xianke had been received by Zhen, he was placed into the family school with the other young men of the clan. The relationship between uncle and nephew was the same as before, but Zhen kept silent about the marriage agreement and Xianke heard no discussion of the matter. He once caught a glimpse of Wushuang through the window. She was as radiant and dazzling as if she were a goddess. Xiangke became crazy and worried that his marriage plan would go awry.

---

[2]Xiang 湘 stands for Xiangyang county which is in modern Hubei province. Deng refers to Deng county which is in modern Honan province. According to the story, the Wang family's hometown was in the Xiang-Deng region, thus Xianke brought his mother's corpse back for proper burial.

[3] According to Hucker, it was the job of the Special Supply Commissioner to sell off court valuables in the wealthy Huai and Yangtze River basins in exchange for grain, which was used for army rations during the period that this story took place. See Charles O. Hucker, *A Dictionary of Official Titles in Imperial China* (Beijing: Peking University Press, 2007), entry 7056, p. 528.

He thus sold his belongings and obtained several million coins in cash. He lavishly bribed the attendants of his uncle and aunt, and even their lowly servants. He also invited them to feasts several times, and thus gained access to the entire inner quarters beyond the middle gate. When he was together with his cousins, he treated them all with respect. And on the occasion of his aunt's birthday, he bought rare and exotic gifts to present to her. He obtained a carved rhinoceros horn and jade which he made into hairpins for her. His aunt was greatly pleased. After about ten days, Xianke sent an old woman to his aunt to broach the issue of his seeking marriage with Wushuang. His aunt said, "This is what I wish for. We should discuss this subject right away." Several evenings later, a maid reported back to Xianke, "Her ladyship just talked to the master about the marriage. The master said, 'I never consented to their marriage, even in the past,' and other such words. I am afraid all may not go to plan." When Xianke heard this, he became frustrated at heart and despondent in spirit. He was sleepless the entire night for worry that his uncle would abandon him. However, he dared not to diminish his attention and service to his uncle's family.

One day, Zhen went to the court, and just after sunrise, came suddenly galloping back on his horseback to his residence. He arrived sweating and breathless, only speaking the words, "Bolt the main gate, bolt the main gate!" The entire family was terror-stricken. They could not figure out the reason for his actions. Only after a long while did Zhen explain, "The soldiers at the Jing-Yuan region[4] rebelled. Yao Lingyan[5] led his troops into the Hanyuan

---

[4]Jing 涇 refers to Baoding prefecture in the Jing region and Yuan 原 refers to Pingliang prefecture in the Yuan region. Both places are located in modern Pingliang district in Gansu province.

[5]Yao Lingyan 姚令言 (d. 784) served as Military Commission of the Jing-Yuan region and was a leading figure during Zhu Ci's rebellion. When the rebel army was later defeated, he was captured and beheaded

hall.[6] The Son-of-Heaven fled through the northern gate of the palace complex and all the other court officials rushed to his assistance. Because I had my wife and daughter on my mind, I returned home briefly to make some arrangements. Summon Xianke immediately to arrange the household matters with me. I will marry off Wushuang to him."

When Xianke heard his uncle's order, he was pleasantly surprised and bowed to express his gratitude. Zhen then packed gold, silver, silk and brocade in sacks that could be carried by twenty horses. He said to Xianke, "Change your clothes, escort these goods out through the Kaiyuan Gate,[7] and find a remote and secluded inn to settle down in. I will leave with your aunt and Wushuang through the Qixia Gate.[8] We will make a detour around the city wall and arrive after you." Xianke followed his instructions. He waited at the inn outside of the city wall for a long time until sunset, but his uncle, aunt, and cousin did not come.

The city gates had been bolted since noon. Xianke looked out southward as far as he could see [but saw no sign of Zhen and his family]. He then mounted a horse, and, holding a torch in his hand, rode around the city wall to the Qixia Gate. The Qixia gate was also bolted. There were several men guarding the gate, bearing white staffs. Some were standing and some were sitting.

---

by the succeeding Military Commissioner of Jing-Yuan. For more information, see his biography in the two official Tang histories.

[6]The Hanyuan 含元 Hall was the main hall of the Daming Palace which was the imperial palace complex of the Tang dynasty. The area of the palace is located northeast of modern Xi'an in Shaanxi province.

[7]The Kaiyuan 開遠 Gate was one of three western gates of the capital and it was located the farthest north among all three gates.

[8]The Qixia 啟夏 Gate was one of three southern gates of the capital and it was located to the farthest east among all three gates.

Xianke dismounted his horse and inquired leisurely, "What happened in the city that brought you all here?" He asked further, "Did anyone come out of the city through this gate today?"

The gate guards said, "Defender-in-Chief Zhu[9] has ascended the throne. Just past noon, there was a man who wore a black hat over his head-covering that came here. He was followed by four or five women, and intended to pass through this gate. People on the street all recognized him and they said he was Minister Liu, the Special Supply Commissioner. The Gate Office dared not let him go. When night fell, the cavalrymen who had been pursuing him arrived and the minister and his family were immediately driven to the north."

Xianke burst into tears and cried bitterly. He returned to the inn. When it was almost past the third watch, the city gate was suddenly opened and torches lit up the night so brightly that it looked as though it were daylight. Soldiers all held their weapons tightly and shouted one after another that the execution commissioner was going out of the city in search of court officials. [Hearing this,] Xianke abandoned all his carriages and belongings and ran away in terror. He returned to Xiangyang where he remained in a village for three years.

Later he learned that the lost territory had been recovered, and order had been restored in the capital. The world was in peace. He then went back to the capital and inquired after news of his uncle's family. When he reached the south street in the Xinchang quarter, he halted his horse, hesitating. A man suddenly bowed in front of his horse. Xianke stared at the man. He was Sai Hong, a former servant of his family. Hong was born in the Wang

---

[9]Zhu Ci 朱泚 (742–784) served as Defender-in-Chief at the time of rebellion. He was supported by the rebels and ascended the throne in 783. When the rebel troops were defeated, he was killed by his subordinates in 784. See his biography in the two official Tang histories.

family. Xianke's uncle often sought Hong's service and found him helpful, and thus kept him in the Liu household. The two men held each other's hands and shed tears.

Xianke asked Hong, "Are my uncle and aunt well?"

Hong replied, "They are all in the residence in the Xinghua quarter."

Xianke was overjoyed and said, "I will go over at once."

Hong said, "I have gained my freedom and am renting a small house. I make a living by selling silk. It is already nighttime, Sir, come stay the night in my rented house. It won't be too late if we go together tomorrow morning."

Hong then took Xianke to where he lived and arranged for a feast for him. Only when it became dark did Xianke hear the true report from Hong. "Because the minister accepted official appointment from the usurping emperor, he and the lady were both executed. Wushuang has already been taken into the inner palace." Xianke was extremely sorrowful and cried so mournfully that even the neighbors felt moved.

Xianke said to Hong, "The world within the four seas is so broad, but I look around and find no relatives. I don't know where I can entrust myself." He further asked, "Who else from the old Liu household is around?"

Hong replied, "There is only Caiping, Wushuang's former maid, who is now in the residence of Wang Suizhong, General of the Imperial Insignia Guard."

Xianke said, "There is certainly no chance for me of meeting Wushuang. But if I could at least see Caiping, I would die content."

Thereafter, he submitted his name card and requested to pay a visit to Suizhong. He met the general, following the rituals of a nephew from the same clan. He related his entire story from beginning to end and expressed his wish to redeem Caiping with a large sum of money. Suizhong found he and Xianke shared a deep, mutual understanding. He was moved by Xianke's experiences and gave consent to his request. Xianke rented a house and lived there with Hong and Caiping.

Sai Hong often said, "Sir, you are getting older and you should seek an official position. You are always melancholy and unhappy. How will you spend your time otherwise?" Xianke was moved by his words. So he appealed to Suizhong and sincerely asked him for help. Suizhong recommended Xianke to Li Qiyun, the Metropolitan Governor. Based on Xianke's previous title, Qiyun appointed him Magistrate of Fuping county,[10] also putting him in charge of the Changle Postal Relay Station.[11]

After several months, there was an unexpected report of an Imperial Commissioner escorting thirty palace maids to the imperial mausoleum. They would be deployed to do cleaning. They were to be lodged at the Changle Postal Relay Station and came in ten carriages with felt awnings. Xianke said to Sai Hong, "I heard that the imperial maids who were selected and sent to the inner palace were mostly daughters from court officials' families. I am afraid that Wushuang is among them. Can you secretly take a look for me?"

Hong said, "There are several thousand imperial maids. How could Wushuang have possibly been chosen?"

Xianke said, "Just go and check. Human matters are hard to predict."

---

[10]Fuping 富平 county was one of the subsidiary counties of the capital city and is still known today by the same name in Shaanxi province.

[11]A postal relay station was set up about every ten miles (thirty *li*) on major routes connecting the capital and other big cities during the Tang dynasty. Lodging and transportation were provided there for officials. The Changle station is located in the east side of modern Xi'an city. It was an important site where people travelling to the east bid farewell to family and friends during the Tang dynasty, and many famous poems were written on the subject.

Accordingly, he ordered Sai Hong to pretend to be a station officer, boiling tea outside of the curtains that enclosed the maids' chamber. Xianke gave him three thousand coins in cash and made an agreement with him, saying, "Attend strictly to your tea utensils and do not leave for a moment. If you see anything peculiar, come to report it immediately."

Sai Hong replied with a respectful, "Yes, yes," and left.

All the imperial maids were behind the curtains and could not be seen. Nothing but the noise of their chatting and talking at night could be heard. When it was late in the night, all the commotion faded to silence. Sai Hong washed his utensils and set up a fire, daring not go to sleep right away.

He suddenly heard a voice from behind the curtain, saying, "Sai Hong, Sai Hong, how did you know that I am here? Is the gentleman in good health?" She began to softly sob after saying these words.

Sai Hong said, "The gentleman is in charge of this station. He suspected that you were here today and ordered Sai Hong to convey his greetings."

Wushuang further said, "I cannot talk long. After I depart tomorrow, come to fetch a letter from under the purple bedding in the chamber of the northeastern residence and give it to the gentleman."

She left immediately after saying these words. Suddenly, a loud clattering noise was heard from behind the curtains. Someone said, "A maid has fainted." The imperial commissioner shouted urgently for medication. The fallen maid turned out to be Wushuang.

Sai Hong reported this to Xianke immediately. Xianke was filled with shock and asked, "Is there any way that I can see her?"

Sai Hong said, "The Wei River bridge is currently under repair. Sir, you can pretend to be the officer in charge of the bridge repair work and stand close to the carriages when they cross the bridge. If Wushuang recognizes you, she will certainly lift the carriage curtain and you should be able to have a glimpse of her." Xianke followed Hong's instructions. When the third carriage arrived, the curtain was indeed lifted. Xianke glanced at the woman and she really was Wushuang. Xianke was struck by such a great sorrow and longing that he could not bear his emotions.

Sai Hong obtained the letter under the bedding in the chamber and delivered it to Xianke. It was composed of five sheets of flowered paper covered in writings in Wushuang's hand. Her words conveyed a deep sadness as she accounted her experiences in full detail. After reading the letter, Xianke became filled with regret and tears poured down his face. They would be parted forever. At the end of her letter, Wushuang wrote, "I often heard the imperial envoy say that Officer Gu from the Fuping county, who is in charge of the imperial insignia, is a man of heart. Can you seek his help?"

Xianke then submitted his resignation to the Superior Prefecture, requesting to be relieved of his duty at the postal relay station, and returned to his original appointment as magistrate of Fuping county. He then searched for Officer Gu and found out that he lived in a village cottage. Xianke went to pay a visit to Gu and met him. Whatever Gu wished for, Xianke would try his best to procure for him. He presented Gu with countless gifts, such as colorful silk and precious jade. For a whole year, Xianke did not ask for anything in return.

When Xianke's term of office ended, he retired to live quietly in the county. One day, Officer Gu suddenly came to his door and said to Xianke, "I, Hong, am only an aging military man. I am no good for any service! Sir, you have made great efforts to gain my favor. Observing your intentions, I realize that you must have some request to make of this old man. This old man is a man of heart. I am moved by your deep kindness and I am willing to repay you even at the sacrifice of a cruel death."

Xianke cried and bowed to him, relating the story to Gu.

Gu looked up toward the sky, tapping his head with his hands several times before saying, "This task is not an easy one by any means. I will try to accomplish it for you, but don't expect results overnight."

Xianke bowed to him and said, "I only wish to see her before I die. How dare I impose a time limit?"

Half a year passed without any news, until one day, a knock on the door announced the delivery of a letter from Gu. The letter read, "The messenger sent to Mt. Mao[12] has returned. Come here immediately."

Xianke mounted his horse and galloped off. When he was received by Gu, Gu did not utter a single word. Xianke then inquired about the messenger.

Gu responded, "I have already killed him. Let's just have tea for now."

Only when it was deep at night, did Gu say to Xianke, "Is there anyone from Wushuang's family who knows her?" Xianke replied that Caiping did and fetched her at once.

Gu looked at her up and down, and with a pleased smile said, "I will borrow and keep her for a few days. Sir, you return home first."

Several days later, an unexpected message came that a high official had stopped by and executed a palace lady of the mausoleum. Xianke was very surprised and ordered Sai Hong to find out who was killed; it turned out to be Wushuang. Xianke cried, letting out a sigh saying "I originally set my hope upon Gu.

---

[12]Mt. Mao 茅 (Reeds Mountain), located to the south of modern Zhenjiang city in Jiangsu province, is a sacred mountain for Daoism. It was the principle seat of the Shangqing (Supreme Clarity) School of Daoism.

She is dead now! What shall I do?" With tears rolling down his cheeks, he sobbed sorrowfully and uncontrollably.

Late that night, he heard someone urgently knocking on his door. When he opened the door, it turned out to be Gu who entered followed by a bamboo sedan chair. He said to Xianke, "This is Wushuang. She is 'dead' now, but her heart is still slightly warm. She will come back to life the day after tomorrow. Feed her a little concoction. And you must keep it quiet and secret."

After Gu finished his words, Xianke carried Wushuang into the chamber and attended to her by himself. When it was dawn, her entire body became warm. Seeing Xianke, she uttered a single cry and fainted. She did not recover until night after she had been treated.

Gu made another request; "I would like to borrow Sai Hong to dig a pit behind the house." When the pit was deep enough, he drew his knife and cut off Sai Hong's head into the pit. Xianke was startled and horrified.

Gu said, "Sir, don't be frightened. Now I have paid back your kindness in full. I heard that a Daoist priest on Mt. Mao had an elixir. Anyone who takes this elixir will die immediately but will revive after three days. I sent someone specially to seek it and obtained one pill. Yesterday I asked Caiping to disguise herself to be a palace envoy, bestowing Wushuang this pill to commit suicide due to her connections with the rebel party. When we arrived at the mausoleum, I, assuming the name of her relative, ransomed her corpse with a hundred bolts of double-weaved silk. I lavishly bribed all the relay stations on the way to make absolutely sure that nothing would leak out. As for the messenger from Mt. Mao and the men who carried the bamboo sedan chair, I executed all of them in the field. This old man will also commit suicide for your sake. You cannot live here any longer. There are five litters with ten bearers, five horses, and two hundred bolts of raw silk. Take Wushuang with you and set off at the fifth watch, change your name and wander around to avoid catastrophe."

After saying these words, Gu raised his knife. Before Xianke could stop him, his head had already fallen. Xianke then covered and buried his head and body. He set off before dawn, passed through the Shu area,[13] flowing down the three gorges, and settled down in Zhugong.[14] When news of danger from the capital gradually subsided, he brought his family to his country residence in the Xiang and Deng region. He grew old together with Wushuang and they had a houseful of children.

Alas! There are numerous separations and reunions in one's life time, but it is rare that something is comparable to this experience. I have always said that there is nothing in history quite like this story. Wushuang suffered from the chaos of her time and was drafted into the imperial service; however, Xianke held fast to his intentions, which did not change even when it meant sacrificing his life. In the end, he encountered Gu who rescued Wushuang with an unusual method, and over a dozen innocent people died. He fled and wandered through dire circumstances before he could return to his hometown. They lived as husband and wife for fifty years. How extraordinary a story indeed!

---

[13]The Shu area is modern Sichuan province.

[14]Zhugong 渚宫 was the name of a palace in the state of Chu during the Spring and Autumn period. It was located in modern Jiangling county in Hubei province.

無雙傳

薛調

　　王仙客者，建中中朝臣劉震之甥也。初，仙客父亡，與母同歸外氏。震有女曰無雙，小仙客數歲，皆幼稚，戲弄相狎。震之妻常戲呼仙客為王郎子。如是者凡數歲，而震奉孀姊及撫仙客尤至。

　　一旦，王氏姊疾，且重，召震約曰：“我一子，念之可知也。恨不見其婚室。無雙端麗聰慧，我深念之。異日無令歸他族。我以仙客為託。爾誠許我，瞑目無所恨也。”震曰：“姊宜安靜自頤養，無以他事自撓。”其姊竟不痊。

　　仙客護喪，歸葬襄鄧。服闋，思念：“身世孤子如此，宜求婚娶，以廣後嗣。無雙長成矣。我舅氏豈以位尊官顯，而廢舊約耶？”於是飾裝抵京師。

　　時震為尚書租庸使，門館赫奕，冠蓋填塞。仙客既覲，置於學舍，弟子為伍。舅甥之分，依然如故，但寂然不聞選取之議。又於窗隙間窺見無雙，姿質明艷，若神仙中人。仙客發狂，唯恐姻親之事不諧也。遂鬻囊橐，得錢數百萬。舅氏舅母左右給使，達於廝養，皆厚遺之。又因復設酒饌，中門之內，皆得入之矣。諸表同處，悉敬事之。遇舅母生日，市新奇以獻，雕鏤犀玉，以為首飾。舅母大喜。又旬日，仙客遣老嫗，以求親之事聞於舅母。舅母曰：“是我所願也。即當議其事。”又數夕，有青衣告仙客曰：“娘子適以親情事言於阿郎，阿郎云：‘向前亦未許之。’模樣云云，恐是參差也。”仙客聞之，心氣俱喪，達旦不寐，恐舅氏之見棄也。然奉事不敢懈怠。

　　一日，震趨朝，至日初出，忽然走馬入宅，汗流氣促，唯言：“鎖卻大門，鎖卻大門！”一家惶駭，不測其由，良久，乃言：“涇原兵士反，姚令言領兵入含元殿，天子出苑北門，百官奔赴行在。我以妻女為念，略歸部署。疾召仙客與我勾當家事。我嫁與爾無雙。”

仙客聞命，驚喜拜謝。乃裝金銀羅錦二十馱，謂仙客曰：“汝易衣服，押領此物出開遠門，覓一深隙店安下。我與汝舅母及無雙出啟夏門，繞城續至。”仙客依所教。至日落，城外店中待久不至。

城門自午後扃鎖，南望目斷。遂乘驄，秉燭繞城至啟夏門。門亦鎖。守門者不一，持白梃，或立，或坐。

仙客下馬，徐問曰：“城中有何事如此？”又問“今日有何人出此？”

門者曰：“朱太尉已作天子。午後有一人重戴，領婦人四五輩，欲出此門。街中人皆識，云是租庸使劉尚書。門司不敢放出。近夜，追騎至，一時驅向北去矣。”

仙客失聲慟哭，卻歸店。三更向盡，城門忽開，見火炬如晝。兵士皆持兵挺刃，傳呼斬斫使出城，搜城外朝官。仙客舍輜騎驚走，歸襄陽，村居三年。

後知剋復，京師重整，海內無事，乃入京，訪舅氏消息，至新昌南街，立馬仿徨之際，忽有一人馬前拜，熟視之，乃舊使蒼頭塞鴻也。鴻本王家生，其舅常使得力，遂留之。握手垂涕。

仙客謂鴻曰：“阿舅舅母安否？”鴻云：“並在興化宅。”仙客喜極云：“我便過街去。”鴻曰：“某已得從良，客戶有一小宅子，販繒為業。今日已夜，郎君且就客戶一宿。來早同去未晚。”

遂引至所居，飲饌甚備。至昏黑，乃聞報曰：“尚書受偽命官，與夫人皆處極刑。無雙已入掖庭矣。”仙客哀冤號絕，感動鄰里。謂鴻曰：“四海至廣，舉目無親戚，未知托身之所。”又問曰：“舊家人誰在？”鴻曰：“唯無雙所使婢採蘋者，今在金吾將軍王遂中宅。”仙客曰：“無雙固無見期。得見採蘋，死亦足矣。”由是乃刺謁，以從姪禮見遂中，具道本末，願納厚價以贖採蘋。遂中深見相知，感其事而許之。仙客稅屋，與鴻蘋居。

塞鴻每言：“郎君年漸長，合求官職。悒悒不樂，何以遣時？”仙客感其言，以情懇告遂中。遂中薦見仙客於京兆尹李齊運，齊運以仙客前銜，為富平縣尹，知長樂驛。

累月，忽報有中使押領內家三十人往園陵，以備灑掃，宿長樂驛。氈車子十乘下訖。仙客謂塞鴻曰：“我聞官嬪選在掖庭，多是衣冠子女。我恐無雙在焉。汝為我一窺，可乎？”鴻曰：“宮嬪數千，豈便及無雙？”仙客曰：“汝但去，人事亦未可定。”因令塞

鴻假為驛吏，烹茗於簾外。仍給錢三千，約曰：“堅守茗具，無暫
捨去。忽有所覩，即疾報來。”塞鴻唯唯而去。

宮人悉在簾下，不可得見之，但夜語喧嘩而已。至夜深，群動
皆息。塞鴻滌器構火，不敢輒寐。忽聞簾下語曰：“塞鴻，塞鴻，
汝爭得知我在此耶？郎健否？”言訖，嗚咽，塞鴻曰：“郎君見知
此驛。今日疑娘子在此，令塞鴻問候。”又曰：“我不久語。明日
我去後，汝於東北舍閣子中紫褥下，取書送郎君。”言訖，便去。
忽聞簾下極鬧，云：“內家中惡。”中使索湯藥甚急，乃無雙也。

塞鴻疾告仙客，仙客驚曰：“我何得一見？”塞鴻曰：“今方
修渭橋。郎君可假作理橋官，車子過橋時，近車子立。無雙若認得，
必開簾子，當得瞥見耳。”仙客如其言。至第三車子，果開簾子，
窺見，真無雙也。仙客悲感怨慕，不勝其情。

塞鴻於閣子中褥下得書送仙客。花箋五幅，皆無雙真跡，詞理
哀切，敘述周盡，仙客覽之，茹恨涕下。自此永訣矣。其書後云：
“常見敕便說富平縣古押衙人間有心人。今能求之否？”

仙客遂申府，請解驛務，歸本官。遂尋訪古押衙，則居於村墅。
仙客造謁，見古生。生所願，必力致之，繒綵寶玉之贈，不可勝紀。
一年未開口。

秩滿，閒居於縣，古生忽來，謂仙客曰：“洪一武夫，年且老，
何所用？郎君於某竭分。察郎君之意，將有求於老夫。老夫乃一片
有心人也。感郎君之深恩，願粉身以答效。”仙客泣拜，以實告古
生。古生仰天，以手拍腦數四，曰：“此事大不易。然與郎君試求，
不可朝夕便望。”仙客拜曰：“但生前得見，豈敢以遲晚為限耶。”

半歲無消息。一日，扣門，乃古生送書。書云：“茅山使者回。
且來此。”仙客奔馬去。見古生，生乃無一言。又啟使者。復云：
“殺卻也。且吃茶。”夜深，謂仙客曰：“宅中有女家人識無雙
否？”仙客以采蘋對。仙客立取而至。古生端相，且笑且喜云：
“借留三五日。郎君且歸。”

後累日，忽傳說曰：“有高品過，處置園陵宮人。”仙客心甚
異之。令塞鴻探所殺者，乃無雙也。仙客號哭，乃歎曰：“本望古
生。今死矣！為之奈何！”流涕歔欷，不能自已。

是夕更深，聞叩門甚急。及開門，乃古生也。領一篼子入，謂
仙客曰：“此無雙也。今死矣。心頭微暖，後日當活，微灌湯藥，
切須靜密。”言訖，仙客抱入閣子中，獨守之。至明，遍體有暖氣。
見仙客，哭一聲遂絕。救療至夜，方愈。

　古生又曰：“暫借塞鴻於舍後掘一坑。”坑稍深，抽刀斷塞鴻頭於坑中。仙客驚怕。古生曰：“郎君莫怕。今日報郎君恩足矣。比聞茅山道士有藥術。其藥服之者立死，三日卻活。某使人專求，得一丸。昨令採蘋假作中使，以無雙逆黨，賜此藥令自盡。至陵下，托以親故，百縑贖其尸。凡道路郵傳，皆厚賂矣，必免漏泄。茅山使者及舁篼人，在野外處置訖。老夫為郎君，亦自刎。君不得更居此。門外有檐子一十人，馬五匹，絹二百匹。五更挈無雙便發，變姓名浪跡以避禍。”

　言訖，舉刀。仙客救之，頭已落矣。遂并尸蓋覆訖。未明發，歷四蜀下峽，寓居於渚宮。悄不聞京兆之耗，乃挈家歸襄鄧別業，與無雙偕老矣。男女成群。

　噫，人生之契闊會合多矣，罕有若斯之比。常謂古今所無。無雙遭亂世籍沒，而仙客之志，死而不奪。卒遇古生之奇法取之，冤死者十餘人。艱難走竄後，得歸故鄉，為夫婦五十年，何其異哉！

Tale 4.26

An Account of the Maid Shangqing

By Liu Cheng
Translated by Yuhua Wen

It was the third month of the *renshen* year in the Zhenyuan period (785–805). Duke Dou,[1] the Minister of the State, lived in his residence located at Guangfu Ward. Once he walked leisurely in the courtyard in a spring evening full of moonlight. His favorite maidservant, Shangqing, said to him, "I have something to report to you, but I dare not speak out unless Your Excellence goes to the hall."

Duke Dou hurriedly went to the hall. Shangqing said, "Someone is hidden in the tree of the atrium, so I request Your Excellence to keep away from him to avoid being scared." Duke Dou said, "Lu Zhi has planned to take my power and position away for a long time.[2] Now an unknown person is hiding himself in the tree, so my calamity is coming. Whether I report the matter to the emperor or not, I would suffer from it, and I am bound to die on the way to exile. You are rare among the maidservants in

---

[1]Dou Shen 竇參 (734–793), styled Shizhong 時中, was appointed minister of the state in the fifth year of Zhenyuan reign under Emperor Dezong of the Tang.

[2]Lu Zhi 陸贄 (754–805), styled Jing Yu 敬輿, was a famous statesman, writer and political commentator of the Tang Dynasty.

the mansion. After my exile and my family members' dispersion, you would certainly be confiscated to serve as a servant in the imperial palace. If there is any chance that the emperor has a talk with you, please speak on my behalf."

Shangqing cried, "If that is the case, I promise to do it even at the risk of my life." Then Dou walked down the steps, shouted, "The gentleman in the tree, you must be sent by Lu Zhi. If you can save an old fellow's life like mine, I will pay a handsome reward to you."

The man in the tree climbed down the tree upon hearing his words, and he turned out to be clothed in sackcloth mourning dress. He said, "My family is required to provide a funeral, but we are too poor to make arrangements. I have heard that you always help the poor sincerely, so I decided to come at night. I hope you will not blame me." Duke Dou said, "I will donate all of my assets, which are just one thousand silk fabrics. I planned to take it as the budget for building my ancestral temple, but now I will give it to you instead — how about that?" The man in mourning dress bowed to express his gratitude, and Duke Dou returned the salute. The man said again, "I would say farewell to you, the prime minister. Please ask your servants to throw my silk fabric out of the wall, and I will wait on the street." Dou did this according to his requests. He also ordered his servants to watch secretly. He dared not go back to his bedroom to sleep until long after the man left his sight.

The next day, the chamberlain for the imperial insignia reported the happening to the emperor, and Duke Dou reported it to the emperor again when summoned to the court. The emperor Dezong snapped, "You are making friendly relations with military commissioners and raising chivalrous assassins! You have the most superior position as the chief bulwark of the state, so what else do you desire?" Dou replied with a kowtow, "Thanks entirely to Your Majesty's appreciation and promotion, but not that of others', I was promoted from the inferior official who dealt with the official documents and correspondence to the superior Grand Councilor. Unfortunately, I am in a difficult situation today, and it is likely that my foe has framed me. If, because of me, Your Majesty flew into a rage, I should be guilty of the crime for which one deserves one thousand deaths." Later the eunuch went out of the court to announce his majesty's order, "You just go home for the moment, waiting for either advancement or retreat."

One month later Duke Dou was demoted to Administrative Aide in Chenzhou.[3] Just as the time when Liu Shining, the military commissioner in Xuanwu area remained in regular contact with Dou, the investigation officer submitted a memorial to the emperor enumerating the facts. Emperor Dezong said, "There is indeed evidence Dou consorted together with the military commissioner in private." He ordered Dou's exile to Huanzhou[4] and the confiscation of family property; not even a hairpin could be taken with him. Before Dou arrived at the place of exile, the emperor ordered him to commit suicide.

As expected, Shangqing was confiscated for the palace. Several years later, because of her excellent skills in communication and making tea, she had served the emperor several times. The emperor Dezong said to her, "There are quite a number of maidservants in the palace, but you are so sensible and thoughtful. From what place did you enter the palace as a maidservant?" Shangqing answered, "I was originally a maidservant of Dou Shen, the former Grand Councilor. His wife passed away in the early years, so I had the chance to keep him company as a maid. After his family declined, I was fortunate

---

[3]Its seat was in modern-day Zhen County, Hunan.

[4]A state of Tang covering Hejing province and the south of Yi'an Province in Vietnam.

enough to come into the palace. Since I started serving Your Majesty, I feel as if I'm in heaven."

The emperor Dezong said, "Dou's crime was not only harboring assassins, but also serious corruption. A lot of silverware found in his house was confiscated." Shangqing said, in tears, "Dou originally was appointed to be the vice censor-in-chief, then an official in the Tax Bureau, the Census Bureau, and the Salt Monopoly Bureau, and finally the Grand Councilor. That was a period of about six years with the monthly income of 100 thousand. The awards he received at various times are numerous. The confiscated silver wares in Chenzhou were all from awards bestowed by Your Majesty. When the confiscated property was registered I was also in Chenzhou and witnessed the officials scraping the signs of royal reward away according to the order of Lu Zhi. The confiscated silver items were then carved with the names and titles of those in the frontier defense command, so a false accusation was lodged that it was booty. I beg Your Majesty to inspect this." Thereupon, the emperor ordered a reexamination of the silverwares confiscated from Dou's house, and the scraping traces on the silverwares were seen to be just as Shangqing said.

It was the 12th year in the Zhenyuan Period then. The emperor asked Shangqing about Dou's affairs in harboring assassins. Shangqing said, "There was indeed no such thing, it was Lu Zhi who instructed others to do it and who framed the accusation." The emperor was then angered by Lu Zhi, saying, "This evil slave, I gave him the privilege of putting on the purple shirt of a high ranking official and taking off the green shirt of a lower ranking official, and often call him Lu the ninth. Though I had been satisfied with the appointment of Dou Shen, I killed him unjustly because of Lu Zhi. The power then came to Lu Zhi, and he handles government affairs in a way as weak and soft as the mud." Then he ordered that Dou be exonerated of unjust charges.

When he heard that Lu Zhi was no longer favored, Pei Yanling⁵ framed him without restraint. Lu Zhi was demoted to somewhere away and banned from going back to the capital. Later Shangqing was granted an imperial edict permitting her to become a Buddhist nun, and she finally married Jin Zhongyi⁶ as his wife. Because quite a lot of Lu Zhi's disciples were illustrious and influential in terms of fame and position, people of the time dared not pass any word about her, so the story of Shangqing is hardly known.

---

⁵Pei Yanling 裴延齡 (728–796) was promoted to the Minister of Revenue in charge of the economic lifeline in 792.

⁶Jin Zhongyi, 金忠義 a famous craftsman in Tang Dynasty. He was promoted to directorate for Imperial Manufactories because of his outstanding craftsmanship.

上清傳

柳珵

　　貞元壬申歲春三月，相國竇公居光福里第，月夜閒步於中庭。有常所寵青衣上清者，乃曰："今欲啟事。郎須到堂前，方敢言之。"竇公亟上堂。

　　上清曰："庭樹上有人，恐驚郎，請謹避之。"竇公曰："陸贄久欲傾奪吾權位。今有人在庭樹上，吾禍將至。且此事將奏與不奏皆受禍，必竄死于道路。汝在輩流中，不可多得。吾身死家破，汝定為宮婢。聖君若顧問，善為我辭焉。"

　　上清泣曰："誠如是，死生以之！"竇公下階，大呼曰："樹上君子，應是陸贄使來。能全老夫性命，敢不厚報！"

　　樹上應聲而下，乃衣繢粗者也。曰："家有大喪。貧甚，不辦葬禮。伏知相公推心濟物，所以卜夜而來，幸相公無怪。"公曰："某罄所有，堂封絹千匹而已。方擬修私廟次。今且輒贈，可乎？"繢者拜謝。竇公答之，如禮。又曰："便辭相公。請左右齎所賜絹，擲於牆外。某先於街中俟之。"竇公依其請。命僕，使偵其絕蹤且久，方敢歸寢。

　　翌日，執金吾先奏其事，竇公得次，又奏之。德宗厲聲曰："卿交通節將，蓄養俠刺。位崇台鼎，更欲何求？"竇公頓首曰："臣起自刀筆小才，官以至貴。皆陛下獎拔，實不由人。今不幸至此，抑乃仇家所為耳。陛下忽震雷霆之怒，臣便合萬死。"中使下殿宣曰："卿且歸私第，待候進止。"

　　越月，貶郴州別駕。會宣武節度劉士甯通好于郴州，廉使條疏上聞。德宗曰："交通節將，信而有徵。"流竇於驩州，沒入家資。一簪不著身，竟未達流所，詔自盡。

379

　　上清果隸名掖庭。後數年，以善應對，能煎茶，數得在帝左右。德宗謂曰：“宮掖間人數不少。汝了事。從何得至此？”上清對曰：“妾本故宰相竇參家女奴。竇某妻早亡，故妾得陪掃灑。及竇某家破，幸得填宮，既侍龍顏，如在天上。”

　　德宗曰：“竇某罪不止養俠刺，亦甚有贓污。前時納官銀器至多。”上清流涕而言曰：“竇某自御史中丞，曆度支，戶部，鹽鐵三使，至宰相。首尾六年，月入數十萬。前後非時賞賜，當亦不知紀極。迺者郴州所送納官銀物，皆是恩賜。當部錄日，妾在郴州，親見州縣希陸贄意旨刮去。所進銀器，上刻作藩鎮官銜姓名，誣為贓物。伏乞陛下驗之。”於是宣索竇某沒官銀器覆視，其刮字處，皆如上清言。

　　時貞元十二年。德宗又問蓄養俠刺事。上清曰：“本實無。悉是陸贄陷害，使人為之。”德宗怒陸贄曰：“這獠奴！我脫卻伊綠衫，便與紫衫著。又常喚伊作陸九。我任使竇參，方稱意次，須教我枉殺卻他。及至權入伊手，其為軟弱，甚於泥團。”乃下詔雪竇參。

　　時裴延齡探知陸贄恩衰，得恣行媒孽。贄竟受譴不迴。後上清特敕丹書度為女道士，終嫁為金忠義妻。世以陸贄門生名位多顯達者，世不可傳說，故此事絕無人知。

The Account of Courtesan Yang

By Fang Qianli
Translated by Scott W. Galer and Trever McKay

Courtesan Yang was a stunningly beautiful girl in the alley brothels in Chang'an. She had a lovely manner and was confident with her enticing looks. Aristocrats and officials, while feasting with their guests, would contend to have her sit at their tables.[1] She could even get teetotalers to fill their cups to the brim and enjoy themselves to the fullest. Many of the young men of Chang'an would happily risk loss of life and fortune to visit her chambers. For these reasons, the courtesan's name was at the head of the registry of courtesans, and she cost a pretty penny.

---

[1]Being a courtesan in the Tang dynasty was much more than our modern concept of a prostitute. To begin with, they were often also entertainers skilled in song, poems, and intellectual conversations. Second, it was a social class and required adding one's name to the official courtesan registry. Lastly, changing occupations (as is indicated later in the story) required formal removal from the registry — something that involved a large sum of money. For a more in-depth look at the life of a courtesan, see Jeanne Larsen, *Brocade River Poems: Selected Works of the Tang Dynasty Courtesan* (Princeton: Princeton University Press, 1987), xiv-xvi *et passim*.

The commander of the land south of the Five Ranges[2] was the son of an aristocrat. His wife, from a family of imperial relatives by marriage, tended to treat the commander rather cruelly. By prior agreement, if either were disloyal, they would die by the blade. The commander was a young noble and liked to enjoy himself. At home, however, he was pained by his wife and thus never paid any attention to her. So, he secretly gave a handsome sum to have Yang removed from the courtesan registry. He then took her to Nanhai,[3] housing her in other quarters. He accompanied her in his leisure hours and returned home only under cover of darkness. The courtesan was intelligent and exceptionally circumspect in serving the commander. During the day, she preoccupied herself with the feminine arts. She was not given to rash speech and was also kind to the commander's attendants. All were fond of her so that the commander loved her all the more.

One year after being together, the commander was stricken with an illness. Near his death, he wanted to see the courtesan one more time. Yet he was too fearful of his wife to act. As the commander had a long and deep friendship with the military inspector, he secretly sent a message conveying his desires and asked him to devise a plan. The military inspector misled the commander's wife, saying, "The general is gravely ill and desires to find someone who is skilled in serving and cooking medicine to look after him. Doing so should speed up his recovery. I have such a servant girl who has long attended upon noble families and who is skilled at meeting people's wishes. If it so pleases my lady, the servant girl could come and attend to the general. What think

---

[2]"South of the Five Ranges" refers to an area comprised of present-day Guangxi, Guangdong, Hainan, Hong Kong, Macau, and potentially northern Vietnam. These five mountain ranges function as the watershed between the Yangtze and Pearl River basins.

[3]Nanhai was the name of a prefecture in what is now the Yuexiu district in Guangzhou.

you?" The commander's wife replied, "As a high official close to the emperor, you are trustworthy. If she turns out to be as you say, I do not see any harm in it. Please have her come promptly."

The military inspector commanded the courtesan to disguise herself as a servant to see the commander. Before the plan could be carried out, however, the truth got out. The commander's wife gathered scores of strong servant girls. They laid out large sticks, heated up a cooking pot in the courtyard, and waited for her. As soon as the courtesan arrived, they would throw her into the boiling cauldron.

The commander was struck with dread when he heard what was happening. He quickly issued an order to stop the courtesan before she arrived. "This was my idea," he said, "and it almost got her killed. Fortunately, I am still alive. I must ensure she escapes the tiger's mouth. If not, it will be too late." Thereupon he sent a house servant with many rare treasures and a light boat, commanding him to protect the courtesan and take her back to the north. From that point on, the commander became increasingly disturbed, and less than ten days later he died.

When the courtesan arrived at Hongzhou,[4] she heard the news of his death. Having sent back all of the valuables the commander had given with the servant, she erected a spirit tablet and cried, saying, "General, you died because of me. With you dead, of what use is life to me? How can I leave you alone over there?" She immediately removed the sacrificial offerings and killed herself.

Courtesans serve others with their beauty. If there is no profit involved they do not act. Yet, Yang repaid the general's kindness by ending her life. This is a gallant act. She also returned the

---

[4]During the Tang dynasty, Hongzhou was at times also known as Yuzhang. It was located in what is now the north part of Jiangxi Province.

valuables given her. This is an act of honesty. Although she was a courtesan, she is deserving of some praise!

楊娼傳

房千里

楊娼者，長安里中之殊色也；態度甚都，復以冶容自喜。王公鉅人享客，競邀致席上。雖不飲者，必為之引滿盡歡。長安諸兒一造其室，殆至亡生破產而不悔。由是娼之名冠諸籍中，大售於時矣。

嶺南帥甲，貴遊子也。妻本戚里女，遇帥甚悍。先約，設有異志者，當取死白刃下。帥幼貴，喜媱，內苦其妻，莫之措意。乃陰出重賂，削去娼之籍，而挈之南海，館之他舍。公餘而同，夕隱而歸。娼有慧性，事帥尤謹。平居以女職自守，非其理，不妄發。復厚帥之左右，咸能得其歡心。故帥益嬖之。

會間歲，帥得病，且不起。思一見娼，而憚其妻。帥素與監軍使厚，密遣導意，使為方略。監軍乃紿其妻曰：“將軍病甚，思得善奉侍煎調者視之，瘳當速矣。某有善婢，久給事貴室，動得人意。請夫人聽以婢安將軍四體，如何？”妻曰：“中貴人，信人也，果然。於吾無苦耳，可促召婢來。”

監軍即命娼冒為婢以見帥。計未行而事泄。帥之妻乃擁健婢數十，列白挺，熾膏鑊於廷而伺之矣。須其至，當投之沸鬲。帥聞而大恐，促命止娼之至。且曰：“此自我意，幾累於渠。今幸吾之未死也，必使脫其虎喙。不然，且無及矣。”乃大遣其奇寶，命家僮傍輕舠，衛娼北歸。自是，帥之憤益深，不逾旬而物故。娼之行，適及洪矣。問至，娼乃盡返帥之賂，設位而哭，曰：“將軍由妾而死。將軍且死，妾安用生為？妾豈孤將軍者耶？”即撤奠而死之。

夫娼，以色事人者也，非其利則不合矣。而楊能報帥以死，義也；卻帥之賂，廉也。雖為娼，差足多乎！

Tale 4.28

The Tale of Feiyan

By Huangfu Mei
Translated by Jing Wang

Wu Gongye of Linhuai[1] served as Administrator of the Personnel Evaluation Section in Henan prefecture[2] during the Xiantong reign (860–873). His favorite concubine was Feiyan (Soaring-mist) with the last name Bu. She was slender and beautiful in her appearance and manner, as if too delicate to bear the weight of her own silk garment. She was good at singing the songs from the Qin region[3] and was fond of literary composition. And she was especially skilled at striking the pitch cups[4] in harmony with the strings and flutes. Gongye favored her very much.

Adjacent to his house was the residence of the Zhao family of Tianshui prefecture,[5] which was also a prominent clan, and thus their names will not be mentioned here. Their son, whose name was Xiang, was handsome and had literary talent. He had just

---

[1] A county in modern Jiangsu province.

[2] In modern Henan province. The site of prefectural administration was in Luoyang during the Tang dynasty.

[3] In modern Shanxi province.

[4] The pitch cups were a popular musical instrument during the Tang dynasty. A dozen cups were filled with water at different levels and were tapped with sticks to make music.

[5] In modern Gansu province.

turned twenty and was in the midst of observing the mourning ritual at the time. One day, he unexpectedly saw Feiyan through a crack in the south wall. He was so dispirited that he was unable to eat or sleep. He therefore lavishly bribed Gongye's gatekeeper, confessing his feelings for the lady within. The gatekeeper's face showed signs of reluctance, but he was eventually won over by the generous bribe. The gatekeeper asked his wife to keep an eye on Feiyan, and tell her all about Xiang's feelings when she found her at leisure.

After Feiyan heard tell of Xiang's intentions, she only smiled slightly and gazed wordlessly at the gatekeeper's wife. The gatekeeper's wife told Xiang all the details of Feiyan's reaction. Xiang went crazy; his heart was dazzled, and he didn't know how to control himself. He then grabbed a piece of vermillion notepaper and wrote a poem, in the cut-off style:

> Upon seeing your beauty that could cause the fall of a city,
> My secular heart is only filled with confusion.
> Do not follow Xiaoshi and take leave,[6]
> But emulate Lan and descend to this world.[7]

He tightly sealed the paper and begged the gatekeeper's wife to take it to Feiyan. After Yan finished reading it, she sighed for a long time, and then said to the old woman, "I also once had a glimpse of Mr. Zhao and found him to be talented and handsome.

---

[6]This line alludes to the anecdote of Nongyu, daughter of Duke Mu of the Qin State. She was good at playing the pipes and her tunes resembled the sound of the phoenix. The emperor built a high terrace for her, naming it after the mythical animal. Nongyu married Xiaoshi, who was skilled at playing the flute and was a descended immortal. The couple later ascended to Heaven on the back of dragons from the terrace.

[7]The allusion of this line is not clear. It might refer to the immortal Du Lanxiang 杜蘭香, who was banished to the human world.

How little fortune I have in this life that I will not be able to be with him." It seemed that she disdained Mr. Wu and considered him coarse and violent — not at all a good match for her. So she reciprocated Xiang's gesture by composing a poem of her own, writing it on a piece of paper with a gold-phoenix pattern. The poem read,

> With dark green furrowed eyebrows, I cannot control myself,
> A result of nothing more than the deep regret expressed in
>   your new poem.
> Sir, your heart should be filled with resentment like the zither
>   tone,
> Loving and longing, to whom shall I convey my spring-like
>   feelings?

She sealed it and entrusted it to the gatekeeper's wife, asking her to give it to Xiang. After Xiang opened the letter, he chanted the poem aloud quite a few times. Clapping his hands, he was pleased and said, "My plan should go smoothly." He then composed a poem to express his gratitude, writing it on a piece of jade-leaf paper made from the water of the Shan creek. The poem read,

> I cherished the fine melody that the beauty sent,
> In the colorful paper and scented ink, our emotions toward
>   each other run deep.
> Thinner than the cicada wing, it is difficult for the paper to
>   hold our regret,
> Densely arranged like the heads of flies, the characters cannot
>   fully express our hearts.
> As a falling flower loses its way in a green cave,
> I can only imagine a light rain sprinkling on my deep emotions.
> Thinking of your messages a hundred times and dreaming a
>   thousand times,

I tailored my thought into a long song to play on the green
zither.[8]

It had been over ten days since the poem was sent to Feiyan,
but the gatekeeper's wife did not come again. Xiang was worried
and afraid that his affair had been disclosed or that Feiyan had
changed her mind. One spring night, he sat in the front yard alone
and composed a poem which read:

The green darkened and the red concealed, dim smoke rose,
With profound regret, I am in the front yard alone.
Heavy and deep, with whom can I talk on this lovely night?
Stars separated by the Milky Way and the moon hanging in the
    center of the sky.

The next morning, while he was chanting poems after getting
up, the gatekeeper's wife came and passed on Feiyan's words to
him, "Don't be surprised that there has been no news for over ten
days, for I felt a little uneasy about this." Then the gatekeeper's
wife gave Xiang a sachet made of brocade as thin as cicada wings
with linked-flower patterns and some green paper tinted with
water moss. The poem on the paper read,

Forcing myself to dress, I lean on the carved window frame.
With unfathomed thoughts, I secretly inscribed a poem on the
    thin brocade.
Recently I have been afflicted with spring-longing sickness,
Like weak willow trees and tilting flowers, I am afraid of the
    morning breeze.

---

[8]Green zither is a short term for green-gauze zither, which was an
archaic fine zither in a dark green color. It later became a symbol for a
fine zither.

Xiang tied the brocade sachet to his underclothes. He read the note closely and worried that Feiyan's deep brooding would make her illness become worse. He then cut a piece of black-lined paper and wrote a note in response:

The spring is gentle and prolonged, and the heart is filled with sadness. Since I caught a glimpse of you, your image has dominated my dreams for a long time. Although it is difficult for us, you as an immortal who can fly with feathered wings and me as a mundane man, to unite in matrimony, I vow with the ultimate sincerity to the bright sun that I want to be with you. Yesterday the blue bird[9] from the Jade Terrace suddenly arrived carrying with it a sincere message. Your gift of the brocade sachet, as thin as cicada wings, filled my breast with a fragrant aroma. My admiration for you deepens and my attachment to you has become more profound. I hear that you are over-burdened with thoughts because of the spring and your delicate body is not well. Your beautiful ice-and-snow-like appearance has diminished and your fragrant, orchid-like charisma has been affected. I was so despondent that I could not fly to your side. I hope that you can temper your heavy thoughts so that you won't become disheartened. Do not ignore my wish expressed in the short poem. I would rather sacrifice further meetings with you [were you to be well]. How can this letter fully express my disconsolate feelings? I enclose this meager poem to respond to your resplendent piece. My only humble wish is that you would direct your sight upon it.

The poem read,

Seeing that you suffered from excessive emotions because of the spring,

---

[9]The blue bird was said to be a messenger for the Divine Mother of the West. It later became a metaphor for a messenger.

Imagining that you knit your dark moth-like eyebrows while
   sealing the brocade sachet as thin as cicada wings.
Bowing to repay the favor that dear Feiyan expressed in her
   poem,
People of supreme talent will suffer the most pain of all.

After the gatekeeper's wife got the reply, she went directly to
Feiyan's chamber for a visit.

Mr. Wu, as an administrator in the prefecture government,
was overwhelmed with business. Sometimes he was on the night
shift once every few days, sometimes he did not return home for
an entire day. It happened at that time that he went to the
government office. Feiyan opened Xiang's letter and was able to
read it carefully to gather all the heart-felt feelings conveyed.
Thereafter, she cast a long sigh and said, "A man's ambition and a
woman's feelings! We are connected in our hearts and souls.
Although we are far apart, it feels as though we are very close."
She then closed the door, lowered the curtains, and wrote a letter
which read:

I, a lowly woman, am unfortunate. I was orphaned when I was
a child. Later I was deceived by a matchmaker and thus
married a vulgar creature. Every time there was a refreshing
breeze and bright moon, I played the zither to relieve my
anxieties. With curtains in cold autumn days and lights in dark
winter nights, I entrusted my regret to the music. Never did I
expect that you, Sir, would send me pleasant notes. When I
sent you the message on the decorated notepaper, my thoughts
flew with it. While I was chanting beautiful lines, I gazed into
the distance. What I hate is that we are separated as if by the
waves of the Luo River[10] and the high wall that prevents me,

---

[10]This alludes to Cao Zhi's (192–232) "Rhapsody on the Goddess of
the Luo River" in which he described his encounter with the Goddess of

like Jia Wu,[11] from seeing my lover. Even if I were to be on a terrace that touches the clouds, it would not be as high as the terrace in the Qin state.[12] Even if I wanted to meet you in my dreams, I would still be too far away from the mountain in the State of Chu.[13] I pray that Heaven will grant my wish of a lifetime and the spirits will give us a meager chance. Bowing to the clear shine of Heaven, I have no regret even if I should die many times. I have also composed a short poem in which I have confided my deep feelings. My only humble wish is that you would lower yourself to read it.

The poem read,

Under the decorated eves, the spring swallows must stay in
    pairs,
On the orchid shore, would the two mandarin ducks fly alone?
I always feel regret for the immortal ladies in the Peach
    Blossom Spring,
Lightheartedly, they saw their gentlemen off in the blooming
    season.[14]

---

the Luo River. His admiration for her went in vain because of the insurmountable barrier between an immortal and a human being.

[11]Jia Wu 賈午 (260–300) fell in love with her father's subordinate Han Shou, who crossed over the wall to meet her in the middle of night.

[12]See note 6.

[13]This alludes to the famous erotic legend of the Goddess of Mt. Wu and the King of Chu. The goddess offered herself to the king in his dream. When the king woke up, he could only remember her farewell message that she resided on the southern side of Mt. Wu in the form of morning mist and evening rain.

[14]The last couplet alludes to the anecdote of Liu Chen 劉晨 and Ruan Zhao 阮肇 of the Han dynasty. They lost their way when picking herbs in Mt. Tiantai and had a romantic encounter with two immortal maidens. When they returned to the human world half a year later, they

After she sealed the letter, she summoned the gatekeeper's wife and asked her to send it to Xiang. When Xiang read the letter and the poem, he believed that Feiyan was sincere in her feelings. He was so pleased that he almost lost control of himself. He went straight to burn incense in a quiet meditation room, praying and waiting.

One day, when dusk was about to fall, the gatekeeper's wife arrived in haste. Laughing and bowing, she said to Xiang, "Does Mr. Zhao want to meet the immortal?" Xiang was surprised and asked her repeatedly what she meant. She passed on Feiyan's words, saying, "It happened that my husband is on duty at the Personnel Evaluation Section tonight. This can be said to be a good time. The backyard of my house adjoins the front wall of your yard. If your affection has not changed, I especially hope that you will come. My mind is tangled with endless thoughts and I could hope for nothing more but to meet and talk with you."

When it was getting dark, Xiang then climbed up the ladder and ascended the wall. Feiyan had already ordered two couches to be stacked on one another beneath the wall. After he descended, he found Feiyan standing in the front of the yard with exquisite make-up and splendid attire. After they bowed to each other, both of them were speechless in their bliss. Hand in hand, they then entered the hall through the back door. The room was decorated with silver candles and silk curtains. They indulged themselves fully in sensual pleasure. Just when the morning bell rang, Feiyan saw Xiang off by the yard wall.

Holding his hand, Feiyan said to Xiang, "It must be our pre-determined fate that we met today. Don't think that I am not as faithful as pure jade and virtuous pine trees and behave in such a

---

found out that seven generations had passed. They eventually left the human world for good and presumably became immortals themselves.

licentious way. It is simply because of your charisma that I could not restrain myself. I hope you understand the situation."

Xiang said, "I have seen your incomparable beauty in this world and your unusual mind that exceeds that of ordinary people. I have already made vows to gods and spirits and wished for us to be happy and harmonious forever." After saying this, Xiang climbed over the wall and returned home. The next day, Xiang asked the gatekeeper's wife to present Feiyan with a poem that read,

> Although the route to the ten grottos and three purity
>   heavens[15] is filled with obstacles,
> One who has the intention can still approach the Jade Terrace.
> The fragrance of the winter daphne brought by the breeze
>   makes me think in the deep night.
> I know that the immortal from the Palace of Stamen[16] has
>   arrived on her ride.

Feiyan smiled as she read the poem and again, in return, wrote a poem which read,

> Yearning for your love, I only feared that we were not
>   acquainted.
> Seeing each other, I still worried that I was to be separated
>   from you.
> I wish that we could be transformed to become cranes in a pine
>   tree,
> In a pair, we would fly into the moving clouds.

She sealed the note, gave it to the gatekeeper's wife, and also asked her to tell Xiang, "It is fortunate that this humble maid has a

---

[15]These are the dwellings of immortals.
[16]A palace of the Daoist immortals.

little knowledge of poetry, otherwise, how could I tell how talented you are?"

After that, they were able to meet in the back yard regularly once every ten days or so, expressing their profound and subtle thoughts and confiding their long-lasting feelings. They thought that their affair was unknown even to ghost birds and that Heaven and the human world were conspiring with them to keep their love a secret. They sometimes gazed at scenes in front of them and chanted poems to express their feelings. Their interactions were so frequent that not all details could be written down. It was like this for a whole year.

Shortly afterwards, Feiyan whipped her maid servant several times because of minor mistakes. The servant secretly held a grudge against her and reported Feiyan's entire affair to Gongye when she got a chance. Gongye said, "You must be cautious and not spread the word. I shall investigate the matter." Later on, the day he was on duty, he secretly reported the situation [to the government] and asked for leave of absence. When night fell, he made as if to head out to the office as usual, but then hid at the gate of his residential quarter. After the street drum for curfew was sounded, he sneaked home secretly. He walked along the wall and came to the back yard. He saw Feiyan was leaning against the door and chanting softly, while Xiang was standing by the wall and glancing sideways at her. Gongye, unable to contain his anger, charged forward in an attempt to catch Xiang. Xiang realized his intention and jumped away. Gongye fought him and ripped his upper coat in half. He then entered the room and called on Feiyan to question her. Feiyan's countenance changed, her voice quivered, but she did not tell the truth. Gongye became more furious. He tied her to a big pillar and whipped her until she bled. Feiyan only said, "Since we could be together when we were alive, I have no regret even if I die."

In the middle of the night, Gongye was tired and took a nap. Feiyan called out to her favorite maid servant and said, "Give me a cup of water." When the water was brought to her, she drank it all and died. When Gongye woke up intending to whip her again, she was already dead. He then untied the rope and carried her to the chamber. He cried out her name several times and claimed that Feiyan had died from an acute disease. After several days, he buried her on Mt. Beimang,[17] but the entire neighborhood knew that she'd died a violent death.

Thereafter, Xiang changed his clothes, adopted the name of Yuan, and fled to the area of the Yangtze River and Qiantang River.

There was a talented scholar from Luoyang who composed "The Tale of Feiyan." In the tale were a Mr. Cui and a Mr. Li who often interacted with Mr. Wu, the administrator. [Each had written a poem after Feiyan's death.] The last couplet of Cui's poem read,

> Just like after a flower-circulating game, when the drinking
>   guests disperse,
> On an empty couch, a branch with the most luxuriant blossoms
>   is left behind.

On the evening [of the day when he wrote the poem], Cui dreamed that Feiyan expressed her gratitude to him, saying, "Although my appearance cannot match up to peach and plum blossoms, I have suffered a more wretched fate. Holding your excellent poem, I can't help but feel ashamed."

---

[17]Mt. Beimang 北邙, located to the northeast of Luoyang, was a burial site for nobles.

The last couplet of Mr. Li read,

If her gorgeous soul and fragrant spirit are still around,
She should be ashamed to meet the maid who threw herself off
  the Terrace.[18]

On the evening [of the day when he wrote the poem], Li dreamt that Feiyan, pointing her finger at him, scolded, "A scholar should possess a hundred virtues. Sir, do you have them all? Why did you have to make arrogant remarks in your couplet and so condemn me? I shall confront you in the underworld and testify to your words in person." After a few days, Mr. Li died. People at the time found it extraordinary.

Yuan later was transferred to Lushan county in Ru prefecture[19] where he was appointed Recorder. Li Yuan from Longxi succeeded him. I succeeded Li Yuan at the end of the Xiantong reign period (860–873). I was on close terms with Yuan when we were young, and therefore knew about his secret affair in Luoyang. Li Yuan also made a record of it and therefore the story was able to be transmitted.

The gentleman from Sanshui[20] commented: Alas! The appearance of enchanting beauty can be found once in a generation, but pure and upright virtue is rarely witnessed. Therefore, if a scholar is arrogant about his talent, then he has little virtue; if a woman flaunts her beauty, then she will have affairs. If they could behave cautiously as if they were holding a full glass of water and standing on the edge of a steep precipice,

---

[18]The maid refers to Green Pearl, a maid servant of Shi Chong (249–300) who was famous for his grand fortune. When a forceful rebel general intended to seize her, she committed suicide by throwing herself off a terrace, showing her devotion and fidelity to her master. Cf. T7.39.

[19]In modern Lushan county in Henan province.

[20]This was the title that the author used to refer to himself.

he would become an upright gentleman and she a virtuous lady. Although Feiyan's crime cannot be excused, if one examines her mind, one will have sympathy for her.

飛烟傳

皇甫枚

　　臨淮武公業，咸通中任河南府功曹參軍。愛妾曰飛烟，姓步氏。容止纖麗，若不勝綺羅。善秦聲，好文筆，尤工擊甌，其韻與絲竹合。公業甚嬖之。

　　其比鄰，天水趙氏第也，亦衣纓之族，不能斥言。其子曰象，秀端有文，纔弱冠矣。時方居喪禮。忽一日，於南垣隙中窺見飛烟，神氣俱喪，廢食忘寐。乃厚賂公業之閽，以情告之。閽有難色，復爲厚利所動。乃令其妻伺飛烟間處，具以象意言焉。飛烟聞之，但含笑凝睇而不答。門媼盡以語象。象發狂心蕩，不知所持，乃取薛濤箋，題絕句曰：

> “一睹傾城貌，塵心只自猜。
> 不隨蕭史去，擬學阿蘭來。”

　　以所題密緘之，祈門媼達飛烟。烟讀畢，吁嗟良久，謂媼曰：“我亦曾窺見趙郎，大好才貌。此生薄福，不得當之。”蓋鄙武生麤悍，非良配耳。乃復酬篇，寫於金鳳箋，曰：

> “綠慘雙娥不自持，只緣幽恨在新詩。
> 郎心應似琴心怨，脈脈春情更擬誰。”

　　封付門媼，令遺象。象啓緘，吟諷數四，拊掌喜曰：“吾事諧矣。”又以剡溪玉葉紙，賦詩以謝，曰：

"珍重佳人贈好音，綵箋芳翰兩情深。
薄於蟬翼難供恨，密似蠅頭未寫心。
疑是落花迷碧洞，只思輕雨灑幽襟。
百回消息千回夢，裁作長謠寄綠琴。"

詩去旬日，門媼不復來。象憂恐事泄，或非烟追悔。春夕，於前庭獨坐，賦詩曰：

"綠暗紅藏起暝煙，獨將幽恨小庭前。
沉沉良夜與誰語，星隔銀河月半天。"

明日，晨起吟際，而門媼來。傳非烟語曰："勿訝旬日無信，蓋以微有不安。"因授象以連蟬錦香囊並碧苔箋，詩曰：

"強力嚴妝倚繡櫳，暗題蟬錦思難窮。
近來贏得傷春病，柳弱花敧怯曉風。"

象結錦香囊於懷，細讀小簡，又恐飛烟幽思增疾，乃剪烏絲簡爲回械，曰：

"春景遲遲，人心悄悄。自因窺覯，長役夢魂。雖羽駕塵襟，難於會合，而丹誠皎日，誓以周旋。昨日瑤臺青鳥忽來，殷勤寄語。蟬錦香囊之贈，芬馥盈懷，佩服徒增，翹戀彌切。況又聞乘春多感，芳履乖和，耗冰雪之妍姿，鬱蕙蘭之佳氣。憂抑之極，恨不翻飛。企望寬情，無至憔悴。莫孤短願，寧爽後期。惝恍寸心，書豈能盡？兼持菲什，仰繼華篇。伏惟試賜凝睇。"

詩曰：

"應見傷情爲九春，想封蟬錦綠蛾矉。
叩頭爲報煙卿道，第一風流最損人。"

閽媼既得迴報，徑詣詣飛烟閣中。武生爲府掾屬，公務繁夥，或數夜一直，或竟日不歸。此時恰值生入府曹。飛烟拆書，得以款曲尋繹。既而長太息曰："丈夫之志，女子之情，心契魂交，視遠如近也。"於是闔戶垂幌，爲書曰："下妾不幸，垂髫而孤。中間爲媒妁所欺，遂匹合於瑣類。每至清風明月，移玉柱以增懷。秋帳

冬釭，泛金徽而寄恨。豈謂公子，忽貽好音。發華緘而思飛，諷麗
句而目斷。所恨洛川波隔，賈午牆高。連雲不及於秦臺，薦夢尚遙
於楚岫。猶望天從素懇，神假微機，一拜清光，九殞無恨。兼題短
什，用寄幽懷。伏惟特賜吟諷也。"

　　詩曰：

　　"畫簾春燕須同宿，蘭浦雙鴛肯獨飛。
　　長恨桃源諸女伴，等閒花裏送郎歸。"

　　封訖，召閬媼，令達於象。象覽書及詩，以飛烟意稍切，喜不
自持，但靜室焚香虔禱以俟息。
　　一日將夕，閬媼促步而至，笑且拜曰："趙郎願見神仙否？"
象驚，連問之。傳飛烟語曰："值今夜功曹府直，可謂良時。妾家
後庭，即君之前垣也。若不渝惠好，專望來儀。方寸萬重，悉候晤
語。"
　　既曛黑，象乃乘梯而登，飛烟已令重榻於下。既下，見飛烟靚
妝盛服，立於庭前。交拜訖，俱以喜極不能言。乃相攜自後門入堂
中，皆銀鮮絹幌，盡繾綣之意焉。及曉鍾初動，復送象於垣下。
　　飛烟執象手曰："今日相遇，乃前生姻緣耳。勿謂妾無玉潔松
貞之志，放蕩如斯。直以郎之風調，不能自顧。願深鑑之。"象曰：
"挹希世之貌，見出人之心。已誓幽庸，永奉歡洽。"言訖，象逾
垣而歸。明日，託閬媼贈飛烟詩曰：

　　"十洞三清雖路阻，有心還得傍瑤臺。
　　瑞香風引思深夜，知是蘂宮仙馭來。"

　　飛烟覽詩微笑，復贈象詩曰：

　　"相思只怕不相識，相見還愁卻別君。
　　願得化爲松上鶴，一雙飛去入行雲。"

　　封付閬媼，仍令語象曰："賴值兒家有小小篇詠。不然，君作
幾許大才面目？"

　　茲不盈旬，常得一期於後庭矣。展幽微之思，罄宿昔之心。以爲鬼鳥不知，人神相助。或景物寓目，歌詠寄情，來往便繁，不能悉載。如是者週歲。

　　無何，飛烟數以細過撻其女奴，奴陰銜之，乘間盡以告公業。公業曰：“汝愼勿揚聲！我當伺察之。”後至當赴直日，乃密陳狀請假。迨夜，如常入直，遂潛於里門。街皷既作，匍伏而歸。循牆至後庭，見飛烟方倚戶微吟，象則據垣斜睇。公業不勝其憤，挺前欲擒。象覺，跳去。業搏之，得其半襦。乃入室，呼飛烟詰之。飛煙色動聲戰，而不以實告。公業愈怒，縛之大柱，鞭楚血流。但云：“生得相親，死亦何恨。”

　　深夜，公業怠而假寐。飛烟呼其所愛女僕曰：“與我一盃水。”水至，飮盡而絕。公業起，將復笞之，已死矣。乃解縛，舉置閤中，連呼之，聲言飛烟暴疾致殞。數日，窆之北邙。而里巷間皆知其強死矣。

　　象因變服，易名遠，竄江浙間。洛中才士有著《飛烟傳》者，傳中崔李二生，常與武掾遊處。崔詩末句云：

　　　“恰似傳花人飮散，空牀抛下最繁枝。”

　　其夕，夢飛烟謝曰：“妾貌雖不迨桃李，而零落過之。捧君佳什，媿仰無已。”李生詩末句云：

　　　“豔魄香魂如有在，還應羞見墜樓人。”

　　其夕，夢飛烟戟手而詈曰：“士有百行，君得全乎？何至務矜片言，苦相詆斥。當屈君於地下面證之。”數日，李生卒。時人異焉。

　　遠後調授汝州魯山縣主簿，隴西李垣代之。咸通末，予復代垣，而與遠少相狎，故洛中秘事，亦知之。而垣復爲手記，故得以傳焉。

　　三水人曰：噫，豔冶之貌，則代有之矣；潔朗之操，則人鮮聞乎。故士矜才則德薄，女衒色則情私。若能如執盈，如臨深，則皆爲端士淑女矣。飛烟之罪雖不可逭，察其心，亦可悲矣。

Tale 4.29

The Tale of the Curly-Bearded Guest

By Du Guangting
Translated by Jing Wang

When Emperor Yang[1] (r. 605–616) of the Sui (569–618) Dynasty favored Jiangdu[2] with a visit, he ordered Yang Su (d. 606),[3]

---

[1]Emperor Yang 煬 of Sui 隋, named Yang Guang 楊廣, was the second son of Emperor Wen of the Sui Dynasty. He had two reign titles, Daye (605–614) and Jianyuan 建元 (615–616) for a total of 12 years. He was killed in 616.

[2]Jiangdu 江都 was a commandery of the Sui Empire. It was located in the northern part of modern Jiangsu province. In the beginning of the Daye reign, it was established as a commandery. Emperor Yang of Sui ordered palaces built there and made it an imperial resort.

[3]Yang Su 楊素 was talented in both literature and military strategies, according to his biography in *Sui shu*. He assisted the emperor of the Northern Zhou 周 (557–589) in destroying the Northern Qi 齊 (550–577), and later joined Yang Jian 楊堅, who usurped the throne of the Northern Zhou and became the first emperor of the Sui. Yang Su aided him in destroying Chen and pacifying the empire. In the closing years of Emperor Wen, he supported the enthronement of Yang Guang and was appointed Minister of Education in 606.

The time frame and the official position of Yang Su are not accurate in this tale. He did not end his official career in the position of the Minister of Works. Moreover, when Emperor Yang visited Jiangdu in 616, Yang Su had been dead for eleven years. It was Prince Yang Tong

Minister of Works, to guard the western capital.[4] Yang Su was arrogant and privileged by his rank. Furthermore, because of the chaotic time, he considered that, among those with great authority and high reputation in the world, none could rival himself. He treated himself extravagantly and neglected to follow the appropriate rituals for a subject. Every time ministers and high-ranking officials came to confer with him, or retainers and guests paid visits, he would always receive them reclining on a couch.[5] He ordered beautiful women to surround him and accompany him when he went out, and maids to line up and wait on him. His practices even exceeded the rituals and privileges of a sovereign. He became even worse in his later years. It never occurred to him that he should shoulder his responsibility and did not have the intention of eliminating danger and upholding the fallen.

One day, Li Jing (570–649),[6] the [future] Duke of Wei, came as a commoner to pay a visit and present extraordinary strategies. Su

楊桐 (r. 618–619) of Yue 越 and Duan Da 段達, Grand Master for Splendid Happiness, who guarded the western capital. The time frame and facts about specific figures in this tale cannot be read as historical records. They only serve to provide a backdrop for the story to develop.

[4]The western capital refers to Chang'an. In the second year of Kaihuang (582) reign period, the capital was moved to Daxing 大興, about five miles southeast of Chang'an.

[5]*Juzuo* 踞坐 (to recline on a couch) literally means to sit with one's legs spread, which is an arrogant and impolite pose.

[6]Li Jing 李靖 (571–649) was a nephew of Han Qinhu 韓擒虎 (538–592), who was a famous general of the Sui dynasty. Li Jing served in the Sui government as Palace Censor. At the end of the Daye reign period, Li Jing served as the Commandery Aide of Ma County 馬邑, which was located about thirty miles northwest of the Yanmen 雁門 Pass in modern Shanxi province. He realized that Li Yuan 李淵 (566–635), who later became Emperor Gaozu 高祖 of the Tang dynasty, intended to rebel. Li Jing planned to report this to Emperor Yang secretly, but was found out and caught by Li Yuan. Li Jing was released right before his execution

as usual received him reclining on a couch. Li Jing stepped forward, bowed to him, and said, "The world is in turmoil at this moment, and heroes have risen to compete for the throne. You, sir, are a mighty minister of the Imperial Court, with heavy responsibilities. You ought to occupy yourself with thoughts about how to congregate and collect extraordinary people. It is inappropriate to receive guests while reclining on a couch." Su assumed a serious expression, rose from his seat, and apologized to the Duke. He conversed with the Duke and was greatly pleased. He accepted the Duke's strategies and retreated [to his private chamber].

While the Duke was convincingly presenting his arguments, there was a singing girl with exceptional beauty present who carried a red whisk in her hand and stood in the front. She looked intently only at the Duke. After the Duke had left, the singing girl with the red whisk stood by the window, pointed at an official and said to him, "Ask the man who is leaving what his rank is and where he lives." The Duke answered in detail. The singing girl repeated it and left.

The Duke returned to where he lodged. That night, at the beginning of the fifth clock, he suddenly heard someone knocking softly on the door. The Duke got up and asked who it was. It was someone in purple clothes, wearing a cap and carrying a sack tied on a stick. The Duke asked who it was. The person said, "I am the singing girl with a red whisk at Yang's residence." The Duke immediately invited her in. Taking off her coat and removing her cap, she appeared to be a beauty of eighteen or nineteen years old. She was in gorgeous clothes with no make-up on her face, and she bowed to him. The Duke was surprised and bowed, following suit.

---

because of his heroic speech. He later became a meritorious official for the establishment of the Tang Dynasty. See Li Jing's biography in the *Jiu Tang shu* and *Xin Tang shu*.

The singing girl said, "I have served Minister of Works Yang for a long time and have seen many people in the world under Heaven. There have been none equal to you. The twining vine cannot live by itself and wishes to cling to a tall tree.[7] This is the reason why I came to you."

The Duke said, "Minister Yang has absolute power in the capital. What can one do about that?"

She said, "He lives like a corpse with only breath left and is not to be feared. There are many singing girls who, knowing that he will not achieve anything, have left him. He did not attempt to chase them, either. I have planned it out meticulously. Please do not doubt me."

He asked for her family name. She answered, "It is Zhang."

He also asked her rank in the family and she replied, "I am the eldest."

Observing her skin and manner, conversation and disposition, it seemed that she was indeed a lady from Heaven. The Duke had not expected to obtain her. But the greater his delight, the greater also his fear. In the twinkling of an eye, he felt himself plunged into thousands of worries and anxieties. He walked back and fro, peeking out of the window unceasingly. After several days, although he heard some news of them being chased or searched, he considered the situation not very serious. Only then did he have her put on men's clothes, mount a horse, and gallop with him out through the gate, planning to return to Taiyuan.

They stopped and lodged at an inn at Lingshi[8] on their way. After setting up the beds, they cooked meat on the stove, and it was about to be ready. Miss Zhang let her long hair drape down to the ground and stood in front of the bed, combing her hair,

---

[7]The image of the vine twined on a tall tree is a metaphor for love and marriage.

[8]Lingshi 靈石 was located about eighty miles southwest of Taiyuan.

while the Duke groomed the horses. Suddenly, a mid-sized man whose red beard was curled like a dragon approached them, riding a lame donkey. He threw his leather sack in front of the stove, fetched himself a pillow, laid down on his side, and watched Miss Zhang comb her hair. The Duke got very angry, but he had not decided what he should do, and still kept currying the horses. Zhang stared at the guest's face for a while. She held her hair with one hand and hid the other hand behind her body, waving and signaling to the Duke not to get enraged. She finished combing her hair in haste, organized herself, and came up to ask for his name.

The reclining guest answered, "My last name is Zhang."

She replied, "My last name is also Zhang. I ought to be your younger sister." She bowed to him immediately and asked for his rank in the family.

He said, "I am the third." He asked the younger sister about her rank.

She replied, "I am the eldest."

Then he said with delight, "It is so fortunate today to meet the first younger sister."

Miss Zhang called out from a distance: "Master Li, come to bow to our third brother!"

The Duke bowed to him at once. Then they sat in a circle and the guest said, "What kind of meat are you boiling?"

The Duke said, "It is lamb. I think it should be ready by now."

The guest said, "I am starving."

The Duke went out to buy some tartar bread. The guest pulled out a dagger from his waist, cut the meat, and ate with them. After they finished eating, he chopped off what was left of the meat and brought it to the donkey to feed it. All this was done quickly.

The guest said, "Master Li, judging from your behavior, you are a poor scholar. How could you obtain such an extraordinary person?"

The Duke said, "Although I am poor, I am also a man with ambition. When I was asked this question by other people, I purposely did not talk about it. But since you, brother, asked about it, I will not conceal it." He explained the reason [for his being with the lady] in detail.

The guest said, "Given this situation, where will you go?"

The Duke said, "We will go to Taiyuan to stay away from trouble."

The guest said, "So that's the case, I was not someone that you would able to obtain." He added, "Is there wine?"

The Duke said, "To the west of the inn is a wine shop." The Duke went to get a pint of wine.

After one round of drinking, the guest said, "I have a little something to go with the wine. Master Li, would you like to share it with me?"

The Duke said, "I dare not [disobey your order]."

At this, the guest opened his leather sack and took out a man's head, heart, and liver. He put the head back into the sack, cut the heart and liver with the dagger, and ate it with the Duke. The guest said, "This is the heart of a person who was unfaithful to the world. I had him on my mind for ten years and was not able to capture him until recently. I am relieved and have no regret anymore." He further said, "Master Li, judging from your appearance and demeanor, you are a real man. Have you also heard of the extraordinary person in Taiyuan?"

[Li] Jing said, "I used to encounter such a person, and I would call him a true man. The rest are only to be generals or ministers."

The guest said, "What is his last name?"

Jing said, "He has the same last name as mine."

The guest said, "How old is he?"

Jing said, "He is only twenty years old."

The guest said, "What is he doing now?"

Jing said, "He is a son of a Commandery General."

The Guest said, "This is close to what I heard. I must see him also. Master Li, can you arrange a meeting for me to see him at once?"

Jing said, "My friend Liu Wenjing knows him intimately. It is possible to see him through Wenjing; however, my elder brother, what do you want to do?"

The guest said, "A man who [excels in] observing the air [of heavenly signs] said that Taiyuan had an extraordinary emanation and asked me to investigate it. Master Li, if you set off tomorrow, when will you arrive in Taiyuan?"

Jing calculated his arrival and concluded that it was a certain date.

The guest said, "The day after your arrival, right at sunrise, wait for me at the Fenyang bridge."

After saying this, he hoisted himself onto the donkey and left as rapidly as if he were flying. He had already disappeared in the distance when they looked back. The Duke and Miss Zhang were both surprised and pleased. After a long while, they said, "A marvelous man does not deceive people, and we have nothing to fear." They spurred their horses with their whips and went on to the west.

When the time for the appointment came, they entered Taiyuan and met the guest as expected. They were greatly pleased and went to visit Mr. Liu together.

The Duke lied to Wenjing, saying, "There is a man who excels in reading faces and longs to meet the gentleman. Please invite him here."

Wenjing had always considered the man extraordinary. Once he knew that there was someone who excelled in reading faces, he immediately sent envoys to invite the gentleman.

Shortly after, the envoy returned and the gentleman arrived. He did not wear a robe or shoes, and was wearing his silk garment which partially covered his fur coat. His spirit was high and his appearance different from ordinary people. The Curly-Bearded Guest sat at the end of the table in silence. When he saw the gentleman, his ambition vanished. After several rounds of drinking, he rose up and waved to Jing to come over, and said, "This is indeed the Son of Heaven!"

Jing told this to Liu. Liu became more pleased and was proud of himself [for recognizing the true lord]. After they had come out of Liu's residence, the Curly-Bearded Guest said, "I am eighty to ninety percent sure of my judgment; however, my Daoist brother has to meet the gentleman. Master Li, you had better go to the capital again with the first younger sister. At the eleventh clock of a certain day, visit me at the wine shop east of the horse market. This donkey and a thin donkey will be outside of the wine shop. My Daoist brother and I will both be at the upper level." He then bid farewell and left. The Duke and Miss Zhang again agreed to his request.

When the Duke paid a visit at the appointed time, he saw the two animals that the Curly-Bearded Guest and the Daoist rode. Lifting the skirt of his garment, he went upstairs. The Curly-Bearded Guest and a Daoist were sitting, facing each other and drinking. When they saw the Duke, they were surprised and pleased, and summoned him to sit. They sat around the table and drank for over a dozen rounds. The guest said, "There is ten thousand cash in the cabinet downstairs. Choose a remote hiding place to lodge my first younger sister. Meet me again at the Fenyang Bridge on a certain day."

When the Duke came at the appointed time, the Daoist and the Curly-Bearded Guest had already arrived. They all went to visit Wenjing, who was playing Go at the time. They bowed to him and told him their real intentions. Wenjing sent a quick message to August [Emperor] Wen[9] and invited him to watch a Go game. The Daoist played the game with Wenjing while the Curly-Bearded Guest and the Duke stood aside and waited upon them.

Shortly after, the August Emperor Wen arrived. His spirit and appearance were astonishingly splendid. He made a long bow and sat down. His charisma was so clear and expression so serene that everyone present was influenced. When he looked around, he was very graceful. As soon as the Daoist saw him, he became very depressed. He put down his chessmen and said, "I have completely lost this game! I have lost it at this point! There is no way to save it! What else can one say!" He quit playing and requested to leave.

After he had got out, he said to the Curly-Bearded Guest, "This world is not your world, sir. In other places, it may be possible. Try your best, and don't burden yourself with this on your mind." Thereafter, they entered the capital together.

The Curly-Bearded Guest said, "Master Li, as I calculate your itinerary, you won't arrive until such-and-such a day. The day after your arrival, you may visit a small residence in a certain quarter with the first younger sister. Master Li, you and the first younger sister have nothing in your possession. I would like my humble wife to pay her respects to you and we could also discuss future plans. Please do not decline." After saying this, he sighed and left.

The Duke whipped his horse and headed back. As soon as he arrived in the capital, he went to visit the Curly-Bearded Guest with Miss Zhang. There was a small plank door. He knocked on the door and someone answered the door and bowed, saying,

---

[9]Wenhuang 文皇 (The August Cultured [Emperor]) refers to Li Shimin 李世民, i.e. Emperor Taizong. "Wen" is the original posthumous title given to Li Shimin following his death in 649.

"The Third Master has ordered me to wait for Master Li and Lady the First for a long time." He invited them to go through several doors, which became grander and grander. Forty maids spread out in front of the yard and twenty male servants led the Duke to enter the east hall. The display of furnishings in the hall was resplendent with extraordinary treasures. Mirrors and jewelry in the chests were so beautiful that they were things that could not have belonged to the human world. After they had washed and organized themselves, they were invited to change into clothes which were again precious and extraordinary. After finishing this, a message was passed to them saying that "The Third Master has arrived." It was the Curly-Bearded Guest, who came in wearing a gauze cap and brown fur coat. He demonstrated the bearing of a dragon and a tiger. He was joyous to see them and urged his wife to come out and bow to them. She was a heavenly person. Then they were invited into the central hall, where a grandiose feast had been set up. Even the households of grand ministers could not reach its splendor. The four of them took seats facing each other. After they ate, twenty female entertainers lined up before them and played music. The music sounded as though it had descended from Heaven, completely out of this world. After eating, wine was served. Meanwhile, the house servants carried out twenty couches from the west hall, each covered with an embroidered brocade cloth. After presenting them, the servants removed all the cloth, and what was left turned out to be registers and keys.

The Curly-Bearded Guest said, "These are all records of my precious treasures and money. I will give all that I have to you. Why did I do this? I originally intended to pursue my career in this world. I would have fought for the throne for a dozen of years and gradually established achievement and merit. Now that there has been a lord, why should I detain myself here? That Mr. Li from Taiyuan will indeed be an eminent ruler. Within three to five years, the world will be at peace. Master Li, with your exceptional talent, you will assist a ruler of serenity and peace. If you exert yourself to perfection, you will certainly reach the highest position of a minister. First younger sister, with her heavenly beauty, possesses aptitude beyond this world. She will become honored through her husband. Her carriages and clothes will be extremely splendid. No one else other than the first younger sister would be able to recognize Master Li, and no one else other than Master Li would find his match with the first younger sister. The precious opportunity of earthshaking changes and the right occasion of encounter [between you and the lord] are determined like this. When a tiger roars, the winds blow; when a dragon bellows, clouds congregate. This is the way it intrinsically should be. Use what I gave you to aid the true lord and to assist you in gaining merit and achievement. Do your best! Ten years hereafter, there will be an extraordinary event in the southeast, several thousand miles away. That is the time when I will realize my ambition. My first younger sister and Master Li may congratulate me by spilling wine onto the ground towards the southeast." He then ordered his servants to line up and bow, saying, "Master Li and the first younger sister are your masters!" After he had said this, he and his wife mounted horses and left, followed by a servant. They disappeared within a few steps.

The Duke occupied this residence and then became a powerful gallant. He was able to use his wealth to assist the August Emperor Wen in founding a new empire and therefore in pacifying the world under heaven. In the tenth year of the Zhenguan (627–649) reign, the Duke was appointed Vice Director of the Left and Manager of Affairs. At that time, the southeast barbican tribe *Man* reported to the court, saying, "There were pirates with over a thousand ships and a hundred thousand armored soldiers entering the Fuyu Kingdom.[10] The leader killed the sovereign and enthroned himself. The state has been settled." The Duke realized that the Curly-Bearded Guest had succeeded. He returned home and told Miss Zhang. They followed the complete set of rituals and bowed in congratulations, dripping wine towards the southeast, and invoking their blessings.

Not until now did we know that the prosperity of a true man is beyond what a hero could anticipate, let alone those who are not heroes! Those among the subjects who wrongly thought of making chaos were like nothing more than a mantis intending to use its legs to repel a running wheel. Our royal house spread its fortune through ten thousand generations. How could this be false! Some say, "Half of the military strategies of the Duke of Wei were imparted from the Curly-Bearded Guest."

Note: This is a revised version of my 2010 rendition in William H. Nienhauser, ed., *Tang Dynasty Tales: A Guided Reader*, pp. 189–232.

---

[10]Fuyu 扶餘 was to the southeast of the Tang Empire. Some scholars argue that it could be read allegorically. The author of this story was warning the rebellious generals who had northern barbarian origins, urging them to go back to the northwest, if they wanted to have their own realm. Southeast should be understood as northwest, its opposite direction.

虬髯客傳

杜光庭

　　隋煬帝之幸江都也，命司空楊素守西京。素驕貴，又以時亂，天下之權重望崇者，莫我若也，奢貴自奉，禮異人臣。每公卿入言，賓客上謁，未嘗不踞床而見，令美人捧出。侍婢羅列，頗僭於上。末年愈甚，無復知所負荷，有扶危持顛之心。

　　一日，衛公李靖以布衣上謁，獻奇策。素亦踞見。公前揖曰：“天下方亂，英雄競起。公為帝室重臣，須以收羅豪傑為心，不宜踞見賓客。”素斂容而起，謝公，與語，大悅，收其策而退。

　　當公之騁辯也，一妓有殊色，執紅拂，立於前，獨目公。公既去，而執拂者臨軒指吏曰：“問去者處士第幾？住何處？”公具以對。妓誦而去。

　　公歸逆旅。其夜五更初，忽聞叩門而聲低者，公起問焉。乃紫衣戴帽人，杖揭一囊。公問誰。曰：“妾，楊家之紅拂妓也。”公遽延入。脫衣去帽，乃十八九佳麗人也。素面畫衣而拜。公驚答拜。曰：“妾侍楊司空久，閱天下之人多矣，無如公者。絲蘿非獨生，願托喬木，故來奔耳。”

　　公曰：“楊司空權重京師，如何？”曰：“彼屍居餘氣，不足畏也。諸妓知其無成，去者眾矣。彼亦不甚逐也。計之詳矣。幸無疑焉。”問其姓。曰：“張。”問其伯仲之次。曰：“最長。”觀其肌膚，儀狀，言詞，氣性，真天人也。公不自意獲之，愈喜愈懼，瞬息萬慮不安。而窺戶者無停履。數日，亦聞追討之聲，意亦非峻。乃雄服乘馬，排闥而去，將歸太原。

　　行次靈石旅舍，既設床，爐中烹肉且熟，張氏以髮長委地，立梳床前。公方刷馬。忽有一人，中形，赤髯而虬，乘蹇驢而來。投革囊於爐前，取枕欹臥，看張梳頭。公怒甚，未決，猶刷馬。張熟視其面，一手握髮，一手映身搖示公，令勿怒。急急梳頭畢，斂衽前問其姓。臥客答曰：“姓張。”對曰：“妾亦姓張。合是妹。”遽拜之。問第幾。曰：“第三。”因問妹第幾。曰：“最長。”遂喜曰：“今多幸逢一妹。”張氏遙呼：“李郎且來見三兄！”公驟拜之。遂環坐。曰：“煮者何肉？”曰：“羊肉，計已熟矣。”客曰：“饑。”公出市胡餅，客抽腰間匕首，切肉共食。食竟，餘肉亂切送驢前食之，甚速。客曰：“觀李郎之行，貧士也。何以致斯異人？”曰：“靖雖貧，亦有心者焉。他人見問，故不言。兄之問，則不隱耳。”具言其由。曰：“然則將何之？”曰：“將避地太原。”曰：“然吾故非君所致也。”曰：“有酒乎？”曰：“主人西，則酒肆也。”公取酒一斗。既巡，客曰：“吾有少下酒物，李郎能同之乎？”曰：“不敢。”

於是開革囊，取一人頭並心肝。卻頭囊中，以匕首切心肝，共食之。曰：“此人天下負心者，銜之十年，今始獲之。吾憾釋矣。”又曰：“觀李郎儀形器宇，真丈夫也。亦聞太原有異人乎？”曰：“嘗識一人，愚謂之真人也。其餘，將帥而已。”曰：“何姓？”曰：“靖之同姓。”曰：“年幾？”曰：“僅二十。”曰：“今何為？”曰：“州將之子。”曰：“似矣。亦須見之。李郎能致吾一見乎？”曰：“靖之友劉文靜者，與之狎。因文靜見之可也。然兄何為？”曰：“望氣者言太原有奇氣，使訪之。李郎明發，何日到太原？”靖計之日。曰：“達之明日日方曙，候我於汾陽橋。”言訖，乘驢而去，其行若飛，回顧已失。公與張氏且驚且喜，久之，曰：“烈士不欺人。固無畏。”速鞭而行，及期，入太原。果復相見。大喜，偕詣劉氏。詐謂文靜曰：“以善相者思見郎君，請迎之。”文靜素奇其人，一旦聞有客善相，遽致使迎之。使迴而至，不衫不履，裼裘而來，神氣揚揚，貌與常異。虬髯默居末坐，見之心死，飲數杯，招靖曰：“真天子也！”公以告劉，劉益喜，自負。既出，而虬髯曰：“吾得十八九矣。亦須道兄見。李郎宜與一妹復入京，某日午時，訪我於馬行東酒樓下。下有此驢及瘦驢，即我與道兄俱在其上矣。到即登焉。”又別而去。公與張氏復應之。

及期訪焉，宛見二乘。攬衣登樓，虬髯與一道士方對飲，見公驚喜，召坐。圍飲十數巡，曰：“樓下櫃中有錢十萬。擇一深隱處駐一妹。某日復會我於汾陽橋。”如期至，即道士與虬髯已到矣。俱謁文靜。時方弈棋，揖而話心焉。文靜飛書迎文皇看棋。道士對弈，虬髯與公傍侍焉。俄而文皇到來，精采驚人，長揖而坐。神氣

清朗，滿坐風生，顧盼煒如也。道士一見慘然，下棋子曰："此局
全輸矣！於此失卻局哉！救無路矣！復奚言！"罷弈而請去。既出，
謂虬髯曰："此世界非公世界。他方可也。勉之，勿以為念。"因
共入京。虬髯曰："計李郎之程，某日方到。到之明日，可與一妹
同詣某坊曲小宅相訪。李郎相從一妹，懸然如磬。欲令新婦祗謁，
兼議從容，無前卻也。"言畢，吁嗟而去。

公策馬而歸。即到京，遂與張氏同往。乃一小版門子，叩之，
有應者，拜曰："三郎令候李郎、一娘子久矣。"延入重門，門愈
壯。婢四十人，羅列庭前。奴二十人，引公入東廳。廳之陳設，窮
極珍異，箱中妝奩冠鏡首飾之盛，非人間之物。巾櫛妝飾畢，請更
衣，衣又珍異。既畢，傳云："三郎來！"乃虬髯紗帽裼裘而來，
亦有龍虎之狀，歡然相見。催其妻出拜，蓋亦天人耳。遂延中堂，
陳設盤筵之盛，雖王公家不侔也。四人對饌訖，陳女樂二十人，列
奏於前，似從天降，非人間之曲。食畢，行酒。家人自東堂舁出二
十牀、各以錦繡帕覆之。既陳，盡去其帕，乃文簿鑰匙耳。

虬髯曰："此盡寶貨泉貝之數。吾之所有，悉以充贈。何者？
欲於此世界求事，當龍戰三二十載，建少功業。今既有主，住亦何
為？太原李氏，真英主也。三五年內，即當太平。李郎以奇特之才，
輔清平之主，竭心盡善，必極人臣。一妹以天人之姿，蘊不世之藝，
從夫之貴，以盛軒裳。非一妹不能識李郎，非李郎不能榮一妹。起
陸之貴，際會如期，虎嘯風生，龍吟雲萃，固非偶然也。持余之贈，
以佐真主，贊功業也，勉之哉！此後十年，當東南數千里外有異事，
是吾得事之秋也。一妹與李郎可瀝酒東南相賀。"因命家童列拜，
曰："李郎一妹，是汝主也！"言訖，與其妻從一奴，乘馬而去。
數步，遂不復見。

公據其宅，乃為豪家，得以助文皇締構之資，遂匡天下。貞觀
十年，公以左僕射平章事。適南蠻入奏曰："有海船千艘，甲兵十
萬，入扶餘國，殺其主自立。國已定矣。"公心知虬髯得事也。歸
告張氏，具衣拜賀，瀝酒東南祝拜之。

乃知真人之興也，非英雄所冀。況非英雄乎？人臣之謬思亂者，
乃螳臂之拒走輪耳。我皇家垂福萬葉，豈虛然哉。或曰："衛公之
兵法，半乃虬髯所傳耳。"

Chapter 5

Tale 5.30

Music from the Netherworld

Anonymous[1]
Translated by Daniel Hsieh

Li Kan, district defender of Lujiang,[2] was a native of Longxi.[3] His home was in the district of Henan by Luoyang. In the early part of the Taihe reign period (827–835) he passed away while in office. He had a mistress surnamed Cui who originally was a singer from the Guangling area.[4] She bore him two daughters, who were thus suddenly fatherless at a young age. The widow raised them with great propriety and care, and now being nearly adults, they took Lujiang as their home. Once Li Kan had passed away, because his family was a very prominent one, they would have nothing to

---

[1]The earliest extant complete version of this story, "Ming yin lu" 冥音錄, is to be found in the tenth-century compendium *Taiping guangji* (*juan* 489). No source or authorship is indicated. Some later collections indicate the Tang poet, Zhu Qingyu 朱慶餘 (*jinshi* 826), as the author, but apparently without any authority; see Li Jianguo, *Tang Wudai zhiguai chuanqi xulu* (vol. 2, p. 571). For an annotated version of this story and thoughtful discussions, see Li Jianguo, ed., *Tang Song chuanqi pindu cidian*, pp. 717–22.

[2]Lujiang 廬江, in present-day Anhui.

[3]Longxi 隴西, in present-day Gansu.

[4]Guangling 廣陵, present-day Yangzhou, Jiangsu.

do with the mother and daughters.[5] The people of Lujiang all sympathized with the fatherless children and their resolve.

Ms. Cui loved music. Although poor she confronted life head on, and would often use the music of strings to comfort and amuse herself. She had a younger sister by the name of Chainu who was as attractive and elegant as herself, and who excelled at playing the cither (*zheng*). Her talent was unparalleled, and her fame spread far and wide. But when she was 17 and not yet married, she passed away; everyone was shocked and saddened by the news. The two daughters, from the time they were young, were taught her art. The eldest daughter married a local citizen by the name of Ding Xuanfu. This eldest daughter was not particularly bright or gifted. When she was younger and being taught, any time she made the slightest mistake, her mother would give her a rap, but in the end she just could not achieve the depths of the art. She would often think of her aunt and say, "I am my aunt's niece; separated by the paths of life and death I have been long cut off from her love. In life she was brilliant; in death must she remain silent? Can she not use her powers to help me and open up my mind and eyes so that I can at least come up to the level of my contemporaries?" During holidays and on the first day of each month she would offer a toast and libation to her aunt, weeping and full of sorrow. This continued for eight years; her mother also mourned on her behalf.

In the fifth year of the Kaicheng reign period (840), on the third day of the fourth month, she was asleep, when she suddenly awoke moaning and crying, and she told her mother, "I just dreamed of my aunt; she took my hand and, weeping, said, 'Since leaving the human realm, I have been attached to the School of Music

---

[5]This sentence can be read in several ways depending on how *sui* 雖 is understood and who are taken to be the subjects and objects of the last phrase. Another possibility: "Once Li Kan had passed away, and, although his family was a very prominent one, the mother and daughters would have nothing to do with them."

and Dance here in the netherworld. I received instruction on various musical works from the Erudite, Li Yuanping.[6] Yuanping repeatedly recommended me to Emperor Xianzong (r. 806–820) who then summoned me to his palace to be in residence for one year. I also served at the palace of Emperor Muzong (r. 821–824) for about a year where I taught cither to the imperial consorts. When God smote Zheng Zhu (an instigator of the bloody Sweet Dew Incident of 835; d. 835), the whole world celebrated with feasting. The palaces of the various Tang emperors selected female performers to offer to the palaces of Gaozu (r. 618–626) and Taizong (r. 626–649), and I came to again serve Xianzong. Within each month, once every five days, I would be on duty at Changqiu Hall. Other than that my days were free to look and roam, though I was not allowed to leave the palace grounds. I indeed knew of your earnest sincerity, but there was no way for me to come to you. Recently however, the Xiangyang Princess has come to regard me as her daughter.[7] She cares for me very much. I visit her residence often, and she has secretly allowed me to return so as to fulfill your wishes. You should immediately make preparations. The laws of the netherworld are strict; if the emperor catches wind of it I will suffer strict punishment and the Princess, my master, will also be implicated.'" Mother and daughter hugged each other and wept.

The next day, after sprinkling some water and sweeping a room, she laid out a place at a table in expectation, providing wine and fruit. Seeming to see something, she seized her cither and took a seat. Closing her eyes she played, her fingering now fluent. Originally, when taught ordinary, mortal tunes, she could not learn a single piece in ten days. Now in one day she mastered ten. The

---

[6]Li Yuanping 李元憑 was the nephew of the Tang general, Li Guangbi 李光弼 (708–764).

[7]Xiangyang 襄陽 Princess (fl. early 9th century) was the daughter of Emperor Shunzong 順宗 (r. 805–806).

names and types of these tunes were not those of the mortal world. The melodies were sad and plaintive. Like the cry of an owl or the wail of a ghost, they were dark and somber. Those who heard them would all sigh and gasp. The tunes included: "Welcoming the Lord" (*zhengshang* mode; 28 refrains); "Oak Grove Lament" (*fensi* mode; 44 refrains); "King Qin Bestowing Gold" (*xiaoshi* mode, 28 refrains); "Guangling Tune" (*zhengshang* mode; 28 refrains); "Hardships on the Path" (*zhengshang* mode; 28 refrains); "Upper River Rainbow" (*zhengshang* mode; 28 refrains); "Jincheng Immortal" (*xiaoshi* mode; 28 refrains); "Bestowing Gold, with String and Wind Instruments" (*xiaoshi* mode, 28 refrains); "Red Window Reflections" (*shuangzhu* mode, 40 refrains).[8]

After she finished teaching her the ten tunes, she sorrowfully explained to her niece, "These are all newly revised works from the palace chambers and especially loved by the Emperor. Tunes such as 'Oak Grove Lament' and 'Red Window Reflections' are performed at every banquet. During drinking games such as 'flying balls and dancing cups' they provide pleasure, encouraging drinking throughout the night. Emperor Muzong ordered the Secretary at the Institute for Literature, Yuan Zhen (779–831), to compose several tens of lyrics to this music, which were exceedingly beautiful.[9] As drinking continues and the parties get late, he has the palace ladies sing them in turn. The Emperor himself would take a jade *ruyi* scepter, beat the rhythm and harmonize with them. The Emperor has jealously guarded these pieces, afraid that other kingdoms might obtain them, thus we dare not reveal them. But in the *sheti* year (846) there will be an important event in the netherworld, and this will provide the means by which this music will be spread to the mortal realm. The

---

[8]The text actually lists only nine tune titles. Several of the titles are quite well known, e.g. "Guangling Tune" and "Hardships on the Path."

[9]Yuan Zhen 元稹, see p. 236, n. 5.

roads of the light and the dark are distinct, mortals and ghosts tread different paths; today for me to be involved with human affairs is something that happens once in 10,000 generations, so it is not an accident. Now is the time to present my ten pieces to the Emperor of the mortal realm, because they must not remain unheard in this brilliant age."

The district administrator thereupon reported this to the prefectural authorities, and they reported it to the superior prefecture authorities. The prefect, Cui Shou, himself summoned and tested the niece. The sounds of her *zheng* playing were clear, crisp and pleasing to the ear. The way in which this music differed from zither (*qin*) tunes and the music of Qin, was that, when combined with other instruments, the tone of the music became quite different. The mother also had the younger daughter pay her respects to her aunt and request that she be taught the ten tunes, so that she also became fairly accomplished at them. In the evening the aunt left, but then a few days later returned and said, "I have heard that the military commissioner of Yangzhou wants to take you. I am afraid you may make some mistakes; review each tune one by one."[10] She also left an additional tune, titled "Longing to Return." Shortly afterwards the prefectural government did order that she be sent to Yangzhou; she played flawlessly. The investigation commissioner and former minister, Li Deyu (787–850), discussed presenting a memorial regarding this event, but the daughter died shortly afterwards.[11]

---

[10]It is not clear whom the "you" refers to, the elder or the younger daughter; but it seems most likely to refer to the younger daughter. The translation reflects the ambiguity of the original text.

[11]Li Deyu 李德裕 was a prominent mid-Tang statesman. The year of his death (AD 850) furnishes some evidence for the dating of this story. Li Jianguo tentatively suggests that it dates from the later part of the Dazhong reign period (847–859). See Li Jianguo, *Tang Wudai zhiguai chuanqi xulu*, vol. 2, p. 572.

冥音錄

缺名

廬江尉李侃者，隴西人，家於洛之河南。太和初，卒於官。有外婦崔氏，本廣陵倡家。生二女，既孤且幼，孀母撫之以道，近於成人。因寓家廬江。侃既死，雖侃之宗親，居顯要者，絕不相聞。廬江之人，咸哀其孤藐而能自強。

崔氏性酷嗜音，雖貧苦求活，常以絃歌自娛。有女弟菂奴，風容不下，善鼓箏，爲古今絕妙，知名於時。年十七，未嫁而卒。人多傷焉。二女幼傳其藝。長女適邑人丁玄夫，性識不甚聰慧。幼時，每教其藝，小有所未至，其母輒加鞭箠，終莫究其妙。每心念其姨曰：“我，姨之甥也，今乃死生殊途，恩愛久絕。姨之生乃聰明，死何蔑然，而不能以力祐助，使我心開目明，粗及流輩哉？”每至節朔，輒舉觴酹地，哀咽流涕。如此者八歲。母亦哀而憫焉。

開成五年四月三日，因夜寐，驚起號泣謂其母曰：“向者夢姨執手泣曰：‘我自辭人世，在陰司簿屬教坊，授曲於博士李元憑。元憑屢薦我於憲宗皇帝。帝召居宮。一年，以我更直穆宗皇帝宮中，以箏導諸妃，出入一年。上帝誅鄭注，天下大酺。唐氏諸帝宮中互選妓樂，以進神堯、太宗二宮。我復得侍憲宗。每一月之中，五日一直長秋殿，餘日得肆遊觀，但不得出宮禁耳。汝之情懇，我乃知也，但無由得來。近日襄陽公主以我爲女，思念頗至，得出入主第，私許我歸，成汝之願。汝早圖之！陰中法嚴，帝或聞之，當獲大譴，亦上累於主。’”復與其母相持而泣。

翼日，乃灑掃一室，列虛筵，設酒果，彷彿如有所見。因執箏就坐，閉目彈之，隨指有得。初授人間之曲，十日不得一曲。此一日獲十曲。曲之名品，殆非生人之意。聲調哀怨，幽幽然鴉啼鬼嘯，聞之者莫不噓唏。曲有《迎君樂》（正商調，二十八疊）、《槲林

424

嘆》（分絲調，四十四疊）、《秦王賞金歌》（小石調，二十八疊）、《廣陵散》（正商調，二十八疊）、《行路難》（正商調，二十八疊）、《上江虹》（正商調，二十八疊）、《晉城仙》（小石調，二十八疊）、《絲竹賞金歌》（小玉調，二十八疊）、《紅窗影》（雙柱調，四十疊）。

　　十曲畢，慘然謂女曰：“此皆宮闈中新翻曲，帝尤所愛重。《榭林嘆》、《紅窗影》等，每宴飲，即飛球舞盞，爲佐酒長夜之歡。穆宗敕修文舍人元稹撰其詞數十首，甚美。宴酣，令宮人遞歌之。帝親執玉如意，擊節而和之。帝祕其調極切，恐爲諸國所得，故不敢泄。歲攝提，地府當有大變，得以流傳人世。幽明路異，人鬼道殊，今者人事相接，亦萬代一時，非偶然也。會以吾之十曲，獻陽地天子，不可使無聞於明代。”

　　於是縣白州，州白府，刺史崔璹親召試之。則絲桐之音，槍鏦可聽，其差琴調不類秦聲。乃以衆樂合之，則宮商調殊不同矣。毋令小女再拜求傳十曲，亦備得之。至暮，訣去。數日復來，曰：“聞揚州連帥欲取汝。恐有謬誤，汝可一一彈之。”又留一曲曰《思歸樂》。無何，州府果令送至揚州，一無差錯。廉使故相李德裕議表其事，女尋卒。

Tale 5.31

A Record of Nocturnal Spirits near Dongyang

Anonymous
Translated by Kelsey Seymour

Wang Zhu, the not-yet-employed presented scholar,[1] had the style name Xueyuan. His family was originally from Langye.[2] He passed the imperial examination in the spring of the thirteenth year of the Yuanhe period (818 CE). Once he was residing at a famous mountain between the Zou and Lu regions in order to study.[3] Zhu said that four years earlier, when he was on his way to the capital [for the examination] based on his registry, he stayed overnight at an inn in Xingyang.[4] It so happened that a student from Pengcheng,[5] Ernest Pretenderson, was staying there as a guest. [Ernest] was unable to go to the imperial examination due to family matters. He said he was returning to his hometown, and

---

[1] *Qian jinshi* 前進士 refers to a scholar who has passed the examination but has not yet received an official appointment.

[2] Langye 琅邪 commandery was located north of modern Linyi in Shandong.

[3] In modern Shandong.

[4] In modern-day Zhengzhou, Henan.

[5] Modern-day Xuzhou, Jiangsu.

by chance he ran into Zhu [there], so they talked about the effort of trudging back and forth [between places].

Ernest's style name was "Delicate Origins,"[6] and he mentioned that he had personally witnessed a strange occurrence in the human realm. That year, on the eighth day of the eleventh month,[7] he was returning east. The next day, he arrived at Weinan County,[8] and it then became so cloudy and dark that he could not tell how late it was. The District Magistrate Li Wei invited him to stay for several rounds of drinks. Counting on the strength of his mount, Ernest then ordered his servants to carry his luggage and go in advance to lodge at the Chishui Inn while he stayed and chatted a bit longer there.

When he left from the eastern gate of the district, an ill wind arose that cut across the ground, and flying snow clouded the sky. He had only gone a few *li* when it became very dark. Since Ernest's servants had all been made to go ahead, and since on the road there were no other travelers, he could not ask for directions. At this point he did not know where he was [going]. The road went south from the Dongyang postal relay station; he searched for the path leading to the mouth of Chishui Valley. He had not gone more than three or four *li* from the station when he came

---

[6]Ernest Pretenderson is Cheng Zixu 成自虛. His name is a hint to his being a fiction or fabrication. Since this hint is not clear when the name is converted to pinyin and we cannot see the Chinese characters, I have instead rendered the name into a Westernized one that captures the suggestion that he is an invention.

[7]The eighth year of the Yuanhe reign period. The Western date is December 4, 813. This follows a parenthetical commentary in the Chinese text. This kind of note is present throughout the Chinese version of the text, as well as in other version like the *Taiping guangji,* and such commentaries are explained in the footnotes of this translation where relevant.

[8]A county in the area surrounding the capital, in modern Linwei district, east of Xi'an, Shanxi.

across a low wall. Through the forest, washed in faint moonlight, he was able scarcely to make out a Buddhist temple. Ernest opened the gate and quickly threw himself inside, just as the snowfall was becoming more intense.

Ernest thought to himself that there would be monks residing at the Buddhist temple, and he could request lodging from them, so he urged his horse through. Only afterwards did he realize that the northern row of rooms was all empty, the rooms silent and unlit. He listened attentively for a long time, and there faintly seemed to be the sound of a person breathing. So he tied his horse to the western pillar and called out: "Abbot, please have mercy and assist me tonight!"

He heard a person answer slowly: "The old, sick Bactrian monk Lofty Wisdom is here. I've just sent the servants out to the village to beg for charity, and I cannot manage to light the candles. With snow like this, and also so deep in the night, why are you here? Where have you come from? Without relatives or friends in the surrounding areas, from whom can you find relief? Tonight, if perhaps you do not fear that I'm sick and dirty, then you can come here and avoid exposure to the outside. I can also offer to divide the straw from this sleeping mat for you to use."

Ernest had no other ideas, so when he heard these words he felt quite happy. Then he asked: "Bactrian Monk, where are you from? Why are you staying here? What was your surname before ordination? Since you have received me with such kindness, I should also learn something more about you."

The monk replied: "As a layperson my surname was Humphrey,[9] and I was born in the western desert region. Originally I

---

[9]The Bactrian monk's name is my rendering of Seng Zhigao 僧智高. In the Chinese text, his lay surname is An 安, which was commonly assigned to people from the Central Asian region of Parthia (*Anxi guo* 安息國). In the case of the monk in this story, there is an additional layer of connotation: *an* is a homophone of *an* 鞍, "saddle," as in *rou an* 肉鞍,

spent my strength [making my living], so I then happened to come to China. Before long, I was here at this weedy temple. You, sir, have dropped by so suddenly; I don't have much to offer you, so I hope you do not mind."

As Ernest and the abbot talked back and forth like this, he rather forgot his previous fatigue. He then said to the Bactrian monk: "I was just thinking about 'searching for the jewels and conjuring a city.'[10] The Buddha did not use metaphors lightly. Now, you are my teacher, Bactrian monk. You are rooted in the Buddhist tradition; indeed you have such a teaching for settling my mind."

Shortly afterwards, there was a *ta-ta-ta-ta*, as if several people were walking together in their direction! Then he heard: "What a tremendous snow! Is the master in?" The Bactrian monk had not yet answered when they heard another person say: "Officer,[11] you go ahead first." Someone else said: "Preford the Eighth, you should go first." Then he heard someone say: "The path is quite

---

"flesh saddle," hinting at his camel hump. Although the text implies that he is Parthian, I have chosen to translate it as Bactrian, since it captures more of his "camel-ness." Likewise, I have rendered his lay name as Humphrey as a hint at his camel form.

[10]The reference is to the Parable of the Conjured City (*Hua cheng yu pin* 化城喻品), a famous parable from the *Lotus Sūtra* (妙法蓮華經, T262, 22a18). In the parable, a group of people is searching for a jeweled city, and when they become exhausted and want to turn back, a conjurer creates a jeweled city for them to rest in. After they have rested, the illusion dissipates, and the group continues onwards towards its true goal. The conjured city represents the "Hīnayāna (*xiaosheng* 小乘)" *nirvāṇa*, and the true jeweled city represents the Mahāyāna (*dasheng* 大乘) goals of true enlightenment and Buddhahood for all sentient beings. The former is an expedient means (*upāya* 方便) to get to the latter.

[11]The *cao* 曹 of *caozhang* 曹長, "officer," is not his name, but part of his title, given to flaunt his office. "Cao 曹" is perhaps a play on *cao* 槽, "trough," where pack animals like donkeys and horses feed.

wide, there's no need to bother yielding. We can all go together!" Ernest thought that it must be several people, and in his mind he gathered courage.

A while later, it seemed that everyone had found a seat. One person among them said: "Master, is there a guest here?" The Bactrian monk replied: "A guest has just arrived to find lodging for the night." Because it was so dark, Ernest could not clearly make out the appearances of the people. He could only see the one who was at the very front stooping under the eaves, reflected by the snow. He seemed to be wearing black fur, and the back and rib areas had added white patches.

This person was the first to ask Ernest: "Why have you braved the snow to come here all by yourself on such a dark night?" Ernest then told him all that had happened. The person then asked Ernest's name, and he replied: "I am the presented scholar Ernest Pretenderson."

Ernest then said to them: "In the dark I cannot greet each of you clearly face to face. Since on another day I may not be able to recount you all for my posterity, may I ask each of you to state your position and name?"

Then he heard one person say: "I am the appointee of the Left Courageous Guard Armorer Administrator of the Troops, Don Pluskey,[12] the previous transport inspector of Heyin.[13]" The next person said: "I am the Vice General of Light Chariots, the guest from Taolin,[14] Oxford Preford VIII."[15] The next person said: "I am

---

[12]This is Lu Yima 盧倚馬. His name is also a pun. When read as "The character *lu* 盧 relying on (*yi* 倚) the character *ma* 馬," it hints that the reader should put these two characters together to make *lü* 驢, "donkey." My Westernized name for him maintains the same wordplay.

[13]Heyin 河陰 is in present-day Henan.

[14]This is an allusion to the *Liji* 禮記 "Yue ji 樂記" chapter, in which King Wu's oxen are set free in the fields of Taolin (牛散之桃林之野).

Cadogan Caanless." [16] The next person said: "I am Roose Goldbird.[17]" Then it seemed everyone had sat down.

Since Ernest had just recently sat for examination, Don turned to a discussion of writing. Don said: "When I was a child, I heard a person chant the Master's 'Poem on Piling Snow into a Mountain.' I can still recall it now. Tonight this scenery is unfolding before our eyes. Master, do you still remember it?" The Bactrian monk said: "How did the words go again? You can try to recite it." Don said: "This is what I remember:

---

[15]This is Zhu Zhongzheng 朱中正, also called Zhu Bazhang 朱八丈 and Zhu Ba 朱八 by his companions. The "bazhang" is his rank, "eighth," rather than a given name. Both are plays on his animal identity. His given name, Zhongzheng, means "the center is correct"; when the "outer" part of the character *zhu* 朱 is removed, and we are left with the "center," we are left with the character *niu* 牛, "ox." Likewise, the *ba* 八 part of his rank is precisely the "outer" part of the character *zhu* 朱, a suggestion towards this wordplay as well. I have tried to maintain something similar for my rendering of the name.

[16]This is Jing Quwen 敬去文, and yet another play on characters. When the character *jing* 敬 is rid of (*qu* 去) the character component *wen* 文, we are left with *gou* 苟, a homophone of *gou* 狗, "dog." Likewise, when we remove certain letters from Cadogan, we are left with his true identity.

[17]This is Xi Ruijin 奚銳金. For the *xi* 奚 part of his name, the *Shuowen jiezi* 說文解字 states that it is pronounced as *ji* 雞, "rooster." The given name Ruijin relies on cosmological associations to hint at his animal identity. Both *rui* and *jin* have the metal component *jin* 金, which, according to Five Phases cosmology (*wuxing* 五行), is associated with the Earthly Branch (*dizhi*) *you* 酉. The Earthly Branches each have an association with one of the twelve animals of the Chinese zodiac. In this case, *you* 酉 is associated with the rooster. His Westernized name tries to maintain some of these associations.

At someone's home the snow is swept, filling the front of the
   courtyard,
In a single fist a thousand peaks and a myriad of dells.
My heart is involuntarily cloaked in frost,
For how many years already have I among these dwelt?"

Ernest appeared blank, with his mouth agape and his eyes
staring vacantly; he seemed not to understand. The Bactrian monk
then said: "Mount Snow was a mountain near my home. In the
past I happened to see children piling up snow very high with
ridges and peaks, just like the shape of a mountain. I looked west
towards my old state forlornly, so I made this poem. The officer is
very bright to thus remember my coarse sentences from so long
ago. If it weren't for the officer's recitation, I truly would have
forgotten it."

Don said: "Master, you have galloped freely in far-off lands
and shed the fetters of your worldly bridle.[18] Your virtue is lofty,
and it can be said that you tower over your peers.[19] As for me, I
rush after the dust behind you. How dare I peep into your
loftiness![20] This spring I went to the city for an official matter, but
the nature I am endowed with is blunt and thick-headed. In the
capital it was extremely difficult. Day and night I travelled
hungrily.[21] Although I worked constantly and diligently, the grain

---

[18]The commentary here notes that *ji* 機, "mental conditions," is a
homophonic pun on *ji* 羈 "bridle."

[19]Or, more literally, his head comes out above his peers, as a camel's
head towers above that of many other kinds of animals.

[20]The commentary here suggests that *he* 曷, "how," is a pun on *he* 褐,
"brown," alluding to the color of his fur, and is being used to ridicule
him.

[21]The commentary here states that "bridle," *ji* 羈, should be "hunger"
ji 饑.

was still meager,[22] and my burden was not light. I feared being blamed and punished. As of recently, thanks to this temple I've changed my title to a nominal one, and my intent rests in painstakingly seeking liberation. Yesterday evening I left my inn at Changle. Grieving at my toil through the dust, I sighed with emotion, longing to [be like] mountain deer and wild roebucks. So entrusting [these feelings] to you all, I composed two coarse poems. For all the present poets, I would like to recite them,[23] but I dare not do it."

Ernest said: "What night is this that we get to hear such wonderful phrases!" Don again said modestly: "[These poems] are less than crude and shallow, not to mention that the Master, a model of literature, is here. How dare I present such clumsiness!" Ernest implored: "We sincerely wish to hear them, we sincerely wish to hear them!" So Don loudly recited his poems:

East of Chang'an on the way to Luoyang,
The cart wheels spin constantly, clouds of dust borne.
Striving for the lead, brandishing the whip,
When we finally meet, we have grown old in the mundane
    world.

Day and night, along the river, without planning a course,
I depart from the pack and travel solo, completely mum.
Because there is green grass along the riverside,
I look forward to the spring to ease the feeling of the bridle.[24]

---

[22]*Liao* 料, "grain," can also mean "salary." He is blurring the line between human and animal compensation for work.

[23]Wang Meng'ou suggests that *kouzhan* 口占 means "compose on the spot with no draft," rather than just "recite."

[24]The commentary here indicates that *weiji* 慰羈, "relaxing the bridle," can also mean *weiji* 餧饑, "feeding one's hunger."

Everyone sitting said: "Sublimely composed!" Don replied modestly: "It is clumsy, it is clumsy."

Oxford said to the Bactrian monk: "I have heard that the scholars from the desert like to cite many of your great verses! Now we are in Yingchuan,[25] and moreover we have just listened to the recitation of Officer Pluskey. It has enlightened me and cleansed me of my ignorance. The intent of the poems is so pleasant and the spirit is so pure. And the innovations are abundant. Now the audience is thirsting for recitations. How could you not reveal two or three more to quench everyone's expectations?" The Bactrian monk requested to wait for another day.

Oxford then said: "How wonderful that these esteemed persons are all here, how can we even be concerned with the Rabbit Garden?[26] Such elegant discussions and lofty conversations are contained within this grand occasion! Now the markets seem distant, and deep in the night we are still [feeling] excited. The wine goblets admittedly cannot be found, and we are unable to produce the feast dishes, leaving us no etiquette between host and guest. What a shame! We can [instead] masticate on our ideas.[27] But if you gentlemen have nothing to fill your bellies tonight, how can we make up for such shame?"

The Bactrian monk said: "I've heard that excellent conversation can allay hunger and thirst. It is just as when Preford the Eighth relied on his strength to help other people. His movements adhered to prior ruts. As for besieging towns and giving tribute to soldiers, this is also what he was good for. But as for the twelve links of

---

[25]Yingchuan 潁川 seems to be a place in present-day Henan. The Ying River 潁水 flows through it. This is perhaps an obscure allusion.

[26]An allusion to *Shiji*, "Liang Xiao Wang shi jia 梁孝王世家." An allusion to knowledge.

[27]The commentary here alludes to the behavior of animals like himself — oxen, donkeys, and camels — which all chew on grasses.

dependent arising, they all begin with 'contact.' [28] The sea of bitterness is boundless, and afflictions are accordingly generated. In what place can we find enlightenment?[29] Through which gates can we leave the burning house?"[30]

Oxford replied: "As for how I understand it, if one follows the track of an overturned cart, he will be reincarnated onto an evil path; as for the successive retribution [he suffers], the matter will be extremely clear. As for making efforts towards practices, this is the point of it."

The Bactrian monk laughed heartily, then said: "The Śākya clan [i.e. Buddhists] value their purity, and when practice is

---

[28]The commentary here suggests chu 觸, "contact," rather than shang 觴 "goblet." Chu is definitely the right choice. In Buddhist philosophy, "contact" is the sixth of the twelve links of dependent arising, the conditions that lead to suffering.

[29]The commentary here notes that the ti of puti 菩提, "Bodhi" or "enlightenment," is homophonic with ti 蹄, "trotters." Wang also suggests the pun is on both syllables of puti 菩提, and should be read as buti 不蹄, "un-trotted," since oxen do not have trotters. He claims that it also refers more generally to the suffering of animal rebirths.

[30]The commentary here suggests that the monk may be ridiculing Zhongzheng (Oxford). The "burning house" refers to the Burning House Parable from the Lotus Sutra. In this parable, a group of children are in a burning house playing games. Their father tries to get them to leave, but they are too absorbed in the game to notice the danger. So the father tempts them into coming out by telling them there are goat-pulled, deer-pulled, and oxen-pulled carts outside that they can play with. Thus they children come out and the danger is averted. However, instead of the promised carts, there is only a cart filled with jewels and pulled by white oxen. The burning house represents suffering in the world, and the jewel-filled cart Buddhahood. The promise of the animal-pulled carts was an expedient means to save the children from suffering and help them reach the jewel-filled cart.

successful, it is then called 'true awakening.'[31] Those who are awakened are Buddhas. As you said just before, you deeply understand this." Don laughed.

Ernest then said: "General Preford has just now repeatedly requested the abbot to compose a new poem. As for me, I would truly like to behold such a treasure. Do you, abbot, scorn me, a guest from afar, because I am not part of the Dharma? What's more, your breadth of knowledge is extraordinary, and your bearing is profound and lofty. [The poem] would certainly be distinctive in rhyme and creative in style, and it would surpass everything. Its beauty and wonder would be innovative, and it would cast away all profane feelings. How can you still hide away this conferral of elocution and not chant one or two verses to open our ears and eyes?"

The Bactrian monk said: "I am deeply burdened by the painful pleas of the fine talent Ernest; his request is difficult to firmly refuse. But this old monk is decrepit, weak, and crippled with disease, and my studies were abandoned long ago. And as for the way of composition, I wasn't even good at it to begin with. The fact is that Preford the Eighth is too nice to nitpick at my shortcomings. But during my illness I coincidentally composed a couple of verses. But could such experts[32] [as you] listen to these?" Ernest said: "I sincerely wish to hear them." His poems were:

> Wearing coarse cloth, hiding my name, my path is not fixed,
> I cross a thousand miles of quicksand with my form growing
>   weak.

---

[31]The commentary here states that *jue* 覺, "awakening," is a pun on *jiao* 角, "horns."

[32]The reference is to Craftsman Shi from *Zhuangzi*, who was able to use his axe to chop a bit of substance the size of a fly's wing off of the tip of a man's nose without harming him.

After transmitting the true mind of the Southern School,[33]
This body should just retire to the Twin Peaks.[34]

Because I care about Jambudvīpa,[35]
I departed from the western state and to Chang'an I tread.
Ever since I lost my strength, I no longer travel on the roads,
I took up the unbridled body of an ascetic monk instead.[36]

The audience all praised the poems as wonderful, which lasted for a long time.

Cadogan suddenly said to everyone in the room: "In former times, Wang Ziyou visited Dai Andao in Shanyin[37] on a bright, snowy night. He went up to the door and then turned around. Thus we have the legend of 'No Need to See Dai.'[38] At that time they all valued unrestrained freedom. Now, Mr. Pretenderson can be said to have made friends through literary pursuits, and he looks down on Yuan An and Jiang Xu.[39] When I was young, I had

---

[33]This probably refers to the Southern School of Chan, established by Huineng 慧能 (638–713), the Sixth Patriarch of Chan Buddhism.

[34]A reference to the location where the Fourth Patriarch of Chan, Daoxin 道信, had his locus of teaching. Daoxin was the teacher of Hongren 弘忍, who taught Huineng. It is also a play on words alluding to the "two peaks" that form the camel's humps.

[35]This is a general reference to the mundane world.

[36]The tuo 陀 in toutuo 頭陀, "ascetic monk," is homophonic with tuo 駝, "camel." The "unbridled body" can also refer to no longer wearing a bridle for the purpose of transporting goods.

[37]Shanyin 山陰 is in present-day northern Shaanxi.

[38]Dai Andao 戴安道 is the famous fourth-century artist Dai Kui 戴逵 (326–396). Wang Ziyou 王子猷 is the scholar Wang Weizhi 王徽之 (338–386), who was famous for his casual behavior and for following his own whims. The story of their *not* meeting is from *Shishuo xinyu* 世說新語.

[39]Yuan An 袁安 (d. 92 CE) and Jiang Xu 蔣詡 (69 BCE–17 CE) were Han dynasty figures known for being upright worthies.

a rather heroic demeanor, and I was endowed with a love of birds of prey.[40] Previously in these times, I rushed around hunting. I am originally from the southeast of Chang'an,[41] in the eastern field of Yusuchuan.[42] On the topic of singing about snowfall, I have one [poem] called 'To Cao Zhoufang.'[43] Now I am attacked by the mania of poetry, so it may sully your lofty perceptions." He then recited this poem:

> I am fond of this flying six-petaled duke,
> In the sky dancing, like jade flecks and willow catkins.
> At that time I was just escorting the counselor-in-chief of Qin,[44]
> Delighting in the north winds, leaping over the rivers and
>   glades.

---

[40]Hinting at his love of hunting.

[41] The directions here are given by associations with the Eight Trigrams rather than cardinal directions. In this case, southeast is *xunwei* 巽維, since the trigram *xun* ☴ is associated with the southeast.

[42]The commentary here states that Yusuchuan 御宿川 is a location in present-day Chang'an. The alternate name, Goujiazui 苟家觜, is a play on words, since the *gou* 苟 in the place name sounds like *gou* 狗, "dog." It is thus a *goujia* 狗家, "dog home."

[43]Based on the text, it seems that Cao Zhoufang 曹州房 is a person. However, Wang Meng'ou interprets this as a location: the "Office of Caozhou." Caozhou 曹州 is in present-day Shandong. According to Wang, the Tang prime minister and general Tang Xiujing 唐休璟 requested ferocious dogs from this region.

[44]The counselor-in-chief of Qin is Li Si 李斯 (284–208 BCE), and this refers to the expression derived from the *Shiji*, *dongmen huangquan* 東門黃犬, meaning "yellow dogs at the eastern gate," or *tan huangquan* 嘆黃犬, meaning "lamenting the yellow dogs." It is an allusion to Li Si's grieving that he would no longer be able to accompany them to chase rabbits with the dogs, said as he was on the brink of execution by waist-cutting after being betrayed by Zhao Gao 趙高.

[Cadogan continued]: "After being offered this poem, Cao Zhoufang quite appreciated it. But then he questioned it by saying: 'Calling the snow a duke, is this not too unrestricted?' So to prove it, I then mentioned that people in ancient times had also called bamboo a lord,[45] and later generations of worthies all thought this was a brilliant expression. Cao Zhoufang was tongue-tied and did not know how to reply. But Cao Zhoufang simply did not understand poetry. [My friend] Crowley[46] once said to me: 'It's hard to come by someone with the same inclinations as oneself.' These words are so true. Now he has become an official in a distant place, participating in military affairs in an eastern state, so we have several thousand [*li*] between us. [Instead there is] 'Bartholo-mew-mew,'[47] who is always being noisy, relying on his kin and seeking out others to undertake tasks. If the state of Lu had no gentlemen, then where could he have acquired this [behavior]?[48]"

Roose said: "What makes you say this? How long since you last saw Mr. Catsby?" Someone said: "It's been ten days. In that

---

[45]Wang notes that one person said this was Wang Ziyou, mentioned above.

[46]This is Wu Da 烏大. He is perhaps a crow.

[47]This is Miao Shi (Miao Ten) 苗十, a nickname of Miao Jieli 苗介立. The commentary says he is called "Ten" because it is the sum of five plus five. The pronunciation of "five-five" (*wuwu* 五五) resembled onomatopoeia for cat sounds, *wuwu* 嗚嗚. Miao 苗, of course, sounds similar to *mao* 貓, "cat." His Westernized name tries to maintain these puns.

[48]Quoted inaccurately from the *Analects* (*Lunyu*). The last character should be 斯 rather than 諸. The quoted phrase originally was used to describe learning good behavior, but here it is used to talk about the cat acquiring bad habits. There is a possibility that there is a textual corruption and something about the rooster is missing, since some of his later dialogue seems out of place. If that is the case, it may still be that it is meant to describe good behavior.

case, where is he?" Cadogan said: "He is probably not far off. If he knows we have gathered here, I reckon he'll join us on his own."

No sooner had he said this than Bartholomew suddenly arrived. Cadogan feigned a happy expression and patted him on the back, saying: "Just what I had been hoping for!" Cadogan then introduced Bartholomew and Ernest to each other. Ernest stated his name first, and Bartholomew said: "I am Bartholomew Catsby."[49] The words exchanged between the hosts and guests were quite superfluous and long-winded.

Roose roosted on the side and said: "Now is the time to painstakingly compose [verses]. Since you have all now arrived, Old Goldbird's habit of poetry has flared up again. How about it?" Ernest said: "I have received deep care from you previously, Mr. Goldbird.[50] How could you still conceal such a treasure and disappoint us so much?" Roose hesitated, but said: "How dare I not give the audience a laugh!" Then he intoned the three verses of his recent poems:

> Dancing in the mirror,[51] my brilliance is comparable to the
> *simurgh*,
> At the battlefield,[52] [the outcome] is decided by my Goshawk
> Fist.[53]

---

[49]See note 47.

[50]Wang says 眷與之分 means 彼此交契之情分. This sentence does not make a lot of sense. Perhaps there is some dialogue or action missing from the rooster in the story.

[51]A reference to the phrase expressing self-appreciation, *shanji wu jing* 山雞舞鏡, meaning "the mountain rooster dances in the mirror." It derives from an account in *Yiyuan* 異苑: Mountain roosters would dance looking at their own reflections in pools of water. When some of these roosters were presented to the court from the south, the emperor also wanted them to dance, so a mirror was installed for them.

[52]I.e., the cockpit, for cockfighting.

I just recall the days in the immortal entourage,
I raise my head in front of the mansion.

Cultivated for battle, my form is like a piece of wood,[54]
During the spring, my physical form is [supple] like mud.
If the wind and rain come, [I can still crow],
Why should I fear to be in a lowly position?

In order to help Tian Wen escape disaster,[55]
I constantly harbored the grace of Ji Juan.[56]
Desiring to understand the conditions of the wild,
I crowed to the abandoned village in the frosty dawn.

When Roose finished chanting, appreciation was loudly heard [from the audience] in the dark.

The Bactrian monk said: "All you worthies should not regard General Preford [just] as a warrior. This gentleman is in fact very proficient in philosophical thinking, and he is also good at literary writing. Although it seems like he says nothing, under his hide he is judging us; isn't that wrong? Moreover, Mr. Pretenderson is our

---

[53]Although goshawks technically have claws, this seems to be meant to sound like a martial arts technique, and so I have translated it this way.

[54]This is an allusion to Ji Shengzi 紀渻子 in Zhuangzi 莊子, who raised roosters for cockfighting for the ruler. According to the story, the roosters are ready to fight when they are "like wood," meaning that they no longer respond to the actions and sounds of other roosters, and the other roosters will dare not challenge them.

[55]Tian Wen 田文 is Meng Changjun 孟嘗君 (d. 279 BCE). When he was staying at Hangu Pass 函谷關, they had a rule that the gates would not open to admit and release guests until the rooster crowed in the morning. He feared that a pursuing army would catch up to him, so he found someone who could imitate rooster calls, and when this person crowed, the roosters in the area also crowed, and the gates opened early, allowing him to escape.

[56]This is again Ji Shengzi, from Zhuangzi.

guest from afar, and we gather [here] on this one night. Just as Buddhist doctrine says, it is a once-in-many-lifetimes opportunity.[57] We are birds nesting in the same tree. In light of this, how could he not leave us with some words to talk about in the future?"

Oxford rose and said: "What our master says puts me in a pickle. But if everyone feels so upset [over this], how dare I not comply with this order! It's just that my composition will only invite trouble, don't you think?" The Bactrian monk said: "All you worthies, please listen silently." Oxford's poems were:

I bore a false reputation to bring disorder to Lu,[58]
When I traveled to Qin I was indebted to Ning Sheng.[59]
While I idled, my wheezing surprised the prime minister,[60]
While working, my mooing was recognized by Ge Lu.[61]
Millet nourishes this agricultural zeal,
I lack the mood to pull the cart.

---

[57]The Chinese here is *duo sheng you yuan* 多生有緣. This is the same as *sansheng you yuan* 三生有緣, "the three lives share the same destiny." The three (or many) lives refer to one's past, present, and future rebirths, which are all predetermined by karmic causes. More generally, it refers to circumstances that are very rare, and thus very special.

[58]This refers to Shusun Muzi's 叔孫穆子 illegitimate child, called Niu 牛, "ox," who rebelled against his father in the state of Lu, from the text *Kongzi jia yu* 孔子家語.

[59]This should be Ning Qi 甯戚, and it should also be the state of Qi 齊, rather than Qin 秦. It refers to a story from *Shiji* in which Ning Qi feeds oxen and is then appointed to office by Duke Huan of Qi.

[60]This refers to Bing Ji 丙吉, who, when witnessing an ox exhausted and sick from being driven too hard, asked about its condition, indicating his awareness of the link between human suffering and agricultural distress.

[61]This refers to the account of Ge Lu 葛盧 going to have an audience at court; upon hearing an ox call out, he understood its offspring would be used in a sacrifice.

Lately I have felt the strength of my muscles declining,
My whole intent rests in returning to the plow.

The Bactrian monk sighed and said: "Preford the Eighth, your words are as ornate as this, yet you still cannot get away from being between posts![62] What kind of person is it that leads you about by the yoke? How unjust, how unjust!"

Don said: "Among my two brothers from Fufeng,[63] [one] is by chance tied up.[64] My family is from Kucha, and our blue-grey [furs] are greatly fading. They revel in clamor and loathe stillness, they are prone to free and easy matters, and they delight in transporting bundles. They are courageous forerunners.[65] You can understand his deep regret that he is not at this gathering."

Cadogan said to Bartholomew: "The von Hodge brothers live near here, but they have not come [to join us]. Where do they use their lofty aspirations? The *Book of Poetry* states: 'Friends from afar gather together.' And as long as they are in the mood for leisure, we ought to send them a letter of invitation. I think they would very much enjoy it."

Bartholomew said: "I had originally been on the way to pay a visit to the elder von Hodge. It's just that I became so caught up in these discussions of literature that I was delayed without realizing it! Mr. Caanless has commanded me, so now I ask that you gentlemen do not rise. I, Bartholomew, will go straight to the von Hodge family and promptly return. How about I just bring the von Hodge brothers here together, might I?" Everyone said: "Of course!" Bartholomew then left.

---

[62]Referring to his official positions, but also to his yoke.

[63]East of Xianyang, in present-day Shanxi. Wang says the surname Ma 馬 is prominent here.

[64]The commentary here states that this refers to Zixu's tied-up horse.

[65]The commentary here says this is a squadron that carries light goods ahead of donkeys.

Before long, Cadogan furtively began to disparage Bartholomew in front of everyone: "What a stupid person, with such claws! I often hear that he is honest and good at managing the storehouse.[66] But there are also rumors of stealing;[67] how can it be difficult to avoid criticism?" He had no idea that Bartholomew had arrived back, along with the von Hodge brothers, and in the doorway he had unexpectedly heard everything [Cadogan] said.

Bartholomew raised his sleeves and angrily said: "I am Bartholomew Catsby, the direct descendent of Dou Bobi.[68] My surname comes from the remote ancestor of Chu, Fen Huangru.[69] His line divided into twenty clans, and we are even mentioned in the records of sacrificial libations from the *Canon of Ritual*.[70] How [dare] you, Cadogan Caanless, a descendent of Panhu[71] who does not make distinctions between elder and younger, and who does not differentiate human relations! You are only suited to tamely play with children, or if fierce-looking, then guard wine shop signs. Your flattery is like a fox-spirit, cozying up near the stove to steal some fat. How dare you comment on the characters of people! If I did not possess any skills whatsoever, Caanless here

---

[66] An apt place for a cat, since it is prone to mice infestations.

[67] This is a reference to the *la* 蜡 sacrifices in the "Jiao te xing 郊特性" section of *Liji*.

[68] Dou Bobi 鬥伯比 was a Spring and Autumn period figure from the state of Chu 楚. He had a son who was abandoned near a pond and who was found and nursed by a tiger.

[69] Fen Huangru 棼皇茹 refers to Miao Benhuang 苗賁皇, a figure from the state of Chu who shares Jieli's surname.

[70] The commentary here notes that this also refers to the *Liji* chapter "Jiao te xing," which elevates cats and tigers.

[71] Panhu 盤瓠 is a mythological dog. When the legendary emperor Di Ku 帝嚳 was suffering from invasions, he offered his daughter in marriage to anyone who could bring him the head of his enemy. Panhu succeeded and won the bride.

would successively say that I have no talents and make all of you despise me hereafter. So now I will recite a verse of rustic poetry for the teacher, and you can then see how it is!" His poem was:

I feel guilty at my master's deep kindness as I eat meat,
Late in the day I lay coiled on a brocade quilt.
I imitate the ambitious people who know black and white,[72]
How will a high position move my heart?

Ernest exclaimed that it was quite wonderful.

Cadogan said [to Bartholomew]: "You don't know me! That's just an enormous amount of nonsense and slander. I am the descendent of Xiang Xu[73] from the Spring and Autumn period. Your taking me as the dregs of Panhu is just like comparing the sun at dawn to the *fang* star.[74] This is widely different from me!"

Oxford felt deeply worried that the two would riposte endlessly, so he said: "I hope that I can act as Yiliao[75] to resolve the resentment between you two — might I? In the past my [ancestor]

---

[72]Wang Meng'ou states that the *zhiren* 志人, "ambitious people," here should be *zhiren* 至人, "Realized Person." Because of this, he claims it is referring to Laozi, and specifically the quotation from *Laozi*, "As for knowing the white and guarding the black, it is the model of all under heaven 知其白，守其黑，為天下式." Cats prowling in the night is like the "guarding the black 守其黑" part. This seems to stretch it a bit.

[73]Xiang Xu 向戌 was a figure from the state of Song 宋 in the Spring and Autumn period. His given name, Xu, denotes the earthly branch that is associated with the dog in the Chinese zodiac.

[74]Wang Meng'ou interprets the "sun at dawn," *chenyang* 辰陽, as actually a place name.

[75]This most likely refers to Yiliao 宜僚, the style name of Ban Yong 班勇 (d. 127 CE), an Eastern Han military officer who united his army with the Kuchean army to fight the Xiongnu and thus strengthened Han power in the Western Regions.

Pang Choufu[76] indeed repeatedly made alliances with the Xiang family and Fenhuang during the Spring and Autumn period. Now we have a respectable guest sitting among us — how can you two slander each other's ancestors? If you accidentally expose our flaws through your words, this will make Mr. Pretenderson scoff at us! Let us just finish our poetry recital; I strongly urge you to stop fighting."

Thereupon Bartholomew introduced the von Hodge brothers and Ernest to each other. At first the brothers, in their ornate attire, seemed to keep to themselves. [Then] the two came to the front, and the first said he was Gourdon von Hodge, and the next one said he was Hatter.[77] Ernest also stated his name. Gourdon also went around the room greeting the other guests: "Esteemed brothers."

Bartholomew then elaborated on the reputation of the von Hodge brothers for the rest of the audience: "Though they hide away in the grassy fields, their reputation has been circulated even to the most famous clans; though above they join with the constellations,[78] the intimacy between them reaches [the closeness of] the liver and gall organs.[79] What's more, the eight rivers of Qin

---

[76]The character *feng* 逢 should be *pang* 逄. Pang Choufu 逄丑父 was a figure from the state of Qi in the Spring and Autumn period. The *chou* 丑 in his name denotes the earthly branch associated with the ox in the Chinese zodiac.

[77]These two are Wei Canghu 胃藏瓠 and Wei Cangli 胃藏立. *Canghu* 藏瓠 is "hiding in the gourd," and Cangli 藏立 is homophonic with *cangli* 藏笠, "hiding in the bamboo hat." Their surname, Wei 胃, is a homophone of *wei* 蝟, "hedgehog." The Westernized versions of their names are an attempt to capture some of these allusions.

[78]This is referring to the lunar mansion *wei* 胃, matching their surname.

[79]In Five Phases cosmology (*wuxing* 五行), the liver and gall bladder are associated with the same phase, wood. Linking them to internal

are linked to the imperial granaries,[80] and the twenty clans of their homeland are mainly [located] around Xianyang.[81] I heard that the younger brother has recently composed a poem describing his old career. It has been considered very beautiful by people. How about we have a listen?"

Gourdon replied: "I have only joined this noble party by accident, and with all you writers gathered here, when I try to issue forth the words from my mouth, I am first filled with shame. Now I have no choice, [though this disgraceful poem] will pollute the senses of you worthy gentlemen." The poem was:

> The [water from] Bird-Mouse Mountain is the river of my homeland,[82]
> In the past, the king of Zhou sought out the worthy [Lü Shang there].[83]
> As soon as I transform from the rat and rabbit,[84]
> I should see the sea becoming a mulberry field.

---

organs also plays on the *cang* 藏 in their given names, since this character has another meaning, "storehouse," that can indicate organs.

[80]One of the eight rivers, the Wei 渭, flows around Chang'an. This is another play on their surname and the word "hedgehog."

[81]In present-day Shanxi, near modern Xi'an.

[82]Bird-Mouse Mountain (Niaoshu shan 鳥鼠山) is the source of the Wei 渭 river, according to *Shanhai jing* 山海經. There is a Niaoshu Mountain in present-day Gansu province.

[83]Lü Shang 呂尚 is Jiang Ziya 姜子牙, who was living in self-imposed exile, fishing on a tributary of the Wei River, when he was found and recruited by King Wen.

[84]*Zi* 子 and *mao* 卯 are the earthly branches representing the rat and the rabbit in the Chinese zodiac, respectively. According to the commentary, rats and rabbits change into hedgehogs.

Bartholomew praised it: "You will certainly gain fame in the coming days! If justice really exists, then this poem will endure forever."

Gourdon bowed and humbly declined: "I am only suited to obscurity and lowliness. It's just that I am fortunate enough to be in the company of this group of accomplished gentlemen. Brother Bartholomew, your praise is too much. I cannot bear these heavy words; it is like bearing thorns and prickles on my back!"[85] The guests all laughed.

Until then, Ernest had listened to all the guests' elegant recitals, but there was no time to read his own work. He only said: "The pure talents of you gentlemen are sublime. You are all examples of 'seeing the ox and [allowing] the knife to travel.'"[86]

Oxford misunderstood this to be ridicule and secretly left. The Bactrian monk looked for him but could not find him. He said: "Why is it that Preford the Eighth has left without a word?" Don replied: "Preford the Eighth has had a hatred for the Pao clan[87] his whole life. He disliked hearing the allusion to the whetstone[88] and he just left." Ernest apologized for his lack of sensitivity.

At that time, Cadogan started a conversation just between himself and Ernest. He said to Ernest: "In general when people do things, gentlemen esteem their virtues. As for wagging one's tail to

---

[85] Of course referring to his spines.

[86] An allusion to the story of Chef Pao Ding 庖丁 from *Zhuangzi*, who is so practiced at butchering oxen, that he no longer sees a whole ox. He never needs to sharpen his knife because the blade glides through the sections with ease. The more general meaning is a reference to astounding skill.

[87] The Pao 炮 here should probably be Pao 庖, as in the Chef Pao Ding.

[88] This also refers to the story of Pao Ding.

beg for food, that is why tigers are criticized.[89] Sometimes we might bark for the ones who know us, but we cannot abandon this righteousness even when the master lacks virtue.[90] I am untalented, but I still have two verses about my determination to present." The poems were:

> Serving my master, I have the same joys and worries [as he],
> I completely cease my intention to quibble over coarse meals.
> If I am not guarding an empty stump waiting for a rabbit,
> Then in the end I should pursue a deer out of the wooded hills.

> When I was young I hoped to be as useful as a starving eagle,[91]
> I never once desired to have the heart of a pampered crane.
> In the autumn grasses I dispel my thoughts of leaving home,
> In the plains my fur and blood stir as I pursue birds.

Ernest expressed his unbounded appreciation, completely forgetting about the [earlier] trouble during the night.

He was just about to boast about poems he had previously composed, when he suddenly heard the stroke of a bell from a distant temple. Then everyone around him abruptly vanished. He looked around intently, but he could not see anything at all; he could only sense the wind and snow coming through the window, and a dirty smell assailing his nose. There was only a *rustle-rustle*, as if there was some movement. But when he called out in a loud

---

[89]Wang Meng'ou thinks *ji* 幾 should be *ji* 譏 here. He states that this is an allusion to a sentence from the biography of Sima Qian in *Hanshu*, in which he says that even a tiger caught in a trap will shake its tail to beg for food. Of course, coming from Quwen (Cadogan), wagging one's tail is certainly also a reference to canine behavior.

[90]These are references to dogs barking, as well as being loyal to their masters.

[91]Perhaps because of their desperation, hungry birds of prey are all the more fierce.

voice, there was no answer at all. He became confused and frightened, and he didn't dare move forward to feel about in the space.

He went back outside to find his tethered horse. It was still bound to the western corner of the building, the saddle blanketed in snow, and the horse standing and gnawing at the pillar. He hesitated for a moment, and the dawn light became bright enough for him to start distinguishing his surroundings.

Then [he saw that] to the north of the wall of the building, there was a camel kneeling down, his belly stuck on the ground, with missing teeth[92] and deaf ears. Ernest thought about the strange things during the night and was finally able to look around everywhere for them. Outside, under the northern corridor, he suddenly also saw a weak and careworn black donkey. Along its back there were three worn-down and exposed spots with white fur growing in to fill them.

He then looked up at the northern arch of the room. It vaguely seemed as though there was a fluttering thing, and then he saw an old rooster perching there. In front, to the north of the seat where the Buddha image was set, there was an open space about several dozen paces apart from east to west. Under each of the lattice windows, there were spaces with colorful paintings such that local people could stack tall barley between them.[93] He saw a big calico cat sleeping on top.

Nearby there was also a broken gourd for holding water for farmhands, and next to it there was a broken, discarded bamboo

---

[92] One version of the Chinese text has 齝, a variant of 齝, "to masticate." I have gone with *tiao* 齠, "to shed teeth," which enhances the vivid description here.

[93] According to the commentary in the *Taiping guangji*, *wen* 穩, should be 麰, "trifles." Wang has *sui* 穗, "spikes or awns of barley," instead of *wen* 穩.

shepherd's hat. Ernest nudged them with his foot, and indeed they were holding two squirming, wriggling hedgehogs.

Ernest looked around everywhere, and all was silent, without a single person. He could no longer stand the coldness of the night, so he seized the reins, shook off the snow, mounted his horse, and left.

[The road] snaked out to the north of a village. On the left of the road, he passed a meager brushwood fence surrounding an old garden, and [in it he] saw an ox lying in the snow, chewing grass. Next to this, not more than a hundred paces, was the place where the whole village all piled manure together. As Ernest passed by it, a group of dogs began barking. In the center there was a dog with fur around its ankles. [94] Its appearance was incredibly strange, and it [seemed to] glare at Ernest.

Ernest urged his horse onwards for a long while and then happened upon an old man coming out of a wooden door, having risen early to clear the path of snow. Ernest stationed his horse and asked him about the area. He replied: "This is the farm of my old friend Peng of the Right Army. Sir, where did you stop last night? You seem to have lost your way during a journey."

Ernest told him what he saw during the night, and the old man leaned against his broom in amazement, saying: "How bizarre, how bizarre! Last night the weather was so windy and snowy. Previously the farmhouse had a sick camel. We thought it was going to die [during the snow], so we took it to the north of the temple, and [sheltered it] under the hall for chanting the name of the Buddha. Several days ago, a messenger from the Heyin office passed by with a tired donkey who could not bear to go

---

[94] Wang suggests luo 猓, "naked," should be huai 踝, "ankle," so "fur reaching down to its ankles." The breed in my imagination is the Chinese Crested Dog, since it is aptly "strange-looking." But this might just be wishful thinking.

forward any longer. I pitied [the donkey's] tenacity despite his cruel life and traded a *hu* full of millet for him. I also did not tether him. That thin and weak ox fenced in over there belongs to the farm. Hearing this story just now, I do not know what reason there is for eerie occurrences like this."

Ernest said: "I was already deprived of my saddle pack last night, so right now I am both extremely hungry and cold. There is no simple explanation for things like this, [but] this is the general idea. It is very difficult to completely describe." Then he urged his horse forward and left.

When he arrived at the Chishui Inn, he saw his servants. [They were] quite bewildered that their master had lost them and had busily started to search for him. Ernest was very emotional, and for several days it was as if he were scared witless.

東陽夜怪錄

缺名

　　前進士王洙，字學源，其先瑯琊人。元和十三年春擢第。嘗居鄒魯間名山習業。洙自云，前四年時，因隨籍入貢，暮次榮陽逆旅。值彭城客秀才成自虛者，以家事不得就舉，言旋故里。遇洙，因話辛勤往復之意。

　　自虛字致本，語及人間目睹之異。是歲，自虛十有一月八日東還（乃元和八年也）。翼日，到渭南縣，方屬陰曀，不知時之早晚。縣宰黎謂留飲數巡。自虛恃所乘壯，乃命僮僕輜重，悉令先於赤水店俟宿，聊踟躕焉。

　　東出縣郭門，則陰風刮地，飛雪霧天。行未數里，迨將昏黑。自虛僮僕，既悉令前去，道上又行人已絕，無可問程。至是不知所屆矣。路出東陽驛南，尋赤水谷口道。去驛不三四里，有下塢。林月依微，略辨佛廟。自虛啟扉，投身突入。雪勢愈甚。

　　自虛竊意佛宇之居，有住僧，將求委焉，則策馬入。其後纔認北橫數間空屋，寂無燈燭。久之傾聽，微似有人喘息聲。遂繫馬於西面柱，連問"院主和尚，今夜慈悲相救。"

　　徐聞人應："老病僧智高在此。適僮僕已出使村中教化，無從以致火燭。雪若是，復當深夜，客何為者？自何而來？四絕親鄰，何以取濟？今夕脫不惡其病穢，且此相就，則免暴露。兼撤所藉芻藁分用，委質可矣。"

　　自虛他計既窮，聞此內亦頗喜。乃問"高公生緣何鄉？何故棲此？又俗姓云何？既接恩容，當還審其出處。"

　　曰："貧道俗姓安（以本身肉鞍之故也），生在磧西。本因捨力，隨緣來詣中國。到此未幾，房院疎蕪，秀才卒降，無以供待，不垂見怪為幸。"

453

自虛如此問答，頗忘前倦。乃謂高公曰："方知探寶化城
（"城"原作"成"，據明抄本改），如來非妄立喻，今高公是我
導師矣。高公本宗，固有如是降伏其心之教。"

俄則沓沓然若數人聯步而至者。遂聞云："極好雪。師丈在
否？"高公未應間，聞一人云："曹長先行。"或曰："朱八丈合
先行。"又聞人曰："路其寬，曹長不合苦讓，偕行可也。"自虛
竊謂人多，私心益壯。

有頃，即似悉造座隅矣。內謂一人曰："師丈，此有宿客乎？"
高公對曰："適有客來詣宿耳。"自虛昏昏然，莫審其形質，唯最
前一人，俯簷映雪，彷彿若見著皂裘者，背及肋有搭白補處。

其人先發問自虛云："客何故瑀瑀（丘圭反）然犯雪，昏夜至
此？"自虛則具以實告。其人因請自虛姓名，對曰："進士成自
虛。"

自虛亦從而語曰："暗中不可悉揖清揚，他日無以為子孫之舊。
請各稱其官及名氏。"

便聞一人云："前河陰轉運巡官、試左驍衛冑曹叅軍盧倚馬。"
次一人云："桃林客副輕車將軍朱中正。"次一人曰："去文，姓
敬。"次一人曰："銳金，姓奚。"此時則似周坐矣。

初，因成公應舉，倚馬旁及論文。倚馬曰："某兒童時，即聞
人詠師丈《聚雪為山》詩，今猶記得。今夜景象宛在目中，師丈有
之乎？"高公曰："其詞謂何？試言之。"倚馬曰："所記云：誰
家掃雪滿庭前，萬壑千峰在一拳。吾心不覺侵衣冷，曾向此中居幾
年。"自虛茫然如失，口呿眸眙，尤所不測。高公乃曰："雪山是
吾家山，往年偶見小兒聚雪，屹有峰巒山狀，西望故國恨然，因作
是詩。曹長大聰明，如何記得？貧道舊時惡句，不因曹長誠念在口，
實亦遺忘。"

倚馬曰："師丈騁逸步於遐荒，脫塵機（"機"當為"羈"）
於維縶，巍巍道德，可謂首出儕流。如小子之徒，望塵奔走，曷
（"曷"當為"褐"，用毛色而譏之）敢窺其高遠哉？倚馬今春以
公事到城，受性頑鈍，闕下桂玉，煎迫不堪。且夕羇（"羇"當為
"饑"）旅，雖勤勞夙夜，料入況微，負荷非輕，常懼刑責。近蒙
本院轉一虛銜（謂空驅作替驢），意在苦求脫免。昨晚出長樂城下
宿，自悲塵中勞役，慨然有山鹿野麋之志。因寄同侶，成兩篇惡詩。
對諸作者，輒欲口占，去就未敢。"

自虛曰：“今夕何夕，得聞佳句。”倚馬又謙曰：“不揆荒淺。況師丈文宗在此，敢呈醜拙邪？”自虛苦請曰：“願聞，願聞！”倚馬因朗吟其詩曰：“長安城東洛陽道，車輪不息塵浩浩。爭利貪前競著鞭，相逢盡是塵中老。”（其一）。“日晚長川不計程，

離群獨步不能鳴。賴有青青河畔草，春來猶得慰（“慰”當作“餧”）羈（“羈”當作“饑”）情。”合座咸曰：“太高作。”倚馬謙曰：“拙惡拙惡！”

中正謂高公曰：“比聞朔漠之士，吟諷師丈佳句絕多，今此是潁川，況側聆盧曹長所念，開洗昏鄙，意爽神清。新製的多，滿座渴詠，豈不能見示三兩首，以沃群矚？”高公請俟他日。

中正又曰：“眷彼名公悉至，何惜兔園。雅論高談，抑一時之盛事。今去市肆苦遠，夜艾興餘，杯觴固不可求，炮炙無由而致。賓主禮闕，憖惡空多。吾輩方以觀心朵頤（謂齕草之性與師丈同），而諸公通宵無以充腹，頹然何補？”

高公曰：“吾聞嘉話可以忘乎饑渴，秖如八郎，力濟生人，動循軌轍，攻城犄士，為己所長。但以十二因緣，皆從觸（明抄本“觸”作“觸”）起；茫茫苦海，煩惱隨生。何地而可見菩提（“提”當作“蹄”）？何門而得離火宅（亦用事譏之）？”

中正對曰：“以愚所謂：覆轍相尋，輪迴惡道，先後報應，事甚分明。引領修行，義歸於此。”

高公大笑，乃曰：“釋氏尚其清淨，道成則為正覺（“覺”當為“角”），覺則佛也。如八郎向來之談，深得之矣。”倚馬大笑。

自虛又曰：“適來朱將軍再三有請和尚新制。在小生下情，實願觀寶。和尚豈以自虛遠客，非我法中而見鄙之乎？且和尚器識非凡，岸谷深峻，必當格韻才思，貫絕一時，妍妙清新，擺落俗態。豈終秘咳唾之餘思，不吟一兩篇以開耳目乎？”

高公曰：“深荷秀才苦請，事則難於固違。況老僧殘疾衰羸，習讀久廢，章句之道，本非所長。卻是朱八無端挑抉吾短。然於病中偶有兩篇自述，匠石能聽之乎？”曰：“願聞。”其詩曰：“擁褐藏名無定蹤，流沙千里度衰容。傳得南宗心地後，此身應便老雙峰。”“為有閻浮珍重因，遠離西國赴咸秦。自從無力休行道，且作頭陀不繫身。”

又聞滿座稱好聲，移時不定。

去文忽於座內云：“昔王子猷訪戴安道於山陰，雪夜皎然，及門而返，遂傳‘何必見戴’之論。當時皆重逸興。今成君可謂以文

會友，下視袁安、蔣詡。吾少年時頗負雋氣，性好鷹鸇。曾於此時，畋遊馳騁。吾故林在長安之巽維，御宿川之東時（此處地名苟家觜也）。詠雪有獻曹州房一篇，不覺詩狂所攻，輒污泥高鑒耳。”因吟詩曰：

> ‘愛此飄颻六出公，輕瓊洽絮舞長空。
> 當時正逐秦丞相，騰躑川原喜北風。’

獻詩訖，曹州房頗甚賞僕此詩，因難云：‘呼雪為公，得無檢束乎？’余遂徵古人尚有呼竹為君，後賢以為名論，用以證之。曹州房結舌，莫知所對。然曹州房素非知詩者。烏大嘗謂吾曰：‘難得臭味同。’ 斯言不妄。今涉彼遠官，糸束州軍事（義見《古今注》），相去數千。苗十（以五五之數故第十）氣候啞吒。憑恃群親，索人承事。魯無君子者，斯焉取諸？

銳金曰：“安敢當。不見苗生幾日？”曰：“涉旬矣。然則苗子何在？”去文曰：“亦應非遠。知吾輩會於此，計合解來。”

居無幾，苗生遽至。去文偽為喜意，拊背曰：“適我願兮！”去文遂引苗生與自虛相揖，自虛先稱名氏，苗生曰：“介立姓苗。”賓主相諭之詞，頗甚稠沓。

銳金居其側曰：“此時則苦吟之矣，諸公皆由，老奚詩病又發，如何如何？”自虛曰：“向者承奚生眷與之分非淺，何為尚吝瑰寶，大失所望？”銳金退而逡巡曰：“敢不貽廣席一噱乎？”輒念三篇近詩云：“舞鏡爭鸞彩，臨場定鶻拳。正思仙仗日，翹首仰樓前。”“養鬥形如木，迎春質似泥。信如風雨在，何憚跡卑棲。”“為脫田文難，

常懷紀涓恩。欲知疎野態，霜曉叫荒村。”銳金吟訖，暗中亦大聞稱賞聲。

高公曰：“諸賢勿以武士見待朱將軍，此公甚精名理，又善屬文，而乃猶無所言，皮裏臧否吾輩，抑將不可。況成君遠客，一夕之聚，空門所謂多生有緣，宿鳥同樹者也。得不因此留異時之談端哉？”

中正起曰：“師丈此言，乃與中正樹荊棘耳。苟眾情疑阻，敢不唯命是聽。然盧探手作事，自貽伊戚，如何？”高公曰：“請諸賢靜聽。”中正詩曰：“亂魯負虛名，遊秦感寧生。候驚丞相喘，用識葛盧鳴。”“黍稷茲農興，軒車乏道情。近來筋力退，一志在

歸耕。”高公歎曰：“朱八文華若此，未離散秩。引駕者又何人哉！屈甚，屈甚！”

倚馬曰：“扶風二兄，偶有所繫，（意屬自虛所乘，）吾家龜茲，蒼文斃甚，樂喧厭靜，好事揮霍，興在結束，勇於前驅（謂般輕貨首隊頭驢）。此會不至，恨可知也。”

去文謂介立曰：“胃家兄弟，居處匪遙，莫往莫來，安用尚志。《詩》云：‘朋友攸攝，’而使尚有遲心。必須折簡見招，鄙意頗成其美。”

介立曰：“某本欲訪胃大去，方以論文興酣，不覺遲遲耳。敬君命予。今且請諸公不起。介立略到胃家即回。不然，便拉胃氏昆季同至，可乎？”皆曰：“諾。”介立乃去。

無何，去文於眾前竊是非介立曰：“蠢茲為人，有甚爪距，頗聞潔廉，善主倉庫。其如蜡姑之醜，難以掩於物論何？”殊不知介立與胃氏相攜而來。及門，瞥聞其說。

介立攘袂大怒曰：“天生苗介立，鬭伯比之直下。得姓於楚遠祖夢皇茹，分二十族，祀典配享，至於《禮經》（謂《郊特牲》八蜡迎虎迎貓也）。奈何一敬去文，盤瓠之餘，長細無別，非人倫所齒，只合馴狎稚子，獷守酒旗，諂同妖狐，竊脂媚竈，安敢言人之長短。我若不呈薄藝，敬子謂我咸秩無文，使諸人異日藐我。今對師丈念一篇惡詩，且看如何？”詩曰：“為慭食肉主恩深，日晏蟠蜿臥錦衾。且學志人知白黑，那將好爵縻吾心。”自虛頗甚佳歎。

去文曰：“卿不詳本末，厚加矯誣。我實春秋向戌之後，卿以我為盤瓠楠，如辰陽比房，於吾殊所華潤。”

中正深以兩家獻酬未絕為病，乃曰：“吾願作宜僚以釋二忿，可乎？昔我逢丑父實與向家夢皇，春秋時屢同盟會。今座上有名客，二子何乃互毀祖宗，語中忽有綻露。是取笑於成公齒冷也。且盡吟詠，固請息喧。”

於是介立即引胃氏昆仲與自虛相見。初襜襜然若自色。二人來前，長曰胃藏瓠，次曰藏立。自虛亦稱姓名。藏瓠又巡座云：“令兄令弟。”

介立乃於廣眾延譽胃氏昆弟：“潛跡草野，行著及於名族；上參列宿，親密內達肝膽。況秦之八水，實貫天府，故林二十族，多是咸京。聞弟新有題舊業詩，時稱甚美。如何，得聞乎？”

藏瓠對曰：“小子謬廁賓筵，作者雲集，欲出口吻，先增慙怍。今不得已，塵污諸賢耳目。”詩曰：“鳥鼠是家川，周王昔獵賢。

一從離子卯（鼠兔皆變為蝟也），應見海桑田。"介立稱好："弟他日必負重名，公道若存，斯文不朽。"

藏瓠斂躬謝曰："藏瓠幽蟄所宜，幸陪群彥。兄揄揚太過。小子謬當重言，若負芒刺。"座客皆笑。

時自虛方聆諸客嘉什，不暇自念己文，但曰："諸公清才綺靡，皆是目牛游刃。"

中正將謂有譏，潛然遁去。高公求之，不得，曰："朱八不告而退，何也？"倚馬對曰："朱八世與炮氏為讐，惡聞發硎之說而去耳。"自虛謝不敏。

此時去文獨與自虛論詰，語自虛曰："凡人行藏卷舒，君子尚其達節，搖尾求食，猛虎所以見幾。或為知己吠鳴，不可以主人無德而廢斯義也。去文不才，亦有兩篇言志奉呈。"詩曰："事君同樂義同憂，那校糟糠滿志休。不是守株空待兔，終當逐鹿出林邱。""少年嘗負饑鷹用，內願曾無寵鶴心。秋草毆除思去宇，平原毛血興從禽。"自虛賞激無限，全忘一夕之苦。

方欲自誇舊制，忽聞遠寺撞鐘，則比膞鏋然聲盡矣。注目略無所睹，但覺風雪透窗，臊穢撲鼻。唯窣颯如有動者，而厲聲呼問，絕無由答。自虛心神恍惚，未敢邃前捫搦。

退尋所繫之馬，宛在屋之西隅，鞍轡被雪，馬則齕柱而立。遲疑間，曉色已將辨物矣。

乃於屋壁之北，有橐駝一，貼腹跪足，儑耳韶口。自虛覺夜來之異，得以遍求之。室外北軒下俄又見一瘁瘠烏驢，連脊有磨破三處，白毛茁然將滿。

舉視屋之北栱，微若振迅有物，乃見一老雞蹲焉。前及設像佛宇塌座之北，東西有隙地數十步。牖下皆有彩畫處，土人曾以麥穩之長者，積於其間，見一大駁貓兒眠於上。

咫尺又有盛餉田漿破瓠一，次有牧童所棄破笠一，自虛因蹴之，果獲二刺蝟，蠕然而動。

自虛周求四顧，悄未有人，又不勝一夕之凍乏，乃攬轡振雪，上馬而去。

周出村之北道，左經柴欄舊圃，睹一牛踏雪齕草。次此不百餘步，合村悉葦糞幸此蘊崇。自虛過其下，群犬喧吠。中有一犬，毛悉齊髴，其狀甚異，睥睨自虛。

　　自虛驅馬久之，值一叟，闢荊扉，晨興開徑雪。自虛駐馬訊焉。對曰：「此故友右軍彭特進莊也。郎君昨宵何止？行李間有似迷途者。」

　　自虛語及夜來之見。叟倚篲驚訝曰：「極差，極差！昨晚天氣風雪，莊家先有一病橐駝，慮其為所斃，遂覆之佛宇之北，念佛社屋下。有數日前，河陰官腳過，有乏驢一頭，不任前去。某哀其殘命未捨，以粟斛易留之，亦不羈絆。彼欄中瘠牛，皆莊家所畜。適聞此說，不知何緣如此作怪。」

　　自虛曰：「昨夜已失鞍馱，今餒凍且甚。事有不可率話者。大略如斯，難於悉述。」遂策馬奔去。

　　至赤水店，見僮僕方訝其主之相失，始忙於求訪。自虛慨然，如喪魂者數日。

Tale 5.32

An Account of Lingying

Anonymous
Translated by Zhenjun Zhang and Yuhua Wen

Twenty *li* east of Jingzhou was the ancient city of Xue Ju,[1] in the corner of which was the Good Woman Pool, which stretched several square *li*. Around clusters of verdant reeds in dark green, old trees grew sparsely. The water in the pool was clear and green, and no one could measure the depth of it. Water creatures and numinous monsters in the pool often appeared. The local people set up an ancestral shrine temple by the pool dedicated to the Deity of the Ninth Lady. At the time of yearly floods or drought, a ceremony for disaster relief would be held, and all went there to pray. There was also another water spirit named after its location — the Deity of Chaona north of Chaona Village, 200 *li* west of Jingzhou. In terms of the efficacy of his miraculous responses to the people's prayers, the Deity of Chaona ranked before that of the Good Woman.

---

[1]Jingzhou 涇州, modern Jingchuan in Gansu. Xue Ju 薛舉 (d. 618), a warlord at the end of the Sui 隋 dynasty, proclaimed himself the emperor of Western Qin in 617.

During the fifth year of the Qianfu reign period (874–879), when the military commissioner Zhoubao[2] garrisoned the city, cloud masses had risen many times from the two pools since the beginning of midsummer, with the shapes of wondrous peaks, beautiful women, rats, and tigers. The air was stirred up into a fierce wind, accompanied by thunder and lightning, which tore the roof and uprooted the trees. In several minutes these phenomena would cease, but they caused countless people to be seriously injured and many crops damaged. Zhou Bao blamed himself for the natural disturbance, saying that he had received these reproaches from the gods because of his inadequate government of the city.

On the fifth day of the six month, during a break from the work in the office, Zhou felt sleepy and wanted to take a nap. He took off his headscarf and lay down on his pillow. Before falling asleep, he saw a warrior standing by the steps of the hall, wearing a helmet and armour, with a broadaxe in his hand, saying, "A female guest is outside the door and would like to pay a visit to you, so I have come for your permission." Zhou Bao asked, "Who are you?" The answer was "I am your gatekeeper, and I have worked and handled affairs for you for many years." Just as Zhou Bao was about to inquire more about the reason, he saw two maidens in black clothes come up on the steps, kneel down in front of him, and say, "Ninth Lady came all the way here from her rural residence, to pay you a visit, so she sent her attendants first to inform you, Sir." Zhou Bao said, "Ninth lady is not my acquaintance, nor my relative, how can we meet casually?"

Before he could finish speaking, he saw auspicious clouds and drizzles with extraordinary fragrance spraying into the air. Shortly after, a 17- or 18-year-old woman with a slim figure in

---

[2]A native of Lulong, Zhou Bao 周寶 (814–887) was the military governor of Qianfu during the reign of Emperor Wuzong 武宗 (r. 841–846). He was made prime minister in 882.

pure white descended from the sky and stood in the corridor between the courtyards. Her manner was graceful and her beauty was matchless, even in all the world. There were more than ten servant maids, all in bright and clean clothes, making the lady appear somewhat like a princess. With gentle and graceful footsteps, she walked slowly to Zhou Bao's bedroom. Zhou intended to withdraw for the moment and hear about her intention first. A servant maid walked quickly into his room and said, "Because you are a man of noble morality to whom she can confide her sincere appeal, the honorable Lady wants to tell you about the injustice and oppression that have been done to her. Can you bear not to save her from her misfortune?"

Zhou Bao asked her to walk up the steps to meet. The host and the guest saluted each other solemnly and respectfully. As she ascended the couch to sit down, they were surrounded by auspicious mist, and purple haze filled the courtyard. She lowered her head in a reserved manner, appearing very sad and full of grief. Zhou Bao ordered wine and dishes and received her in a generous manner. A moment later, she drew back her sleeves and left the banquet, walking back and forth, and said, "Because I live in the outskirts of the city, I have enjoyed the grace of the sacrifices, wine and food, for many years, and the favour I have received is indeed generous.. Although I am willing to live a solitary life until I die, as a solitary woman I entrusted myself to your place, and I feel deeply in debt. Just because this visible world and the invisible underworld are fundamentally different, our behaviours do not coincide with each other, so I have never visited you. Today I am forced by some special reasons — how can I conceal my thoughts? If you can understand my unspoken mind, I would dare to expose my feelings." Zhou Bao said, "I'd like to hear your story. Particularly I hope I can know about your family background. If I can help you, how dare I take the difference between this world and the underworld as an excuse? A gentleman can sacrifice even his life for the sake of benevolence, and can devote himself to righteousness resolutely and unyieldingly. It is my wish to help wash away unjust grievances even if I have to leap into boiling water or burning flames."

She answered, "My family had lived in Mao County of Guiji Prefecture for generations. The clan made its home in a deep pool connected to the East Ocean and has lived and increased greatly there for more than one hundred generations. Later, my family suffered from unpropitious times, and calamities befell the whole household. Over 500 people in the clan were burned to death by the fire started by a man surnamed Yu, and the clan was almost exterminated. I couldn't bear the deep rancour against the enemy, so I fled and hid myself in a secluded mountain cave, but the long-standing grievances cannot be washed away.

"In the middle of Tianjian's reign period (502–520) in the Liang Dynasty, Emperor Wu lived, and he was fond of rare treasures. He sent someone to communicate with the Dragon King's Palace, and he then entered Withered Mulberry Island. With the help of the roasted swallows, he won the favour of the seventh daughter of the treasurer of Lord Dongting, in order to seek rare treasures. Then I heard that Yu Piluo, a descendant of our enemy, had lost his official position and insignia as a White River Gentleman in Mao County. He wished to accept Emperor Wu's summons to go to the Dragon King's Palace, but he harboured evil intentions, so that, if he were sent to the Dragon Palace, he would like to destroy our entire clan under the cover of looking for rare treasures. Owing to his sensitivity, Lord Jie was aware that Yu had requested the mission with selfish intent, and that his unscrupulous actions would harm innocent people, and he was afraid that he would bring trouble and even shame to the mission of the monarch. He therefore reported the situation to Emperor Wu. Emperor Wu prevented him from going and sent

Luo Zichuan from the Ouyue area in Luoli County of Hepu Commandery on the mission, instead of Yu.

"My ancestor, ashamed of living in the same world as Yu, and worried about any future trouble he might cause, led all the people of the whole clan to hide their strengths and to cover all the traces of their existence by changing their names and moving to the An Village in Zhenning County of Xinping. There they could avoid meeting the enemy, and there hazelnut bushes were cleared, foundations dug, and houses built. The place where our ancestors originally lived later became irrelevant, since one group was then located in the South and the other in the north. We have lived here for the last three generations. Then my ancestor was granted the title of the Lord of Miraculous Responses. Later, because he helped the people in the world by the hidden spirit, and his merit and grace reached to all the ordinary people, he was named the King of Universal Salvation. His prestige and virtue were known by all. All people in the world attached great importance to him.

"I am the ninth daughter of the King of Universal Salvation, and I married the youngest son of the Stone Dragon clan in Xiang County when I came to the age of fifteen. My husband had inherited a violent character and, very young and full of sap, was disobedient to laws and regulations, and even his strict father could not curb him. He dealt with everything cruelly, and disdained all etiquette. Accordingly, in less than a year, my husband received his punishment from heaven — his clan became extinct, his children were dead, his title was cut off, and his name was removed from the register. I was the only one who survived intact. My parents wanted me to remarry. But I didn't agree. The noble families came around to make offers, with carriages following one another in a steady stream. I would rather mutilate my nose than yield, since my conviction was sincere and firm. My parents, angry with my determination, sent me away to live in another town in the area. I have had no news of them for three dozen years now. I can no longer see my parents, so the tender feeling between a mother and a daughter has long gone. It is exactly what I wanted: to live alone away from the crowd.

"In a recent year, there appeared a little dragon of Chaona. Since his youngest brother was not married, he secretly sent a handsome bride-price and said sweet words to arrange our marriage, and he even returned again after my refusal. I would never have accepted that proposal even though he were to eliminate my life and destroy my physical body. Then Chaona wanted to achieve his purpose through cultivating a friendly relationship with my parents. So he let his youngest brother temporarily move to the west of my father's domain in order to achieve marriage through bribery. My father knew that my will could not be changed, so he instigated a plan whereby Chaona would compel me by force. But I led more than 50 servants in my family, armed with weapons, to fight back, and we started the fighting on a plain in the outskirts of the city. Outmatched in number, three times we fought and three times we were defeated. The soldiers were too exhausted to be able to rely on each other and help each other. So I prepared to gather up the remainder of the soldiers to make the last battle. But I was also worrying about the larger situation, as Jinyang was flooded and Taicheng was burned.[3] Once defeated and captured, I would be disgraced by this renegade man. If one day I were to go to the underworld after death, I would be ashamed to face my husband.

"Therefore the *Classic of Odes* says,

It floats about, that boat of cypress wood,
There in the middle of the Ho.

---

[3]Jinyang 晉陽, modern Taiyuan, was flooded by Zhibo 智伯 of Jin during the Spring and Autumn period. Taicheng 臺城, north of modern Nanjing, was burned by Hou Jing 侯景, the rebel.

With his two tufts of hair falling over his forehead,
He was my mate;
And I swear that till death I will have no other,
O mother, O Heaven,
Why will you not understand me?[4]

This poem is the oath from the widow of the heir of the Wei state. Another poem in *the Classic of Odes* reads,

Who can say that the rat has no teeth?
How else could it bore through my wall?
Who can say that you did not get me betrothed?
How else could you have urged on this trial?
But, though you have forced me to trial,
I still will not follow you."[5]

This indicates that, when Duke Shao was dealing with lawsuits, decadent and chaotic customs arose, and the teaching of integrity and faithfulness diminished. [But still] a violent man could not violate a chaste woman.

"Now, your teachings can reach both this visible world and the dark underworld, and serve as a model for the past as well as the present. Your teaching of chastity and faithfulness is not inferior to that of Jirong's [Duke Shao's]. I hope that, with a little of your strength, I can borrow some weapon from you to frustrate that fierce and arrogant man, to enable widowers and widows to live, to fullfil my life's pledge, and to show your wish to help those in calamity. What I have said is only my sincerest wish. Please don't refuse me."

---

[4]James Legge, *The Chinese Classics IV* (Hong Kong University Press, 1960), 73.

[5]Ibid., 27–8.

While in his mind he had already promised to fullfil her wishes, Zhou Bao, being amazed at her eloquence and erudition, still seemed to reject her, offering other excuses in order to hear what she would say. Thus he said, "There are too many affairs on the border, and the smoke and dust of the battle may appear in no time. Because the western border is being occupied by the enemy, more than thirty states have fallen, and the imperial court is planning to take up arms to recover the lands. I've been waiting for orders day and night, and I dare not be sluggish. Tonight or tomorrow morning, the vanguard is going to leave. I can only express my indignation and grief in vain, but I don't have time to do as you request."

She answered, "In the past, King Zhao of Chu took the mountain ranges of Fangcheng as the city wall and the Han River as the moat. But he completely occupied the land of Jing and Man. Relying on the wealth left by his father and brother, he made alliances with other powerful states outside and received assistance from the three loyal ministers inside. But as soon as the State of Wu attacked, the army of Chu collapsed like birds scattering and clouds vanishing, running away as fast as running rabbits, with no time to defend their cities. The precious jade was taken away, the ancestral temples were trampled, and the power of a state with ten thousand carriages [drawn by four horses each] was not even able to protect the rotten bones of their previous kings. When Shen Baoxu sought troops from the King of Qin, he shed tears with blood over the court of the Qin State. He cried for seven days without ceasing. Duke Qin, who pitied his country for its disasters and being defeated, sent troops to help him restore Chu and defeat Wu, so the endangered country was preserved. The Mi clan of Chu was powerful in the Spring and Autumn Period, and Shen Baoxu was a grandee of the declining Chu State. However, when the bows and arrows were used up and the troops were exhausted, he could humble himself, give up his usual grace, and was even willing to die the cruellest death for his lord, so that eventually he moved the powerful king of Qin. In comparison, I'm just a weak woman. My parents are blaming me for my chastity, and this demented man is bullying me for being lonely and powerless. I'm being trapped in a critical situation. How can such dire experience not even slightly move a benevolent man?"

Zhou Bao said, "The Ninth Lady belongs to the realm of the spirit, whose breathing can bring wind and clouds. We humble human beings are certainly under your control. How can you show us mortals your weakness and push yourself in such a dilemma?" She answered, "The reputation of my clan is known all over the world. Around Pengli Lake and Dongting Lake, for example, live my maternal grandfathers; around the Ling River and Luo River are my cousins; there are more than 100 close and distant relatives who live in the Wu and Yue areas, scattered in their own lands; and half of the people in charge of eight major lakes in the capital of Xianyang are the relatives of my family. If I send a messenger to deliver a letter quickly to Pengli Lake and Dongting Lake, summoning the Ling River and Luo River, they would lead the light troops around Yangzhou, command the mighty warriors of the eight major rivers, and then pass an official call to arms to the spirit of rivers, Ping Yi, persuade the giant spirit to agitate Wu Zixu's[6] revenging waves, and mix the devils of the spirit of waves Yang hou, drive out the lightning spirit Lieque, command the thunder spirit Feng long, raising swift gusts and stirring violent tides. A hundred branches of troops would set out together, the six divisions would march forward accompanying

---

[6]Wu Zi Xu 伍子胥 (d. 484 BCE), a minster of the state of Wu during the Spring and Autumn period. He led the attack on Chu to avenge his father, who was unjustly killed by King Ping of Chu (r. 528–516 BCE). As he was awarded the land of Shen, he was also called Shen Xu 申胥.

the sound of drums, and then success would come after only one battle. In this case, Chaona, the scaled creature, would be smashed into fine powder. Within a thousand miles of Jingzhou would be nothing but a dirty pond. What I said could be seen in no time — how would I dare lie to you! Previously, the Lord of Jingyang and my maternal grandfather in Dongting Lake had been related in marriage for generations. But because of the problem between the husband and wife, the young wife was abandoned. This caused Lord Qiantang's anger. He killed the living creatures and harmed the crops. The tumultuous water surrounded the mountains and flooded the hills, and the little dragon of the Jing River was killed by my grandfather's teeth. Now the ruts of carriage wheels and tracks of horses left during the battle are still on the banks of Jing River, and detailed historical records are still extant, which is surely not wrong. In addition, I have offended Heaven because of the affair of my husband's clan, and I have not yet been forgiven by God, so I hid from the public and suffered from such a plight. If you can't understand my sincere pleading and take multiple affairs as your reasoning, what I just said will occur, and I would dare not avoid the god's punishment." Therefore Zhou Bao consented to her request. After they finished drinking wine and cleared away the dishes, she bowed to him twice, and left.

When Zhou Bao woke up, it was almost evening. What he had heard and seen seemed still to be in front of her eyes. The next day, he dispatched 1,500 soldiers to be on guard by the temple of the Good Woman Pool. On the seventh day of this month, one morning when the roosters began to crow, Zhou Bao was about to get up while it was still dark outside the windows. Suddenly a man walked through the tapestry curtains and a profile appeared on the curtain, looking like a servant maid who assisted him in washing and combing. Zhou Bao ordered her to strike a light, but there was no reply. Only when he shouted out at her did she say, "The underworld and this world are separated from each other. I wish you would not threaten me with light." Zhou Bao then realized that something was unusual, so he held his breath, then said slowly and tentatively, "Are you the Ninth Lady?" The answered was, "I am a servant of the Ninth Lady. Yesterday you kindly lent us soldiers to rescue us from danger. But because of the difference between the hidden and the visible worlds, they cannot be commanded by us. If you intend to keep your original promise, please resolve this situation." In a short while, it became bright outside the gauze window. Zhou Bao watched through the windows, but he saw nobody there. Zhou Bao considered the situation for a long time before he understood what the servant meant. Then he quickly summoned the official under him and ordered him to select 500 cavalry and 1500 infantry from the list of dead soldiers. From the list, the sheriff Meng Yuan was selected as the commanding officer ordered to send the official documents to the deity of Good Woman Pond.

On the eleventh day of this month, Zhou Bao withdrew the soldiers who guarded the temple and met them in front of his office. Suddenly, an armoured soldier fell onto the ground. While his mouth could move and his eyes could blink, he could not answer questions, nor did he appear to have died of a sudden illness. He was then placed in the outer corridors and didn't wake up until dawn. Then Zhou Bao sent someone to ask him questions, and he answered: "At first I saw a person coming from the east in a black gown, who was very polite to me, and he said to me, 'Our honourable lady has received the greatest favour from your master, which saved us from flood and fire. But still he has not yet exhausted all the means. We hope to rely on your sharp eyes and quick mind, once again to convey a message about our secretive and unspeakable pleading, please do not refuse and try your best.' When I hastily tried to find an excuse to refuse him, he pulled me by grabbing my sleeve, so that I became faint and fell down. After that I only felt I was following the person in the black gown. After a while, we came to a temple, and he urged me to take quick steps and walk quickly to a curtain. Behind it the honourable lady said to me, 'Thanks to your master's taking pity on me for my helplessness in danger yesterday, he sent you to guard our humble town. Marching back and forth on the way, how could you not be tired? Recently, your master lent me the soldiers again. I am very pleased with his sincerity. I have observed that those soldiers and horses are trained and strong, and their armour [firm and weapons] sharp, but Sheriff Meng Yuan, untalented and lowly, knew nothing about strategy. On the ninth day of this month, more than 3,000 wandering soldiers came to plunder my borders. Then I ordered Meng Yuan to lead the newly-arrived troops to intercept the enemy on the plain. He planned an ambush but it was not kept confidential, so, unexpectedly, he was defeated by the invading troops. I'm longing for a general who is good at strategy. Please go back quickly and bring my message to your master.' After she finished her words, I said goodbye and left. I was dizzy as if drunk. I can't remember anything else."

Zhou Bao checked what he said and confirmed that it coincided with his dream. Intending to verify what had happened previously, he sent Zheng Chengfu, the commander of the Zhisheng Pass, to replace Meng Yuan. In the evening of the thirteenth day of that month, he burned incense and sprinkled wine on the football field behind his office complex, and issued the official documents to request the Ninth Lady to accept and administer them. On the sixteenth day, the Zhisheng Pass reported: "At the midnight of the thirteenth day of this month, the commander of the pass suddenly passed away." Zhou Bao sighed in surprise, and then sent someone on horseback to see about it. When the horseman arrived, he found the commander was truly dead, but his stomach pit and back were still not cold, and the corpse was not decayed even though it had been placed there [awaiting burial] in the summer months. His family felt it was very strange.

Suddenly one night, a fierce chilly wind blew up sand and carried away stones, tore the roof from houses and uprooted trees, and the crops all fell down to the ground. When it stopped at dawn, clouds and fog were spread all around and did not disperse for the whole day. In the evening, a sudden clap of thunder sounded as if the heaven were being ripped apart. Zheng Chengfu was then heard moaning several times in the coffin. His family cut open the coffin and examined him. It took quite a long time for him to become conscious. That night, all his relatives and neighbours gathered around with sadness and happiness. In two consecutive nights, he had recovered to the state he had been in before his supposed death.

When the family inquired about the reason, he said, "At the beginning, I saw a man in a garment with a purple sash, riding a black horse and followed by more than ten people. He dismounted at the door and ordered me to meet him. After a moment of courtesy, he handed me a document with both of his hands and said, 'The honourable lady had a dream in which wind blew away all the dust, knowing that you have great talent capable of governing the world.[7] She intends to follow the practice in the story that took place in Nanyang,[8] in order to exterminate the foe of the state. She sent me, this humble subject, with these gifts and money to show her respect to you in the hope that you will help us to

---

[7]It is said that the Yellow Emperor had such a dream, following which he obtained a talented prime minister. See Sima Qian, *Shiji* (Beijing: Zhonghua shuju, 1959), 1, pp. 6–8.

[8]Referring to the emperor of Shu 蜀, Liu Bei 劉備 (162–223), who visited Zhuge Liang's 諸葛亮 home in Nanyang 南陽 three times to invite him to be his prime minister.

revive our state. We would be fortunate if we don't have to visit you three times.'[9]

"I had no time to say anything else except that I did not deserve this. During our courtesy exchanges, I saw the presents for hiring were already being displayed side by side below the steps: Horses with saddles, weapons and armour, brocade silk, precious playthings, and the case for arrows, were all spread in the hall. I tried to decline politely but they insisted on offering; thus I bowed twice and accepted. Right then he urged me to mount a chariot. The horses we rode on were exceptionally handsome and tall, with bright and clean decorations and tidy, solemn servants and drivers. In a moment we had driven more than a hundred *li*, when around 300 armoured horsemen came to welcome us by running ahead and after us, with the equipage fit for a grand general, and I was greatly pleased.

"Not long afterwards, I saw a great city with towering parapet walls and deep moats. Confused, I didn't know where I was. Soon, tents were set up on the outskirts, music was arranged and a feast was prepared. After the banquet, we entered the city. The crowd who watched us formed a wall of people, and among them the petty officials rushed hastily to deliver messages. I cannot remember how many doors I passed through. When I arrived at a place like a government office, the attendants around me told me to dismount my horse, change my clothes, and go to meet the honourable lady quickly. The lady sent orders that we meet in the courtesy for the host and the guest. I said to myself that since I had accepted the official documents and the equipment for battle such as weapon and armour, I was her subject; thus I firmly disagreed with her suggestion, and I got in and met the honourable lady in my military uniform. The honourable lady sent orders to ask me remove my arrow case [in

---

[9]See above footnote.

order to show her respect], though she agreed to meet me with a lower level of courtesy than that between the host and the guest.

"Then I removed my weapons, walked in with small and quick steps, and saw the honourable lady sitting in the hall. I bowed to her just as a subject does to his lord. After that, she asked me to ascend the platform repeatedly. Then I bowed again and got on the stairs from the west steps. I saw dozens of beauties in red, with black eyebrows and hair coils in the shape of dragon and phoenix, stood on both sides in attendance. There were another several dozens of girls who, wearing colourful flowers and fantastic clothing, served there by playing stringed instruments and flutes. There were several women who, wearing gold girdles, purple robes, ornament sashes and hairpins, walked quickly to the corner. Many more girls, who wore light furs and grand belts and with white jade around their waists, stood below the steps. Then the honourable lady ordered five or six female guests, each with more than ten attendants, who came into the hall while jostling each other in a crowd. Lowering my head, I made a deep bow with my hands clasped in front, daring not to kowtow. After everyone was seated, several colonels were also ordered to sit by my side. Then music began and wine was served.

"When the wine came, the honourable lady tidied her sleeves, raised her cup, and was about to explain why she had recruited me, but suddenly we heard the fire of battles being lit up all around and among the uproar someone shouted loudly, 'Several dozen thousands of Chaona's bandit troops captured our fortification at dawn today. Now they have crossed the border, marched forward together in several groups, and the fire and smoke are seen everywhere. Please send out troops to aid and support us.' Those seated in service looked at each other, and their faces turned pale. Having no time to say goodbye, those women scattered disorientedly. When the colonels descended the steps to say thanks and stood waiting for orders, the honourable lady approached the balustrade and told me, "I received an extraordinary favour from your master, who had pitied me for being solitary and helpless, and sent out troops repeatedly to rescue me from disasters. However, due to the disadvantages of our vehicles and armours, we have to consider attaching importance to strategy and tactics. Without minding the crumbling of our area, your master sent you here as general, exactly to help us out of this dangerous situation. I hope you won't take the remoteness of our area as an excuse, and correct us whenever we cannot do well." Thus she conferred upon me two extra battle horses, a set of golden armour, banners and flags, a military pennant, and a long-handled axe, as well as treasures and utensils, which filled the courtyard and the eyes of people, too many to be counted. Two palace girls in colourful clothes presented me with the commander's tally, as well as a handsome award. I kowtowed and then went out, holding the commander's tally with both of my hands. I summoned the generals to take command of the troops, and they responded consistently from inside to outside.

"That night we went out of the city, and the scouts reported similar information respectively that the enemy's force was gradually becoming stronger. I had long been familiar with those hills and streams, as well as the general terrain of the area, which was isolated desert, so I led the troops to set out at night, scattered the army in the key points about 100 *li* away from the city, clearly announced the rewards and punishments, and ordered the three armies to set up three ambush sites to wait for the enemy. At dawn, everything for the battle was completed. Relying on their previous victory, the enemy felt overconfident and marched rashly. They still thought that Meng Yuan was commanding my troop. I personally led the light cavalry, climbing high to watch the enemy's movements. I found only smoke and dust rising everywhere, and the enemy's formation for the battle was in strict order. I sent the light troops first to challenge them, and then pretended to be weak to lure them. When we started fighting at close quarters, we kept withdrawing while fighting against the enemy. The sound of metal and leather resounded loudly, as if the heaven ripped and earth fell apart. Pretending to be defeated, I led my troops withdrawing, and the enemy made every effort to pursue with all of their picked troops. While drums and whoops burst out suddenly, our troops in ambush all arose at the same time. Within the ten-*li* range of the battle, we fought from one place to another and attacked the enemy in all directions. The enemy's army was crushed and the dead were countless.

"In the second battle, the enemy was defeated again and ran away. Chaona, the sly thug, escaped from the mesh of swords and fled, but with no more than ten people escorting him. I selected thirty swift steeds for horsemen to chase him. In the end, he was captured alive and brought back under the commanding flag. As a result of this fierce battle, the grass and bushes were stained with blood and flesh, and the plain was smeared with fat and grease. The stink of corpses floated in the air, and weapons and armours were piled up like mountains. The enemy's commander-in-chief was quickly brought to the honourable lady by a light cart, and the lady ascended the Pavilion of Pacifying the North (*Pingshuo*) to accept him. Officials and commoners of the state all came together. Chaona was taken to the front of the pavilion and accused of violating the social norms. Chaona said nothing but 'I deserve death.' The honourable lady thus ordered him to be taken to the capital for execution. As the order was being carried out, however, a messenger from the King [of Universal Salvation] arrived in a special carriage from a post station. He held an urgent imperial order which urged that the criminal be pardoned, saying, "The crime of Chaona is my own crime. You may forgive him thereby to reduce my guilt." The lady was very happy to hear from her parents again. She addressed all the generals, 'The rash action of Chaona was directed by my father's order. Now I am asked to pardon him, also directed by my father's order. I refused to obey my parents' order in the past because of my will to keep my chastity; now if I refuse to obey my father's order again, it won't be auspicious.' She thus ordered Chaona's bonds untied and sent a knight soldier to escort him in going back home. But before his return to the town of Chaona, he died in shame on the way.

"Because of my meritorious deeds in crushing the enemy, I was greatly favoured and rewarded. Soon afterwards, I was appointed the Grand General of Pacifying Calamities with complete ceremony, enjoying the emolument of 13,000 households in the north. I was also awarded houses each with a yard, carriages and horses, precious utensils, clothes, servant boys and maids, gardens and parks, an official residence in the capital, banners, and armour. She then rewarded the other generals with different gifts according to their ranks. The next day, there was a big banquet. Only five or six guests were invited. Six or seven ladies I saw previously came to sit with me, and their beauty and charm were even more alluring. We drank our fill the whole night and were extremely joyful. When wine was served, the Ninth Lady raised her cup, saying, 'I was unfortunate to be widowed young. I was born to be arrogant and chaste in nature, disobeying the orders of my strict father. I have lived here in seclusion for three dozen years. Disheartened, with disordered hair, I yet managed to be alive. But when my neighbor urged me [to marry him] by force, I was almost ruined. If it were not for the special favour of your master and the mighty power of you, the General, I would, like the silent widow of the State of Xi [who was forced into marriage],[10] have become the prisoner of that fellow Chaona. I will never forget your favour for the rest of my life.' So she picked up a cup decorated with seven treasures filled with wine and had it presented to me, General Zheng. So I left my seat, bowed twice, and then drank it up. From that moment, I quite desired to go home. Since the rationale of my request was convincing and my words sincere, she gave me leave to go for a month. After the feast, I left the palace. The next day, after saying thanks and bidding farewell, I returned home with more than thirty men under my banner. Along the way, when I heard the crow of cocks and the bark of dogs, I felt sad. Shortly, I arrived home, seeing all my family crying. A casket under the canopy was solemnly set up. One of my attendants urged me to enter the coffin through a crack. When I intended to go forward, I was lifted up by people on both sides. Then I heard a loud peal of thunder and woke up."

From that day on Zheng Chengfu no longer engaged in managing his family's property; the only thing he did was to entrust his funeral affairs to his wife and children. As expected, he died without any illness at the end of the month. Before he died suddenly, he told those close to him, "I was originally employed for my military tactics, and I kept my integrity in the army. Although I did not make outstanding contributions, I showed my talent in my service. But when I was implicated in calamities, I was degraded to such a low position, that I became melancholy in my life and could not fulfil my ambition. A great man should stir up the fierce wind, push forward great waves, lift Mount Tai to strike at the eggs, draw water from the Eastern Sea to douse fireflies, arouse within himself an ambition as in hawks and hounds to right wrongs for others. I shall receive an appointment

---

[10]When King Wen 文 of Chu destroyed the State of Xi 息, he brought Duke Xi's wife to his palace, but she never spoke, even after she had given birth to two children. See *Zuo zhuan*, Zhuanggong 14.

[for such opportunities] very soon, and the time to part from you is just around the corner."

On the thirteenth day of that month, someone set out early from Xueju City. When he had walked more than ten *li*, it was dawn, and he saw the dust of carriages rise ahead of him. There were also bright, dazzling banners and hundreds of cavalry in armour. The man at the center of the others appeared quite arrogant and complacent. When he approached them to look, it turned out that that great man was Zheng Chengfu. Standing on the left side of the road, the man stood in astonishment for a long while. While he watched, he saw the troops marching swiftly like clouds and winds, and then suddenly disappear when they reached the Pool of Good Woman.

靈應傳

缺名

涇州之東二十里，有故薛舉城。城之隅有善女湫，廣袤數里，兼葭叢翠，古木蕭疏。其水湛然而碧，莫有測其淺深者。水族靈怪，往往見焉。鄉人立祠於旁，曰"九娘子神"，歲之水旱祓禳，皆得祈請焉。又州之西二百餘里，朝那鎮之北有湫神，因地而名，曰"朝那神"。其肸蠁靈應，則居善女之右矣。

乾符五年，節度使周寶在鎮日，自仲夏之初，數數有雲氣，狀如奇峰者，如美女者，如鼠，如虎者，由二湫而興。至於激迅風，震雷電，發屋拔樹，數刻而止。傷人害稼，其數甚多。寶責躬勵己，謂為政之未敷，致陰靈之所譴也。

至六月五日，府中視事之暇，昏然思寐，因解巾就枕。寢猶未熟，見一武士，冠鍪被鎧，持鉞而立於階下，曰："有女客在門，欲申參謁，故先聽命。"寶曰："爾為誰乎？"曰："某即君之閽者，效役有年矣。"寶將詰其由，已見二青衣歷階而昇，長跪於前曰："九娘子自郊墅特來告謁，故先使下執事致命於明公。"寶曰："九娘子非吾通家親戚，安敢造次相面乎？"

言猶未終，而見祥雲細雨，異香襲人。俄有一婦人，年可十七八，衣裙素淡，容質窈窕，憑空而下，立庭廡之間。容儀綽約，有絕世之貌。侍者十餘輩，皆服飾鮮潔，有如妃主之儀。顧步徊翔，漸及臥所。寶將少避之，以候期意。侍者趨進而言曰："貴主以君之高義，可申誠信之託，故將冤抑之懷，訴諸明公。明公忍不救其急難乎？"

寶遂命升階相見。賓主之禮，頗甚肅恭。登榻而坐，祥煙四合，紫氣充庭，斂態低鬟，若有憂戚之貌。寶命酌醴設饌，厚禮以待之。俄而斂袂離席，逡巡而言曰："妾以寓止郊園，綿歷多祀，醉酒飽德，蒙惠誠深。雖以孤枕寒床，甘心沒齒，煢嫠有托，負荷逾多。但以顯晦殊途，行止乖互。今乃迫於情禮，豈暇緘藏？倘鑒幽情，當敢披露。"寶曰，"願聞其說。所冀識其宗系，苟可展分，安敢以幽顯為辭？君子殺身以成仁，狥其毅烈；蹈赴湯火，旁雪不平，乃寶之志也。"

對曰："姜家世會稽之鄮縣，卜築於東海之潭，桑榆墳隴，百有餘代。其後遭世不造，畂室貽災，五百人皆遭庾氏焚炙之禍。纂紹幾絕，不忍戴天，潛遁幽岩，沈冤莫雪。

"至梁天監中，武帝好奇，召人通龍宮，入枯桑島，以燒燕奇味，結好於洞庭君寶藏主第七女，以求異寶。尋聞家仇，庾毗羅自鄮縣自水郎棄官解印，欲承命請行，陰懷不道，因使得入龍宮，假以求貨，覆吾宗嗣。賴傑公敏鑒，知渠挾私請行，欲肆無辜之害。慮其反貽伊戚，辱君之命，言於武帝，武帝遂止。乃令合浦郡落黎縣歐越羅子春代行。

"姜之先宗，羞共戴天，慮其後患，乃率其族，韜光滅跡，易姓變名，避仇於新平真寧縣安村。披榛鑿穴，築室於茲，先人弊廬，殆成胡越。今三世卜居，先為靈應君，尋受封應聖侯。后以陰靈普濟，功德及民，又封普濟王。威德臨人，為世所重。

"姜即王之第九女也，笄年配於象郡石龍之少子。良人以世襲猛烈，血氣方剛，憲法不拘，嚴父不禁，殘虐視事，禮教蔑聞。未及期年，果貽天譴，覆宗絕嗣，削跡除名。唯妾一身，僅以獲免。父母抑遣再行，姜終違命。王侯致聘，接軫交轅。誠願既堅，遂欲自劌。父母怒其剛烈，遂遣屏居於茲土之別邑。音問不通，於今三紀。雖慈顏未復，溫凊久違，離群索居，甚為得志。

"近年為朝那小龍，以季弟未婚，潛行禮聘。甘言厚幣，峻阻復來。滅性毀形，殆將不可。朝那遂通好於家君，欲成其事。遂使其季弟權徙居於王畿之西，將貨於我王，以成姻好。家君知妾之不可奪，乃令朝那縱兵相逼。姜亦率其家僮五十餘人，付以兵仗，逆戰郊原。眾寡不敵，三戰三北，師徒倦弊，掎角無怙。將欲收拾餘燼，背城借一，而慮晉陽水急，台城火炎，一旦攻下，為頑童所辱。縱沒於泉下，無面石氏之子。故《詩》云：'泛彼柏舟，在彼中河。髧彼兩髦，實維我儀。之死矢靡他。母也天只！不諒人只！'此衛世子媚婦自誓之詞。又云：'誰謂鼠無牙，何以穿我墉？誰謂女無家，何以速我訟？雖速我訟，亦不女從。'此邵伯聽訟，衰亂之俗興，貞信之教微，強暴之男，不能侵凌貞女也。

　　　"今則公之教，可以精通幽顯，貽範古今。貞信之教，故不為姬嫄之下者。幸以君之餘力，少假兵鋒，挫彼凶狂，存其鰥寡。成賤妾終天之誓，彰明公赴難之心。輒具志誠，幸無見阻。"

　　　寶心雖許之，訝其辨博，欲拒以他事，以觀其詞。乃曰："邊徼事繁，煙塵在望。朝廷以西郵陷虜，燕沒者三十餘州。將議舉戈，復其土壤。曉夕恭命，不敢自安。匪夕伊朝，前茅即舉。空多憤悱，未暇承命。"

　　　對曰："昔者楚昭王以方城為城，漢水為池，盡有荊蠻之地。籍父兄之資，強國外連，三良內助。而吳兵一舉，鳥迸雲奔，不暇嬰城，迫於走兔。寶玉遷徙，宗社凌夷。萬乘之靈，不能庇先王之朽骨。至申胥乞師於嬴氏，血淚污於秦庭，七日長號，晝夜靡息。秦伯憫其禍敗，竟為出師，復楚退吳，僅存亡國。況芊氏為春秋之強國，申胥乃衰楚之大夫，而以矢盡兵窮，委身折節，肝腦塗地，感動於強秦。矧妾一女子，父母斥其孤貞，狂童凌其寡弱，綴旒之急，安得不少動仁人之心乎？"

　　　寶曰："九娘子靈宗異派，呼吸風雲，蠢爾黎元，固在掌握。又焉得示弱於世俗之人，而自困如是者哉？"對曰："妾家族望，海內咸知。只如彭蠡洞庭，皆外祖也；陵水羅水，皆中表也。內外昆季，百有餘人，散居吳越之間，各分地土。咸京八水，半是宗親。若以遣一介之使，飛咫尺之書，告彭蠡洞庭，召陵水羅水，率維揚之輕銳，征八水之鷹揚。然後檄馮夷，說巨靈，鼓子胥之波濤，混陽侯之鬼怪，鞭驅列缺，指揮豐隆，扇疾風，翻暴浪，百道俱進，六師鼓行。一戰而成功，則朝那一鱗，立為齏粉；涇城千里，坐變污潴。言下可觀，安敢謬矣。頃者，涇陽君與洞庭外祖世為姻戚。后以琴瑟不調，棄擲少婦，遭錢塘之一怒，傷生害稼，懷山襄陵。涇水窮鱗，尋斃外祖之牙齒。今涇上車輪馬跡猶在，史傳具存，固非謬也。妾又以夫族得罪於天，未蒙上帝昭雪，所以銷聲避影，而自困如是。君若不悉誠款，終以多事為詞，則向者之言，不敢避上帝之責也。"寶遂許諾。卒爵撤饌，再拜而去。

　　　寶及晡方寤，耳聞目覽，怳然如在。翼日，遂遣兵士一千五百人，戍於湫廟之側。是月七日，雞初鳴，寶將晨興，疎牖尚暗。忽於帳前有一人，經行於帷幌之間，有若侍巾櫛者。呼之命燭，竟無酬對，遂屬而叱之。乃言曰："幽明有隔，幸不以燈燭見迫也。"寶潛知異，乃屏氣息音，徐謂之曰："得非九娘子乎？"對曰："某即九娘子之執事者也。昨日蒙君假以師徒，救其危患，但以幽

顯事別，不能驅策。苟能存其始約，幸再思之。”俄而紗窗漸白，
注目視之，悄無所見。寶良久思之，方達其義。遂呼吏，命按兵籍，
選亡沒者名，得馬軍五百人，步卒一千五百人；數內選押衙孟遠，
充行營都虞候，牒送善女湫神。

是月十一日，抽回戍廟之卒。見於廳事之前，轉旋之際，有一
甲士仆地，口動目瞬，問無所應，亦不似暴卒者。遂置於廊廡之間，
天明方悟。遂使人詰之。對曰：“某初見一人，衣青袍，自東而來，
相見甚有禮。謂某曰：‘貴主蒙相公莫大之恩，拯其焚溺。然亦未
盡誠款。假爾明敏，再通幽情。幸無辭，勉也。’某急以他詞拒之。
遂以袂相牽，懵然顛仆。但覺與青衣者繼踵偕行，俄至其廟。促呼
連步，至於帷薄之前。見貴主謂某云：‘昨蒙相公憫念孤危，俾爾
戍於弊邑。往返途路，得無勞止？余蒙相公再借兵師，深愜誠願。
觀其士馬精強，衣甲銛利，然都虞候孟遠才輕位下，甚無機略。今
月九日，有游軍三千餘，來掠我近郊。遂令孟遠領新到將士，邀擊
於平原之上。設伏不密，反為彼軍所敗。甚思一權謀之將。俾爾速
歸，達我情素。’言訖，拜辭而出，昏然似醉，餘無所知矣。”

寶驗其說，與夢相符。意欲質前事，遂差制勝關使鄭承符以代
孟遠。是月三日晚，衙於後球場，瀝酒焚香，牒請九娘子神收管。
至十六日，制勝關申云：“今月十三日夜，三更已來，關使暴卒。”
寶驚嘆息，使人馳視之。至則果卒。唯心背不冷，暑月停屍，亦不
敗壞。其家甚異之。

忽一夜，陰風慘冽，吹砂走石，發屋拔樹，禾苗盡偃，及曉而
止。雲霧四布，連夕不解。至暮，有迅雷一聲，劃如天裂。承符忽
呻吟數息。其家剖棺視之，良久復蘇。是夕，親鄰咸聚，悲喜相仍，
信宿如故。

家人詰其由，乃曰：“余初見一人，衣紫綬，乘驪駒，從者十
餘人，至門，下馬，命吾相見。揖讓周旋，手捧一牒授吾云：“貴
主得吹塵之夢，知君負命世之才，欲遵南陽故事，思殄邦仇。使下
臣持茲禮幣，聊展敬於君子，而冀再康國步。幸不以三顧為勞也。’

“余不暇他辭，唯稱不敢。酬酢之際，已見聘幣羅於階下，鞍
馬器甲錦彩服玩橐鞬之屬，咸布列於庭。吾辭不獲免，遂再拜受之。
即相促登車，所乘馬異常駿偉，裝飾鮮潔，仆御整肅。倏忽行百餘
里，有甲馬三百騎已來，迎候驅殿，有大將軍之行李，余亦頗以為
得志。

"指顧間，望見一大城，其雉堞穹崇，溝洫深浚。余惚恍不知所自。俄於郊外備帳樂，設享。宴罷入城，觀者如堵，傳呼小吏，交錯其間。所經之門，不記重數。及至一處，如有公署。左右使余下馬易衣，趨見貴主。貴主使人傳命，請以賓主之禮見。余自謂既受公文器甲臨戎之具，即是臣也。遂堅辭，具戎服入見。貴主使人復命，請去櫜鞬，賓主之間，降殺可也。

"余遂舍器仗而趨入，見貴主坐於廳上，余拜謁，一如君匡之禮。拜訖，連呼登階。余乃再拜，昇自西階。見紅妝翠眉，蟠龍髻鳳而侍立者，數十餘輩。彈弦握管，穠花異服而執役者，又數十輩。腰金拖紫，曳組攢彎而趨隅者，又非止一人也。輕裘大帶，白玉橫腰，而森羅於階下者，其數甚多。次命女客五六人，各有侍者十數輩，差肩接跡，累累而進。余亦低視長揖，不敢施拜。坐定，有大校數人，皆令預坐，舉酒進樂。

"酒至，貴主斂袂舉觴，將欲興詞，敘向來徵聘之意。俄聞烽燧四起，叫噪喧呼云：'朝那賊步騎數萬人，今日平明攻破堡寨，尋已入界。數道齊進，煙火不絕。請發兵救應。'侍坐者相顧失色，諸女不及敘別，狼狽而散。及諸校降階拜謝，佇立聽命。貴主臨軒謂余曰：'吾受相公非常之急，憫其孤煢，繼發師徒，拯其患難。然以車甲不利，權略是思。今不棄弊陋，所以命將軍者，正為此危急也。幸不以幽僻為辭，少匡不逮。'遂別賜戰馬二疋，黃金甲一副，旌旗旄鉞珍寶器用，充庭溢目，不可勝計。彩女二人，給以兵符，錫賚甚豐。余拜捧而出，傳呼諸將，指揮部伍，內外響應。

"是夜出城，相次探報，皆云，'賊勢漸雄。'余素諳其山川地里，形勢孤虛。遂引軍夜出，去城百餘里，分佈要害。明懸賞罰，號令三軍。設三伏以待之。遲明，排布已畢。賊汰其前功，頗甚輕進，猶謂孟遠之統眾也。余自引輕騎，登高視之，見煙塵四合，行陣整肅。余先使輕兵搦戰，示弱以誘之。接以短兵，且戰且行。金革之聲，天裂地坼。余引兵詐北，彼亦盡銳前趨。鼓噪一聲，伏兵盡起。千里轉戰，四面夾攻。彼軍敗績，死者如麻。

"再戰再奔，朝那狡童，漏刃而去。從亡之卒，不過十餘人。余選健馬三十騎追之，果生擒於麾下。由是血肉染草木，脂膏潤原野，腥穢盪空，戈甲山積。賊帥以輕車馳送於貴主，貴主登平朔樓受之。舉國士民，咸來會集，引於樓前，以禮責問。唯稱死罪，竟絕他詞。遂令押赴都市腰斬。臨刑，有一使乘傳，來自王所，持急詔，令促救之。曰：'朝那之罪，吾之罪也。汝可赦之，以輕吾

過。’貴主以父母再通音間，喜不自勝，謂諸將曰：‘朝那妄動，
即父之命也；今使救之，亦父之命也。昔吾違命，乃貞節也；今若
又違，是不祥也。’遂命解縛，使單騎送歸。未及朝那，已羞而卒
於路。

　　“余以克敵之功，大被寵錫。尋備禮拜平難大將軍，食朔方一
萬三千戶。別賜第宅，輿馬，寶器，衣服，婢僕，園林，邸第，旌
旛，鎧甲。次及諸將，賞賚有差。明日，大宴，預坐者不過五六人，
前者六七女皆來侍坐，風姿艷態，愈更動人。竟夕酣飲，甚歡。酒
至，貴主捧觴而言曰：‘妾之不幸，少處空閨。天賦孤貞，不從嚴
父之命。屏居於此三紀矣。蓬首灰心，未得其死。鄰童迫脅，幾至
顛危。若非相公之殊恩，將軍之雄武，則息國不言之婦，及為朝那
之囚耳。永言斯惠，終天不忘。’遂以七寶鍾酌酒，使人持送鄭將
軍。余因避席再拜而飲。余自是頗動歸心，詞理懇切，遂許給假一
月，宴罷，出。明日，辭謝訖，擁其麾下三十餘人，返於來路，所
經之處，聞雞犬，頗甚酸辛。俄頃到家，見家人聚泣，靈帳儼然。
麾下一人，令余促入棺縫之中。余欲前，而為左右所聳。俄聞震雷
一聲，醒然而悟。”

　　承符自此不事家產，唯以後事付妻挈。果經一月，無疾而終。
其初欲暴卒時，告其所親曰：“余本機鈴入用，效節戎行。雖奇功
蔑聞，而薄效粗立。洎遭釁累，譴謫於茲。平生志氣，郁而未申。
丈夫終當扇長風，摧巨浪，摧太山以壓卵，決東海以沃螢。奮其鷹
犬之心，為人雪不平之事。吾朝夕當有所受，與子分襟，固不久
矣。”

　　其月十三日，有人自薛舉城晨發十餘里，天初平曉，忽見前有
車塵競起，旌旗煥赫，甲馬數百人。中擁一人，氣概洋洋然。逼而
視之，鄭承符也。此人驚訝移時，因佇於路左，見譬如風雲，抵善
女湫。俄頃，悄無所見。

Chapter 6

Tale 6.33

Leftover Record of the Sui Dynasty (A)

By Yan Shigu
Translated by Alister Inglis

In the twelfth year of the Daye reign period (616), as he was about to visit the Riparian Capital,[1] Emperor Yang ordered the Prince of Yue, Yang You, to safeguard the Eastern Capital.[2] Half the palace women were instructed not to accompany the imperial carriage, so they tearfully vied to detain His Majesty, arguing that Liaodong was a miniscule kingdom unworthy of the imperial presence. Pleading that a general be appointed to pacify the region instead, they clambered onto his carriage so as to hold it back, while blood from their fingers stained the leather reins. Yet the emperor's resolve could not be shaken. On a length of silk, he playfully wrote twenty characters which he gave the women who were to remain:

> My dream of Jiangnan has been fine, likewise
> The conquest of Liao is but a twist of fate.
> Be sure not to change your features fair,
> Only for this year need we separate.

---

[1]Jiangdu, modern Yangzhou.
[2]Modern Luoyang.

A million troops formed a vanguard as the imperial carriage got under way. Since the Great Bridge had not yet been constructed, the emperor ordered his general, Ma Shumou, to divert water from the Yellow River into the Bian Dike so as to render it navigable by large vessels. Ma carried out his orders callously, using wooden geese with iron-feet to measure the water's depth. When the wooden geese ceased to move, he considered the corvée laborers disloyal and so drowned an entire gang in the river. Even to this day, whenever crying children hear the phrase "Ma the Barbarous is coming," they immediately cease. Such are the tales about his fearful reputation.

Ten days after his departure from the capital, the emperor condescended to ride in an ox-drawn carriage contributed by He Tuo of Song. The carriage's front wheels were high with a wide circumference and fitted with sharp spikes. The rear wheels were made of soft elm and positioned low to the ground so as to prevent sluggish movement. It was harnessed to a team of oxen. (In regard to the carriage's name, see He Tuo's biography.) On the journey from the capital to Bian commandery, daily tribute was made of women for the imperial carriage. The carriage was curtained in gossamer netting interwoven, here and there, with small jade bells. The bells would ring with the motion of the carriage in the hope that the sound of laughter from within would not be heard by those milling around without.

Chang'an had made a tributary gift of Almaia Yuan as an imperial carriage attendant. She was but fifteen years (*sui*) of age. She had a slim waist and an expressive, naïve demeanor. The emperor doted on her. At the time, Luoyang made tribute of twin flowers on a single stem known as Greeting the Imperial Carriage, said to have come from a valley at the foot of Mount Song. People did not know their name. Those who picked the flowers considered them exotic and so presented them as tribute. As the emperor's carriage had just arrived, they named them Greeting the Imperial Carriage. The petal's extremities were an intense magenta. Their middle was smooth and fragrant, the color of undyed silk. The stamens were covered in pollen, while the very center was a deep crimson. Two flowers sat side by side on a stem of lush green, not unlike that of the rice-paper plant. They bore no thorns. Their thin leaves were long and oval in shape. Their heady fragrance was such that it would not fade throughout an entire day were one's sleeve to touch them. Inhaling their bouquet would frequently prevent one from sleeping. The emperor commanded Almaia to carry them. After this, she became known as Keeper of the Flowers.

When the emperor commanded Yu Shinan to draft the "Virtuous Admonition Regarding the Conquest of the Liao Kingdom" in the imperial presence, Almaia stared at him for a great length of time. The emperor then said to Yu, "It has long been said that Flying Swallow could dance on one's palm. We have often considered this literary embellishment by men-of-letters. After all, who could do such a thing, eh? Now that we have Almaia, I can see that she is living proof of the story. She has such a naïve air about her and now she turns her attention to you. You're a man of talent. Compose something to poke fun at her!"

Yu Shinan obeyed the command with a quatrain:

Behold a half-master of cosmetics, though she would her brows
      adorn,
With shoulders double-layered and trailing sleeves, much
      naivity is born.
Yet it's thanks to such naivity that she wins her sovereign's
      care,
Flowers beside the travelling cart will she henceforth bear.

The emperor was greatly pleased.

Upon reaching the Bian River, the emperor took command of the Dragon Barge whereas Consort Southernwood rode aboard the Phoenix Boat. Replete with brocade sails and hawser cables made of colored silk, they were the epitome of extravagance. In the forecastle stood a stage, while hanging from the stage was an awning to block the sunlight. The awning was a tributary gift from the Kingdom of Puze. Threads as fine as mosquito antennae had been sewn into a base-fabric of lotus-root silk from which small pearls had been strung. Even the fierce rays of the morning sun could not pierce it. A thousand stunning serving-women, all tall and fair, had been selected for each boat. Carrying carved oars decorated with golden filigree, they were known as "imperial foot-servants."

One day, when the emperor was about to board the Phoenix Boat, he steadied himself on the shoulder of a foot-servant known as Scarlett Wu. He reveled in her soft beauty that was so unlike her peers. Captivated, he remained there a long time without moving. Scarlett was skilled at painting long eyebrows so that the emperor could not contain his lust. He summoned her after his return to the imperial capital and would have appointed her Instructress of Palace Ladies had it not been for her marriage to the jade-carver, Wan Qun. He could not, on this account, bring his plan to fruition. After the emperor had shared his bed with her, he appointed her Chief Oar-Bearer for the Dragon Barge with the title Lady of the Grotto. Henceforth the foot-servants competed among themselves to emulate her manner of painting long eyebrows.

Palace attendants daily supplied five bushels of kohl made from aquatic snails. This was termed "viridian eye-liner." The kohl came from Persia and every cake was worth ten pieces of gold. Later, supply could not meet demand and so it was adulterated with copper-based kohl. Only Scarlett continued to receive an inexhaustible supply of the aquatic snail variety. The emperor would lean toward the blind and gaze at her for ages without moving. He would then say to those waiting on him, "The ancients said that one may dine on beauty. One such as

Scarlett could certainly cure hunger." He therefore recited "Holding the Oars," which he gave her. It read:

> Old songs praise Lady Peach Leaf
> New fashion surpasses falling plum blossoms;
> She rests her body on the lightweight oar,
> Knowing she will cross to the river's other shore.

He bade the thousand foot-servants sing it.

At that time, Yuexi presented tribute in the form of "radiant satin." The fabric would, for a time, sparkle with lustrous colors if suddenly creased. The people of Yue ride swift-moving skiffs to the base of Stone Sail Mountain. There they collect cocoons in the wild which they process. One night, a woman silk-worker dreamed of a deity who told her, "King Yu's Cave opens but once every three thousand years. The cocoons you harvested are silverfish transformed from *Jiang Yan's Collected Poetical Works*. If you weave silk [from these cocoons] into clothing, you will be sure to achieve a remarkable pattern." When they had completed their weaving, the finished cloth substantiated the woman's dream. The people therefore made a gift of it. The emperor bestowed it solely on Scarlett and the Keeper of the Flowers, neglecting the other waiting ladies. This provoked Consort Southernwood's unrelenting jealousy. The two ladies' intimacy with the emperor was, thereafter, somewhat curtailed.

The emperor would often rove drunk throughout the whole harem. Once he happened to flirt with a palace attendant named Silky. Fearful of Consort Southernwood, Silky dared not welcome the emperor's attentions. She excused herself from his bed on the grounds that her time of the month had arrived. The emperor therefore teased her:

> What can one do in the face of such curvaceous eyes,
> Across your broad forehead, fine brows from kohl are dyed;

With good grace would I have you accompany me in a dream,
Yet you refuse me, now what could this mean?

Ever since the emperor reached Guangling,[3] members of the
palace all emulated the local *Wu* dialect, hence he used it in the
poem.[4]

Extremely muddleheaded, the emperor was given to women
and sensual pleasure, and often haunted by malicious spirits. He
once visited Poultry Terrace at the residence of the Duke of Wu.
There, in a trance-like state, he met the Last Ruler of the Chen
dynasty. The Last Ruler still referred to the emperor as "Your
Majesty." He wore a bandana of light, black silk, a long black robe
with wide sleeves, and purple-patterned, square-nosed shoes with
a green brocade border. Several dozen or more dancing women
were arrayed to left and right. Among them was one of
uncommon beauty whom the emperor looked at several times.
The Last Ruler asked him, "Does Your Majesty not know her? She
is none other than Ayana. I often recall how, with Mount Peach
Leaf ahead of me, I crossed with her to the north side of the river
aboard a warship. How she detested that time. She had just
reclined beside the Hall of Purveying Spring and, using a purple
rabbit-hair brush on polished red silk, she was responding to
Magistrate Jiang [Zong]'s verse, "Jade Moon." Before she could
finish, we saw Han the Tiger-Catcher mounted on a white charger
leading a rushing onslaught of ten thousand men-at-arms. They
spared neither those who remained nor those who fled. And here
we are today."

---

[3]Modern Yangzhou.

[4]The term *nong* 儂 used in the original may denote either the first or
second person pronoun and is distinctive of the *Wu* 吳 dialect; i.e., that
spoken in Zhejiang province, Shanghai, southern Jiangsu province and
environs. This does not, however, translate into English.

Shortly after, the emperor was invited to partake of newly brewed, red-sorghum wine served in green-patterned, conch-shell cups. The emperor drank with relish. He therefore asked Ayana to dance "Jade-Tree Flowers in the Rear Garden." She declined, pleading that her performance would not have the beauty of former times as she was long out of practice; besides, her waist was inflexible having had to climb from a well.[5] The emperor pressed her repeatedly, after which she slowly rose and completed one movement. The Last Ruler asked the emperor, "How does she compare with Consort Southernwood?" The emperor replied, "A spring orchid and an autumnal chrysanthemum each have their own season." The Last Ruler then composed ten or more poems. The emperor could not remember them all, only "Little Window" and "To the Maid, Green Jade" did he love. "Little Window" is as follows:

Waking late from an afternoon nap
My unpopulated dream gives me fright.
The evening sun appears sentient,
Beside the little window bright.

"Sending the Green Jade" runs:

Having parted, I felt as though my heart should shatter,
My pining bones dissolve away.
So that melancholy clouds may above me scatter;
I rely on bidding you to stay.

Bowing before the emperor, Ayana requested that he compose a poem. He declined, pleading his inability. Laughingly, she retorted, "I have heard the lines: 'If you don't keep me here, there

---

[5]The consort was forced to hide from marauding soldiers in a well.

will be a place to keep me, dear.' How can you say you cannot?"
The emperor reluctantly applied himself to the writing tablets.

> There is nothing improper in our rendezvous,
> Yet I've known your reputation for a good while.
> Sitting there, your many charms beguile,
> Verily you are a kindred spirit true.

As Ayana held the poem, her brow creased in displeasure. The
Last Ruler asked the emperor, "Is the voyage of the Dragon Barge
pleasurable? Initially I considered Your Majesty's governance to
be above that of Yao and Shun, yet you now embark on this
leisurely journey. More or less everyone seeks their own pleasure
in life. Why, in former times, did I taste your wrath so keenly? Six
and thirty letters [did you write]. Even today they leave a bitter
taste in one's mouth."

The emperor suddenly awoke. He cursed the Last Ruler,
saying, "For what reason do you address me as 'Your Majesty'
today while asking about the past?" With the roar of the
emperor's voice, they disappeared.

隋遺錄卷上

顏師古

大業十二年，煬帝將幸江都，命越王侑留守東都。宮女半不隨駕，爭泣留帝。言遼東小國，不足以煩大駕，願擇將徵之。攀車留措，指血染靸。帝意不回，因戲以帛題二十字賜守宮女，云："我夢江南好，徵遼亦偶然。但存顏色在，離別只今年。"

車駕既行，師徒百萬前驅。大橋未就，別命雲屯將軍麻叔謀，浚黃河入汴堤，使勝鉅艦。叔謀銜命，甚酷，以鐵腳木鵝試彼淺深，鵝止，謂浚河之夫不忠，隊伍死水下。至今兒啼，聞人言"麻胡來"即止。其訛言畏人皆若是。

帝離都旬日，幸宋何妥所進牛車。車前只輪高廣，疏釘爲刃，後只輪庳下，以柔榆爲之，使滑勁不滯，使牛御焉（車名見《何妥傳》）。自都抵汴郡，日進御車女。車幰垂鮫綃網，雜綴片玉鳴鈴，行搖玲瓏，以混車中笑語，冀左右不聞也。

長安貢御車女袁寶兒，年十五，腰肢纖墮，騃冶多態，帝寵愛之特厚。時洛陽進合蒂迎輦花，云得之嵩山塢中，人不知名。採者異而貢之。會帝駕適至，因以迎輦名之。花外殷紫，內素膩菲芬，粉蕊，心深紅，跗爭兩花。枝幹烘翠，類通草，無刺，葉圓長薄。其香濃芬馥，或惹襟袖，移日不散，嗅之令人多不睡。帝命寶兒持之，號曰"司花女"。

時詔虞世南草《徵遼指揮德音敕》於帝側，寶兒注視久之。帝謂世南曰："昔傳飛燕可掌上舞，朕常謂儒生飾於文字，豈人能若是乎？及今得寶兒，方昭前事。然多憨態。今注目於卿，卿才人，可便嘲之。"世南應詔爲絕句曰："學畫鴉黃半未成，垂肩軃袖太憨生。緣憨卻得君王惜，長把花枝傍輦行。"上大悅。

　　至汴，上御龍舟，蕭妃乘鳳舸，錦帆彩纜，窮極侈靡。舟前爲舞臺，臺上垂蔽日簾，簾即蒲澤國所進，以負山蛟睫紉蓮根絲，貫小珠，間睫編成，雖曉日激射，而光不能透。每舟擇妍麗長白女子千人，執雕板鏤金楫，號爲殿腳女。

　　一日，帝將登鳳舸，憑殿腳女吳絳仙肩，喜其柔麗，不與羣輩齒，愛之甚，久不移步。絳仙善畫長蛾眉。帝色不自禁，回輦召絳仙，將拜婕妤。適值絳仙下嫁爲玉工萬羣妻，故不克諧。帝寢興罷，擢爲龍舟首楫，號曰“崆峒夫人。”由是殿腳女爭效爲長蛾眉。

　　司宮吏日給螺子黛五斛，號爲“蛾綠螺子”。黛出波斯國，每顆直十金。後徵賦不足，雜以銅黛給之。獨絳仙得賜螺黛不絕。帝每倚簾視絳仙，移時不去，顧內謁者云：“古人言‘秀色若可食。’如絳仙，真可療飢矣。”因吟《持楫篇》賜之，曰：“舊曲歌桃葉，新妝豔落梅。將身倚輕楫，知是渡江來。”詔殿腳女千輩唱之。

　　時越溪進耀光綾，綾紋突起，時有光彩。越人乘樵風舟，泛於石帆山下，收野蘭繰之。繰絲女夜夢神人告之：“禹穴三千年一開。汝所得野繭，即江淹文集中壁魚所化也。絲織爲裳，必有奇文。”織成果符所夢，故進之。帝獨賜司花女洎絳仙，他姬莫預。蕭妃恚妒不懌，由是二姬稍稍不得親倖。

　　帝常醉遊諸宮，偶戲宮婢羅羅者。羅羅畏蕭妃，不敢迎帝，且辭以有程妃之疾，不可薦寢。帝乃嘲之，曰：“個人無賴是橫波，黛染隆顱簇小峨。幸好留儂伴成夢，不留儂住意如何？”帝自達廣陵，宮中多效吳言，因有儂語也。

　　帝昏涵滋深，往往爲妖祟所惑。嘗遊吳公宅雞臺，恍惚間與陳後主相遇，尚喚帝爲殿下。後主戴輕紗皂幘，青綽袖，長裾，綠錦純緣紫紋方平履。舞女數十許，羅侍左右。中一人迥美，帝屢目之。後主云：“殿下不識此人耶？即麗華也。每憶桃葉山前，乘戰艦與此子北渡。爾時，麗華最恨。方倚臨春閣，試東郭逡紫毫筆，書小硏紅綃，作答江令“璧月”句。詩詞未終，見韓擒虎躍青驄駒，擁萬甲，直來沖人，都不存去就，便至今日。”

　　俄以綠文測海蠡，酌紅梁新醞勸帝。帝飲之，甚歡，因請麗華舞《玉樹後庭花》。麗華辭以拋擲歲久，自井中出來，腰肢依拒，無復往時姿態。帝再三索之，乃徐起，終一曲。後主問帝：“蕭妃何如此人？”帝曰：“春蘭秋菊，各一時之秀也。”後主復詩十數篇，帝不記之，獨愛《小窗》詩及《寄侍兒碧玉》詩。《小窗》云：“午睡醒來晚，無人夢自驚。夕陽如有意，偏傍小窗明。”《寄碧玉》云："離別腸應斷，相思骨合銷。愁雲若飛散，憑仗一相招。"
麗華拜帝，求一章。帝辭以不能。麗華笑曰："嘗聞'此處不留儂，
會有留儂處。'安可言不能？"帝強爲之操觚，曰："見面無多事，
聞名爾許時。坐來生百媚，實個好相知。"麗華奉詩，嚬然不懌。
後主問帝："龍舟之遊樂乎？始謂殿下致治在堯舜之上，今日復此
逸遊。大抵人生各圖快樂，曩时何見罪之深耶？三十六封書，至今
使人怏怏不悅。"

　　帝忽悟，叱之云："何今日尚目我爲殿下，復以往事訊我耶？"
隨叱聲恍然不見。

Tale 6.34

Leftover Record of the Sui Dynasty (B)

By Yan Shigu
Translated by Alister Inglis

The emperor visited Moon-Viewing Palace, which overlooked a springtime scene under clear skies. In the middle of the night, alone but for the company of Consort Southernwood, he rose to look down from the front verandah. The blinds remained unopened while all else was at rest. Leaning on his Consort's shoulder, the emperor reminisced about the time when he was a crown prince. Just then, hidden in some rose bushes, there happened to be a young eunuch flirting with a palace lady. His sash had become entangled in one of the bushes and the sound of her laughter poured forth unceasingly. In view of her slim waist, the emperor thought it was Almaia having an affair. Throwing on a light robe, he rushed out to catch them, yet it proved to be the servant, Miss Elegantia. Once he had returned to his bedchamber, Consort Southernwood was unable to contain her teasing laughter. He therefore explained, "When I had that secret affair with Miss Prim, it was just like this. At times such as these we don't care about our very existence. Later I had Luna. She drove me crazy. Yet what I felt for her at the time was in no way less than the love I now feel for you, my dear. I once imitated Liu Xiaochuo's poem, "Random Memories," and would often recite it to you. Do you remember?" With this, Consort Southernwood instantly intoned:

I recall when I went to sleep,
I would wait for you to come;
But then you wouldn't.
It was only once I'd removed my make-up
Would you seek me as your mate.
How you would then press me to remove my jewelry!
The mountain-shaped incense-burner recalls our entangled
    dream;
The aloeswood inside the burner has still not turned to dust.

She also chanted:

I remember when we rose,
Petition-holders announced the dawn.
The quilt spoiled my fragrant eyebrows,
The pillow hid my wispy golden pins.
Our laughter disturbed sylvan denizens,
And scattered the avian keepers of the morn.

The emperor listened. He then sighed and said, "How time
has passed. That was a good many years ago." The Consort
replied, "I have heard that there are many bandits abroad. I do
wish that Your Majesty would make a plan!" The emperor replied,
"All my family business has been entrusted to Yang Su. For how
long might a lifetime endure? Even were some crisis to occur, in
the end I can at least become another Last Ruler. Don't talk to me
of the situation outside [the palace]!"

The emperor once visited Prince Zhaoming's Anthology of
Literature Hall. Before the imperial carriage had arrived, several
thousand palace ladies had been ordered to ascend the upper
stories and welcome its arrival. A gentle breeze then arose from
the east. The ladies' dresses were caught in its gusts and flapped
against their necks and shoulders. The emperor's lust burned with
even greater intensity as he surveyed the scene. He therefore
constructed the Maze Tower and selected elegant, pubescent girls

among the commoner-classes to reside therein. He had them wear single-layered garments of lightweight silk and, when viewed leaning against the balustrade, they appeared as if in flight. Prized incense was also placed in all four corners. The incense smoke perpetually billowed and seethed as though the morning mist had not lifted. It would not be an exaggeration to say that it was an immortal realm. The upper floors were draped with four valuable wall-hangings, each of which bore a special name. One was called Purging Spring Sorrow. The second was named Forgetting to Return when Drunk. The third was called Sweet Nocturnal Fragrance, while the fourth was Prolonging the Autumn Moon. Each was equipped with unique sets of toiletry cases and sleeping garments.

Once the emperor reached Guangling, he sunk into moral turpitude. Whenever he slept, he needed to shake his four limbs or else sing and play drums before he could reach the land of dreams. The lady-in-waiting, Bonita Han, was especially favored. Without fail, the emperor would summon her to massage him every time he retired. After that he was able to sleep. He bestowed on her the nick-name "Dream-Trigger." Consort Southernwood once secretly questioned her, "His Imperial Majesty has frequently been unwell. What special allurements do you possess that can put him at his ease?" In awe of the Consort, Bonita explained, "As I accompanied His Imperial Majesty from the capital, I noticed that he often rode in He Tuo's carriage. The carriage bounces unevenly when it moves and the ladies inside sway with the movement. His Imperial Majesty takes pleasure in their swaying motion. Thanks to Your Majesty's grace that allows me to serve the imperial bedchamber, I surreptitiously imitate the rocking inside the carriage so as to put His Imperial Majesty at ease. I have no other allure."

On another day, Consort Southernwood dismissed her on trumped up charges and the emperor was unable to prevent it.

During a day of leisure, he climbed the Maze Tower and thought of her. He then wrote two poems on the south-eastern column which read:

> Sorrow darkly invades my bones,
> I feel an illness binding, creeping.
> You must know that even Pan Yue's hoary side-whiskers,[1]
> Were mostly caused by failed feeling.

Another read:

> I cannot believe my long-held longing,[2]
> White silk-floss from my temples spring.
> Beside the tower, idly standing
> I henceforth look out as I lodge my feeling.

Ever since their arrival in Guangling, the foot-servants had all been ordered to make ready the Moon-Viewing Palace. From that time onward, Scarlett and her fellows had been unable to serve the imperial bed-chamber. It was then that a commandant of militia arrived from Gua prefecture where he had been issuing proclamations. He proffered the throne a container of double-clustered fruit. The emperor ordered a young eunuch ride post-haste so as to deliver a pair to Scarlett. Unfortunately, it broke apart due to the horse's speed. Scarlett bowed to receive the imperial favor and sent her thanks on a scroll of small, red writing tablets.

---

[1] Pan Yue 潘岳 (247–300) was a famous poet and lover of the Western Jin dynasty (265–316). The hair on his temples was said to have turned white when he was thirty.

[2] "Longing" here refers to the emperor's feelings for Bonita.

An express rider brought me fruit in a joined-pair,
Deeply grateful as I am for my sovereign's kindness.
I would rather know why since parting from His Imperial
    Highness,
Our hearts will nevermore so pair.

The emperor read the letter with displeasure. He held the messenger in his gaze and asked, "How does Scarlett do? Why is it that she sends such a resentful note?" Fear-struck, the young eunuch prostrated himself and explained, "The container was buffeted with the motion of the horse. By the time I reached Moon Viewing Palace, the fruit had already broken apart and was no longer paired." The emperor's mood remained unchanged. He therefore remarked, "Scarlett not only possesses a lovely face; her poetry, too, is deep and cutting. She is a female Sima Xiangru. Indeed, she is in no way inferior to Exalted Consort Zuo.[3]

On one occasion the emperor held a modest banquet in the palace at which the company engaged in character-riddles; that is, characters were broken up and reassembled. Miss Seclusa was waiting on him at the time. The emperor announced, "I will take the character for "seclusa" to make "ten" and "eight" "days." Miss Seclusa responded by breaking the character "silk-gauze" into "four" "ropes." The emperor regarded Consort Southernwood and asked, "Are you able to dissect the character for the imperial 'We'? If not, you must drink a cup of wine as a forfeit." The Consort languidly responded: "Isn't it simply a matter of transposing the left for the right to make 'cataract?'" At the time, people throughout the realm were all hoping to be ruled by the Duke of Tang.[4] The emperor was unhappy on hearing this. He

---

[3] Zuo Fen 左棻 (253–300) was the literarily talented consort of Emperor Wu (r. 265–290) of the Jin dynasty.

[4] "Cataract" was the personal name of the Tang dynasty's founding emperor, Li Yuan (r. 618–626), referred to here as the Duke of Tang.

replied, "I wouldn't know about that. Does this mean I'm not a sage-like ruler?"

And so traitors arose from within while bandits swarmed without. A Duty Officer of the Palace Gate Guards, Pei Qiantong, Imperial Marshal Sima Deqin, and others inveigled the general of the Left and Right Encampment Guards, Yuwen Huaji, to plot a rebellion. A petition was therefore sent requesting that the palace attendants be disbanded in stages. After approving the petition, the emperor delivered the following proclamation to the women:

> Our servants! Heat and cold alternate so that the annual harvest may attain fruition. Similarly, the sun and moon share the task of illuminating the earth so that people's labor and leisure may be equally divided. Therefore, gentleman may speak of repose and play while farmers have rest-giving festivals. Eunuchs and palace ladies, your duties have been onerous. Yet you have not been remiss in your labor, to the extent that dirt has filled your fingernails and hair while lice have bred beneath your caps. We are thoroughly sympathetic with your plight. Therefore, We will enable you to attain rest from the ranks and live according to your own proclivity. Ah! Without emulating the antics of Dongfang Shuo,[5] We will approve the document presented to Us by the guardsman. Let it be said that We have been gracious in Our treatment of you, Our servants. Let this business be conducted according to precedent."

This was followed by the Rebellion of the Burning Thatch.[6]

---

[5]A statesman and thinker of the Western Han dynasty, Dongfang Shuo (fl. late second century BCE) was, among other things, known for his comical manner of remonstrating with the emperor.

[6]This is the name of the rebellion that overthrew the Sui dynasty, so called because those in league with the rebels concealed the consequent

In regard to the *Leftover Record of the Daye Reign Period* recorded above,[7] the Liang dynastic rulers constructed a hall for the Temple of the Terracotta Coffin, located in the former capital of the southern dynasties in Shangyuan County. There were twin wings on each corner of its southern façade. These had been closed for so many years that people had forgotten exactly how many. During the *huichang* period (841–846), an edict was promulgated ordering the dissolution of the Buddhist church. The wings were, therefore, reopened. Over a thousand *xun* brushes were found, inside which a book had been concealed. Although it fell apart with the touch of a hand, the characters were still recognizable. It proved none other than a draft of the *Sui Dynastic History*. Inside were several sheets of shiny white rattan paper titled *A Record of Beauties from the Southern Region*. The monk, Zhiche, received it. When all the Buddhist sutras were burned, the monks were loath to destroy the scroll-holders made from fragrant wood. They therefore frantically tore the paper from the holders. When they looked at them, they found that all had been personally inscribed by Duke Yan, Loyal Bard of Lu Commandery."[8] We may be certain that these were written using the aforementioned *xun* brushes. Zhiche was therefore able to record events of former times. When he was able to collate the record with [a current copy of] the *Sui Dynastic History*, many instances of abstruse phraseology corresponded perfectly, yet narrated events were somewhat abridged or missing. Might this not be because, at a time when our dynastic founding fathers strove to rule in the mold of the ancient sage kings, Duke Yan partially erased the record to avoid appearing tainted by the

---

tumult by telling Emperor Yang it was due to thatched roofs burning in the city.

[7]This was the original title of the current narrative.

[8]This refers to the statesman and man-of-letters, Yan Shigu (581–645), purported author of the current text.

extravagance of former times? Nowadays the spirit of King Yao has returned and imperial rule charts its proper course. Nevertheless, I regret that this work alone has been forgotten and, as a consequence, is unable to provide a subject of conversation for men of letters and learning. I have, therefore, edited it as *Leftover Record of the Daye Reign Period*. Seven or eight tenths of the original text was missing, but I have supplemented it all.

隋遺錄卷下

顏師古

帝幸月觀，煙景清朗。中夜，獨與蕭妃起臨前軒。簾掩不開，左右方寢。帝憑妃肩，說東宮時事。適有小黃門映薔薇叢調宮婢，衣帶爲薔薇冒結，笑聲吃吃不止。帝望見腰肢纖弱，意爲寶兒有私。帝披單衣丞行擒之，乃宮婢雅娘也。回入寢殿，蕭妃誚笑不知止。帝因曰：“往年私幸妥娘時，情態正如此。此時雖有性命，不復惜矣。後得月賓，被伊作意態不徹。是時儂憐心，不減今日對蕭娘情態。曾效劉孝綽爲《雜憶》詩，常念與妃。妃記之否？”蕭妃承問，即念云：“憶睡時，待來剛不來。卸妝仍索伴，解珮更相催。博山思結夢，沉水未成灰。”又云：“憶起時，投籤初報曉。被惹香黛殘，枕隱金釵嫋。笑動上林中，除卻司晨鳥。”

帝聽之，諮嗟云：“日月遄逝，今來已是幾年事矣。”妃因言：“聞說外方羣盜不少，幸帝圖之。”帝曰：“儂家事，一切已託楊素了。人生能幾何？縱有他變，儂終不失作長城公。汝無言外事也！”

帝嘗幸昭明文選樓，車駕未至，先命宮娥數千人升樓迎侍。微風東來，宮娥衣被風綽，直拍肩項。帝睹之，色荒愈熾。因此乃建迷樓，擇下俚稚女居之，使衣輕羅單裳，倚檻望之，勢若飛舉。又爇名香於四隅，煙氣霏霏，常若朝霧未散，謂爲神仙境不我多也。樓上張四寶帳，帳各異名：一名散春愁，二曰醉忘歸，三曰夜酣香，四曰延秋月。妝奩寢衣，帳各異制。帝自達廣陵，沉湎失度。每睡，須搖頓四體，或歌吹齊鼓，方就一夢。侍兒韓俊娥尤得帝意，每寢必召，令振簹支節，然後成寢，別賜名爲“來夢兒”。蕭妃常密訊俊娥曰：“帝常不舒，汝能安之，豈有他媚？”俊娥畏威，進言：“妾從帝自都城來，見帝常在何妥車。車行高下不等，女態自搖。

506

帝就搖怡悅。妾今幸承皇后恩德，侍寢帳下，私效車中之態以安帝耳，非他媚也。"他日，蕭后誣罪去之，帝不能止。暇日登迷樓，憶之，題東南柱二篇云："黯黯愁侵骨，綿綿病欲成。須知潘岳鬢，強半爲多情。"又云："不信長相憶，絲從鬢裏生。閒來倚樓立，相望幾含情。"

殿腳女自至廣陵，悉命備月觀行宮，由是絳仙等亦不得親侍寢殿。有郎將自瓜州宣事回，進合歡水果一器。帝命小黃門以一雙馳騎賜絳仙，遇馬急搖解。絳仙拜賜私恩，因附紅箋小簡上進曰："驛騎傳雙果，君王寵念深。寧知辭帝裏，無複合歡心。"帝省章不悅，顧黃門曰："絳仙如何？何來辭怨之深也？"黃門懼，拜而言曰："適走馬搖動，及月觀，果已離解，不復連理。"帝意不解，因言曰："絳仙不獨貌可觀，詩意深切，乃女相如也。亦何謝左貴嬪乎？"

帝於宮中嘗小會，爲拆字令，取左右離合之意。時杏娘侍側。帝曰："我取'杏'字爲十八日。"杏娘復解"羅"字爲四維。帝顧蕭妃曰："爾能拆朕字乎？不能當醉一杯。"妃徐曰："移左畫居右，豈非淵字乎？"時人望多歸唐公，帝聞之不懌，乃言："吾不知此事，豈爲非聖人耶？"

於是奸蠹起於內，盜賊生於外，直閣裴虔通、虎賁郎將司馬德勤等，引左右屯衛將軍宇文化及將謀亂，因請放官奴分直上下。帝可奏，即宣詔云："門下，寒暑迭用，所以成歲功也。日月代明，所以均勞逸也。故士子有遊息之談，農夫有休勞之節。咨爾髡衆，服役甚勤，執勞無怠。埃塗溢於爪髮，蟣蝨結於兜鍪。朕甚憫之，俾爾休番從便。億戲！無煩方朔滑稽之請，而從衛士遞上之文。朕於侍從之間，可謂恩矣。可依前件事！"是有焚草之變。

右《大業拾遺記》者，上元縣南朝故都，樑建瓦棺寺閣，閣南隅有雙閣，閉之，忘記歲月。會昌中，詔拆浮圖，因開之，得苟筆千餘頭。中藏書一帙，雖皆隨手靡潰，而文字可紀者，乃《隋書》遺稿也。中有生白藤紙數幅，題爲《南部煙花錄》，僧志徹得之。及焚釋氏羣經，僧人惜其香軸，爭取紙尾，拆去視軸，皆有魯郡文忠顏公名，題云：手寫，是錄即前之苟筆，可不舉而知也。志徹得錄前事，及取《隋書》校之，多隱文，特有書符會，而事頗簡脫。豈不以國初將相，爭以王道輔政，顏公不欲華靡前跡，因而削乎？今堯風已遵，德車斯駕，獨惜斯文湮沒，不得爲辭人才子談柄，故編云《大業拾遺記》，本文缺落几十七八，悉從而補之矣。

Tale 6.35

Record of the Oceans and Mountains of Emperor Yang of the Sui (A)

Anonymous
Translated by Graham Sanders

My family has been fond of amassing old books and artifacts for generations. We have particularly detailed accounts regarding Emperor Yang [of the Sui dynasty] not found in any other books.[1] So, I have compiled these passages into this record, which I pass on to fellow enthusiasts, so that they may hear of past matters they may not have heard of before.

When Yangdi was born in the second year of the Renshou era,[2] rays of red light shot up into the sky, and those in the imperial palace were utterly astonished. Even the oxen and horses all sounded forth at that moment. Prior to this, Yangdi's mother

---

[1]Emperor Yang 煬 (given name Guang 廣), who lived from 569 to 618, was the last ruler of the Sui dynasty, reigning from 604 to 618. His extravagant lifestyle and violent demise were often held up as minatory examples, warning against the dangers of being a decadent and profligate ruler. I will refer to him as Yangdi (Emperor Yang) throughout the translation even though he was not technically emperor until 604.

[2]The Renshou era ran from 601 to 604, during the reign of Emperor Wen of Sui, but Yangdi was actually born in 569, the fourth year of the Tianhe era during the reign of Emperor Wu of the Northern Zhou.

dreamed that a dragon had emerged from within her body, soared for miles into the sky, then fell to the earth, snapping off its tail. When she informed [Yangdi's father], Emperor Wen, he pondered it silently for a long time, but made no reply.[3]

Yangdi was given the name Guang [Expansive].[4] When he was two years old,[5] he was at play in front of Wendi, who scooped him up in his arms before the balustrade and teased him affectionately. He held him close for a long while, then said: "This young boy has such a noble bearing, I fear he will be the destruction of my dynasty!" From then on, even though Wendi was still fond of the boy, he did not make plans for him. By the time Yangdi was nine years old, he was an avid reader of books and records, both old and new, on topics as varied as medicine, astronomy, geography, craftsmanship, and thaumaturgy, and he gained a thorough knowledge of all of them. However, it was his nature to be particularly ruthless, and prone to secrecy and paranoia, which served him well in probing the depths of other people's psychologies.

At that time, Yang Su had earned outstanding military merit for the dynasty, and enjoyed a powerful position at court — so

---

[3]Emperor Wen (given name Jian 堅, hereafter Wendi) lived from 541 to 604, and was the founder and first ruler of the Sui dynasty, from 581 to 604. He had two sons Yong (d. 604) and Guang (Yangdi). Wendi initially appointed Yong as Crown Prince, but was displeased by his son's decadent tendencies, and instead installed Guang as Crown Prince in 600, placing Yong under house arrest.

[4]The text erroneously records Yang Guang's given name as Yong, which was the name of his older brother. I have emended it to Guang.

[5]According to Chinese custom, infants are one *sui* at birth, so, although the text says Yangdi was three *sui* old, he would have been closer to two years in modern nomenclature.

Yangdi made every effort to befriend him.[6] Wendi had fallen ill, but no one inside or outside the palace knew of it. The Empress was not feeling well either at the time, and it had been over ten days since either had heard how the other was faring. Yangdi was situated in adjacent quarters, to which he summoned Su to confer with him, saying: "As a senior statesman of our dynastic house, you are the one who is truly able to settle our family affairs." Yangdi then personally took hold of Su's hands and told him, "If you enable me to achieve my ambition, then I will be in your debt for the rest of my life." Su replied, "Leave it to me. I will have a plan."

Su then entered the palace to inquire after the health of Wendi. When Wendi saw Su, he sat up and said to him, "I held a sharp sword in my own hand for a long time, braved slings and arrows, risked life and death — with you at my side — and so today we enjoy nobility. Yet, I believe I cannot escape this illness, so I am no longer able to govern the empire. Should the unspeakable befall me, you shall install my son Yong as emperor. If you go against my words, then I will kill you even if I have already left this world. I have spoken of this to no one else. If you install any other member of my clan, I will not be able to close my eyes even in death."[7] Wendi grew enraged at [the prospect of] this, and bellowed to his attendants, "Summon my son Yong here!" But the exertion caused him to choke, and he turned his face away, unable to speak another word. Su made his exit and informed

---

[6]Yang Su 楊素 (d. 606) was a general who was instrumental in helping Wendi to defeat the forces of the Northern Qi dynasty and establish the Sui dynasty in 581 as a successor state to the Northern Zhou dynasty. I refer to him as Su throughout the translation.

[7]Rumours at the time said that Yangdi tried to rape the favored consort of his ailing father, which caused Wendi to consider releasing his eldest son Yong 勇 from house arrest and restoring the title of Crown Prince to him instead. See *Zizhi tongjian* (*juan* 180).

Yangdi, "The matter is not yet settled; just wait a little longer." Before long, court attendants arrived and reported to Su, "The Emperor is not responding to our shouts, and there is nothing more than a faint bleating coming from his throat." Yangdi bowed to Su, and said, "I wish to entrust my entire future to you." Su then hurried back to the palace. Wendi had already perished, but they did not reveal his death at first.[8]

The next day, Su tucked into his sleeve a final imperial edict announcing the installation of [Guang] as emperor. None of the court officials knew anything of the matter, when Su, holding the jade scepter in his hand, addressed them as follows, "This is Wendi's final imperial edict, installing the new emperor. All those who fail to obey this order, will be put to death on the spot!" The attendants supported Yangdi by his arms as he ascended the basilica, but his legs were weak and, after nearly falling several times, he was unable to mount the platform.[9] Su came down and shooed away the attendants, then extended his hand to support Yangdi. Yangdi took hold of Su's hand and was finally able to ascend. Every one of the court officials sighed at this. When Su returned home afterward, he said to his family members, "I have raised this young boy to be the emperor, but I am not sure if he will be able to manage it."

Su presumed on his merits, and he often addressed Yangdi simply as "young fellow" when he met with him. Once, when Su was attending a banquet in the Inner Palace, one of the palace maids was careless and knocked over a wine goblet, staining Su's

---

[8]Wendi's death in his summer palace of Renshou was kept secret for eight days. Yangdi reportedly sent Yang Su's brother Yang Yue back to the capital with a forged edict commanding Yong to commit suicide. When Yong refused to do so, Yang Yue allegedly strangled him, clearing the way for Yangdi to be the uncontested successor to the throne.

[9]Yangdi seems to be putting on a show of weakness from worry and grief over his father's death.

robes. Su was furious and shouted for the attendants to drag the maid from the basilica and have her flogged. Yangdi was very resentful toward him over this, but he bided his time and did not reveal his true feelings.

On another day, Yangdi was fishing with Su in a pond, sitting by his side, with the attendants extending a shade overhead to protect them from the sunshine. When Yangdi rose to relieve himself, he turned back and saw Su seated there beneath the russet sunshade, with a graceful and imposing bearing, cutting a striking figure of dignified majesty. Yangdi grew even more suspicious and jealous of him.

Yangdi had many desires, but he could not realize all of them, because they were kept in check by Su's entreaties. As a result, Yangdi was even more of a mind to bring harm to him. When Su was on his deathbed, Yangdi said, "If Su does not die, I will exterminate his entire clan." Prior to this, when Su was preparing to attend court, he left his home and saw [an apparition of] Wendi holding a golden battle-axe, chasing after him, saying, "You bandit! I did not wish to install Guang as the ruler,[10] but you did not heed my words. Now I will kill you!" Su cried out in fear and ran back into his house, where he summoned two of his sons and told them, "I will surely die soon, for I have just witnessed Wendi saying so." Before long, Su did indeed die.

After Su's death, Yangdi became increasingly unrestrained. He cleared out a plot of land two hundred *li* in circumference to make a West Pleasure Park, employing the constant labour of millions of his people.[11] Within the park, he erected sixteen walled

---

[10]Again, the original text mistakenly records Yong instead of Guang, and I have emended it.

[11]During the Sui, a *li* = 459m = 502 yards, so 200 *li* would be approximately 57 miles in circumference, or 259 square miles in area, which is roughly 200 times the size of Central Park in Manhattan. These figures may have been exaggerated for dramatic effect.

courtyards, amassed earth and stone into mountains, and excavated ponds to make five great lakes and four seas. Then he decreed that specimens of every bird, beast, plant, and tree in the empire be conveyed forthwith to the capital.

Tongtai presented sixteen varieties of pears: yellow pears, purple pears, jade nipple pears, blushing pears, birchleaf pears, easy-dissolve pears, honey-flavored pears, drop-water pears, round pears, woody mottled pears, seat-of-realm pears, empire pears, water-whole pears, snowflake pears, sand-savor pears, and fire-hue pears.[12]

Chenliu presented ten varieties of peaches: golden peaches, glossy peaches, silver peaches, black honey peaches, pancake peaches, rosy peaches, rouge peaches, winter-welcome peaches, Kunlun peaches, and freestone brocade stripe peaches.

Qingzhou presented ten varieties of dates: triple-heart dates, purple stripe dates, perfect love dates, three inch dates, golden mallet dates, toothsome dates, phoenix eye dates, sour dates, honey ripple dates, (and one missing variety).

Nanliu presented five varieties of cherries: pink cherries, wax cherries, purple cherries, vermilion cherries, and large and small woody cherries.

Caizhou presented three varieties of chestnuts: giant chestnuts, purple chestnuts, and tiny chestnuts.

Suanzao presented ten varieties of plums: jade plums, criss-cross plums, honey-sweet plums, oxheart plums, green stripe plums, half-catty plums, red-droop plums, wheat-ripe plums, purple hue plums, and never-ripe plums.

Yangzhou presented bayberry and loquat fruit.

Jiangnan presented gingko and torreya.

---

[12]The translations of the plant names in these lists are tentative, as some of them seem to be in regional dialect, and may have their names as much for the sound of the characters as for their meaning.

Hunan presented three varieties of apricot plums: red stripe plums, fancy yellow plums, and double circle plums.

Minzhong presented five varieties of lychees: green lychees, purple stripe lychees, russet hue lychees, clove lychees, and pale yellow lychees.

Guangnan presented eight varieties of other trees: longan trees, shuttle trees, laurel-fig trees, sour peel tangerine trees, rouge trees, cinnamon trees, sweet orange trees, and sweet peel tangerine trees.

Yizhou presented twenty-four varieties of variegated peonies: reddish-browns, russet woodies, orange-reds, earth brown, pale reds, flying reds, Yuan family reds, Qizhou reds, drunken consort reds, take-the-stage reds, cloudy reds, beyond heaven yellows, single brush yellows, soft stem yellows, crown yellows, Yan'an yellows, early spring reds, and trembling graces, [among others].

All the flowers, plants, trees, birds, beasts, fish, and insects presented from across the empire were countless in number and will not be fully enumerated here.

Yangdi decreed the construction of sixteen walled courtyards in West Park: Shining Sunlight, Welcoming Radiance, Roosting Simurgh, Morning Rays, Glowing Clouds, Kingfisher Glory, Cultured Peace, Heaped Gems, Shadow Weaving, Regal Bearing, Kind Wisdom, Pure Practice, Treasure Forest, Gentle Brightness, Tracery Brightness, and Scarlet Sunlight. All of these names were personally fashioned by Yangdi himself. Every courtyard was replete with twenty women, all selected from among the prettiest, most circumspect and honest beauties of the palace. And in each courtyard, the beauty who was most favored by Yangdi was put in charge. Each courtyard also had a eunuch, who managed the comings and goings and provisions.

Five lakes were also excavated, each lake being forty square *li*.[13] To the south was Welcoming Sunlight Lake, to the east was Halcyon Radiance Lake, to the west was Golden Light Lake, to the north was Clear Water Lake, and in the center was Expansive Light Lake. In the middle of each lake, earth and stone was piled up into mountains, and pavilions were erected in elaborate, winding configurations, extending to thousands of spans, more resplendent than anything in the world.

And a North Sea was excavated, forty *li* around.[14] There were three mountains situated in it—in imitation of the fabled islands of Penglai, Fangzhang, and Yingzhou[15] — and on top of each mountain was a terraced pavilion, surrounded by winding verandas. The water in the sea was several fathoms deep, and canals were opened to connect the five lakes and four seas, all large enough to admit the imperial Dragon and Phoenix Barge. Yangdi often liked to drift in his barge on the East Lake, so he composed a series of eight lyrics on the topic, called "Airs on the Lake, Gazing at the Southlands":

The moon on the lake
shines especially on these arrayed immortals.
Water refreshes the cool rays: unfurling ivory mats,
waves stir clear reflections: running golden serpents,
truly apt for the divine floating raft.

The scene is fair,
as pale colors slant into view.

---

[13] Approximately 3.25 square miles in area.

[14] Approximately 11.4 miles around, or 10.3 square miles in area, assuming a roughly circular shape.

[15] Mythical homes of the Immortals in the East Sea. The first Emperor of Qin (r. 246–210 BCE) reportedly sent an expedition to these islands to retrieve an herb of immortality.

Clear dew coldly soaks silver shadows of the lunar hare,
a west wind fells blossoms from the moon's cinnamon tree,
let us feast with boundless feeling!

Willows on the lake
cannot help but bend in the mist.
Night dew washes clear their bright, alluring eyes,[16]
an east wind playfully caresses their slender waists,
a misty rain suits them even more.

Along the winding shores,
sheltering shade hangs over painted bridges.
Tendrils brush passersby at the end of a spring evening,
fluff floats in the warm breeze as shining snow,
a serene mood lingers in their gentle swaying.

Snow on the lake
falls even more in surging wind.
Slight flakes sometimes knock on bamboo gates,
white blossoms noiselessly enter the clear waves,
in misty waters, flecks of jade rub against each other.

The lake goes on forever,
the colors of sky and earth blend together.
Looking upward, no one recalls the rhapsody on Liang Park,[17]
the court worthies instead listen to the jade beauties sing,
save for being drunk, how could we respond to this?

Grasses on the lake,
waves cut channels through their blue and green.

---

[16]The term "willow eyes" refers to willow leaves just beginning to unfurl, which are said to resemble eyes opening.

[17]This might refer to a rhapsody (*fu*) on the famous Hare Garden (*Tu yuan* 兔苑) constructed by Prince Xiao 孝 of Liang 梁 (ca. 184–144 BCE) during the Han dynasty.

Their tapering bands may not be sashes for dancers,
spread so thickly, they would make mats for drunken guests,
but they have no mind to line fragrant quilts.

After the skies clear,
their complexions are all refreshed.
Floating seeds do not return, sprouting up everywhere,
fine beauties entrust their distant mood to green spring,
leaving behind poems, unable to tell their woes in the end.

Flowers on the lake,
divine blossoms moistened by Heaven's waters.
Wet buds at water's edge: jade powder sprinkled all around,
dew-soaked sepals beyond the sky: cut from glowing rosy
    clouds,
existing only in the residences of these arrayed immortals.

An unfurling riot of colors,
pinned over ears in layer after layer.
Spring chill in the water-borne palace subtly cools its elegance,
fresh radiance at the jade balustrade warmly augments its
    splendor,
in such a scene of prized elegance, how can our thoughts
    diminish?

Women on the lake,
selected just so for their pleasing figures.
To lighten the regrets of leaving palace companions,
they set out together as these lotus-picking girls,
with clear-toned singing filling their numbers.

It is fine within the imperial coach,
frolicking they go down to Dragon Ford.
Jade flutes and vermilion strings are heard day and night,
grassy strolls and "flower fights" are their springtime tasks,
in the jade chariot are these gathered perfections.

Wine on the lake
helps us to refined enjoyment the whole day through.
Rosewood clappers sound softly, silver strings warm up,
spring rice floats in the cooling froth of unfiltered wine,
we look at each other furtively with drunken eyes.

Day breaks over the Hall of Spring,
as enchanting beauties proffer cups and platters.
In the mist on the lake, the light plays delightfully,
in the land of intoxication we relax between Heaven and Earth,
it is precisely here where the emperor finds peace and calm.

Waters of the lake,
flow all around this forbidden park.
The setting sun warmly stirs fresh green hues to swaying,
amidst the languid scent of falling blossoms, myriad patterns
　　　redden,
a cool breeze rises from the tips of the floating duckweed.

Let your eyes travel as far as they can,
fish leap east of the tiny lotus flowers.
Drifting currents lightly rock the moored magnolia boat,
the celestial palace is reflected on the coolness of deep waters,
our lofty mood grows ever more profound.

When Yangdi was on his regular outings on the lake, he
would often command the palace beauties to sing these songs.

隋煬帝海山記上

缺名

　　余家世好蓄古書器，惟煬帝事詳備，皆他書不載之文。乃編以成記，傳諸好事者，使聞其所未聞故也。

　　煬帝生於仁壽二年，有紅光竟天，宮中甚驚，是時牛馬皆鳴。帝母先是夢龍出身中，飛高十餘里，龍墜地，尾輒斷。以其事奏於帝，帝沈吟默塞不答。

　　帝名廣，三歲，戲於文帝前。文帝抱之臨軒愛玩，親之甚久，曰：“是兒極貴，恐破吾家。”文帝自茲雖愛而不意於廣。帝十歲，好觀書，古今書傳，至於藥方天文地理伎藝術數，無不通曉。然而性偏忍，陰默疑忌，好用鉤賾人情深淺焉。

　　時楊素有戰功，方貴用，帝傾意結之。文帝得疾，內外莫有知者。時后亦不安，旬餘日不通兩宮安否。帝坐便室，召素謀曰：“君國之元老，能了吾家事者君也。”乃私執素手曰：“使我得志，我亦終身報公。”素曰：“待之。當自有謀。”

　　素入問疾，文帝見素，起坐，謂素曰：“吾常親鋒刃，冒矢石，出入死生，與子同之，方享今日之貴。吾自惟不免此疾，不能臨天下。倘吾不諱，汝立吾兒勇為帝。汝背吾言，吾去世亦殺汝。此事吾不語人，汝立吾族中人，吾之死目不合。”帝因憤懣，乃大呼左右曰：“召吾兒勇來！”力氣哽塞，回面向內不言。素乃出語帝曰：“事未可，更待之。”有頃，左右出報素曰：“帝呼不應，喉中呦呦有不足。”帝拜素：“願以終身累公。”素急入，帝已崩已，乃不發。

　　明日，素袖遺詔立帝。時百官猶未知，素執圭謂百官曰：“文帝遺詔立帝。有不從者，戮於此！”左右扶帝上殿，帝足弱，欲倒者數四，不能上。素下，去左右，以手扶接帝。帝執之，乃上。百官莫不嗟歎。素歸，謂家人輩曰：“小兒子吾已提起，教作大家。即不知了當得否？”

素恃有功，見帝多呼為郎君。侍宴內殿，宮人偶覆酒汙素衣，素怒，叱左右引下殿，加撻焉。帝頗惡之，隱忍不發。

一日，帝與素釣魚於池，與素並坐，左右張傘以遮日色。帝起如廁，回見素坐赭傘下，風骨秀異，堂堂然。帝大疑忌。

帝多欲，有所不諧，為素請而抑之，由是愈有害素意。會素死，帝曰：“使素不死，夷其九族。”先，素欲入朝，出，見文帝執金鉞，逐之曰：“此賊！吾不欲立廣，汝竟不從吾言。今必殺汝！”素驚呼入室，召子弟二人而語之曰：“吾必死，以見文帝出語也。”不移時，素死。

帝自素死，益無憚，乃辟地，周二百里，為西苑，役民力常百萬數。苑內為十六院，聚土石為山，鑿池為五湖四海。詔天下境內所有鳥獸草木，驛至京師。

銅臺進梨十六種：黃色梨、紫色梨、玉乳梨、臉色梨、某棠梨、輕消梨、蜜味梨、墮水梨、圓梨、木唐梨、坐國梨、天下梨、水全梨、玉沙梨、沙味梨、火色梨。

陳留進十色桃：金色桃、油光桃、銀桃、烏蜜桃、餅桃、粉紅桃、胭脂桃、迎冬桃、昆侖桃、脫核錦紋桃。

青州進十色棗：三心棗、紫紋棗、圓愛棗、三寸棗、金槌棗、牙美棗、鳳眼棗、酸味棗、蜜波棗、（缺）。

南留進五色櫻桃：粉櫻桃、蠟櫻桃、紫櫻桃、朱櫻桃、大小木櫻桃。

蔡州進三種栗：巨栗、紫栗、小栗。

酸棗進十色李：玉李、橫枝李、蜜甘李、牛心李、緣紋李、半斤李、紅垂李、麥熟李、紫色李、不知熟李。

楊州進：楊梅、枇杷。

江南進：銀杏、榧子。

湖南進三色梅：紅紋梅、弄黃梅、二圓成梅。

閩中進五色荔枝：綠荔枝、紫紋荔枝、赭色荔枝、丁香荔枝、淺黃荔枝。

廣南進八般木：龍眼木、梭木、榕木、橘木、胭脂木、桂木、棍木、柑木。

易州進二十四相牡丹：赭紅、赭木、橙紅、坏紅、淺紅、飛來紅、袁家紅、起州紅、醉妃紅、起臺紅、雲紅、天外黃、一拂黃、軟條黃、冠子黃、延安黃、先春紅、顫風嬌。

天下共進花卉草木鳥獸魚蟲，莫知其數，此不具載。

詔起西苑十六院：景陽一、迎暉二、棲鸞三、晨光四、明霞五、翠華六、文安七、積珍八、影紋九、儀風十、仁智十一、清修十二、寶林十三、和明十四、綺明十五、絳陽十六。皆帝自製名。院有二十人，皆擇宮中嬪麗謹厚有容色美人實之，每一院，選帝常幸御者為之首。每院有宦者，主出入市易。

又鑿五湖，每湖方四十里：南曰迎陽湖，東曰翠光湖，西曰金明湖，北曰潔水湖，中曰廣明湖。湖中積土石為山，構亭殿，曲屈盤旋廣袤數千間，皆窮極人間華麗。

又鑿北海，周環四十里。中有三山，效蓬萊、方丈、瀛洲，上皆臺榭回廊。水深數丈，開溝通五湖四海。溝盡通行龍鳳舸。帝常泛東湖。帝因製《湖上曲・望江南》八闋：

湖上月，偏照列仙家。水浸寒光鋪象簟，浪搖晴影走金蛇。偏稱泛靈槎。　光景好，輕彩望中斜。清露冷侵銀兔影，西風吹落桂枝花。開宴思無涯。

湖上柳，煙裏不勝垂。宿露洗開明媚眼，東風搖弄好腰肢。煙雨更相宜。　環曲岸，陰覆畫橋低。線拂行人春晚後，絮飛晴雪暖風時。幽意更依依。

湖上雪，風急墮還多。輕片有時敲竹戶，素華無韻入澄波。煙水玉相磨。　湖水遠，天地色相和。仰面莫思梁苑賦，朝尊且聽玉人歌。不醉擬如何？

湖上草，碧翠浪通津。修帶不為歌舞綴，濃鋪堪作醉人茵。無意襯香衾。　晴靄後，顏色一般新。遊子不歸生滿地，佳人遠意寄青春。留詠卒難伸。

湖上花，天水浸靈葩。浸蓓水邊勻玉粉，濃苞天外剪明霞。只在列仙家。　開爛熳，插鬢若相遮。水殿春寒微冷艷，玉軒清照暖添華。清賞思何賒。

湖上女，精選正宜身。輕恨昨離金殿侶，相將今是采蓮人。清唱
滿頻頻。　軒內好，嬉戲下龍津。玉琯朱弦聞畫夜，踏青鬥草事
青春。玉輦是群真。

湖上酒，終日助清歡。檀板輕聲銀線暖，醅浮春米玉蛆寒。醉眼
暗相看。　春殿曉，仙艷奉杯盤。湖上風煙光可愛，醉鄉天地就
中寬。帝主正清安。

湖上水，流繞禁園中。斜日暖搖清翠動，落花香緩眾紋紅。萍末
起清風。　閒縱目，魚躍小蓮東。泛泛輕搖蘭棹穩，沈沈寒影上
仙宮。遠意更重重。

帝常遊湖上，多令宮中美人歌此曲。

Tale 6.36

Record of the Oceans and Mountains of Emperor Yang of the Sui (B)

Anonymous
Translated by Graham Sanders

In the sixth year of the Daye reign (610), the plants, trees, birds and beasts of Rear Park were flourishing, narrow pathways criss-crossed beneath the peach and plum trees, and under the blue-green shade of their interlocking branches, golden gibbons and black deer thronged together freely. A roadway for the imperial carriage was opened up from the main palace directly to West Park, and planted on both sides with upright pines and towering willow trees. Yangdi was prone to making frequent visits to the park at any time. He would often go there in the middle of the night, so a large complement of sentries was usually stationed along the roadway the whole night through.

One evening, Yangdi was floating on his barge in the North Sea, with only a few dozen palace ladies in attendance. He climbed up to the mountain pavilion overlooking the sea, just as the moon shone hazily, the evening breeze fluttered gently, the drifting waves were noiseless, and the sounds of nature were hushed. Suddenly, a tiny craft appeared on the water, just big enough to hold two people, and Yangdi took it to be two beauties from one of the sixteen courtyards in West Park. When the boat arrived, one person came ashore first to proclaim, "The Last Ruler of the Chen

Dynasty presents himself to Emperor Yang."[1] Yangdi's mind was in a bit of trance, and he did not recall that the Last Ruler of Chen had already died. Yangdi had been on very close terms with him during his childhood, so he immediately rose to receive him.

The Last Ruler bowed twice to Yangdi, who bowed to him in return. After they were seated, the Last Ruler said to him, "Do you remember the old days, when we used to play together as a pair, and we loved each other more than brothers? And now you enjoy the wealth of the world and command the admiration of all. In the beginning, you claimed you would exert your administration to the utmost, beyond that even of the Three Kings of ages past.[2] But now, you are intent on taking your pleasure while you can to give yourself a lifetime of ease. This too can be a very fine thing! Since I left, you have opened up the Sui Canal, to draw in water from the great Yellow River to allow travel eastward all the way to Yangzhou. I have written a poem about it, which I come to offer to you now." Then he withdrew a poem manuscript from his robes, and presented it to Yangdi. And this is how the poem went:

> The House of Sui opened up this waterway,
> planning a grand project from the start.
> A thousand leagues of human toil,
> a million sighs from the common folk.
> The water-borne palace no longer returns,
> the dragon ship rises and is well on its way.

---

[1] Chen Shubao 陳叔寶 (553–604 CE, r. 582–589 CE) was the ruler of the Southern Chen dynasty when it was conquered by Wendi of the Sui, reuniting north and south China in 589. He was well liked by Wendi, who continued to protect him during the Sui. He died soon after Yangdi ascended the Sui throne.

[2] The term Three Kings traditionally refers to the first rulers of China's earliest dynasties — Xia, Shang, and Zhou — who were lauded as exemplars of kingly virtues.

The Heron Boat surges forth on white waves,
striking breakers, it spits forth yellow sands.
Two figures greet travelers upstream,
in the third month fluff flies from the willows.
Rays of the setting sun sink beyond the clouds,
dusky crows caw in the elm branches.
Nowadays all your desires are satisfied,
in other days you would not even have a home.
Just enjoy the vistas of this mortal world,
and search no more for the celestial raft.[3]
A hubbub to the East as we moor the boat ashore,
the wind slackens, brocade sails fall askew.
Do not claim there is no benefit for those who follow,
it will strengthen the capital for all time.

Yangdi read the poem, and said in fury and annoyance, "To live or die is by Heaven's decree. To flourish or perish is a matter of destiny. How do you know that my opening up the waters of the Yellow River will benefit those who come *after* me?" In a state of rage, he reviled the Last Ruler of Chen. The Last Ruler replied, "For how long can you maintain such a vigorous spirit? In the end, you will be no better off than me." Yangdi rose to his feet to chase him away. The Last Ruler fled, while saying, "I'm leaving! I'm leaving! But within a year, we will meet again below Duke Wu's Terrace."[4] With these words, he threw himself into the water. Only then did Yangdi recall that the Last Ruler was already dead — he sat there, stunned and beside himself, trembling in his heart for some time.

---

[3]A reference to a story recorded in a collection of strange tales called *Bowu zhi*, by Zhang Hua (232–300 BCE), which tells of a man who rode a raft up to the Milky Way, the celestial home of gods and immortals.

[4]Duke Wu's Terrace was a historical site near Yangzhou, where the Chen dynasty general Wu Mingche 吳明徹 (512–578) launched a siege against the forces of Northern Qi that helped to expand the territory under Chen control.

One day, Lady Yang, a beauty of Glowing Clouds courtyard, excitedly reported to Yangdi, "The jade plum trees presented by Suanzao suddenly shot up in a single night, and now they are giving acres of shade!" Yangdi pondered this in silence for a time, then said, "How is it that these trees suddenly grew so lush?" Lady Yang replied, "In the evening, everyone in the courtyard heard a sound as though thousands of voices in the air were whispering, 'The plum trees shall flourish.'[5] When the morning came, and we looked at the plum trees, they had already grown as lush as they are now." Yangdi wanted to have the plum trees razed to the ground, but one of his attendants counseled him, "This surely corresponds to the potency of the trees aiding Your Majesty."

The next day, Lady Zhou of Morning Rays courtyard came and reported to Yangdi, "The bayberry trees suddenly grew luxuriant in the space of one night."[6] Yangdi was delighted and asked, "How does the lushness of the bayberries compare to the jade plums?" Someone replied, "The bayberries may be lush, but in the end they cannot rival the flourishing jade plums." Yangdi went to see the courtyards for himself, and personally witnessed just how luxuriant the jade plums were. Later, both the bayberry and plum trees bore fruit at the same time, and the courtyard ladies presented them to the emperor. Yangdi asked which of the two fruits was superior, and the ladies replied, "The bayberries are nice, but their flavor is a bit sour and cannot really measure up to the sweetness of the jade plums. Most everyone in the park

---

[5]The term "jade plum" (*yuli* 玉李) contains the surname of Li Yuan, the founder and first ruler (Emperor Gaozu, r. 618–626) of the Tang dynasty, which supplanted the Sui dynasty. The flourishing plum trees are an omen of the Li clan's rise to power.

[6]The word for "bayberry" (*yangmei* 楊梅) contains Yangdi's own surname of Yang, and thus corresponds to the ruling clan of the Sui dynasty.

prefers the jade plums." Yangdi sighed, and said, "They hate the bayberries (*yang*) and love the plums (*li*). How can this just be a matter of human sensibilities? This is the will of Heaven!" Later, when Yangdi was on his deathbed in Yangzhou, a courtyard lady came one day to report that the bayberry trees had all withered and died. And Yangdi indeed ended up passing from this earth there in Yangzhou. How strange it is!

On another day, a fisherman on the Luo River caught a live carp, which had golden scales and a red tail, and was very lively and attractive.[7] Yangdi inquired as to the fisherman's name, and was told that his surname was Xie 解, but that he had no given name. Yangdi used red ink to write the phrase "release alive" (*jiesheng* 解生) as a mark on the fish's forehead, then had it released into the North Sea.[8] Later, when Yangdi was boating on the North Sea, this carp, which had grown to more than ten feet long, rose to the surface of the water to meet Yangdi and would not go back down. Yangdi saw it together with Lady Xiao at that time, and it still had some characters in red ink remaining on its forehead. But half of the character for "release" (*jie* 解) had faded and they could only faintly make out the part of the character that means "horn" (*jiao* 角) remaining. Lady Xiao then said, "A carp with horns is actually a dragon."[9] Yangdi responded, "I am the sovereign. How can I fail to see the meaning here?" Then he

---

[7]The word for "carp" (*li* 鯉) is a homophone for the surname of the ascendant Li clan.

[8]The surname Xie is written with the same character as the word "to release" (*jie*). The practice of releasing captured animals (normally called *fangsheng* 放生 rather than *jiesheng* 解生) was a means of accumulating good merit.

[9]The dragon (*long* 龍) in Chinese mythology is a sinuous, scaly, bewhiskered creature with horns, and is strongly associated with water as well as celestial and imperial power.

seized his bow and arrow and shot the fish, which promptly sank back into the water.

In the fourth year of the Daye reign (608), Daozhou presented to the court a dwarf by the name of Wang Yi, who had thick eyebrows and charming eyes, and was very shrewd in answering questions. Yangdi grew particularly fond of him. Wang Yi would follow Yangdi on his outings, but he was never permitted to enter the palace. Yangdi said to him, "You are not something that is suitable for the palace." So Wang Yi castrated himself.[10] Yangdi favored him even more as a result, and Wang Yi was able to come and go as he pleased. When Yangdi was sleeping in his inner chambers, Wang Yi would often sleep right at the foot of his bed. And when Yangdi returned after touring the lakes and oceans of West Park, Wang Yi would often spend the night with him in the sixteen courtyards.

One night, Yangdi stole quietly into Roosting Simurgh courtyard. The summer heat was at its height just then, and Lady Niu Qing'er was sleeping beneath a gauze curtain. The light of the newly risen moon shone into the window, illuminating everything brightly. Qing'er cried out in a nightmare as though her spirit were leaving her. Yangdi had Wang Yi rouse Qing'er, and Yangdi himself held her in his arms, but it was some time before she was fully awake. Yangdi asked, "What was it in your dreams that upset you so?" Qing'er replied, "I was dreaming peacefully as usual. Your Majesty took me by the arm to visit the sixteen courtyards. When we got to the tenth courtyard, Your Majesty went in and took your place on the basilica, but it suddenly caught fire and I fled. I looked back to see Your Majesty seated in the midst of the inferno, and I shouted for someone to come rescue Your Majesty. But it was a long time before I could

---

[10]Eunuch attendants were the only males allowed access to the inner palace, as they posed no threat to the chastity of the imperial harem.

wake up." It was Yangdi's nature to seek to bolster himself, so he interpreted the dream as follows: "You dreamed of my staying alive in the face of death. Fire has a formidable power, and my dwelling within in it means that I availed myself of that power." In the tenth year of the Daye reign (614), the Sui dynasty was destroyed and Yangdi took refuge in the tenth courtyard, amidst flames, just as this dream had predicted.

The dragon boat [of Yangdi] was burned by Yang Xuangan.[11] Afterward, Yangdi issued an edict for the Governor of Yangzhou to construct another boat for him, except of dimensions even more magnificent, and longer and wider than before. When the boat was presented to him, Yangdi set out on an eastward journey to Yangzhou, with the imperial harem of the sixteen courtyards accompanying him. The warden of West Park, Ma Shouzhong, bid farewell to Yangdi, saying, "I pray for Your Majesty's speedy return to the capital. I will prepare West Park for the arrival of Your Majesty's imperial carriage. The scenery and structures of West Park are of such splendor, how could Your Majesty not miss them when leaving this place to roam afar?" After he said this, there were tears streaming down his face. Yangdi was also very much struck with sorrow, and said to Shouzhong, "Take good care of West Park for me, lest those who come after mock me for not understanding how to fashion elegant vistas." Even the attendants around him all felt bewildered and shocked at what he said. When Yangdi was traveling aboard his dragon boat, midway through his journey, he heard someone singing a mournful tune at the stroke of midnight. The lyrics of the song said:

My elder brother marched to Liaodong,[12]

---

[11]Yang Xuangan 楊玄感 was Yang Su's son, who raised forces to rebel against the Sui dynasty during its decline.

[12]Key strategic location in Yangdi's repeated campaigns against the Goguryeo kingdom of Korea.

and starved to death at the foot of green mountains.
And now I am hauling an imperial dragon barge,
exhausted on the embankments of the Sui causeway.
Nowadays the entire world goes hungry,
and I have no provisions for the road.
Thirty stages of the journey lie ahead,
and I don't know how my body will last.
Cold bones rankle on the sandy wastes,
dark specters weep in the misty grasses.
Mourning the loss of my wife in her quarters,
I have ceased hoping to grow old at home.
Where can I find a righteous man,
who might pity this lordless corpse?
To guide this lonely soul in its return,
to carry these white bones back home.

After Yangdi heard this song, he sent someone to find the singer, but even after a search until dawn he could not be found. Yangdi was very uneasy and did not sleep for the entire night. In Yangzhou, Yangdi held court with every rank of official, but not a single envoy arrived bearing tribute from anywhere in the empire. Some of them had been waylaid en route by soldiers who plundered the gifts. Yangdi consulted with the assembled officials, and issued an edict to raise an army from the thirteen circuits to execute anyone who had failed to offer tribute. He understood that auspicious times for his dynasty had already passed, and planned to decamp to Yongjia, but his various officials were not willing to follow him.

In the days leading up to his demise, Yangdi came to understand a bit about celestial omens, and took to getting up during the night to observe the sky. He summoned the Court Astronomer, Yuan Chong, and asked him, "How do the celestial omens appear to you?"[13] Yuan Chong prostrated himself on the ground and lamented, "The star signs portend great evil. A rogue comet is encroaching with great swiftness on the Imperial Constellation.[14] I fear it means a disaster is imminent, so I pray that Your Majesty would rectify his moral conduct straightaway to eliminate this impending catastrophe." Yangdi was displeased and sprang to his feet, rushing into the adjacent hall, where he sat, clasping his knees and hanging his head, without saying a word. Then, he looked back at Wang Yi and asked, "Did you know that the empire was slipping into chaos? Why did you keep quiet about it and not tell me?" Wang Yi sobbed and replied, "I am just a deformed person from a remote area who has benefited from Your Majesty's kindness. Ever since I was admitted to the inner palace, I have long received Your gracious favor. I even castrated myself so that I may remain close to Your Majesty. The great chaos in the empire certainly did not just arise in recent days. To move from frost to solid ice takes a long spell of cold. I have been anticipating this great calamity, but there is no way to resolve these events now." Yangdi asked, "Why didn't you try to enlighten me earlier?" Wang Yi replied, "I did not speak of it earlier, for if I had, it would have meant my death long ago." Tears streamed down Yangdi's face at these words, and he said, "Try to explain to me the principles of success and failure, for I value your knowledge." The next day, Wang Yi submitted a memorial to the emperor, which read:

> Your servant originally came from the lowly, impoverished region of Southern Chu, during Your era of enlightened rule over the empire. I did not seek to preserve myself, but instead

---

[13]Yuan Chong 袁充 (544–618 CE) was a diviner and astronomer who served both the Chen and Sui dynasties, and was favored by both Wendi and Yangdi, with whom he perished.

[14]Roughly corresponding to the constellation of Hercules.

was willing to obey Your command to arrive at the imperial court as tribute. I am really nothing but a dwarf, and a particularly dim-witted one, but ever since I was able to attend court these past years, I have benefited profoundly from Your sagely grace, far exceeding my lifelong wishes. I have even attended upon the imperial carriage as it made its rounds of the government bureaus in every region of this land. Although I am very ignorant, I love studying the classics in depth, and thus I do know something of the sources of good and evil, and have gained some understanding of what leads to the rise and fall of kingdoms. And in my dealings with the common folk, I have learned quite a bit of what causes benefit or harm among them. Only as I have solemnly received Your request for counsel, will I dare to set forth my views…

Ever since Your Majesty inherited the imperial seal, You have practiced Your rule with your great capacities, making decisions solely with Your sagely wisdom, never once heeding the remonstrations of Your subordinates, only putting Your farsighted strategies into effect, not admitting any proposals from others. You have undertaken vast constructions in West Park; twice You have sent forces to Liaodong; Your dragon ships exceed ten thousand in number; Your palaces blanket the empire; You have conscripted an army of millions; and Your subjects extend even into mountains and valleys. Of all those who served in Your campaigns to Liaodong, fewer than a tenth have survived, and fewer than one in ten of the dead have received a proper burial. The imperial treasury is utterly empty, and grain has shot up in price. And still Your Majesty wants to take Your carriage out on pleasure excursions, riding here and there at Your whim, with a customary entourage of armed soldiers exceeding ten thousand in number. This causes everyone in all four corners of the land to lose hope, and it turns Your empire into a wasteland.

Nowadays, the remaining taxes to be collected from the common folk are [so low] as to be easily reckoned. Their sons and younger brothers have died in military service. Their elderly and young are trapped in a barren wilderness. The corpses of fallen soldiers pile into mountains. The bodies of those who have starved to death fill the open fields. Wild dogs and swine are feasting on human flesh. Hawks arrive to consume the remains. The rotting stench can be smelled for hundreds of miles. Bones are heaped into high hills. The fat and blood of the dead serve to nourish grasses in the fields. Foxes and rodents are all growing fat. An ill wind blows through deserted wastelands, and ghosts wail in the withered grasses. When gazing out across the open country, the smoke of a hearth cannot be seen for hundreds of miles. The survivors have all fallen into ruin, barely able to make it through each day. Fathers leave behind infant sons, and wives weep bitterly for fallen husbands. So many people suffer alone, especially in these times of famine. This catastrophe has only just begun — who knows when one will live or die? If a ruler loves His people, how could He let them come to this?

Yet, Your Majesty is resolute by nature, so who would dare to submit a remonstration to You? Moreover, You would command the suicide of anyone who did speak plainly to You. Your other officials would all stare at one another, and keep their mouths shut in order to preserve themselves. Even if Guan Longfeng came back to life, would he dare to offer his opinion?[15] All Your close courtiers in high positions flatter and toady, cater to Your Majesty's way of thinking, and concoct excuses for You to reject any criticism. Everyone who follows this path meets with riches and rank. When Your Majesty makes a harmful mistake, how would You ever get to hear of it?

Now, Your forces were just defeated in Liaodong, and yet Your Majesty continues with more pleasure excursions to the east land, even when the imperial altars are as precarious as snow in spring, when weapons of war blanket the four corners

---

[15]Guan Longfeng 閔龍逢 served as an advisor to the tyrannical last king of the Xia 夏 dynasty, King Jie 傑 (r. 1728–1675 BCE), and dared to remonstrate with him even though he knew it meant he would be executed.

of the land, when the common folk are thrown into the mud and burning charcoals — and still Your officials dare not speak their minds. Consider it for Yourself, Your Majesty — what recourse do You have? Does Your Majesty want to make an excursion to Yongjia simply to delay the inevitable march of time? Has the divine might and imposing dignity of Your forebears completely melted away?

Your Majesty wishes to raise more troops, yet Your soldiers and officials will not heed your commands. You wish to make a tour of the empire, yet Your imperial bodyguard will not accompany You. At such a time as this, how might Your Majesty conduct Yourself? Your Majesty may be fiercely determined to amend Your moral character, and to redouble Your efforts to care for the people. Your sagely wisdom and benevolence may be the key to curing the ills of our time. But it is already too late for the empire to be restored. The grand potential to do so has been lost, and the time will not come again. The great edifice is about to crumble, and a single log cannot support it. The mighty river has burst its banks, and a handful of mud will not repair it.

Your servant is just a person from a remote place, who does not understand what he should avoid saying. But when things have reached this point so quickly, how can I dare not to speak out? If I am not to die today, then I will surely die later at the hands of rebel soldiers, so I dare to submit this memorial. I stretch out my neck and await my end.

When Yangdi read Wang Yi's memorial, he said, "Since ancient times, when has there been a kingdom that has not fallen? When has there been a ruler who has not perished?" Wang Yi replied, "Your Majesty would still cover up Your own mistakes? Has Your Majesty not always said that You would surpass the Three Sovereigns, exceed the Five Emperors, look down upon the Shang and Zhou, and ensure that the next ten thousand generations could never measure up to You?[16] Then what do You make of present circumstances? Can You really restore the might of the imperial capital on Your own?"

At this, tears started to stream down Yangdi's face, and he sighed over and over again. Wang Yi continued, "I never spoke of this in the past because, in truth, I was too fond of staying alive. Now that I have laid out everything for You in my memorial, I wish to atone for my crimes with my death. The empire is slipping into a great chaos. I beg Your Majesty to take good care of Yourself." After a moment, the court attendants reported to the emperor, "Wang Yi has just cut his own throat." Yangdi was overcome with grief, and issued a special order that Wang Yi be buried with full honors. Before even a few days had passed, Yangdi was to meet his own demise.

It was in the middle of the night, when Yangdi heard low voices whispering outside. He hurried to his feet, put on his robes and cap, and made his way to the audience hall. He was not seated there for long when hidden soldiers suddenly rose up from both sides. Sima Kan wielded a blade and confronted Yangdi.[17] Yangdi roared at him, "I have spent years supporting you with a generous salary, and have never treated you unfairly, so how can you betray me?" One of Yangdi's favorite palace ladies, Zhu Gui'er, stood beside Yangdi and said to Sima Kan, "Just three days ago, His Majesty was concerned that the clothing of His imperial bodyguard was too thin for the cold weather. So, He issued an edict that the ladies of the palace all sew cotton-padded tunics and trousers. His Majesty personally went to supervise

---

[16]The Three Sovereigns and Five Emperors have been variously identified, but the terms are used in general to refer to the great sage rulers of high antiquity.

[17]Sima Kan 司馬戡 here refers to Sima Dekan 司馬德戡 (580–618 CE), a commander of Yangdi's forces who organized the fatal coup against him in response to Yangdi's misrule of the dynasty in its waning days.

them, and several thousand items of clothing were completed within two days. The day before yesterday, they were bestowed upon you. How could you not be mindful of this? How could all of you here dare to harass and threaten His Majesty?" Then she roundly cursed Sima Kan.

Sima Kan said, "It is true that I have betrayed Your Majesty, but the two capitals have already been occupied by rebels. There is no road by which Your Majesty can return. Even my death would not provide a way out for You. The seeds of rebellion have been planted in my mind, and though we may wish to, it is no longer possible to return to the way things were before. I wish to take Your Majesty's head to make amends to the empire." And with that, Sima Kan raised his sword and mounted the basilica. Yangdi shouted at him, "How can you not know that spilling the blood of even a feudal lord upon the ground will give rise to a great drought in the land, let alone the blood of the ruler of men?" So, Sima Kan presented a silken cord to the emperor, who went into the inner chambers and put an end to himself. Gui'er kept cursing Sima Kan all the while, until she was finally killed by the rebel soldiers.

隋煬帝海山記下

缺名

　　大業六年，後苑草木鳥獸繁息茂盛。桃蹊李徑，翠蔭交合，金猿青鹿，動輒成羣。自大內開為御道，通西苑，夾道植長松高柳。帝多幸苑中，無時，宿御多夾道而宿，帝往往中夜即幸焉。

　　一夕，帝泛舟遊北海，惟宮人數十輩。帝升海山殿，是時月初朦朧，晚風輕軟，浮浪無聲，萬籟俱息。俄水上有一小舟，只容兩人。帝謂十六院中美人。泊至，有一人先登贊道，唱："陳後主謁帝。"帝意恍惚，亦忘其死。帝幼年於後主甚善，乃起迎之。

　　後主再拜，帝亦鞠躬勞謝。既坐，後主曰："憶昔與帝同隊戲，情愛甚於同氣。今陛下富有四海，令人欽服。始者謂帝將致理於三王之上，今乃甚取當時樂以快平生，亦甚美事。離陛下已開隋渠，引洪河之水，東遊維揚，因作詩來奏。"乃探懷出詩，上帝。詩曰：

> 隋室開茲水，初心謀太奢。一千里力役，百萬民吁嗟。
> 水殿不復反，龍舟興已遐。鸂流催白浪，觸浪噴黃沙。
> 兩人迎客溯，三月柳飛花。日腳沈雲外，榆梢噪暝鴉。
> 如今投子欲，異日便無家。且樂人間景，休尋漢上槎。
> 東喧舟艤岸，風細錦帆斜。莫言無後利，千古壯京華。

　　帝觀書，拂然慍曰："死生，命也。興亡，數也。爾安知吾開河為後人之利？"帝怒叱之。後主曰："子之壯氣，能得幾日？其終始更不若吾。"帝乃起而逐之。後主走，曰："且去！且去！後一年，吳公臺下相見。"乃投於水際。旁方悟其死。帝兀坐不自知，驚悸移時。

一日，明霞院美人楊夫人喜報帝曰："酸棗邑所進玉李，一夕忽長，陰橫數畝。"帝沈默甚久，曰："何故而忽茂？"夫人云："是夕，院中聞空中若有千百人，語言切切，云：'李木當茂。'洎曉看之，已茂盛如此。"帝欲伐去。左右或奏曰："木德來助之應也。"

又一夕，晨光院周夫人來奏云："楊梅一夕忽爾繁盛。"帝喜，問曰："楊梅之茂，能如玉李乎？"或曰："楊梅雖茂，終不敵玉李之盛。"帝自於兩院觀之，亦自見玉李至繁茂。後梅李同時結實，院妃來獻。帝問二果孰勝，院妃曰："楊梅雖好，味清酸，終不若玉李之甘。苑中人多好玉李。"帝嘆曰："惡楊好李，豈人情哉，天意乎！"後帝將崩揚州，一日，院妃報楊梅已枯死。帝果崩於揚州。異乎！

一日，洛水漁者獲生鯉一尾，金鱗赤尾，鮮明可愛。帝問漁者之姓。姓解，未有名。帝以朱筆於魚額書"解生"字以記之，乃放之北海中。後帝幸北海，其鯉已長丈餘，浮水見帝，其魚不沒。帝時與蕭院妃同看，魚之額朱字猶存，惟"解"字無半，尚隱隱"角"字存焉。蕭後曰："鯉有角，乃龍也。"帝曰："朕為人主，豈不知此意？"遂引弓射之。魚乃沈。

大業四年，道州貢矮民王義，眉目濃秀，應對甚敏。帝尤愛之。常從帝遊，終不得入宮。帝曰："爾非宮中物。"義乃自宮。帝由是愈加憐愛，得出入。帝臥內寢，義多臥榻下；帝遊湖海回，義多宿十六院。

一夕，帝中夜潛入棲鸞院。時夏氣暄煩，院妃牛慶兒臥於簾下。初月照軒，頗明朗。慶兒睡中驚魘，若不救者。帝使義呼慶兒，帝自扶起，久方清醒。帝曰："汝夢中何苦如此？"慶兒曰："妾夢中如常時。帝握妾臂，遊十六院。至第十院，帝入坐殿上。俄而火發，妾乃奔走。回視帝坐烈焰中，妾驚呼人救帝。久方睡覺。"帝性自強，解曰："夢死得生。火有威烈之勢，吾居其中，得威者也。"大業十年，隋乃亡。入第十院，帝居火中，此其應也。

龍舟為楊玄感所燒。後勅揚州刺史再造，制度又華麗，仍長廣於前舟。舟初來進，帝東幸維揚，後宮十六院皆隨行。西苑令馬守忠別帝曰："願陛下早還都輦，臣整頓西苑以待乘輿之來。西苑風景臺殿如此，陛下豈不思戀，舍之而遠遊也？"又泣下。帝亦愴然，謂守忠曰："為吾好看西苑，無令後人笑吾不解裝景趣也！"左右亦疑訝。帝御龍舟，中道，夜半，聞歌者甚悲。其歌曰：

我兄征遼東，餓死青山下。今我挽龍舟，又困隋堤道。
方今天下饑，路糧無些少。前去三十程，此身安可保。
寒骨慨荒沙，幽魂泣煙草。悲損閨內妻，望斷吾家老。
安得義男兒，憫此無主屍。引其孤魂回，負其白骨歸。

　　帝聞其歌，遂遣人求其歌者，至曉不得其人。帝頗徊徨，通夕不寢。揚州朝百官，天下朝貢無一人至。有來者在路，乃兵奪其貢物。帝猶與群臣議，詔十三道起兵，誅不朝貢者。帝知世祚已去，意欲遂幸永嘉，群臣皆不願從。
　　帝未遇害前數日，帝亦微識玄象，多夜起觀天。乃召太史令袁充，問曰：「天象如何？」充伏地泣涕曰：「星文太惡，賊星逼帝坐甚急。恐禍起旦夕，願陛下遽修德滅之。」帝不樂，乃起，人便殿挽膝俯首不語。乃顧王義曰：「汝知天下將亂乎？汝何故省言而不告我也？」義泣對曰：「臣遠方廢民，得蒙上恩，自入深宮，久膺聖澤。又常自宮，以近陛下。天下大亂，固非今日，履霜堅冰，其來久矣。臣料大禍，事在不救。」帝曰：「子何不早教我也？」義曰：「臣不早言。言，即臣死久矣。」帝乃泣下，曰：「卿為我陳成敗之理。朕貴知也。」翌日，義上書云：

　　「臣本出南楚卑薄之地，逢聖明為治之時。不愛此身，願從入貢。臣本侏儒，性尤蒙滯。出入金馬，積有歲華，濃被聖私，皆逾素望，侍從乘輿，周旋臺閣。臣雖至鄙，酷好窮經，頗知善惡之本源，少識興亡之所自。還往民間，頗知利害。深蒙顧問，方敢敷陳。
　　自陛下嗣守元符，體臨大器，聖神獨斷，諫諍莫從，獨發睿謀，不容人獻。大興西苑，兩至遼東，龍舟逾於萬艘，宮闕遍於天下，兵甲常役百萬，士民窮乎山谷。征遼者百不存十，沒葬者十未有一。帑藏全虛，穀粟踴貴。乘輿竟往，行幸無時，兵士時從，常逾萬人。遂令四方失望，天下為墟。
　　方今百姓之賦，存者可計。子弟死於兵役，老弱困於蓬蒿，兵屍如嶽，餓殍盈郊，狗彘厭人之肉，鳥鳶食人之餘。聞臭千里，骨積高山，膏血野草，狐鼠盡肥，陰風無人之墟，鬼哭寒草之下。目斷平野，千里無煙。殘民削落，莫保朝昏，父遺幼子，妻號故夫。孤苦何多，饑荒尤甚。亂權方始，生死孰知。人主愛人，一何如此？

陛下情性毅然，孰敢上諫？或有鯁言，又令賜死，臣下相顧，鈐結自全。龍逢復生，安敢議奏？上位近臣，阿諛順旨，迎合帝意，造作拒諫。皆出此途，乃逢富貴。陛下過惡，從何得聞？

方今又敗遼師，再幸東土，社稷危於春雪，干戈遍於四方，生民方入塗炭，官吏猶未敢言。陛下自惟，若何為計？陛下欲幸永嘉，坐延歲月。神武威嚴，一何消爍？

陛下欲興師則兵吏不順，欲行幸則侍衛莫從。帝當此時，如何自處？陛下雖欲發憤修德，特加愛民。聖慈雖切救時，天下不可復得。大勢已去，時不再來。巨廈將顛，一木不能支；洪河已決，掬壤不能救。

臣本遠，不知忌諱。事忽至此，安敢不言？臣今不死，後必死兵。敢獻此書，延頸待盡。”

帝省義奏，曰：“自古安有不亡之國，不死之主乎？”義曰：“陛下尚猶蔽飾己過。陛下平日常言：‘吾當跨三皇，超五帝，下視商周，使萬世不可及。’今日其勢如何？能自復回都輦乎？”

帝乃泣下，再三加歎。義曰：“臣昔不言，誠愛生也；今既具奏，願以死謝也。天下方亂，陛下自愛。”少選，報云：“義已自刎矣。”帝不勝悲傷，特命厚葬焉。不數日，帝遇害。

時中夜，聞外切切有聲。帝急起，衣冠御內殿。坐未久，左右伏兵俱起，司馬戡攜刃向帝。帝叱之曰：“吾終年重祿養汝。吾無負汝，汝何負我！”帝常所幸朱貴兒在帝旁，謂戡曰：“三日前，帝慮侍衛薄衣小寒，有詔：宮人悉絮袍褲。帝自臨視之。數千袍兩日畢工。前日賜公。第豈不知也？爾等何敢逼脅乘輿？”乃大罵戡。

戡曰：“臣實負陛下，但目今二京已為賊據，陛下歸亦無路，臣死亦無門。臣已萌逆節，雖欲復已，不可得也。願得陛下首以謝天下。”乃攜劍上殿。帝復叱曰：“汝豈不知諸侯之血入地尚大旱，況人主乎？”戡進帛。帝入內閣自絕。貴兒猶大罵不息，為亂兵所殺耳。

Tale 6.37

The Mansion of Enchantment

Anonymous
Translated by Zhenzhen Lu

In his old age, Emperor Yang was especially taken by the pleasures of women.[1] One day, he regarded his attendants and said: "A ruler of men may enjoy the wealth of Heaven and Earth, yet he desires as well to relive the raptures of his youth and see his wants to satisfaction. Now that all under heaven is peaceful and prosperous, without incursions from beyond, I may finally pursue these delights. Though the palace is grand and magnificent, it lacks secluded residences with intimate chambers, and shady corridors with low balustrades. If these may be had, I shall await my old age within it."

The emperor's attendant Gao Chang reported: "Your servant, I, have a friend by the name of Xiang Sheng, who is a man of Zhe. He claims to be capable of building palaces." The emperor summoned the man the next day and questioned him. Sheng said: "Your servant begs to first submit a blueprint."

After several days, the blueprint was presented. Looking over it, the emperor was greatly pleased. On the very same day, he commanded officials to supply Sheng with building materials.

---

[1]The historical Emperor Yang, the last emperor of the Sui dynasty who reigned from 605 to 618 AD. See T6.35, n. 1.

With laborers numbering several tens of thousands, the structure was built in a year's time. Its pavilions stood low and tall; its windows appeared assorted against each other. There were secluded residences and deep inner chambers, jade balustrades and vermillion railings. The structures were connected to each other in interlocking patterns, so that they formed a maze leading in from the outside. The myriad doors and entrances were decked with jade and gold. Golden dragons reclined beneath the beams; jade beasts squatted by the doorways. The walls and steps shone brightly, while sunlight penetrated through the intricately latticed windows. The artisanship was fine to the extreme; nothing of the kind was ever seen before. The gold and jade lavished on it depleted the treasury. As for those who had accidentally entered the place, they could not find their way out even in a day's time. When the emperor made his visit, he was greatly pleased, and said to his attendants: "Even if a true immortal is sent to wander inside, he would become so enchanted that he would lose his way. It may be called 'the Mansion of Enchantment.'" He thereby commanded an official of the fifth rank to reward Sheng with a thousand bolts of silk from the palace treasury. Then he ordered several thousand girls from the palace's inner quarters, who came from good, ordinary families, to be selected to reside in the mansion. With every visit, he would remain inside for as long as a month.

One day, the minister He Chou presented a Girl-Child's Cart to the emperor. The dimensions of the cart were extremely small, with space for only one person. It contained mechanical devices within it, with which one could obstruct the limbs of a girl, so that she could not move in the slightest. The emperor tried the cart with virgin girls, and was extremely pleased. He summoned He Chou and said to him: "What fine thought has gone into this! How did you invent something so marvelous?" He gave the minister a thousand catties of gold as reward for his skills. After

He Chou left, he relayed to others the fine workings of the apparatus. Those discerning ones said: "This is not an object of virtue."

He Chou further presented the emperor with a Pulley Cart. When it is pulled on, it can ascend a tower as if traveling on land. When one makes love to a girl inside it, it would rock by itself. The emperor was especially delighted by it. He said to He Chou: "What name does this cart have?" He Chou replied: "Your servant made it as he pleased; it does not yet have a name. Would your Highness be so kind as to bestow on it a name?" The emperor said: "You have made the cart as you pleased, after that fine mind of yours; now that I have received it, I can delight myself as I please. It can be called the 'Cart of Doing-as-one-pleases.'" He Chou left after bowing twice.

The emperor had commanded painters to make several dozen paintings of scenes of sexual consort, which were hung up in the chambers. At that time the official Shangguan Shi had received a replacement for his post and returned from Jiangnan. He ordered eight panels of brass doors to be cast, each five feet tall and three feet wide, which were then polished into mirrors; together they formed a screen which could be placed in a circle in the bedchamber. He brought them to the palace and presented them to the emperor, who had them placed inside the Mansion of Enchantment. Making love to girls inside them, he found every detail to be visible in the mirrors. Greatly pleased, the emperor said: "paintings may capture the shape of a person, and yet these can seize her true likeness. They exceed paintings by ten thousand times." He further rewarded Shangguan Shi with a thousand catties of gold.

The emperor indulged himself day and night in the Mansion of Enchantment. Exhausting what energies he had, often he felt weary. He said to his attendants: "When I had first ascended the throne, I often suffered from sleeplessness; only by cuddling a woman could I shut my eyes. Just as I would drift into dream, I would wake again. But now, when I sleep, I fall into a heavy slumber, knowing no return. With sex I feel weary. Why is this?"

One day, the midget Wang Yi presented himself to the emperor and said: "Your humble servant is a useless man from the countryside, incompetent in every matter. Born in a desolate, faraway realm, I was fortunate to have been presented as tribute, and given the duty of cleaner in the palace's inner quarters. Your Highness had especially favored me; I thus castrated myself to better serve Your Highness. Since then, serving you in the sleeping chambers and accompanying you around the palace, I have gained more of your trust than anyone. I have taken advantage of this to secretly read the learned books of the palace; contemplating them over and over again, I have obtained some humble insights.

"I have heard that the sense faculties of men are founded on the *qi* borne of the vital essence.[2] In the time before you succeeded to the throne, the former emperor was diligent and frugal. You rarely touched the sensual pleasures, and every day you were in the proximity of virtuous men. Inside, your vital essence was strong; outside, your spirit was pure. Thus you were sleepless day and night. For several years now, Your Highness has indulged countless times in sensual pleasures, gratifying yourself in the palace's inner quarters. There you have reveled day and night. Apart from the Day of the Prime and major festivals,[3] when have you made your way to the palace's front hall? Most of the time, you do not conduct meetings with the court officials. Even if Your Highness were to receive visitors from faraway, or during occasional celebrations, you would either hold court fairly late or take leave for the concubine quarters without so much as having

---

[2]*Jing* 精 (vital essence) is semen in its most physical form.

[3]The Day of the Prime is the first day of the lunar new year.

sat down for a little while. To devote one's limited body to satiating limitless desire, I know it is certainly exhausting.

"I have heard that in ancient times there was a rustic old man who sang and danced by himself on a great rock. A passerby asked: 'How come you are so happy all by yourself?' The old man replied: 'Would you like to know my three joys?' 'And what are they?' The old man said: 'In life it is rare to come across peaceful times. I see no war and strife in this day: this is one joy. In life it is rare to possess a complete body. I am not crippled: this is my second joy. In life it is rare to live to old age. Now I am eighty years old already, and this is my third joy.' The passerby left sighing with admiration.

"Your Highness, you possess the wealth of the world; you have the noblest disposition and the loftiest countenance, and yet you do not take care of yourself. You are certainly not as thoughtful as that rustic old man. Your humble servant, I, have only my feeble body and trivial life to give to requite Your Highness. I fear I have spoken what is forbidden, and have committed a great offense."

Wang Yi prostrated himself and wept. The emperor commanded him to rise. The next day, he summoned Wang Yi and said to him: "I contemplated your words last night; you are completely right. You truly care for me." He asked Wang Yi to select a quiet room in the inner quarters of the palace, and stayed inside it. None of the palace girls were allowed to enter. After two days, the emperor emerged angrily, and said: "How can I stay pent up like this? If I were to live this way, even if I live for ten thousand years, it is of no use." Then he returned to the Mansion of Enchantment.

There were so many girls in the palace that the ones who were not chosen to go into the Mansion were numerous. One day, Lady Hou of the palace's inner quarters, who possessed great beauty, was found having hung herself on the beams. A brocade satchel was attached to her arm; there were writings inside it. The attendants took them and presented them to the emperor, who found them to be verses. There were three poems entitled "Laments":

> (the first poem)
> In the courtyard his royal carriage leaves not a trace
> While the green grasses have grown tall
> I hear the faint sound of flute and drums –
> Where does he bestow his affections now?

> (the second)
> My sorrow would yield no tears, though tears are wanting
> As grief surges inside me, I could but force a song
> The flowers in the yard have burst into bloom this season;
> How helpless I am against the spring!

> (the third)
> In spring's boundless radiance
> What sends her to pace alone?
> The idle willows and blossoms are better fated
> To collect the dew and raindrops[4]

Then there was "Gazing at Plum Blossoms," with two poems:

> (the first poem)
> When is the day when the snow shall melt?
> I roll up the curtains, and grimace to myself –
> The blossoming plum in the yard pities me and shows
> An inkling of spring at the tips of her bough

> (the second poem)
> Her fragrant beauty is borne of the cold
> Her grace comes not from artifice

---

[4]The rain and dew are a metaphor for the emperor's favors.

Sunny days shall arrive after her blossoms cease
And toss spring among the myriad flowers

There was a poem entitled "I have adorned my face":

I have adorned my face, and gaze at myself
Sweet be my dreams, they have grown into grief
I envy the carefree willow catkins in the spring
Drifting here, there, everywhere

Another poem, "A Plaint," went like this:

Deep in the secret cavern, a divine flower blooms –
Latched behind latticed windows is a beauty of a woman
Sir Mao truly deserves to be slain for what he did:
He wouldn't paint the true likeness of Zhaojun![5]

And then there was "Elegy for myself":

I remember still, my first night in the palace
The sounding of the midnight hours in its depths.
In the seven or eight long years since,
I have not seen His Majesty's face.
I can feel the spring night's chilling
As I lie in my room, alone in my grief.
Restless I rise, stepping into the garden,
Feeling only sorrow heaving in my chest.
I have made myself beautiful all these years, awaiting

[5]This refers to the story of Wang Zhaojun 王昭君, a palace girl in the time of emperor Yuandi of the former Han dynasty, who was given as a bride to a Xiongnu chieftain. As legend has it, the court painter Mao Yanshou 毛延壽 would not paint Zhaojun in her true likeness for lack of a bribe, and the emperor saw, only too late, her exceeding beauty. Historically, Mao Yanshou was executed by the court, but the association between it and Wang Zhaojun is questionable.

What promised to be an extraordinary fate.
Yet who knew I would be abandoned
To a destiny of immeasurable woe!
Your Majesty, you kept me ever at a distance;
Your concubine, piteous, has known no peace.
It is not that I have no loved ones at home –
My old mother and I are especially close
If only I would grow wings on this body, to
bring me above these imposing walls!
Life is to be treasured:
To renounce it is a shame.
As I hang the silk noose on the vermillion beam,
I am toiling, toiling inside –
I put my head in it, and yet I hesitate
For something tugs softly at my heart –
Enough! I shall die, my mind is made,
And henceforth call home the Land of Shades!

When the emperor read Lady Hou's poems, he was stirred
again and again. He went to examine her corpse, and upon seeing
it, he said to himself: "she is dead, and yet she looks as beautiful
as a fresh plum on the trees." He immediately summoned the
eunuch Xu Tingfu. He said to Xu: "I have always sent you to
select the girls from the inner quarters for the Mansion of
Enchantment. Why did you alone neglect her?" Then he had
Tingfu put in jail, and ordered him to commit suicide. Lady Hou
was given an elaborate burial. Day after day the emperor recited
her poems; adoring them, he had the Bureau of Music set them to
song. He further went to the palace's inner quarters to personally
select one hundred girls for the Mansion of Enchantment.

In the eighth year of the Reign of Great Attainment, the
wizard Qian[6] presented the Great Elixir at court. After ingesting it,
the emperor felt his desire for sex to be ever insatiable, so that he

---

[6]The first character of his name is missing in the text.

would consort with several dozen girls in a day. When it came to be summer, he constantly felt restless, and though he would drink several hundred cups of water a day, his thirst could not be quenched. The imperial physician Mo Junxi presented himself to the emperor and said: "Your Highness, your heart pulses with agitation, and your primal *qi* is extremely weak. If you drink often, you will incur a great illness." Then he presented the emperor with a tonic as a cure. He further asked for plates of ice to be brought, and implored the emperor to gaze at them from morning to evening. This was another way of treating his agitation. From then on, the beauties of the various palace quarters competed to purchase ice to be gathered into plates, in the hope that the emperor would visit them. As a result, the price of ice in the capital became exorbitant, and those households that stored it all reaped thousands of catties of gold in profit.

In the ninth year of the Reign of Great Attainment (605–618), the emperor was going to revisit Jiangdu.[7] One still night, a girl from the Mansion of Enchantment was heard singing in a soaring voice:

> South of the river the willow flowers are wilting
> North of the river the plum trees are in bloom
> Where will the willow catkins drift to, as they drift away?
> The plum trees will bear fruit in nature's time.

Having heard her sing, the emperor put on his robes and rose to listen. He summoned the girl and asked her: "Who told you to sing it? Or did you compose the ditty yourself?"

The girl replied: "My brother learned it from the ordinary folk. He said that the children on the way all sang it."

---

[7]Jiangdu 江都, see p. 403, n. 2.

The emperor grew silent. After a long time, he said: "Heaven portends it! The words of men portend it!" He had wine brought, and sang to himself:

In the shady groves of the palace, swallows flit from tree to tree
Somber is the fate of every dynasty through the ages
I see the Mansion of Enchantment splendid one day
Beaming with beauty, in the red of flames

Upon singing the last notes, he was overcome with grief. His attendants asked: "Why is Your Highness so despondent all of a sudden, and why do you sing? We beg your pardon." The emperor replied: "Ask me not. One day you shall understand by yourselves."

Later on, the emperor made his visit to Jiangdu. The ruler of the Tang occupied the capital with his troops; at the sight of the Mansion of Enchantment, he was appalled, and said: "This is built with the blood and toil of the people!" He ordered it to be burned to the ground; the flames would not cease after a month.

Both the ditty and the poem have predicted this. One learns therein that the rise and fall of dynasties do not happen by chance.[8]

---

[8]Historically, the Sui dynasty fell in 618, with the assassination of Emperor Yang in Jiangdu and the rise to power of Li Yuan, founding ruler of the Tang dynasty. The earlier ditty can be read as a prophecy, with willow (*yang*) being a homonym for Emperor Yang and plum (*li*) alluding to Li, the surname of the Tang rulers.

迷樓記

缺名

　　煬帝晚年，尤沉迷女色。他日，顧謂近侍曰："人主享天地之富，亦欲極當年之樂，自快其意。今天下安富無外事，此吾得以遂其樂也。今宮殿雖壯麗顯敞，苦無曲房小室，幽軒短檻。若得此，則吾期老於其中也。"

　　近侍高昌奏曰："臣有友項昇，浙人也，自言能搆宮室。"翌日，召而問之。昇曰："臣先乞奏圖。"

　　後數日，進圖。帝披覽，大悅。即日詔有司，供其材木。凡役夫數萬，經歲而成。樓閣高下，軒窗掩映。幽房曲室，玉欄朱楯，互相連屬，迴環四合，曲屋自通。千門萬戶，上下金碧。金虯伏於棟下，玉獸蹲乎戶旁，壁砌生光，瑣窗射日。工巧云極，自古無有也。費用金玉，帑庫爲之一虛。

　　人誤入者，雖終日不能出。帝幸之，大喜，顧左右曰："使真仙遊其中，亦當自迷也。可目之曰迷樓。"詔以五品官賜昇，仍給內庫帛千疋賞之。詔選後宮良家女數千，以居樓中。每一幸，有經月不出。

　　是月，大夫何稠進御童女車。車之制度絕小，祇容一人，有機處于其中，以機礙女子手足，纖毫不能動。帝以處女試之，極喜。召何稠語之曰："卿之巧思，一何神妙如此？"以千金贈之，旌其巧也。何稠出，爲人言車之機巧。有識者曰："此非盛德之器也。"

　　稠又進轉關車，用挽之，可以升樓閣如行平地。車中御女則自搖動，帝尤喜悅。帝語稠曰："此車何名也？"稠曰："臣任意造成，未有名也。願帝賜佳名。"帝曰："卿任其巧意以成車，朕得之，任其意以自樂，可名任意車也。"何稠再拜而去。

帝令畫工繪士女會合之圖數十幅，懸於閣中。上官時自江外得替回。鑄烏銅扉八面，其高五尺而闊三尺，磨以成鑑，爲屏，可環於寢所，詣闕投進。帝以屏內迷樓，而御女於其中，纖毫皆入於鑑中。帝大喜曰：“繪畫得其象耳。此得人之真容也，勝繪畫萬倍矣。”又以千金賜上官時。

帝日夕沉荒於迷樓，罄竭其力，亦多倦怠。顧謂近侍曰：“朕憶初登極日，多辛苦無睡，得婦人枕而藉之，方能合目。纔似夢，則又覺。今睡則冥冥不知返，近女色則憊，何也？”

它日，矮民王義上奏曰：“臣田野廢民，作事皆不勝人。生於恩薄絕遠之域，幸因入貢，得備後宮掃除之役。陛下特加愛遇，臣嘗一自宮以侍陛下。自茲出入臥內，周旋宮室，方今親信，無如臣者。臣由是竊覽殿中簡編，反覆玩味，微有所得。

“臣聞精氣爲人之聰明。陛下當龍潛日，先帝勤儉，陛下鮮親聲色，日近善人。陛下精實於內，神清於外，故日夕無寢。陛下自數年聲色無數，盈滿後宮，陛下日夕遊宴於其中。非元日大辰，陛下何嘗御前殿？其餘多不受朝。設或引見遠人，非時慶賀，亦日宴坐朝，曾未移刻，則聖躬起入後宮。夫以有限之體而投無盡之慾，臣固知其憊也。

“臣聞古者有野叟獨歌舞於盤石之上，人詢之曰：”子何獨樂之多也？‘叟曰：‘吾有三樂，子知之乎？’‘何也？’叟曰：‘人生難遇太平世。吾今不見兵革，此一樂也。人生難得支體全完。吾今不殘疾，此二樂也。人生難得老壽。吾今年八十矣，此三樂也。’其人歎賞而去。

“陛下享天下之富貴，聖貌軒逸，章龍姿鳳，而不自愛重，其思慮固出於野叟之外。臣蕞爾微軀，難圖報效，罔知忌諱，上逆天顏。”

因俯伏泣涕。帝乃命引起。翌日，召義語之曰：“朕昨夜思汝言，極有深理。汝真愛我者也。”乃命義後宮擇一靜室，而帝居其中，宮女皆不得入。居二日，帝忿然而出曰：“安能悒悒居此乎？若此，雖壽千萬歲，將安用也！”乃復入迷樓。

宮女無數，後宮不得進御者亦極衆。後宮女侯夫人有美色，一日，自經於棟下。臂懸錦囊，中有文。左右取以進帝，乃詩也。《自感》三首云：

庭絕玉輦跡，芳草漸成科。隱隱聞簫鼓，君恩何處多？
欲泣不成淚，悲來翻強歌。庭花方爛熳，無計奈春何。
春陰正無際，獨步意如何？不及閛花柳，翻承雨露多。

《看梅》二首云：

砌雪無消日，捲簾時自鼛。庭梅對我有憐意，先露枝頭一點春。
香清寒豔好，誰識是天真。玉梅謝後陽和至，散與羣芳自在春。

《粧成》云：

粧成多自惜，夢好卻成悲。不及楊花意，春來到處飛。

《遣意》云：

秘洞扃仙卉，雕窗鎖玉人。毛君真可戮，不肯寫昭君。

《自傷》云：

初入承明日，深深報未央。長門七八載，無復見君王。
春寒人骨清，獨臥愁空房，颯履步庭下，幽懷空感傷。
平日新愛惜，自待聊非常。色美反成棄，命薄何可量？
君恩實疏遠，妾意徒彷徨。家豈無骨肉，偏親老北堂。
此身無羽翼，何計出高牆？性命誠所重，棄割良可傷。
懸帛朱棟上，肝腸如沸湯。引頸又自惜，有若絲牽腸。
毅然就死地，從此歸冥鄉！

帝見其詩，反覆傷感。帝往視其屍，曰：“此已死，顏色猶美如桃李。”乃急召中使許廷輔曰：“朕向遣汝入後宮擇女入迷樓，何故獨棄此人也？”乃令廷輔就獄，賜自盡，厚禮葬侯夫人。帝日誦詩，酷好其文，乃令樂府歌之。帝又於後宮親擇女百人入謎樓。

大業八年，方士口千進大丹，帝服之，蕩思愈不可制，日夕御女數十人。入夏，帝煩躁，日引飲數百杯，而渴不止。醫丞莫君錫上奏曰：“帝心脈煩盛，真元太虛，多引飲，即大疾生焉。”因進劑治之。仍乞置冰盤於前，俾帝日夕朝望之，亦治煩躁之一術也。

自茲諸院美人各市冰以爲盤，望行幸，京師冰爲之踊貴，藏冰之家，皆獲千金。

大業九年，帝將再幸江都。有迷樓宮人靜夜抗歌云：

河南楊柳謝，河北李花榮。楊花飛去去何處？李花結果自然成。

帝聞其歌，披衣起聽，召宮女問之云：“孰使汝歌也？汝自歌之耶？”

宮女曰：“臣有弟，民間得此歌，曰：‘道途兒童多唱此歌。’”

帝默然久之，曰：“天啓之也，人啓之也！”帝因索酒，自歌云：

宮木陰濃燕子飛，興衰自古漫成悲。
它日迷樓更好景，宮中吐豔變紅輝。

歌竟，不勝其悲。近侍奏：“無故而悲，又歌，臣皆不曉。”帝曰：“休問。它日自知也。”

後帝幸江都。唐帝提兵號令入京，見迷樓，大驚曰：“此皆民膏血所爲也！”乃命焚之。經月火不滅。

前謠前詩皆見矣。方知世代興亡，非偶然也。

Tale 6.38

Records of Constructing the Grand Canal

Anonymous[1]
Translated by Weiguo Cao

There was an emanation of a king coming out of Suiyang.[2] The imperial astrologer Geng Chunchen reported it to the emperor, predicting that a Son of Heaven would rise to power over there in five hundred years. Emperor Yang (r. 604–618),[3] having been fatuous and licentious, did not believe this.

One time, while the emperor amused himself in the Magnolia Courtyard, he asked Yuan Bao'er to sing a song to the tune of "Song of Willow Branch." Upon seeing a painting of Guangling[4] on the palace wall, he stared at it, unable to move his feet for a while. At that time, Empress Xiao (567–647) was next to him. She asked the emperor, "I don't know what kind of painting this is.

---

[1]It is generally believed that the author of this tale is unknown, although some editions attribute it to Han Wo 韓偓 (844–923). See the endnote for its date.

[2]*Wang qi* 王氣 might also be translated as "an auspicious aura befitting of a king," or simply "kingly aura." Suiyang 睢陽 is in modern day Shangqiu, Henan.

[3]The second and last emperor of the Sui dynasty. Yang 煬 was his posthumous title which carried the following meanings: to lust after women, abandon ritual and defy Heaven. See Victor Xiong, p. 227.

[4]In modern Yangzhou city, Jiangsu province.

How could Your Majesty care about it so much?" The emperor said, "I am not particularly fond of this painting; it is just that it makes me think of a place I visited in the old days." At this, the emperor placed his left hand on the shoulder of the empress and used his right hand to point at the mountains, rivers, households, villages and temples on the painting. All of these were shown vividly before his eyes. He said to the empress, "When I was the prince of Chen, I garrisoned Guangling.⁵ Day and night I took pleasant excursions there. At that time, I regarded clouds and mists as beautiful scenery, and viewed wealth and honor as abyss.⁶ I didn't expect that sitting on the throne for a long time and dealing with thousands of state affairs would make me unable to let my sentiments roam about at will." Having said this, grief was mapped on his face. The empress said, "If Your Majesty wants to be in Guangling, how about favoring the place with an imperial tour?" Having heard this, the emperor was suddenly enlightened.

The next day, the emperor discussed this issue with his ministers. He intended to go on a giant boat from the Luo River⁷ to the Yellow River, from the Yellow River to the sea, from the sea to the Huai River, and finally to reach Guangling. The ministers all said a journey like this would cover more than five thousand kilometers. Furthermore, the water flow at Mengjin (Meng Ford) was treacherous; the waves of the boundless sea were deep. If the

---

⁵Li Jianguo argued that the text might have been corrupted here. According to historical records, the emperor once served as the King of Jin 晉 but he had never served as the King of Chen. However, he had led troops to attack and conquer the state of Chen in the past.

⁶It seems the word *shen yuan* 深冤 (deep injustice) is odd here. The original word might have been *shen yuan* 深淵 (abyss). The usage of the word *yuan* 淵 was a taboo during the Tang dynasty since the name of the founding father of the dynasty is Li Yuan.

⁷Nearby his capital, Luoyang.

emperor went on a giant boat to those places, an accident might happen. The Grandee Remonstrant and Consultant, Xiao Huaijing (he was a younger brother of Empress Xiao),[8] suggested to the emperor, "Your servant has heard that at the time of the First Emperor of Qin (r. 220–210 B.C.), an emanation of a king appeared in Jinling.[9] He sent someone to cut off the Dizhu Mountain,[10] and subsequently the emanation of a king was exterminated. Now an emanation of a king has appeared in Suiyang. In the meantime, Your Majesty intends to go southeast, but Your Majesty is also concerned about the danger of passing through Meng Ford on a boat. I happen to know there is an old river course northwest of Daliang. This is the place where Wang Li, the general of Qin, diverted the water to flood Daliang.[11] I would like to beg Your

---

[8]According to *Sui shu* (*History of Sui*), Xiao Huaijing 蕭懷靜 once served as Army-inspecting Censor (*jianjun yushi* 監軍御使). There was no record indicating he was the younger brother of the empress. See *Sui shu*, 76.1633.

[9]In modern Nanjing city, Jiangsu province.

[10]Dizhu is the name of a mountain (in the shape of a pillar) located in the midstream of the Yellow River. Legend has it the Great Yü 禹 cut off the Dizhu mountain in order to channel the watercourse of the Yellow River. According to Sima Qian's account in his *Grand Scribe's Records*, when the First Emperor learned about the emanation of the Son of Heaven, he took a tour of inspection to the southeast to repress it. There is no mentioning of Dizhu Pillar. See William H. Nienhauser, Jr., ed., *The Grand Scribe's Records* (Bloomington: Indiana University Press, 2002), 2:17. Since Dizhu Mountain is far away from Jinling, this might suggest that the author might not have known the exact location of the mountain.

[11]According to the *Grand Scribe's Records* (1:134), in 225 B.C., the Qin General Wang Ben 王賁 diverted the water to flood Daliang and caused the city walls to be ruined. Wang Ben was actually Wang Li's father. The confusion of the names of Wang Ben and Wang Li again suggests the author lacks the knowledge of historical facts. The parallel accounts in *Xingshi hengyan* 醒世恆言 continued this mistake but the translators

Majesty to collect a large number of soldiers and corvée laborers to dig a canal starting from Daliang. From west in Heyin, the water of Mengjin will be diverted to the canal. When it reaches its conjunction with the Huai River in the east, the water of Mengjin will be released [to the Huai River]. The distance between these two places is less than five hundred kilometers. Furthermore, the canal will pass through the territory of Suiyang. On the one hand, the canal can fulfill your wish to reach Guangling; on the other hand, it will cut off the emanation of a king." When the emperor heard this suggestion, he was greatly pleased. All the ministers became silent.

The emperor then issued an imperial order: "if anyone remonstrates in the imperial court, asking me not to construct the canal, he will be decapitated." He issued an edict, appointing Ma Shumou,[12] the Superior Commander of the Northern Expedition, to be the Commissioner of the Canal Construction; appointing Li

---

(p. 550) corrected this mistake in their English translation without giving a note. Yang Xianyi (p. 229) mistakenly put the name of the general as "Wang Fen."

[12] Ma Shumou 麻叔謀 is a half-historical, half-fictional character. There is no mentioning of Ma Shumou in official histories. Lu Xun, based on *Zixia ji* 資暇集, a work compiled during the late Tang dynasty, speculated that the character was based on Ma Hu 麻祜, a general of Sui. It was indicated in *Zi Xiaji* that Ma Hu was tyrannical and therefore it became a custom for people to use his name to scare children. There was even a temple for him in Suiyang, the place where he was killed according to this tale. Lu Xun also pointed out that even in modern times, people used Ma Huzi 麻鬍子 to scare children. This might suggest stories about this character had been widely circulated in oral tradition for a long time. As Lu Xun points out, "The accounts in this tale certainly came from story transmission from mouth to ear" 此篇所記，固亦得之口耳之傳.

Yuan (566–635),[13] the General Who Quells Bandits, to be the Vice-Commissioner. But Li Yuan did not go to his post, pleading illness. Thus Linghu Xinda,[14] the General of Left Encampment Guards, was made the Vice-Commissioner and Chief Superintendent to replace Li Yuan. Since the project started from Daliang, a new government office was established to the north of Yuetai (Music Tower). The canal was named Bian Canal (in ancient times this place was simply called Bian. The city of Kaifeng was called Bian Town[15]). Accordingly, the government office was called the Post Station of the Upstream of Bian Canal (a post station was a place which provided lodging for government messengers. The Bian Canal started from here, and therefore it was called the Upstream of the Bian Canal). An edict was issued to raise the corvée laborers of the greater area: males over fifteen years old must come.[16] For those who went into hiding, he and his three kindred[17] would be exterminated. Because the canal passed by Bian, the emperor granted the water radical to be added to the character Bian.[18] In total there were 3,600,000 corvée laborers. Furthermore, five

---

[13]Li Yuan later on rebelled against Sui and established the Tang Dynasty.

[14]Li Jianguo (p. 902) argued this was the same person as Linghu Xingda 令狐行達, who later murdered Emperor Yang according to the historical accounts in *Sui shu*.

[15]This is again not historically true. The ancient Bian 卞 Town was not in Kaifeng, rather it was located in a remote place in modern Shandong.

[16]Some editions read "males above fifteen years old and below fifty years old must come."

[17]There are different opinions concerning the meaning of the term "three kindred," one of which claims it refers to parents, brothers and wife.

[18]This means the character of Bian was changed from 卞 to 汴. A Chinese radical is a component of a Chinese character usually indicating the meaning of the character. 氵 is the water radical.

households should provide one person each, either young, old, male or female, to supply food and drinks. He also ordered 50,000 young and valiant soldiers to supervise the workers, in the capacity of officers, company leaders, and the like, each carrying a cudgel. The total number was over 5,430,000. Then Ma Shumou gave an order to take one third of the workforce to start from the Upstream and move west to Heyin, connecting the ancient river course (in the place where Wang Li flooded Daliang). The canal would wind its way to Chousi tai (Tower of Gloomy Moods) and then go further north. He also ordered the other two-thirds of the corvée laborers to start from the Upstream Post Station and then go east.

This was during the fifth year of the Daye reign (609).[19] Early in the eighth month the project was set up. Buckets and spades were all gathered together. The labor force stretched from west to east for thousands of kilometers.

After the digging started, no sooner than it reached ten feet or so deep, they found an ancient hall with several rooms. It was glittering, solemn and clean. Lamps lighted by paint[20] sparkled. It was so bright that it looked as if it were under daylight. Walls on the four sides were all decorated with colorful paintings, with images of flowers, bamboo, dragons and ghosts. In the middle there was a coffin, resembling those buried in the luxurious tombs. The foreman then reported this to Shumou, who ordered the coffin to be opened. Inside the coffin there was a man who appeared as if he were alive. His skin was clean white like jade, and he was plump. His hair came out of his head, covered his face, passed his chest and belly, wrapped his feet below, and then grew

---

[19] This is not historically accurate. The project of Grand Canal construction started in the first year of the Daye reign (605).

[20] According to Chinese legends, *qideng* 漆燈 (lamps lighted by paint) were used in the tombs.

upwards in an opposite direction, until it reached his back under his body. They found a stone inscription. The characters on it looked like the "seal characters" in the shape of bird tracks invented by Cang Jie.[21] Then Ma Shumou summoned the laborers and announced: if anyone could read these characters, his labor service would be exempted. A man from Xiapi read it, saying,

> I am the Great Gold Immortal.
> I have been dead for one thousand years.
> It is preordained that when the term of one thousand years is
>   fulfilled,
> there will be a flowing spring under my back.
> I will be able to encounter Ma Shumou,
> who will bury me in the highland.
> My hair will grow and reach my brain.
> I need to wait for another one thousand years,
> only then will I be able to ascend the Tushita Heaven.

Thus Shumou personally prepared coffin and buried him at the west side of the city (it is located in the current Great Buddha Temple).

Next they constructed the canal at Chenliu. The emperor sent a messenger carrying the imperial prayer[22] signed by himself, as well as a pair of white jade discs. They prepared pig and sheep to offer as a sacrifice at the Temple of the Marquis of Liu[23] in order to

---

[21]A legendary hero who was claimed to have invented the Chinese characters.

[22]*Yuzhu* 玉祝, literally meaning "jade prayer," is a very uncommon word. It probably derived from the word *yuyin* 玉音 (literally, "jade sound") which was used to refer to what the emperor said. Yang Xianyi (p. 231) translated it as "a jade tablet inscribed with his blessing."

[23]Marquis of Liu 留 is Zhang Liang 張良 (ca. 250–186 B.C.). He was a great strategist who made great contributions to the establishment of the

beg his permission to go through this route. After the sacrifice was completed, suddenly a gust of strong wind came out of the windows in the hall of the temple, blowing in the face of the musicians.[24] The imperial messenger withdrew. They finally constructed the canal from Chenliu and moved east. People carrying loads or dragging shovels came and went, swift as the wind and quick as lightening. People far and near trod on the earth, like a gathering of bees and assembling of ants.

In several days, they reached Yongqiu. At that time there was a laborer from Zhongmu, who just so happened to suffer from the illness of bended-back. He was unable to move forward like others and thereby lagged behind the team, walking alone by himself. On that night, it was peacefully quiet with clear moonlight. Then he heard very rigorous shouts to clear the road for an official. The laborer bowed and waited on the left side of the road. After a long while, he saw bailiffs in charge of road clearance continuously coming, along with guards of honor beyond description. Among them there was a noble lord, wearing a hat of the marquis and the clothes of a king, riding on a white horse. This lord ordered his attendants to summon the laborer to come forward and told him, "Speak on my behalf to your Twelfth Lord: '[I] return a pair of white jade discs [to you]; you should be a guest in the Heaven' (Emperor Yang possessed the world for

---

Han dynasty. They had to offer sacrifice to Zhang Liang presumably because the latter's tomb was on their way to build the canal.

[24]Another edition read *chui shuo ren mian* 吹鑠人面 for *chui yue ren mian* 吹樂人面. Yang Xianyi (p. 232), possibly based on this textual variant, translated it as "(the wind is) like shrapnel across the faces." However, *Shuo* means "melted metal." It does not mean "shrapnel." Since the melted metal would cause excruciating pain, it seems the word *shuo* here simply means "to cause excruciating pain as if being burned by melted metal."

twelve years)."[25] After finishing speaking, he took out the jade discs and gave them to the laborer, who knelt and received them. When he tried to further prostrate himself, the noble lord galloped his horse and went westward. When the laborer reached Yongqiu, he presented the jade discs to Commissioner Ma, who, upon close examination, found that these were none other than the jade discs the emperor presented to the Marquis of Liu. He questioned the laborer, who told him everything in detail. Shumou was greedy by nature, so he hid the jade. However, he did not understand the words of the Marquis of Liu. He was worried that the laborer might divulge the incident to outsiders, so he beheaded him to keep it a secret.

Afterwards the construction began at Yongqiu. Upon arriving at a large area of woods, the project leaders found a small temple in the woods. Shumou visited it and asked an elder of the village about it, who said, "Ancient legend has it that this was called the tomb of a recluse. His spirit is immensely magical." Shumou did not believe his words, and thus he had his men dig in the tomb area. They dug for several feet until all of a sudden they reached an empty cave. A group of laborers went down to take a peek, and they found that there were glimmering lights inside. No one dared to enter the place, so [Shumou] directed his officers to go. Di Quxie, the Commandant of Martial Pacification, volunteered to enter the cave to explore it. Shumou said happily, "You are truly a brave man like Jing Ke and Nie Zheng."[26] He had the waist of Quxie tied and cast him down. Quxie did not reach the ground until he went down for about several hundred feet. He untied the knot, walked for about one hundred paces, and entered a stone room. In the north and east there were four stone pillars in each

---

[25]This statement is not historically true. Emperor Yang was in his reign for fourteen years.

[26]Both are famous assassins during the Warring States period.

direction. A beast was tied by two iron chains. It was as big as an ox. Upon close examination, he found out that it was none other than a giant rat. After a short while, in the west of the stone room a stone gate was wide open. A child came out, saying, "Aren't you Di Quxie?" He said, "Correct." The child said, "Lord Huangfu has already been sitting [and waiting for you] for a long time."[27] So the child led him in. He saw a man wearing red clothes and a hat of cloud,[28] presiding high above in a great hall. Quxie prostrated himself on the ground a couple of times. That man did not speak, nor did he return the salute. An official in green clothes led Quxie to stand under the western terrace of the hall. After a long time, the person above in the hall called the strongmen to fetch A Mo by a tether (A Mo was the childhood name of Emperor Yang).[29] Several warriors, who looked monstrous and burly in appearance, drove the giant rat he saw earlier, and arrived. Quxie was originally a court official, and he knew the childhood name of the emperor. He was not clear about the ins and outs of the matter, so he just held his breath, standing there. The person above in the hall censured the rat, saying, "I send you to temporarily shed your hair and skin to be the ruler of the country. Why do you abuse people and ruin properties, without adhering to the way of Heaven?" The rat just nodded his head and wagged his tail, nothing more. The man sitting above in the hall became more enraged. He ordered his warrior to strike his brain with a big stick. With one strike, a sound suddenly broke out just as if a wall was collapsing. The rat roared like a clap of thunder. Just when the warrior was about to raise the stick to strike again, a child descended holding the credentials of Heaven. Startled, the person

---

[27]Some editions read 皇甫君望子已久 (Lord Huangfu has been expecting you for a long time) for 皇甫君坐來已久 (Lord Huangfu has been sitting for a long time).

[28]This is the kind of hat worn by monks, Taoist priests and recluses.

[29]Emperor Yang was also born in the year of rat.

above in the hall jumped from his seat, walked down the steps, prostrated himself and listened to the order. The child then proclaimed the edict from Heaven, "A Mo was originally destined to rule for twelve years. Up to now it has been seven years.[30] In five more years, he should die with a white scarf tied around his neck."[31] After the child left, the person above in the hall again gave the order to tie the rat in the old room. He said to Quxie, "Speak to Ma Shumou for me, 'Thank you for not attacking my territory. Next year I will offer you two golden knives as a gift. Please do not regard this as a meager reward.'" After he finished speaking, the official in green clothes led Quxie to go out through another door.

He walked for more than ten *li* before he entered an area of woods. He traveled around, stepping on rocks and dragging rattans. When he looked back, the envoy had already disappeared. After he traveled for three more *li* or so, he saw a thatched cottage. An old man was sitting on an earthen bed. He inquired about the place. The old man said, "You are at the foot of Shaoshi [32] Mountain south of Mt Song." The old man asked where Quxie had been. Quxie told him everything in detail. Subsequently the old man gave Quxie a detailed explanation. Quxie then realized that Emperor Yang would not live for long. The old man further said, "If you can abandon your official position, you will be able

---

[30]It was indicated in the passage above that the construction of the canal began in the fifth year of the emperor's reign. The statement here implied it took two years for the construction work to reach Yongqiu. Li Jianguo (p. 901) claimed the record here was mistaken because the distance between Kaifeng and Yongqiu was only about 90 miles.

[31]This statement implied that the emperor would be strangled to death later.

[32]The Shaoshi Mountain is part of Mt. Song 嵩 located northwest of modern Dengfeng City in Henan province. It is home to the famous Shaolin 少林 Temple.

to extricate yourself from the tiger's mouth." Quxie then travelled west. When he looked back, he could no longer find where the thatched cottage was.

At that time Commissioner Ma had already reached Ningyang County.[33] Quxie went to see Shumou and told him the matter in detail. It turned out that after Quxie entered the tomb, the tomb collapsed by itself. Everyone originally thought Quxie had already died, so no one expected him to come today. Shumou did not believe his words and thought he was a madman. Quxie then pretended that he suffered the illness of mental disorder and went to live in seclusion in Zhongnan Mountains.[34] At that time Emperor Yang had not held a court for over a month because he suffered a headache. When Quxie inquired about the reason, everyone said the emperor had a dream in which his brain was struck by someone. Subsequently he was stricken with pain for several days. The day [when the emperor had the dream] was none other than the day Quxie saw the rat.

After Shumou reached Ningling county, he suffered the illness of pruritus and his movements were impaired. The

---

[33] There is a textual error concerning the name of the county. Ningyang 寧陽 county is under the jurisdiction of modern Tai'an County in Shandong province. It was very far away from Yongqiu, the last construction site where Ma Shumou was said to be. The text below stated that Ma Shumou had reached Ningling 寧陵, which was not far away from Yongqiu. Thus, Ningyang must be a textual error for Ningling. The parallel text in *Sui Tang yan i* 隋唐演義 (*Romance of Sui and Tang Dynasties*) also read Ningling for Ningyang.

[34] Located in the middle branch of the Qin 秦 Mountains in Shanxi province. It was considered a sacred place for the Taoist religion and many Taoist hermits chose to live there.

emperor ordered Chao Yuanfang,[35] an imperial physician, to go there to treat his illness. He said, "The malady has entered your skin and flesh, the disease is in your chest. You should use fat and young sheep with tender meat. After the meat was fully steamed, mix it with medicine. Take this and you will recover from your illness." Shumou fetched lamb half a year old, killed it, and added medicine to its body cavity.[36] Before he had finished taking the medicine, he recovered from his illness. Afterwards he often gave orders to kill more lambs. Every day he took the medicine with lamb several times. He steamed the lamb with almond paste, added condiments to produce five flavors.[37] He placed the lamb meat in a plate. He himself pulled apart the meat into small slices with his hands and ate it. He called it "meat pasties." Every day thousands of people in the villages presented lamb to him.[38] He rewarded all of them generously so that his reward exceeded the value of the lamb.

Tao Lang'er, a native of Xiama Village of Ningling County, was from a very rich family. His brothers were all fierce and malicious. Because the tomb area of his ancestors was only a dozen feet away from the canal route, he was worried that Ma Shumou would dig into the tomb. So he stole a child from another family, who was three or four years old. He killed the child, removed the head and feet, steamed the meat fully, and presented it to Shumou. When the latter chewed on the meat, he felt it was lusciously delicious, and it was completely different from the taste of lamb. He admired it very much, so he summoned and

---

[35] A famous physician in the Sui dynasty. He was the compiler of *Zhu bing yuan hou lun* 諸病源候論 (*Treatise on the Origin and Symptoms of Diseases*).

[36] I.e., after the internal organs were removed, the meat was in the shape of the cavity.

[37] I.e, sweet, sour, bitter, spicy, and salty flavors.

[38] This is clearly an exaggeration.

questioned Lang'er about it, who divulged the matter while being drunk. When he sobered up, Shumou gave him ten taels of gold. He also ordered his officers and laborers to make a roundabout of the canal route in order to protect his ancestors' tomb area. Afterwards, Lang'er and his brothers often stole children and presented them to Shumou. By doing this they obtained great profit.

When other poor people learned about it, they scrambled to loot other families' children and presented them to Shumou so as to seek bounty. Hundreds of children were lost in Xiangyi, Ningling and Suiyang. The lament of mournful sorrow could be heard day and night without end. Duan Da (d. 621), the Commandant Brave as Tigers, served as Secretary of the Middle Gate, [39] in charge of handling memorials submitted from all quarters far and near. Shumou asked Huang Jinku, his house servant, to bring a large amount[40] of gold and present it to him. For all those who submitted memorials to bring accusations on the

---

[39] *Zhongmenshi* 中門使. It seems this official title only appeared during the Five Dynasties period. A search of the Academic Sinica database reveals *Zhongmenshi* only appeared in the *Jiu Wudai shi* 舊五代史 and *Xin Wudai shi* 新五代史. Wang Fengxiang 王鳳翔 also maintained that *Zhongmenshi* was a unique official title during the Five Dynasties period. According to his study, this was a very important position, especially in the Later Tang dynasty. See Wang Fengxiang. "Wudai Shiguo shiqi de Zhongmenshi" 五代十國時期的中門使, in *Shixue yuekan* 12(2003):120–121. This might suggest the tale was written neither in the Tang or Song dynasty, as previous scholars debated. The tale might have been written in a period between these two dynasties.

According to historical records, Duan Da's official position was Left General of Standby Guards.

[40] The original text read *yi lie* 一埒. The word *lie* might have been used to refer to a measurement unit, but the exact quantity is not clear. The parallel text in *Sui Yangdi yanshi* 隋煬帝豔史, in order to avoid this difficult word, changed the text to "one thousand taels of white gold."

grounds that their children were eaten, their cases would not be investigated. They would instead all be flogged on their backs forty times and driven out of Luoyang under escort. About seventy to eighty percent of them died on their way back home.

At this time Linhu Xinda came to know about it. He secretly asked people to collect the bones of those slaughtered children. In just a few days, the bones filled an entire carriage. Because of this, every family in the cities and villages who had children made a wooden cabinet, using iron to cover the seams. Every night, mother and child would be placed and locked in the cabinet. The entire family, holding the candles, surrounded and guarded the cabinet. At dawn, when they opened the cabinet and found the child was there, everyone in the house, young and old, congratulated each other.

When the canal work reached the boundary of Suiyang, Chen Bogong, a Superintendent of Trenches and Stockades Construction,[41] said that if this canal route took a straight way, it would cut through the city of Suiyang; if the city was to be spared, then one must ask for permission from the emperor. Shumou was angry with him for talking about "sparing the city," so he gave an order to push him out to be cut in half at the waist, but Linhu Xinda saved him. At this time there were one hundred eighty

---

[41]Haozhaishi 濠寨使. Yang Xianyi (p. 238) mistakenly translated it as "village bailiff." As Li Jianguo (p. 28) pointed out, this official position did not exist in Sui dynasty. It first appeared at the end of Tang dynasty.

According to *Chen Shu* 陳書 (*History of Chen*), Chen Bogong was the King of Jin'an 晉安 in the Southern Chen Dynasty (557–589). After Chen was conquered by Sui, he served as a Chamberlain for Ceremonials (*taichangqing* 太常卿) during the beginning of the Daye reign period. According to legends, Chen went to the Jiugong 九宮 Mountain, established nine palaces there, and taught a group of Daoist disciples martial arts. Hence the mountain was called Jiugong, which means "nine palaces."

households of gentry in Suiyang. They were all afraid that their houses and tomb areas would be dug through. They pooled three thousand taels of gold and were about to present it to Shumou, but they could not find a person who could serve as a go-between.

The canal work quickly made its way through and reached a large area of woods, in which there was a tomb. As ancient legends had it, this was the tomb of Hua Yuan, the Marshal of the state of Song.[42] They dug through a stone room. In the room there were things such as lamps lighted by paint, a coffin, and a tent. When they met with the wind they were all transformed into ashes. They found a stone inscription, saying,

> The earth level of Suiyang is high.
> The Bian River can be used as a trench.
> If you do not shy away.
> I will offer two golden knives as a gift.

Shumou said, "This is a trick. It is unbelievable." On that day, Shumou dreamed that an envoy summoned him to a palace. There was a man wearing clothes in red silk, and a "hat of presenting the worthy."[43] Shumou greeted him by prostrating himself twice. The king also returned the greeting. After finishing the greeting, the king said, "This lonely one, I, am Duke Xiang of Song (r. 650–637 B.C.). It has been two thousand years since the Supreme Deity made it clear that I should guard this place. If you, general, could lend a hand and spare this city, people of the entire city, old and young, would feel grateful for your kindness."

---

[42]The state of Song (1114 B.C.–286 B.C.) was a feudal state during the Zhou dynasty. The capital of Song was located exactly in Suiyang where the canal construction was taking place.

[43]Victor Xiong (p. 134) noted that this was a special kind of hat worn by civil officials at court. It originally was matched to a complicated outfit with a variety of ornaments.

Shumou did not accede to this request. The king again said, "The matter of sparing this city we discussed just now is not just an idea of this lonely one. I actually made the request according to the order from the Supreme Deity, who said that in five hundred years, a king will appear in this place and lay out the foundation of a dynasty which will last for ten thousand generations. How can the emanation of a king be dug through just because [the current emperor] indulges himself in pleasure trips?" Shumou again did not accede to the request. After a long time, a servant came in and reported, "Hua Yuan, the Grand Marshal,[44] has arrived." The attendants led a man in, who wore purple clothes and a "hat of presenting the worthy." He prostrated himself before the king to pay his respects. The king then recounted the matter of protecting the city. This person erupted in fury, saying, "This is an order from the Supreme Deity. It is not just our intention [to protect the city]. Shumou is a man of ignorance. He does not understand the mandate of Heaven." He cried out aloud to the attendant, ordering them to prepare for implements for punishment. The king said, "As for the matter of torture, which method can cause the most pain?" The man in purple clothes said, "Pouring melted copper liquor into his mouth can decompose his intestines and stomach. This is the number one method." The king consented to it. Then several warriors dragged Shumou, stripped off his clothes, leaving only his underwear on. They bound him to an iron pillar, intending to pour the melted copper liquor to his mouth. Shumou was scared out of his wits. The person above in the palace hurriedly stopped the warriors, saying, "How about the matter of protecting the city?" Shumou said repeatedly, "I will respectfully follow the order of Your Highness." Subsequently the king gave the order to release him and give back his clothes and

---

[44] Yang Xianyi (p. 238) mistakenly translated the name as Sima Huayuan.

hat. The king gave an order to lead him away. When he was about to leave, the man in purple clothes said, "The Supreme Deity bestows three thousand taels of gold on Shumou. He will take this from common folk." Shumou was greedy by nature. He asked an attendant, saying, "The Supreme Deity bestows gold on me. What is this about?" The attendant said, "Some common people in Suiyang will present it to you, the general. This is called 'for something ordained in the underworld, you will receive it in the mortal world.'" In a trance it seems he woke up from the dream. He just felt as if his spirit did not reside in his body.

People of Suiyang indeed bribed Huang Jinku. Through him they presented to Shumou three thousand taels of gold. Shumou thought about the matter in the dream, so he received it. He immediately summoned Chen Bogong, ordering him to make the canal pass through the west of Suiyang, then take a roundabout by going the direction of north and south, and then go east, pass Liu-Zhao Village, and then move ahead continuously. When Linhu Xinda learned about it, he sent memorials to the imperial throne several times. They were all withheld by Duan Da, who did not present the memorials to the throne.

When the canal work reached Pengcheng, on its way it passed through a large area of woods, where there was a tomb of King Yan.[45] They dug for several feet, then they were unable to dig further because they hit copper or iron. After they dug away the earth from four sides, only iron was revealed beneath the earth. Next to the tomb a stone gate was installed. It was tightly locked. By employing a plan from a person of Zanyang, they broke open the gate of the tomb. Shumou entered the tomb by himself. After he walked for over one hundred paces, two children stood in front

---

[45]He was the ruler of the state of Xu 徐 during the Western Zhou period. There are many legendary stories about the king. One source claimed that he was born from an egg.

of him, saying, "King Yan has been respectfully waiting for you for a long time." Then he followed them and entered the place. He saw a palace. There was a man in red silk clothes, sitting above in the palace, wearing a "hat connected to Heaven." Shumou prostrated himself to pay his respects, the king also prostrated himself, saying, "The tomb area of me, this lonely one, obstructs the canal route. Now I am offering you, the general, a piece of precious jade which can cause you to possess the world. It would be a blessing to my tomb if you could protect it." Shumou acceded to it. The king then ordered an attendant to hold a jade seal and give it to Shumou. He took a close look. The inscription read, "The jade seal for emperors of hundreds of generations who received the mandate of Heaven." Shumou was greatly pleased. The king further said, "Please take great care of it. This is the omen of knife, knife." ("knife, knife" is a riddle. It carries the same meaning as "two golden knives.") When Shumou went out, he ordered his soldiers and laborers to protect the tomb on a daily basis.

At this time Emperor Yang was in Luoyang. He suddenly lost his imperial seal. He had people search everywhere in his palace, but no one knew its whereabouts. He made this a secret and did not announce it. The emperor made an urgent request to speed up the canal construction. So starting from Xuzhou, Shumou asked his men to work day and night, without any rest. He had already lost over one and a half million conscribed laborers. In the places where he camped, the field was filled with dead bodies.

Once the emperor read books at the Palace of Observing Culture. When he was perusing the *Grand Scribe's Records*,[46] he learned about how the First Emperor of Qin (r. 247–210 B.C.) constructed the Great Wall. He told Yuwen Shu (546–616), his prime minister, "It has been about one thousand years from the

---

[46]The first comprehensive history of China, written by Sima Qian.

time of the First Emperor until now.[47] I assume that the Great Wall should have already been ruined." Yuwen Shu, catering to the idea of the emperor, said, "Your Majesty accidentally has the inspiration of continuing the undertaking of the emperor of Qin and establishing an enterprise lasting for ten thousand generations. It is a great idea to repair the wall and make it more solid." The emperor was greatly pleased. So he issued an edict, appointing Heruo Bi (544–607),[48] the Duke of the state of Shu, to be the Commissioner of Repairing the Great Wall; appointing Gao Jiong (541–607), the Grand Master of Remonstrance,[49] to be the Vice Commissioner. 1,200,000 laborers, from the prefectures of Jiang, Huai, Wu, Chu, Xiang, Deng, Chen, Cai, Bing, Kai and Tuo,[50] were to be conscripted to repair the Great Wall. When the edict was issued, Bi remonstrated, saying, "Your subject has heard that the First Emperor constructed the Great Wall at the remote fortresses. It was continuously meandering for three thousand miles. As a result, men died and women were deserted. Wives became widows and children became orphaned. The emperor and his son both died while the wall was not yet finished. Your Majesty intends to listen to the words of a madman and learn

---

[47]The time span between the First Emperor to Emperor Yang is actually about eight hundred years.

[48]Yang Xianyi (p. 242) mistakenly put his name as He Ruobi. Actually Heruo is his surname and Bi is his given name. According to *Sui shu* (52.1345), he was enfeoffed as Duke of the state of Song rather than the state of Shu.

[49]According to *Sui shu* (4.70), Gao Jiong's 高熲 official position during the reign of Emperor Yang was Chamberlain for Ceremonials.

[50]The Prefecture of Kai was located in the Sichuan province and thereby was far away from the other states in the list. The Prefecture of Tuo probably never existed. A possible solution to the problem is to treat *kaituo* as a word and translate *kai tuo zhu zhou* 開拓諸州 as "the prefectures which have just been established."

from the wrongdoings of perished Qin. I am afraid that the altar of the soil and grain[51] will disintegrate and collapse, just in the same way as it did in the Qin era." The emperor was enraged and did not speak a word. At this time Yuwen Shu was at his side, so he fanned the flames by saying, "You are just a presumptuous soldier from the military. What kind of wisdom do you have to make you even want to disrupt our great plan?" Bi grew angry. He hit Yuwen Shu with his ivory tablet.[52] The emperor also grew angry, so he put [Heruo] Bi under house arrest. On that night he drank poisoned wine and died. Gao Jiong also refused to go. Then Yuwen Shu recommended Yuwen Bi, the Chamberlain of Agriculture,[53] to be the Commissioner of Repairing the Great Wall; Yuwen Kai, Vice Minister of the Ministry of Revenue,[54] to be the Vice Commissioner.[55]

---

[51]The emperor used the altar to offer sacrifices to the gods of soil and grain. Thus the term was used to refer to a country.

[52]The tablet was held by ministers who were present at the imperial court.

[53]This is inaccurate according to historical records. Yuwen Bi 宇文弼 was actually killed together with Hero Bi and Gao Jiong, and he never held the position of Minister of Agriculture.

[54]According to historical records, Yuwen Kai 宇文愷 was a specialist in construction engineering. He held the official position in the Ministry of Works rather than Ministry of Revenue.

[55]In the middle of his account of the canal construction, the author switched to the account of repairing the Great Wall. It may seem to be a diversion of the main plot. However, the author clearly attempted to establish a link between Emperor Yang and the First Emperor of Qin: while the First Emperor caused his empire to perish by building the Great Wall, Emperor Yang ruined his country by building the canal. Thus, the story to a certain extent could be put in the same category as the story of Lady Meng Jiang 孟姜女. Both stories used fictional and exaggerated accounts to criticize the despotic rulers who exhausted the national resources through their extravagant projects.

At this time Shumou was constructing the Bian Canal to fill the canal bed at Guankou.[56] Upon examining his laborers, he found out that he had lost about 2,500,000 men. Originally the soldiers and officers he commanded numbered about 50,000. 23,000 of them were lost. After the construction was completed, he submitted a report to the Emperor, requesting him to send people to breach the Yellow River to pour the water into the Bian Canal.

The emperor moved from Luoyang to Daliang.[57] He issued an edict ordering the prefectures of Jiang and Huai, and others, to build five hundred large boats. The order arrived in an extremely urgent manner. There were people among the common folks who used up all of their family property, but still it was not enough to build one ship they were assigned to. As a punishment, cangue[58] was put around their necks and they were flogged on their backs. Afterwards they sold boys and girls in order to pay for the government duties they were burdened with.

When the dragon boats were completed, they floated along the Yangtze and Huai rivers and eventually reached Daliang, where they were further decorated with various gems, gold, jade and so on. Five hundred women, around fifteen to sixteen years

---

[56]The modern vernacular translation treated Guankou as the name of a place, which is located southwest of modern Chizhou 池州 city in Anhui province. This is problematic because Guanhou actually was not located on the route of the Bian Canal. It seems Guankou here might not be used as a place name. The word *guan* means "to pour water," and *kou* means "a hole or opening." Thus *guan kou* might just literally mean "to pour water into an opening."

[57]The text here reads *da qu* 大渠 (large canal). This might have been a textual error for Daliang, given the fact that the text below indicated the emperor arrived at Daliang. The characters *qu* 渠 and *liang* 梁 looked similar and therefore could easily be confused.

[58]Cangue was a device for punishment in ancient China. The word "cangue" is French, which means "yoke."

old, were recruited from the Wu and Yue region. They were called "women of palace foot,"[59] serving as the "imperial paddle" of the dragon boat. Every boat was equipped with ten towlines made of silk of various colors. For each towline, ten "women of palace foot" and ten young sheep were assigned to drag it. The "women of palace foot" were ordered to walk in tandem with the sheep while towing the boat. For fear that the summer was too hot at this time, Yu Shiji, an Academician of the Imperial Academy, presented a plan, requesting that drooping willow be planted along both banks of the Bian Canal. First of all, the roots of the trees would be scattered all around to protect the canal bank; secondly, people who towed the boat could stay cool under the cover of trees; thirdly, the sheep which led the boat could eat their leaves. The Sovereign was greatly pleased. He issued an edict to award a bolt of fine silk to those among the common folks who contributed a willow tree. The common people scrambled to present the trees. He also issued an order asking people to plant the trees by themselves. The emperor personally planted a tree. Then the ministers planted the trees in a proper order. Only then was the turn of the common people. At this time there was a ballad, saying, "The Son of Heaven planted first; and then all the people planted."[60] After the planting was completed, the emperor wrote in his imperial pen to grant the surname Yang to the drooping willow,[61] thus it was called Yang willow.

---

[59]They were named in such a way because they were assigned to tow the dragon boats, so that it seemed as if they became the feet of the palace by making the boat move on the river.

[60]The word zai 栽 (to plant) has the same pronunciation as zai 災 (disaster). Thus, it was a pun and the hidden meaning of this line is: "The Son of Heaven suffered the disaster first, and then all the people suffered the disaster."

[61]Yang 楊 was the surname of the emperor.

At this time, the fleet from stem to stern wound its way for a thousand *li*. From Daliang to its confluence to the Huai River, it marched on in an unbroken line. When the boats with their sails of brocade passed by, the fragrance could be smelled far and wide. After the fleet passed Yongqiu, it gradually reached the territory of Ningling. The current of the canal gradually became treacherous and the movements of the dragon boats were hindered, so much so that people started to feel it was more strenuous to tow the boats. At this time Xianyu Juluo,[62] the Commandant Brave as Tigers, served as Superintendent of Boat Towing. He reported to the emperor saying that it became extremely difficult to move the boats because the water was shallow and the canal was narrow. The Sovereign asked Yu Shiji about this, who replied, "Please make a wooden swan with iron feet twelve feet long, and send it down from the upper reaches. If the wooden swan stops, then we can tell the water is shallow." The emperor followed his suggestion. So he ordered Liu Cen, the Right General of Standby Guards, to detect places where the water was shallow. He found 129 such places from Yongqiu to Guankou. The emperor was enraged and gave an order to thoroughly investigate the names of people and officials responsible for the construction in those places. In the places where the wooden swan stopped, workers from both sides of the canal were tied and buried upside down under the shore. The emperor said, "Let them serve as workers constructing the canal when they are alive, and become ghosts embracing the sand when

---

[62] There was no record of Xianyu Juluo in historical records. However, there were records of Yu Juluo 魚俱羅 (d. 613) in *Sui shu* (78.2641). Yu was a Sui general famous for his great strength and thunderous voice. The character of Yu Juluo was further developed in the later vernacular novel *Xing Tang zhuan* 興唐傳.

they are dead." He further buried more than fifty thousand people.[63]

After he reached Suiyang, he asked Shumou, saying, "How many neighborhoods and households were affected by the canal digging?" Shumou said, "The land of Suiyang is of divine nature, and therefore cannot be violated. If I dig the land, it will surely produce an ominous result. Your servant has already spared the city." The emperor grew angry and ordered Liu Cen to take a small boat to thoroughly investigate the roundabouts of the canal route. It was about 20 *li* longer than the straight route. The emperor became even more angry, so he had Shumou arrested and imprisoned in the rear cell. He immediately sent an envoy to summon Linghu Xinda to get to the bottom of this whole affair.

Xinda reported to the emperor, "Shumou started to engage in lawless activities ever since he arrived at Ningling. In the beginning he ate lamb. Later he devoured babies. Furthermore, he kept a thief Tao Lang'er to steal other people's children. Upon receiving three thousand taels of gold, he took the liberty of changing the canal route in Suiyang." Then he took the bones of children and presented them to the emperor. The emperor said, "Why didn't you send a memorial reporting this?" Xinda said, "I submitted memorials several times, but they were withheld by Duan Da and thereby were unable to be delivered to the throne."

The emperor had someone search Shumou's bag. They found the gold the people of Suiyang presented to him. Furthermore, they found the white jade discs that the Marquis of Liu returned to him, as well as the imperial jade seal for emperors who received the Mandate. The Sovereign was astonished and said to Yuwen

---

[63]A similar account can be found in another tale, "Sui yi lu" (T6.33–34). However, according to that tale, it was Ma Shumou who sent the wooden swan and killed those who were responsible for causing the shallow places in the canal.

Shu, "The gold and jade are both insignificant things, but where did he get the precious seal from me, this lonely one?" [Yu]wen Shu said, "He must have sent a thief to steal it." The emperor glared and said, "Today Shumou steals my precious seal. Tomorrow he will plunder my head." Xinda, while being at his side, reported, "Shumou often sends Tao Lang'er to steal other people's children. I am afraid that the imperial precious seal was stolen by Lang'er."

The Sovereign became even more angry. He sent Lai Hu'er (d. 618), the Duke of Glorifying the Nation,[64] Li Baiyao (564–648), a palace eunuch,[65] Yang Yichen (546–617), Chamberlain for the Imperial Stud,[66] to interrogate Shumou. Their office was established in Suiyang. Moreover, the entire family of Tao Lang'er was imprisoned. Lang'er was ordered to confess in detail the matter of entering the palace to steal the imperial seal. Lang'er couldn't endure the harshness of torture, so he confessed to everything he was charged with. In addition, Duan Da was accused of not submitting to the throne the memorials he received from Linghu Xinda. After the case was concluded they reported it to the Sovereign. The emperor asked the Prime Minister, Yuwen Shu, who said, "Shumou has committed four great crimes: eating children of other people; accepting gold from other people; sending a thief to steal the imperial seal; altering the route of canal construction without authorization. Please execute him in a severe

---

[64]According to *Sui shu* (64.1516), Lai Hu'er 來護兒 was not enfeoffed as the Duke of Glorifying the Nation until the seventh year of the emperor's reign (611).

[65]According to *Sui shu* (72.2571), Li Baiyao 李百藥 served at various local offices during the Sui dynasty, but he was never a palace eunuch. He composed *Qi shu* 齊書 (*History of Qi*) at the beginning of Tang dynasty.

[66]According to *Sui shu* (63.1500), Yang Yichen 楊義臣 reached this position around the third year of the emperor's reign (607).

manner. As for how to handle his descendants, we will follow your instruction." The emperor said, "Shumou has committed great crimes. However, because he has rendered meritorious services in the canal construction, his descendants will be exempt from punishment." He only gave the order to cut Shumou at the waist next to the canal.

At the time when Lai Hu'er received the emperor's order but still did not come, Shumou in his dream saw a child descending from Heaven, saying, "Duke Xiang of Song, along with the Grand Marshal Hua Yuan, express gratitude to you, the general, for your kindness of protecting the city. In the past they promised to offer you two golden knives. Now they are paying you back." Shumou then woke up and said, "According to this omen, I will be in bad luck. It will be difficult to keep my head and waist." Before he finished speaking, Lai Hu'er came. He drove him to the northern shore of the canal, and cut him into three pieces. Lang'er and his four brothers, as well as Shumou's house servant Huang Jinku were all flogged to death. Duan Da, the Secretary of the Middle Gate, was exempt from the death penalty. His official position was demoted to that of chief of gate guards in Luoyang.

Note: Lu Xun claimed that this tale was written during the Song dynasty, whereas Li Jianguo argued it was written during the Tang dynasty. Based on the mentioning of Zhongmenshi 中門使 in this tale, it seems the tale might have been written during the Five Dynasties. Zhongmenshi was a unique official title which only appeared in the Five Dynasties (see further discussion of this issue in n. 39 above). One of the reasons Li Jianguo claimed the tale was written during the Tang dynasty was because this tale, as well as several other tales recording stories of Emperor Yang, observed a taboo on using the names of the Tang emperors. It should be pointed out that the rulers of Later Tang 後唐 dynasty claimed they were the legitimate successors of the Tang dynasty, so it would not be hard to imagine that they would also have the taboo on using the names of the Tang emperors. It is also noteworthy that among all the five dynasties, the official position of Zhongmenshi played the most important role in the Later Tang court. Thus, the tale might have been written during the Later Tang dynasty.

This tale has had tremendous influence on the literary depiction of Emperor Yang of Sui in novels of later ages, notably *Sui Yangdi yan shi* and *Sui Tang yanyi*.

開河記

缺名

睢陽有王氣出，占天耿純臣奏後五百年當有天子興。煬帝已昏淫，不以為信。

時遊木蘭庭，命袁寶兒歌《柳枝詞》。因觀殿壁上有《廣陵圖》，帝瞪目視之，移時不能舉步。時蕭后在側，謂帝曰："知他是甚圖畫，何消皇帝如此掛意。"帝曰："朕不愛此畫，只為思舊遊之處。"於是帝以左手憑后肩，右手指圖上山水及人煙村落寺宇，歷歷皆如目前。謂后曰："朕為陳王時，守鎮廣陵，旦夕遊賞。當此之時，以雲煙為美景，視榮貴若深冤。豈期久有臨軒，萬機在務，使不得豁於懷抱也。"言訖，聖容慘然。后曰："帝意欲在廣陵，何如一幸？"帝聞，心中豁然。

翌日與大臣議，欲泛巨舟自洛入河，自河達海入淮，方至廣陵。群臣皆言似此程途，不啻萬里，又孟津水緊，滄海波深，若泛巨舟，事有不測。時有諫議大夫蕭懷靜（乃蕭后弟）奏曰："臣聞秦始皇時，金陵有王氣，始皇使人鑿斷砥柱，王氣遂絕。今睢陽有王氣，又陛下意在東南，欲泛孟津，又慮危險。況大梁西北有故河道，乃是秦將王離畎水灌大梁之處。欲乞陛下廣集兵夫，於大梁起首開掘，西自河陰，引孟津水入，東至淮口，放孟津水出。此間地不過千里，況於睢陽境內過，一則路達廣陵，二則鑿穿王氣。"帝聞奏大喜，羣臣皆默。

帝乃出敕，朝堂如有諫朕不開河者，斬之。詔以征北大總管麻叔謀為開河都護，以蕩寇將軍李淵為副使。淵稱疾不赴，即以左屯衛將軍令狐辛達代李淵為開渠副使都督。自大梁起首，於樂臺之北建修渠新所署，命之為卞渠（古祇有此卞字，開封城乃卞邑），因名其府署為卞渠上源傳舍也。（傳舍，驛名。因卞渠此處起首，故

號卞渠上源也。）詔發天下丁夫，男年十五以上者至，如有隱匿者
斬三族。帝以河水經於卞，乃賜卞字加水。丁夫計三百六十萬人。
乃更五家出一人，或老、或少、或婦人等供饋飲食。又令少年驍卒
五萬人，各執杖為督工夫，如節級隊長之類，共五百四十三萬餘人。
叔謀乃令三分中取一分人，自上源而西至河陰，通連古河道（乃王
離浸城處），迤邐趨愁思臺而至北去。又令二分丁夫，自上源驛而
東去。

其年乃隋大業五年，八月上旬建功。畚鍤既集，東西橫布數千
里。

纔開斷未及丈餘，得古堂室，可數間，瑩然肅靜。漆燈晶煌，
照耀如晝。四壁皆有彩畫花竹龍鬼之像。中有棺柩，如豪家之葬。
其促工吏聞於叔謀。命啟棺，一人容貌如生，肌膚潔白如玉而肥。
其髮自頭而出，覆其面，過腹胸下裹其足，倒生而上，及其背下而
方止。搜得一石銘，上有字如蒼頡鳥跡之篆。乃召夫中有識者免其
役。有一下邳民，讀曰：

> 我是大金仙，死來一千年。數滿一千年，背下有流泉。得逢麻叔
> 謀，葬我在高原。髮長至泥丸。更候一千年，方登兜率天。

叔謀乃自備棺槨，葬於城西隅之地（今大佛寺是也）。

次開掘陳留，帝遣使持御署玉祝，並白璧一雙，具少牢之奠，
祭於留侯廟以假道。祭訖，忽有大風，出於殿內窗牖間，吹樂人面。
使者退。自陳留果開掘東去，往來負擔拖鍬者，風馳電激。遠近之
人，踐踐如蜂屯蟻聚。

數日，達雍邱。時有一夫，乃中牟人。偶患傴僂之疾，不能前
進，墮於隊後，伶仃而行。是夜月色澄靜，聞呵殿聲甚嚴。夫鞠躬
俟道左，良久，見清道繼至，儀衛莫述。一貴人戴侯冠，衣王者衣，
乘白馬。命左右呼夫至前，謂曰：「與吾言你十二郎，還白璧一雙。
爾當賓於天（煬帝有天下十二年）。」言畢，取璧以授。夫跪受訖，
欲再拜，貴人躍馬西去。屆雍邱，以獻於麻都護，熟視，乃帝獻留
侯物也。詰其夫，夫具道。叔謀性貪，乃匿璧。又不曉其言，慮夫
洩於外，乃斬以滅口。

然後於雍邱起工。至大林，林中有小祠廟。叔謀訪問村叟，曰：
「古老相傳，呼為隱士墓，其神甚靈。」叔謀不以為信，將塋域發
掘。數尺，忽鑿一竅嵌空，群夫下窺，有燈火熒熒。無人敢入者。

乃指使將官武平郎將狄去邪者，請入探之。叔謀喜曰："真荊聶之輩也。"命繫去邪腰，下釣，約數十丈，方及地。去邪解其索，行約百步，入一石室。東北各有四石柱，鐵索二條繫一獸，大如牛。熟視之，一巨鼠也。須臾，石室之西有一石門洞開。一童子出，曰："子非狄去邪乎？"曰："然也。"童子曰："皇甫君坐來已久。"乃引入。見一人朱衣，頂雲冠，居高堂之上。去邪再拜。其人不言，亦不答拜。綠衣吏引去邪立於堂之西堦下。良久，堂上人呼力士牽取阿麼來（阿麼，煬帝小字）。武夫數人，形貌醜異魁奇，控所見大鼠至。去邪本乃廷臣，知帝小字，莫究其事，但屏氣而立。堂上人責鼠曰："吾遣爾暫脫皮毛，為中國主。何虐民害物，不遵天道？"鼠但點頭搖尾而已。堂上人益怒，令武士以大捧撾其腦。一擊，摔然有聲如墻崩，其鼠大叫若雷吼。方欲舉杖再擊，俄一童子捧天符而下。堂上驚躍，降階俯伏聽命。童子乃宣言曰："阿麼數本一紀，今已七年。更候五年，當以練巾繫頸死。"童子去，堂上人復令繫鼠於舊室中。堂上人謂去邪曰："與吾語麻叔謀：「謝你不伐吾域，來歲奉爾二金刀，勿謂輕酬也。」"言訖，綠衣吏引去邪於他門出。

約行十數里，入一林，躡石攀藤而行。回顧，已失使者。又行三里餘，見草舍，一老父坐土榻上。去邪訪其處，老父曰："此乃嵩陽少室山下也。"老父問去邪所至之處。去邪一一具言。老父遂細解去邪。去邪知煬帝不永之事。且曰："子能免官，即脫身於虎口也。"去邪東行，回視茅屋，已失所在。

時麻叔謀已至寧陽縣。去邪見叔謀，具言其事。元來去邪入墓後，其墓自崩。將謂去邪已死，今曰卻來。叔謀不信，將謂狂人。去邪乃托狂疾，隱終南山。時煬帝以患腦痛，月餘不視朝。訪其因，皆言帝夢中為人撾其腦，遂發痛數日。乃是去邪見鼠之日也。

叔謀既至寧陵縣，患風痒，起坐不得。帝令太醫令巢元方往治之。曰："風入腠理，病在胸臆。須用嫩羊肥者蒸熟，糝藥食之，則瘥。"叔謀取半年羊羔，殺而取腔，以和藥，藥未盡而病已痊。自後每令殺羊羔，日數枚。同杏酪五味蒸之，置其腔盤中，自以手臠掣而食之，謂曰含酥臠。鄉村獻羊羔者日數千人，皆厚酬其直。

寧陵下馬村民陶郎兒，家中巨富，兄弟皆兇很。以祖父塋域傍河道二丈余，慮其發掘。乃盜他人孩兒年三四歲者，殺之，去頭足，蒸熟，獻叔謀。咀嚼香美，迥異於羊羔，愛慕不已。召詰郎兒，郎兒乘醉泄其事。及醒，叔謀乃以金十兩與郎兒，又令役夫置一河曲以護其塋域。郎兒兄弟自後每盜以獻，所獲甚厚。

貧民有知者，競竊人家子以獻，求賜。襄邑、寧陵、睢陽所失孩兒數百，冤痛哀聲，旦夕不輟。虎賁郎將段達為中門使，掌四方表奏事，叔謀令家奴黃金窟將金一埒贈與。凡有上表及訟食子者，不訊其詞理，並令笞背四十，押出洛陽。道中死者，十有七八。

時令狐辛達知之，潛令人收孩骨，未及數日，已盈車。於是城市村坊之民有孩兒者，家做木櫃，鐵裹其縫。每夜，置母子於櫃中，鎖之，全家秉燭圍守。至天明，開櫃見子，即長幼皆賀。

既達睢陽界，有濠寨使陳伯恭言此河道若取直路，徑穿透睢陽城，如要回護，即取令旨。叔謀怒其言回護，令推出腰斬。令狐辛達救之。時睢陽坊市豪民一百八十戶，皆恐掘穿其宅並塋域，乃以釀金三千兩，將獻叔謀，未有梯媒可達。

忽穿至一大林，中有墓，故老相傳云宋司馬華元墓。掘透一石室，室中漆燈棺柩帳幕之類，遇風皆化為灰燼。得一石銘，曰：“睢陽土地高，汴水可為濠。若也不迴避，奉贈二金刀。”

叔謀曰：“此乃詐也，不足信。”是日，叔謀夢使者召至一宮殿上，一人衣絳綃，戴進賢冠。叔謀再拜，王亦答拜。拜畢，曰：“寡人宋襄公也。上帝明鎮此方，二千年矣。倘將軍借其方便，迴護此城，即一城老幼皆荷恩德也。”叔謀不允。又曰：“適來護城之事，蓋非寡人之意。況奉上帝之命，言此地候五百年間，當有王者建萬世之基。豈可偶為逸遊，致使掘穿王氣。”叔謀亦不允。良久，有使者入奏云：“大司馬華元至矣。”左右引一人，紫衣，戴進賢冠，拜覲於王前。王乃敘護城之事。其人勃然大怒曰：“上帝有命，臣等無心。叔謀愚昧之夫，不曉天命。”大呼左右，令置拷訊之物。王曰：“拷訊之事，何法最苦？”紫衣人曰：“銅汁灌之口，爛其腸胃，此為第一。”王許之。乃有數武夫拽叔謀，脫去其衣，惟留犢鼻，縛鐵柱上，欲以銅汁灌之。叔謀魂膽俱喪。殿上人連止之曰：“護城之事如何？”叔謀連聲言：“謹依上命。”遂令解縛。與本衣冠。王令引去，將行，紫衣人曰：“上帝賜叔謀金三千兩，取於民間。”叔謀性貪，謂使者曰：“上帝賜金，此何言也？”使者曰：“有睢陽百姓獻與將軍，此陰注陽受也。”忽如夢覺，但覺神不住體。

　　睢陽民果賂黃金窟而獻金三千兩。叔謀思夢中事，乃收之。立召陳伯恭，令自睢陽西穿渠，南北回屈，東行過劉趙村，連延而去。令狐辛達知之，累上表，亦為段達抑而不獻。

　　至彭城，路經大林中，有偃王墓。掘數尺，不可掘，乃銅鐵也。四面掘去其土，唯見鐵。墓旁安石門，扃鎖甚嚴。用酂陽民計，撞開墓門。叔謀自入墓中，行百餘步，二童子當前云：“偃王顒候久矣。”乃隨而入。見宮殿，一人戴通天冠，衣絳綃衣，坐殿上。叔謀拜，王亦拜，曰：“寡人塋域，當于河道。今奉與將軍玉寶，遣君當有天下。倘然護之，丘山之幸也。”叔謀許之。王乃令使者持一玉印與叔謀。又視之，印文乃『百代帝王受命玉印』也。叔謀大喜。王又曰：“再三保惜，乃刀刀之兆也。”（刀刀者，隱語，亦二金刀之意也。）叔謀出，令兵夫日護其墓。

　　時煬帝在洛陽，忽失國寶，搜訪宮闈，莫知所在，隱而不宣。帝督功甚急。叔謀乃自徐州，朝夕無暇，所役之夫已少一百五十餘萬，下寨之處，死屍滿野。

　　帝在觀文殿讀書，因覽《史記》，見秦始皇築長城之事，謂宰相宇文述曰：“始皇時至此已及千年，料長城已應摧毀。”宇文述順帝意，奏曰：“陛下偶然續秦皇之事，建萬世之業，莫若修其城，堅其壁。”帝大喜。乃詔以舒國公賀若弼為修城都護，以諫議大夫高熲為副使，以江淮吳楚襄鄧陳蔡並開拓諸州丁夫一百二十萬修長城。詔下，弼諫曰：“臣聞始皇築長城於絕塞，連延一萬里，男死女曠，婦寡子孤，其城未就，父子俱死。陛下欲聽狂夫之言，學亡秦之事，但恐社稷崩離，有同秦世。”帝大怒，未發其言。宇文述在側，乃掇曰：“爾武夫狂卒，有何知，而亂其大謀？”弼怒，以象簡擊宇文述。帝怒，令囚若弼於家，是夜飲酖死。高熲亦不行。宇文述乃舉司農卿宇文弼為修城都護，以民部侍郎宇文愷為副使。

　　時叔謀開汴渠盈灌口，點檢丁夫，約折二百五十萬人。其部役兵士舊五萬人，折二萬三千人。工既畢，上言於帝。遣決汴口，注水入汴渠。

　　帝自洛陽遷駕大渠。詔江淮諸州造大船五百隻。使命至，急如星火。民間有配蓋造船一隻者，家產破用皆盡，猶有不足，枷項笞背，然後鬻貨男女，以供官用。

　　龍舟既成，泛江沿淮而下。至大梁，又別加修飾，砌以七寶金玉之類。於吳越間取民間女年十五六歲者五百人，謂之殿腳女。至於龍舟禦艫，即每船用彩纜十條，每條用殿腳女十人，嫩羊十口，令殿腳女與羊相間而行，牽之。時恐盛暑，翰林學士虞世基獻計，請用垂柳栽於汴渠兩隄上。一則樹根四散，鞠護河隄；二乃牽船之人，護其陰涼；三則率舟之羊食其葉。上大喜，詔民間有柳一株，賞一縑。百姓競獻之。又令親種，帝自種一株，羣臣次第種，方及百姓。時有謠言曰："天子先栽，然後萬姓栽。"栽畢，帝御筆寫賜垂楊柳姓楊，曰楊柳也。

時舳艫相繼，連接千里，自大梁至淮口，聯緜不絕。錦帆過處，香聞千里。既過雍邱，漸達寧陵界。水勢漸緊，龍舟阻礙，牽駕之人，費力轉甚。時有虎賁郎將鮮于俱羅為護纜使，上言水淺河窄，行舟甚難。上以問虞世基。曰："請為鐵腳木鵝，長一丈二尺，上流放下。如木鵝住，即是淺。"帝依其言，乃令右翊將軍劉岑驗其水淺之處。自雍邱至灌口，得一百二十九處。帝大怒，令根究本處人吏姓名。應是木鵝住處，兩岸地分之人皆縛之，倒埋於岸下，曰："令教生為開河夫，死作抱沙鬼。"又埋却五萬餘人。

既達睢陽，帝問叔謀曰："坊市人煙，所掘幾何？"叔謀曰："睢陽地靈，不可干犯。若掘之，必有不祥。臣已迴護其城。"帝怒，令劉岑乘小舟根訪屈曲之處，比直路較二十里。帝益怒，乃令擒出叔謀，囚於後獄。急使宣令狐辛達詢問其由。

辛達奏：自寧陵便為不法，初食羊攢，後啗嬰兒；養賊陶郎兒，盜人之子；受金三千兩，於睢陽擅易河道。乃取小兒骨進呈。帝曰："何不達奏？"辛達曰："表章數上，為段達扼而不進。"

帝令人搜叔謀囊橐間，得睢陽民所獻金，又得留侯所還白璧及受命寶玉印。上驚異，謂宇文述曰："金與璧皆微物。寡人之寶，何自而得乎？"文述曰："必是遣賊竊取之矣。"帝瞠目而言曰："叔謀今日竊吾寶，明日盜吾首矣。"辛達在側，奏曰："叔謀常遣陶郎兒盜人之子，恐國寶郎兒所盜也。"

上益怒，遣榮國公來護兒，內使李百藥，太僕卿楊義臣推鞠叔謀，置臺署於睢陽。並收陶郎兒全家，令郎兒具招入內盜寶事。郎兒不勝其苦，乃具事招款。又責段達所收令狐辛達奏章即不奏之罪。案成進上，帝問丞相宇文述。述曰："叔謀有大罪四條：食人之子，受人之金，遣賊盜寶，擅移開河道。請用峻法誅之。其子孫取聖旨。"帝曰："叔謀有大罪。為開河有功，免其子孫。"只令腰斬叔謀於河側。

時來護兒受敕未至間，叔謀夢一童子自天而降，謂曰："宋襄公與大司馬華元遣我來，感將軍護城之惠意，往年所許二金刀，今曰奉還。"叔謀覺，曰："據此先兆，不祥。我腰領難存矣。"言未畢，護兒至，驅於河之北岸，斬為三段。郎兒兄弟五人，並家奴黃金窟並鞭死。中門使段達免死，降官為洛陽監門令。

Chapter 7

Tale 7.39

The Tale of Green Pearl

by Yue Shi
Translated by Jing Wang

Lüzhu (Green Pearl), whose last name was Liang, was a native from Bobai county in Bai prefecture.[1] Bai prefecture was also referred to as Nanchang commandery. In ancient times, it first belonged to the territory of Yue, then to Xiang commandery during the Qin dynasty (221 BCE–207 BCE), and later to the territory of Hepu county during the Han dynasty (202 BCE–220 AD). At the beginning of the Wude era (618–626) of the Tang dynasty (618–907), after defeating and pacifying the army of Xiao Xian (583–621), the Tang court established Nan prefecture, whose name soon after was changed to Bai prefecture after the River Bai. Mt. Bobai, River Bobai, Coiling Dragon Cave, Mt. Fang, Mt. Dual Horns, and Mt. Great Wilderness were within this region. At the top of Mt. Great Wilderness was a pond in which there were Bondmaid Concubine Fish. Lüzhu was born at the foot of Mt. Dual Horns. She was beautiful and enchanting. According to a

---

[1]Bobai 博白 county was the governing seat of Bai prefecture. It was located in modern Bobai in Guangxi province, about one hundred and twenty miles southeast of the provincial capital Nanning. The use of geographical terms of Song indicates that the text was written during the early Song dynasty.

certain Yue custom, because pearls were the most precious treasure, if one had a daughter, she would be named Pearl Girl; if one had a son, he would be named Pearl Boy. Following this tradition, Lüzhu was given the name Green Pearl.

When Shi Chong (249–300)[2] of the Jin dynasty (265–420) was the Investigatory Commissioner of Jiaozhi prefecture, he obtained Lüzhu with three bushels of pearls.[3] Chong owned a villa at the Jingu (Golden Valley) Brook, south of the Yellow River. In the valley, there was the Golden River that originated from the Taibai Plateau. Chong built a garden residence along the brook and the mountain. Lüzhu played the flute, and she was good at performing the "Mingjun" dance. Mingjun was a consort of an emperor during the Han dynasty. During the reign of Emperor Yuan (76 BCE–33 BCE) of Han, the *Chanyu*, the ruler of the northern nomadic *Xiongnu* people, came to pay homage to the Han court. The emperor issued an imperial edict to order Wang Qiang — also known as Zhaojun — to marry him. Prior to her departure, Zhaojun entered the court to bid the emperor farewell.

---

[2] Shi Chong's 石崇 biography can be found in *Jin shu*. It is attached to that of his father Shi Bao 石苞. Shi Chong, agnomen Jilun 季倫, was intelligent and courageous when he was young. He earned a reputation as a capable man when he served as a magistrate in his twenties. He ascended the social ladder because of his military merit, his own talent, and family connections. He was famous for his grand fortune, which he accumulated by robbing merchants when he was governor of Jingzhou 荊州. There are many anecdotes about his showing off his wealth and competing with his contemporaries on who could live the more luxurious life. He was beheaded at the age of fifty-two by Sima Lun 司馬倫 (d. 301), King of Zhao 趙, during the Rebellion of Eight Kings (291–306).

[3] Jiaozhi 交趾 prefecture, during the Jin dynasty, covered the northern part of modern Vietnam. The title of Investigatory Commissioner was used only during the Tang–Song period and did not exist in the Jin.

Her glorious beauty was dazzling to all that beheld her. The Son of Heaven regretted seeing her go, but he could not change his decision. Sympathizing with her because her marriage would take her far away, a man of the Han composed the "Mingjun" song in her honor. Chong taught Lüzhu the tune, and composed new lyrics to go with it:

> I was originally the child of a respectable family,
> Who was to marry into the court of the *Chanyu*.
> Before I could finish bidding farewell,
> The forerunner of the troops had already raised their flag.
> The carriage driver departed and wept with tears flowing
>   down his face,
> The lead horse gave a melancholy cry.
> My sorrow and anguish harm me from inside,
> My tears wet the pearl jewelry.
> Marching on and on, every day I was farther away,
> Then I arrived at the city of the *Xiongnu*.
> The *Chanyu* stood waiting by the tent,
> And he bestowed upon me the title *Yanzhi*.[4]
> Among people of a different category I could not feel at ease,
> Although my status was noble, it was not what I took pride in.
> Bullied and insulted by father and son,[5]
> I was ashamed and alarmed by the situation I faced.
> It was indeed not easy to commit suicide,
> In silence, I carried on living an ignoble life.
> In such an ignoble life what could I count on?
> My mind is constantly filled with accumulated thoughts.

---

[4]*Yanzhi* 閼氏 was the title of the empress and imperial wife of a certain prince of the *Xiongnu*. Zhaojun was given the title "Ninghu yanzhi" 寧胡閼氏. See *Hanshu*, 94.3806.

[5]After Huhanye *chanyu* 呼韓邪單于 — Zhaojun's first husband — died in 31 BCE, she asked the Han court for permission to return home; instead, she was ordered to adhere to the *Xiongnu* custom and marry his oldest son, who succeeded the throne. See *Hou Han shu*, 89.2941.

I wish I could borrow the wings of a flying goose,
Ride it and travel afar.
The flying geese do not turn to look at me,
I stand here bewildered and hurt.
In the past, I was jade in a box,
At present, I am a flower above excrement.
Morning blossoms are not good enough to please people,
I am willing to stay side by side with the autumn grass.
Pass on the word to later generations:
Marrying afar is harsh for one's emotions.

Chong also composed the "Melody of Worry and Sorrow" and gave it to Lüzhu.

Chong had over one thousand beautiful and enchanting entertainer-concubines. He selected several dozen and dressed them up in the same way, so that, at a glance, no one could tell the difference between them. Chong ordered that some jade be carved into pendants with coiling dragon designs and that gold be melted to make phoenix-shaped hairpins. His ladies tied their sleeves and danced around the pillars of the hall. When Chong wanted to summon one of the women, he did not call her by name; instead, he listened to the sound of the pendants and looked at the color of the hairpins. Those whose pendants made lighter sound stayed in the front, and those whose hairpins were brighter in color stayed in the back. They lined up and advanced in this order.

When Sima Lun (d. 301), King of Zhao, disrupted the order of the dynasty, his fellow rebel Sun Xiu (d. 301) sent someone to seek out Lüzhu.[6] When Sun Xiu's envoy arrived, Chong had just

---

[6]Sun Xiu 孫秀, agnomen Junzhong 俊忠, was a practitioner of *Wudoumi Dao* 五斗米道 (Way of the Five Bushels of Rice), a Daoist sect that originated in the Sichuan area in the mid-second century. He later played a vital role in Sima Lun's rebellion and controlled the court administration after Sima Lun ascended the throne.

ascended the Terrace of Coolness and was looking down at a clear river with his ladies waiting on him. The envoy reported the message. Chong asked several hundred of his serving maidens to come out and presented them to the envoy. All of them wore fragrance of orchids and musk and were dressed in delicate silk. Chong said to the envoy, "Choose whomever you like." The envoy responded, "Your Lord's serving maidens are indeed magnificent; however, I was ordered to seek only after Lüzhu. I don't know which one she is." Shi Chong was enraged and said, "Lüzhu is the only one that I love. You are not permitted to take her." From then on, Sun Xiu slandered Shi Chong in front of the King of Zhao and spoke of exterminating his clan. When the troops that Sun Xiu sent to arrest Shi Chong arrived at his residence unannounced, Chong said to Lüzhu, "Now I have committed a crime because of you." Lüzhu cried and declared, "Sir, I am willing to die in front of you" Chong attempted to stop her, but she threw herself off of the terrace and died. Chong was then executed, and his corpse was abandoned in the East Market. People at the time named the terrace "Green Pearl Terrace." The terrace was located in the Buguang Ward close to the Di Spring[7] which was to the east of the Royal City.[8] Lüzhu had a disciple, Song Yi, who was known throughout the state for her beauty, and she was good at playing the flute. She later entered the harem of Emperor Ming 明 (299–325) of the Jin dynasty.

Today, in Bai prefecture, there is a tributary called the Green Pearl River that originates from Mt. Double Horn and merges into the Rongzhou River. Similarly, in Guizhou, there are places named Zhaojun Beach, Zhaojun Village, and Zhaojun Square; in

---

[7]Buguang 步廣 Ward was located in the northern part of Luoyang. The Di Spring 狄泉 was also named the Zhai Spring 翟泉 (Shuijing zhu, 16.128).

[8]Zhengcheng 正城 should be Wangcheng 王城 (Royal City); it refers to Luoyi 雒邑 in modern Luoyang.

the Wu area, there are Xi Shi Valley and the Pond of Rouge and Powder.[9] In short, each of these places is named after the origin of a beautiful woman. At the foot of Mt. Double Horn, there is also the Green Pearl Well. Among the wise elders a rumor circulated: "Those who drank from this well would most likely give birth to beautiful girls. The wise men in the village thought beauty was not beneficial to society, and so covered up the well with a giant stone. Henceforth, although some women still gave birth to graceful and beautiful girls, most of them were born with physical defects in their limbs or faces." How extraordinary this was! The mountains and the rivers made matters this way! When a girl was born in the Zhaojun Village, people always burned and damaged her face. Therefore Bo Juyi (772–846) composed a poem on this phenomenon that reads:

> If one does not learn from the past,
> It will probably bring misfortune to the generations to come.
> Up to now the faces of the village girls
> have been burned so that they are covered with scars.

The poet was sympathetic toward the girls because of their physical defects.[10]

Niu Sengru (779–847)[11] wrote in his tale "Zhou Qin xingji" (A Record of Travels through Zhou and Qin)[12]:

---

[9]Xi Shi was a famous beauty of ancient China. She lived during the end of the Spring and Autumn period (770 BCE–476 BCE) and was a native of the State of Yue 越.

[10]This rendering is based on the text in the *Shoufu* and the *Linlang mishi congshu*. The original Chinese reads 又以不完具而惜焉. See Li Jianguo, *Songdai chuanqi ji*, p. 19, note 27.

[11]Niu Sengru, agnomen Si'an 思黯, served three Tang emperors as Chancellor: Emperor Muzong 穆宗 (r. 820–824), Emperor Jingzong 敬宗 (r. 824–826) and Emperor Wenzong 文宗 (r. 827–840). He was the

When I stayed overnight at the Temple of Empress Dowager
Bo (d. 155 BCE),[13] I met Lady Qi (221 BCE–194 BCE),[14] Wang

---

leader of one of the political factions — later known as the "Niu
Faction" — during the Niu–Li Factional Struggle. Niu Sengru started
his career in the government after passing the *Jinshi* Civil Service
Examination in 805; he held a series of important offices throughout
his career. An influential political leader, he was also a talented writer.
Lu Xun regards his work *Xuanguai lu* 玄怪錄 (*Records of the Mysterious
and Strange*) as the most magnificent among numerous collections of
tales from the Tang dynasty.

[12]"Zhou Qin xingji" T4.21 is a first-person narrative written from
Niu Sengru's perspective. It recounts Niu's extraordinary experience as
he departs from the capital after failing the *Jinshi* examination during the
Zhenyuan 貞元 era (785–805). He gets lost at dusk and, by chance, enters
Empress Dowager Bo's sacrificial temple. According to this account,
upon his arrival, Empress Dowager Bo summons several beautiful
women, all of whom were consorts of emperors in the past, to feast and
exchange poetry with him. He even spends the night with Zhaojun. Niu
leaves the next morning; upon returning at a later time, he finds the
temple to be nothing but an inaccessible ruin. The authorship of this tale
is under debate. Because the protagonist's encounter with the imperial
ladies, his behavior, and his speech are all considered extremely
inappropriate, many scholars argue that this text is a product of the
factional struggle at the time, that Niu Sengru's political rivals wrote it to
slander him.

[13]Empress Dowager Bo was a consort of the founding emperor of
the Han dynasty — Emperor Gaozu (256 BCE–195 BCE) — and the
mother of Emperor Wen (r. 179 BCE–155 BCE). Records about her life are
preserved in "Waiqi shijia" 外戚世家 (Hereditary Houses of the Imperial
Maternal Relatives) in *Shiji*, and also in the "Waiqi zhuan" 外戚傳
(Biographies of the Imperial Maternal Relatives) in *Hanshu*.

[14]Lady Qi was a consort of Emperor Gaozu of the Han dynasty.
Empress Lü (241 BCE–180 BCE) was extremely resentful of her — the
emperor was particularly fond of Lady Qi, and she also schemed to
replace the Heir, Empress Lü's son, with her own son. Following

Qiang, Consort Taizhen (719–756),[15] and the Virtuous Consort Pan (d. 453).[16] Each one of them composed poems to express their

---

Emperor Gaozu's death, Empress Lü sent her to prison. At the Empress' command, an attendant "cut off Lady Qi's hands and feet, removed her eyes, cauterized her ears, caused her to drink a drug that rendered her mute, and sent her to live in the privy, calling her 'the human hog.'" See "Empress Dowager Lü, Basic Annals 9" in William H. Nienhauser, Jr., trans., ed., *The Grand Scribe's Records: The Basic Annals of Han China* (Bloomington: Indiana University Press, 2002), vol. 2, p. 111.

[15]Consort Taizhen, i.e. Precious Consort Yang, was a consort of Emperor Xuanzong of the Tang dynasty. She was the daughter of the Revenue Manager of Shu Prefecture, which is now known as Sichuan Province. Taizhen was orphaned at an early age and was raised by her uncle, who worked at the Levied Service section in the government of Henan Prefecture. She was originally married to Emperor Xuanzong's son Li Mao (720–775), Prince of Shou, in 735, but later, Emperor Xuanzong took a fancy to her. In order to take her as his own consort and prevent criticism, the emperor arranged for her to become a Daoist nun with the tonsure name Taizhen before reentering the palace as his imperial consort. The emperor was so fond of her that he bestowed imperial titles and high official positions on many of her relatives. After the capital fell into the hands of rebels during the An Lushan (703–757) rebellion in 755, Emperor Xuanzong fled to Shu with Precious Consort Yang. When they reached the Mawei courier station, the imperial guards pressured the emperor into killing his consort. She eventually hanged herself. See records about her life in "The Biographies of Empresses and Consorts" 后妃傳 in *Xin Tang shu* and *Jiu Tang shu*. See also T3.17, T7.40–41 in this volume.

[16]Virtuous Consort Pan was a consort of Emperor Wen (r. 424–453) of the Song dynasty during the Southern Dynasties period. See records about her life in *Song shu* 宋書 (*History of Song*) and in *Nan shi* 南史 (*History of the Southern Dynasties*). Although Pan entered the emperor's harem because of her beauty, she initially failed to earn his favor. It is said that the emperor habitually rode past the residences of his consorts in a goat cart. Accordingly, Pan soaked the ground with saltwater so that

intentions. There was also a woman who excelled in playing the flute. Her hair was tucked into a small bun, and she wore a tight-fitting shirt and a belt. She was quite beautiful and came together with Consort Pan. Empress Dowager made her sit at the servant seat and ordered her to play the flute. From time to time, she was also offered wine. Empress Dowager turned to me and asked, "Do you know this woman? She is Lüzhu from the Shi household. Consort Pan kept her as a younger sister." Empress Dowager said, "How could Lüzhu not come up with a poem?" Lüzhu apologized and composed a poem which read:

> This person today is not the one in the past,
> In the sound of the flute, I resent King of Zhao in vain.
> The red blossoms withered, and the hairpin shattered under
>   the flower terrace,
> Spring will not come to the Golden Valley for a thousand years.

The Empress Dowager said, "Scholar Niu came from afar, so who will accompany him today?" Lüzhu said, "Chamberlain Shi,[17] as a person, was strict and jealous. I would rather die today than get involved in any molestation."

Although such events were strange and abnormal, they could, to some extent, be used to make people laugh.

Alas, although Shi Chong's demise started with Lüzhu, it happened gradually over time. When Shi Chong governed Jing prefecture, he not only robbed and plundered the envoys sent to

---

the goat would stop and lick it. Ultimately, she captured the emperor's attention and won his affection thereafter. She was resented by the Crown Prince, whose mother, the Empress, died of jealousy. The Crown Prince, together with Consort Pan's son, started a rebellion and killed both Emperor Wen and Consort Pan.

[17]This refers to Shi Chong who was once appointed Chamberlain.

the court from afar, but also drowned and murdered traveling merchants to gain enormous wealth. He also sent a poisonous bird[18] to Wang Kai,[19] and later collaborated with him on plots to poison others. He had such schemes in mind. Furthermore, every time he invited guests to a feast, he ordered beautiful maids to serve wine to each guest. If a guest did not finish the wine, he would order the Imperial Gate Keepers to behead the maids. Counselor-in-Chief Wang[20] and the General-in-Chief[21] once came

---

[18] *Zhenniao* 鴆鳥 was a poisonous bird that was said to live in southern China and prey on poisonous snakes. People in ancient China used its feathers, soaking them in wine, to make poisonous wine. This poisonous wine was both colorless and odorless. There are numerous records in ancient Chinese history and tales about murders involving this type of toxic substance.

[19] A brief record of Wang Kai's 王愷 life is kept in "Biographies of the Imperial Maternal Relatives" on *Jin shu* 93.2412. Wang Kai, cognomen Junfu 君夫, was talented and strong when he was young. He received many imperial titles and was appointed General because of his military prowess. He maintained a luxurious lifestyle. Anecdotes about his competing with Shi Chong to prove his wealth can be found in "Chitai" 侈汰 (Sybaritism) in Liu Yiqing's *Shishuo xinyu*.

[20] Counselor-in-Chief Wang refers to Wang Dao 王導 (276–339), agnomen Maohong 茂弘, one of the major contributors to the founding of the Eastern Jin dynasty. He served as Counselor-in-Chief for three emperors of the Eastern Jin, i.e. Emperor Yuan 元帝 (r. 317–323), Emperor Ming 明帝 (r. 323–325), and Emperor Cheng 成帝 (r. 325–342). See his biography in *Jin shu*.

[21] General-in-Chief Wang Dun 王敦 (266–324), agnomen Chuzhong 處仲, was Counselor-in-Chief Wang Dao's cousin. He also married Emperor Wu's daughter, Princess Xiangcheng 襄城. He became a powerful general for assisting Emperor Yuan in founding the Eastern Jin dynasty. In 322, Wang Dun started a rebellion and led his army to attack the capital city. He died of an illness in 324, and the rebellion was quenched. His corpse was excavated and abused, and his head was severed and hung for public display. See his biography in *Jin shu*.

together to visit Chong. Normally, the Counselor-in-Chief did not drink; on this occasion, however, he forced himself to drink the wine and became deeply intoxicated. The General-in-Chief, however, deliberately refused to drink to observe Chong's reaction, [even after] three women had already been beheaded.[22] The Gentleman said, "There is no entrance to catastrophe or fortune. It only happens to the person who causes it." Chong was not a righteous person at heart, and he murdered people at will. How could he not face retribution? If it were not for Lüzhu, Shi Chong's execution would not have been expedited; if it were not for Shi Chong, Lüzhu's name would not have become famous.

Lüzhu threw herself off of the terrace, thus becoming a maid of chastity and principle. A comparable example of a virtuous woman in ancient times was a woman named Liuchu. Liuchu was a servant girl of Wang Jinxian[23] — the consort of Crown Prince Min (278–300)[24] of the Jin dynasty. When chaos ensued in the

---

[22]This anecdote is based on a record in Chapter "Chitai" in the *Shishuo xinyu*. The account of the execution is incomplete, and the original text reads: "Although Shi Chong had already sentenced three women to execution, the General-in-chief did not change his expression and remained unwilling to drink."

[23]Wang Jinxian, agnomen Huifeng 惠风, was the youngest daughter of Grand Guardian Wang Yan 王衍 (256–311). She was selected by Empress Jia 贾 (257–300) to marry the Crown Prince, Minhuai 愍懷 (278–300). When the Crown Prince was framed and banished, Wang Yan submitted a written request to the emperor, asking for a divorce for his daughter. Jinxian cried and returned home. What is presented in this tale slightly departs from Jinxian's brief biography in the *Jin shu*. In her official biography, Liu Yao 劉曜 (d. 329) kidnapped her and gave her, as a gift, to his commanding officer, General Qiao Shu 喬屬. Jinxian resisted when the general tried to rape her, and therefore he killed her. See "Lienü zhuan" 列女傳 (Biographies of Exemplary Women) in *Jin shu*.

[24]Crown Prince Min refers to Crown Prince Minhuai — also known as Sima Yu 司馬遹 with cognomen Xizu 熙祖 — whose biography is

capital, Luoyang, [25] Shi Le (274–333) [26] kidnapped Jinxian and crossed the Yellow River at Mengjin. [27] He tried to rape her, but Jinxian scolded him, saying, "I am the wife of the royal Crown Prince and daughter of a minister. You are a little barbarian fellow, how dare you humiliate me?" After these words, she threw herself into the Yellow River. Liuchu said, "The one at a higher position has taken action, and the one at a lower position should do the same." So she threw herself into the Yellow River as well.

---

preserved in *Jin shu*. He was the only son of Emperor Hui 惠 of the Jin dynasty (r. 290–307) and was made the Crown Prince once his father ascended the throne in 290. According to his biography, he had a good reputation at a young age, but gradually lost it as he matured in age and began to indulge himself in entertainment. He was resented and later framed by Empress Jia; she took advantage of his inebriated state and lured him into copying a statement that he had attempted to usurp the throne. The Crown Prince was then deposed and reduced to commoner status. A year later, in 300, Empress Jia oversaw his assassination.

[25]Led by Shi Le, Liu Yao, and several others, the army of the Kingdom of Han 漢 defeated the Jin army and captured the capital city, Luoyang, in 311, the fifth year of the Yongjia 永嘉 reign (307–313). Numerous people, including officials, were slaughtered; the palace was burned down; and Emperor Huai of Jin 晉懷帝 (284–313) was abducted. This is the so-called "The Chaos of Yongjia," (永嘉之亂) which marked the end to the Western Jin dynasty. See "Xiao Huaidi ji" 孝懷帝紀 (The Annals of Emperor Huai) in *Jin shu*.

[26]Shi Le 石勒, agnomen Shilong 世龍, was a native of the northern nomadic group *Jie* 羯 and was the founding emperor of the Later Zhao 後趙 (319–351) dynasty during the period of the Sixteen Kingdoms. See his biography in *juan* 104 and 105 in *Jin shu*.

[27]Mengjin is an important ferry crossing on the Yellow River. The ferry is located about twenty miles northeast of Luoyang in Henan Province.

There was also a woman named Yaoniang, who was the favorite maid of Qiao Zhizhi (d. 697)[28] during the reign of Empress Wu (r. 690–705) of the Zhou dynasty. Yaoniang was magnificently beautiful and was exceptionally skilled in singing and dancing. Zhizhi taught her to read, and she excelled in writing; thus, Zhizhi loved and favored her greatly. At that time, Wu Chengsi (649–698) was arrogant and aristocratic.[29] He drank wine at a royal feast, became intoxicated, and forced Zhizhi to wager Yaoniang in exchange for some gold and jade. When Zhizhi lost the game, Chengsi sent some people to his household and took Yaoniang by force. Zhizhi was resentful of Chengsi and regretted his actions, so he composed "Lüzhu pian" (A Poem on Lüzhu) to express his resentment. The lyrics read:

The Shi family of the Golden Valley valued new melodies,
He spent ten bushels of bright pearls to purchase the graceful girl.
That day was so lovely that no other time could compare,
That moment was so pleasant that it won everybody's heart.

---

[28]Qiao Zhizhi's brief biography is preserved in "Wenyuan" 文苑 (Biographies of Literary Figures) in *Jiu Tang shu*. His father, Qiao Shiwang 喬師望, married Princess Luling 廬陵, daughter of Emperor Gaozu (566–635) of Tang. Qiao Zhizhi and his two brothers were all famous for their literary writings. He was appointed Right Rectifier of Omissions and later promoted to Director of the Left Office of the Department of Affairs during the reign of Empress Wu 武 (624–705).

[29]Wu Chengsi's biography is kept in "Biographies of the Imperial Maternal Relatives" in *Jiu Tang* shu, and in *Xin Tang shu*. Wu Chengsi, agnomen Fengxian 奉先, was the nephew of Empress Wu of the Tang dynasty. He was appointed to a series of high official positions and inherited the title Duke of Zhou 周國公 because of his connection to Empress Wu. He tried to persuade the empress to pronounce him Crown Prince but eventually failed.

The lady's chamber in your gentleman's household was never
  difficult to access,
He frequently invited people to watch her singing and
  dancing.
The wealthy and heroic were not people who could be
  reasoned with,
The arrogant and noble used their power tyrannically to
  interfere.
She could not bear to say farewell and leave the gentleman,
In vain, the woman cried with her face covered up and felt
  melancholy.
The eternal parting took place at the high terrace,
All of a sudden, the beauty reached the end of her life for the
  gentleman.

Zhizhi privately entrusted the poem to a eunuch-servant in
Chengsi's household to pass it onto Yaoniang. When Yaoniang
received the poem, she grieved, cried, and later committed suicide
by throwing herself into a well. Chengsi ordered people to drain
the well and retrieve her corpse. He found the poem amongst her
clothes and whipped the eunuch-servant to death. Chengsi, then,
through a remonstrance official, set Zhizhi up and went so far as
to have him murdered.

How sad is this! The two men showed their favorite
concubines to others and brought about fatal catastrophes to
themselves; this is what is referred to as, "Holding the sword of
Tai'e by the blade and giving others the handle." According to the
Yi jing, "the careless placement of things excites robbery, as a
woman's adorning of herself excites lust." Are these sorts of
situations not the types of scenarios to which this saying applies?
After Lüzhu's death, poets who wrote about singing and dancing

courtesans all named their characters after Lüzhu. Yu Jianwu's (487–ca. 552) poem read:[30]

> Honored guests arrive at the Orchid Hall.
> Elegant music is played on the zither at the splendid feast.
> I compose "The poem on Mingjun,"
> And ask Lüzhu to dance to it.

Li Yuancao's[31] poem read:

> The beautiful maid Jiangshu[32] waves the dancing fan,
> The girl from the Golden Valley dances to start the feast.
> Their silk sleeves sweep over the returning guests
> Who stay to seek pleasure and become drunk with the jade goblets.

---

[30]Yu Jianwu 庾肩吾, agnomen Zishen 子慎, was a native of Nanyang 南陽 in modern Henan Province. He was an important poet and scholar of calligraphy of the Liang 梁 dynasty during the Southern Dynasties period. See Yu Jianwu's biography in *Nan shi*.

[31]Li Yuancao's 李元操 given name was Xiaozhen 孝貞. He was said to be diligent when he was young and excelled at literature. He served in the Northern Qi 北齊 and the Northern Zhou 北周 of the Northern Dynasties, as well the Sui 隋 dynasty. See his biography in *Sui shu* 隋書 (*History of Sui*).

[32]Jiangshu 絳樹 (Crimson Tree) is the name of a legendary girl who was extremely beautiful and talented at singing and dancing. She is mentioned in numerous poems and prose from ancient times.

Jiang Zong's (519–594) poem read:[33]

> Lüzhu danced with tears in her eyes,
> Sun Xiu invited her against her will.

It has been several hundred years since Lüzhu's death; however, poets still ceaselessly chant praises in her name. What is the reason behind this? As a maidservant, Lüzhu was not well versed in books, yet she was able to appreciate her master's kindness, and did not hesitate to sacrifice her life for him. Her will [to sacrifice herself] was unyielding and awe-inspiring. She was indeed good enough to make later generations admire her character and sing in praise of her actions. Those who enjoy large salaries and steal high positions know neither benevolence nor righteousness. They have no loyalty in their hearts and act fickle. They only seek their own profit. Their character cannot hold a candle even to that of a woman's — how ashamed they should feel! The reason that I composed this tale is not only to narrate a story about beauty and to eliminate the sources of such catastrophes, but also to punish and admonish the kind of people who are dismissive of the generosity bestowed upon them as well as those who turn against righteousness.

Ten days after Shi Chong's death, Sima Lun, King of Zhao, was defeated. Zhao Quan, General of the Left Guard, beheaded

---

[33]Jiang Zong, agnomen Zongchi 總持, was a famous poet during the Southern Dynasties. He was especially good at composing regulated poetry and was considered one of the best writers of Palace-Style poetry. His poems were criticized for being superficial and flamboyant. He served in three different dynasties: the Liang and the Chen 陳 of the Southern Dynasties, and the Sui dynasty. He was a favored minister of the last emperor of the Chen dynasty and was notorious for his neglect of the state administration and indulgence in entertainment with the emperor. See his biography in *Chen shu* 陳書 (*History of Chen*).

Sun Xiu at the Secretariat. The military officer Zhao Jun cut open Sun Xiu's chest and ate his heart. Sima Lun was imprisoned in the city of Jinyong [34] and on him was bestowed gold-flake wine. [35] Sima Lun felt ashamed of himself, covered his face with his head scarf, and said, "Sun Xiu led me astray." He drank the gold-flake wine and died. His family and clan were exterminated. The Scholar from Nanyang speculated, "This was vengeance as ordered from Heaven; otherwise, how did the execution happen immediately?"

Note: This is a revised version of my 2017 rendition in Zhenjun Zhang and Jing Wang, *Song Dynasty Tales: A Guided Reader* (Singapore: World Scientific, 2017, pp. 199–234), where much more detailed annotations and commentary are provided.

---

[34]Jinyong City was a small walled city of about 3.5 acres located in the northwestern corner of Luoyang in the fourth century, about fifteen miles to the east of modern Luoyang. It was built during the reign of Emperor Ming of Wei 魏明帝 (r. 226–239), and was not only a separate imperial residence but also an important military site. It later became a place for kings and emperors to reside following their abdication.

[35]In ancient China, emperors used *jinxie jiu* 金屑酒 (gold-flake wine), poisonous wine also known as golden wine or golden flakes, to put officials and imperial family members to death.

綠珠傳

樂史

　　綠珠者，姓梁，白州博白縣人也。州則南昌郡，古越地，秦象郡，漢合浦縣地。唐武德初，削平蕭銑，於此置南州；尋改為白州，取白江為名。州境有博白山，博白江，盤龍洞，房山，雙角山，大荒山。山上有池，池中有婢妾魚。綠珠生雙角山下，美而艷。越俗以珠為上寶，生女為珠娘，生男為珠兒。綠珠之字，由此而稱。

　　晉石崇為交趾采訪使，以真珠三斛致之。崇有別廬在河南金谷澗。澗中有金水，自太白源來。崇即川阜置園館。綠珠能吹笛，又善舞《明君》。明君者，漢妃也。漢元帝時，匈奴單於入朝，詔王嬙配之，即昭君也。及將去，入辭，光彩射人，天子悔焉，重難改更，漢人憐其遠嫁，為作此歌。崇以此曲教之，而自制新歌曰：

“我本良家子，將適單於庭。
辭別未及終，前驅已抗旌。
仆禦流涕別，轅馬悲且鳴。
哀鬱傷五內，涕泣霑珠纓。
行行日已遠，遂造匈奴城。
延佇於穹廬，加我閼氏名。
殊類非所安，雖貴非所榮。
父子見凌辱，對之慚且驚。
殺身良不易，默默以苟生。
苟生亦何聊，積思常憤盈。
願假飛鴻翼，乘之以遐征。
飛鴻不我顧，佇立以屏營。
昔以匣中玉，今為糞上英。
朝華不足歡，甘與秋草并。

608

傳語後世人：遠嫁難為情。"

崇又制《懊惱曲》以贈綠珠。

崇之美艷者千余人，擇數十人，裝飾一等，使忽視之，不相分別。刻玉為倒龍佩，縈金為鳳凰釵，結袖繞楹而舞。欲有所召者，不呼姓名，悉聽佩聲，視釵色。佩聲輕者居前，釵色艷者居後，以為行次而進。

趙王倫亂常，賊類孫秀使人求綠珠。崇方登涼觀，臨清水，婦人侍側。使者以告，崇出侍婢數百人以示之，皆蘊蘭麝而披羅縠。曰："任所擇。"使者曰："君侯服禦，麗矣。然受命指索綠珠。不知孰是？"崇勃然曰："吾所愛，不可得也。"秀因是譖倫族之。收兵忽至，崇謂綠珠曰："我今為爾獲罪。"綠珠泣曰："願效死於君前。"崇因止之，於是墜樓而死。崇棄東市。時人名其樓曰綠珠樓。樓在步庚里，近狄泉。狄泉在正城之東。綠珠有弟子宋禕，有國色，善吹笛。後入晉明帝宮中。

今白州有一派水，自雙角山出，合容州江，呼為綠珠江。亦猶歸州有昭君灘，昭君村，昭君場；吳有西施谷，脂粉塘，蓋取美人出處為名。又有綠珠井，在雙角山下。耆老傳云："汲此井飲者，誕女必多美麗。里閭有識者以美色無益於時，因以巨石鎮之。爾後雖有產女端妍者，而七竅四肢多不完具。"異哉！山水之使然。昭君村生女皆炙破其面，故白居易詩曰："不取往者戒，恐貽來者冤。至今村女面，燒灼成瘢痕。"又以不完具而惜焉。

牛僧儒《周秦行記》云："夜宿薄太后廟，見戚夫人，王嬙，太真妃，潘淑妃，各賦詩言誌。別有善笛女子，短鬢窄衫具帶，貌甚美，與潘氏偕來。太后以接坐居之，令吹笛，往往亦及酒。太后顧而謂曰：'識此否？石家綠珠也。潘妃養作妹。'太后曰'綠珠豈能無詩乎？'綠珠拜謝，作曰：'此日人非昔日人，笛聲空怨趙王倫。紅殘鈿碎花樓下，金谷千年更不春。'太后曰：'牛秀才遠來，今日誰人與伴？'綠珠曰：'石衛尉性嚴忌。今有死，不可及亂。'"然事雖詭怪，聊以解頤。

噫，石崇之敗，雖自綠珠始，亦其來有漸矣。崇常刺荊州，劫奪遠使，沈殺客商，以致巨富。又遺王愷鴆鳥，共為鴆毒之事。有此陰謀，加以每邀客宴集，令美人行酒，客飲不盡者，使黃門斬美人。王丞相與大將軍嘗共訪崇，丞相素不能飲，輒自勉強，至於沈醉。至大將軍，故不飲以觀其變，已斬三人。君子曰："禍福無門，

惟人所召。"崇心不義，舉動殺人，烏得無報也。非綠珠無以速石
崇之誅，非石崇無以顯綠珠之名。

綠珠之墜樓，侍兒之有貞節者也。比之於古，則有曰六出。六
出者，王進賢侍兒也。進賢，晉愍太子妃。洛陽亂，石勒掠進賢渡
孟津，欲妻之。進賢罵曰："我皇太子婦，司徒公女。胡羌小子，
敢干我乎？"言畢投河。六出曰："大既有之，小亦宜然。"復投
河中。

又有窈娘者，武周時喬知之寵婢也。盛有姿色，特善歌舞。知
之教讀書，善屬文，深所愛幸。時武承嗣驕貴，內宴酒酣，迫知之
將金玉賭窈娘。知之不勝，便使人就家強載以歸。知之怨悔，作
《綠珠篇》以敘其怨。詞曰：

"石家金谷重新聲，明珠十斛買娉婷。
此日可憐無復比，此時可愛得人情。
君家閨閣未曾難，嘗持歌舞使人看。
富貴雄豪非分理，驕矜勢力橫相干。
辭君去君終不忍，徒勞掩面傷紅粉。
百年離別在高樓，一旦紅顏為君盡。"

知之私屬承嗣家閹奴傳詩於窈娘。窈娘得詩悲泣，投井而死。
承嗣令汲出，於衣中得詩，鞭殺閹奴。諷吏羅織知之，以至殺焉。

悲夫，二子以愛姬示人，掇喪身之禍。所謂倒持太阿，授人以
柄。《易》曰："慢藏誨盜，冶容誨淫，"其此之謂乎。其後詩人
題歌舞妓者，皆以綠珠為名。庾肩吾曰："蘭堂上客至，綺席清弦
撫。自作《明君辭》，還教綠珠舞。"李元操云："絳樹搖歌扇，
金谷舞筵開。羅袖拂歸客，留歡醉玉杯。"江總云："綠珠含淚舞，
孫秀強相邀。"

綠珠之沒已數百年矣，詩人尚詠之不已，其故何哉？蓋一婢子，
不知書，而能感主恩，憤不顧身，其志烈懍懍，誠足使後人仰慕歌
詠也。至有享厚祿，盜高位，亡仁義之性，懷反覆之情，暮四朝三，
惟利是務，節操反不若一婦人，豈不愧哉。今為此傳，非徒述美麗，
室禍源，且欲懲戒辜恩背義之類也。

季倫死後十日，趙王倫敗。左衛將軍趙泉斬孫秀於中書，軍士
趙駿剖秀心食之。倫囚金墉城，賜金屑酒。倫慚，以巾覆面曰：

“孫秀誤我也。”飲金屑而卒。皆夷家族。南陽生曰：此乃假天之報怨。不然，何梟夷之立見乎！

Tale 7.40

Unofficial Biography of Yang the Grand Verity (A)

By Yue Shi
Translated by Xin Zou

Precious Consort Yang, pet name Yuhuan, was a native of Huayin in Hongnong.[1] Her ancestors moved to Puzhou Prefecture and lived in Dutou Village of Yongle County. The consort's great-great-grandfather was Lingben, a Prefect of Jinzhou prefecture. Her father Xuanyan was Revenue Manager of the Shu Prefecture. The Precious Consort was born in Shu. She once accidentally fell into a pond, which later was called "The Pond of the Fallen Consort," and it is located on the frontier of Daojiang County. (This is like the case that Wang Zhaojun was born in Xiazhou Prefecture, and now Zhaojun Village is named after her; likewise, Lüzhu was born in Baizhou Prefecture, and so there is now a Lüzhu River in her honor.) The consort became orphaned at a young age, and she was raised in the home of her paternal uncle, Xuanjiao, a clerk in the Bureau of Works of Henan Metropolitan Prefecture. In the eleventh lunar month of the twenty-second year of the Kaiyuan Era (734), she married into the family of Prince Shou. In the tenth lunar month of the twenty-eighth year,

---

[1]Huayin 華陰, in Hongnong 弘農, is southwest of modern Huayin, Shanxi.

612

Emperor Xuazong graced *Wenquan gong* (Palace of Hot Spring Water) with his presence (since the tenth lunar month of the sixth year of the Tianbao Era (745), the palace had been renamed back to *Huaqing gong* [the Palace of Splendor and Purity]). He sent Gao Lishi to take Lady Yang from Prince Shou's residence, converted her into a Taoist priestess, now known as Taizhen, and housed her in the Taizhen Temple within the Forbidden Palace. In the seventh lunar month of the fourth Tianbao year (744), the emperor ordered the daughter of Wei Zhaoxun, General of the Left-Side Military Guard, to marry Prince Shou instead. That same month, in the Garden of Phoenix, the emperor conferred upon Lady Yang, then a Taoist Priestess of the Taizhen Temple, the title of Precious Consort, allowing her to enjoy clothing and articles half that of an empress.

On the day the consort was received by the emperor, the suite "Rainbow Skirt and Feather Vestments" was played. (The song was composed by Emperor Xuanzong, after he ascended the Sanxiang post-station[2] and gazed upon Nǚ'ji Mountain. Thus, Liu Yuxi (772–842) later composed a poem that reads:

> I, a minor official, respectfully read Emperor Xuanzong's poem on gazing at the Nǚ'ji Moutain, and a multitude of feelings surged.

> The Son of Heaven, during his "Opened Prime," was content in all affairs,
> Regretting only the swift passage of time.
> At the top of the Sanxiang post-station, he gazed at the mountain of transcendence,
> And coming back, he composed the tune "Rainbow Skirts and Feather Vestments."

---

[2] The Sanxiang post-station 三鄉驛 is near present-day Yiyang, Henan.

From then on, his heart was fascinated with the Chalcedony
  Pool,
And he was followed by the Three Clarities and Eight
  Phosphors.
One day he rode a white cloud in the sky and went off,
In this world, here remains only the lyrics of "The Autumn
  Wind."[3]

Yishi (Lost History) also has it: Luo Gongyuan served
Emperor Xuanzong at the beginning of the Tianbao Era. On the
fifteenth night of the eighth lunar month, while enjoying viewing
the moon, Luo said to the emperor: "Would Your Majesty follow
me to roam on the moon?" Then he tossed a branch of Osmanthus
into the air, which turned into a bridge, shining like silver. He
invited the emperor to ascend the bridge with him. After walking
for roughly several tens of *li*, they reached a great watchtower.
Gongyuan observed, "This is the Moon Palace." There were fairy
women counted in the hundreds, all wearing loose garments of
white silk and dancing in a spacious courtyard. His Highness
stepped forward and asked, "What tune is this?" The answer was,
"It is the tune 'Rainbow Skirt and Feather Vestments.'" His
Highness secretly memorized the sound of its melody. When the
emperor and Gongyuan returned onto the bridge, and looked
back, the bridge vanished step by step behind them. The next

---

[3]This translation is based on Paul Kroll's translation with minor
modification. Kroll also notes that Yao chi (Chalcedony Pool) is the
Queen Mother of the West's hunt on her cosmic mountain of Kunlun
崑崙. The Three Clarities 三清 refer to the Great Clarity, Highest Clarity
and Jade Clarity in the Daoist Heaven, and the Eight Phosphors, the
bright spirits of the eight directions of space. Kroll also convincingly
associates "the lyrics of the autumn wind" to a poem by Wudi of the
Han dynasty, which also mourns the passage of time. For details, see
Paul Kroll, "Nostalgia and History in Mid-Ninth Century Verse: Cheng
Yŭ's Poem on the 'Chin-Yang Gate,'" *T'oung Pao* 89 (2003): 357–58.

morning, the emperor instructed the court musician to reproduce the sound of that melody, in effect composing the tune of "Rainbow Skirt and Feather Vestments." Because these two accounts above differ, I recorded them both here.) That evening, the emperor presented to Precious Consort golden hairpins and an inlaid box. He came to the consort's dressing-room, and personally placed in the hair on her temples a dangling hair ornament carved out of top-grade gold from the warehouse of Lishui Town. The emperor was extremely pleased [to see the consort wearing this hairpin], and he commented to the attendants of the inner palace: "For me, having Precious Consort Yang with me is like obtaining the most precious treasure." Thus, he composed a tune and named it "Obtaining Treasure," also called "Obtaining *bengzi*."

Before that, at the beginning of the Kaiyuan Era, Emperor Xuanzong had both Gracious Consort Wu and Empress Wang. The empress had no sons. The Gracious Consort, however, begot a son, and was also beautiful. Thus, favored in the harem, she monopolized the emperor's attention. By the thirteenth year [of the Kaiyuan Era] (726), after the empress was demoted, none of the other imperial concubines could compete with Gracious Consort. In the eleventh month of the twenty-first year (733), Consort Wu passed away. Although the imperial harem had many young women from good families, there was no one else who could please the eyes of the emperor. His Highness's heart was filled with sorrow. But now that the emperor had obtained the Precious Consort, he doted on her, even more than he once had on Consort Wu. The Precious Consort had three elder sisters, all fine-looking: plump and voluptuous, tall and tidy. They were especially witty and flirtatious and could interpret the emperor's intentions and cater to his taste. Each time they entered the palace, they never emerged before the shadows on the sundial shifted.

The Precious Consort was called his "wife" in the palace, and the courtesy she received was the same as that of an empress.

On the day she formally had the title Precious Consort conferred upon her, her father Xuanyan was posthumously presented with the title of Governor of Jiyin, and her mother, née Li, was enfeoffed as Lady of Longxi Prefecture. Later, Xuanyan was granted the title of Minister of War, and her mother, Lady of Liang State. Her paternal uncle Xuangui was elevated to President of the Board of Imperial Banquets and received the [honorary] rank of Grand Master of Imperial Entertainments with Silver Seal and Blue Ribbon. Further, her paternal elder cousin Zhao had conferred upon him the title of Vice Director and held several concurrent posts. Additionally, her elder cousin, Xian, held a high position at the imperial court; her younger cousin, Qi, married the Princess Taihua, Gracious Consort Wu's daughter. Because of her mother, the treatment of this princess surpassed that of other princesses. She was presented with a mansion directly connected to the Forbidden City. Since then, the Yang family held sway over the entire empire: every time they had requests, court departments and divisions, prefectures and districts all obeyed with the majesty accorded imperial mandates. Every day, young servants would race down the roads on horseback to bring rare goods from the four regions to their doors.

At that time, An Lushan was Military Commissioner of Fanyang; His Highness called him his "son" and deeply favored him. He often joined the emperor and the consort at the Palace Hall for Casual Affairs for feasting and entertainment. Each time Lushan took his seat, he would not do obeisance to the emperor, but, rather, to the Precious Consort. The emperor turned to him and asked, "Why do you not do obeisance to me, but to my consort? Why is this?" Lushan replied: "Those of us from foreign realms do not know our father, and only know our mother." The emperor laughed and pardoned him. The emperor also ordered those who were younger than Yang Xian to treat Lushan as a sibling. Whenever Lushan came to or left the capital, they would invariably give him welcome or farewell banquets. Although in the beginning their sworn brotherhood was rather deep, they later became formidable adversaries and no longer at all in harmony.

In the seventh month of the fifth year [of Tianbao] (746), the Precious Consort offended the emperor due to her "jealousy and ferociousness." The emperor ordered Gao Lishi to send the consort back in a single carriage to her elder cousin Yang Xian's home. By noon, the emperor was already missing her terribly and could not swallow anything. He would fly into a rage on the slightest provocation. Lishi ascertained the emperor's intentions and asked the emperor if he could bring back the consort. He then sent to the consort clothing and articles suitable for ladies in the court, as well as rice, wheat flour, food and drink from the National Granaries. These goods filled more than a hundred cartloads. At first, the consort's elder sisters and [her elderly cousin] Xian were all terrified and wept together. As the offerings gradually increased and imperial meals also arrived, they were only then slightly pacified and consoled. When the consort had just been sent away, the emperor became listless. Eunuchs who merely quickly passed before his eyes would likely be whipped and flogged. The situation was so tense that some even died from fear. Thus, Lishi requested the emperor to summon the consort back. When it was dark, he opened the gate of Anxing Ward, and led the consort through the residence of Prince of Taihua into the inner palace. At dawn, Xuanzong was greatly pleased to see her when he came to the inner palace. The Precious Consort made an obeisance to him, sobbed, and apologized for her transgressions. The emperor convened miscellaneous performances from the two markets (i.e. the Eastern and Western Markets of Chang'an) to entertain the consort. The consort's sisters all brought forth food and roistered with her. From then on, the imperial favor to the consort deepened daily. None of the other ladies in the harem had an opportunity to obtain the imperial favors anymore.

In the seventh year [of Tianbao] (748), Zhao was further promoted to be Censorate, served as acting Metropolitan Governor and was given the name *Guozhong*. The emperor conferred on the Precious Consort's eldest sister the title of Lady of the Han State; on her third sister, Lady of the Guo State, and on her eighth sister, Lady of the Qin State — all three were enfeoffed on the same day and given cash of 100,000 each month for their rouge and power. However, the Lady of the Guo State did not like to apply rouge and powder. She was confident in her glamor and beauty, and she would often present her face to the emperor in its natural form and without any makeup. At that time, Du Fu composed a poem:

> The Lady of Guo received our lord's graciousness.
> At dawn, she mounted a horse and entered the palace gate.
> Disliking the rouge and powder that spoiled her beauty,
> she lightly brushed her brows to face the most revered man.

The emperor further gave the Lady of the Guo State night-shining pearls, the Lady of the Qin State a seven-leaf crown, and Guozhong a gold thread tent. These were all rare treasures, well demonstrating his favor towards the Yang family. Xian was awarded [the honorary rank of] Grand Master of Imperial Entertainments with Silver Seal and Blue Ribbon, and Director of the Board of Ceremonial towards Foreigners, enjoying the honor of displaying halberds in front of his entourage when going out. He had been especially awarded the title of "Imperial Pillar of the State," and had even received three imperial edicts in one day to summon him to court. Together with Guozhong, the five families [namely, those of the three sisters, the elder brother Xian, and cousin Yang Guozhong] lived in the Xuanyang Ward, with the gates of their splendid mansions wide open. Their mansions were, inappropriately, comparable to the imperial palace in its splendor. Their carts, horses, servants, and chariots were so spectacular that they illuminated the entire capital. They boasted to one another of their pre-eminence and extravagance. Every time they constructed a building, the expenses would exceed ten million in cash. If they saw a mansion built on a grander scale, they would tear down and rebuild their own. Their construction projects were carried on day and night. Imperial meals from the emperor and tributes from outside were all allotted and bestowed upon the five families. Ever since the Kaiyuan era, no family was comparable to the Yang clan in power and splendor.

Every time His Highness went on a journey, he invariably had the Precious Consort accompany him. When the consort was about to mount a horse, Lishi would hold the reins and hand over the whip to her. There were about seven hundred people in the palace who supplied weaving and embroidery for the Precious Consort, and several hundred more carved and molded for celebrations of her birthday and seasonal festivals. Moreover, the emperor ordered prefects from Yang and Yi prefectures to Lingnan to seek rare and novel objects as offerings to the court. Zhang Jiuzhang, Military Commissioner of Lingnan, and Wang Yi, Chief Administrator of Guangling, were both promoted for this reason: the rare objects and unusual clothing they offered to the Precious Consort on Dragon Boat Festival stood above the congratulatory offerings from other prefectures. Jiuzhang was awarded [the honorary rank of] Grand Master of Imperial Entertainments with Silver Seal and Blue Ribbon, and Yi was promoted to be Vice Director of the Ministry of Revenue respectively.

In the second month of the ninth Tianbao year (750), His Highness stayed in his old "Five Princes' Tent" with his brothers, sharing a long pillow and an extra-large quilt. Not long after, the consort stole Prince Ning's purple jade lute and played it. Thus, the poet Zhang You wrote these lines:

> Among pearl blossoms, in a quiet courtyard, where no one can
>   see her,
> she takes Prince Ning's flute and plays it at her leisure.

Because of this, the consort, once again, offended the emperor, and was sent out of the palace. At the time, Ji Wen was on good terms with powerful eunuchs in the palace. Deeply concerned, the consort's brother, Yang Guozhong, sought advice from Ji Wen. Thus, Ji Wen entered the court to memorialize the throne, saying, "The consort is merely a woman without much wisdom or knowledge. She has disobeyed Your Majesty and deserves the penalty of death. Yet, given the fact that she was once highly favored, it is only appropriate she die within the palace walls. Why would Your Majesty begrudge a small space to receive her execution? How can you bear to exhibit her shame to the outside world?" The emperor replied, "I did not employ you, Sir, because of my consort [so you have no obligation to intercede for her]." Earlier, the emperor ordered eunuch Zhang Taoguang to escort the consort back to her brother's residence, where the consort said to Taoguang in tears, "Please kindly help me memorializing the emperor: This concubine deserves to die ten thousand times for her offense. Besides her clothing, everything else was bestowed upon her by the grace of His Majesty. Only her hair and skin were given by her parents. Now she is about to die, she has nothing to thank His Highness but this one gift." With this comment, she drew out a knife, cut off and gave one lock of her hair as her offering to the emperor. Meanwhile, after expelling the consort, His Highness was dejected. When Taoguang came in the palace to recount the consort's words, with her hair hanging over his shoulder, the emperor was startled and compassionate, and he immediately sent Lishi to summon the consort back to the palace.

Since then, the emperor favored her even more deeply. He further appointed Guozhong as Military Commissioner of Jiannan, commanding this region in absentia.

On the night of the Lantern Festival in the tenth Tianbao year (751), the five households of the Yang clan went out to enjoy the spectacle. They competed with Princess Guangning's horse guards to get through the West Market gate. A servant of the Yang clan flourished his whip and accidently hit the princess' clothing, causing her to fall from her horse. The imperial son-in-law Cheng Changyi helped her up, and therefore also received several blows from the whip. The princess memorialized in tears the emperor about this incident. His Highness ordered an immediate execution of the servant and the suspension of the imperial son-in-law Changyi from office, thus not allowing him to attend court assembly, or pay obeisance. From then on, the Yang clan grew more arrogant than ever. They would not be questioned when entering or leaving through the gate of the Forbidden Palace, causing other officials in the capital to look askance at them. A popular proverb at the time goes: "Do not feel saddened when you give birth to a daughter, and do not be overjoyed when you give birth to a son," and continued: "Men are no longer granted a rank of nobility, but girls may become the emperor's consort. See! It is your daughter who became the door lintel of your house [bringing honor and grace to her family]. The hearts of people under heaven were all filled with admiration and envy [of the Yang clan] in this way.

One morning, His Highness went up to the *Qinzheng* (Diligent Administration) Tower and set up music for entertainment. At the time, there was a Madam Wang from the Imperial Music Academy, who could balance a very tall pole of a hundred *chi* on her head with a platform in the shape of the sacred

Mounts Yingzhou and Fangzhang at the top.[4] She could further have a little child hold a red tally, come and go between these two miniature mountains while she herself was dancing below. At the time, a prodigy, Liu Yan, became a Proofreader at the Imperial Library. At the age of ten, he far exceeded others in intelligence. His Highness summoned this boy to the Qinzheng Tower. The Precious Consort placed him on her lap, putting makeup on him, tidying his scarf, and combing his hair. She then asked the boy to compose a poem on Madam Wang's holding the pole on her head. Yan immediately orally composed:

> In front of the Tower a hundred shows are striving for novelty,
> Yet only the tall pole is astounding beyond imagination.
> Who would expect a woman wearing delicate silk to be so
>   strong:
> As if the tall pole is not heavy enough, she adds to its top
>   another man!

This brought down the house — His Highness, Precious Consort, and other attendants all laughed heartily for a long time. Their voices were so loud that they could be heard from outside the tower. The emperor thus ordered an ivory scepter and an embroidered yellow gown for this boy.

On another occasion, His Highness gave a banquet for his brothers at the *Mulan dian* (Magnolias Hall). At the time, magnolias were in full bloom, yet His Highness seemed not in the right mood. Half drunk, the consort rose to dance to the tune "Rainbow Skirt and Feather Vestments," and the emperor was greatly pleased. Only then did he realize that a dance as elegant and smooth as "snow whirled by the driving wind" could be so

---

[4]Together with Mount Penglai 蓬萊, Fangzhang 方丈 and Yingzhou 瀛洲 were believed to be the three sacred mountains in the sea where immortals reside.

powerful as to reverse the rotation of the sky and earth. His Highness once dreamed of ten fairies, and composed a melody titled, "Return of the Purple Clouds." (Emperor Xuanzong once dreamed that more than ten fairies descended from the sky on the clouds, each playing an instrument in midair. The melody was clear and far-reaching — indeed the sound was from the celestial realm. One of the fairies said, "This 'Return of the Purple Cloud' was composed by the immortal, and now it will be passed on to Your Majesty as the orthodox music." His Highness was delighted and accepted it. After he woke up from the dream, the sound of the tune still lingered on. The next morning, he immediately asked people to bring him his jade flute for practicing this melody from memory, and completely mastered the rhythm.) He also dreamed of a dragon king's daughter, and he composed "Riding the Waves." (Emperor Xuanzong was once at the Eastern Capital Luoyang. One night, he dreamed of a girl who was extraordinarily beautiful and resplendent: her hair was in a delicate double-bun style, and she wore a loose garment with wide sleeves. She made an obeisance in front of the emperor's bed. His Highness asked, "Who are you?" She answered, "I, your servant, am the dragon king's daughter from Your Majesty's *Lingbo chi* (the Pond of Wave-Riding). As a matter of fact, I also rendered some service in protecting this palace and escorting Your Majesty. Now that Your Majesty has a clear knowledge of the heavenly music, I beg you to compose one piece for me, which will bring great honor to my clan." In the dream, His Highness, playing a *huqin* (a two-stringed bowed instrument), and combining melodies old and new, composed this "Riding the Waves." The dragon daughter bowed twice before she left. After he woke up, the emperor quickly wrote down the melody. He then gathered his musicians, and he himself played the *pipa* to practice and adapt this melody. After several rehearsals, he summoned his civil and military officials to the palace and played this newly composed melody in front of the

Wave-Riding Pond. Suddenly, waves surged from the pond, and a goddess emerged from in its center. This girl was none other than the one in the emperor's dream. His Highness was greatly pleased and asked his Chief Minister to build a shrine for the dragon daughter on the pond. Each year, he would order the public to offer sacrifice (for the dragon daughter). Once these two pieces of music were completed, the emperor gave them to the disciples of *Yichun Yuan* (Harmonizing with the Spring Court) and *Liyuan* (Pear Garden) as well as his own brothers.[5]

At the time, a female dancer, Xie Aman, had just been presented from Xinfeng to the emperor. She excelled in dancing. Both His Highness and the Precious Consort doted on her, so they kept her in the palace. One time, the emperor arranged a special performance in the Qingyuan Palace Hall, where Prince Ning played the flute; His Highness, the drum; the Consort the *pipa*, and Ma Xianqi the *fangxiang* metallophone; Li Guinian, the Tartar pipe (bamboo wind instrument with a reed mouthpiece); Zhang Yehu *konghou* (a plucked stringed instrument), and He Huaizhi beat time with clappers. They played from morning to noon, indulging in their joyful and harmonious performances. Nobody but the consort's younger sister, Lady of the Qin State, could sit there and enjoy this performance. Afterwards, the emperor playfully remarked, "Aman (His Highness referred to himself as Aman in the palace), as a registered entertainer, had this honor to serve you, Madam. I beg for an embroidered headband.[6] The Lady

---

[5]During Xuanzong's time, *jiaofang* 教坊 (the Court Entertainment Bureau) became the official academy dedicated to singers and housing dancers. Particularly talented women from the outer *jiaofang* would be selected for the *Yichun yuan* 宜春院. *Liyuan* 梨園 was the acting and musical academy during Xuanzong's reign, which later became the emblematic term for the popular entertainments of that reign.

[6]*Chantou*, or the embroidered headband, was often given to a dancer or singer as a reward for an outstanding performance.

of the Qin State said, "How could I, the sister-in-law of the Son of Heaven of our Great Tang, have no money to spare!" With that, she immediately furnished cash of three million for the expenses of this performance show.

Their instruments used in this performance could not have been found elsewhere. A cool breeze passed over them as they started to play, and the sound of their music travelled far beyond the skies. The consort's *pipa* was made of a hard sandalwood from Tibet, brought to the palace as a tribute by Eunuch Bai Jizhen from a mission to Shu. The surface of the wood was fine — as smooth as jade, and as shining and bright as a looking glass. On the *pipa* there was a beautiful gold and scarlet grain that resembled twin-phoenixes. The strings were tribute from Kasmira (in northern India) during the first year of the Yongtai Era (498).[7] They were made of silk and washed with water to become glossy like strings of pearls. The purple jade flute was believed to have once been owned by the Moon Lady Heng'e. An Lushan also presented three hundred wind instruments to the Emperor, all made of fine jade. The princes, princesses, and the consort's sisters all took the Precious Consort as their master and studied *pipa* under her. Each time they learned a melody, they would compete in presenting the consort with expensive gifts. That day, after the performance, the consort said to Xie Aman, "You, poor girl, must be unable to afford any gift to your mentor, so let me give you something instead." She told her maid, Hongtaoniang, to bring a red-jade golden grain arm bracelet. The consort was also good at playing *qing* (a percussion instrument made of stone or jade pieces), with which she was able to produce a crisp sharp sound. She produced

---

[7]Here Yongtai could refer to the reign period of Xiao Luan 蕭鸞 (452–498), Emperor Gaozong 高宗 (r. 494–498) of the Southern Qi 南齊, or the reign period of Li Yu 李豫 (726–779), Emperor Daizong 代宗 (r. 762–779) of the Tang, who succeeded to the throne after Lady Yang's death. If the last, then this must be an anachronism.

many new tunes with the *qing*, and even the professionals in the Court of Imperial Sacrifices and the Imperial Orchestra were no match for the consort. His Highness ordered for her a special *qing* carved out of green jade from Lantian. He also directed his staff to build a wooden frame for the *qing*, with tassels decorated in gold, pearls, and jade, and two cast gold lions as a pedestal. The frame was elaborately painted and decorated, making it without equal at the time.

Early in the Kaiyuan period, gardens in the Forbidden Palace valued *mu shaoyao* (tree peonies), more generally known as *mudan* (peonies) nowadays. (*Records of Flowers and Trees of The Kaiyuan-Tianbao Era* states: "In the Forbidden Palace, *mu shaoyao* were called *mudan*). The emperor obtained several types of these peonies — red-purple, light red, and white and moved them in front of the *Chenxiang ting* (Eaglewood Pavilion) east of the Xingqing Pond. It happened one day the peonies bloomed in a roaring blaze, while His Highness rode his horse, Dazzling White, followed by the consort, on a sedan chair. The emperor ordered his staff to select the best among the students of the Pear Garden and found sixteen musicians. At the head of this group stood Li Guinian, who enjoyed fame in his time as a great singer. With clapper in hand, Li Guinian was about to sing when the emperor asked, "What's the use of these old lyrics in front of these beautiful flowers and in the presence of my Precious Consort?" Thus, he ordered Guinian to bring some royal golden flower writing paper to Li Bai, a Hanlin Academician, and asked Li to compose immediately three verses to the tune of "Qingpingle." As he received this imperial decree, Li Bai's mind was still clouded from last night's heavy drinking, yet he picked up a brush and wrote:

Verse One:
Clouds remind me of her clothes, and flowers her face.

Spring wind caresses the railings of the garden and dew is
  thick on the peonies.
If you cannot find her by the Mountain of Numerous Jewels,
  head for the Jasper Terrace,
you may meet her beneath the moon.

Verse Two:
A branch of red flowers, dews congealed her perfume,
The goddess who came as clouds and rains on Wu Mountain,
  broke her heart in vain.
If I may ask who in the palaces of the Han can be compared to
  her,
It would be the dear Flying Swallow, just decked out in her
  new powder and rouge.[8]

Verse Three:
Famous flowers laugh with the radiant beauty,
  the monarch watches them both with beaming.
The flowers dispel the endless regrets brought by the spring
  wind.
North of the Eaglewood Pavilion, they lean on the railing.[9]

Guinian presented with both of his hands the newly written
verse to Xuanzong, who ordered disciples from the Pear Garden
to set the lyrics to music. While they played the music, the
emperor strongly urged Guinian to sing along with it. The consort
held a crystal glass decorated with seven treasures, drank grape
wine from the West Liangzhou, and enjoyed the lyrics with
gratitude. His Highness accompanied the tune on his jade flute,

---

[8]Zhao Feiyan, Empress Xiaocheng 孝成皇后 of the Han dynasty,
was known for her beauty, dancing and slender build in popular
narratives.

[9]I mainly consulted Elling Eide's translation in Victor Mair, ed., *The
Short Columbia Anthology of Traditional Chinese Literature* (New York:
Columbia University Press, 2000), pp. 147–9.

slowly ending the note of each verse to please her. When she finished her wine, the consort tidied her embroidered scarf and bowed with her palms together twice to the emperor. After that, His Highness placed Li Bai far above his peers in the Hanlin Academy. Gao Lishi, nonetheless, still harbored resentment towards Li Bai since the poet had made Gao take off his boots for him that day [before composing the lyrics]. On another day, when the consort was reciting these verses, Lishi cut in with a jibe: "I thought you would bitterly hate Li, how come you admire him like this?" [Having heard Lishi's false charge,] the consort was astonished and responded, "How could Scholar Li insult me to that extent?" Lishi continued, "He compares you to a Flying Swallow; what is more deprecating?" The consort was swayed. On three occasions His Highness wished to confer upon Li Bai an official title, but eventually had to give it up because of the consort's opposition.

One day, His Highness was reading the "The Unofficial Biography of Emperor Cheng of the Han" in an attached palace of the Hundred Flowers Courtyard. A little later, the consort came. She smoothed the emperor's collar with her hands and asked, "What are you reading?" His Highness replied with a smile, "You'd better not ask, or you will pester me again!" She took the book from him anyway and found the following text:

> When Emperor Cheng of the Han obtained Flying Swallow, she was extremely slim and light, as if she could not bear the wind. Lest she might be blown away, the emperor had a crystal tray made for her. The maids would carry the tray for her to sing and dance upon. Moreover, he built a seven-gem pedestal for her. It was lined with burning incense to [detect] and protect her delicate limbs [from the wind].

His Highness turned to the consort and bantered, "As for you, no strong wind can carry you away." Perhaps because the consort was a little plump, His Highness made fun of her with this remark. The consort replied, "But my dance of 'Rainbow Skirt and Feather Vestments' eclipses all those beauties in the past." His Highness said, "See? I am just joking, and you are not going to be mad, are you? Well, I recall I once had a fine screen. It must still be somewhere, so let me have them find and give it to you as recompense," coaxed the emperor. The screen took its name from the rainbow. It was carved with figurines of great beauties of the past, each about three inches tall. Their jewelry, artware, and clothes were made from an assortment of treasures. The screen, made of crystal, was intricately edged with tortoise shell and horn, and twined with rustling pearls. It was so exquisite that even the most skilled craftsmen could not produce it. This screen was made in response to the order of Emperor Yang of the former Sui dynasty and was later given to Princess Yicheng [as her dowry] and followed her to the realm of the northern "barbarians." In the early years of the Zhenguan Era (627–649), the northern "barbarians" were vanquished, and Empress Xiao was returned with the screen to the "Central States" (*i.e.* the Tang court). Therefore, the emperor was able to give it to his consort.

(When the consort returned home to visit the Duke of the Wei State (*i.e.* her brother, Yang Guozhong), she brought the screen with her and set it on a high tower. Before the consort had time to carry it back to the palace, Guozhong took a nap in the tower one day at noon. As he reached his bed, he saw the screen standing there. Just as he put his head on his pillow, the beauties on the screen suddenly all walked down to the foot of his bed. They began informing him of their sobriquets (literary names) one by one: "I am called 'the person who loves the sound of breaking tabby silk.'"[10] "I am 'the person from Dingtao.'"[11] "'I am 'the one

---

[10]This lady is most likely Meixi 妹喜, the consort of Jie 桀, the last emperor of the Xia dynasty.

who dwelt in a domed tent.'"[12] "I am 'the one in the wine-shop.'"[13]
"I am 'the person who brought down the Kingdom of Wu.'"[14] "I
am 'the one walking on the golden water lily.'"[15] "I am 'the one
from the Peach Blossom Spring.'" [16]"I am 'the one whose tears
spotted the bamboo trees.'" [17] "I am 'the one who served the
Gentlemen of Household for All Purposes.'"[18] "I am 'the one with

---

[11]Lady Qi 戚夫人, the favorite consort of Liu Bang, Emperor Gaozu
of the Han dynasty.

[12]Wang Zhaojun was a beauty from the harem of the Emperor Yuan
of the Han (r. 48–32 BCE). She was chosen as consort for Huhanye, the
chanyu or leader of Xiongnu. "The domed tent," as seen in this sentence,
was traditionally inhabited by these nomadic tribes.

[13]Zhuo Wenjun, who, after she eloped with Sima Xiangru (179–117
BCE), had to sell alcohol in a "wine-shop" to support her family.

[14]Xi Shi 西施, who was sent by her king to seduce an enemy
monarch, King Fuchai of Wu 吳王夫差 (r. 495–473).

[15]This self-identification may refer to Yaoniang 窅娘, a consort of Li
Yu 李煜 (r. 961–976), emperor of the Southern Tang. Yaoniang came from
a humble origin and once picked lotus seed for a living. She was known
for her skillful dancing and reportedly invented the dance of the "golden
lotus"; this sobriquet may also refer to Pan Yuer 潘玉儿, the favorite
consort of Xiao Baojuan 蕭寶卷 (r. 498–501), emperor of the Southern Qi
南齊. Xiao ordered his people to carve golden water lilies and
proclaimed that "water lilies blossom under each of his consort's
graceful steps."

[16]This refers to the female immortal in the legend of Liu Chen and
Ruan Zhao of the later Han.

[17]Ladies of the Xiang, legendary sisters who were married to the
Sage King Shun 舜. After Shun's death, the two ladies wept so copiously
that their tears spotted the bamboo trees along the Xiang river.

[18]This refers to Lady Zhen, wife of Cao Pi (r. 220–226), the first ruler
of the Wei state during the Three Kingdoms Period; Lady Zhen first
married Yuan Xi 袁熙, but after the Yuan clan was defeated, she was
married to Cao Pi, who at the time was serving as Gentlemen of
Household for All Purposes (*wuguan chonglang jiang* 五官中郎將).

smooth and warm skin.'"[19] "I am 'the girl from Cao family who threw herself into the river.'"[20] "I am 'the one without any rivals for whom the emperor burned incense to summon her spirit.'"[21] "I am 'the one picking up the feathers of green birds.'"[22] "I am 'the one who stole the aromatic.'"[23] "I am 'the one who was put in a golden house.'"[24] "I am 'the one who gave away her pendants by the Han River.'"[25] "I am 'the one who becomes clouds in the

---

[19]This most likely refers to Zhao Hede 趙合德, the younger sister of Zhao Feiyan and also a woman greatly favored by Emperor Cheng of the Han (r. 33–7 BCE). See T8.43.

[20]This probably refers to Cao E 曹娥, or Maiden Cao, whose father's boat was swamped by a large wave. Cao E waited for her father many days and eventually drowned herself. Several days later, she was found with her father's body clasped in her arms.

[21]This refers to Lady Li, the favorite consort of Liu Che 劉彻 (156–87 BCE), Emperor Wu of the Han dynasty 漢武帝. Unable to bear the sorrow of the death of Lady Li, the emperor asked his people to recall her soul back to the palace by burning incense.

[22]This allusion's exact reference is unclear, though it is generally believed women would pick up the feathers of green birds to serve as their jewelry during the springtime.

[23]This refers to Jia Wu 賈午 (260–300), who stole the rare aromatic that the emperor had bestowed upon his father. Jia Wu gave the aromatic to her lover Han Shou 韓壽.

[24]This refers to A Jiao 阿嬌, the first wife of Emperor Wu of the Han Dynasty. The emperor swore he would marry A Jiao one day and build a golden house for her while they were both still very young.

[25]This probably refers to a legend in which Zheng Jiaofu 鄭交甫 of the Zhou dynasty once met two goddesses by the Han River. He took delight in them and asked for their pendants. The goddesses took off and gave their pendants to him. Zheng happily accepted their gifts only to see the pedants suddenly disappear just as he took a few steps away from the goddesses.

morning [and passing rain in the evening].'" [26] "I am Dong Shuangcheng."[27] "I am 'the one who turned into mist.'"[28] "I am 'the one who was good at painting long eyebrows.'" [29] "I am 'the one who played the pipes.'"[30] "I was 'the one who once laughed at a cripple.'"[31] "I was 'the one who was trapped in Gaixia.'"[32] "I am

---

[26]This refers to the goddess of Mount Wu, who had a romantic relationship with the King of Chu when he roamed the region. She later told the king upon her returning to Mount Wu that she lived on the sunlit side of the mountain. At dawn she becomes morning clouds, and in the evening, appears as passing rain.

[27]Dong was known as an attendant of Xiwangmu, the legendary Queen Mother of the West.

[28]This refers to Ziyu 紫玉, the daughter of the King of Wu 吳王 during the Spring and Autumn period (722–468 BCE), who fell in love with Han Zhong 韓重 and pledged to marry him. Her father did not approve, however, and Ziyu died of grief.

[29]This refers to Wu Jiangxian 吳絳仙, a consort of Emperor Yang of the Sui (r. 604–618), known for her eyebrow makeup. Since she enjoyed the emperor's favor, the other ladies in the imperial harem all followed her style.

[30]Possibly, it refers to Nongyu, one of Duke Mu of Qin's (682–621 BCE) daughters who fell in love with Xiao Shi, a master of the pipes. It was said that Xiao Shi taught Nongyu birdcalls and later drew the auspicious phoenix. It was said that, years later, the couple flew off with the phoenixes.

[31]This refers to a concubine of Lord Pingyuan 平原君 of Zhao in the Warring States period (403–221 BCE), who was known for his appreciation of highly talented men. It was said that one of his concubines once laughed at a cripple. On account of this comment, the lord beheaded her to show that he valued talents far more than sensual beauty.

[32]This possibly refers to Consort Yu 虞姬, the favorite concubine of Xiang Yu (232–202 BCE). Consort Yu committed suicide at Gaixia 垓下 to demonstrate her loyalty to her lord.

Xu Feiqiong."[33] "I am Zhao Feiyan."[34] "I am 'the one who resided in the Garden of the Golden Valley.'"[35] "I am 'the one with beautiful temple hair.'"[36] "I am 'the one with glossy hair.'"[37] "I am Xue Yelai."[38] "I am 'the one who resided in the Jieqi Pavilion.'" "I am 'the one who resided in the Linchun Pavilion.'"[39] "I am the woman from Fufeng."[40]

Although Guozhong's eyes were wide open and clearly saw all that was happening in front of him, he could not move his

---

[33]Xu was also an attendant of Xiwagmu, mentioned above.

[34]See note 43 above.

[35]This refers to Lüzhu, the favorite concubine of Shi Chong (249–300), a wealthy man in the Western Jin 西晉. When Sun Xiu 孫秀 sent troops to seize Lüzhu, she leapt to her death from a high tower in the "Garden of the Golden Valley."

[36]This perhaps refers to Wei Zifu 衛子夫, the second empress of Emperor Wu of the Han dynasty.

[37]This most likely refers to Lady Li, the younger sister of Li Shi 李勢 (r. 343–347), the last ruler of Shu 蜀. When Huan Wen 桓溫 conquered Shu, he took Lady Li as a concubine and treated her with great favor. It was said that Huan's wife, the Princess of Nankang 南康, decided to kill Lady Li. Yet, when the princess arrived, she saw Lady Li combing her hair and was deeply touched by her beauty. She instead befriended Lady Li.

[38]Xue Yelai 薛夜來, or Xue Lingyun 薛靈芸, was Cao Pi's 曹丕 favorite concubine, known for her beauty and needlework.

[39]The Jieqi Pavilion 結綺閣 and the Linchun Pavilion 臨春閣, together with the Wangxian Pavilion 望仙閣 were all built by Chen Shubao 陳叔寶 (r. 583–589), the last lord of the Chen dynasty, for his favorite consorts — Zhang Lihua 張麗華, Consort Kong 孔 and Consort Gong 龔.

[40]This might refer to the female historian, Ban Zhao 班昭 (45?–117?), or Meng Guang 孟光, the wife of Liang Hong 梁鴻 (23–220). They both came from Fufeng 扶風. Alternatively, the term *fufeng* may also mean a delicate lady who moves like "a pliant willow swaying in the wind" 弱柳 扶風.

body, nor could he speak. These beautiful women all found something to sit on and sat in a row. Shortly thereafter, about ten courtesans, all slim-waisted, came forward and said to him: "We are 'stepping and singing women' from the state of Chu." With that said, they then stood arm in arm and started to sing: "The three lotuses [on the screen] were no other than us, (the screen) was built by the elder Yang (*i.e.* Emperor Yang of the Sui dynasty), now possessed by the younger Yang (*i.e.* Consort Yang)." Then another two or three courtesans came forward and announced: "We are the bow-waist dancing women from the Chu Palace.[41] Didn't you see there is a line in the unofficial preface to the *Chuci* that reads: 'Her poise is charming, her bearing graceful, just like a flower; her waist bends like a bow, and her skin shines like jade'? With these words, each of these dancing ladies came to offer their specific skills. When their performance ended, they returned to the screen one by one." It was not until then that Guozhong woke up. Terrified, he hurried downstairs and ordered his staff people to immediately put away and lock up the screen. Having heard about this incident, the Precious Consort decided she, too, would not see the screen again. The screen survived the An Lushan Rebellion (755–763) and found its way into the household of Chief Minister Yuan Zai (713–777). Since then, however, no one knows its whereabouts.)

Note: I am indebted to Professor Zhenjun Zhang, Dr. Chen Wu, and Mr. Charles Rippin for their gracious help and insightful comments for corrections and improvement. I would also like to thank Mr. Yibing Zuo of Peking University for providing helpful references to various terms and allusions.

---

[41]*Gongyao* 弓腰, literally, "bow-waist," is most likely a highly skilled movement in which the dancer bends her head back so that her hair touches the ground and her bent waist looks just like a bow.

楊太真外傳（上）

樂史

　　楊貴妃，小字玉環，弘農華陰人也。後徙居蒲州永樂之獨頭村。高祖令本，金州刺史。父玄琰，蜀州司戶。貴妃生於蜀。嘗誤墜池中，後人呼爲落妃池。池在導江縣前。（亦如王昭君生於峽州，今有昭君村；綠珠生於白州，今有綠珠江。）妃早孤，養於叔父河南府士曹玄璬家。開元二十二年十一月，歸於壽邸。二十八年十月，玄宗幸温泉宮（自天寶六載十月，復改爲華清宮），使高力士取楊氏女於壽邸，度爲女道士，號太真，住內太真宮。天寶四載七月，册左衛中郎將韋昭訓女配壽邸。是月，於鳳凰園册太真宮女道士楊氏爲貴妃，半后服用。

　　進見之日，奏《霓裳羽衣曲》。（《霓裳羽衣曲》者，是玄宗登三鄉驛，望女几山所作也。故劉禹錫詩有云：伏覩玄宗皇帝《望女几山》詩，小臣斐然有感：

> “開元天子萬事足，惟惜當時光景促。
> 三鄉驛上望仙山，歸作《霓裳羽衣曲》。
> 仙心從此在瑤池，三清八景相追隨。
> 天上忽乘白雲去，世間空有秋風詞。”

　　又《逸史》云：“羅公遠天寶初侍玄宗，八月十五日夜，宮中翫月，曰：‘陛下能從臣月中游乎？’乃取一枝桂，向空擲之，化爲一橋，其色如銀。請上同登，約行數十里，遂至大城闕。公遠曰：‘此月宮也。’有仙女數百，素練寬衣，舞於廣庭。上前問曰：‘此何曲也？’曰：‘《霓裳羽衣》也。’上密記其聲調，遂回橋，却顧，隨步而滅。且諭伶官，象其聲調，作《霓裳羽衣曲》。”以

635

二説不同，乃備録於此。)是夕，授金釵鈿合。上又自執麗水鎮庫紫磨金琢成步摇，至粧閣，親與插鬢。上喜甚，謂後宫人曰："朕得楊貴妃，如得至寶也。"乃製曲子曰《得寶子》，又曰《得鞛(方孔反)子》。

先是，開元初，玄宗有武惠妃、王皇后。后無子。妃生子，又美麗，寵傾後宫。至十三年，皇后廢，妃嬪無得與惠妃比。二十一年十一月，惠妃即世。後庭雖有良家子，無悦上目者，上心凄然。至是得貴妃，又寵甚於惠妃。有姊三人，皆豐碩修整，工於謔浪，巧會旨趣，每入宫中，移晷方出。宫中呼貴妃爲娘子，禮數同於皇后。

册妃日贈其父玄琰濟陰太守，母李氏隴西郡夫人。又贈玄琰兵部尚書，李氏涼國夫人。叔玄珪爲光禄卿，銀青光禄大夫。再從兄釗拜爲侍郎，兼數使。兄銛又居朝列。堂弟錡尚太華公主，是武惠妃生，以母見遇過於諸女，賜第連於宫禁。自此楊氏權傾天下，每有囑請，臺省府縣，若奉詔勑。四方奇貨，僮僕駞馬，日輸其門。

時安禄山爲范陽節度，恩遇最深，上呼之爲兒。嘗於便殿與貴妃同宴樂，禄山每就坐，不拜上而拜貴妃。上顧而問之："胡不拜我而拜妃子？意者何也？"禄山奏云："胡家不知其父，只知其母。"上笑而赦之。又命楊銛以下，約禄山爲兄弟姊妹，往來必相宴餞。初雖結義頗深，後亦權敵，不叶。

五載七月，妃子以妬悍忤旨。乘單車，令高力士送還楊銛宅。及亭午，上思之不食，舉動發怒。力士探旨，奏請載還，送院中宫人衣物及司農米麪酒饌百餘車。諸姊及銛初則懼禍聚哭，及恩賜浸廣，御饌兼至，乃稍寬慰。妃初出，上無聊，中官趨過者，或笞撻之，至有驚怖而亡者。力士因請就召，既夜，遂開安興坊，從太華宅以入。及曉，玄宗見之内殿，大悦。貴妃拜泣謝過。因召兩市雜戲，以娱貴妃，貴妃諸姊進食作樂。自兹恩遇日深，後宫無得進幸矣。

七載，加釗御史大夫、權京兆尹，賜名國忠。封大姨爲韓國夫人，三姨爲虢國夫人，八姨爲秦國夫人。同日拜命，皆月給錢十萬，爲脂粉之資。然虢國不施粧粉，自衒美艷，常素面朝天。當時杜甫有詩云：

"虢國夫人承主恩，平明上馬入宫門。
却嫌脂粉涴顏色，淡掃娥眉朝至尊。"

又賜虢國照夜璣，秦國七葉冠，國忠鏒子帳，蓋希代之珍，其恩寵如此。銛授銀青光禄大夫、鴻臚卿，列棨戟，特授上柱國，一日三詔。與國忠五家於宣陽里，甲第洞開，僭擬宮掖，車馬僕從，照耀京邑。遞相誇尚，每造一堂，費逾千萬計，見制度宏壯於己者，則毀之復造，土木之工，不捨晝夜。上賜御食，及外方進獻，皆頒賜五宅。開元已來，豪貴榮盛，未之比也。

上起動必與貴妃同行，將乘馬，則力士執轡授鞭。宮中掌貴妃刺繡織錦七百人，雕鏤器物又數百人，供生日及時節慶。續命楊益往嶺南。長吏日求新奇以進奉。嶺南節度張九章，廣陵長史王翼，以端午進貴妃珍玩衣服，異於他郡，九章加銀青光禄大夫，翼擢爲户部侍郎。

九載二月，上舊置五王帳，長枕大被，與兄弟共處其間。妃子無何竊寧王紫玉笛吹。故詩人張祜詩云："梨花静院無人見，閑把寧王玉笛吹。"因此又忤旨，放出。時吉温多與中貴人善，國忠懼，請計於温。遂入奏曰："妃，婦人，無智識。有忤聖顔，罪當死。既嘗蒙恩寵，只合死於宮中。陛下何惜一席之地，使其就戮？安忍取辱於外乎？"上曰："朕用卿，蓋不緣妃也。"初，令中使張韜光送妃至宅，妃泣謂韜光曰："請奏：妾罪合萬死。衣服之外，皆聖恩所賜，唯髮膚是父母所生。今當即死，無以謝上。"乃引刀剪其髮一繚，附韜光以獻。妃既出，上憮然。至是，韜光以髮搭於肩上以奏，上大驚惋，遽使力士就召以歸，自後益嬖焉。又加國忠遥領劍南節度使。

十載上元節，楊氏五宅夜遊，遂與廣寧公主騎從爭西市門。楊氏奴揮鞭誤及公主衣，公主墮馬。駙馬程昌裔扶公主，因及數撾。公主泣奏之，上令決殺楊家奴一人，昌裔停官，不許朝謁。於是楊家轉橫，出入禁門不問，京師長吏，爲之側目。故當時謡曰："生女勿悲酸，生男勿喜歡。"又曰："男不封侯女作妃，君看女却是門楣。"其天下人心羡慕如此。

上一旦御勤政樓，大張聲樂。時教坊有王大娘，善戴百尺竿，上施木山，狀瀛洲、方丈，令小兒持絳節，出入其間，而舞不輟。時劉晏以神童爲祕書省正字，十歲，惠悟過人。上召於樓中，貴妃坐於膝上，爲施粉黛，與之巾櫛。貴妃令詠王大娘戴竿，晏應聲曰："樓前百戲競争新，唯有長竿妙入神。誰謂綺羅翻有力，猶自嫌輕更著人。"上與妃及嬪御皆歡笑移時，聲聞于外，因命牙笏、黄紋袍賜之。

上又宴諸王於木蘭殿，時木蘭花發，皇情不悦。妃醉中舞《霓裳羽衣》一曲，天顏大悦，方知迴雪流風，可以迴天轉地。上嘗夢十仙子，乃製《紫雲迴》（玄宗嘗夢仙子十餘輩，御卿雲而下，各執樂器，懸奏之。曲度清越，真仙府之音。有一仙人曰：“此神仙《紫雲迴》。今傳受陛下，爲正始之音。”上喜而傳受。寤後，餘響猶在。旦，命玉笛習之，盡得其節奏也。）并夢龍女，又製《凌波曲》。（玄宗在東都，夢一女，容貌艷異，梳交心髻，大袖寬衣，拜於床前。上問：“汝何人？”曰：“妾是陛下凌波池中龍女。衛宮護駕，妾實有功。今陛下洞曉鈞天之音，乞賜一曲，以光族類。”上於夢中爲鼓胡琴，拾新舊之曲聲，爲《凌波曲》。龍女再拜而去。及覺，盡記之。會禁樂，自御琵琶，習而翻之。與文武臣僚，於凌波宮臨池奏新曲，池中波濤湧起，復有神女出池心，乃所夢之女也。上大悦，語於宰相，因於池上置廟，每歲命祀之。）二曲既成，遂賜宜春院及梨園弟子并諸王。

時新豐初進女伶謝阿蠻，善舞。上與妃子鍾念，因而受焉。就按於清元小殿，寧王吹玉笛，上羯鼓，妃琵琶，馬仙期方響，李龜年觱篥，張野狐箜篌，賀懷智拍。自旦至午，歡洽異常。時唯妃女弟秦國夫人端坐觀之。曲罷，上戲曰：“阿瞞（上在禁中，多自稱也），樂籍，今日幸得供養夫人。請一纏頭！”秦國曰：“豈有大唐天子阿姨，無錢用耶？”遂出三百萬爲一局焉。

樂器皆非世有者，才奏而清風習習，聲出天表。妃子琵琶邏逤檀，寺人白季貞使蜀還獻。其木溫潤如玉，光耀可鑒，有金縷紅文，蹙成雙鳳。絃乃末訶彌羅國永泰元年所貢者，渌水蠶絲也，光瑩如貫珠瑟瑟。紫玉笛乃姮娥所得也。禄山進三百事管色，俱用媚玉爲之。諸王，郡主，妃之姊妹，皆師妃，爲琵琶弟子，每一曲徹，廣有獻遺。妃子是日問阿蠻曰：“爾貧，無可獻師長，待我與爾爲。”命侍兒紅桃娘取紅粟玉臂支賜阿蠻。妃善擊磬，拊搏之音泠泠然，多新聲，雖太常梨園之妓，莫能及之。上命採藍田緑玉，琢成磬。上方造簨，流蘇之屬，以金鈿珠翠飾之，鑄金爲二獅子，以爲跌，綵繪縟麗，一時無比。

先，開元中，禁中重木芍藥，即今牡丹（《開元天寶花木記》云：“禁中呼木芍藥爲牡丹也”）。得數本紅紫淺紅通白者，上因移植於興慶池東沉香亭前。會花方繁開，上乘照夜白，妃以步輦從。詔選梨園弟子中尤者，得樂十六色。李龜年以歌擅一時之名，手捧檀板，押衆樂前，將欲歌之。上曰：“賞名花，對妃子，焉用舊樂

詞爲？"遽命龜年持金花牋，宣賜翰林學士李白立進《清平樂詞》
三篇。承旨，猶苦宿醒，因援筆賦之。第一首：

"雲想衣裳花想容，春風拂檻露華濃。
若非羣玉山頭見，會向瑤臺月下逢。"

第二首：

"一枝紅艷露凝香，雲雨巫山枉斷腸。
借問漢宮誰得似？可憐飛燕倚新粧。"

第三首：

"名花傾國兩相歡，長得君王帶笑看。
解釋春風無限恨，沉香亭北倚欄干。"

龜年捧詞進，上命梨園弟子略約詞調，撫絲竹，遂促龜年以歌。
妃持玻璃七寶杯，酌西涼州葡萄酒，笑領歌，意甚厚。上因調玉笛
以倚曲，每曲遍將換，則遲其聲以媚之。妃飲罷，斂繡巾再拜。上
自是顧李翰林尤異於他學士。會力士終以脫靴爲恥，異日，妃重吟
前詞，力士戲曰："始爲妃子怨李白深入骨髓，何翻拳拳如是耶？"
妃子驚曰："何學士能辱人如斯？"力士曰："以飛燕指妃子，賤
之甚矣。"妃深然之。上嘗三欲命李白官，卒爲宮中所捍而止。
上在百花院便殿，因覽《漢成帝內傳》，時妃子後至，以手整
上衣領，曰："看何文書？"上笑曰："莫問。知則又殢人。"覓
去，乃是："漢成帝獲飛燕，身輕欲不勝風。恐其飄蕩，帝爲造水
晶盤，令宮人掌之而歌舞。又製七寶避風臺，間以諸香，安於上，
恐其四肢不禁"也。上又曰："爾則任風吹多少。"蓋妃微有肌也，
故上有此語戲妃。妃曰："《霓裳羽衣》一曲，可掩前古。"上曰：
"我纔弄，爾便欲嗔乎？憶有一屏風，合在，待訪得，以賜爾。"
屏風乃虹霓爲名，雕刻前代美人之形，可長三寸許。其間服玩之器、
衣服，皆用衆寶雜厠而成。水精爲地，外以玳瑁、水犀爲押，絡以
珍珠瑟瑟。間綴精妙，迨非人力所製。此乃隋文帝所造，賜義成公
主，隨在北胡。貞觀初，滅胡，與蕭后同歸中國，因而賜焉。
（妃歸衛公家，遂持去。安於高樓上，未及將歸。國忠日午偃
息樓上，至牀，覿屏風在焉。纔就枕，而屏風諸女悉皆下牀前，各

通所號，曰："裂繒人也。""定陶人也。""穹廬人也。"
"當壚人也。""亡吳人也。""步蓮人也。""桃源人也。"
"班竹人也。""奉五官人也。""溫肌人也。""曹氏投波人
也。""吳宮無雙返香人也。""拾翠人也。""竊香人也。"
"金屋人也。""解佩人也。""爲雲人也。""董雙成也。"
"爲煙人也。""畫眉人也。""吹簫人也。""笑躄人也。"
"垓中人也。""許飛瓊也。""趙飛燕也。""金谷人也。"
"小鬟人也。""光髮人也。""薛夜來也。""結綺人也。"
"臨春閣人也。""扶風女也。"國忠雖開目，歷歷見之，而身體
不能動，口不能發聲。諸女各以物列坐。俄有纖腰妓人近十餘輩，
曰："楚章華踏謠娘也。"迺連臂而歌之，曰："三朵芙蓉是我流，
大楊造得小楊收。"復有二三妓，又曰："楚宮弓腰也。何不見
《楚辭別序》云'婷約花態，弓身玉肌'？"俄而遞爲本藝。將呈
訖，一一復歸屏上。國忠方醒，惶懼甚，遽走下樓，急令封鐍之。
貴妃知之，亦不欲見焉。祿山亂後，其物猶存。在宰相元載家，自
後不知所在。）

Tale 7.41

Unofficial Biography of Yang the Grand Verity (B)

By Yue Shi
Translated by Chen Wu

At the end of the Kaiyuan Era, Jiangling[1] had presented milky tangerines as a tribute to the court. His Highness had ten of them planted in the Penglai Palace. When it came to the ninth lunar month in the autumn of the tenth year of the Tianbao Era (751), the trees yielded fruit. Emperor Xuanzong summoned his ministers and bestowed the tangerines upon them, saying, "Not long ago I had several tangerine trees planted in the palace grounds. This autumn they yielded over a hundred and fifty tangerines, which taste no different than those presented from Jiangnan or through the road from Shu. This indeed can be regarded as something special." The ministers submitted a memorial and congratulated him, "We humbly reckoned that those nurtured by Heaven could not change their constant nature. If events unprecedented since ancient times occur, then they can be said to have reacted to something in an unusual way. Thus we know that when the sage takes charge of things, he allows [nature's] primordial *qi* to spread peacefully and the Great Way to

---

[1]Jiangling 江陵 is located in modern Jingzhou in Hubei Province.

operate with the right timing. In this way, various aspects can be coordinated and harmonized. As for the growing of tangerines and pomelos, their different names in the north and south are actually due to nature's original endowment — not because of the change of *yin/yang*. Your Majesty's non-interfering governance and purifying principles unite all under Heaven as one family. Rain and dew sprinkle evenly, and all get moistened in different Heavenly districts. Grass and trees have their nature, secretly interconnecting with one another through earthly vapor. As a result, this precious fruit grown beyond the Yangtze River has its good harvest within the royal garden. Their green stems are covered with frost; their fragrance permeates the gorgeous palace; their golden skin reflects the sunlight; and their color beautifies the glowing red court." Then Emperor Xuanzong had the tangerines distributed to and bestowed upon the great ministers. There was also a "fruit of concordant joy" (i.e. a twin tangerine). His Highness and the consort held and played with it together. His Highness said, "This fruit seems to know people's minds. You and I are essentially one body, so we have this concordant joy." Thereupon, they sat close to each other and ate the fruit together, and the emperor ordered their images to be painted, hoping it would be passed down to later generations.

The consort was born in Shu and had a craving for lychees. Lychees from the Southern Seas were better than those from Shu, and thus every year they were presented to the palace, delivered by post horses. However, lychees ripen only in hot summer weather and lose their flavor overnight. People of later generations had no way of knowing this fact. His Highness was once playing a dice game with the consort. He was about to lose and only throwing double four dots would turn the tables for him. He kept shouting as the dice rolled — and they settled on the double four dots. Following this he ordered Gao Lishi to bestow red color on the four dots, and since then this custom has never changed. Guangnan[2] presented a white parrot that had a clear knowledge of words and was called "Snow-Coated Maiden." One morning, the bird flew onto the consort's dressing table and spoke to itself, "The Snow-Coated Maiden was struck by a ferocious bird in her dream last night." His Highness ordered the consort to teach the parrot the "Heart Sutra" (Prajñāpāramitāhṛdaya Sutra) which the parrot learnt by heart and was able to recite fluently. Later on, His Highness and the consort went on an excursion to another palace. They brought the Snow-Coated Maiden and placed it on the pole of the sedan chair. They saw a hawk swoop down and strike the parrot to death. His Highness and the consort sighed for a long time. Then they had the bird buried in a grave in the imperial garden and named it the "Parrot's Mound." Once Vietnam presented to the court "dragon camphor" as a tribute. The camphor had the shape of cicada silkworm and numbered fifty pieces. The Persians claimed that this "dragon camphor" was produced only by the knots of aged camphor trees. People in the imperial palace called it the "auspicious dragon camphor." His Highness bestowed ten pieces of the dragon camphor upon the consort. The consort secretly sent bright camel emissaries (The bright camel emissaries had fur under their bellies, which could be luminous in the night. They could run five hundred *li* per day) to carry three pieces as a gift to An Lushan. The consort also often gave An Lushan gold-inlaid army appliances, jade cases, and gold-inlaid iron-coated bowls.

In the eleventh year of the Tianbao Era (752), Li Linfu died. Emperor Xuanzong then appointed Yang Guozhong as his Chief Minister, and he held over forty other positions as well. In the twelfth year of the Tianbao Era (753), Yang Guozhong was granted the title Minister of Works. His eldest son, Yang Xuan,

---

[2]Guangnan 廣南 is located in the northeastern region of modern Wenshanzhou 文山州 in Yunnan Province.

first married Commandery Princess Yanhe, and then was appointed the Grand Master of Imperial Entertainments with Silver Seal and Blue Ribbon, Chamberlain for Ceremonials, and concurrently the Vice Director of the Ministry of Revenue. His youngest son, Yang Fei, married Princess Wanchun. The consort's cousin, Yang Jian, who was the Vice Director of the Palace Library, married Commandery Princess Chengrong. Because there was one Precious Consort, the Yang family married two Princesses and three Commandery Princesses, and there were thus three entitled Ladies. In the thirteenth year (754), the consort's father, Yang Xuanyan, was awarded the posthumous titles of Defender in Chief and Duke of Qi State. Her mother was named again Lady of Liang State. The government built a memorial temple for her parents, and His Highness drafted the tablet inscription and handwrote it. The consort's uncle, Yang Xuangui, was also appointed the Imperial Secretary of the Ministry of Works. The daughter of Cui Xun, Lady of Han State's husband and the Vice Director of the Palace Library, was selected as Emperor Daizong's (r. 762–779) consort. Pei Hui, Lady of Guo State's son, married Emperor Daizong's daughter, Princess Yanguang. The daughter of Lady of Guo became the daughter-in-law of the resigned emperor.[3] Liu Jun, the son of Lady of Qin State and her husband Liu Cheng, married District Princess Changqing. Liu Cheng's younger brother Liu Tan married Emperor Suzong's daughter, Princess Hezheng.

Every winter in the tenth lunar month, His Highness would grace the Huaqing Palace with his imperial presence and often spend the entire winter there before he made his way back to the palace [in the capital]. Whenever he went, he would ride with the consort in the same carriage. The Duanzheng Tower (Tower of

---

[3] Here the resigned emperor refers to Li Xian 李憲 (679–742), Emperor Xuanzong's elder brother.

Uprightness and Integrity) was within the Huaqing Palace, and it was the place where the Precious Consort washed and dressed herself. There was also the Lianhua Thermae (Thermae of Lotus Flowers), and it was at the location where the Precious Consort took her bath. Yang Guozhong's imperially bestowed residence was on the south side of the east palace gate, opposite to Lady of Guo State's residence. The rafters and ridgepoles of the residences of the Lady of Han State and Lady of Qin State adjoined one another. Whenever His Highness graced one of these residences with his imperial presence, he would always visit and bestow banquets and music on all five families. When they escorted [the imperial carriage], each family would send out a line of honored guards dressed in uniforms of the same color. The colors of the five family escort teams reflected upon each other, as if hundreds of flowers were in full bloom. [After they had passed], their left-behind hairpins, fallen shoes, turquoise gems, pearls and jade glittered on the road, and these could be collected by the handfuls. Once a person bent over to peek into the carriage, the fragrance lingered around him for several days. Over a thousand camels and horses were led by the flags and tallies of the honored guards from the Jiannan Military Commissioner. When the escorts set out, there would be a farewell feast; when they returned, there would be a reception banquet. Valuable curios, dogs, and horses came as gifts from near and afar. Eunuchs and singing girls formed an endless stream on the road.

After Lady of Qin State passed away first, Lady of Guo State, Lady of Han State, and Yang Guozhong flourished. Also, Lady of Guo State had an affair with Yang Guozhong. They broke all the rules and were undisciplined. Whenever they entered the court to pay respect to the emperor, Yang Guozhong, Lady of Han State, and Lady of Guo State harnessed their horses side by side, brandished their whips and galloped around, chatting and joking [all the way]. Their entourage and serving maids rode over a hundred horses and held so many candles that the night was lit up like daytime. They were gaily dressed in stunning clothes and did not bother to hide themselves [from the public]. The crowd of spectators stood around the street like a wall, all exclaiming and feeling astonished. All marriages in the household of the ten princes needed to be arranged by Lady of Han State and Lady of Guo State, who acted as go-betweens and collected one thousand strings of cash from each person. Only then did His Highness approve the marriage.

On the first day of the sixth lunar month in the fourteenth Tiaobao year (755), His Highness graced the Huaqing Palace with his imperial presence. It was the Precious Consort's birthday. He ordered the Minor Group Orchestra (The so-called "Minor Group" was organized by the Regulation Department of the Pear Garden. There were thirty people in total, all under fifteen years of age) to perform a new tune in the Changsheng Palace Hall (Palace Hall of Eternal Life). The music did not have a title yet, and just then a tribute of lychees was presented from the Southern Seas to the court, so they named the tune "Aroma of Lychee." All the attendants cheered, and their loud applause shook the mountains and valleys [surrounding the Huaqing Palace].

In the eleventh lunar month of that same year, An Lushan rebelled in Youling.[4] (An Lushan, originally named Ya Luoshan, was a hybrid barbarian. His mother used to be a witch. Lushan became increasingly overweight in his later years. His belly hung over his knees. He weighed himself at three hundred and fifty catties. [Yet when] he danced the Sogdian Whirl in front of His Highness, [his dance steps] were as fast as a gust of wind. Once His Highness had golden-cockerel screens set up throughout the east wing room of the Qinzheng Tower and placed a large couch with the curtain scrolled up. He ordered Lushan to sit on the

---

[4]Youling 幽陵 is located within the modern Beijing area.

couch. Acrobatics were performed downstairs while His Highness and Lushan watched together on the tower. The future Emperor Suzong (r. 756–762) remonstrated, "Throughout history, I have never heard of any subject sitting together with his sovereign to watch acrobatics." His Highness said, "He has an unusual appearance. I do this because I want to exorcise his potential harm." On another occasion, His Highness and Lushan were enjoying together an evening feast. An Lushan lay down drunkenly and was transformed into a pig but with a dragon's head. The attendants immediately reported this spectacle to His Highness, who commented, "He is just a piggish dragon and can do nothing [harmful]." He didn't kill Lushan in the end, and the latter eventually drove the central plains into disorder.) An Lushan [rebelled] under the pretext of eradicating Yang Guozhong. People all said it was the fault of Yang Guozhong, Lady of Guo State, and the Precious Consort, but none dared to report this to His Highness. His Highness intended the Crown Prince to take charge of the national administrations, probably planning to pass on the power to his son and lead the troops into battle [to quell the rebellion] himself. He discussed this plan with Yang Guozhong, who was extremely terrified. Guozhong returned home and told his sisters, saying, "We are on the verge of death. Now that the East Palace will take charge of the national administrations, you ladies and I will all lose our lives." The Yang sisters cried out to the Precious Consort and the consort held a piece of dirt in her mouth and pleaded on their behalf to Emperor Xuanzong. Only then was the plan put off.

In the sixth lunar month of the fifteenth Tianbao year (756), Tongguan Pass fell to the rebels. His Highness made his way to Ba Shu, and the Precious Consort followed. When they reached the

Mawei Post Station,[5] Chen Xuanli, Commander on the Right of the Militant as Dragon Army, fearing the army's revolt, declared to his soldiers, "Now the whole world has fallen apart, and the imperial authority is shaken. Didn't Yang Guozhong's exploitation of common people bring about this bad situation? If we don't execute him, how could we then apologize for the offence to the world?" The public responded, "We have been yearning for this for a long time." At that time, an ambassador from Tibet happened to stop Yang Guozhong at the post station gate to discuss matters with him, and the soldiers shouted, "Yang Guozhong is plotting treason with Tibetans!" The soldiers then besieged the post station and killed Yang Guozhong, his son Yang Xuan, and several others. (Yang Guozhong's previous name was Yang Zhao. He was originally Zhang Yizhi's son. During the Tianshou Era (690–692), Yizhi enjoyed incomparable imperial favor. After he returned to his personal residence, the imperial decree always commanded him to stay in the tower. Moreover, the ladder to his room was removed, and the tower was enclosed by thistles and thorns, with no female servants attending him. But his mother was afraid the Zhang family might have no offspring, so she hid a serving maid named Pin Shu between the double walls of the tower. Thereafter, the maid became pregnant and bore Yang Guozhong. She was later married into the Yang family.)

His Highness had no choice but to come out to the entrance of the post station and reward the Six Armies. The Six Armies refused to raise the siege. His Highness turned to his attendants and asked why. Gao Lishi replied, "Yang Guozhong committed a crime, so these generals punished him. The Precious Consort is Yang Guozhong's sister, and she still remains at Your Majesty's side. How can the ministers be free of fear and concern? We beg

---

[5]Mawei 馬嵬 is located about 50 kilometers north of modern Xi'an in Shaanxi Province.

Your Majesty to consider this fact and make a decision."
(According to another edition, [The soldiers said,] "The root of the
thief is still here. How do we dare dissolve?" They were actually
scolding the Precious Consort.) His Highness walked back into the
post station. There was a small lane next to the post station gate.
His Highness could not bear to go back to his temporary palace,
so he stood alone in the lane, leaning on a stick and bending his
head on his chest. The sage emperor felt dizzy and kept silent, and
for a long time he did not move forward. Wei E, the Metropolitan
Record Keeper (He was Wei Jiansu's son), remonstrated, "We beg
Your Majesty to give up personal affection and bear the pain to
make a decision, so as to bring peace to the nation." After a short
while, His Highness entered the temporary palace. With his hand
on the consort's back, he gently took her out through the gate of
the hall, reached the horse track before the north wall, bid her
farewell and sent Gao Lishi to end her life. Choking with tears in
her throat, the consort was devastated with grief when she made
this speech. She said, "I hope Your Majesty will take good care of
yourself. I have indeed failed to live up to the expectations of the
nation and have no regrets that I shall die. I beg to be allowed to
pay my respects to the Buddha." The emperor replied, "I hope
you will be reincarnated to a good place in your next life." Then
Gao Lishi strangled her under a pear tree in front of the Buddhist
worship hall. When she had barely expired, a tribute of lychees
was presented from the south. Seeing the lychees, His Highness
gave several loud wails. He ordered Gao Lishi, saying, "Offer
sacrifice to her on my behalf." After the sacrifice, the Six Armies
still did not raise the siege. With an embroidered quilt covering
her in a bed, [the consort's body] was placed in the post station's
courtyard. By imperial order, Chen Xuanli and several other
officers entered the post station to check on the consort. Xuanli
lifted her head and knew she was dead. He said, "It is true." Then
the siege was raised. The consort was buried in a pit north of the

road about one *li* away from the west outer wall of the town. She was then thirty-eight years old. On horseback and holding the lychees in his hand, His Highness said to Zhang Yehu, "All the way from here to Jianmen,[6] those twittering birds and fallen flowers, clear waters and green mountains will do nothing but cause me to grieve over my consort."

Earlier, when His Highness was at the Huaqing Palace, he rode a horse and exited the palace gate, intending to grace Lady of Guo State's residence with his imperial presence. Chen Xuanli said to him, "Having not yet announced the imperial order or notified the subjects, the Son of Heaven should not be too careless about his leaving or staying." Because of this comment, His Highness pulled the horse's head around [and returned to the palace]. In another year when the emperor was at the Huaqing Palace and the Shangyuan Festival (the fifteenth day of the first lunar month, also known as the Lantern Festival) was approaching, he intended to go on a night excursion. Chen Xuanli remonstrated, "Outside the palace is wilderness, so the trip has to be well prepared ahead of time. If Your Majesty would like to go on a night excursion, I suggest doing that after returning to the capital." Again, His Highness could not disobey Chen Xuanli's remonstration. From earlier cases to this execution at Mawei, all benefited from the fact that Chen Xuanli dared speak out.

In an earlier time, Li Xiazhou, a geomancer, composed this poem,

> The men from Yanshi all left;
> The horses didn't return from the Hangu Pass.
> If you ever meet a ghost under the hill,
> [You will see] a silk dress hanging on a ring.

---

[6]Jianmen 劍門 is located in modern Guangyuan in Sichuan Province.

"The men from Yanshi all left" suggests that An Lushan was an officer from Jimen. "The horses didn't return from the Hangu Pass" refers to Ge Shuhan's defeat at the Tongguan Pass. In "if you ever meet a ghost under the hill," the character "wei" [which consists of a "shan" (hill) on the top and a "gui" (ghost) at the bottom] represents the Mawei Post Station. In "a silk dress hanging on a ring," the "ring" indicates the Precious Consort's pet name Yuhuan, which means "jade ring"; the silk dress symbolizes the piece of silk cloth Gao Lishi used to strangle the consort when she was at the end of her life. Further, the consort often wore a false bun as headwear and liked to wear yellow skirts. In the later years of the Tianbao Era, a children's song in the capital recited, "The false bun is thrown into the river, and the yellow skirt flows with the water." Now this prophecy came true. Earlier, when An Lushan was called before His Highness, he responded with wisecracks and jokes. The consort was often present, and An Lushan was tempted by her. When An Lushan learned of the consort's death at Mawei, he sighed with regret for several days. Although [he rebelled because] Linfu appeased him and Yang Guozhong infuriated him, there was additionally a more personal reason for him to do it.

At that time, Lady of Guo State first entered a government-operated store in Chencang.[7] Then the news of Yang Guozhong's death arrived. The County Magistrate Xue Jingxian led officers to run after her. She ran into a bamboo grove and, thinking the rebel army was approaching, first killed her son, Pei Hui, and then her daughter. Yang Guozhong's wife, Pei Rou, asked, "Lady, why not do me a favor?" Therefore the Lady killed her and her daughter. After doing so, she cut her own throat, but did not die, and was carried into a prison. There she continued to ask, "Was this due to a government decision or the rebels?" The prison guard replied,

---

[7]Chencang 陳倉 is located in modern Baoji in Shanxi Province.

"Both are involved." The blood clogged her throat and thus she died. All the bodies were buried in a pit under a poplar tree north of the road and a few steps east of the town's outer wall.

His Highness set off from Mawei, and when he arrived in the Fufeng Circuit,[8] he saw flowers on the side of the road and a Chinese photinia tree clustered about a temple. The emperor admired and enjoyed it, and therefore called it "The Tree of Uprightness and Integrity." He probably had something [related to his lost love] on his mind. Then they arrived at an entrance of a sloping valley, where it had been drizzling over the past ten days. As the emperor was walking on the plank road in the rain, he heard ringing bells resounding across the mountains. Since His Highness was mourning the Precious Consort, he composed a tune named "Ringing Bells in the Rain" by mimicking the sound of the bells in order to express his regret.

In the second year of the Zhide Era (757), since the Western Capital had been recaptured, in the eleventh lunar month, His Highness returned from Chengdu. [On his way back], he ordered his people to offer sacrifice for the late Consort Yang. Later, he wished to move her tomb, but Li Fuguo and others all disagreed with him. At the time, Li Kui, the Vice Minister of Rites, presented a memorial, proclaiming, "Generals and soldiers of the Dragon Army killed Yang Guozhong because of his treason. Now if you move the late consort's tomb, I fear they would become suspicious and frightened." Therefore, Emperor Suzong stopped the plan. [Emperor Xuanzong, now] the Emperor Emeritus, secretly ordered his eunuchs to stealthily move Consort Yang's tomb to another place. In her original tomb, her body was wrapped with a purple quilt. At the time of reburial, her flesh had decomposed and only the brocade perfume satchel still remained on her chest. After the reburial, the eunuchs presented the satchel to the

---

[8]Fufeng 扶風 is also located in modern Baoji in Shanxi Province.

Emperor Emeritus who put it in his sleeve. He also ordered a painter to draw a portrait of the late Precious Consort and hang it on the wall inside a rest palace. There he gazed at the portrait day and night, sighing in tears.

After the Emperor Emeritus moved into the Southern Inner Palace (i.e. the Xingqing Palace, or the Palace of Ascendant Felicity), late one night he ascended the Qinzheng Tower. He leaned on its banister and looked southward into the distance. Mist and the moon met his eyes. His Highness then sang to himself, "The *qi* tree[9] in front of my courtyard can already be climbed, but the soldiers beyond the Great Wall have yet to return." Having finished this song, he heard a faint sound of singing from a nearby ward. He turned to Gao Lishi and asked, "Is that one of the former performers in my Pear Garden? You'd better go and find him for me tomorrow." The next day, Lishi secretly searched in the wards, found the man, and summoned him to go back with him. As expected, the man was once a disciple in the Pear Garden. After that, His Highness and the consort's serving maid Hongtao were there [on the Qinzheng Tower]. Hongtao sang the lyric of "The Liang Prefecture," the Precious Consort had composed. His Highness himself played the jade flute to accompany the music. After the performance ended, they gazed at each other, and both covered their faces as they wept. His Highness then embellished the song, which the one circulating in the Liang Prefecture nowadays further expanded.

During the Zhide Era (756–758), [Emperor Xuanzong] again graced the Huaqing Palace with his imperial presence. Most of those in his entourage of officials and palace maids were no longer acquainted with him. At the bottom of the Wangjing Tower (Tower of Gazing at the Capital), His Highness ordered Zhang Yehu to play "Ringing Bells in the Rain." In the middle of the

---

[9]The *qi* tree resembles a willow and bears green pearl-like fruit.

song, His Highness looked around, felt dreary and could not help but weep. His attendants also felt sorry for him. Xie Aman, a female performer from Xinfeng, was good at dancing to the melody "Over the Waves." She was once a frequent visitor to the imperial harem, and the Precious Consort treated her generously. On that day, she was asked to dance under imperial order. After the performance, Aman took the opportunity to present a gold-grained arm bracelet to His Highness, explaining, "This was bestowed upon me by the Precious Consort." His Highness held it, sadly shed tears, and said, "This is one of the two treasures my grandfather, the great emperor, obtained when he conquered Korea. One was the purple gold belt, and the other was this red jade arm bracelet. I bestowed the gold belt upon Prince Qi for the 'Dragon Pond' piece that he presented, and bestowed the red jade arm bracelet on the consort. Later when Koreans learned that these treasures now belonged to me, they sent a memorial, saying, 'Since our nation lost these treasures, we are having abnormal weather, our people are displaced, and our military power weakened.' I often thought we should not value this kind of things, so I ordered the return of their purple gold belt, but I kept the bracelet. Now that you obtained it from my consort, when I see it again today, it just awakens my sad feelings." When he finished speaking, he shed tears again.

When it came to the first year of the Qianyuan Era (758), He Huaizhi further addressed His Highness, "Once in a summer, Your Majesty was playing chess with a prince, ordering me to play *pipa* solo. (The slot of his *pipa* was made of stone, its strings made of crane tendons, and an iron pick was used to play it.) The Precious Consort was standing in front of the chessboard and watching. When Your Majesty was counting chess pieces on the chessboard and about to lose the game, the Precious Consort set free a dog from the State of Kang, which hopped onto the chessboard and upset it. Your Majesty was greatly pleased. At that moment, a gust of wind blew off her silk scarf, catching on my turban and remaining there for quite a while. The scarf fell down only when she turned back. When I returned home, I found there was a fragrant smell all over my body. Then I took off the turban and placed it in a brocade bag. Today I present to you this turban that I kept all this time." The Emperor Emeritus opened the bag and said, "This is the fragrance of the 'auspicious dragon camphor.' I once applied it on the jade lotus flowers in the hot-spring pool. When I revisited the place, the fragrant smell was still distinct. Won't delicate and smooth silk keep it even better?" Then he looked extremely mournful. Since then, his heart was constantly disturbed, only chanting this verse,

> Carving the wood and pulling the strings one makes an old puppet man.
> His wrinkled face and grey hair look no different than a real man.
> After the play was soon finished, with nothing to do, I feel lonely.
> It was just like one's life journey in this world."[10]

There was a Daoist named Yang Tongyou who came from Shu. He knew the Emperor Emeritus was longing for Precious Consort Yang, and he claimed himself to have Li Shaojun's Daoist arts.[11] The Emperor Emeritus was greatly delighted and ordered

---

[10]*Quan Tang shi* 全唐詩 reads "*shi*" 世 (world) as "*meng*" 夢 (dream). The line can thus be translated alternatively as "It was just like one's life journey in a dream." See Peng Dingqiu 彭定求 (1645–1719) et al., eds., *Quan Tangshi* (Beijing: Zhonghua Shuju, 1960), 3.42. The idea of human life being like a dream was popular in the Tang; cf. Zhenjun Zhang, *Buddhism and Tales of the Supernatural in Early Medieval China* (Brill, 2014), pp. 189–90.

[11]Li Shaojun 李少君, a Han Daoist, who summoned Lady Li's soul back to meet Emperor Wu of Han, who missed her so much after her

Yang to summon the consort's spirit. The geomancer therefore exhausted all his arts to call for her, but she did not come. He was also able to roam about the spiritual world and drive the pneuma, so he ascended to the Heavenly realm and submerged to the underworld kingdom to search for her, but in the end he could not see her. He then conducted further searches from top to bottom through the Four Voids.[12] He went to the eastern extremity where the sea ends, stepped over the Mountain of Penglai Pot,[13] and suddenly saw the highest mountain with many towers and pavilions on its top. When he reached it, he saw in the west chamber a deep-set room with its doors closed facing eastward and labeled "The Courtyard of the Jade Consort Grand Verity." When the geomancer pulled out his hairpin to knock on the door leaf, a young girl with a double-knot hairstyle came out and answered the door. Things happened so quickly that the geomancer had no time to speak before the double-knot girl went back in. Soon, a maid in green clothes came to the door and asked him where he came from. The geomancer then explained that he was the envoy of the Son of Heaven, and he took out the imperial order. The green-clothed maid said, "The Jade Consort has just fallen asleep, so please wait a bit." After a long while, the green-clothed maid invited him in and guided his way, saying, "The Jade Consort has come out." [The Precious Consort] was crowned with a gold lotus, draped in purple silks, wearing red jade and scuffing along in phoenix slippers. There were seven or eight

---

death. See "Xiaowu benji 孝武本紀" [Basic Annual of the Filial and Martial Emperor] in the *Shi ji*, 12. 453–5.

[12]Here "Four Voids" refers to the four directions and four sides of the sky.

[13]According to Wang Jia's 王嘉 (d. 390) *Shiyi ji* 拾遺記, the Mountain of Penglai Pot is one of the three mountains on the sea. The other two mountains are Mountain of Fangzhang Pot 方壺 and Mountain of Yingzhou Pot 瀛壺. All the three mountains look like pots.

attendants at her side. She bowed to the geomancer and asked if the emperor was well. She next inquired about what had happened after the fourteenth year of the Tianbao Era. When the geomancer finished speaking, she grieved and became silent. Then she directed the green-clothed maid to fetch a gold hairpin and an inlaid case, and then she broke each in half. She handed [the halves] to the envoy, saying, "Thank the Grand Emperor Emeritus for me. I present these objects to His Highness in memory of our former affection." The geomancer was about to leave, but he appeared to be not fully satisfied. The Jade Consort therefore inquired about his intentions. He again knelt, moved forward and addressed her, "I request to be informed about one thing at that time, which was not known by others, to check with the Grand Emperor Emeritus; otherwise, I'm afraid the gold hairpin and inlaid case will carry the deceit of Xin Yuanping."[14] The Jade Consort stepped back and stood blankly, as if she were thinking of something. Then she slowly stated, "Formerly, in the tenth year of the Tianbao Era, I attended the imperial carriage as we went up to the Palace on Mount Li to avoid the summer heat. It was the seventh lunar month in the autumn and the night when the Cowherd and the Weaving Maiden met each other. His Highness stood with his arm around my shoulders. Looking up to Heaven, we sighed over the affair of the Cowherd and the Weaving Maiden, and secretly vowed to one another our desire to be husband and wife generation after generation. After saying these vows, we held each other's hands and sobbed. This is only known by our lord." She thus felt sorrow and said, "Because of

---

[14]Xin Yuanping 新垣平 was a person from Zhao 趙 in the time of Emperor Wen of Han 漢文帝 (i.e. 180 B.C.–157 B.C.). He did all kinds of evil under the pretense that he had the art of *wang qi* 望氣 (observing the air currents). He was then defamed and sentenced to death. See "Xiaowen Benji 孝文本紀" [Basic Annual of the Wen the Filial] in the *Shi ji*, 10. 175–7.

this single thought, I would no longer live here, but shall descend to the lower world again and then recast our later relation. Either in Heaven or the human world, I'm determined to meet him again and be coupled with him as before." She then added, "The Grand Emperor Emeritus is also not long for this world. I hope he can just take comfort rather than become depressed."

When the envoy returned and reported to the Grand Emperor Emeritus in detail [on his meeting with the consort], the Sovereign was astonished with grief. When he moved into the Ganlu Palace Hall (Palace Hall of Sweet Dew) in the inner palace, he lamented over his late consort every single day. Thereafter, he abstained from cereals and took air as his food. Empress Zhang presented cherries and sugarcane juice to him, but the sage emperor did not touch them. He often played a purple jade flute. Once, as he played a few sounds, a pair of cranes landed in the courtyard and lingered for a while and then flew off. The sage emperor remarked to his serving maid Gong Ai that, "I have been acting under the order of the Heavenly God to be the Real Man of Original Commencement and Grand Ascent, giving me hope to see my consort again. This flute is not what you cherish, so you may give it to Dashou (Dashou was Emperor Daizong's pet name)." Then he ordered her to prepare the bath water and told her, "If I fall asleep, be careful not to disturb me." When Gong Ai heard him making a noise in his sleep, she felt terrified and went to check. He had already passed away.

On the day of the consort's death, an old woman at Mawei obtained a silk stocking [that the consort left behind]. It was said that she charged one hundred cash for passers-by who wished to fondle it. [As a result], from beginning to end, she made a great fortune from it.

Alas! After Emperor Xuanzong had been on the throne, he became tired of numerous official duties. He often felt that the way his ministers responded to him was too conservative and restrained, making it hard for him to satisfy his personal desires. Since he had Li Linfu, he entrusted all administrative affairs to him. He thereby blocked all unpleasant criticism and was able to indulge himself in banquets and music. He did not follow moral scruples in choosing his sex mates and did not consider it shameful. These behaviors were all due to Li Linfu's encouragement. His Highness was put to flight; the royal government fell; hundreds of officials surrendered to the rebels; the consort and princes were executed; wars broke out everywhere; and calamities spread within the four seas. All these catastrophes were brought about by Yang Guozhong.

The historian says that, ritual is what is used to distinguish noble from humble and to manage the household and the state. If a ruler does not act like a ruler, how could he rule his nation? If a father does not act like a father, how could he regulate his family? [Any emperor] who fails to perform well in either case will inevitably let his nation perish. The Brilliant Emperor Xuanzong made this error and disgraced himself in front of the nation. Therefore, An Lushan rebelled in the name of punishing the three people (i.e. Yang Guozhong, Consort Yang, and Lady of Guo State). Now I write this unofficial biography not only to collect Consort Yang's old anecdotes, but also to admonish people to guard against originating such disasters.

楊太真外傳(下)

樂史

　　初，開元末，江陵進乳柑橘，上以十枚種於蓬萊宮。至天寶十載九月秋，結實。宣賜宰臣，曰："朕近於宮內種柑子樹數株，今秋結實一百五十餘顆，乃與江南及蜀道所進無別，亦可謂稍異者。"宰臣表賀曰："伏以自天所育者，不能改有常之性。曠古所無者，乃可謂非常之感。是知聖人御物，以元氣布和，大道乘時，則殊方叶致。且橘柚所植，南北異名，實造化之有初，匪陰陽之有革。陛下玄風真紀，六合一家。雨露所均，混天區而齊被；草木有性，憑地氣以潛通。故茲江外之珍果，為禁中之佳實。綠蒂含霜，芳流綺殿；金衣爛日，色麗彤庭。"云云。乃頒賜大臣。外有一合歡實，上與妃子互相持翫。上曰："此果似知人意，朕與卿固同一體，所以合歡。"於是促坐同食焉。因令畫圖，傳之於後。

　　妃子既生於蜀，嗜荔枝。南海荔枝，勝於蜀者，故每歲馳驛以進。然方暑熱而熟，經宿則無味。後人不能知也。上與妃采戲，將北，唯重四轉敗為勝。連叱之，骰子宛轉而成重四。遂命高力士賜緋，風俗因而不易。廣南進白鸚鵡，洞曉言詞，呼為雪衣女。一朝飛上妃鏡臺上，自語："雪衣女昨夜夢為鷙鳥所搏。"上令妃授以《多心經》，記誦精熟。後上與妃遊別殿，置雪衣女於步輦竿上同去。瞥有鷹至，搏之而斃。上與妃嘆息久之，遂瘞於苑中，呼為鸚鵡塚。交趾貢龍腦香，有蟬蠶之狀，五十枚。波斯言老龍腦樹節方有。禁中呼為瑞龍腦，上賜妃十枚。妃私發明馳使（明馳使腹下有毛，夜能明，日馳五百里），持三枚遺祿山。妃又常遺祿山金平脫裝具、玉合、金平脫鐵面椀。

　　十一載，李林甫死。又以國忠為相，帶四十餘使。十二載，加國忠司空。長男暄，先尚延和郡主，又拜銀青光祿大夫、太常卿，兼户部侍郎。小男朏，尚萬春公主。貴妃堂弟祕書少監鑑，尚承榮郡主。一門一貴妃、二公主、三郡主、三夫人。十三載，重贈玄琰太尉、齊國公。母重封梁國夫人。官為造廟，御製碑及書。叔玄珪又拜工部尚書。韓國婿祕書少監崔峋女為代宗妃；虢國男裴徽尚代宗女延光公主，女為讓帝男妻。秦國婿柳澄男鈞尚長清縣主，澄弟潭尚肅宗女和政公主。

上每年冬十月，幸華清宮，常經冬還宮闕，去即與妃同輦。華清宮有端正樓，即貴妃梳洗之所；有蓮花湯，即貴妃澡沐之室。國忠賜第在宮東門之南，虢國相對。韓國、秦國，甍棟相接。天子幸其第，必過五家，賞賜燕樂。扈從之時，每家為一隊，隊著一色衣。五家合隊相映，如百花之煥發。遺鈿、墜舄、瑟瑟、珠翠，燦於路岐，可掬。曾有人俯身一窺其車，香氣數日不絕。馳馬千餘頭匹，以劍南旌節器仗前驅。出有餞飲，還有軟腳。遠近餉遺珍玩狗馬，閹侍歌兒，相望于道。

及秦國先死，獨虢國、韓國、國忠轉盛。虢國又與國忠亂焉，略無儀檢。每入朝謁，國忠與韓虢連轡，揮鞭驟馬，以為諧謔。從官嬪娥百餘騎，秉燭如晝，鮮裝袨服而行，亦無蒙蔽。衢路觀者如堵，無不駭嘆。十宅諸王男女婚嫁，皆資韓虢紹介；每一人納一千貫，上乃許之。

十四載六月一日，上幸華清宮，乃貴妃生日。上命小部音聲（小部者，梨園法部所置，凡三十人，皆十五己下）於長生殿奏新曲，未有名，會南海進荔枝，因以曲名《荔枝香》。左右歡呼，聲動山谷。

其年十一月，祿山反幽陵。（祿山本名軋犖山，雜種胡人也。母本巫師。祿山晚年益肥，垂肚過膝，自秤得三百五十斤。於上前胡旋舞，疾如風焉。上嘗於勤政樓東間設大金雞障，施一大榻，卷去簾，令祿山坐。其下設百戲，與祿山看焉。肅宗諫曰：“歷觀今古，未聞臣下與君上同坐閱戲。”上私曰：“渠有異相，我禳之故耳。”又嘗與夜燕，祿山醉臥，化為一猪而龍首。左右遽告帝。帝曰：“此猪龍，無能為。”終不殺。卒亂中國。）以誅國忠為名，咸言國忠、虢國、貴妃三罪，莫敢上聞。上欲以皇太子監國，蓋欲傳位，自親征。謀於國忠，國忠大懼，歸謂姊妹曰：“我等死在旦夕。今東宮監國，當與娘子等併命矣。”姊妹哭訴於貴妃。妃銜土請命，事乃寢。

十五載六月，潼關失守，上幸巴蜀，貴妃從。至馬嵬，右龍武將軍陳玄禮懼兵亂，乃謂軍士曰：“今天下崩離，萬乘震蕩，豈不由楊國忠割剝甿庶，以至於此？若不誅之，何以謝天下？”眾曰：“念之久矣。”會吐蕃和好使在驛門遮國忠訴事。軍士呼曰：“楊國忠與蕃人謀叛！”諸軍乃圍驛四合，殺國忠并男暄等。（國忠舊名釗，本張易之子也。天授中，易之恩幸莫比，每歸私第，詔令居樓，仍去其梯，圍以束棘，無復女奴侍立。母恐張氏絕嗣，乃置女奴媵姝于樓複壁中。遂有娠，而生國忠。後嫁于楊氏。）

上乃出驛門勞六軍。六軍不解圍，上顧左右責其故。高力士對曰：“國忠負罪，諸將討之。貴妃即國忠之妹，猶在陛下左右，群臣能無憂怖？伏乞聖慮裁斷。（一本云：“賊根猶在，何敢散乎？”蓋斥貴妃也。）上迴入驛，驛門內傍有小巷，上不忍歸行宮，於巷中倚杖欹首而立。聖情昏默，久而不進。京兆司錄韋鍔（見素男也）進曰：“乞陛下割恩忍斷，以寧國家。”逡巡，上入行宮。撫妃子出于廳門，至馬道北墻口而別之，使力士賜死。妃泣涕嗚咽，語不勝情，乃曰：“願大家好住。妾誠負國恩，死無恨矣。乞容禮佛。”帝曰：“願妃子善地受生。”力士遂縊于佛堂前之梨樹下。纔絕，而南方進荔枝至。上覩之，長號數息，使力士曰：“與我祭之。”祭後，六軍尚未解圍。以繡衾覆牀，置驛庭中，勅玄禮等入驛視之。玄禮擡其首，知其死，曰：“是矣。”而圍解。瘞于西郭之外一里許道北坎下。妃時年三十八。上持荔枝於馬上謂張野狐曰：“此去劍門，鳥啼花落，水綠山青，無非助朕悲悼妃子之由也。”

初，上在華清宮日，乘馬出宮門，欲幸虢國夫人之宅。玄禮曰：“未宣勅報臣，天子不可輕去就。”上為之迴轡。他年，在華清宮，逼上元，欲夜遊。玄禮奏曰：“宮外即是曠野，須有預備，若欲夜遊，願歸城闕。”上又不能違諫。及此馬嵬之誅，皆是敢言之有便也。

先是，術士李遐周有詩曰：“燕市人皆去，函關馬不歸。若逢山下鬼，環上繫羅衣。”“燕市人皆去”，祿山即薊門之士而來；“函關馬不歸”，哥舒翰之敗潼關也；“若逢山下鬼”，“嵬”字即馬嵬驛也；“環上繫羅衣”，貴妃小字玉環，及其死也，力士以羅巾縊焉。又妃常以假髻為首飾，而好服黃裙。天寶末，京師童謠曰：“義髻拋河裏，黃裙逐水流。”至此應矣。初，祿山嘗於上前應對，雜以諧謔。妃常在座，祿山心動。及聞馬嵬之死，數日嘆惋。雖林甫養育之，國忠激怒之，然其有所自也。

是時，虢國夫人先至陳倉之官店。國忠誅問至，縣令薛景仙率吏人追之。走入竹林下，以為賊軍至，虢國先殺其男徽，次殺其女。國忠妻裴柔曰：「娘子何不借我方便乎？」遂并其女殺之，已而自刎，不死。載于獄中，猶問人曰：「國家乎？賊乎？」獄吏曰：「互有之。」血凝其喉而死。遂併坎于東郭十餘步道北楊樹下。

上發馬嵬，行至扶風道。道傍有花，寺畔見石楠樹團圓，愛玩之，因呼為端正樹，蓋有所思也。又至斜谷口，屬霖雨涉旬，於棧道雨中聞鈴聲隔山相應。上既悼念貴妃，因採其聲為《雨霖鈴》曲，以寄恨焉。

至德二年，既收復西京。十一月，上自成都還，使祭之。後欲改葬，李輔國等皆不從。時禮部侍郎李揆奏曰：「龍武將士以楊國忠反，故誅之。今改葬故妃，恐龍武將士疑懼。」肅宗遂止之。上皇密令中官潛移葬之于他所。妃之初瘞，以紫褥裹之，及移葬，肌膚已消釋矣，胸前猶有錦香囊在焉。中官葬畢以獻，上皇置之懷袖。又令畫工寫妃形於別殿，朝夕視之而歔欷焉。

上皇既居南內，夜闌登勤政樓，凭欄南望，煙月滿目。上因自歌曰：「庭前琪樹已堪攀，塞外征人殊未還。」歌歇，聞里中隱隱如有歌聲者。顧力士曰：「得非梨園舊人乎？遲明為我訪來。」翌日，力士潛求於里中，因召與同去，果梨園弟子也。其後，上復與妃侍者紅桃在焉，歌《涼州》之詞，貴妃所製也。上親御玉笛，為之倚曲。曲罷相視，無不掩泣。上因廣其曲。今《涼州》留傳者益加焉。

至德中，復幸華清宮。從官嬪御，多非舊人。上於望京樓下命張野狐奏《雨霖鈴》曲。曲半，上四顧淒涼，不覺流涕。左右亦為感傷。新豐有女伶謝阿蠻，善舞《凌波曲》，舊出入宮禁，貴妃厚焉。是日，詔令舞。舞罷，阿蠻因進金粟裝臂環，曰：「此貴妃所賜。」上持之，淒然垂涕曰：「此我祖大帝破高麗，獲二寶：一紫金帶，一紅玉支。朕以岐王所進《龍池篇》，賜之金帶。紅玉支賜妃子。後高麗知此寶歸我，乃上言：『本國因失此寶，風雨愆時，民離兵弱。』朕尋以為得此不足為貴，乃命還其紫金帶。唯此不還。汝既得之於妃子，朕今再覩之，但興悲念矣。」言訖又涕零。

至乾元元年，賀懷智又上言曰：「昔上夏日與親王某，令臣獨彈琵琶（其琵琶以石為槽，鵾雞筋為絃，用鐵撥彈之），貴妃立於局前觀之。上數抨子將輸，貴妃放康國猧子上局亂之，上大悅。時風吹貴妃領巾於臣巾上，良久，迴身方落。及歸，覺滿身香氣，乃卸頭幘，貯於錦囊中。今輒進所貯幞頭。”上皇發囊，且曰：“此瑞龍腦香也。吾曾施於暖池玉蓮朵，再幸尚有香氣宛然，況乎絲縷潤膩之物哉？”遂淒愴不已。自是聖懷耿耿，但吟：“刻木牽絲作老翁，雞皮鶴髮與真同。須臾舞罷寂無事，還似人生一世中。”

有道士楊通幽自蜀來，知上皇念楊貴妃，自云有李少君之術。上皇大喜，命致其神。方士乃竭其術以索之，不至。又能遊神馭氣，出天界，入地府求之，竟不見。又旁求四虛上下，東極，絕大海，跨蓬壺。忽見最高山，上多樓閣。洎至，西廂下有洞戶，東向，闔其門，額署曰“玉妃太真院”。方士抽簪叩扉，有雙鬟童女出應門。方士造次未及言，雙鬟復入。俄有碧衣侍女至，詰其所從來。方士因稱天子使者，且致其命。碧衣云：“玉妃方寢，請少待之。”逾時，碧衣延入，且引曰：“玉妃出。”冠金蓮，帨紫綃，佩紅玉，拽鳳舄，左右侍女七八人。揖方士，問皇帝安否，次問天寶十四載已還。言訖憫然，指碧衣女取金釵鈿合，折其半授使者曰：“為我謝太上皇。謹獻是物，尋舊好也。”方士將行，色有不足。玉妃因徵其意，乃復前跪致詞：“請當時一事，不聞于他人者，驗於太上皇。不然，恐金釵鈿合，負新垣平之詐也。”玉妃忙然退立，若有所思，徐而言曰：“昔天寶十載，侍輦避暑驪山宮。秋七月，牽牛織女相見之夕，上憑肩而望。因仰天感牛女事，密相誓心，願世世為夫婦。言畢，執手各嗚咽。此獨君王知之耳。”因悲曰：“由此一念，又不得居此，復墮下界，且結後緣。或為天，或為人，決再相見，好合如舊。”因言：“太上皇亦不久人間，幸惟自愛，無自苦耳。”

使者還，具奏太上皇。皇心震悼。及至移入大內甘露殿，悲悼妃子，無日無之。遂辟穀服氣，張皇后進櫻桃蔗漿，聖皇並不食。常玩一紫玉笛，因吹數聲，有雙鶴下於庭，徘徊而去。聖皇語侍兒宮愛曰：“吾奉上帝所命，為元始孔昇真人，此期可再會妃子耳。笛非爾所寶，可送大收（大收，代宗小字）。”即令具湯沐。“我若就枕，慎勿驚我。”宮愛聞睡中有聲，駭而視之，已崩矣。

妃之死日，馬嵬媼得錦袎襪一隻。相傳過客一玩百錢，前後獲錢無數。

悲夫！玄宗在位，倦於萬機，常以大臣接對拘檢，難徇私欲。自得李林甫，一以委成，故絕逆耳之言，恣行燕樂。衽席無別，不以為恥，由林甫之贊成矣。乘輿遷播，朝廷陷沒，百僚繫頸，妃主被戮，兵滿天下，毒流四海，皆國忠之召禍也。

　　史臣曰：夫禮者，定尊卑，理家國。君不君，何以享國？父不父，何以正家？有一于此，未或不亡。唐明皇之一誤，貽天下之羞，所以祿山叛亂，指罪三人。今為外傳，非徒拾楊妃之故事，且懲禍階而已。

Chapter 8

Tale 8.42

The Record of the Drifting Red Leaf

By Zhang Shi
Translated by Zhenjun Zhang

During the Xizong reign period (874–888) of the Tang dynasty,[1] a Confucian scholar named Yu You was once taking an evening stroll along a broad road in the imperial city.[2] The season was late fall, when all things on earth were withering and falling in the autumnal wind; it was about sunset, increasing his sorrow as a traveler.

Watching the Royal Canal, Yu You saw drifting leaves continuously flowing down. He approached the canal to wash his hands.[3] A while later, he saw one fallen leaf a little larger than the others. From a distance, it appeared that there were traces of ink on it. The floating red leaf drifted leisurely and seemed to bear endless affection from afar. Yu You picked it up, examined it, and found a quatrain written on it, which read:

---

[1]Xizong 僖宗, named Li Xuan 李懁 (r. 874–888), was an emperor of the late Tang.

[2]Information about Yu You's 于祐 life is not available.

[3]During the Tang dynasty, water was drawn from Mount Zhongnan 終南山 to Chang'an, flowing through the royal palace. It was called *yugou* 御溝 (the Royal Canal) or *jingou* 禁溝 (Forbidden Canal).

Why does the water flow so fast?
In the deep palace I am leisurely all day long.
Ardently I bid farewell to this red leaf,
and wish you safe arrival to the human world.

Yu You took the leaf and hid it in a bookcase, reciting and savoring the poem all day long. He liked the novelty and beauty of the lines but wondered who composed and inscribed them on the leaf. Considering that the water in the Royal Canal flows out from the imperial palace, the poem must have been composed by a palace beauty. Yu You treasured the leaf merely as a souvenir, yet from time to time he also spoke of it to those who had nothing better to do. Thenceforth, Yu You always ruminated over the anonymous author of the poem, exhausting both his energy and spirit.

One day, a friend saw him and said, "Why are you so thin? There must be a reason. Tell me please!" Yu You said, "I have lost both my appetite and sleep for several months." Then Yu told his friend about the red leaf and the lines on it.

His friend laughed loudly at him, saying, "Why have you become so stupid? It's not as if the lady wrote this poem especially for you. You obtained it by chance. Why do you care so much? Though you have been secretly loving her for so long, she is deep in the imperial palace. Even if you had wings, you would not dare venture there. Your stupid enthusiasm is ridiculous."

Yu You said, "Though Heaven is high above, he is aware of everything below. If one has a will, Heaven will certainly grant his wish. I have heard the story of Niu Xianke encountering Liu Wushuang.[4] In the end they obtained a clever strategy from Scholar Gu 古 and married. Things are intrinsically unpredictable; the only thing one needs to worry about is not having ambition."

---

[4]Niu Xianke 牛仙客 is a mistake for Wang Xianke.

Yu You still could not stop ruminating and worrying, so he further composed two lines and wrote them on a red leaf, which read:

I have learned of the sorrow of a beauty, written on a leaf,
After writing the poem on the leaf, to whom did you intend to send it?

He placed the red leaf on the flowing water of the upper reaches of the Royal Canal, enabling it to drift into the palace. Some laughed at him for this but he was also praised by some enthusiastic ones. Someone presented a poem to him as a gift, which read:

The imperial favor did not stop the east-flowing water,
The grief of a palace girl flowed through this ditch.

Afterward, Yu You took the imperial examination several times but never passed. He became tired of the life he lived, so he sought refuge with Han Yong, a noble of the Hezhong prefect,[5] and lodged in his guest room. Having earned barely enough money and silk to support himself, he had no intention to seek an official rank anymore.

Quite a while later, Han Yong called Yu You in and told him, "In the imperial palace more than three thousand women have had some demerits. The emperor allowed all of them to marry. Lady Han, who shares a surname with me, was in the palace for a long time. Now she has left the imperial palace and lives at my residence. Currently, you are not married and have passed the prime of your life. You have been suffering from privation, achieving nothing and living alone. I feel extremely sorry for you.

---

[5]Hezhong 河中, also known as Puzhou 蒲州. Its seat was located in present-day Yongji County, Shanxi province.

Now Lady Han has no less than a thousand strings of cash in her suitcase; besides, she was originally from a good family, now is only thirty years old, and she is extremely beautiful. I'll talk with her and convince her to marry you. How does this sound?"

Yu You left his seat, knelt down onto the ground and said, "As a poverty-stricken scholar, I have sponged off you under your roof. In the daytime I have enough food to eat and at night I have a warm place to sleep. It has been quite a long time since I have received your favor. I regret that I have no special skills and therefore cannot repay your kindness. I feel ashamed and terrified from morning to evening, not knowing what to do. How could I dare have such an absurd hope?"

Han Yong ordered that the marriage be proposed in a message through a matchmaker. He aided Yu You in purchasing and forwarding betrothal gifts, such as a lamb and a swallow, completing the process of the six marriage rites and intertwining the happiness of the two families.[6] On the evening of his wedding day, Yu You was extremely delighted. The next morning, he found that the dowry in Lady Han's boxes was handsome, and her appearance gorgeous. As Yu You had never dared to have such an extravagant hope, he thought that he had entered the land of immortals by accident, and he went into ecstasies.

A short while later, Lady Han saw the red leaf in Yu You's bookcase. She said with astonishment, "This is the poem I composed. How did you acquire it?" Yu You told her what happened. Lady Han said further, "I also received a red leaf. I wonder who wrote the poem on it." Then she opened her suitcase and took the red leaf out; it was exactly the poem composed by Yu You. Face to face, they sighed in astonishment and wept emotionally for quite a while. Both asked, "How could this have happened by accident? Is it possible that it was destined?"

---

[6]*Liu li* 六禮, six rites, see footnote 15 in tale 2.10.

Han said, "When I first got the leaf, I composed a poem, which is now still in my suitcase." She took it out and showed Yu You. The poem read:

> Walking alone on the bank of the Royal Canal,
> It was then I approached the flowing water and acquired the leaf.
> Such a feeling, who could understand?
> Simply a poetic couplet that broke my heart!

Those who heard their story all sighed in wonder and amazement.

One day, Han Yong held a banquet in honor of Yu You and Lady Han. Yong said, "Today you two may want to say thanks to your matchmaker."

Lady Han replied with a smile, "The marriage of You and I was made by Heaven, not a matchmaker."

Han Yong asked, "Why do you say that?"

Lady Han asked for a brush and composed a poem, which read:

> A good couplet was written for [dropping into] the flowing water,
> Ten years' secret feeling satisfied my long-cherished wish.
> Today we have become husband and wife,
> Thus I know the red leaf was a good matchmaker.

Han Yong said, "Now I know that nothing in the world happens by chance."

Later when Emperor Xizong visited Shu,[7] Han Yong ordered Yu You to lead a hundred servant boys to march out front.

---

[7] Xizong fled from the capital, Chang'an, to Shu (present-day Sichuan) in 880 because the rebels led by Huang Chao 黄巢 had seized the capital.

Because she used to be a palace girl, Lady Han was able to see the emperor and told him the whole story about her marriage with Yu You. The emperor replied, "I have also heard a bit of it." Then he called Yu You in and said with a smile, "You have been an old guest of mine." Yu You prostrated himself on the ground and kowtowed, apologizing for his offense.

When the emperor returned to the Western Capital,[8] because of his accompanying the emperor, Yu You obtained a position as an official and became an inspector in the Army of Inspired Strategy. Lady Han gave birth to five sons and three daughters. Their sons all became officials because of their diligent studying, and their daughters all married into famous families. Because Lady Han had regulated her family well, she was given a title as a woman by the emperor that she retained all her life. The Prime Minister Zhang Jun (?–904) composed a poem for the couple,[9] which read:

> In Chang'an there are millions of households,
> Day by day the imperial river flows eastwards.
> On the river there are numerous red leaves,
> You were the only one who got the good lines.
> Then you wrote on the fallen leaf,
> Let it flow into the imperial residence.
> Deep in the palace, where the women numbered thousands,
> The leaf drifts only to Lady Han.
> Three thousand ladies leaving the forbidden city,
> Lady Han is recorded as one of them.
> Recalling the past, she thanks the imperial favor,

---

[8]The Western Capital refers to Chang'an, while the Eastern Capital refers to Luoyang.

[9]Zhang Jun 張濬, styled Yuchuan 禹川, a native of Hejian 河間 commandery. During the Xizong reign, he was the *Tong zhongshu menxia pingzhangshi* 同中書門下平章事 (Jointly Manager of Affairs with the Secretariat-Chancellery). His biography is found in *Jiu Tangshu* (p. 183) and *Xin Tangshu* (p. 185).

Shedding tears like a rain of rouge.
Lodging in the home of a nobleman,
Thereupon she met you.
Communicating through a matchmaker and completing the six
    rites,
You become husband and wife forever.
Sons and daughters crowd before your eyes,
Men in green and purple robes fill your home.[10]
Such a thing has never happened in the past,
It can be spoken of for thousands of years.

Commentary: Flowing water is unfeeling, and red leaves are unfeeling too. Absurdly, [Lady Han's] entrusting an emotionless substance onto another emotionless substance to seek for an enchanted ends with the emotionless substance being obtained by the enchanted and, further, she married the enchanted. This is indeed something I have never heard of. Those who follow the principles of heaven can love each other and be wed, even if they live far apart; but those who reject these principles can do neither, even if they are close neighbors. After reading this story, those who rejoice in what they have and those who crave to gain more should draw a lesson from it.

Note: This tale, T8.46, and T8.48 are revised from my 2017 renditions in *Song Dynasty Tales: A Guided Reader*, pp. 33–54, 299–316 & 145–172.

---

[10]*Qingzi* 青紫, Green and purple: colors of the ribbons attached to the seals held by high-ranking officials of Han, and the colors of clothing worn by high-ranking officials of Tang.

流紅記

張實

唐僖宗時，有儒士于祐，晚步禁衢間。於時萬物搖落，悲風素秋，頹陽西傾，羈懷增感。視御溝，浮葉徐徐而下。祐臨流浣手。久之，有一脫葉，差大於他葉，遠視之，若有墨跡載於其上。浮紅泛泛，遠意綿綿。祐取而視之，果有四句題於其上。其詩曰：

"流水何太急，深宮盡日閑。
殷勤謝紅葉，好去到人間。"

祐得之，蓄於書笥，終日詠味，喜其句意新美，然莫知何人作而書於葉也。因念御溝水出禁掖，此必宮中美人所作也。祐但寶之，以為念耳，亦時時對好事者說之。祐自此思念，精神俱耗。

一日，友人見之，曰："子何清削如此？必有故，為吾言之。"祐曰："吾數月來，眠食俱廢。"因以紅葉句言之。

友人大笑曰："子何愚如是也！彼書之者，無意於子。子偶得之，何置念如此？子雖思愛之勤，帝禁深宮，子雖有羽翼，莫敢往也。子之愚，又可笑也。"

祐曰："天雖高而聽卑，人苟有志，天必從人願耳。吾聞牛仙客遇無雙之事，卒得古生之奇計。但患無志耳，事固未可知也。"

祐終不廢思慮，復題二句，書於紅葉上云："曾聞葉上題紅怨，葉上題詩寄阿誰？"置御溝上流水中，俾其流入宮中。人為笑之，亦為好事者稱道。有贈之詩者，曰："君恩不禁東流水，流出宮情是此溝。"

祐后累舉不捷，跡頗羈倦，乃依河中貴人韓泳門館，得錢帛稍稍自給，亦無意進取。

　　久之，韓泳召祐謂之曰：“帝禁宮人三千餘得罪，使各適人。有韓夫人者，吾同姓，久在宮。今出禁庭，來居吾舍。子今未娶，年又踰壯，困苦一身，無所成就，孤生獨處，吾甚憐汝。今韓夫人篋中不下千緡，本良家女，年纔三十，姿色甚麗。吾言之，使聘子，何如？”

　　祐避席伏地曰：“窮困書生，寄食門下，晝飽夜溫，受賜甚久。恨無一長，不能圖報，早暮愧懼，莫知所為。安敢復望如此！”

　　泳令人通媒妁，助祐進羔雁，盡六禮之數，交二姓之歡。祐就吉之夕，樂甚。明日，見韓氏裝橐甚厚，姿色絕艷。祐本不敢有此望，自以為誤入仙源，神魂飛越。

　　既而韓氏於祐書笥中見紅葉，大驚曰：“此吾所作之句，君何故得之？”祐以實告。韓氏復曰：“吾於水中亦得紅葉，不知何人所作也。”乃開笥取之，乃祐所題之詩。相對驚嘆感泣久之。曰：“事豈偶然哉？莫非前定也。”

　　韓氏曰：“吾得葉之初，嘗有詩，今尚藏篋中。”取以示祐。詩云：

　　“獨步天溝岸，臨流得葉時。
　　此情誰會得？腸斷一聯詩。”

　　聞者莫不嘆異驚駭。

　　一日，韓泳開宴召祐泊韓氏。泳曰：“子二人今日可謝媒人也。”

　　韓氏笑答曰：“吾為祐之合，乃天也，非媒氏之力也。”

　　泳曰：“何以言之？”

　　韓氏索筆為詩，曰：

　　“一聯佳句題流水，十載幽思滿素懷。
　　今日卻成鸞鳳友，方知紅葉是良媒。”

　　泳曰：“吾今知天下事無偶然者也。”

　　僖宗之幸蜀，韓泳令祐將家童百人前導。韓以宮人得見帝，具言適祐事。帝曰：“吾亦微聞之。”召祐，笑曰：“卿乃朕門下舊客也。”祐伏地拜，謝罪。

帝還西都，以從駕得官，為神策軍虞候。韓氏生五子三女。子
以力學具有官，女配名家。韓氏治家有法度，終身為命婦。宰相張
浚作詩曰：

"長安百萬戶，御水日東注。
水上有紅葉，子獨得佳句。
子復題脫葉，流入宮中去。
深宮千萬人，葉歸韓氏處。
出宮三千人，韓氏籍中數。
回首謝君恩，淚灑胭脂雨。
寓居貴人家，方與子相遇。
通媒六禮具，百歲為夫婦。
兒女滿眼前，青紫盈門戶。
茲事自古無，可以傳千古。"

議曰："流水，無情也；紅葉，無情也。以無情寓無情而求有
情，終為有情者得之，復與有情者合，信前世所未聞也。夫在天理
可合，雖胡越之遠，亦可合也；天理不可，則雖比屋鄰居，不可得
也。悅於得，好於求者，觀此，可以為誡也。"

Tale 8.43

Separate Traditions of Empress Zhao, "the Flying Swallow"

Qin Chun[1]
Translated by Shengyu Wang

A young scholar surnamed Li lived in my native place. For generations, his family had engaged in Confucian scholarship. I visited Li one day, but by that time his family's fortunes had considerably dwindled. In the corner of his room, I spotted a shabby basket containing several bundles of ancient texts, among which was a copy of the "Separate Traditions of Empress Zhao."[2]

---

[1] A native of Qiaochuan 譙川 in present-day Bozhou, Anhui province, Qin Chun 秦醇, courtesy name Zifu 子複, was a writer of the Northern Song dynasty (960–1127 CE) to whom are attributed this and three other surviving tales, namely, "Wenquan ji 溫泉記," "Lishan ji 驪山記," and "Tanyige ji 譚意哥記."

[2] The term *biezhuan* 別傳 (separate traditions) designates a form of unofficial historiography that often records anecdotal accounts of historical figures. Empress Zhao here refers to Zhao Feiyan 趙飛燕 (45–1 BCE), who was made empress by Emperor Cheng of Han (51–7 BCE) two years after his first wife Empress Xu was deposed in 18 BCE. In "Waiqi zhuan" 外戚傳 (traditions of the imperial in-laws) of the *Hanshu* (the History of the Han), we find one of the earliest accounts of Zhao Feiyan's life recorded in official historiography. However, this tale is not so much influenced by the *Hanshu* as by other sources, such as Ge

Though some parts were missing and the rest was out of order, the text still rewarded even a cursory examination; I therefore implored Li to allow me to take it home. Subsequently I made additions and corrections to make the *Traditions* complete, so that it can be passed onto those interested in the affair.

Empress Zhao was blessed with a slender waist and delicate bones. She was adept at walking in slow, graceful steps, swinging her upper body as if she were a quivering flower branch grasped in someone's hand.[3] No one could mimic her gait. While serving in the Princess' household, she earned herself the nickname of "the Flying Swallow."[4]

After she entered the imperial palace, Zhao also recommended her younger sister to the throne. Her sister won the favor of the emperor and was promoted to the rank of Zhaoyi

---

Hong's (283–343 CE) *Xijing zaji* 西京雜記 (Miscellaneous Records of the Western Capital) and "Zhao Feiyan waizhuan 趙飛燕外傳" (The Esoteric Traditions of Zhao Feiyan), attributed to Ling Xuan 伶玄 of the Western Han dynasty.

[3]In the original text, Empress Zhao is said to walk in "*jubu* 踽步," which some scholars choose to gloss as "walking slowly," though its exact meaning remains unclear. Another version of the text, included in the Qing dynasty *Hongyao shanfang* 紅藥山房 manuscript edition of *Qingsuo gaoyi*, uses the term *yubu* 禹步, literally "the pace of Yu 禹," referring to the legendary flood-taming sage in antiquity. According to "Junzhi 君治" of the pre-Han text *Shizi* 尸子 (Master Shi), Yu, crippled by years of hard work, had to walk in small steps, with "one foot never passing the other 步不相過." It is also worth mentioning that Qin Chun's description here appears to allude to a passage in Ge Hong's *Xijing zaji*, which writes: "Empress Zhao had a light body and slender waist. She was good at walking back and forth 趙后體輕腰弱, 善行步進退."

[4]According to the *Hanshu*, Zhao was formerly an entertainer in the service of Princess Yang'e 陽阿.

(Lady of Illustrious Deportment).[5] Skilled in playful repartee, Zhaoyi was born with skin smooth as silk and a graceful form. In all the land, none surpassed the two sisters in beauty, and they eclipsed all the ladies in the Imperial palace.

From the time Zhaoyi entered the palace, the emperor seldom visited the Eastern Palace, the residence of the empress. Zhaoyi occupied the Western palace, and the Empress Dowager lived in the Central Palace. Day and night, Empress Zhao dwelt on the idea of giving birth to a son, in order to secure her power in the long term. She often sent calf-drawn carts to smuggle young men into the Palace and sleep with them.[6]

Once, when the emperor chanced to visit the Western Palace with a small entourage of three or four attendants, the empress was committing adultery with a lover. Urgently alerted by her attendants, the panic-stricken empress hastened outside to greet the emperor. But with her hair tousled and headdress awry, she babbled nonsensically and aroused the suspicion of the emperor. Not long after the emperor had taken his seat, he heard coughing from behind the wall hanging and left the Eastern Palace.[7] From then on, the emperor nursed the intention to inflict punishment on the empress, which he suppressed for the sake of Zhaoyi.

But one day, while drinking with Zhaoyi, the emperor suddenly pulled up his sleeves, his wide-open eyes blazing at Zhaoyi, and his formidable visage contorted in anger. She sprang up terrified from the floor mat and prostrated herself on the bare

---

[5]During Emperor Cheng's reign, when this tale is set, the term Zhaoyi refers to the highest-ranking imperial concubine, whose bureaucratic degree is equivalent to that of the imperial chancellor.

[6]Ge Hong's *Xijing zaji* also mentions that Empress Zhao committed adultery with "frivolous young men 輕浮少年," who were secretly taken into the palace in "carriages drawn by a pair of horses 駢車."

[7]*Biyi* 壁衣, literally "wall attire," refers to the fabrics that hung in front of bare walls inside the palace.

floor, entreating him: "I, your subject and concubine, come from an unremarkable commoner's clan and have no close relatives. Since I was added to Your Majesty's retinue in the palace, I have been the unexpected object of your undivided imperial favor. Blessed by Your Majesty's fond devotion, I proudly stand above the rest of the ladies. Relying on your imperial favor, I have competed for increasing affection from Your Majesty. But this gave rise to the slanders that multiply against me. What is more, not knowing what is prohibited, I must have unwittingly provoked Your Majesty to this fury. I beg Your Majesty be kind in bestowing upon me an immediate death, so that Your Majesty may be released from this consuming passion." With these words, Zhaoyi sobbed, and her tears flowed in streams.

The emperor himself went to pull up Zhaoyi by the arm. "Take a seat and let me speak to you," said the emperor, "You are free of blame. But that is not the case of your sister! How my imperial person wishes to have her head chopped off, her limbs cut apart, and her body thrown into a dunghill. Only then will my imperial person be satisfied!"

"But how did my sister offend Your Majesty?" inquired Zhaoyi.

The emperor told her about the affair behind the wall hanging at the Eastern palace.

Zhaoyi pleaded: "Without the empress, I would not have entered the place. Were the empress to die, how could I alone endure the shame of living? Besides, if Your Majesty decreed the execution of the empress without explanation, then all manner of unruly subjects in the empire would have an excuse to cast their eye upon the throne. Please let me suffer the four cruelest tortures on the empress' behalf!" Saying this, she burst into loud weeping and threw herself onto the floor.

The startled emperor stood up to raise Zhaoyi. "For your sake, I was not going to prosecute the empress anyway; just now I was talking idly, no more. Why do you blame yourself so harshly?"

But it was some time before Zhaoyi finally returned to her seat and inquired about the man behind the wall hanging. The emperor's retainers had secretly uncovered his identity, and he turned out to be the son of the imperial guard Chen Chong. The emperor then sent men to kill the adulterer in the Chen residence, and demoted Chen Chong to the rank of a commoner.

Later, Zhaoyi paid the empress a visit in the Eastern Palace, and she relayed what the emperor had said, further adding: "Dear sister, do you not remember the times when our destitute family provided us with neither food nor warmth? In those days we had no one to depend upon. You let me join the neighbors' girls to make straw sandals and sell them in the market for the money to buy rice. One day, we brought rice home, but a storm came and dampened the firewood for cooking, making it impossible for us to light the stove. Starved and freezing, we two could not fall asleep. Sister, you let me huddle with you, and that night we two sobbed together. Have you already forgotten this? Now, with all these luxuries at our disposal, we are second to none. But you yourself are ruining your reputation. If a second offence were to provoke the emperor's anger, the damage would be beyond repair. You would face not only capital punishment, but the derision of all under heaven. Today, I can still come to your rescue. But life is precarious; if I died first, to whom would you turn for help?" Zhaoyi could not stop weeping after uttering these words, and the empress also burst into tears.

Since the incident, the emperor had ceased to honor the empress with his visits. He favored no one except Zhaoyi. One day, Zhaoyi was taking a bath, and the emperor peeked at her. The maids informed Zhaoyi of the emperor's presence, and she hurried to hide from the candlelight. Seeing this, the emperor was dazzled and even more beguiled.

On another day, Zhaoyi was again taking a bath, and the emperor gave her maids money to keep quiet. He peeped through the gap between the screen panels and saw Zhaoyi resting in the tub, with glimmering ripples of floral bathwater around her naked body. She reminded him of a piece of translucent jade lying beneath three feet of icy spring water.[8] The emperor was carried away by passion.[9]

He told his close attendant that "Since ancient times, no lord of men has had more than one empress at a time; but if there were such a precedent, my imperial person would have established Zhaoyi as my second empress." His words reached the ears of empress Zhao, who was aware that the emperor's affection for Zhaoyi had deepened after seeing her in her bath. She therefore also arranged a hot bath and invited the emperor to come over and watch. When the emperor arrived, she entered the bath naked and playfully splashed him with water. But the more she tried to seduce the emperor, the unhappier he became. The emperor left before they could get intimate, and the empress said in tears: "His majesty bestows his affection upon one person alone. There is nothing I can do."

---

[8] The Ming dynasty scholar Hu Yinglin (1551–1602 CE) highly praised the vivid depiction of Zhaoyi taking a bath. He wrote in the "Jiuliu xulun xia 九流緒論下" of his *Shaoshi shanfang bicong* (Notes from the Mountain Villa of Shaoshi), it "may suddenly enthuse readers even a hundred generations later 百世下讀之尤勃然興."

[9] An analogous scene is found in "Wenquan ji" (Records of the Hot Spring Bath), also attributed to Qin Chun, which uses similar phrasing to describe the main character's romantic dream of being invited by the famous imperial consort Yang Yuhuan of Tang dynasty to a bath at the Lishan hot spring. According to anecdote, Emperor Xuanzong was instantly smitten with Yang when he caught sight of her emerging from the hot spring.

On the day of Empress Zhao's birthday, Zhaoyi went to the celebration, together with the emperor. In the middle of the feast, the empress, seeking to regain her husband's sympathy, let streams of tears run down her cheeks.

Seeing this, the emperor said: "Everyone radiates happiness with a cup in hand, while you alone look distressed. Is there anything that does not satisfy you?"

The empress replied: "In the days when I, your subject and concubine, was a bondservant at my former mistress' palace, Your Majesty once graced her residence with a royal visit. I was standing behind my lady, and Your Majesty's eyes often lingered on me. My mistress realized what you desired, so she sent me to serve Your Majesty. I thus had the greatest honor of assisting Your Majesty to change clothes. The [blood from] my lower body left a stain on your royal robe, and I was eager to wash it off. Your Majesty said 'let it be kept as a remembrance'. A few days later, when I was selected to enter the royal palace, my neck still bore the marks from Your Majesty's love bites. When all these reminiscences came back to me today, tears had already flooded my eyes before I realized it."

Those words triggered the emperor's own memories of the past and aroused his sympathy. With his affection for the empress renewed, he turned his head and heaved a sigh. Zhaoyi sensed that the emperor intended to stay, so she excused herself and departed. Indeed, the emperor stayed in the palace of the empress until almost dusk.

Since she was favored by the emperor, the empress devised a treacherous scheme to pursue further gains. Three months later, she submitted a memorial to the emperor, falsely claiming to have become pregnant:

Your Majesty appointed me to the inner court a long time ago. I was first graced by your imperial favor, and then Your Majesty conferred upon me the grand title of empress. So it has been for several years. Recently, I was blessed with your good wishes during my birthday. Your Majesty showed me the greatest favor in riding the royal carriage to visit the Eastern Wing of the palace. I had the honor of serving you at the banquet for a considerable time and of being once again the object of your affection. In the past few months, my womb has been filled with your seed, and my menstrual cycle has ceased. Food and drink brought me the same pleasure and delight as before. I know the future emperor is within me. As a rainbow crossing the sun is a rare propitious sign, so is the dragon occupying my bosom a good omen for blissful prosperity.[10] In eager anticipation, I look forward to the day I give birth to the child that continues your divine lineage. I will carry him in my arms, and traverse the courtyard to pay respect to his sage and brilliant father.[11] In a rush to receive Your Majesty's congratulations, I submit this memorial to report this joyful event.

The emperor was in the Western palace when the letter arrived, and the good news lit up his face with joy. He replied:

Your letter brings me happiness doubled with felicity. Husband and wife form an intimate union and partake in the

---

[10]According to Zhang Zhenjun, the phrase *hongchu guanri* 虹出貫日 may be a conflation of two images: one is the rainbow as the harbinger of the birth of an emperor, and the other is a white rainbow either crossing the sun or arching over the city wall, which is interpreted as a bad omen. See Zhenjun Zhang and Jing Wang, *Song Dynasty Tales: A Guided Reader* (World Scientific, 2017), note 21.

[11]The term *quting* 趨廳 (traversing the courtyard with quickened steps) derives from the phrase "*qu er guoting* 趨而過廳," which was originally used to describe Kongli's respectful behavior in front of his father Kongzi (Confucius) in "Jishi 季氏" of the *Lunyu* (the *Analects*). In later times, the condensed version of this phrase, *guoting* 過廳, became an idiom to describe a son receiving his father's instruction.

same responsibilities. The continuation of my throne carries more weight than all other state affairs. Now that you are early in pregnancy, taking good care of yourself is essential. Stay away from potent medicine but indulge yourself with harmless food. Whenever you have a request, there is no need to submit a written memorial; it is permitted that you send a courier to deliver the message orally.

Both the empress dowager and Zhaoyi sent their greetings. The couriers they dispatched arrived one after another.

The empress feared that during the occasions of conjugal fulfillment the emperor might discover her fraud, she therefore consulted the courtier Wang Sheng for a strategy by which to protect herself.

Wang Sheng advised the empress: "Why not use the excuse that a pregnant woman should not go near men, as the contact triggers aversion, which may in turn cause a miscarriage?"

Accordingly, the empress sent Wang Sheng to deliver the message to her husband. From then on, the emperor refrained from seeing the empress in person and only dispatched envoys to inquire about her well-being.

When the time of the expected birth drew near, the emperor arranged the "Baby Bath Ceremony." The empress summoned Wang Sheng (and the other eunuchs) and said to him: "You came to the forbidden quarters as a eunuch.[12] Thanks to me, you and your father enjoy wealth and power. Seeking a strategy to secure my long-term interests, I made up the story of my pregnancy. Now that the day of expectancy is approaching, can you come up with a plan to cover up for me? If your plan works, you will be rewarded handsomely from generation to generation."

---

[12]The words in parentheses, absent in some versions of the tale, are not in keeping with the context and may be the result of scribal error.

Wang Sheng replied: "I, your servant, will find a commoner's newborn and smuggle it into the palace to be Your Highness' son. However, this must be kept secret." The empress approved.

Outside the precinct of the capital city, Wang Sheng bought a newborn at the price of some hundred taels. He hid the baby in a capsule and brought it to the palace. But by the time they opened the capsule, the baby had already died.

Startled, the empress said: "Now the baby is dead, how can it help us?"

Wang Sheng replied: "I see why: the container was airtight, so the baby suffocated. Let me find another baby and put it in a container with punched holes. Since air can go through the holes, the baby will survive."

Wang Sheng obtained another infant. But when he was approaching the palace gate, the baby cried loudly. He did not dare to enter. A while later, he re-approached the palace gate; but the same thing happened again. In the end, Wang Sheng did not dare smuggle the baby into the palace. (The imperial palace was tightly guarded. After the incident in the Eastern palace, the emperor decreed stricter surveillance.)[13] Meeting with the empress, Wang Sheng told her about the baby's crying. The empress wept and said, "Now what can be done?"

After twelve lunar months, the empress still had not given birth. The emperor grew very suspicious. Someone submitted a memorial to offer an explanation: "It took fourteen lunar months for King Yao to be born. Clearly, the empress must be bearing a sage."[14]

---

[13] The text in parentheses is likely to be an in-text commentary mistaken for the main text when it was being transcribed.

[14] Yao 堯 is one of the three legendary sage-kings in ancient times, together with Shun 舜 and Yu 禹.

In the end, the empress had no way to cover up her fraud other than to send a courier to inform the emperor [, saying]: "In my dream last night I saw a dragon lying still. Sadly, the sage emperor's offspring was not born."

The emperor only lamented, but Zhaoyi saw through the lie. She sent a courier to reproach the empress: "Why was the sage emperor's son not born? Is it really because time was not ripe? How could you attempt to deceive the lord with a puny lie that would not fool even a child three-feet tall? If one day the lie were to be discovered, I dare not predict what end my sister will meet."

One day, a maid surnamed Zhu, who served tea for the palace ladies, gave birth to a child. When the eunuch Li Shouguang reported this to the emperor, he was dining with Zhaoyi. Bursting into a rage, Zhaoyi confronted the emperor: "Your Majesty claimed earlier to have visited the empress dowager; now the Zhou woman has given birth to a son. How did she get pregnant?" Zhaoyi then threw herself onto the floor and cried loudly.

The emperor personally helped Zhaoyi back to her seat. Zhaoyi summoned the palace official Zhai Gui and commanded: "Hurry, go and fetch that infant." When Zhai Gui brought the child and presented it to Zhaoyi, she said to him: "Kill it for me." Zhai Gui hesitated. Zhaoyi reproached him in anger: "I have made you rich. Will you make yourself useful now? If you disobey, I will kill you together with the baby."

Gui threw the baby against a pillar base in the palace and killed it. He then disposed of the body in the inner palace. From then on, every pregnant maid had to be killed.

As time passed, the emperor began to walk with difficulty. With his vitality waning, he became impotent. A master of esoterica presented him with a powerful cinnabar that had come out of the kiln after a hundred days of firing: first, water was poured into a jar until it was full, and then the cinnabar was dropped into the water; as soon as the water boiled, it would be poured out and replaced with fresh water. This was repeated for ten days, after which the water no longer boiled. The cinnabar was then ready for consumption.

Taking one cinnabar each day, the emperor became again capable of making love to Zhaoyi.

One time, the emperor was spending the evening at the Hall of Grand Celebration, and a tipsy Zhaoyi presented him with ten cinnabar pills all at once. [15] Early in the night, the emperor continually let out laughing groans while he held Zhaoyi in a bed covered with brown satin drapes. By midnight, however, he began to feel dizzy. Knowing something was wrong, he tried to sit up but failed; he would either fall face down or onto his back. Zhaoyi immediately got up to hold a light to the emperor, and saw that semen was oozing out of him like a bubbling spring. In a short while, the emperor was dead.[16] The empress dowager sent officials to question Zhaoyi about the cause of death. Zhaoyi committed suicide.

Empress Zhao in the Eastern palace had long been neglected by the emperor. One evening, she cried with grief in her sleep for a long time, until she was woken up by the attending maids. "In my dream just now the emperor disappeared," she recalled, "I saw the emperor appear in the clouds and offer me a seat. When

---

[15]There was no building in the Han-dynasty palace known as the Daqing Hall 大慶殿, literally "Hall of Grand Celebration"; this was, on the other hand, the name of the main hall in the Northern-Song imperial palace. The character *tai* 太, which was used interchangeably with *da* 大, appears in some other versions of the text.

[16] The passage borrows plot and language from "Zhao Feiyan waizhuan," which also contains a startling scene of the emperor emitting an unstoppable overflow of semen. This constitutes one of the earliest depictions in literature of a character dying from sexual exhaustion due to an overdose of aphrodisiacs.

he ordered his attendants to serve her tea, they disobeyed, saying 'she who did not serve Your Majesty with respect before deserves no tea.' I was displeased and asked, 'Where is Zhaoyi?' The emperor replied, 'Because she murdered several of my sons, she was condemned to become a giant softshell turtle. In the North Sea, she resides in the cave of dark streams and suffers from the perpetual cold of icy water.' This is the reason I cried in deep grief."

Later, while hunting at sea, the king of the northern state of Greater Yue saw a giant turtle emerging from a cave.[17] On its head the turtle wore a jade hairpiece. She gazed at the waves, seemingly with a yearning for the human world. The king sent an envoy to Emperor Wu of Liang to inquire about the matter and was told the story of Zhaoyi.[18]

---

[17]The northern state *Dayue* 大月 appears as *Da yuezhi* 大月支 (the Greater *Yuezhi*) in other versions, which may be a variant way of writing *Da yuezhi* 大月氏, the Chinese name for a confederacy of nomadic (possibly Indo-European) tribes who migrated from their putative homeland at the edge of the Gobi desert in present-day Gansu province to the Ferghana valley in modern Uzbekistan. A branch of the *Yuezhi* confederation later established the Kushan Empire around 50 CE.

[18]Emperor Wu of Liang (464–549 CE) was the founding emperor of the Liang dynasty; by the time of his reign, however, the Kushan empire had already been divided and conquered by neighboring empires.

趙飛燕別傳

秦醇

余里有李生，世業儒術。一日，家事零替。余往見之。牆角破筐中有古文數冊，其間有趙后別傳，雖編次脫落，尚可觀覽。余就李生乞其文以歸，補正編次以成傳，傳諸好事者。

趙后腰骨尤纖細，善踽步行。若人手執花枝，顫顫然，他人莫可學也。生在主家時，號爲飛燕。入宮復引援其妹，得幸，爲昭儀。昭儀尤善笑語，肌骨秀滑。二人皆天下第一，色傾後宮。

自昭儀入宮，帝亦希幸東宮。昭儀居西宮，太后居中宮。后日夜欲求子，爲自固久遠計，多用小犢車載年少子與通。帝一日惟從三四人往后宮，后方與人亂，不知。左右急報，后遽驚出迎帝。后冠發散亂，言語失度，帝固亦疑焉。帝坐未久，復聞壁衣中有人嗽聲，帝乃出。由是帝有害后意，以昭儀隱忍未發。

一日，帝與昭儀方飲，帝忽攘袖嗔目，直視昭儀，怒氣怫然不可犯。昭儀遽起，避席伏地，謝曰：“臣妾族孤寒下，無強近之愛。一旦得備後庭驅使之列，不意獨承幸御，濃被聖私，立於衆人之上。恃寵邀愛，衆謗來集。加以不識忌諱，冒觸威怒。臣妾願賜速死以寬聖抱。”因淚交下。

帝自引昭儀曰：“汝復坐，吾語汝。”帝曰：“汝無罪，汝之姊，吾欲梟其首，斷其手足，置於溷中，乃快吾意。”昭儀曰：“何緣而得罪？” 帝言壁衣中事。昭儀曰：“臣妾緣后得備後宮。后死，則妾安能獨生？陛下無故而殺一后，天下有以窺陛下也。願得身實鼎鑊，體膏斧鉞。”因大慟，以身投地。帝驚，遽起持昭儀曰：“吾以汝之故，固不害后，第言之耳，汝何自恨若是？”久之，昭儀方就坐，問壁衣中人。帝陰窮其跡，乃宿衛陳崇子也。帝使人就其家殺之，而廢陳崇。

昭儀往見后，言帝所言，且曰：“姊曾憶家貧飢寒無聊，姊使我與鄰家女爲草履，入市貨履市米。一日得米歸，遇風雨無火可炊。飢寒甚，不能成寐，使我擁姊背，同泣。此事姊豈不憶也？今日幸富貴，無他人次我，而自毀如此。脫或再有過，帝復怒，事不可救，身首異地，爲天下笑。今日，妾能拯救也。存殁無定。或爾妾死，姊尚誰攀乎？”乃涕泣不已，后亦泣焉。

自是帝不復往后宮，承幸御者，昭儀一人而已。昭儀方浴，帝私視。侍者報昭儀，昭儀急趨燭後避。帝瞥見之，心愈眩惑。他日昭儀浴，帝默賜侍者，特令不言。帝自屏罅覘，蘭湯灔灔，昭儀坐其中，若三尺寒泉浸明玉，帝意思飛蕩，若無所主。

帝語近侍曰：“自古人主無二后，若有，則吾立昭儀爲后矣。”趙后知帝見昭儀浴，益加寵幸，乃具湯浴，請帝以觀。既往，后入浴。后裸體，以水沃帝，愈親近而帝愈不樂，不終幸而去。后泣曰：“愛在一身，無可奈何。”

后生日，昭儀爲賀，帝亦同往。酒半酣，后欲感動帝意，乃泣數行。帝曰：“它人對酒而樂，子獨悲，豈不足耶？”后曰：“妾昔在主宮時，帝幸其第。妾立主後，帝時視妾不移目，甚久。主知帝意，遺妾侍帝，竟承更衣之幸。下體嘗污御服，妾欲爲帝浣去，帝曰：‘留以爲憶。’不數日，備後宮。時帝齒痕猶在妾頸。今日思之，不覺感泣。”帝惻然懷舊，有愛后意，顧視嗟歎。昭儀知帝欲留，昭儀先辭去。帝逼暮方離后宮。

后因帝幸，心爲姦利，上器主受，經三月，乃詐託有孕，上箋奏云：

> “臣妾久備掖庭，先承幸御，遣賜大號，積有歲時。近因始生之日，復加善祝之私，特屈乘輿，俯臨東掖，久侍宴私，再承幸御。臣妾數月來，內宮盈實，月脈不流，飲食甘美，不異常日。知聖躬之在體，辨天日之入懷。虹初貫日，應是珍符，龍據妾胸，茲爲佳瑞。更期蕃育神嗣，抱日趨庭，瞻望聖明，踊躍臨賀。謹此以聞。”

帝時在西宮，得奏，喜動顏色，答云：

> “因閱來奏，喜慶交集。夫婦之私，義均一體，社稷之重，嗣續其先。姙體方初，保綏宜厚。藥有性者勿舉，食無毒者可親。有懇來上，無煩箋奏，口授宮使可矣。”

兩宮候問，宮使交至。

后慮帝幸，見其詐，乃與宮使王盛謀自爲之計。盛謂后曰：“莫若辭以有姙者不可近人，近人則有所觸焉，觸則孕或敗。”后乃遣王盛奏帝。帝不復見后，第遣使問安否。

而甫及誕月，帝具浴子之儀。后召王盛及宮中人曰：“汝自黃衣郎出入禁掖，吾引汝父子俱富貴。吾欲爲自利長久計，託孕乃吾之私意，實非也。言已及期。子能爲吾謀焉？若事成，子萬世有後利。”盛曰：‘臣爲后取民間才生子，攜入宮爲后子。但事密不洩，亦無害。”后曰：“可。”

盛于都城外有生子者，纔數日，以百金售之。以物囊之，入宮見后。既發器，則子死。后驚曰：“子死，安用也？”盛曰：“臣今知矣。載子之器氣不泄，此子所以死也。臣今求子，載之器，穴其上，使氣可出入，則子不死。”盛得子，趨宮門欲入，則子驚啼尤甚，盛不敢入。少選，復攜之趨門，子復如此，盛終不敢入宮。

（後宮守門吏甚嚴密。因向壁衣事。故帝令加嚴之甚。）

盛來見后，具言驚啼事。后泣曰：“爲之奈何？”

時已踰十二月矣。帝頗疑訝。或奏帝曰：“堯之母十四月而生堯，后所姙當是聖人。”后終無計，乃遣人奏帝云：“臣姜昨夢龍臥，不幸聖嗣不育。”帝但歎惋而已。昭儀知其詐，乃遣人謝后曰：“聖嗣不育，豈日月不滿也？三尺童子尚不可欺，況人主乎？一日手足俱見，妾不知姊之死所也。”

時後庭掌茶宮女朱氏生子，宦官李守光奏帝，帝方與昭儀共食，昭儀怒，言於帝曰：“前者帝言自中宮來。今朱氏生子，從何而得也？”乃以身投地，大慟。帝自持昭儀起坐。昭儀呼宮吏祭規曰：“急爲取子來！”規取子上。昭儀謂規曰：“爲我殺之。”規疑慮。昭儀怒罵曰：“吾重祿養汝，將安用也？不然，吾併戮汝。”規以子擊殿礎死，投之後宮。宮人孕子者盡殺之。

後帝行步遲澀，頗氣憊，不能御昭義。有方士獻大丹，其丹養于火百日，乃成。先以甕貯水，滿，即置丹于水中，即沸，又易去，復以新水。如是十日，不沸，方可服。帝日服一粒，頗能幸昭儀。

一夕，在大慶殿，昭儀醉進十粒。初夜，絳帳中擁昭儀，帝笑聲吃吃不止。及中夜，帝昏昏，知不可，將起坐，夜或仆臥。昭儀急起，秉燭自視帝，精出如泉溢。有頃，帝崩。太后遣人理昭儀且急，窮帝得疾之端，昭儀乃自絕。

后居東宮，久失御。一夕后寢，驚啼甚久，侍者呼問，方覺。乃言曰：“適吾夢不見帝。帝自雲中賜吾坐。帝命進茶，左右奏帝：‘后向日侍帝不謹，不合啜此茶。’吾意既不足，吾又問：‘昭儀安在？’帝曰：‘以數殺吾子，今罰爲巨黿，居北海之陰水穴間，受千歲冰寒之苦。’”乃大慟。

後北鄙大月王獵於海，見一巨黿出於穴上，首猶貫玉釵，顒望波上，惓惓有戀人之意。大月王遣使問梁武帝，武帝以昭儀事答之。

Tale 8.44

The Tale of Tan Yige

by Qin Chun
Translated by Jing Wang

Tan Yige, who had the childhood name Yingnu, was born in Yingzhou[1] where her parents resided. After her father passed away, she wandered, homeless, in Changsha, which is now known as Tanzhou.[2] When she was eight years old, her mother also died, and Yige was entrusted to the household of a minor craftsman, Zhang Wen, who earned a living by making bamboo utensils.

One day, a government courtesan,[3] Ding Wanqing, visited Wen's household and thought to herself, "If I could get custody of

---

[1]Yingzhou 英州 was located about ninety miles north of modern Guangzhou in Guangdong province.

[2]Tanzhou 潭州 was modern Changsha in Hunan province.

[3]Courtesans in the Tang and Song were divided into two major categories. The first category was *guanji* 官妓 (government courtesans), who were on the government register and were responsible for providing entertainment at official banquets and other official occasions. A special group in this category was *yingji* 營妓 (barracks courtesans), or *junji* 軍妓 (army courtesans) established in the Song, who mainly served military commanders. The second category was independent or private courtesans, which included housemaids and those in marketplace brothels.

694

Yige, she would definitely make me rich." She then invited Wen for a drink, but did not say anything about her potential plans and left. On another day, she sent Wen money and cloth, and lavished gifts on him. Wen then said to her, "I am only a lowly market craftsman, but you have bestowed your generosity on me. I am poor and have nothing with which to repay you. I do not know what your intentions are. If there is anything you wish to request of me, please let me know. I am willing to repay you with all of my stupidity for your generosity." Wanqing said, "I didn't mention anything for a long time, fearing that I would enrage a gentleman like you. Now, only after you have spoken to me in such a sincere way do I dare initiate this conversation. I privately know that Yige is not your child. I admire her complexion and appearance. If you sell her to me, I will not only pay you a large amount today, but you will also benefit greatly in the future. Do not make her stay in your household and suffer in vain from cold and hunger. What do you say?" Wen responded, "I have suspected your intentions for a long time and had planned to broach the subject first. Given this situation, how dare I not oblige you!" Yige was only ten years old at the time. When she realized the intentions of Wen and Wanqing, she berated Wen furiously, saying, "I am not your child. How can you live with abandoning me to that house of prostitution? If I can be married off — even into a poor household — that is what I wish." Wen eventually sent Yige to Wanqing.

When Yige entered Wanqing's household, she screamed and cried, "I am alone and wretched, wandering around in this world without any strong family connections. I am young, have no one who cares for me and who would come to my rescue, and have no way of marrying a respectable man." People who heard her all sighed and felt deeply sad for her. Wanqing cajoled Yige every day with a myriad plans, decorated her hair with pearls and jade jewelry, covered her body with light and warm clothes, and satiated her appetite with delicious and fresh food. Wanqing's hospitality only became more earnest with time, as she treated Yige as an affectionate mother would treat her baby. Day and night, Yige was showered with such care and attention that she gradually changed her opinion because of such love, and she took on a new attitude due to the benefits she received. Yige forgot about her initial ambition.

Before Yige reached the age of maturity at fifteen, Wanqing chose a fine match for her. Yige's skin was pure, and her figure was elegant: her hair was dark in color; her eyes were long; her grass-blades-like hands were tender and slim; and her waist was slender and flexible like that of a palace lady.[4] By that time, her beauty was incomparable. The carriages and horses of visiting patrons regularly overflowed the front of her gate, and her residence was as crowded as a market. Furthermore, Yige was bright, quick-witted, and intelligent in nature. She was educated in music and was especially talented at writing poetry and prose. Young men competed with each other bestowing thousands of pieces of gold to win a smile from this spring-wind-like girl, and they only feared being left behind. When the prefecture officials held feasts or gatherings, they sent carriages to fetch her.

When Master Zhou, [5] Fiscal Commissioner and Deputy Governor of Tanzhou at the time, invited guests to a gathering in

---

[4] The "Jian'ai" 兼愛 (Universal Love) Chapter in the *Mo zi* 墨子 records an anecdote about King Ling of Chu 楚靈王 (r. 540 BCE–529 BCE). The King liked slender waists, so all of his subjects only had one meal a day. They tied their belts after exhaling and could not stand up without leaning against the wall.

[5] Master Zhou, i.e. Zhou Kang 周沆, served as Fiscal Commissioner of Southern Jing Hu Circuit 荊湖南路 in 1046 after the imperial army was defeated several times by the local rebels. He proposed military strategies to the court and successfully subdued the rebellion. He was then appointed Governor of Tanzhou.

his residence, Yige was the first to arrive. The Erudite for General Medicine,[6] Ji, also arrived at Zhou's residence on business, and he went into the hall to pay his respects to the Master. Ji had a fine beard and was handsome, prompting the Master to laugh and say, "I have the first line to a couplet. Can you come up with a matching line?" Ji responded, "I would like to hear it." The Master said, "When the gentleman of medicine bowed, his beard touched the floor." Before Ji could respond, Yige chimed in, "I would like to respond to the line on behalf of the Erudite." The Master replied, "It is permissible." Yige said, "At the place where the Marquise of the prefecture feasted, his curtains reached the sky." The Master was greatly delighted by her wit.

After Yige recovered from an illness and once again went to visit the government officials in their courtyard,[7] she often claimed herself to be "Half a Prefect" of poetry and wine. When Jiang Tian[8] saw these words, he laughed heartily and asked her to produce a matching line to a couplet. He pointed at her face and said, "Gourds after the fall mist become whiter and whiter." Yige then picked up the sleeve of his official garment and responded,

---

[6] Erudite for General Medicine was a local medical official in a prefecture in charge of medical treatment and administration. The most skillful doctor in the prefecture was selected to fulfill the position. This position was established only in the capital and the upper prefectures in the early Song and was later regularized throughout the state during the Chongning 崇寧 (1102–1106) reign of Emperor Huizong 徽宗 (1082–1135). When the story took place, Tan prefecture, as one of the upper prefectures, had this medical position.

[7] Yi's illness is out of context and not addressed in the previous text. There is a gap in the narrative, and some of the text may be missing.

[8] No historical record about Jiang Tian is available. Based on the text, he was most likely a subordinate official in the local government.

"Dates with the coming of autumn also wear the color of red."[9] The gentleman was both embarrassed and pleased, and the people around all praised her and sighed with admiration.

When Grand Master of Remonstrance Wei Guan[10] served as Governor of Changsha, he paid a visit to Marchmount Hill.[11] Yige followed him in his entourage. The Master knew that Yige could write poetry, so he summoned her and said, "Can you come up with a line and complete my couplet?" The Master said, "Led by an official in crimson garment, she climbs up the green screen." Yige responded, "Supported by the hands of a lady with red sleeves, he steps down from the white clouds." Because the Master was pleased with her response, he gave her the name Wenwan (Literate and Graceful) with the cognomen Caiji (Talented Charmer). Yige bowed twice and said, "I am a person of low birth, but the Master has given me a name and a cognomen. This honorable bestowal is worth more than a million pieces of gold."

When Grand Chancellor Liu Hang[12] (995–1060) governed Changsha, he ascended the Bixiang Gate[13] one day to enjoy the

---

[9]Officials with the rank of five or six wore red garments in the Song dynasty.

[10]Wei Guan was Governor of Tanzhou during the first three years of the Qingli reign of Emperor Renzong, i.e. from 1041 to 1043. He was said to be meticulous and circumspect when handling lawsuits, and skilled in government administration.

[11]Marchmount Hill, or the Yuelu 嶽麓 Mountain, is located on the west bank of the Xiang River in modern Changsha. It is not only a sacred mountain in Daoism, but also important in the history of Chinese philosophy. The Yuelu Academy, established in 976, was one of the most prestigious institutions of learning. It attracted many important philosophers to come and teach, such as Zhu Xi 朱熹 (1130–1200) and Wang Yangming 王陽明 (1472–1529).

[12]Grand Chancellor Liu, referred to as Liu Hang 劉沆, served as Governor of Tanzhou twice, i.e. in 1042 and again from 1043 to 1045. He quelled the rebellion of the "Yao Barbarians" in Hunan. He failed the

cool air. His subordinate officials followed him there. The Master summoned Yige, requesting that she produce a matching line to his couplet. Yige said, "I am a person of dishonorable birth. Sir, how dare I compete with your talent? However, you gave the order, so I dare not refuse." At that time, they wandered around and looked afar at the small islands of the Xiang River. There were bamboo houses, thatched huts, and a fisherman carrying a pair of fish while entering a narrow alley. The Grand Chancellor said, "A pair of fish entered the deep alley." Yige responded, "A foot of silk was sent to whose household?"[14] Master Liu was pleased and praised her talent for a long time.

On another day, she again followed Master Liu to visit Marchmount Hill. They traveled to the Baohuang Cave[15] and the Gazing-Hill Pavilion, where the Master chanted poems and the guests all produced echoing verses. Yige wrote a poem to present to the Master, which read:

It has been a millennium since the real immortal left,[16]
Here a precipitous pavilion was built, looking around at the openness.
The trace of spirituality was almost lost among the three-island-roads.

Civil Service Examination the first time, but he passed in the second place in 1030. He was said to be unreserved and straightforward in personality and was skilled in government administration.

[13]Bixiang Gate was the southern gate of Changsha.

[14]Both a pair of fish and a foot of silk are metaphors for letters.

[15]The Baohuang Cave is located in a valley of Marchmount Hill. Legend has it that during the Xiangfu 祥符 reign (1008–1016) a Daoist practitioner named Zhang Baohuang 張抱黃 practiced Daoist techniques in the cave and eventually achieved transcendence. Therefore, the cave was named after him. After his departure, the cave was said to be occupied by a python, thus also earning the name "Python Cave."

[16]The "real immortal" refers to the Daoist Zhang Baohuang.

Climbing high, we contemplate in vain the five-cloud
carriage.[17]
The apes' clear whistles at the moon alert a thousand cliffs.
The ancient trees chant at the wind along a winding road.
When will the one flying on the crane return to his
homeland?[18]
In the town on the riverside, there should remain few old
households.

When the Master saw this poem, he was even more astounded.
The seated guests passed the poem around, and everyone came to
sincerely admire her. The Master said, "This is a demonic poet."
When the Master asked her of her origin, Yige replied with the
truth, and the Master was saddened and felt deep sympathy for
her. Yige then told him, "It has been years since I was registered
as a government courtesan and began providing services to
the marquise. I dare not complain of being tired. Today, I am
fortunate to meet you, Master. If I could be released from the
courtesan registers and marry and labor for a respectable
commoner, I would definitely be grateful to you, even if I should
die." The Master agreed that she be released. On another day,
Yige visited the Master and submitted the application, and the
Master approved her request.

Yi then sought a good match but, for a long time, did not find
one. It happened that, at that time, Zhang Zhengyu, a man from

---

[17]The "five-cloud carriage" is the vehicle of an immortal. It was said
that at the seventh quarter in the evening on the seventh day of the
seventh month, the Queen Mother arrived at Emperor Wu's palace on a
cloud carriage.

[18]The phrase "flying on the crane" alludes to the Ding Lingwei 丁令
威 anecdote in *Soushen ji*. Ding Lingwei studied Daoist techniques at
Lingxu 靈虛 Mountain. Later he transformed into a crane and returned
to his hometown. He rested on the pillar at the city gate. When a young
fellow raised his bow and intended to shoot at it, the crane flew away.

Ruzhou,[19] was serving as the Tea Official[20] of Tanzhou. As soon as Yige met him, she told people, "I have found my husband." When people inquired about it, Yige stated, "The character, temperament, talent, and intelligence of that man all satisfy my expectations." When Zhang heard about this, he in turn expressed his interest in Yige.

One day, Zhang invited Yige to meet him at the riverside pavilion. At that time, the pavilion was located high in the light breeze, and the moon shone over the open river. Tassels hung from the upright canopy, and the clear breeze blew in through the window. Moonlight penetrated the loose bamboo curtains, and the silver incense burner in the shape of a mandarin duck released fragrance. A pair of jade pillows were arranged next to one another on the bed, and embroidered quilts were drawn back halfway. Intimate, sweet words were exchanged between the two, and their loving hearts were like flying willow catkins in the spring. Zhang and Yige were like two immortal flowers of the same root and a pair of fish swimming in the same spring. The ecstasy that they experienced with one another would never end, even after death. The next day, Yige took all of her belongings and married Zhang. An emotional person wrote a poem for them:

Satisfaction achieved only when talent and beauty meet.
It is an especially fine matter when the romantic and the
    elegant interface.

---

[19]Ruzhou 汝州 was located about fifty miles southeast of Luoyang in Henan province.

[20]In 1111, the Song court established the Tea and Salt Supervisorate in each of the six circuits in tea and salt producing areas to strengthen the central government's monopoly on those commodities. Previously, Circuit Supervisors exercised control over these areas on a part-time basis. Each was headed by a Tea and Salt Monopoly and the Supervisory Commissioner was chosen by the central government.

The peony was transplanted to the immortal capital,
There would not be any beautiful flowers at the East Xiang
    River thereafter.

Two years later, Zhang was transferred to another official
post. Before his departure, he again went to see Yige. Yige then
prepared his luggage for him and set up a feast in the suburbs to
bid him farewell. Just as Zhang was about to set off on his journey,
Yige took his arm and said to him, "You originally come from a
prestigious family, but I belong to the courtesan class. It is
certainly not a good marriage when a lowly person is matched
with a noble one. In addition, you do not have a wife who can
preside over the ancestral sacrificial rituals in the household, and
you have parents with white hair in the family hall. We will never
meet again after we are separated from each other today." Zhang
said, "The words of our oath to love one another are as brilliant as
the sun and the moon. If I ever turn against them, the gods and
the spirits are not to be fooled." Yige responded, "I have been
pregnant with your child for several months. He will share your
blood. You should think of him." Both of them were extremely
sad, and Zhang left with reluctance.

[After his departure,] Yige kept her house gate closed and
would not go out. Even her neighbors did not see her face. After a
long time, Yige wrote a letter to Zhang. The letter read:

> Winter has passed and spring has returned. As one sits and
> waits, the seasons come and go. The birds and the fish that
> carry letters for people hide their traces in their nests and at the
> bottom of the lake. We have not exchanged any news. The
> weather of early spring changes abruptly between cold and
> warm, so please do take good care of yourself. You are
> traveling in the capital and must have seen a lot; however, the
> person who lives in this isolated and distant place is restless in
> her heart. She yearns for your carriage to return. Every day is
> like a year to her. So I have written a little poem to send to the

one I miss. Furthermore, take care of yourself, a thousand times over.

Her poem read:

On the rivers Xiao and Xiang one detects the return of spring,
The winter ice has completely melted, and the plum blossoms
   have all fallen.
I wish to have a husband who is similar to the spring
That comes back once a year.

A year had passed, but Zhang still had not returned. Yige also had not heard that Zhang had married. Yige wrote another letter, which read:

Another year is upon us since we separated. The land to the east of River Xiang is warm, and spring is especially vibrant here. The jade-like blossoms of the plum trees by the creek have fallen, and the apricot trees at the rails are bursting with red buds. Last year's swallows have just returned, and orioles that feel the warmth have burst out in their first song. All that lies in front of me is the same as before; moved by human affairs, I feel sorrowful for myself. Sometimes I force myself to talk and laugh, but before I realize it, tears are flowing down my face. In recent months, I have lost my appetite. I am not really ill, but feel as if I am and cannot recover from this alone. Our little child is doing well, so do not trouble yourself and worry about him.

What I told you in person in the past was not meant to fool myself. Sir, you can neither disobey the words of your parents nor let go of the woman you love to form relations with a prestigious family. Isn't this a hopeless situation? If you were to lower your status by tying yourself to a woman as trivial and lowly as me and make sacrifices to stay loyal to our relationship from beginning to end, even to the end of my days, how could I repay you for all that you have done to marry me?

Even if I were to die, I would feel as if I were still alive. Even if I wore myself out from head to toe, it would still not be enough to recompense your kindness. When I think it over, even if I were to write with ten rabbit hair brushes until they went bald and use up all of the paper produced in the Three-River area,[21] my words would not be able to clarify my deeply tangled feelings for you and would only sully your ears. When I picked up my brush to write this letter, my tears had fallen into the ink stone on the table before I realized it. I could not control myself and fell into a melancholy mood. Please take care of yourself, a thousand times over, as the seasons change. Do not think too much of these matters. I have written two short lyric songs. They are not what a gentleman would chant, but I simply want to express my emotions.

The first of Yige's lyric songs was composed to the tune of "Jixiangsi ling" (Extreme Yearnings):

> The land to the east of River Xiang is the earliest to welcome
>   spring,
> The warm air feels like silk.
> The Qingming tomb sweeping festival has passed,
> In the alleys with faded flowers,
> One can still see the swing.
>
> Facing the scenery and moved by the change of seasons, my
>   feelings are in chaos,
> These intimate emotions, in vain the emerald wings of a bird
>   carry to convey.
> Facing the wind, under the moonlight,
> The season of blooming flowers and the never-ending day.

---

[21]The Three-River area refers to the Dongting Lake and Tanzhou in the northern part of modern Hunan province. The three rivers may be the Xiang River, the Yuan River 沅江, and the Zi River 資江, all of which flow into the Dongting Lake from different directions.

Tears pouring down, I don't know what to say.

She also wrote a second lyric song to the tune of "Chang xiangsi ling" (Eternal Yearnings):

Last year's swallows just returned,
The pear blossoms filled the courtyard.
Gradually the weather became warm and pleasant.
On this new sunny day, in the alleys,
In this place there are light carriages, arrogant horses,
Drinking parties and musical entertainment by the river.[22]
Old scenes remain the same while people have changed,
Facing the fine occasions,
I always feel more sorrow than happiness.
Deep and profound, my thoughts for the one far away,
In the secluded boudoir, I frown alone.

I am at the moment speechless because of sorrow and
    frustration,
Climbing high, I feel that the thoughts for the one far away
were entrusted to the misty waves in vain.
The joyous time of lovers has always been
Dictated by Heaven which, for whatever reason,
Separates and tortures them.
I force myself to laugh
At the clothes that have become loose on me recently.
The emotions so devastate me like this
That I have been wan and haggard,
Alas! For you it is all worthwhile!

---

[22]*Qi* 禊 or *fuqi* 祓禊 was originally a riverside sacrificial ceremony held on the *shangsi* day, i.e. the third day of the third month, to cleanse and get rid of all sinister forces. It later became a festival, when people would go on outings and hold drinking parties by the river.

When Zhang received Yige's letter and poems, he was unhappy for a long time. He secretly showed her letter to his close friends. All of those who were emotional sighed over Yige's words. Zhang was facing such internal pressure from the dictates of his parents and external pressure from criticism of his actions that he became a subject of popular disapproval. A month passed, and by then his parents had already arranged his marriage with the daughter of Palace Administration Aide Sun Shi. Betrothal gifts were sent; the woman's name and date of birth were obtained; the agreement for marriage was settled. The matchmaker urged him to select an auspicious wedding date. Within the next few days, he would go over to get the bride. Zhang was devoured by anxiety and sorrow, and tears flowed down his face. Though it was a nice day with beautiful scenery, what he felt was sadness in the face of a joyous event. He climbed high and looked afar in dismay, forcing himself to control his grief in silence. In the end, he dared not write a letter to Yige and notify her of his impending marriage.

Another year passed before Yige heard the news. She wrote the following letter which read:

> I clearly recognize my own lowliness and vulgarity. Every decision lies in your hands, Sir — how dare I inquire further about your choice? Once I entered the boudoir of your household, I diligently fulfilled my duty as a wife. I was respectful and obedient to you from dawn to dusk — how dare I complain about my adversity? It has been three years since I held a broom and a dustpan and served in your household. If I was not meeting your expectations in any way, you could have lowered yourself to teach me and correct my behavior. However, you abruptly abandoned me, leaving me with no one to rely on. If we judge this situation with regard to human emotions, your behavior can be considered ruthless and cruel. If one speculates from the perspective of heavenly principles, it is also impermissible. I have already entrusted myself to you,

Sir, and therefore I shall not blame others for my mistake. I always believed in what the ancient books said — that if there is righteousness between a man and a woman, then they can be united.[23] I have now, however, been estranged from you for no reason, and I feel deeply hurt by how weak I am and by how worthless I am to you. If oaths were to be broken, there would be nothing to say.

Our little child is already three years old. He just took his first steps. I expect that he will grow up to be a gentleman. At least, this is what I can hope for. I still have several hundred strings of coins in my coffers, with which I will purchase land in the suburbs. I will cultivate crops and garden with old peasants every day; rest in a leaky cottage and cover myself with a coarse wool blanket; and dig wells to water the vegetable garden. I will instruct my son to learn lessons from *The Book of Poetry* and *The Book of Documents*, and to know the importance of ritual and righteousness. I hope he achieves success so that I will be protected and taken care of for the rest of my life. I only hope for this and nothing more.

As for other things such as light breezes, grand buildings, the bright moon and terraces of pavilions, and all of those pleasant moments and felicitous moods, I have not enjoyed them to my heart's content for a long time. You certainly will not understand what I am saying today. Wait until a later time, and you will then understand what I feel now. Sir, you are

---

[23] Righteousness here may be an allusion to the righteousness between husband and wife as defined in "Hunyi" 婚義 (The Meaning of the Marriage Ceremony) in the *Liji*. The original *Liji* text reads: "The respect, the caution, the importance, the attention to secure correctness in all the details, and then (the pledge of) mutual affection — these were the great points in the ceremony, and served to establish the distinction to be observed between man and woman, and the righteousness to be maintained between husband and wife." (James Legge, *Sacred Books of China: The Texts of Confucianism*. Part IV, *The Li Ki* [Oxford: Clarendon Press, 1885], p. 430)

newlywed, and it is natural to be filled with joy; however, like the uprooted autumn sunflowers scattered over the field,[24] it is useless for me to have a heart that follows the sun. Ever since I was abandoned, I dare not climb high. My thoughts wander up to the white clouds, and my soul travels through to the edge of heaven. Deep feelings have accumulated in my bosom, and they cannot be exhausted. Where do you hold your official position? Ask the wind to send your news to me. I do not have any other intentions — only to know your whereabouts. I wept as I wrote this letter, and my heart's distress knows no bounds. Please do take good care of yourself.

When Zhang received the letter from Yige, he sighed and moaned day and night.

Three years later, Zhang's wife, the lady from the Sun family, passed away. The news did not reach the lands beyond the Dongting Lake. It happened that a visitor — whose official position had been reassigned — returned from Changsha to the capital. Zhang ran into him at the clergy office in the Department of State Affairs and inquired about Yige's whereabouts. The visitor clapped his hands and scolded in a loud voice, "Scholar Zhang is a wooden man with a stone heart. If he was to be judged by an emotional person, he would be guilty of crimes for which even the death penalty would be insufficient." Zhang asked, "Why do you say this?" The visitor said, "Since Zhang left, Yige has closed her doors and will not go out. Even her neighbors have

---

[24] "Biographies of Reasonable Officials" in *Shiji* records a short anecdote about an academician named Gongyi Xiu, Prime Minister of the State of Lu. When he ate some home-grown vegetables and found them tasty, he immediately pulled up all of them from his garden and threw them away. He set an example to stop government officials from scrambling for profit in competition with the common people. So the author uses a pun in the story and artfully combines the historical allusion and the description of the courtesan's feelings.

not seen her face. When she heard that Zhang had married another woman, Yige was even more resolved to maintain her solitude. She recently bought a hundred *mu* of land in the suburbs to support herself. She managed the household in an honest and strict way and would not allow any miscellaneous ideas to encroach on the family. She educated her son herself. In my opinion, the daughter of Li Zhuman in the ancient times cannot surpass her. If I ever see Zhang, I would spit in his face and cross-examine him." Zhang felt ashamed for a long time. He invited the visitor for a drink at a wine shop and said, "I am scholar Zhang, and what you have accused me of is all correct. You did not know, however, that I had parents at home and that I was forced to act as I did due to the nature of the situation." The visitor said, "I did not know that you were Gentleman Zhang." They did not leave the shop for a long time.

Scholar Zhang then went to Changsha and arrived a few days later. He wandered incognito in the market and inquired about Yige's behavior and activity. Those who talked about Yige's virtue would not allow others to interrupt. Zhang also secretly inquired of Yige's neighbors about Yige, but none of them had seen her. The entrance to her house was sedate and elegant, and the courtyard was clean and well-maintained. Upon seeing it, Zhang already felt melancholy.

When Yige caught sight of Zhang, she immediately shut the gate and refused to step out. Zhang said, "There is no other reason for me to wade several rivers, climb over high mountains, and walk several thousand miles. My heart has always been with you. Why do you so stubbornly refuse to see me? Is it because I treated you badly in the past?" Yige said, "You already have a wife. I behave in an upright, pure way to preserve my long-cherished reputation. You should leave and not damage my name." Zhang continued, "My wife already died. Please do not let past events linger in your mind. You will understand my actions if you think and reason about them. If I cannot have you, I swear I will die in this place." Yige responded, "I have always admired you, but if I enter your household in a rush, you will more easily abandon me. If you do not want to abandon me again, you should communicate with a matchmaker and arrange a wedding ceremony for me. Only after this do I dare follow your orders. Otherwise, we will never meet again." In the end, she did not come out. Zhang then did as she requested — he sent Yige betrothal gifts and asked the matchmaker to inquire about her name and date of birth. Everything was done exactly as in a formal marriage ritual. When the procedures were completed, he brought Yige with him to return to the capital.

Yige managed the household and boudoir strictly with ritual and regulation. She got along with his relatives and clansmen, and treated them with favor and kindness. There was harmony among the people inside and outside of the family, and an appropriate management of the household was finally achieved. Yige later gave birth to another son, who passed the Civil Service Examination. Yige received an imperial title from the emperor and maintained that status throughout her life. Yige and Zhang grew old together, and their sons and grandsons were all prosperous. Oh, she was indeed a virtuous woman!

Note: This is also a revised version of my 2017 rendition in *Song Dynasty Tales: A Guided Reader*, pp. 79–116.

譚意歌傳

秦醇

　　譚意歌小字英奴，隨親生於英州。喪親，流落長沙，今潭州也。年八歲，母又死，寄養小工張文家。文造竹器自給。一日，官妓丁婉卿過之，私念苟得之，必豐吾屋。乃召文飲，不言而去。異日復以財帛賕文，遺頗稠疊。文告婉卿曰：“文廛市賤工，深荷厚意。家貧，無以為報。不識子欲何圖也？子必有告。幸請言之。願盡愚圖報，少答厚意。”婉卿曰：“吾久不言，誠恐激君子之怒。今君懇言，吾方敢發。竊知意歌非君之子。我愛其容色。子能以此售我，不惟今日重酬子，異日亦獲厚利。無使其居子家，徒受寒饑。子意若何。”文曰：“文揣知君意久矣，方欲先白。如是，敢不從命。”是時方十歲，知文與婉卿之意，怒詰文曰：“我非君之子，安忍棄於娼家乎？子能嫁我，雖貧窮家，所願也。”文竟以意歸婉卿。過門，意哥大號泣曰：“我孤苦一身，流落萬里，勢力微弱，年齡幼小。無人憐救，不得從良人。”聞者莫不嗟憫。

　　婉卿日以百計誘之。以珠翠飾其首，輕煖披其體，甘鮮足其口，既久益勤，若慈母之待嬰兒。辰夕浸沒，則心自愛奪，情由利遷。意哥忘其初志，未及笄，為擇佳配。肌清骨秀，髮紺眸長，黃手纖纖，宮腰搦搦，獨步於一時。車馬駢溢，門館如市。加之性明敏慧，解音律，尤工詩筆。年少千金買笑，春風唯恐居後，郡官宴聚，控騎迎之。時運使周公權府會客，意先至府，醫博士及有故至府，升廳拜公。及美髯可愛，公因笑曰：“有句，子能對乎？，及曰：“願聞之。”公曰：“醫士拜時鬚拂地。’及未暇對答，意從旁曰：“願代博士對。”公曰：“可。”意曰：“郡侯宴處幕侵天。”公大喜。意疾既愈，庭見府官，多自稱詩酒於刺。蔣田見其言，頗笑之。因令其對句，指其面曰：“冬瓜霜後頻添粉。”意乃執其公裳

711

袂，對曰：“木棗秋來也著緋。”公且慚且喜，眾口嗡然稱賞。魏
諫議之鎮長沙，遊嶽麓時，意隨軒。公知意能詩，呼意曰：“子可
對吾句否？”公曰：“朱衣吏，引登青障。”意對曰：“紅袖人，扶
下白雲。”公喜，因為之立名文婉，字才姬。意再拜曰：“某，微
品也。而公為之名字，榮踰萬金之賜。”劉相之鎮長沙，云一日登
碧湘門納涼，幕官從焉。公呼意對。意曰：“某，賤品也，安敢敵
公之才？公有命，不敢拒。”爾時迤邐望江外湘渚間，竹屋茅舍，
有漁者攜雙魚入脩巷。公相曰：“雙魚入深巷。”意對曰：“尺素寄
誰家。”公喜，贊美久之。他日，又從公軒遊岳麓，歷抱黃洞望山
亭吟詩，坐客畢和。意為詩以獻曰：

> 真仙去後已千載，此構危亭四望賒。
> 靈跡幾迷三島路，凭高空想五雲車。
> 清猿嘯月千巖曉，古木吟風一徑斜。
> 鶴駕何時還古里，江城應少舊人家。

公見詩愈驚歎，坐客傳觀，莫不心服。公曰：“此詩之妖也。”
公問所從來，意哥以實對。公愴然憫之。意乃告曰：“意入籍驅使
迎候之列有年矣，不敢告勞。今幸遇公，倘得脫籍為良人箕帚之役，
雖死必謝。”公許其脫。

異日，詣投牒，公諾其請。意乃求良匹，久而未遇。會汝州民
張正字為潭茶官，意一見謂人曰：“吾得婿矣。”人詢之，意曰：
“彼風調才學，皆中吾意。”張聞之，亦有意。一日，張約意會於
江亭。於時亭高風怪，江空月明。陡帳垂絲，清風射牖，疎簾透月，
銀鴨噴香。玉枕相連，繡衾低覆，密語調簧，春心飛絮。如仙葩之
並蒂，若雙魚之同泉，相得之歡，雖死未已。翌日，意盡攜其裝囊
歸張。有情者贈之詩曰：

> 才識相逢方得意，風流相遇事尤佳。
> 牡丹移入仙都去，從此湘東無好花。

後二年，張調官，復來見。意乃治行，餞之郊外。張登途，意
把臂囑曰：“子本名家，我乃娼類，以賤偶貴，誠非佳婚。況室無
主祭之婦，堂有垂白之親。今之分袂，決無後期。”張曰：“盟誓
之言，皎如日月，苟或背此，神明非欺。”意曰：“我腹有君之息

數月矣。此君之體也，君宜念之。"相與極慟，乃捨去。意閉戶不出，雖比屋莫見意面。既久，意為書與張云：

陰老春回，坐移歲月。羽伏鱗潛，音問兩絕。首春氣候寒熱，切宜保愛。逆旅都輦，所見甚多。但幽遠之人，搖心左右，企望回轅，度日如歲。因成小詩，裁寄所思。茲外千萬珍重。

其詩曰：

瀟湘江上探春回，消盡寒冰落盡梅。
願得兒夫似春色，一年一度一歸來。

逾歲，張尚未回，亦不聞張娶妻。意復有書曰：

相別入此新歲，湘東地煖，得春尤多。溪梅墮玉，檻杏吐紅，舊燕初歸，煖鶯已囀。對物如舊，感事自傷。或勉為笑語，不覺淚泠。數月來頗不喜食，似病非病，不能自愈。孺子無恙（意子年二歲），無煩流念。向嘗面告，固匪自欺。君不能違親之言，又不能廢己之好，仰結高援，其無□焉。或俯就微下，曲為始終，百歲之恩，沒齒何報。雖亡若存，摩頂至足，猶不足答君意。反覆其心，雖禿十兔毫，磬三江楮，亦不能□茲稠疊，上浼君聽。執筆不覺墮淚几硯中。鬱鬱之意，不能自已。千萬對時善育，無或以此為至念也。短唱二闋，固非君子齒牙間可吟，蓋欲攄情耳。

曲名《極相思令》一首：

湘東最是得春先，和氣煖如綿。清明過了，殘花巷陌，猶見鞦韆。對景感時情緒亂，這密意，翠羽空傳。風前月下，花時永晝，灑淚何言。

又作《長相思令》一首：

舊燕初歸，梨花滿院，迤邐天氣融和。新晴巷陌，是處輕車轎馬，褉飲笙歌。舊賞人非，對佳時，一向樂少愁多。遠意沉沉，幽閨獨自顰蛾。　正消黯無言，自感凭高遠意，空寄烟波。從來美事，因甚天教兩處多磨？開懷強笑，向新來寬卻衣羅。似恁地人懷憔悴，甘心總為伊呵。

張得意書辭，情悰久不快，亦私以意書示其所親，有情者莫不
嗟嘆。張內逼慈親之教，外為物議之非，更莘月，親已約孫貴殿丞
女為姻。定問已行，媒妁素定，促其吉期，不日佳赴。張回腸危結，
感淚自零。好天美景，對樂成悲，憑高悵望，默然自已。終不敢為
記報意。逾歲，意方知，為書云：

> 妾之鄙陋，自知甚明。事由君子，安敢深扣。一入閨帷，克勤婦
> 道，晨昏恭順，豈敢告勞。自執箕帚，三改歲□。苟有未至，固
> 當垂誨。遽此見棄，致我失圖。求之人情，似傷薄惡，揆之天理，
> 亦所不容。業已許君，不可貽咎。有義則企，常風服於前書，無
> 故見離，深自傷於微弱。盟顧可欺，則不復道。稚子今已三歲。
> 方能移步。期於成人，此猶可待。妾囊中尚有數百緡，當售附郭
> 之田畝，日與老農耕褥別穰，臥漏復甍，鑿井灌園。教其子知詩
> 書之訓，禮義之重。願其有成，終身休庇妾之此身，如此而已。
> 其他清風館宇，明月亭軒，賞心樂事，不效如心久矣。今有此言，
> 君固未信，俟在他日，乃知所懷。燕爾方初，宜君子之多喜，拔
> 葵在地，徒向日之有心。自茲棄廢，莫敢凭高。思入白雲，魂遊
> 天末。幽懷蘊積，不能窮極。得官何地，因風寄聲。固無他意，
> 貴知動止。飲泣為書，意緒無極。千萬自愛。

張得意書，日夕歎悵。後三年，張之妻孫氏謝世，湖外莫通信
耗。會有客自長沙替歸，遇於南省書理間。張詢客意哥行沒。客撫
掌大罵曰：“張生乃木人石心也。使有情者見之，罪不容誅。”張
曰：“何以言之？”客曰：“意自張之去，則掩戶不出，雖比屋莫
見其面。聞張已別娶，意之心愈堅，方買郭外田百畝以自給。治家
清肅，異議纖毫不可入。親教其子。吾謂古之李住滿女，不能遠過
此。吾或見張，當唾其面而非之。”張慚忸久之，召客飲於肆，云：
“吾乃張生。子責我皆是。但子不知吾家有親，勢不得已。”客曰：
“吾不知子乃張君也。”久乃散。張生乃如長沙。數日，既至，則
微服遊於肆 ，詢意之所為。言意之美者不容刺口。默詢其鄰，莫
有見者。門戶瀟灑，庭宇消肅。張固已側然。意見張，急閉戶不出。
張曰：“吾無故涉重河，跨大嶺，行數千里之地，心固在子。子何
見拒之深也，豈昔相待之薄歟？”意云：“子已有室，我方端潔以
全其素志。君宜去，無浼我。”張云：“吾妻已亡矣。囊者之事，
君勿復為念，以理推之可也。吾不得子，誓死於此矣。”意云：
“我向慕君，忽遽入君之門，則棄之也容易。君若不棄焉，君當通

媒妁，為行吉禮，然後妾敢聞命。不然，無相見之期。"竟不出。
張乃如其請，納采問名，一如秦晉之禮焉。事己，乃挈意歸京師。
意治閨門，深有禮法。處親族皆有恩意，內外和睦，家道已成。意
後又生一子，以進士登科，終身為命婦。夫婦偕老，子孫繁茂。嗚
呼，賢哉！

Tale 8.45

The Record of Wang Youyu

By Liu Shiyin
Translated by Jing Wang

Lady Wang's given name was Zhenji (Perfected Charmer). Her childhood name was Youyu (Young Jade) and one of her cognomens was Xiancai (Immortal Talent). She was originally a native of the capital, but she followed her father when he wandered and drifted toward the area south of Lake Dongting.[1] Lady Wang and her two adopted sisters — one older, one younger — were all famous courtesans in Heng prefecture. Their stunning appearance and talents in singing and dancing set them apart from the rest of their female peers, and other courtesans dared not compete with them. Youyu was even superior to her two sisters, and those with whom she associated were all literati and ranking officials. Aside from these, even the wealthiest merchants and rich traders could not arouse her interest.

When Xia Gongyou[2] visited Hengyang,[3] the Commandery Marquis hosted a feast for him. Gongyou inquired, "I heard that

---

[1] Lake Dongting is the third largest lake in China and is located in the northern part of modern Hunan province.

[2] Xia E 夏噩, agnomen Gongyou, was a native of Guiji 會稽, which is modern Shaoxing city in Zhejiang province. He was recommended by court officials to attend the special Degree Examination of Direct Speech and Full Remonstrance in 1057 and was appointed Assistant Director of

there is a singing girl named Wang Youyu in Hengyang. She sings and dances splendidly and is exceedingly beautiful. Which one is she?" Upon hearing his question, the Commandery Marquise, Director Zhang Gongji,[4] ordered Youyu to come forward and bow to him. After Gongyou saw her, he sighed, saying, "If you lived in the Eastern or the Western Capital,[5] you would have been equal in fame with the capital's famous courtesans. Now that you dwell in this place, your name will never be made known to the world." He turned to the servants at his side for a piece of writing paper and composed a poem for Youyu. His poem read:

> The Perfected Lord has an impartial heart,
> The myriad things manifest themselves in various forms.
> I sigh for your orchid-like nature,
> for you are far away from the greenness of the secluded valley.
> The clear breeze secretly adds to your elegance.
> The rain and dew highlight your loveliness.
> If one day you dwell in the imperial garden,
> The peach and plum blossoms will yield to your fragrance.

From then on, Youyu's reputation became even more glorious. Despite this, however, in her spare time, she was always lonesome

---

the Court of Imperial Entertainment and Magistrate of Changzhou county. He was removed from his official position in 1061 for secretly charging for unlawful loans to people.

[3]Hengyang 衡陽 was the seat of Heng prefecture. It was located in modern Hengyang in Hunan province, about one hundred miles south of the provincial capital Changsha.

[4]Zhang Gongji 張公紀 passed the Civil Service Examination during the Jingyou reign period (1034–1038) of Emperor Renzong. He was the governor of Heng Prefecture from 1063 to 1065.

[5]The Eastern Capital refers to the capital city Bianliang 汴梁, which is modern Kaifeng in Henan province, and the Western Capital refers to Luoyang which is also in Henan province.

and melancholy, like a bright flower in seclusion, or a budded blossom holding back her fragrance with coldness. When some people inquired of Youyu about her behavior, she answered, "This path is not my ambition." When further prompted to explain herself, she replied, "Nowadays, a craftsman, a merchant, a peasant, a businessman, a Daoist, or a Buddhist monk, each can support himself. Only the women of my class make money by pleasing people with rouge and powder on our faces, and with flattering words and intriguing appearances. When I think about this, I feel endless shame and blush. I was coerced by my parents and siblings, and I have had no way of escaping from this way of life. If I could marry a respectable man,[6] stay at home to wait on my parents-in-law, preside over family ancestral sacrifices, and be identified by others as "that woman is the man's wife," then I would have a piece of land on which I could bury my bones after I die."

It happened that there was an extraordinary and talented man named Liu Fu, agnomen Runqing, who came from the Eastern Capital. The first time she set her eyes on him, Youyu declared, "That man will be my husband." Fu also had the intention of making her his wife. At that time, he was tired of traveling around. They always held hands, deeply in love with one another, when indulging in romantic moments in the breeze and under the moonlight, and they could not bear to part from each other. After a long time, Youyu's younger sister secretly became aware of their relationship. One day, she scolded Fu with the following words: "If you continue to behave the same way you did in the past, I will not let it go, but will immediately report

---

[6]"A respectable man" refers to a commoner whose social status was different from that of a servant or a prostitute. The term was also a form of address a woman used for her husband.

you to the government." From that moment, Fu no longer went to see Youyu.

One day, he encountered Youyu at the river. Weeping, she said, "It was not I who made the mistake. Sir, you should have reasoned this out. I was fortunate to have a marriage agreement with you in the past. Let's not make ourselves regret what happens today." They drank together on the river, and Youyu said, "Someday, my bones will rest in the graveyard of your ancestors." She then added, "Among the courtesans that I have known in my lifetime, many were separated from their lovers and then later reunited. Although they talked about their love for their suitors sincerely, their true intent was to take their wealth, and they would never fully entrust themselves to others. My hair is so long that it touches the ground; I cherish it as if it were gold and jade. Other men would dare not peek at it. However, I am more than willing to spare it for you." She then loosened her chignon and cut a strand of hair to give to Fu. Fu was deeply moved and pleased. After he left, he resented the fact that they could not meet again and suffered from this lingering thought. Because of this, he fell ill and took to his bed. Youyu thought of him day and night and sent people to attend to him. After he recovered, Fu composed a long song to give to Youyu, which read:

In the Purple Palace,[7] terraces and chambers sit high against each other,

---

[7]The Purple Palace is where the Daoist immortals dwell. In the Daoist canon *Baopuzi* 抱樸子 (*Master Who Embraces Simplicity*) written by Ge Hong (283–343), there is an anecdote about a Daoism follower named Xiang Mandu who narrates to his family his journey to Heaven to meet the Heavenly God. The text reads, "When we arrived at Heaven, we first passed the Purple Palace where the gold couch and jade table were shining and sparkling."

Over the golden and jade-colored doors and windows, red
halos rise.

Those who rest peacefully among them are all immortals.

Their gorgeous appearance is peerless in this world.

By chance, she thought to enter the dusty world.

Yet after a few years she was banished to the market in
Hengyang.

The imperial maid Ajiao[8] flew down from the ninth heaven,

She grew up in a courtesan house by chance.

Her heavenly demeanor and talent are unmatchable,

Prevailing over a myriad of women dressed in brocade from
the flower street.

Her dark hair is piled up like the clouds of the Wu Gorge,[9]

The glittering of her dark eyes is like the river water in autumn.

Her white fingers are long and full,

Like spring bamboo shoots pointed up to blue clouds in the
sky.

Embroidered shoes with flower patterns hold her narrow bow-
shaped feet,

---

[8]Ajiao 阿嬌 refers to Empress Chen 陳, the first empress of Emperor
Wu of Han (157 BCE–8 BCE). Her real given name is not recorded in
history, but she is referred to as Ajiao because of a fictional account in
the *Hanwu gushi* (*Precedents of Emperor Wu of the Han*), a collection of
records of anomalies, written by an anonymous writer. When Emperor
Wu was still a child, he was asked if he would like to marry Ajiao. He
made a gallant remark that "if Ajiao were to be my wife, I would build a
golden house and treasure her there." This is the origin of the phrase
jinwu cangjiao 金屋藏嬌 (Hiding Ajiao in a golden house). Ajiao was later
used as a term to refer to beautiful young women.

[9]Wu Gorge 巫峽 is one of the three gorges of the Yangtze River. It is
at the border of modern Hubei and Sichuan province. The image of
"clouds of the Wu Gorge" refers to women's beautiful hair. Using clouds
to describe women's hair originates from the poem "Going Out of the
East Gate" 出其東門 (Mao #93) in the *Book of Poetry*: I went out of the east
gate, where the girls were in clouds.

The phoenix ornaments raise their heads from below her red
    skirt.[10]
Sometimes she leans against the small rail and smiles, and
The peach blossoms are speechless, their petals falling down.
Grandsons of noble scions seem to lose their souls when gazing
    at her.
The daughter of the eastern neighbor is utterly shamed upon
    seeing her.[11]
Henceforth the young fellows of wealthy and powerful
    families,
Summoning servant boys and bridling their horses, pursuing
    her.
A thousand pieces of gold buys one song from her,
Their exuberant love is endless, like rain at dusk and clouds at
    dawn.[12]

---

[10] These two couplets are quite erotic with phallic images and descriptions of brocade slippers and feet. The phrase "narrow bow" seems to suggest the courtesan's bound feet.

[11] "Eastern neighbor" 東鄰 is a metaphor for beautiful women that first appears in Song Yu's (ca. 298 BCE–ca. 222 BCE) "The Poetic Exposition on Deng Tuzi's Lust" 登徒子好色賦. In the work, Deng Tuzi accuses the rhetorician Song Yu of lust or passionate desire. Song Yu responds that he is free of lust because his eastern neighbor, one of the most beautiful women in the world, has been eyeing him for three years, and he has not succumbed to her charms."

[12] The phrase "clouds at dawn and rain at dusk" 暮雨朝雲 alludes to Song Yu's "Rhapsody of Gaotang." When Song Yu traveled with King Xiang of Chu (d. 263 BCE) to the terrace at Cloud-Dream Marsh, the King was confused about the cloud of mist over the shrine that transformed endlessly. Song Yu explained to the king by telling him of a romantic encounter between a former king who roamed there and a goddess. The goddess dwelled on the south side of Wu Mountain. In the dawn she became a cloud of morning, in the evening, a passing shower. The phrase appears frequently in later literature to refer to sexual intercourse between a man and a woman.

That young man from the imperial capital is Gentleman Liu,
He has a charming demeanor and has everything he desires.
At first sight, Youyu paid special attention to him.
With attentive eagerness, she sent a matchmaker to make a
    request.
The blue birds[13] flew with a message to the window of her
    secluded residence,
That the gentleman only bitterly regretted the many
    restrictions.
Hiding her traces and evading her parents,
She secretly spent a night with the talented man at the river
    pavilion.
Still fearing his affection was not firm enough,
She loosened her chignon in front of him.
With golden scissors, she cut a single cloud-like strand.
Their two hearts grow more intimate, their bond dense as
    damask.
Since ancient times, the road to happiness is destined to be
    strewn with obstacles.
With no fixed date, their intentions are suspending and
    dangling.
In the clear night, she lets out a long sigh under the moonlight.
During the blossoming season, she sheds tears facing the east
    wind.
Her resentment enters the zither tune, almost causing the
    string to snap.
Her pearl-like tears fall, one after another.
Standing alone on the towering terrace with no one who
    understands her,
To whom should she entrust her newly written letter
    expressing her resentment?
What should Youyu do? She has a mother at home,

---

[13]The legendary blue birds were said to be messengers of the Queen
Mother of the West.

When she found out about the traces of Youyu's affair, she was
   furious.
Spending a thousand pieces of gold on wine, Youyu turned to
   her servant for help.
Her secret arrangements and stealthy pleasures were
   constantly foiled.
Knives are held in hand to cut the intertwined branches of the
   tree,
Bows are poised to shoot at the birds flying wing to wing.
The immortal mountains are located only in the center of the
   sea,
Due to headwind and high waves, there are no boats that sail.
The route to the Peach Spring[14] is cut off by mist and clouds.
Lying only a foot away from the dust of the world,[15] it is not to
   be found.
Both the man's heart and Youyu's affection are sincere and
   eager.
Together, they made an oath to the pine trees and the bamboo,
   and their attachment is even stronger.
May the gentleman swear until death not to change his heart.
In the world of human beings, they will meet each other when
   the time comes.
One day in the future should the man come back,
They will mount the path of mist and clouds hand in hand.

Because Fu had been traveling for a long time, his parents
urged him to return home. Youyu went secretly to bid him
farewell, and they drank together in a village shop. Youyu said,

---

[14]Peach Spring alludes to Tao Qian's (d. 427) "Record of the Peach
Blossom Spring." In this poem, Tao Qian creates a utopian world in
which people live in harmony and cut off their connection to the outside
world. It is accidentally found by a fisherman. When he leaves, he marks
the route to return, and reports it to the local governor. However, they
fail to find the way back.

[15]Dust is a metaphor for the mundane world.

"You have a pure talent, and I am beautiful. It is nature's way that talent and beauty make the right match, and we must swear not to give up on each other. It has been a long time since we have pledged to the deities and spirits, and our hearts have been intertwined for eternity like the pine trees and the bamboo. You must return to the Xiaoxiang[16] region in the future. I will wait for you." With that, the two of them took an oath, burned incense, and poured the incense powder into the wine, which they drank together. They then spent the night together on the river. The next day, Fu composed a lyric song to bid Youyu farewell. The title of the song was "Zui gaolou" (Intoxicated on the Lofty Terrace). The lyrics read:

> The bitterest thing in the human world,
> Is the bitterness of separation.
> She loves me,
> I am fond of her.
> On the riverbank with green grass, she stands alone.
> As the painted boat goes east, the sound of the oars grows
>   distant.
> The sky in the Chu region is so low,[17]
> When I look back,
> Sorrowfully, we long for each other.
> Though a future meeting is what we both wish,
> we don't yet know what day will be the right time.
> Things on my heart,
> Are tangled up like threads.
> Beautiful days and fine nights pass in vain,
> That sense of abandonment

---

[16]Xiaoxiang 瀟湘 refers to the Xiao and the Xiang rivers in modern Hunan province.

[17]Heng prefecture, where Liu Fu and Youyu met, belonged to the State of Chu in the Spring and Autumn and Warring States period (770 BCE–221 BCE).

is what both our hearts feel.
I wish that for you,
The intimate feelings remain,
Like paired birds we will fly.

Fu sang the song while drinking wine. The melody and the lyrics filled him with such sadness that he could not finish the song. They then stopped drinking and cried with great sorrow. Then Fu stepped onto the boat.

After Fu returned to the capital, because his parents were old and he had to attend to a number of matters in his household, he could not keep his earlier promise to go back to visit Youyu. He could only shed tears in front of the mirror. It happened that there was a visitor who came from Hengyang. He delivered a letter from Youyu and informed Fu that Yuoyu had been bedridden recently. Fu immediately opened her letter and quickly read through it. There was a couplet at the end of the letter which read:

The spring silkworm will not stop spinning its threads until its
    death,
The candle's wick will not dry up its tears until it burns to
    ashes.[18]

Fu was greatly saddened at heart. He sent her a letter in response to express his feelings. The letter read:

When I recall our past encounter in the Xiaoxiang region, it makes me sorrowful. I once wanted to take a boat and float back along the river to visit you so that I could renew our earlier oath and resume our old bond as in the past. This would compensate for your earnest affection for me and also provide me with a lifetime of happiness. However,

---

[18]This is the second couplet from Li Shangyin's 李商隱 (813–858) poem "Untitled."

unfortunately, because my parents are old and I bear the heavy responsibility of presiding over my clan, my heart's wish has been overtaken by other affairs. I admired your gracefulness and thought about you over and over. I could do nothing but remain alone and silent.

In the fine moments in the wind and under the moonlight and at famous places with poetry chanting and wine drinking, all those around me are happy and content, but only I remain in a trance, as if I have lost something. Sometimes I relied on wine for a sense of relief, but when I became sober, my emotions and longing were even more troubling, to the point that I almost had no hope to continue living. As for lovers in ancient times, perhaps their circumstances were to one lover's satisfaction, while the other was left to dissatisfaction. Then, it was easy for them to seek for ways to get together. Now, for you and me, neither of us is content with our circumstances, and it is difficult for us to seek reunion. Please wait a little longer, because matters are hard to predict and the future should turn out as we wish. If not, then heavenly principle and human affairs are not in harmony — though the divine maiden from beyond the heavens and the transcendent traveler from the immortal isles may still meet. If we two humans alone cannot follow them, how can this be anything but fate!

You should force yourself to eat, and not let the true essence of your being be depleted and evaporate. If you damage your own health and cannot meet me again, what can I hope for? Let me build on the two lines at the end of your letter and finish the poem for you:

> Staying by the river and facing the moon, my hidden grief is bitter.
> Standing frailly in the east wind, I am frightened of the chill.
> The beautiful lady from the Xiang River is reported to be ill,
> The talented gentleman in the imperial capital is also not at ease.

> The spring silkworm will not stop spinning its threads
> until its death,
> The candle's wick will not dry up its tears until it burns to
> ashes.
> There is no way of crossing the ten thousand miles of
> clouds and mountains.
> My dreaming soul crosses the Xiang River in vain.

One day as the setting sun sank lower in the west and before his loosely woven curtains were rolled up, Fu stood alone in his parents' room. He saw half of a face appear from between the room dividers. Fu took one look at it, and it was Youyu's face. Youyu said, "I fell ill from longing to see you. I have already died and transcended this world. I wanted to see you one last time, so I made this trip. Because I committed no evil deeds during my life, I did not sink into a gloomy hell. The day after tomorrow, I will be reborn into Zhang Sui's household at the west gate of Yanzhou,[19] again as a woman. The Zhang family sells cakes for a living. If you haven't forgotten about our past relationship, you can come over and see me there. Although I will not know what happened in my previous life, your emotion for me should be as always. I left something with my maidservant; you can retrieve it and use it as testimony to what I said. Please do take care." She then suddenly disappeared. Fu was astonished, but in the end, sighed and felt sympathy for her. Later, on another day, a visitor came from Hengyang. He said that Youyu had died, and he heard that before her death, she told her maidservant, "I was not able to see my gentleman and I will die with this regret. He used to love my hands, hair, eyebrows and eyes. Since I can't entrust these to you, I will only leave a single strand of hair and several fingernails.

---

[19] Yanzhou 兖州 was located in modern Yanzhou in Shandong province, about eighty miles south of Ji'nan.

When the gentleman comes to visit me, please give them to him." After a few days, Youyu died as expected.

The author comments, "As for the courtesans today, they all come and go to seek profit, and nothing else can arouse their interest. I have been searching for stories like that of Lady Xiao[20] and Lady Huo,[21] but have not heard of anything of the kind. Now Youyu loves Gentleman Liu — how deep is her affection! Any emotional man who reads this cannot but be heartbroken. Those who are talented in music can turn their stories into a song, and it can circulate widely in the world and pass on through spoken word. In this way, although Youyu dies, she will never be truly dead. It is for this purpose that I narrated this story."

Note: This is again a revised version of my 2017 rendition in *Song Dynasty Tales: A Guided Reader*, pp. 117–44.

---

[20]The story of Lady Xiao refers to the "Transformation of Yuxiao" in Fan Shu's 范攄 (fl. 875–888) *Yunxi youyi* 雲溪友議.

[21]Lady Huo, i.e. Huo Xiaoyu, is the courtesan protagonist in the famous Tang tale named after her (see T2.10 in Chapter 2 of this anthology).

王幼玉記

柳師尹

　　王生名真姬，小字幼玉，一字仙才，本京師人。隨父流落於湖外，與衡州女弟女兄三人皆為名娼，而其顏色歌舞，甲於倫輩之上。群妓亦不敢與之爭高下。幼玉更出於二人之上，所與往還皆衣冠士大夫。舍此，雖巨商富賈，不能動其意。夏公酉（夏賢良名噩，字公酉）遊衡陽，郡侯開宴召之，公酉曰："聞衡陽有歌妓名王幼玉，妙歌舞，美顏色，孰是也？"郡侯張郎中公起乃命幼玉出拜。公酉見之，嗟吁曰："使汝居東西二京，未必在名妓之下。今居於此，其名不得聞於天下。"顧左右取箋，為詩贈幼玉。其詩曰：

　　"真宰無私心，萬物逞殊形。
　　嗟爾蘭蕙質，遠離幽谷青。
　　清風暗助秀，雨露儒其泠。
　　一朝居上苑，桃李讓芳馨。"

　　由是益有光，但幼玉暇日常幽艷愁寂，寒芳未吐。人或詢之。則曰："此道非吾志也。"又詢其故。曰："今之或工或商或農或賈或道或僧，皆足以自養。惟我儕塗脂抹粉，巧言令色，以取其財。我思之愧赧無限。逼於父母姊弟，莫得脫此。倘從良人，留事舅姑，主祭祀，俾人回指曰：'彼人婦也。'死有埋骨之地。"會東都人柳富字潤卿，豪俊之士。幼玉一見曰："茲吾夫也。"富亦有意室之。富方倦遊，凡於風前月下，執手戀戀，兩不相捨。既久，其妹竊知之。一日，訴富以語曰："子若復為響時事，吾不捨子，即訟子於官府。"富從是不復往。

一日，遇幼玉於江上。幼玉泣曰：“過非我造也。君宜以理推之。異時幸有終身之約，無為今日之恨。”相與飲於江上，幼玉云：“吾之骨，異日當附子之先隴。”又謂富曰：“我平主所知，離而復合者甚眾。雖言愛勤勤，不過取其財帛，未嘗以身許之也，我髮委地，寶之若金玉，他人無敢窺覦，於子無所惜。”乃自解鬟，剪一縷以遺富。富感悅深至，去又羈思不得會為恨，因而伏枕。幼玉日夜懷思，遣人侍病。既愈，富為長歌贈之云：

紫府樓閣高相倚，金碧戶牖紅暉起。
其間燕息皆仙子，絕世妖姿妙難比。
偶然思念起塵心，幾年謫向衡陽市。
陽嬌飛下九天來，長在娼家偶然耳。
天姿才色擬絕倫，壓倒花衢眾羅綺。
紺髮濃堆巫峽雲，翠眸橫剪秋江水。
素手纖長細細圓，春筍脫向青雲裹。
紋履鮮花窄窄弓，風頭翅起紅裙底。
有時笑倚小欄杆，桃花無言亂紅委。
王孫逆目似勞魂，東鄰一見還羞死。
自此城中豪富兒，呼僮控馬相追隨。
千金買得歌一曲，暮雨朝雲鎮相續。
皇都年少是柳君，體段風流萬事足。
幼玉一見苦留心，殷勤厚遣行人祝。
青羽飛來洞戶前，惟郎苦恨多拘束。
偷身不使父母知，江亭暗共才郎宿。
猶恐恩情未甚堅，解開鬟髻對郎前。
一縷雲隨金剪斷，兩心濃更密如綿。
自古美事多磨隔，無時兩意空懸懸。
清宵長歎明月下，花時洒淚東風前。
怨入朱弦危更斷，淚如珠顆自相連。
危樓獨倚無人會，新書寫恨托誰傳。
奈何幼玉家有母，知此端倪蓄嗔怒。
千金買醉囑傭人，密約幽歡鎮相誤。
將刃欲加連理枝，引弓欲彈鶼鶼羽。
仙山只在海中心，風逆波緊無船渡。
桃源去路隔煙霞，咫尺塵埃無覓處。
郎心玉意共殷勤，同指松筠情愈固。
願郎誓死莫改移，人事有時自相遇。
他日得郎歸來時，攜手同上烟霞路。

富因久遊，親促其歸。幼玉潛往別，共飲野店中。玉曰："子有清才，我有麗質。才色相得，誓不相捨，自然之理。我之心，子之意，質諸神明，結之松筠久矣。子必異日有瀟湘之遊，我亦待君之來。"於是二人共盟，焚香，致其灰於酒中，共飲之。是夕同宿江上。翌日，富作詞別幼玉，名《醉高樓》，詞曰：

> 人間最苦，最苦是分離。伊愛我，我憐伊。青草岸頭人獨立，畫船東去櫓聲遲。楚天低，回望處，兩依依。　後會也知俱有願，未知何日是佳期。心下事，亂如絲。好天良夜還虛過，辜負我，兩心知。願伊家，衷腸在，一雙飛。

富唱其曲以沽酒，音調辭意悲惋，不能終曲。乃飲酒，相與大慟。富乃登舟。富至輦下，以親年老，家又多故，不得如約，但對鏡洒涕。會有客自衡陽來，出幼玉書，但言幼玉近多病臥。富遽開其書疾讀，尾有二句云：

> 春蠶到死絲方盡，蠟燭成灰淚始幹。

富大傷感，遺書以見其意，云：

> 憶昔瀟湘之逢，令人愴然。嘗欲拏舟，泛江一往。復其前盟，敘其舊契。以副子念切之心，適我生平之樂。奈因親老族重，心為事奪，傾風結想，徒自瀟然。風月佳時，文酒勝處，他人怡怡，我獨惚惚如有所失。憑酒自釋，酒醒，情思愈仿徨，幾無生理。古之兩有情者，或一如意，一不如意，則求合也易。今子與吾，兩不如意，則求偶也難。君更待焉，事不易知，當如所願。不然，天理人事，果不諧，則天外神姬，海中仙客，猶能相遇，吾二人獨不得遂，豈非命也。子宜勉強飲食，無使真元耗散，自殘其體，則子不吾見，吾何望焉。子書尾有二句，吾為子終其篇。云：

> > 臨流對月暗悲酸，瘦立東風自怯寒。
> > 湘水佳人方告疾，帝都才子亦非安。
> > 春蠶到死絲方盡，蠟燭成灰淚始乾。
> > 萬裏雲山無路去，虛勞魂夢過湘灘。

一日，殘陽沉西，疏簾不捲，畜獨立庭幃，見有半面出於屏間。富視之，乃幼玉也。玉曰："吾以思君得疾，今已化去。欲得一見，故有是行。我以平生無惡，不陷幽獄，後日當生兗州西門張遂家，復為女子。彼家賣餅。君子不忘昔日之舊，可過見我焉。我雖不省前世事，然君之情當如是，我有遺物在侍兒處，君求之以為驗。千萬珍重。”忽不見。富驚愕，但終嘆惋。異日有過客自衡陽來，言幼玉已死，聞未死前囑侍兒曰：“我不得見郎，死為恨。郎平日愛我手髮眉眼。他皆不可寄附，吾今剪髮一縷，手指甲數箇，郎來訪我，子與之。”後數日，幼玉果死。

　　議曰：今之娼，去就狥利，其他不能動其心。求瀟女霍生事，未嘗聞也。今幼玉愛柳郎，一何厚耶？有情者觀之，莫不愴然。善諧音律者廣以為曲，俾行於世，使係於牙齒之間，則幼玉雖死不死也。吾故敘述之。

Tale 8.46

Wang Xie

Anonymous[1]
Translated by Zhenjun Zhang

Wang Xie of the Tang dynasty was a native of Jinling.[2] His family possessed immense wealth, and they had for generations been in the profession of navigation.

One day, Xie prepared a huge boat, planning to go to Arabia. After the boat had traveled for over a month on the ocean, a fierce gale started blowing. Terrifying waves crested over the skyline, with dark clouds that seemed like black ink and surges that

---

[1]This tale is found in volume four of Liu Fu's *Qingsuo gaoyi* [bieji 別集], titled "Wang Xie" 王榭, with a note "fengtao piaoru wuyi guo" 風濤飄入烏衣國. An excerpt of this tale from *Zhiyi* 摭遺 is found in Zeng Zao's *Leishuo*, titled "Wuyi guo" 烏衣國. Neither *Qingsuo gaoyi* nor *Leishuo* mention its author. Based on Yan Youyi's 嚴有翼 *Yiyuan cihuang* 藝苑雌黃 and Wu Zeng's 吳曾 *Nenggaizhai manlu* 能改齋漫錄, the original title should be "Wuyi zhuan" 烏衣傳, and the author should be northern Song scholar Qian Yi. See Li Jianguo, *Songdai zhiguai chuanqi xulu* 宋代志怪傳奇敘錄 (Tianjin: Nankai daxue chubanshe, 1997), 60–61.

[2]Of *Wang Xie* 王謝, Xie was originally *xie* 榭 in *Leishuo*, *Zhi yi* 摭遺 and *Liuchao shiji leibian* 六朝事蹟類編. But *Ganzhu ji, Shihua zonggui* 詩話總龜, *Nenggaizhai manlu*, etc. all read *xie* 謝. Since the story was derived from the line, "舊時王謝堂前燕," in Liu Yuxi's 劉禹錫 poem at the end of the story, 王謝 makes more sense.

resembled floating mountains. Whales and turtles appeared and disappeared randomly, while fish and dragons were hidden or visible, blowing the waves and pushing the surges — in countless numbers. The wind's momentum became stronger and stronger. When a gust hit, one's body seemed to be thrown up to the Ninth Heaven; when the gust returned, the boat seemed to sink to the bottom of the ocean. Everyone in the boat was tossed up, dropped, and then crashed down. Not long afterwards, the boat was destroyed. Only Wang Xie was left clinging to a piece of plank, drifting through the wind and waves. As soon as he opened his eyes, Wang Xie saw that fish monsters had appeared on his left and marine beasts floated on his right, staring at him with mouths agape as if about to devour him. Wang Xie could do nothing but close his eyes, waiting for death.

Three days later, Wang Xie had drifted to an island. He threw away the wood board and crawled ashore. After a hundred or so steps, he saw an old man and old woman both wearing black and they appeared to be over seventy years old. Upon seeing Wang Xie, the old couple exclaimed in pleasant surprise, "This is our young master. How did he come to be here?" Wang Xie truthfully told them what had befallen him; thereupon the elderly couple brought Wang Xie to their own home. After sitting for a while, they said, "Coming from afar, our master must be very hungry." Then they offered him a meal completely of seafood.

Only after about a month did Wang Xie finally recover with his appetite back to normal. The old man said to him, "Those who come to our country must first see the king. Before, you were too exhausted and so could not go. Now, you can." Wang Xie agreed, and the old man led him forth. They walked three *li*, passing the flourishing downtown residential area. A little further, they crossed a long bridge before seeing the palaces and pavilions connected together that seemed like the residences of the princes and nobility. When they arrived before the gate of a large hall, the gatekeeper went in to report their arrival to the king. Soon after, an ornately dressed woman walked out and relayed the message, "The king summons you inside to meet with him."

With female attendants standing to his left and right, the king sat in the great hall, wearing a black robe and black crown. Wang Xie approached the hall's steps. The king announced, "You have come across the ocean from the north and have a different etiquette, so you need not bow." Wang Xie replied, "Since I am here in your country how can I not bow to pay my respects?" The king, seeing Wang Xie bow down, also bowed in response to his gratitude. The king was pleased, so he summoned Wang Xie up into the hall, granted him a seat, and said, "This is a humble distant country. How did you come to be here?" Wang Xie told him that he unwittingly arrived there because the wind and storm had destroyed his ship and that he asked only for the king's pity.

The king asked, "Where are you staying?"

Wang replied, "I am now staying in the home of an elderly man."

The king commanded for the man to be summoned quickly. When the old man arrived he said to the king, "This is my master from my homeland. Let him do as he wishes on all matters." The king said, "If you have any requests, just speak them." The old man then led Wang Xie home again, where Wang Xie continued to reside.

The old man had a very beautiful daughter. At times, she served refreshments, sometimes peeking through the curtain or window, and she was not at all evasive. One day, the old man invited Wang Xie to drink with him. After drinking and becoming half-inebriated, Wang Xie confided in the old man, saying, "I am residing in a foreign land and only survived with your assistance. I feel as if I were at home. Your kindness is too great. But being solitary by myself over ten thousand *li* away from home, lonely and pitiful, not finding sleep restful and food appetizing, I feel depressed everyday. I am afraid that I will soon be confined to bed and hence become a burden to you."

The old man said, "I was just about to mention it to you but was afraid it would be too abrupt. I have a daughter who is seventeen years old and was born on your estate. I want her to marry you to make you a little happier during your sojourn. What do you think?"

Wang Xie replied, "Wonderful!"

The old man then picked an auspicious day to hold the wedding. The king also sent wine, delicacies, and betrothal gifts to help them form a union of conjugal happiness.

After the marriage, Wang Xie looked closely at his wife and found that she had pretty eyes, a slender waist, an apricot-shaped face, and raven black hair. Her body was so light that it seemed as if she were about to fly away; her demeanor was bewitching. When Wang Xie inquired about the name of the country, she said it was called "The State of Black Clothes." Wang queried, "Your father always addresses me as young master, but I do not know him and he is not my servant. Why does he call me master?" His wife answered, "You will understand in time."

Afterwards, they frequently held feasts. Lying down to sleep, his wife often had a tearful frightened look with her brows tightly locked in sorrow. Wang Xie asked her, "What is the matter?" She responded, "I am afraid that before long we will be separated from each other."

Wang said, "Even though I drifted here and am temporarily residing in this place, after acquiring you I have completely forgotten about returning home. Why do you speak of separation?"

His wife replied, "All things in life are already determined by a hidden fate, beyond the control of man."

One day, the king invited Wang Xie to the Precious Ink Palace for a banquet. The decorations and utensils were all black-colored. Even the instruments in the hands of the musicians below the pavilion were black-colored. While they were drinking, the accompanying music sounded clear and sweet, though the name of the tune played was unknown.

The king ordered that a black jade cup be fetched and urged Wang Xie to drink, saying, "Only two people have come to my country from ancient times to present day. The first was Mei Cheng of the Han dynasty, the other one is you.[3] I hope you present us with a poem so that our meeting will become a popular anecdote in the future."

When paper was brought to him, Wang Xie wrote a poem that read:

> Building large boats has been the foundation of my ancestors,
> Having navigated ten thousand *li*, I am used to being a traveler.[4]
> All of a sudden, my fortune declined this year,
> Halfway I encountered this calamity by chance.
> The swift gale resembled pursuing troops,
> Thousand-layered dark clouds like black ink.
> Fish and dragons blew up waves, the fishy scent covered my face,
> Everyone in the boat ended up buried in the residence of fish and dragons.
> Dark fire streaking the sky and purple flames flying,
> I suspected that the waves were clapping with the heaven.
> Lights of whales' eyes lit up the half-red sea,

---

[3]Mei Cheng 梅成 of the Eastern Han was a native of Lujiang 廬江 who rebelled against Cao Cao and was finally killed by Zhang Liao 張遼 (see Pei Songzhi 裴松之, *Sanguo zhi* 三國志 (Beijing: Zhonghua shuju, 1959), 17. 517–20). Nothing is known about his travels overseas. The author probably refers to Mei Cheng 枚乘 (d. 140 BCE) here, whose "Qi fa" 七發 includes descriptions of extensive travels.

[4]*Tihang* 梯航, ladders and boats — i.e. tools for mountain climbing and traveling on the sea; here it refers to the navigation of boats.

Waves pushed by turtle heads surging into the white sky.
The mast fell and broke and the sea floor opened,
Sounding like thunder, the boat departed [from the world
   above the sea].
Assisted by the deity accompanying me, I did not sink,
Clinging to a board, I drifted to this side of the cliffs.
Though Your Majesty's favor is heavy, offering feasts
   frequently,
As a traveler I myself feel sorrow.
Craning my neck to watch my homeland, I shed tears,
I regret that my body cannot grow wings.

After reading the poem the king was very happy, saying,
"Your poem is very good. Don't bitterly lament your
homesickness, because soon you will be allowed to return.
Although I cannot make you grow wings, I can still let you soar
over the clouds and ride through the mist."

After returning from the feast, everyone composed an
answering poem. Wang Xie's wife asked, "Why does the last line
ridicule me?"[5] Wang Xie did not understand what she meant. Not
long after, the wind above the ocean became mild and the day
sunny. Wang Xie's wife wept, saying, "Soon you will return." The
king sent someone to tell Wang Xie, "On a certain day you will be
returning home, so you should bid your family farewell."

His wife prepared wine to see him off. Sorrowfully shedding
tears, she was unable to speak. She looked like a fragile flower
after a rain shower or a delicate willow branch laden with dew.
The green branch seemed pitiful, the red flower anxious; the
fragrance was reduced, and the flesh thin. Wang Xie was also
saddened. His wife composed a parting poem that read:

---

[5]The people in the Black-Clothing State are all birds and of course
have wings, so Wang Xie's wife felt he was ridiculing her.

> Oftentimes, people worry only that happy gatherings are too
>   short,
> Since ancient times love is rare, after all.
> Tonight, a single bed-curtain should bear a thousand year's
>   regret,
> My dream soul is going to fly chasing the north wind.

She also declared, "From now on I won't cross the ocean to travel north anymore. If I let you see my appearance different from what it is today, you will loathe me. How could you still love me? My heart will also grow jealous if I see you again. So from now on I will not travel north, wishing only to die of old age in my homeland. All the things that we have used here you cannot take with you. This is not because I am stingy."

She asked her maidservant to take out an elixir, [6] and explained, "This elixir can bring back a person's spirit. As long as the person has not been dead for more than a month, this elixir can bring him or her to life again. The way it works is to place a mirror on the deceased's chest, place the elixir on his or her neck, then perform moxibustion using moxa sticks made from moxa branches found in the southeast regions. The person should immediately regain life. This kind of elixir is secretly collected and treasured by the ocean god; if it is not kept in a box made of jade from Mount Kunlun, then there is no way to carry it across the ocean."

It just so happened there was such a box. With the elixir inside, she tied the box to Wang Xie's left arm. Crying aloud, they parted. The king said, "My country does not have anything valuable to give you as a gift." So he fetched a piece of paper and wrote a poem that read:

---

[6] It seems that *shizhong* 侍中 is a mistake for *shi'er* 侍兒, "maidservant."

Previously you floated on a big boat toward the southern sea,
Drifting along, you became a guest of our homeland by
    accident.
From now on we cannot expect to see each other again,
Separated by clouds, water, and ten thousand *li* of smoke that
    dissipate with the wind.

Wang Xie bowed in thanks and took his leave. The king ordered the Flying Cloud Carriage to be brought. It turned out to be a black felt sedan chair. The king instructed Wang Xie to sit inside, and ordered the pool water that could transform things to wings to be brought, and sprinkled on top of the felt sedan chair. In addition, the king summoned an old man and an old woman and had them stand on either side to assist Wang Xie's return home. The king warned Wang Xie, "You must shut your eyes and you will be home shortly; otherwise, you will fall into the ocean."

Wang Xie closed his eyes but heard the sound of the wind whistling and the rushing of the surging waves. After quite a long while, Wang Xie opened his eyes and saw that he was already home. He was sitting in the main room with no one around him and only a pair of swallows on the roof beam twittering. Wang Xie looked upward and suddenly realized that the country he had been to was the country of the swallows.

Soon, his family came out and consoled with him. His family all said, "We heard that your ship was destroyed by the wind and waves and that you had already died. How did you suddenly come back?"

Wang Xie explained, "I was the only one who clung to a wooden board and so survived." He did not tell them about the country where he had stayed.

Wang Xie had only one son who was only three years old when he left. Not seeing him present, Wang Xie asked his family about him. His family replied, "He died just half a month ago."

Wang Xie wept in pain and grief. He then remembered the words regarding the elixir and so asked for the coffin to be opened and the body retrieved. He performed moxibustion on the deceased according to the instructions. As expected, his son regained life.

When autumn arrived, the pair of swallows on the beams about to fly away mournfully chirped in front of the courtyard doors. Wang Xie beckoned to them by waving his hand, thus they both flew to alight on his arm. Wang Xie used tiny characters to write a quatrain on the paper that he then tied to the swallow's tail. The poem read:

> By mistake I entered the State of Dreamland,[7]
> The jade girl deeply loved my talent all along.[8]
> Since drifting away in the cloud carriage I have heard nothing
>   from her,
> Some hundred times I shed tears against the wind.

The next spring a swallow returned, alighting on Wang Xie's arm with a small piece of paper tied to its tail. Removing the paper, Wang Xie saw that it was a quatrain which read:

> We met in the past because our fates truly matched,
> But now, our separation is to part alive.
> Even if you have love poems next spring,
> In the third month no swallows will fly back from the south.

Wang Xie felt deeply regretful. And the next year, the swallow really did not return.

---

[7]*Huaxu guo* 華胥國 refers to dreamland. Its origin is found in the "Huangdi" 黃帝 chapter of *Lie zi* 列子. See Lionel Giles, trans., *The Book of Lieh Tzu* (London: John Murray, 1912), 2. 37–8.

[8]*Yuren* 玉人, literally "jade girl," refers to one's lover — a beautiful girl.

This adventure was circulated among the people and passed on orally, and thus everyone came to call the place Wang Xie lived "Black-Clothing Lane."[9] Liu Yuxi's (772–842) "Five Poems on Jinling" includes a poem titled "Black-Clothing Lane" that reads thus:

By the Red Sparrow Bridge weeds and wildflowers grow,[10]
Above the entrance to the Black-Clothing Lane the setting sun shines.
The swallows that once flew in front of the halls of Wang and Xie,[11]
now enter the homes of commoners.

From this it can be seen that Wang Xie's adventure was not false.

---

[9]*Wuyi xiang* 烏衣巷, "Black-Clothing Lane," located on the southern bank of the Qinhuai 秦淮 River in modern Nanjing. It is so-called because it was a camp of Kingdom Wu's 吳 (222–280) army during the Three Kingdoms period (220–280) and all the soldiers at that time wore black garments. It became the residence of the noble and influential families during the Eastern Jin dynasty (317–420).

[10]*Zhuque qiao* 朱雀橋, "Red Sparrow Bridge," a noted bridge across the Qinhuai River connecting Black-Clothing Lane and the downtown area of Jinling.

[11]Wang Xie 王謝, Wang Dao and Xie An 謝安. Wang Dao, styled Maohong 茂弘, was the Counselor-in-chief of Emperor Yuan, Emperor Ming 明 (323–325), and Emperor Cheng 成 (326–342) respectively. His power overwhelmed almost all the powerful ministers at the time, and the Wang Clan became one of the two most distinguished clans, Wang and Xie, in southern China. (See his biography in *Song shu*, 42.1311–27; *Nan shi*, 21.569–72.)

Xie An, styled Anshi 安石, was the governor-general of military affairs in five states and vice director of the Jin Department of State Affairs. In 383, under his direction his brother Xie Shi 謝石 (327–388) and nephew Xie Xuan 謝玄 (343–388) defeated the invasion of the Former Qin in the battle of Fei 淝 River. He was posthumously entitled grand tutor. His biography is in *Jin shu*, 79. 2072–77.

王榭傳

缺名

唐王榭，金陵人，家巨富，祖以航海為業。

一日，榭具大舶，欲之大食國。行踰月，海風大作，驚濤際天，陰雲如墨，巨浪走山。鯨鰲出沒，魚龍隱現，吹波鼓浪，莫知其數。然風勢益壯，巨浪一來，身若上於九天；大浪既回，舟若墜於海底。舉舟之人，興而復顛，顛而又仆。不久，舟破。獨榭一板之附，又為風濤飄蕩。開目則魚怪出其左，海獸浮其右，張目呀口，欲相吞噬。榭閉目待死而已。

三日，抵一洲。舍板登岸。行及百步，見一翁媼，皆皂衣服，年七十餘，喜曰：“此吾主人郎也！何由至此？”榭以實對，乃引到其家。坐未久，曰：“主人遠來，必甚餒。”進食，□肴皆水族。

月余，榭方平復，飲食如故。翁曰：“□吾國者，必先見君。向以郎□倦，未可往。今可矣。”榭諾，翁乃引行三里，過闤闠民居，亦甚煩會。又過一長橋，方見宮室，台榭，連延相接，若王公大人之居。至大殿門，閽者入報。不久一婦人出，服頗美麗，傳言曰：“王召君入見。”

王坐大殿，左右皆女人立。王衣皂袍，烏冠。榭即殿階。王曰：“君北渡人也，禮無統制，無拜也。”榭曰：“既至其國，豈有不拜乎？”王亦折躬勞謝。王喜，召榭上殿，賜坐，曰：“卑遠之國，賢者何由及此？”榭以風濤破舟，不意及此，惟祈王見矜。曰：“君舍何處？”榭曰：“見居翁家。”王令急召來，翁至，□曰：“此本鄉主人也，凡百無令其不如意。”王曰：“有所須但論。”乃引去，復寓翁家。

翁有一女甚美色。或進茶餌，簾牖間偷視私顧，亦無避忌。翁一日召榭飲，半酣，白翁曰：“某身居異地，賴翁母存活，旅況如不失家，為德甚厚。然萬里一身，憐憫孤苦，寢不成寐，食不成甘，使人鬱鬱。但恐成疾伏枕，以累翁也。"

翁曰："方欲發言，又恐輕冒。家有小女，年十七，此主人家所生也。欲以結好，少適旅懷，如何？"榭答："甚善。"乃擇日備禮，王亦遺酒肴彩禮，助結婚好。

成親，榭細視女，俊目狹腰，杏臉紺鬢，體輕欲飛，妖姿多態。榭詢其國名。曰："烏衣國也。"榭曰："翁常目我為主人郎，我亦不識者，所不役使，何主人云也？"女曰："君久即自知也。"

后常飲燕，衽席之間，女多淚眼畏人，愁眉蹙黛。榭曰："何故？"女曰："恐不久暌別。"榭曰："吾雖萍寄，得子亦忘歸。子何言離意？"女曰："事由陰數，不由人也。"王召榭宴於寶墨殿，器皿陳設俱黑，亭下之樂亦然。杯行樂作，亦甚清婉，但不曉其曲耳。王命玄玉杯勸酒，曰："至吾國者，古今止兩人：漢有梅成，今有足下。願得一篇，為異日佳話。"給箋。榭為詩曰：

> 基業祖來興大舶，萬裡梯航慣為客。
> 今年歲運頓衰零，中道偶然罹此厄。
> 巨風迅急若追兵，千疊雲陰如墨色。
> 魚龍吹浪洒面腥，全舟靈葬魚龍宅。
> 陰火連空紫燄飛，直疑浪與天相拍。
> 鯨目光連半海紅，鰲頭波涌掀天白。
> 桅檣倒折海底開，聲若雷霆以分別。
> 隨我神助不沈淪，一板漂來此岸側。
> 君恩雖重賜宴頻，無奈旅人自悽惻。
> 引領鄉原常涕零，恨不此身生羽翼。

王覽詩欣然，曰："君詩甚好！無苦懷家，不久令歸。雖不能羽翼，亦令君跨煙霧。"宴回，各人作□詩。女曰："末句何相讖也？"榭亦不曉。不久，海上風和日暖。女泣曰："君歸有日矣！"王遣人謂曰："君某日當回，宜與家人敘別。"

女置酒，但悲泣，不能發言，雨洗嬌花，露沾弱柳，綠慘紅愁，香消膩瘦。榭亦悲感。女作別詩曰：

> 從來歡會惟憂少，自古恩情到底稀。
> 此夕孤幃千載恨，夢魂應逐北風飛。

又曰：“我自此不復北渡矣。使君見我非今形容，且將憎惡之，何暇憐愛。我見君亦有嫉妒之情。今不復北渡，願老死於故鄉。此中所有之物，郎俱不可持去。非所惜也。”令侍中取丸靈丹來，曰：“此丹可以召人之神魂，死未逾月者，皆可使之更生。其法用一明鏡致死者胸上，以丹安於項，以東南艾枝作柱炙之，立活。此丹海神秘惜，若不以崑侖玉盒盛之，即不可逾海。”

適有玉盒，併付以擊榭左臂，大慟而別。王曰：“吾國無以為贈。”取箋，詩曰：

昔向南溟浮大舶，漂流偶作吾鄉客。
從茲相見不復期，萬裡風煙雲水隔。

榭辭拜。王命取“飛雲軒”來。既至，乃一烏氈兜子耳。命榭入其中，復命取化羽池水，洒之其氈乘。又召翁嫗，扶持榭回。王戒榭曰：“當閉目，少息即至君家。不爾，即墮大海矣。”

榭合目，但聞風聲怒濤。既久，開目，已至其家，坐堂上。四顧無人，惟梁上有雙燕呢喃。榭仰視，乃知所止之國，燕子國也。

須臾，家人出向勞問，俱曰：“聞為風濤破舟，死矣！何故遽歸？”榭曰：“獨我附板而生。”亦不告所居之國。榭惟一子，去時方三歲。不見，乃問家人。曰：“死已半月矣！”榭感泣，因思靈丹之言，命開棺取尸，如法炙之，果生。

至秋，二燕將去，悲鳴庭戶之間。榭招之，飛集於臂，乃取紙細書一絕，系於尾云：

誤到華胥國裡來，玉人終日重憐才。
雲軒飄去無消息，淚洒臨風幾百回。

來春燕來，徑泊榭臂，尾一小束。取視，乃詩也。□有一絕雲：

昔日相逢真數合，而今睽隔是生離。
來春縱有相思字，三月天南無燕飛。

榭深自恨。明年，亦不來。其事流傳眾人口，因目榭所居處為《烏衣巷》。劉禹錫《金陵五詠》，有烏衣巷詩云：

朱雀橋邊野草花，烏衣巷口夕陽斜。
舊時王榭堂前燕，飛入尋常百姓家。

即知王榭之事非虛矣。

Tale 8.47

The Tale of Concubine Plum[1]

Anonymous
Translated by Wilt L. Idema and Beata Grant

Concubine Plum's surname was Jiang and she was a native of Putian. Her father Zhongxun had followed the family profession of physician. At the age of nine she was able to recite the first two sections of the *Book of Odes*. She said to her father: "I may be only a girl, but I hope to model my behavior on (the examples of yielding wifehood in) these poems." Her father was filled with admiration and called her Caipin.

During the reign period Reopened Beginning (Kaiyuan, 713–741), (the eunuch) Gao Lishi was sent to the area of Min and Yue (in search of women for the Inner Palace).[2] The concubine had by then reached marriageable age, and when Gao saw her youthful beauty, he selected her for induction into the Inner Palace. She subsequently served Emperor Xuanzong, and greatly enjoyed his loving affection.

---

[1] We have consulted the following annotated editions: Zhang Youhe 張友鶴, *Songdai chuanqi xuan* 唐宋傳奇選 (Beijing: Renmin, 1979) and Xue Hong 學洪, Mou Qing 牟青, Li Shi 李實, and Ma Lan 馬蘭, *Songdai chuanqi xuan* 宋代傳奇選 (Changsha: Hunan renmin, 1985). For the end note we have consulted Cheng Jie 程傑, "Guanyu Meifei yu Meifei zhuan" 關於梅妃与梅妃傳, *Nanjing shifan daxue wenxueyuan xuebao* 2006.3: 125–29.

[2] "Min and Yue" 閩粵 refers to China's southeasterly coastal regions. Putian 莆田 is located in Fujian province.

The three palaces of Chang'an (Danei, Daming, and Xingqing) and the two palaces of the Eastern Capital (Danei and Shangyang) had a total population of about forty thousand women, but from the moment the emperor acquired this concubine, he regarded the others like dust and dirt. The women in these palaces also felt that they were not her equal. She was expert in literary composition and compared herself to Xie Daoyun.[3] With her light makeup and elegant gowns her appearance was brighter and more excellent than any brush could paint.

The concubine loved plum blossoms and planted plum trees all along the railings of her residence, which the emperor then named the Plum Pavilion. Whenever the blossoms of the plum trees opened, she would write appreciative poems, and she would even remain lovingly gazing up at the flowers until after midnight unable to tear herself away. Because of this infatuation, the emperor jokingly called her Concubine Plum. The concubine wrote the following seven rhapsodies: "The Fragrant Orchid," "The Pear Garden," "The Plum Blossoms," "The Phoenix Flute," "The Glass Cup," "The Pair of Scissors," and "The Gauze Window."

At that time the country had been at peace for many years and there was no fighting anywhere in the world. The emperor was extremely caring and loving towards his brothers; each day he treated them to a festive banquet, with the concubine always in attendance at his side. Once he ordered her to peel an orange and distribute it among the princes. When she came to the Prince of Han, he secretly placed his foot on her slipper. She immediately retired to her residence. The emperor had her summoned repeatedly, but each time she sent the messenger back, saying: "Just now the knot in the

---

[3]Xie Daoyun 謝道韞 (second half of the fourth century) was famous for her literary talents. See Wilt Idema and Beata Grant, *The Red Brush: Writing Women of Imperial China* (Cambridge, Mass.: Harvard University Asia Center, 2004), 136–44.

string of pearls on my slipper became undone. I will come as soon as they have been restrung." When after a long time (she had still not returned), the emperor himself went to fetch her. With trailing gown, she welcomed the emperor and informed him that her whole body was aching and that she was truly unable to return to the banquet. And in the end she did not put in an appearance. This shows the extent to which she presumed on the emperor's doting affection.

On a later occasion, when the emperor and the concubine were engaged in a tea-tasting competition, he jokingly said to the princes: "She must be a plum sprite! When I played the jade white flute and she performed the dance of the startled goose, everyone there was overwhelmed by her brilliance. And now she beats me again in tasting tea!" Immediately she replied: "In games that have to do with grasses and plants I may happen to beat Your Majesty, but when it comes to the harmonizing of all within the four seas and preparing the offerings in the sacrificial tripods, Your Majesty has his own canonical norm—how would I be able to compete with you in those matters!" The emperor was greatly pleased (by her answer).

But when Yang Taizhen was inducted into the Inner Palace to serve the emperor, every day she appropriated more and more of the emperor's love and affection. The emperor had no intention of abandoning Concubine Plum, but the two women were jealous of each other, and kept as much distance between themselves as possible. The emperor once compared the two of them to Nüying and Ehuang,[4] an assessment not shared by others who knew that they were totally dissimilar and secretly laughed at the emperor (for his foolishness). Yang Taizhen was jealous and cunning, but Concubine Plum was submissive and accommodating, and so

---

[4]The two sisters Nüying 女英 and Ehuang 娥皇, daughters of the mythical emperor Yao, were the perfect wives of Yao's successor Shun. Upon his death they drowned themselves in Dongting Lake.

lacked the means to beat Lady Yang at her game. Eventually, Lady Yang had her transferred to the eastern Shangyang Palace.

Once, sometime later, the emperor started to think about Concubine Plum, and had a young eunuch secretly, with his lamp extinguished, bring her on one of his circus horses to the western Cuihua Pavilion. As they gave expression to their old love, they were overcome by emotion and as a result, the emperor overslept. A frightened attendant reported to him: "Lady Yang is already waiting for you outside the pavilion. What should we do?" The emperor threw on his robes, grabbed Concubine Plum in his arms and hid her between the double curtains. The moment Lady Yang entered, she asked: "Where is that plum sprite?" The emperor replied: "She is at the eastern palace." Lady Yang then said: "Please be so good as to summon her, so today we may bathe in the hot spring bath together." The emperor replied: "The woman has already been discarded. Why would you want to go together with her!" When Lady Yang became even more insistent, the emperor looked to his attendants speechlessly for help. The enraged Lady Yang said: "You have had a fine banquet here, and a woman has left her slippers by Your Majesty's bed. With whom did you engage in drunken revelry on this couch last night, such that you are not yet holding audience although the sun has risen? Your Majesty should go out and receive your ministers. I will await your return here in this pavilion." Deeply ashamed, the emperor pulled the bedcovers up, turned his face to the wall, and pretended to sleep, saying: "I am feeling ill today, I cannot hold audience." Lady Yang was furious and returned straightaway to her private quarters. When after a while the emperor looked for Concubine Plum, he found that she had already been escorted out by the young eunuch and ordered to return on foot to the eastern palace. The enraged emperor had him beheaded. He also ordered the slippers and the filigree hair ornaments she had left behind to be bundled up and returned to her. She said to the messenger: "Must the emperor go to this extreme to get rid of me?" The messenger replied: "It is not that the emperor is getting rid of you, it is just that he is really afraid of the foul temper of Lady Yang." Concubine Plum said with a smile: "If he is afraid that by loving me he will provoke the foul temper of that fat bitch, then of course he is getting rid of me."

Hoping to win back the emperor's love, Concubine Plum gave rich treasure to Gao Lishi and asked him to locate a poet just like Sima Xiangru who would be able to write her a *Rhapsody of the Long Gate Palace*.[5] Lishi at the time supported Lady Yang and also feared her power, so he said to her: "There is no one who can write such a rhapsody." And so Concubine Plum wrote a *Rhapsody on the East of My Residence* herself, which briefly reads:

> The jade mirror is covered with dust,
> The perfume in the toilette case has evaporated.
> Too listless to artfully comb my cicada locks,
> Or to put on gold-threaded gowns of light silk,
> Suffering a silent solitude in this fragrant palace,
> My thoughts converge on the orchid hall.
> Truly, I am the plum blossom about to fall,
> But hidden behind the long gate, I go unnoticed.
>
>   Moreover,
> The flower-hearts display their grief,
> The willow-eyes exhibit their sorrow,
> The gentle breezes sough and sigh,
> The spring birds chirp and wail.

---

[5]When Empress Chen, the first wife of Emperor Wu of the Han dynasty (r. 140–87 BCE) had lost his favor and had been banished to the Long Gate Palace, she paid the poet Sima Xiangru to give expression to her desolation and abiding love in a long poem, hoping in this way to regain her husband's affection. For a translation of Sima Xiangru's rhapsody, see David Knechtges, "Ssu-ma Hsiang-ju's *Tall Gate Rhapsody*," *Harvard Journal of Asiatic Studies* 41.1 (1981), 47–64.

In my room when dusk descends,
I hear the phoenix-pipes and turn around;
Under dark clouds as evening falls,
I intently gaze at the white moon.
No more visits to the hot springs—
I recall our past pleasures in Shicui Hall;
Forever locked away in Long Gate Palace—
I bemoan the long absence of the imperial carriage.
        I recall
The clear waves of the Taiye Pond,
A shimmering light flitting on the water,
The music and songs of a festive banquet
And me at the side of His Imperial Majesty.
Musicians played marvelous tunes of dancing phoenixes,
And we rode a fairy boat with painted rocs.[6]
Your love for me was ardent and passionate,
You fully expressed your burning devotion,
You swore it would last forever like mountain and sea,
Would be like the sun and moon without end!

        But alas,
That jealous beauty spared no effort,
The blasts of envy raged uncontrolled:
She robbed me of your love and favor
And banished me to this gloomy abode.
Longing for past pleasures, now beyond reach,
I relive them in stubborn dreams, all misty and vague.
I spend the flowery mornings and moonlit nights
Too ashamed and listless to face the spring winds.
I had hoped that a Xiangru might present his rhapsody
But nowadays there are none who possess his skill.
Before I have finished composing my sorrowful lay,

---

[6]The roc or *peng* is a mythical bird mentioned in the opening chapter
of the *Zhuangzi*, where it is described as being so large that its wings
darken heaven when it rises to the sky.

The ringing of the distant bell resounds.
To no avail I heave a sigh, hiding my face in my sleeve,
As I pace up and down to the east of my room.

When Lady Yang heard about this, she complained to Emperor Xuanzong: "That Concubine Jiang is too vulgar and common! Now she voices her resentment in these pathetic words! May You most graciously allow her to die!" But the emperor remained silent.

Once, when the emperor was at the Flower Bud Tower and barbarian envoys arrived, he ordered ten pecks of the pearls (they had offered in tribute) bundled up and secretly sent to Concubine Plum. She refused them, and handed the messenger a poem, ordering him to present it to His Majesty. The poem read:

My willow-leaf brows I've long left unpainted,
Rouge mixed with tears has dyed my silks red.
The Long Gate Palace is not a place for dressing up:
What need have I of precious pearls to allay my grief!

When the emperor read this poem, he felt desolate and overcome by sadness. He ordered the Music Bureau to put the poem to music using a new tune to which was given the title of "Ten Pecks of Pearls." This is how that tune got its name.

Later, after An Lushan occupied the capital and the emperor fled to Sichuan, Lady Yang met her death. When the emperor returned to the capital, he searched for Concubine Plum, but she was nowhere to be found. In his distress, believing that she might have drifted off somewhere else after the fighting, the emperor issued an edict, stating that the person who located her would be rewarded with an office of the second rank and a monetary award of one million cash. But despite the most extensive search, her whereabouts remained a mystery. The emperor also ordered a shaman to release his spirit and, riding his vital energy, make a secret search of both heaven and earth. However, he too was unable to find her.

When a eunuch presented a painted portrait of Concubine Plum to the emperor, he noted that the likeness was perfect, the only difference being that it was not alive. On the portrait was inscribed the following poem:

> When long ago this concubine lived in these Purple Halls,
> She had no need for rouge and powder to enhance her looks.
> This white silk may have captured her as she was then,
> Except that her dancing eyes do not follow where you go.

Upon reading this, the emperor dissolved in tears, and he ordered the portrait copied and then carved in stone.

Later, as the emperor once lay dozing on a hot summer day, he seemed vaguely to see Concubine Plum crying behind the bamboo. Holding back her tears and hiding her face behind a sleeve, she resembled a flower bathed by misty dew. She said: "When not too long ago Your Majesty suffered the dust of the road, I was killed by mutinous troops. Some people took pity on me and buried my bones by the side of a plum tree to the east of the pond." The startled emperor woke up in a sweat, and immediately ordered (his servants) to go to the Taiye Pond and dig her up.

However, they did not find her body, and the emperor grew even more disconsolate. Suddenly he remembered that by the side of the hot springs pond, there were more than ten plum trees—could that be the place? The emperor went out there himself and ordered the body to be dug up. After digging around a few of the trees, they found the corpse. It had been wrapped in a brocade coverlet, placed in a wine vat, and then covered with more than three feet of earth. The emperor was greatly moved, and none of his entourage could bear to look up. When they inspected her wounds, they found she had been stabbed in the side by a sword.

The emperor himself composed a dirge to lament her, and he had her reburied with the full rites befitting an imperial concubine.

The *Evaluation* reads:

Emperor Minghuang was renowned for his bold behavior and imposing air ever since he served as administrative aide for Luzhou; galloping on horseback and hunting with dogs in the area of Hu and Du districts, he associated with young bravos, and because of this he ascended the imperial throne though only the son of a concubine. For more than fifty years he enjoyed the veneration of all under heaven, exhausting the utmost luxury and extravagance. His sons and grandsons numbered more than a hundred. The beauties from the myriad regions he enjoyed were numerous indeed. Late in life he obtained Lady Yang. Changing and altering the three mainstays, he precipitated the whole world into chaos; when he lost his position, the state was humiliated. But when he pondered this, he did not show the slightest remorse. This must be because she truly was capable of hitting his heart and satisfying his desires. Concubine Jiang followed and preceded her and was deeply hated by her because of her beauty, so it is even more evident that she could please the emperor. Those who discuss their fates, say that the one destroyed her clan and the other died without a fault and that this was all brought about by jealousy. But they certainly ignore the fact that Minghuang in his dotage became suspicious and cruel, to the extent that in one day he killed three sons, as if lightly ending the lives of ants.[7] When he returned after his hasty flight, he was controlled by dimwitted ingrates, and when he searched for his palace ladies, he found that they had all disappeared as they had been beheaded or had fled. Impoverished and alone, he had barely managed to survive and

---

[7]When the Crown Prince Li Ying 李瑛, the Prince of E 鄂 Li Yao 李瑤, and the Prince of Guang 光 Li Ju 李琚 were slandered by one of Xuanzong's concubines they were degraded to the status of commoners and later all killed on the same day.

all under heaven pitied him. The *Commentary* states, "Because of those he didn't love he hurt those he loved."[8] That must have been the way in which Heaven punished him. The rule of revenge and retribution does not allow for the slightest mistake — how could it only have been the crime of these two women?

In the early years of the Han dynasty, the *Annals of Spring and Autumn* was venerated and scholars competed for victory in showing their knowledge of the *Gong Yang* and *Gu Liang* commentaries. But the *Zuo Commentary* remained hidden and found no distribution, and only emerged at the very end.[9] There are indeed many ancient books that were only transmitted after a long time! Now, on those prints of recent times that depict a beauty holding a sprig of plum blossoms, the lady's name is given as "Concubine Plum," and it is usually said that she was "a person of the time of Emperor Xuanzong," although her origin is unknown. Now, Lady Yang is blamed for Emperor Xuanzong's loss of his state, and that is why poets love to write about her story. But Concubine Plum was

---

[8]This is not a quotation from the *Zuo Commentary*, but from Mencius.

[9]The *Annals of Spring and Autumn* (Chunqiu), a chronicle of events in the state of Lu for the period 722–481 BCE), was one of the Five Classics. It was generally believed that the text had been written, or at least edited, by Confucius. Two of the early commentaries to this text, the *Gong Yang Commentary* (Gong Yang zhuan) and the *Guliang Commentary* (Guliang zhuan) focus on the way Confucius expressed his moral verdict on actions and persons by his subtle choice of words. The third commentary, the *Zuo Commentary* (Zuozhuan), provides a detailed account of the political and military history of China during the centuries covered by the *Annals of Springs and Autumn* and may well originally have been compiled as an independent work (its account of affairs is often at variance with the text of the classic). This, and its late appearance has given rise to considerable scholarly controversy from the Tang dynasty onward.

only a lesser concubine of exceptional beauty, so it is perfectly understandable that the one became famous and the other not at all.

This tale was acquired from the house of "Ten Thousand Scrolls" Zhu Zundu. It had been copied in the Seventh Month of the second year of the reign period Great Center (Dazhong, 847–859), and the calligraphy was charming and fine, although the wording was occasionally somewhat vulgar. Afraid that history might overlook her tale, I have slightly improved the style but, fearful of distorting the facts, adhered closely to the original phrases. Only Ye Shaoyun[10] and I have this tale, so the transmission to later generations most likely will depend on these copies. So I have also recorded their origin.

Note: In the middle of the eighth century Emperor Xuanzong almost brought down the Tang dynasty because of his infatuation with a single woman, the Exalted Concubine Yang (Yang Guifei). Yang Yuhuan began her palace career as the spouse of one of Xuanzong's many sons. But when one day her elderly father-in-law became aware of the full extent of her physical attractions as she emerged from the hot springs at Huaqing Palace, he forced her to divorce her husband, enter a Buddhist nunnery (the Taizhen Convent), and then return again to lay life as his own concubine. Yang Yuhuan made a name for herself as a musician and dancer, and she has left us a single quatrain in praise of a fellow-dancer:

For the Dancer Zhang Yunrong
Gauze sleeves that spread their endless fragrance:
Red lotuses that sway softly in the autumn mists—
A weightless mountain cloud caught in a sudden wind,
A drooping willow by the pond caressing its first waves.

The new favorite made sure she enjoyed the emperor's undivided attention. She also had her distant cousin Yang Guozhong appointed prime

---

[10] Ye Shaoyun 葉少蘊 is the well-known official and author Ye Mengde 葉夢得 (1077–1148).

minister. Then, in 755, a Sogdian general in Chinese service by the name of An Lushan led a rebellion in northeast China and after a lightning campaign threatened the capital itself. Emperor Xuanzong hastily fled to the southwest with the Exalted Concubine and Yang Guozhong. When they were only one day away from the capital, however, the imperial guards who were escorting them killed Yang Guozhong, whom they blamed for the debacle, and then insisted on taking the life of the Exalted Concubine as well. The frightened emperor had no choice but to agree. One year later, after his son and successor Suzong (r. 756–762), with the aid of Uighur cavalry, had expelled An Lushan and his troops from the capital, Emperor Xuanzong also returned to Chang'an. Having abdicated by this time, he spent his final years reminiscing over his life with Lady Yang.

Before long, the elderly emperor's incestuous and disastrous passion for the beautiful and plump Exalted Concubine Yang became one of the most celebrated tragic love stories in all of Chinese literary history. Each detail of their relationship was elaborated on by later poets, dramatists, and novelists, who returned to the story time and again. One of the products of this fascination was the *Tale of Concubine Plum* (*Meifei zhuan*), which presents a perfect mirror image of the Exalted Concubine Yang in the person of Concubine Plum (the surname Yang means "poplar," and Mei [plum] is also a common surname). While Lady Yang is depicted as a jealous woman who bewitches the emperor with her "barbarian whirling dance," Concubine Plum is regarded as the embodiment of wifely virtues: she is literate, modest, and so utterly loyal in love that, it is suggested, she preferred death to rape. And, of course, Concubine Plum expressed her enduring fidelity to her lord in appropriate verses.

The earliest preserved text of the *Tale of Concubine Plum* is found in the *Shuofu*, a huge compendium in one hundred chapters of diverse materials, originally compiled by the late Yuan scholar Tao Zongyi. For many decades this collection was transmitted only in manuscript and for printed versions we have to wait until the late Ming. The text was already quoted, however, in the middle of the twelfth century. The text is accompanied by a note of an anonymous editor (often suspected of being the author) who claims that the text as we have it is his revision of a manuscript of 848 that had belonged to the tenth-century bibliophile Zhang Zhundu. Some versions of the *Shuofu* ascribe the original text to the ninth-century poet Cao Ye, but this can only be guesswork. While there are some scholars who trust the editor's claim to have based his edition on a Tang-dynasty manuscript, the majority follow Lu Xun in ascribing the composition of this text to the Song dynasty. Tang-dynasty sources never mention Concubine Plum and her story reads like a patchwork of themes and motifs from earlier stories and legends about abandoned concubines. Yet another reason to date this text to the Song dynasty is the harsh judgment on Emperor Xuanzong in the "Evaluation" at the end of the *Tale of Concubine Plum*. Some scholars argue more specifically that the text must date from the earliest decades of the Southern Song.

Concubine Plum's fictionality has not prevented her from making an appearance in later dramatic and novelistic adaptations of the romance of Emperor Xuanzong and the Exalted Concubine Yang, as well as in anthologies of women's poetry.

This is a revised version of our 2004 rendition in Wilt L. Idema and Beata Grant, *The Red Brush: Writing Women of Imperial China* (Cambridge Mass: Harvard University Asia Center, 2004), pp. 100–07.

梅妃傳

缺名

　　梅妃，姓江氏，莆田人。父仲遜，世爲醫。妃年九歲，能誦《二南》。語父曰：“我雖女子，期以此爲志。”父奇之，名曰採蘋。

　　開元中，高力士使閩越，妃笄矣。見其少麗，選歸，侍明皇，大見寵幸。長安大内、大明、興慶三宫，東都大内、上陽兩宫，幾四萬人，自得妃視如塵土。宫中亦自以爲不及。妃善屬文，自比謝女。淡妝雅服，而姿態明秀，筆不可描畫。

　　性喜梅，所居闌檻，悉植數株，上榜曰“梅亭”。梅開賦賞，至夜分尚顧戀花下不能去。上以其所好，戲名曰“梅妃”。妃有《蕭蘭》、《梨園》、《梅花》、《鳳笛》、《玻盃》、《剪刀》、《絢窗》七賦。

　　是時承平歲久，海内無事。上於兄弟間極友愛，日從燕間，必妃侍側。上命破橙往賜諸王。至漢邸，潛以足躡妃履，妃登時退閣。上命連宣，報言“適履珠脫綴，綴竟當來”。久之，上親往命妃。妃曳衣迓上，言胸腹疾作，不果前也。卒不至，其恃寵如此。

　　後上與妃鬥茶，顧諸王戲曰：“此‘梅精’也，吹白玉笛，作驚鴻舞，一座光輝。鬥茶今又勝我矣。”妃應聲曰：“草木之戲，誤勝陛下。設使調和四海，烹飪鼎鼐，萬乘自有憲法，賤妾何能較勝負也。”上大悅。

　　會太真楊氏入侍，寵愛日奪，上無疏意。而二人相疾，避路而行。上嘗方之英、皇，議者謂廣狹不類，竊笑之。太真忌而智，妃性柔緩，亡以勝。後竟爲楊氏遷於上陽東宫。

　　後上憶妃，夜遣小黃門滅燭，密以戲馬召妃至翠華西閣，敘舊愛，悲不自勝。既而上失寤，侍御驚報曰：“妃子已屆閣前，當奈何？"上披衣，抱妃藏夾幌間。太真既至，問："'梅精'安在？"
上曰："在東宮。"太真曰："乞宣至，今日同浴溫泉。"上曰：
"此女已放屏，無並往也。"太真語益堅，上顧左右不答。太真大
怒，曰："肴核狼藉，御榻下有婦人遺舄，夜來何人侍陛下寢，歡
醉至於日出不視朝？陛下可出見羣臣。妾止此閣以俟駕回。"上愧
甚，曳衾向屏假寐，曰："今日有疾，不可臨朝。"太真怒甚，徑
歸私第。上頃覓妃所在，已爲小黃門送令步歸東宮。上怒斬之。遺
舄並翠鈿命封賜妃。妃謂使者曰："上棄我之深乎？"使者曰：
"上非棄妃，誠恐太真惡情耳！"妃笑曰："恐憐我則動肥婢情，
豈非棄也？"

妃以千金壽高力士，求詞人擬司馬相如爲《長門賦》，欲邀上
意。力士方奉太真，且畏其勢，報曰："無人解賦。"妃乃自作
《樓東賦》，略曰：

> "玉鑑塵生，鳳奩香殄。懶蟬鬢之巧梳，閒縷衣之輕練。苦寂寞
> 於蕙宮，但凝思乎蘭殿。信摽落之梅花，隔長門而不見。況乃花
> 心颺恨，柳眼弄愁，暖風習習，春鳥啾啾。樓上黃昏兮聽風吹而
> 回首，碧雲日暮兮對素月而凝眸。溫泉不到，憶拾翠之舊遊；長
> 門深閉，嗟青鸞之信修。憶太液清波，水光蕩浮，笙歌賞宴，陪
> 從宸旒。奏舞鸞之妙曲，乘畫鷁之仙舟。君情繾綣，深敘綢繆。
> 誓山海而常在，似日月而無休。奈何嫉色庸庸，妒氣沖沖，奪我
> 之愛幸，斥我乎幽宮。思舊歡之莫得，想夢著乎朦朧。度花朝與
> 月夕，羞懶對乎春風。欲相如之奏賦，奈世才之不工。屬愁吟之
> 未盡，已響動乎疏鍾。空長嘆而掩袂，躊躇步於樓東。"

太真聞之，訴明皇曰："江妃庸賤，以廋詞宣言怨望，願賜
死。"上默然。

會嶺表使歸，妃問左右："何處驛使來，非梅使耶？"對曰：
"庶邦貢楊妃荔實使來。"妃悲咽泣下。

上在花萼樓，會夷使至，命封珍珠一斛密賜妃。妃不受，以詩
付使者，曰："爲我進御前也。"曰："柳葉雙眉久不描，殘妝和
淚濕紅綃。長門自是無梳洗，何必珍珠慰寂寥。"

上覽詩，悵然不樂。令樂府以新聲度之，號《一斛珠》，曲名
始此也。

後祿山犯闕，上西幸，太真死。及東歸，尋妃所在，不可得。
上悲謂兵火之後，流落他處。詔有得之，官二秩，錢百萬。訪搜不

知所在。上又命方士飛神御氣，潛經天地，亦不可得。有宦者進其畫真，上言甚似，但不活耳。詩題於上，曰：

> "憶昔嬌妃在紫宸，鉛華不御得天真。
> 霜綃雖似當時態，爭奈嬌波不顧人。"

讀之泣下，命模像刊石。

後上暑月晝寢，彷彿見妃隔竹間泣，含涕障袂，如花濛霧露狀。妃曰："昔陛下蒙塵，妾死亂兵之手。哀妾者埋骨池東梅株旁。"上駭然流汗而寤。登時令往太液池發視之，不獲。

上益不樂。忽悟溫泉湯池側有梅十餘株，豈在是乎？上自命駕，令發現。才數株，得屍，裹以錦裀，盛以酒槽，附土三尺許。上大慟，左右莫能仰視。視其所傷，脅下有刀痕。

上自制文誄之，以妃禮易葬焉。

贊曰：

明皇自爲潞州別駕，以豪偉聞。馳騁犬馬鄠杜之間，與俠少遊。用此起支庶，踐尊位，五十餘年，享天下之奉，窮極奢侈，子孫百數，其閱萬方美色衆矣。晚得楊氏，變易三綱，濁亂四海，身廢國辱，思之不少悔。是固有以中其心，滿其欲矣。江妃者，後先其間，以色爲所深嫉，則其當人主者，又可知矣。議者謂或覆宗，或非命，均其媢忌自取。殊不知明皇耄而忮忍，至一日殺三子，如輕斷螻蟻之命。奔竄而歸，受制昏逆，四顧嬪嬙，斬亡俱盡，窮獨苟活，天下哀之。《傳》曰："以其所不愛及其所愛"，蓋天所以酬之也。報復之理，毫髮不差，是豈特兩女子之罪哉！

漢興，尊《春秋》，諸儒持《公》《穀》角勝負，《左傳》獨隱而不宣，最後迺出。蓋古書歷久始傳者極衆。今世圖畫美人把梅者，號梅妃，泛言唐明皇時人，而莫詳所自也。蓋明皇失邦，咎歸楊氏，故詞人喜傳之。梅妃特嬪御擅美，顯晦不同，理應爾也。

此傳得自萬卷朱遵度家，大中二年七月所書，字亦媚好。其言時有涉俗者。惜乎史逸其説。略加脩潤而曲循舊語，懼没其實也。惟葉少蘊與余得之，後世之傳，或在此本。又記其所從來如此。

Tale 8.48

An Unofficial Biography of Li Shishi

Anonymous
Translated by Zhenjun Zhang

Li Shishi was the daughter of Wang Yin, a dyer of a dyehouse at the Yongqing Ward in the Second Eastern Zone of the Capital Bian.[1] Shortly after giving birth to her daughter, Yin's wife died. Yin used bean starch as milk to feed his daughter, so she was able to escape death and never cried in her infancy.

According to local Bian customs, after the birth of a boy or a girl, to show affection toward their child, the parents must send the baby as a devotee to a Buddhist temple. Yin loved his daughter, so he sent her to the Baoguang Monastery. At that time, the girl was just able to laugh. An old monk looked at her and said, "What kind of place is this? Why did you come here?" Upon hearing this, the girl suddenly began to cry. The old monk stroked the top of her head, and she stopped crying. Yin secretly felt happy, saying, "This girl is truly a disciple of Buddha!" Since Buddhist disciples were commonly known as *shi* (master), Yin named his daughter "Shishi."

When Shishi was only four years old, Yin committed a crime, was imprisoned, and died. Shishi became homeless, and Mother

---

[1] The city of Bianliang 汴梁, capital of the Northern Song (960–1127), is the modern city of Kaifeng, Henan.

Li, a registered courtesan, adopted Shishi as her daughter. When Shishi was grown up, both her beauty and artistic skills were matchless, so she was well-known at all the brothels.

When Emperor Huizong (r. 1101–1125) ascended the throne, he enjoyed pursuing an extravagant lifestyle.[2] In the name of continuing a previous policy, those imperial officials, such as Cai Jing (1047–1126), Zhang Dun (1035-1105), and Wang Fu (1079–1126),[3] urged the emperor to reinstate the Green Sprouts Policy as well as other laws.[4] The capital was made to have a simulated ambience of prosperity and happiness.[5] Alcohol taxes collected daily from the market amounted to ten thousand strings of coins; gold, jade, and silk overfilled the government repository.

---

[2]Huizong 徽宗, named Zhao ji 趙佶 (1082–1135), was the eighth emperor of the Northern Song. He was given to painting, calligraphy, wine, and women, but failed at governing. In 1127, he and his son Qinzong 欽宗 (r. 1126–1127) were captured by Jin 金 (Jurchen) troops and brought back to Manchuria as prisoners; and he died there in disgrace eight years later. See *Song shi* 宋史 (Beijing: Zhonghua shuju, 1977), 19–23: 357–438, and the most recent study in English by Patricia Buchley Ebrey, *Emperor Huizong* (Cambridge, MA: Harvard University Press, 2014).

[3]Cai Jing 蔡京 was the Grand Councilor under Huizong; Zhang Dun 章惇 was the preceding Grand Councilor from 1084 to 1100; and Wang Fu 王黼 was the Vice Grand Councilor under Huizong. All of them are considered evil vassals in the official history. See *Song shi*, 471–472. 13697–741.

[4]Under Huizong's father, Emperor Shenzong 神宗 (r. 1067–1085), the Grand Councilor-in-chief Wang Anshi 王安石 (1021–1086) enforced a set of laws in his reform, including the *Qingmiao fa* 青苗法 (Green Sprouts Policy), a loan program aimed at helping poor peasants.

[5]*Chang'an*, the capital of the Tang dynasty; but here it refers to the capital of Bian.

Thereupon, Tong Guan (1054–1126),[6] Zhu Mian (1075–1126),[7] and others akin to them further enticed Huizong with the pleasures of music, women, hounds, horses, palaces, and imperial gardens. They searched and collected almost all the rare flowers and strange stones within the Four Seas. They built a separate imperial palace to the north of the capital of Bian, and named it Genyue, or Northeast Peak.

Having stayed inside this palace and enjoyed various kinds of pleasure for a long time, Emperor Huizong became tired of it. Further, he longed to wear commoner's clothes in order to secretly visit the courtesan district.

Zhang Di, the Administrative Aid of the Palace Domestic Service, was the emperor's favorite eunuch. Before being mutilated to become a eunuch, he was a patron of brothels in the capital, frequenting various of them. As a result, he was on good terms with Mother Li. When Zhang Di told the emperor of the matchless beauty and arts of Shishi, the girl from the famous Longxi clan, the emperor started to admire her. The next day, the emperor ordered Zhang Di to take out from the inner storage two *pi* of purple velvet, two *duan* of rosy-cloud felt, two *sese* pearls,[8] and twenty *yi* of silver. He claimed himself to be Zhao Yi 趙乙, a wealthy businessman, who would like to pay a visit to Shishi's residence. Greedy for the silver, Mother Li agreed delightedly.

---

[6]Tong Guan 童貫 was a court eunuch, military general, and advisor of Emperor Huizong. He is portrayed as the enemy of the Liang Mountain heroes in Shi Nai'an's *Shuihu zhuan* (Water Margin).

[7]Zhu Mian 朱勔, a native of Suzhou 蘇州, was a high court official under Emperor Huizong. He was executed when Emperor Qinzong was enthroned.

[8]*Sese zhu* 瑟瑟珠, also called *tianzhu* 天珠, is a precious man-made diamond.

At dusk, the emperor changed his clothes, blended among more than forty eunuchs, and left through the Donghua Gate.[9] After walking for about two *li*, they arrived at Zhen'an Ward, where Mother Li was living. The emperor stopped the rest of the men with a wave of his arm and quickly stepped in with only Zhang Di. Both the main room and door were small and low. Mother Li came out to receive her guests. The host and the guests stood opposite in the guest room to greet one another, paying respects to each other properly and thoughtfully. Mother Li presented several kinds of seasonal fruit: fragrant snow lotus roots, crystal apples, and fresh dates as big as eggs. None of the fruit was provided by the food supply official in the imperial palace.[10] The emperor tasted one of each type of fruit. Again, the old lady chatted with and entertained him cordially for quite a long while, but she did not see Shishi come out of her room to greet her guest.[11] The emperor stood there waiting for her for a long time.

By that time Zhang Di had withdrawn. Mother Li led the emperor to a small room. Inside the room, a torreya wood tea table was placed by the window; above it were a few books. Outside the window, the shadows of a cluster of newly sprouted bamboo were dancing up and down. Relaxed, the emperor sat upright, and his mind was at ease. But he did not see Shishi come out to serve him.

Not long afterward, Mother Li led the emperor to the back hall, where a variety of dishes were displayed: roast venison, vinegar-glazed chicken, finely minced fish and fried lamb, along with fragrant rice. The emperor ate the meal for Mother Li's sake.

---

[9]Donghua 東華 Gate, east gate of the Capital Bian.

[10]*Taiguan* 太官, the official in charge of the imperial court's food supply from the Qin 秦 (221–207 BC) to Tang, but only in charge of sacrificial materials after the Song. It is misused here.

[11]It is customary to greet guests when they arrive.

Mother Li served him by his side and talked with him intimately for a long time, but in the end Shishi did not come out to see him.

The emperor was perplexed when Mother Li suddenly asked him to take a bath. The emperor declined her request. Mother Li approached the emperor and whispered in his ear, "This girl likes cleanness by nature, please do not displease her."

The emperor had no choice but to follow Mother Li to the bathroom in a small two-story building. When the emperor finished bathing, Mother Li led him again to sit in the back hall. A variety of dishes and fruit were set up again, and the cups on the table were new and clean. Mother Li urged the emperor to drink his fill, but in the end Shishi did not show up.

After a long while, with a candle in hand Mother Li led the emperor to the bedroom. The emperor lifted the curtain and entered. There he saw only a dim light, without a single trace of Li Shishi. The emperor became even more perplexed. He paced back and forth between the tea table and the bed. After another long while, the emperor saw Mother Li supporting a young girl with her hands and walking out slowly. The girl wore light makeup and a plain white silk outfit. Having just finished bathing, she was as tender and beautiful as a lotus flower rising from the water. Looking at the emperor, Shishi seemed to disdain him. She appeared quite arrogant, and she did not greet him. Mother Li then whispered into the emperor's ear, "This girl has a stubborn temperament, please do not blame her!"

The emperor then fixed his eyes upon Shishi to examine her under the light. She had a graceful demeanor and elegant personal aura; her eyes were bright and dazzlingly radiant. The emperor asked Shishi her age, but she did not answer. When he grudgingly repeated his question, she simply moved her seat away. Mother Li whispered again into the emperor's ear, "This girl is by nature fond of sitting quietly, I know she may come off as rude but please do not blame her." She then lowered the curtain and left the room. Shishi then stood up, removed her black silk jacket, underneath which she wore only a light soft silk shirt. She then rolled up her right sleeve, took her lute off the wall, sat down beside a narrow table, and started playing the tune "Geese Descending onto the Flat Sands." She pressed the strings lightly and plucked slowly; the smooth melody sounded leisurely and otherworldly.[12] Unknowingly, the emperor listened so attentively to the music that he forgot his tiredness.

When the music had been played three times, the rooster began to crow. The emperor hastily lifted the curtain and went out. Hearing this, Mother Li also got up and presented him with snacks such as almond syrup, steamed date cakes, and noodle soup. The emperor drank about a cup of almond syrup, then stood up and left. The eunuchs who were hidden outside waiting all night quickly encircled and escorted him back to the palace. This event occurred on the seventeenth day of the eighth month in the third year of the Daguan reign (1107–1110).

[After the emperor's departure] Mother Li asked Shishi privately, "Neither Zhao's gift nor his affection for you was stingy. Why were you so aloof and unsociable?"

Shishi angrily replied, "He is merely a trading flunkey! What kind of person *am* I?"

Mother Li laughed, saying, "My daughter's neck is so unyielding![13] You could hold the office of an Acting Investigating Censor."

---

[12]*Danyuan* 淡遠, leisurely/indifferently and otherworldly.

[13]*Qiangxiang* 強項, "unyielding neck." During the Eastern Han (25–220) dynasty, the Magistrate of Luoyang, Dong Xuan 董宣, executed the evil servant of Princess Huyang 湖陽; Emperor Guangwu 光武 (劉秀, r. 25–57) ordered Dong to bow to the princess as an apology but Dong resolutely refused to do so, risking his life. Consequently, Dong was later known as the "Unyielding Neck Magistrate." See his biography in *Hou Han shu*, 77. 2489–90.

At that time, however, people in the capital began to talk one after another about the affair, and everyone knew that the emperor had favored Shishi, the courtesan from the Li clan of Longxi. Hearing about this, Mother Li was terrified. She did nothing but weep day and night.

While she cried, Mother Li said to Shishi, "If the man truly was the emperor, our entire clan will be exterminated!"

Shishi replied, "Don't be frightened! Since the emperor was willing to come see me, how could he bear to kill me? Furthermore, during that night, the emperor did not force me to do anything. He must have affection for me in his heart. The only thing that makes me sorrowful and regretful is that my fate is so different from that of others. I fell to such a humble and disgraceful status, causing the most revered and respected man to bear a blemished fame. Even my death would not be enough to expiate such a crime. As for the emperor becoming angry and executing us unreasonably, this will certainly not occur; because it is related to patronizing a brothel, he will avoid it as a serious taboo. We should have no worries."

During the first month of the next year, the emperor sent Zhang Di to bestow upon Li Shishi a snakeskin-patterned lute as a gift. This snakeskin-patterned lute was an antique: the body of the lute was black and yellow, the stripes on the lute resembling the decorative pattern on a snake's belly. This lute was likely a treasure of the inner palace. In addition, the emperor sent Shishi fifty *liang* of silver.

In the third month, the emperor dressed in commoners' clothing to visit Li Shishi again. Wearing light makeup and dressed in white clothes, Shishi then knelt down with her forehead touching the ground on the steps by the gate of her house, waiting for the emperor's arrival. The emperor was pleased, so he held Shishi's hand and let her stand up. The emperor found that the living room and the door had suddenly become magnificent and spacious. All the places where he had previously sat at were covered with silk embroidered with dragons. Additionally, the small room had been transformed into a large pavilion with patterned beams and painted red banisters, but completely losing the ambience of refined seclusion. Seeing the emperor's arrival, Mother Li hid to avoid him. When the emperor summoned her, her body was shaking so much that she could barely stand properly, displaying none of her previous demeanor when she intimately inquired about his well-being. The emperor was unhappy but he still smiled and addressed her as "old mother." He also said to her, "We are members of the same family, please do not be ill-at-ease or nervous." Mother Li bowed to show her gratitude, then led the emperor to the big building.

The building was newly built. Shishi prostrated herself on the ground, begging the emperor to name it on a horizontal inscription board. At this time the apricot tree flowers in front of the building were in full bloom, so the emperor wrote three words for her, "Zui xing lou" (Drunk Apricot Chamber). Shortly, a feast was prepared. Shishi served the emperor at his side, and Mother Li prostrated herself on the ground to pass a cup of wine to toast the emperor on his health. The emperor asked Shishi to sit beside him and ordered her to play the "Meihua sandie" (Three Variations of the Plum Blossom Melody) on her snakeskin-patterned lute.[14] Holding a wine cup to his mouth, the emperor enjoyed the wine while listening to the music; he praised Shishi over and over. However, the emperor saw that the sumptuous foods that were provided were all shaped like a dragon or phoenix, some carved and some painted, closely resembling the style of food in the palace. He inquired accordingly and learned that the dishes were prepared by the imperial kitchen chef and

---

[14]"Meihua sandie" 梅花三疊, also called "Meihua sannong," 梅花三弄.

that Mother Li paid for them. The emperor was displeased. He told Mother Li that in the future, she should prepare everything as she did before, and avoid showing off or indulging in extravagance. Consequently, before the feast ended the emperor returned to the palace.

The emperor once visited the Art Academy, giving the painters a line of poetry to test their painting talents. Only a couple of painters could pass the test each year. During this year's ninth month, the emperor gave Shishi a painting with the following calligraphy lines written on it: "A horse with a golden bridle neighing on the grassland and a man inside a jade chamber drunk while apricot flowers blossom." He also bestowed upon her the following: ten pieces each of the silk lotus lantern, warm snow lantern, fragrant barley lantern, and the lantern shaped like a flaming phoenix holding a pearl in its mouth; ten pieces each of the cormorant cup, amber cup, glass cup, and carved golden flagon; over a hundred *jin* of moon-shaped brick tea, phoenix-patterned brick tea, and Meng Mountain tea, etc.; several boxes each of soup noodles, fried noodles,[15] and cheese and meat filled pancakes. He also sent her one thousand *liang* each of gold and silver. At this time, the affair between the emperor and Shishi was widely circulated in the imperial palace. Empress Zheng heard about it and remonstrated with the emperor, saying, "A prostitute is too lowly to serve Your Majesty. Moreover, while visiting her in commoners' clothes at night, dangerous accidents could befall you as well. I wish Your Majesty would respect yourself." The emperor promised her by nodding his head. For the next two years, the emperor did not leave the palace to meet Shishi, but his inquiries, greetings, and gifts to her never stopped.

---

[15]*Hanju* 寒具, fried sticky-rice noodle, also called *sanzi* 饊子. It is often served as a meal when cooking is forbidden during the Cold Food Festival.

In the second year of the Xuanhe reign (1119–1125), the emperor again visited Li [Shishi] of Longxi. Seeing the painting he sent to Shishi hanging in the Drunk Apricot Chamber, he admired and appreciated it for a long time. When the emperor turned his head around and suddenly saw Shishi, he teased her, saying, "I called the beautiful girl in the painting, has she truly emerged from it?!" That day, the emperor granted Shishi a cold-proof gold coin, a moonlight-reflecting pearl ring, a simurgh-dancing green mirror, and a golden young dragon incense pot. The next day the emperor granted Shishi a phoenix-mouth inkstone made in Duanxi,[16] Li Tinggui's ink,[17] a jade shaft Xuanzhou brush,[18] and the finest calligraphy paper, made in Shanxi.[19] He also gave Mother Li a hundred thousand strings of coins.

Privately, Zhang Di said to the emperor, "While visiting the girl of Longxi, Your Majesty must wear commoners' clothes and walk late at night, so you cannot go frequently. Now, east of the separate Palace at Gen Yue there is a piece of land spanning two to three *li* that is directly connected to the Zhen'an Ward. If a tunnel is built there, it will be extremely convenient for Your Majesty to go and return." The Emperor replied, "You can prepare

---

[16]Duanxi 端溪, located by Mount Lanke 爛柯, west of the modern city of Zhaoqing 肇慶, Jiangxi, is famous for its inkstones. *Fengzhou yan* 鳳咮硯, "phoenix-mouth inkstone," an inkstone crafted from a piece of stone found at a special spot on the phoenix-shaped Mount Longbei 龍焙 in Fujian. It was named by Su Shi in his poem "Longwei yange bing xu" 龍尾硯歌並序. See *Su Dongpo quanji* 蘇東坡全集 (Qianji 前集; Beijing: Zhongguo shudian, 1986), 14. 196.

[17]Li Tinggui 李廷珪 was a noted Southern Tang 南唐 (937–958) ink official.

[18]Xuanzhou 宣州, modern Xuancheng 宣城, Anhui, has been famous for its brushes.

[19]Shanxi 剡溪, modern Sheng 嵊 county, Zhejiang, was noted for its paper.

for it." Hence, Zhang Di and others submitted a memorandum to the emperor, which read:

> The palace guards on duty at night have long been sleeping outside. For the convenience of night guarding, your humble subjects are willing to donate a certain amount of money to build a few hundred rooms as well as construct extensive enclosing walls.

The emperor approved the petition. Thus the imperial army, patrol army, etc., extended their garrison duty to Zhen'an Ward and consequently the pedestrians disappeared from the area.

In the third month of the fourth year, the emperor visited the girl of Longxi for the first time by tunnel. He granted Shishi game appliances for *zangjiu* and *shuanglu*, etc.,[20] and also gave her a jade flake chessboard, green and white-colored jade stones (in a *go* game), a palace fan made by the Imperial Fine Art Academy, a foldable bamboo mat featuring five flowers, a grass mat with fish scale patterns, a patterned curtain made from the mottled bamboo of Lady Xiang, and multicolored coral hooks. On this day, the emperor played *shuanglu* backgammon with Shishi but he did not win. He lost again when they played *go*. Thus, he gave Shishi two thousand *liang* of silver. After that, on Shishi's birthday, the emperor granted her a pair of pearl hairpins, two gold bracelets, a box of pearl strings, several *duan* of fine brocade, one hundred *pi* of heron-feather-colored white silk, emerald-colored satin, and another thousand *liang* of silver.

Later, to celebrate the termination of Liao (916–1125),[21] the emperor handsomely awarded each prefecture and commandery,

---

[20] *Zangjiu* 藏闥 and *shuanglu* 雙陸, both are gambling games.

[21] A state established by the Qidan 契丹 tribe in the north. It had long been an enemy state of Song before being defeated by Jin 金 (1115–1234) and Song troops in 1123.

and offered additional favor to the local government. Hence, the emperor gave Shishi a violet thin silk curtain with multicolored tassels, a silk sheet divine brocade quilt with a dustproof brocade mattress, one thousand *liang* of gold pieces, and good wine that included brand names such as the Sweet-scented osmanthus syrup, Floating rosy cloud, Fragrant honey, etc. In addition, he gave Mother Li ten thousand strings of coins from the imperial treasury. Counting from beginning to end, the gifts he granted them, including gold and silver coins, silk and clothing, utensils and food, amounted to no less than one hundred thousand *liang* of silver.

The emperor once called together his concubines and other palace girls for a feast. Imperial Consort Wei asked him privately, "What kind of creature is the girl from the Li family? Why does Your Majesty dote on her so much?"

The emperor replied, "It is exactly like this: if I ask a hundred of you to replace your gaudy dresses with black and white clothing and let this girl be mixed among you, she would be utterly different from you all. Her graceful carriage and elegant charm essentially lie beyond her beauty and that is all."

Not long afterwards, the emperor abdicated the throne to the crown prince. He claimed himself to be the "Patriarch and Sovereign of the Dao," withdrew, and relocated to Taiyi Palace. From then on, his interest in patronizing brothels diminished.

Shishi said to Mother Li, "Both of us are now living happily, not realizing that misfortunes are imminent."

"Then what can we do?" Mother Li asked.

Shishi replied, "Don't ask too much, just let me deal with it."

At that moment, the Jurchen army had just started to invade the south and the state of Hebei reported that it was in a state of emergency. Shishi collected the money that the emperor had previously given her and submitted a letter to the governor of

Kaifeng,[22] saying that she was willing to donate the money to the government for military expenses to assist Hebei. She also bribed Zhang Di and others, asking them to beg the former emperor Huizong on her behalf to allow her to abandon her family to become a Daoist nun. The emperor approved her request and granted her the "Ciyun guan" (Ciyun Daoist Monastery) outside of the northern city wall to live in.

Not long afterwards, the Jurchen army breached the capital of Bian. [23] Their Commander-in-chief, Talan, searched for Shishi, saying, "The ruler of Jin has heard of Shishi's name, so he surely wants to capture her alive." He searched for her for many days but could not find her. The Song chancellor, Zhang Bangchang (1081–1127), and others traced Shishi and prepared to bring her to the Jurchen camp.[24]

Shishi cursed them, saying, "Though I am but a humble prostitute, I have received the favor of the emperor. I have no other wish but to die! You men are all high officials with lofty salaries. How did the imperial court treat you so badly, such that all you plan is to terminate the royal house's ancestral temple? Now you have surrendered and are serving the ugly barbarians, hoping to use this opportunity as a stepping stone to gain a promotion. How could I be willing to be the lamb and goose [on your list of gifts]?"

Then Shishi removed her golden hairpin and stabbed her own throat, but she still lived. She broke the hairpin, swallowed it, and died.

---

[22]Kaifeng, another name for the capital Bian.

[23]This event occurred in the first year of Jingkang 靖康 (1126).

[24]Zhang Bangchang 張邦昌, an evil vassal. His biography is found in the "Biographies of Evil Vassals" of *Song shu*, 475. 13789–793.

At that time, the former emperor and Patriarch of the Dao was at the City of Five Kingdoms.[25] Hearing of how Shishi died, he could not help but shed tears like rain.

Commentary: Li Shishi was just a lowly prostitute, but unexpectedly, she had a bizarre fate; this is called "staying where one does not belong." Nevertheless, judging from her integrity in her final moments, she was heroic, bearing the spirit of a knight errant. No one can say that she was not outstanding among ordinary people. The Patriarch of the Dao was extravagant and excessive, and this ultimately led to the disaster in which he was trapped in the north;[26] so he deserves it.

---

[25] Wuguo cheng 五國城, located in present-day Heilongjiang or Liaoning.

[26] *Bei yuan zhi huo* 北轅之禍, the disaster of lodging (being trapped) in the northern states. *Yuan* 轅, temporary lodge.

李師師外傳

缺名

李師師者，汴京東二廂永慶坊染局匠王寅之女也。寅妻既產女而卒，寅以菽漿代乳乳之，得不死，在襁褓未嘗啼。

汴俗，凡男女生，父母愛之，必為捨身佛寺。寅憐其女，乃為捨身寶光寺。女時方知孩笑。一老僧目之曰："此何地，爾乃來耶？"女至是忽啼。僧為摩其頂，啼乃止。寅竊喜，曰："是女真佛弟子。"為佛弟子者，俗呼為師，故名之曰師師。

師師方四歲，寅犯罪繫獄死。師師無所歸，有娼籍李姥者收養之。比長，色藝絕倫，遂名冠諸坊曲。

徽宗帝即位，好事奢華，而蔡京、章惇、王黼之徒，遂假紹述為名，勸帝復行青苗諸法。長安中粉飾為饒樂氣象。市肆酒稅，日計萬緡；金玉繒帛，充溢府庫。於是童貫、朱勔輩，復導以聲色狗馬宮室園囿之樂。凡海內奇花異石，搜采殆徧。築離宮於汴城之北，名曰艮嶽。帝般樂其中，久而厭之，更思微行，為狹邪游。

內押班張迪者，帝所親幸之寺人也。未宮時為長安狎客，往來諸坊曲，故與李姥善。為帝言隴西氏色藝雙絕，帝艷心焉。翼曰，命迪出內府紫茸二匹，霞氊二端，瑟瑟珠二顆，白金廿鎰，詭云大賈趙乙，願過廬一顧。姥利金幣，喜諾。

暮夜，帝易服雜內侍四十餘人中，出東華門二里許，至鎮安坊。鎮安坊者，李姥所居之里也。帝麾止餘人，獨與迪翔步而入。堂戶卑庳。姥出迎，分庭抗禮，慰問周至。進以時果數種，中有香雪藕、水晶蘋婆，而鮮棗大如卵，皆大官所未供者。帝為各嘗一枚。姥復款洽良久，獨未見師師出拜。帝延佇以待。

時迪已辭退，姥乃引帝至一小軒。棐几臨窗，縹緗數帙。窗外新篁，參差弄影。帝翛然兀坐，意興閒適，獨未見師師出侍。

少頃，姥引帝到後堂。陳列鹿炙、雞酢、魚膾、羊簽等肴，飯以香子稻米，帝為進一餐。姥侍旁，款語移時，而師師終未出見。帝方疑異，而姥忽復請浴，帝辭之。姥至帝前，耳語曰：“兒性好潔，勿忤。”

帝不得已，隨姥至一小樓下湢室中浴竟。姥復引帝坐後堂，肴核水陸，杯盞新潔，勸帝歡飲，而師師終未一見。

良久，姥纔執燭引帝至房，帝搴帷而入，一燈熒然，亦絕無師師在。帝益異之，為徒倚几榻間。又良久，見姥擁一姬姍姍而來。淡妝不施脂粉，衣絹素，無艷服。新浴方罷，嬌艷如出水芙蓉。見帝意似不屑，貌殊倨，不為禮。姥與帝耳語曰：“兒性頗愎，勿怪。”

帝於燈下凝睇物色之，幽姿逸韻，閃爍驚眸。問其年，不答。復強之，乃遷坐於他所。姥復附帝耳曰：“兒性好靜坐，唐突勿罪。”遂為下帷而出。師師乃起解玄絹褐襖，衣輕綈，捲右袂，援壁間琴，隱几端坐而鼓《平沙落雁》之曲。輕攏漫然，流韻淡遠。帝不覺為之傾耳，遂忘倦。

比曲三終，雞唱矣。帝急披帷出。姥聞亦起，為進杏酥飲，棗糕餶飿諸點品。帝飲杏酥盃許，旋起去。內侍從行者皆潛候於外，即擁衛還宮。時大觀三年八月十七曰事也。

姥語師師曰：“趙人禮意不薄，汝何落落乃爾？”師師怒曰：“彼賈奴耳，我何為者？”姥笑曰：“兒強項，可令御史裏行也。”

而長安人言籍籍，皆知駕幸隴西氏。姥聞大恐，日夕惟啼泣。泣語師師曰：“洵是，夷吾族矣。”師師曰：“無恐，上肯顧我，豈忍殺我？且疇昔之夜，幸不見逼，上意必憐我。惟是我所竊自悼者，實命不猶，流落下賤，使不潔之名，上累至尊，此則死有餘辜耳。若夫天威震怒，橫被誅戮，事起佚游，上所深諱，必不至此，可無慮也。”

次年正月，帝遣迪賜師師蛇跗琴者。蛇跗琴者，琴古而漆黦，則有紋如蛇之跗，蓋大內珍藏寶器也。又賜白金五十兩。

三月，帝復微行如隴西氏。師師仍淡妝素服，俯伏門階迎駕。帝喜，為執其手令起。帝見其堂戶忽華廠，前所御處，皆以蟠龍錦繡覆其上。又小軒改造傑閣，畫棟朱闌，都無幽趣。而李姥見帝至，亦匿避。宣至，則體顫不能起，無復向時調寒送暖情態。帝意不悅，為霽顏，以老娘呼之，諭以一家子無拘畏。姥拜謝，乃引帝至大樓。

樓初成，師師伏地叩帝賜額。時樓前杏花盛放，帝為書"醉杏樓"三字賜之。少頃置酒，師師侍側，姥匍匐傳樽為帝壽。帝賜師師隅坐，命鼓所賜蛇跗琴，為弄《梅花三弄》。帝銜杯飲聽，稱善者再。然帝見所供肴饌皆龍鳳形，或鏤或繪，悉如宮中式。因問之，知出自尚食房廚夫手，姥出金錢倩製者。帝亦不懌，諭姥今後悉如前，無矜張顯著。遂不終席，駕返。

帝嘗御畫院，出詩句試諸畫工，中式者歲間得一二。是年九月，以"金勒馬嘶芳草地，玉樓人醉杏花天"名畫一幅賜隴西氏。又賜藕絲燈、煖雪燈、芳苡燈、火鳳銜珠燈各十盞；鸝鸕盃、琥珀盃、琉璃盃、縷金偏提各十事；月團、鳳團、蒙頂等茶百斤；餺飥寒具、銀壇餅數盒；又賜黃白金各千兩。時宮中已盛傳其事。鄭后聞而諫曰："妓流下賤，不宜上接聖躬。且暮夜微行，亦恐事生叵測。願陛下自愛。"帝頷之。閱歲者再，不復出。然通問賞賜，未嘗絕也。

宣和二年，帝復幸隴西氏。見懸所賜畫於醉杏樓，觀玩久之，忽回顧見師師，戲語曰："畫中人乃呼之欲出耶？"即日，賜師師辟寒金鈿、暎月珠環、舞鸞青鏡、金虯香鼎。次日，又賜師師端溪鳳味硯、李廷珪墨、玉管宣毫筆、剡溪綾紋紙。又賜李姥錢百千緡。

迪私言於上曰："帝幸隴西，必更服夜行，故不能常繼。今艮嶽離宮東偏有官地袤延二三里，直接鎮安坊。若於此處為潛道，帝駕往還殊便。"帝曰："汝圖之。"於是迪等疏言："離宮宿衛人，向多露處。臣等願出貲若干，於官地營室數百楹，廣築圍牆，以便宿衛。"帝可其奏。於是羽林巡軍等，布列至鎮安坊止，而行人為之屏跡矣。

四年三月，帝始從潛道幸隴西，賜藏闐雙陸等具。又賜片玉棊盤，碧白二色玉棊子，畫院宮扇，九折五花之簟，鱗文蓍葉之蓆，湘竹綺簾，五綵珊瑚鉤。是日，帝與師師雙陸不勝，圍棊又不勝，賜白金二千兩。嗣後師師生辰，又賜珠鈿金條脫各二事，璣琲一篋，氈錦數端，鷺毛繒翠羽緞百匹，白金千兩。后又以滅遼慶賀，大賚州郡，加恩宮府，乃賜師師紫綃絹幕、五彩流蘇、冰蠶神錦被、卻塵錦褥，麩金千兩，良醞則有桂露流霞香蜜等名，又賜李姥大府錢萬緡。計前後賜金銀錢、繒帛、器用、食物等，不下十萬。

帝嘗於宮中集宮眷等讌坐。韋妃私問曰："何物李家兒，陛下悅之如此？"帝曰："無他，但令爾等百人，改艷妝，服玄素，令此娃雜處其中，迥然自別。其一種幽姿逸韻，要在色容之外耳。"

　　無何，帝禪位，自號為道君教主，退處太乙宮。佚游之興，於是衰矣。

　　師師語姥曰："吾母子嘻嘻，不知禍之將及。"姥曰："然則奈何？"師師曰："汝第勿與知，唯我所欲。"是時金人方啟釁，河北告急。師師乃集前後所賜金錢，呈牒開封尹，願入官，助河北餉。復賂迪等代請於上皇，願棄家為女冠。上皇許之，賜北郭慈雲觀居之。

　　未幾，金人破汴，主帥闥孄索師師，云："金主知其名，必欲生得之。"乃索之累日不得，張邦昌等為蹤迹之，以獻金營。

　　師師罵曰："吾以賤妓，蒙皇帝眷，寧一死無他志。若輩高爵厚祿，朝廷何負於汝，乃事事為斬滅宗社計？今又北面事醜虜，冀得一當，為呈身之地。吾豈作若輩羔雁贄耶？"乃脫金簪自刺其喉，不死；折而吞之，乃死。

　　道君帝在五國城，知師師死狀，猶不自禁其涕泣之氾瀾也。

　　論曰：李師師以娼妓下流，猥蒙異數，所謂處非其據矣。然觀其晚節，烈烈有俠士風，不可謂非庸中佼佼者也。道君奢侈無度，卒召北轅之禍，宜哉。

Chinese Dynasty Chronology

Shang	ca. 1554–1045 BCE
Western Zhou	ca. 1045–771 BCE
Eastern Zhou	770–222 BCE
Spring and Autumn Period	770–476 BCE
Warring States Period	475–222 BCE
Qin	221–207 BCE
Western Han	206 BCE–8 CE
Xin	9–25 CE
Eastern Han	25–220
Three Kingdoms	220–280
Wei	220–265
Shu	221–263
Wu	222–280
Western Jin	265–316
Eastern Jin	317–420
Southern and Northern Dynasties	386–589

Southern Dynasties	420–589
[Liu] Song	420–479
Southern Qi	479–502
Southern Liang	502–557
Southern Chen	557–589
Northern Dynasties	386–534
Northern Wei	386–534
Eastern Wei	534–550
Western Wei	535–556
Northern Qi	550–577
Northern Zhou	557–581
Sui	581–618
Tang	618–907
Five Dynasties	907–960
Northern Song Dynasty	960–1126
Southern Song Dynasty	1126–1279
Yuan Dynasty	1279–1368
Ming Dynasty	1368–1644
Qing Dynasty	1644–1911

List of Abbreviations

BSOAS	*Bulletin of the School of Oriental and African Studies*
CLEAR	*Chinese Literature: Essays, Articles, Reviews*
comp.	compiler
Hanyu da cidian	*Hanyu da cidian* 漢語大詞典. 13v. 5th printing, Shanghai: Hanyu Da Cidian Chubanshe, 1995.
HJAS	*Harvard Journal of Asiatic Studies.*
Hucker	Charles O. Hucker. *A Dictionary of Official Titles in Imperial China.* Stanford: Stanford University Press, 1985.
Jiu Tang shu	*Jiu Tang shu* 舊唐書. 20v. Beijing: Zhonghua, 1975.
JAOS	*Journal of the American Oriental Society*
JAS	*Journal of Asian Studies*
JOS	*Journal of Oriental Studies*
MS	*Monumenta Serica*
n. (nn.)	note(s)
no.	number

OE	*Oriens Extremus*
des Rotours	Robert des Rotours. *Traité des fonctionnaires et Traité de l'armée.* 2v. Leiden: E. J. Brill, 1947.
Shiji	*Shiji* 史記. 10v. Beijing: Zhong hua, 1959.
TkR	*Tamkang Review*
TP	*T'oung Pao*
TPGJ	*Taiping guangji* 太平廣記. 10v. Beijing: Renmin Chubanshe, 1961.
Tan Qixiang	Tan Qixiang 譚其驤 (1911–1992). *Zhongguo lishi ditu ji* 中國歷史地圖集. 8v. Shanghai: Zhong guo Ditu Chubanshe, 1982.
TS	*T'ang Studies*
v. (vv.)	volume(s)
Wang Meng'ou	Wang Meng'ou 王夢鷗 (1907–2002). *Tangren xiaoshuo jiaoshi* 唐人小說校釋. 2v. Taibei: Zhengzhong 正中 Shuju, 1983.
WYYH	*Wenyuan yinghua* 文苑英華. Rpt.; Taipei: Huawen Shuju 華文書局 1965.
Xin Tang shu	*Xin Tang shu* 新唐書. 20v. Beijing: Zhonghua, 1975.

Bibliography

Texts

Lu Xun 魯迅 (1881–1936), ed. *Tang Song chuanqi ji* 唐宋傳奇集. Beijing: Beixin 北新 shuju, 1927–1928.

——. *Tang Song chuanqi ji.* Shanghai: Lianhua 聯華 shuju, 1934.

——. *Tang Song chuanqi ji.* Shanghai: Lu Xun quanji chubanshe, 1938, 1941, 1947, 1948.

——. *Tang Song chuanqi ji.* Hangzhou: Zhejiang guji chubanshe, 1941.

——. *Tang Song chuanqi ji.* Zuojia shuwu, 1948.

——. *Tang Song chuanqi ji.* Beijing Renmin wenxue chubanshe 1952, 1956, 1973.

——. *Tang Song chuanqi ji.* Beijing: Wenxue guji kanxingshe, 1956, 1958.

——. *Tang Song chuanqi ji.* Hong Kong: Datong 大通 shuju, 1959.

——. *Tang Song chuanqi ji.* Hong Kong: Xinyi 新藝 chubanshe, 1967, 1971, 1973.

——. *Tang Song chuanqi ji.* Hong Kong: Jindai tushu gongsi, 1964, 1968.

——. *Tang Song chuanqi ji.* Changsha: Yuelu shushe, 1995, 2014.

——. *Tang Song chuanqi ji.* Shanghai: Shanghai guji chubanshe, 1998.

——. *Tang Song chuanqi ji.* Beijing: Hualing chubanshe, 2002.

——. *Tang Song chuanqi: Zhencang ban.* Changchun: Jilin sheying chubanshe, 2003.

——. *Tang Song chuanqi ji*. Changchun: Jilin sheying chubanshe, 2003.

——. *Tang Song chuanqi ji*. Haerbin: Beifang wenyi chubanshe, 2006.

——. *Tang Song chuanqi ji*. Beijing: Zhaohua chubanshe, 2018.

Cai Yijiang 蔡義江 and Cai Wanruo 蔡宛若, trans. Baihua quanben *Tang Song chuanqi ji* 白話全本唐宋傳奇集. Shanghai: Guji chubanshe, 1995.

——, trans. *Tang Song chuanqi ji*. HangZhou: Zhejiang wenyi chubanshe, 2013, 2018.

Cheng Xiaoming 程小銘, Yuan Zhengqian 袁政謙, Qiu Ruixiang 邱瑞祥, eds. *Tang Song chuanqi ji quanyi* 唐宋傳奇集全譯［修訂版］. Guiyang: Guizhou chuban jituan, Guizhou renmin chubanshe, 2007, 2009.

Du Dongyan 杜东嫣, trans. *Tang Song chuanqi ji quanyi* 唐宋傳奇集全譯. Shanghai: Shanghai guji chubanshe, 2014.

Wang Zhongli 王中立, annot. & trans. *Tang Song chuanqi ji*. Tianjin: Tianjin guji chubanshe, 2002.

Primary Sources

Chao Zaizhi 晁載之 (fl. 11th century). *Xu tanzhu* 續談助. *Congshu jicheng chubian* 叢書集成初編. Shanghai: Shangwu yinshuguan, 1939.

Hu Ting 胡珽 (1822–1861). *Linlang mishi congshu* 琳琅秘室叢書. Taibei: Yiwen chubanshe, 1967.

Li Fang 李昉 (925–966) *et al.*, comp. *Taiping guangji* 太平廣記. 500 *juan*. Beijng: Zhonghua shuju, 1961.

Liu Fu 劉斧 (fl. 1073), comp. *Qingsuo gaoyi* 青鎖高議. *Song Yuan biji congshu* 宋元筆記叢書. Shanghai: Shanghai guji chubanshe, 1983.

Luo Ye 羅燁 (13th century). *Zuiweng tanlu* 醉翁談錄. Taibei: Shijie shuju, 1965.

Qinhuai yuke 秦淮寓客 (17th century), ed. *Lüchuang nüshi* 綠窗
女史. Ming Chongzhen 明崇禎 edition. Available through
Harvard-Yenching Library Chinese Rare Books Digitalization
Project.

T'ang-tai ts'ung shu 唐代叢書. Shanghai: Jinchang tushuju, 1921.

Tao Zongyi 陶宗儀 (1329–c. 1410), ed. *Shuo fu* 說郛. Shanghai:
Shanghai guji chubanshe, 1988.

Wang Shizhen 王世貞 (1526–1590), ed. *Yen-i pien* 艷異編. Shanghai:
Shanghai guji chubanshe, 2014.

Wenyuan yinghua 文苑英華. Rpt.; Taibei: Huawen Shuju, 1965.

Wuchao xiaoshuo 五朝小說. Taibei: Guangwen shuju, 1979.

Wu Zengqi 吳曾祺, ed. *Chiu-hsiao-shuo* 舊小說. Shanghai: Shangwu
yinshuguan, nd.

Yu chu zhi 虞初志. Rpt.; Taipei: Xingxing shuju, 1956.

Zeng Zao 曾慥 (1091–1155), comp. *Leishuo* 類說. *Beijing tushuguan
guji zhenben congkan* 北京圖書館古籍珍本叢刊 62. Beijing:
Shumu wenxian chubanshe, 1988.

Modern Selections

Bian Xiaoxuan 卞孝萱 and Zhou Qun 周群. *Tang Song chuanqi
jingdian* 唐宋傳奇經典. Shanghai: Shanghai shudian
chubanshe, 1999.

Cai Shouxiang 蔡守湘. *Tangren xiaoshuo xuanzhu* 唐人小說選注. 3v.
Taibei: Liren Shuju, 2002.

Cheng Yizhong 程毅中. *Guti xiaoshuo chao: Song Yuan juan* 古體小
說鈔：宋元卷. Beijing: Zhonghua shuju, 1995.

Li Jianguo 李劍國, ed. *Songdai chuanqi ji* 宋代傳奇集. Beijng:
Zhonghua shuju, 2001.

——. *Tang wudai chuanqi ji* 唐五代傳奇集. 6v. Beijing: Zhonghua
shuju, 2015.

Li Shiren 李時人. Quan Tang Wudai xiaoshuo 全唐五代小説. Xi'an:
Shanxi renmin chubanshe, 1998.

Xue Hong 學洪, Mu Qing 牟青, Li Shi 李實 and Ma Lan 馬蘭. *Songdai chuanqi xuan* 宋代傳奇選. Changsha: Hunan renmin, 1985.

Wang Meng'ou 王夢鷗, *Tang ren xiaoshuo jiao shi* 唐人小說校釋, 2 vols. Taipei: Zhengzhong shuju, 1983.

Wang Pijiang 汪辟疆. *T'ang-jen hsiao-shuo* 唐人小說. Hong Kong: Chonghua shuju,1958.

Wang Rutao 王汝濤. *Quan Tang xiaoshuo* 全唐小説. Ji'nan: Shandong wenyi chubanshe, 1993.

Xu Shinian 徐士年, ed. *Tangdai xiaoshuo xuan* 唐代小說選, Zhongzhou shuhuashe, 1982.

Yao Song 姚松, ed. *Songdai chuanqi xuanyi* 宋代傳奇選譯. Nanjing: Fenghuang chuban chuanmei jituan, Fenghuang chubanshe, 2011.

Zhang Wenqian 張文潛 *et al.*, *Tang Song chuanqi xuan zhuyi ben* 唐宋傳奇選注譯本. Fuzhou: Fujian Jiaoyu Chubanshe, 1983.

Zhang Youhe 張友鶴, ed. *Tang Song chuanqi xuan* 唐宋傳奇選. Beijing: Zhonghua shuju, 1979.

Zhou Peiguang 周培光, ed. Lidai biji xiaoshuo jicheng 歷代筆記小說集成. vol. 4, *Songdai biji xiaoshuo* 宋代筆記小說. Shijiazhuang: Hebei jiaoyu chubanshe, 1994.

Translations

Belpaire, Bruno. *T'ang kien wen tse, Florilége de littérature des T'ang.* 2v. Paris: Editions Universitaires, 1959.

Chai, Ch'u and Winberg Chai. *A Treasury of Chinese Literature.* New York: Van Rees Press, 1965.

Châu, Hải Đường, trans. *Đường Tống truyền kỳ.* Hà Nội: Nhà xuất bản Hội nhà văn, 2017.

Ditter, Alexei Kamran, Jessey Choo, and Sarah M. Allen. *Tales from Tang Dynasty China: Selections from the* Tangping guangji. Indianapolis/Cambridge: Hackett Publishing, Inc., 2017.

Dudbridge, Glen. *The Tale of Li Wa*. London: Ithaca Press, 1983.

Edwards, Evangeline Dora. *Chinese Prose Literature of the T'ang Period A.D. 618–906*. 2v. London: Probsthain, 1937–1938.

Hsu Sung-nien, trans. *Contes choisis des T'ang*. Pekin: Imprimerie de la politique de Pekin, 1935.

Inglis, Alister D., trans. *The Drunken Man's Talk*. Seattle and London: University of Washington Press, 2015.

Kao, Karl S. Y., ed. *Classical Chinese Tales of the Supernatural and Fantastic*. Bloomington: Indiana University Press, 1985.

Levenson, Christopher. *The Golden Casket: Chinese Novellas of Two Millennia*. Translated from Wolfgang Bauer's and Herbert Franke's German version of the original Chinese. Penguin Classics, 1964.

Lévy, André. *Histoires extraodinaires et récits fantastiques de la Chine ancienne*. Paris: Flammarion, 1993.

Ma, Y. W. and Joseph S. M. Lau. *Traditional Chinese Stories: Themes and Variations*. New York: Columbia University Press, 1987.

Maeno Naoaki 前野直彬, ed. *Tōdai denki shu* 唐代伝奇集. 2 vols. Tokyo: Heibon sha, 1964.

Mair, Victor H. *The Columbia Anthology of Traditional Chinese Literature*. New York: Columbia University Press, 1994.

Nienhauser, William H., Jr., *Tang Dynasty Tales: A Guided Reader*. 2v. Singapore: World Scientific, 2010, 2016.

Reed, Carrie E. *Chinese Chronicles of the Strange. The "Nuogao ji."* New York: Peter Lang, 2001.

Uchida Sennosuke 内田泉之助 and Inui Kazuo 乾一夫, eds. *Tōdai denki* 唐代伝奇. Tokyo: Meiji Shoin, 1971.

Wang Chi-chen. *Traditional Chinese Tales*. New York: Columbia University Press, 1944.

Wang, Elizabeth Te-chen, trans. *Ladies of the Tang*. Taibei: Heritage Press, 1961.

Yang, Xianyi and Gladys Yang. *The Dragon King's Daughter*. Beijing: Foreign Language Press, 1954.

——. *Tang Dynasty Stories*. Peking: Chinese Literature Press, 1986.

——, and Huang Jun, trans. *Selected Chinese Short Stories of the Tang and Song Dynasties*. Beijing: Foreign Language Press, 2001.

Zhang, Zhenjun and Wang Jing, *Song Dynasty Tales: A Guided Reader*. Singapore: World Scientific, 2017.

Special Studies

Adkins, Curtis P. "The Hero in T'ang *ch'uan-ch'i* Tales," in *Critical Essays on Chinese Fiction* pp. 17–46. Winston L. Y. Yang and Curtis P. Adkins, eds. Hong Kong: Chinese University Press, 1980.

Allen, Sarah M. *Shifting Stories: History, Gossip, and Lore in Narratives from Tang Dynasty China*. Cambridge, Mass.: Harvard University Asia Center, 2014.

Anderson, Poul. *The Demon Chained under Turtle Mountain: The History and Mythology of the Chinese River Spirit Wuzhiqi*. Berlin: G+H Verling, 2001.

Bian Xiaoxuan 卞孝萱. "Tangdai xiaoshuo yu zhengzhih" 唐代小說與政治. In *Tangdai wenshi luncong* 唐代文史論叢, pp. 48–67. Taiyüan: Shansi renmin chubanshe, 1986.

——. *Tang chuanqi xintan* 唐傳奇新探. Nanjing: Jiangsu jiaoyu chubanshe, 2001.

Cheng Guofu 程國賦. *Tangdai xiaoshuo shanbian yanjiu* 唐代小説嬗變研究. Guangzhou: Guangdong renmin chubanshe, 1997.

——. *Tangdai xiaoshuo yu zhonggu wenhua* 唐代小説與中古文化. Taibei: Wenjin chubanshe, 2000.

Cheng Jie 程杰. "Guanyu Meifei yu Meifeizhuan" 關於梅妃与梅妃傳. *Nanjing shifan daxue wenxueyuan xuebao* 2006. 3: 125–29.

Chen Jue. "History and Fiction in the *Gujing ji* (Record of an Ancient Mirror)," *MS* 52 (2004): 161–97.

——. "A Supplement to Jian Zong's 'Biography of a White Ape,'" *Renditions* 49 (Spring 1998): 76–85.

——. "Revisiting the Yingshe Mode of Representation in Supplement to Jiang Zong's 'Biography of a White Ape,'" *Oriens extremus* 44 (2003–2004): 155–78.

Chen Wenxin 陳文新. "Tang ren chuanqi zhong haoxia xingxiang de yanbian" 唐人傳奇中豪俠形象的演變, *Gudian wenxue zhishi* 古典文學知識 2 (1995).

Chen Xiaolian 陳曉連 and Hu Ruijuan 胡睿娟. "Nüxing zhuyi piping shijiao xia jiedu 'Lüzhu zhuan' zhong de Lüzhu xingxiang" 女性主義批評視角下解讀《綠珠傳》中的綠珠形象, *Mingzuo xinshang* 名作欣賞, 1 (2014): 136–7.

Cheng Yizhong 程毅中. "Lun Tangdai xiaoshuo de yanjin zhi ji". *Wenxue yichan* 1987. 5: 44–53.

——. "Shen Yazhi jiqi 'Sanmeng ji'" 沈亞之及其三夢記. *Tangdai wenxue luncong* 唐代文學論叢 5 (1984): 183–87.

——. *Tangdai xiaoshuo shi* 唐代小説史. Beijing: Renmin wenxue chubanshe, 2003.

——. *Yuan xiaoshuo yanjiu* 宋元小說研究. Nanjing: Jiangsu guji chubanshe, 1999.

Chen Yinque. "Han Yu and the T'ang Novel," James Ware, translator, *HJAS* 1 (1936): 39–43.

Cutter, Robert Joe. "History and 'The Old Man of the Eastern Wall,'" *Journal of the American Oriental Society* 106.3 (1986): 503–528.

Dai Wangshu 戴望舒. *Xiaoshuo xiqu lunji* 小說戲曲論集. Beijing: Zuojia chubanshe, 1958.

Dong Shangde 董上德. "Meifei xingxiang de shenceng yiyi: Yangguifei wenxueshi shang de yige zhongyao gean" 梅妃形象的深層意義 — 楊貴妃文學史上的一個重要個案, *Zhongguo wenxue lunji* 中國文學論集 33 (Dec. 2004), 91–104.

Dudbridge, Glen. "The Tale of Liu Yi and Its Analogues," in Eva Huang, ed., *Paradoxes of Traditional Chinese Literature*. Hong Kong: The Chinese University Press, 1994, pp. 61–88.

Hammond, Charles. "T'ang Legends: History and Hearsay," *Tamkang Review*, 20.4 (Summer 1990): 359–82.

Fan Xiaoqing 樊小青. "'Huo Xiaoyu zhuan' yu 'Tan Yige ji' nüxing xingxiang de yitong" 《霍小玉傳》與《譚意哥記》女性形象的異同, *Journal of Honghe University* 紅河學院學報, 11.3 (2013): 37–40.

Fu Xiren 傅錫壬. *Niu-Li dangzheng yu Tangdai wenxue* 牛李黨爭與唐代文學. Taibei: Dongda Tushu Gongsi 東大圖書公司, 1984.

He Xinling 何新嶺. "Songdai chuanqi zhong de 'jieji' jiqi chengyin" 宋代傳奇中的 "節妓" 及其成因, *Zhongguo gudai wenxue yanjiu* 中國古代文學研究, 6 (2009): 37–8.

Hightower, James Robert. "Fiction in the Literary Language," *Topics in Chinese Literature*. Revised edition; Cambridge, Mass.: Harvard University Press, 1965, pp. 76–83.

——. "Yüan Zhen and 'The Story of Ying-ying,'" *HJAS* 33 (1973): 90–123.

Hou Zhongyi 侯忠義. *Zhongguo wenyan xiaoshuo shigao* 中國文言小說史稿. Beijing: Beijing daxue chubanshe, 1990.

Hsieh, Daniel. "Induced Dreams, Reading, and the Rhetoric of 'Chen chung chi,'" *Tamkang Review* 27. 1 (1996): 63–102.

——. "Wen and Wu in T'ang Fiction," *Tamkang Review* 31. 3 (spring 2001): 99–135.

Huang Guohua 黃國華. "Yetan Meifei zhimi" 也談梅妃之謎. *Meizhou ribao* 湄洲日報, August 5, 2002.

Huo Shixiu 霍世休. "Tangdai chuanqi wen yu Yindu gushi" 唐代傳奇文與印度故事, *Wenxue* 文學 2. 6 (June 1, 1934): 1051–1066.

Jiang Guoxing 江國興. "Meifei que you qiren" 梅妃確有其人 (The Plum-Blossom Consort Existed Indeed). *Renmin zhengxie bao* 人民政協報, April 29, 2003.

Knechtges, David. "Dream Adventure Stories in Europe and Tang China," *Tamkang Review* 4: 2 (October 1973), 101–119.

Kroll, Paul W. "Po Chü-i's 'Song of Lasting Regret': A New Translation," *T'ang Studies* 8–9 (1990–91): 97–105.

Lau, Joseph S. M. "Love and Friendship in Tang *Chuanqi*," *MS* 37 (1986–87).

Li Fengmao 李豐楙. *You yu you: Liuchao Sui Tang xiandao wenxue* 憂與遊：六朝隋唐仙道文學. Beijing: Zhonghua shuju, 2010.

Li Jianguo 李劍國. *Tang wudai zhiguai chuanqi xulu* 唐五代志怪傳奇叙錄. Tienjin: Nankai daxue chubanshe, 1993.

——. *Songdai zhiguai chuanqi xulu* 宋代志怪傳奇敘錄. Tianjin: Nankai daxue chubanshe, 1997.

——. ed. *Tang Song chuanqi pindu cidian* 唐宋傳奇品讀詞典. Beijing: Xinshijie chubanshe, 2007.

——. "Qin Chun 'Zhao Feiyan biezhuan kaolun'" 秦醇趙飛燕別傳考論, *Guyuan shizhuan xuebao* 固原師專學報, 1 (2001): 1–9.

——. "'Daye shiyiji' deng wupian chuanqi xuezuo shidai de zai taolun" 《大業拾遺記》等五篇傳奇寫作時代的再討論, *Wenxue yichan* 文學遺產, 1 (2009): 21–28.

——. *Gubai doushao lu — Li Jianguo zixuan ji* 古稗斗筲錄 — 李劍國自選集. Tianjin: Nankai daxue chubanshe, 2004.

Li Jing 李菁. "Tang chuanqi wen 'Yangdi kai he ji' yanjiu" 唐傳奇文煬帝開河記研究, *Xiamen daxue xuebao* 2012.2: 32–38.

Li Shiren 李時人. "Song Dai lishi wenhua yu wenyan duanpian xiaoshuo de liubian" 宋代歷史文化與文言短篇小說的流變, *Qiushi xuekan* 求是學刊, 2 (2011): 125–32.

Li Yuan 李源. "Liuye qiangu zong qianqing — Songdai chuanqi 'Liuhong ji' jiqi zai Yuan Ming shidai de chuanbo" 流葉千古總牽情 — 宋代傳奇《流紅記》及其在元明時代的傳播, *Yindu xuekan* 殷都學刊, 1 (2003): 85–88.

Liu, James J. Y. *The Chinese Knight-errant*. Chicago: University of Chicago Press, 1967.

Liu K'ai-jung 劉開榮. *T'ang-tai hsiao-shuo yen-chiu* 唐代小說研究. Shanghai: Shangwu yinshuguan, 1947.

Liu Yinbo 劉蔭柏. *Zhongguo wuxia xiaoshuo shi* 中國武俠小說史. Shijiazhuang: Huashan wenyi chubanshe, 1992.

Lu Xun 魯迅. *Zhongguo xiaoshuo shilue* 中國小說史略. Beijing: Renmin wenxue chubanshe, 1973.

Lu Zhaoyin 卢兆荫. "Meifei qiren bian" '梅妃' 其人辨. *Xuelin manlu* 学林漫录 9 (1984): 161.

Luo Manling. *Literati Storytelling in Late Medieval China*. Seattle: University of Washington Press, 2015.

——. "The Seduction of Authenticity: 'The Story of Yingying,'" *Nannü: Men, Women, and Gender in China* 7, no. 1 (2005): 40–70.

Ma, Y. W. "Fact and Fantasy in Tang Tale." *CLEAR* 2 (1980): 167–81.

Mair, Victor H. *The Columbia History of Chinese Literature*. New York: Columbia University Press, 2001.

——. "The Narrative Revolution in Chinese Literature: Ontological Presuppositions," *CLEAR* 5 (1983): 1–27.

Miao Guisong 苗貴松. "Tang Song xiaoshuo de shiqing yu huayi — yi 'You xianku' 'Hongxian' 'Wang Youyu ji' 'Li Shishi waizhuan' deng weili" 唐宋小說的詩情與畫意 — 以《遊仙窟》《紅線》《王幼玉記》《李師師外傳》等為例, *Lilun jie* 理論界, 1 (2013): 146–8.

Ni Haoshi 倪豪士. *Chuan-chi yü hsiao-shuo: Tangdai wenxuebijiao lunji* 傳記與小說：唐代文學比較論集. Taibei: Southern Materials, 1995; Beijing: Zhonghua, 2007.

Nienhauser, William H., Jr. "Creativity and Storytelling in the Chiuan-ch'i: Shen Ya-chih's T'ang Tales," *CLEAR* 20 (1998): 31–70.

——. "A Third Look at 'Li Wa zhuan,'" *T'ang Studies* 25 (2008): 91–110.

Owen, Stephen. "Romance," "Conflicting Interpretations: 'Yingying's Story,'" in *The End of the Chinese "Middle Ages."* Stanford University Press, 1996, pp. 130–176.

Sun, Kang-I Chang, and Owen, Stephen. *The Cambridge History of Chinese Literature*. Cambridge: Cambridge University Press, 2010. "Miscellanies and anecdotal collections" in vol. I, pp. 454–60.

Yang Hsien-i and Gladys Yang, trans. *A Brief History of Chinese Fiction*. Peking: Foreign Language Press, 1964.

Qi Shuhui 齊淑慧. "Tang mo chuanqi wen 'Yangdi kai he ji' yanjiu" 唐末傳奇文煬帝開河記研究, *Yunnan shehui zhuyi xueyuan xuebao* 2014.1: 415–416.

Uchiyama Chinari 內山知也. *Zuy To shosetsu kenkyu* 隋唐小說研究. Tokyo: Mokujisha, 1977, pp. 412–446.

Wang Jue 王珏. *Tang Song chuanqi shuowei* 唐宋傳奇說微. Chengdu: Sichuan jiaoyu chubanshe, 2003.

Wang Meng-ou 王夢鷗. *T'ang-jen hsiao-shuo yen-chiu er-chi* 唐人小說研究二集. Taipei: Yiwen yinshuguan, 1973.

Wang Rutao 王汝濤. *Tangdai xiaoshuo yu Tangdai zhengzhi* 唐代小說與唐代政治. Changsha: Yuehlu Shushe 岳麓書社, 2005.

Wang Qingzhen 王慶珍. "Songdai chuanqi yanjiu" 宋代傳奇研究. PhD diss., Ha'erbin Normal University, 2013.

Wang Xiujuan 王秀娟. "Songdai wenyan xiaoshuo xushi yanbian yanjiu" 宋代文言小說叙事演變研究. PhD diss., Nankai University, 2013.

Wei Xiangqiu 韋湘秋. "Lüzhu ji youguan qi shihua" 綠珠及有關其詩話, *Guangxi shehui kexue* 廣西社會科學, 3 (1988): 169–185.

Wu Zhida 吳誌達. *Zhongguo wenyan xiaoshuo shi* 中國文言小說史. Jinan: Qi Lu shushe, 1994.

Xia Guangxing 夏廣興. *Fojiao yu Sui Tang wudai xiaoshuo* 佛教與隋唐五代小說. Xi'an: Shanxi renmin chubanshe, 2004.

Xia Xiying 夏習英. "Xi Jin zhi Nanbeichao shiqi de Lüzhu xingxiang lunxi" 西晉至南北朝時期的綠珠形象論析, *Mingzuo xinshang* 名作欣賞, 5 (2011): 27–8.

——, "Tangdai shiwen zhong Lüzhu gushi de wenhua yiyun tanxi" 唐代詩文中綠珠故事的文化意蘊探析, *Xue Lilun* 學理論, 15 (2011): 187–9.

——, "Lüzhu gushi de yanbian jiqi wenhua neihan" 綠珠故事的演變及其文化內涵, *Xiamen jiaoyu xueyuan xuebao* 廈門教育學院學報, 6 (2009): 5–11.

——, "Lüzhu gushi de yanbian yu zhiyu qingjie" 綠珠故事的演變與知遇情節, *Xue Lilun*, 32 (2014): 123–4, 140.

——, "Lüzhu gushi de yanbian yu meinü huoshui lun" 綠珠故事的演變與美女禍水論, *Jiujiang xueyuan xuebao* 廈門教育學院學報, 2 (2012): 29–33.

Xiao Xiangkai's 蕭相愷. *Song Yuan xiaoshuo shi* 宋元小說史. Hangzhou: Zhejiang guji chubanshe, 1997.

Xu Ganli 徐贛麗. "Minjian chuanshuo yu defang renting — yi Guangxi Bobai Lüzhu chuanshuo weili" 民間傳說與地方認同 — 以廣西博白綠珠傳說為例, *Guangxi shifan xueyuan xuebao* 廣西師範學院學報, 2 (2011): 1–7.

Xue Hongji 薛洪勣. "*Li Shishi waizhuan* shi shi Mingmo zuopin" 《李師師外傳》應是明末作品, in *Ming Qing xiaoshuo yanjiu* 明清小說研究 3–4 (1990): 181–89.

Xue Keqiao 薛克翹. "Du Qingsuo gaoyi zatan" 讀《青鎖高議》雜談, *Nanya yanjiu* 南亞研究, 2(1998): 65–68.

Xue Shiping 薛世平. "Meifei youwu qiren" 梅妃有無其人 (Was the Plum-Blossom Consort A Real Person?) in Shi Xuanyuan 施宣圓, ed. *Zhongguo wenhua zhimi* 中國文化之謎. Shanghai: Xuelin chubanshe, 1988.

Yang Guo 楊果 & Fang Yuan 方圓, "Wang Kui fu Guiying" gushi zai Songdai de bianqian jiqi zhengzhi daode yihan 《王魁負桂英》故事在宋代的變遷及其政治道德意涵, *Guoji zhehui kexue zazhi* 国际社会科学杂志, 4(2011): 151–5.

Yang Jingmin 楊敬民. "Lun Shihua zonggui dui Qingsuo gaoyi de caizhi" 論《詩話總歸》對《青鎖高議》的採摭, *Guji zhengli yanjiu xuekan* 古籍整理研究學刊, 11(2013): 5–11.

Yang Yi 楊義. "Tang chuanqi de shiyun lequ." 唐代傳奇的詩韻樂趣 *Zhongguo shehui kexue* 6 (1992).

Yim, Sarah Macmillan. "Structure, Theme, and Narrator in T'ang *ch'uan-ch'i*." Unpublished PhD dissertation, Yale University, 1979.

Yu Dan 余丹. "Songdai wenyan xiaoshuo chuangzuo yu shidai sixiang wenhua" 宋代文言小說創作與時代思想文化. PhD diss., Shanghai Normal University, 2005.

Yuan Lükun 袁閭琨 and Xue Hongji 薛洪勣, ed. *Tang Song chuanqi zongji: Nan Bei Song* 唐宋傳奇總集：南北宋. Luoyang: Henan renmin chubanshe, 2002.

Zhang Chang 張萇. "Luelun gudai xiaoshuo zhong de renshen lian gushi 略論古代小說中的人神戀故事," *Xinan shida xuebao* 西南師範大學學報, 1 (1991): 94–99.

Zhang Changgong 張一弓. *Tang Song chuanqi zuozhe jiqi shidai* 唐宋傳奇作者暨其時代. Shanghai: Shangwu yinshuguan, 1951.

Zhang Chengjian 張乘健. "'Changhen ge' yu 'Meifei zhuan': Lishi yu yishu de weimiao chongtu" 《長恨歌》與《梅妃傳》：歷史與藝術的微妙沖突, *Wenxue yichan*, 1 (1992): 51–58.

Zhang Peiheng 章培恒. "'Daye shiyiji,' 'Meifei zhuan,' deng wupian chuanqi de xiezuo shidai" 大業拾異記、梅妃傳等五篇傳奇的寫作時代, *Shenzhen daxue xuebao* 深圳大學學報, 1 (2008): 106–10.

Zhang Songhui 張松輝. "Daojiao yu Tang chuanqi" 道教與唐傳奇. *Zongjiaoxue yanjiu* 1 (1997).

Zhang Xuan 張玄. "Song chuanqi nüxing zhuti yishi de juexing: cong 'Huo Xiaoyu zhuan' dao 'Tan Yige ji'" 宋傳奇女性主體意識的覺醒：從《霍小玉傳》到《譚意歌記》, *Yibin xueyuan xuebao* 宜賓學院學報, 3 (2007): 13–15.

Zhao Xiupei 趙修霈. "'Meifei zhuan' zhongde jingxiang tuoyu shoufa" 〈梅妃傳〉中的鏡像托喻手法. *Zhengda zhongwen xuebao* 政大中文學報, 19(2013): 193–218.

Zhao Zhangchao 趙章超. "Songdai wenyan xiaoshuo yanjiu" 宋代文言小說研究. PhD diss., Sichua University, 2003.

Zhou Shaoliang 周紹良, "'Dong cheng laofu zhuan' jian zheng" 東城老父傳箋證, *Wen shi* 文史 1983, no. 17: 167–181.

——. *Tang chuanqi jianzheng* 唐傳奇箋證. Beijing: Renmin wenxue chubanshe, 2000.

Zhang Zhenjun 張振軍. *Chuantong xiaoshuo yu Zhongguo wenhua* 傳統小説與中國文化. Guilin: Guangxi shifan daxue chubanshe, 1996.

——. "Lun Daojiao dui Zhongguo chuantong xiaoshuo zhi gongxian" 論道教對中國傳統小説之貢獻. *Daojia wenhua yanjiu* 道家文化研究 9 (1996): 332–46.

Zhu Lili 朱麗麗. "Cong shehui biange kan Song Ming xiaoshuo zhong de jinü congliang zhi lu" 從社會變革看宋明小說中的妓女從良之路, *Qingnian zuojia* 青年作家, 4 (2015): 39, 74.

Background Studies

Barrett, Timothy H. *Taoism under the T'ang: Religion and Empire during the Golden Age of Chinese History.* London: Wellsweep Press, 1996.

Benn, Charles. *Daily Life in Traditional China: The Tang Dynasty.* Westport, Conn.: Greenwood Press, 2002.

Benn, James A. *Burning for the Buddha: Self-immolation in Chinese Buddhism.* Honolulu: University of Hawaii Press, 2007.

Bol, Peter K. *"This Culture of Ours": Intellectual Transitions in T'ang and Sung China.* Stanford: Stanford University Press, 1992.

Bossler, Beverly. *Courtesans, Concubines, and the Cult of Female Fidelity.* Cambridge: Harvard University Press, 2012.

Cahill, Suzanne. "The Word Made Bronze: Inscriptions on Medieval Chinese Bronze Mirrors," *Archives of Asian Art*, vol. 39 (1986): 62–9.

Cai Chongbang 蔡崇榜. "Songdai yiliao qianshuo" 宋代醫療淺說. *Sichuan daxue xuebao* 四川大學學報, 1998(04), pp. 92–100.

Chaffee, John W., and Denis Twitchett, eds. *The Cambridge History of China*, vol. 5, pt. 2, *The Five Dynasties and Sung China, 960–1279 AD*. Cambridge: Cambridge University Press, 2015.

Chen Bangxian 陳邦賢. *Zhongguo yixue shi* 中國醫學史 (History of Chinese Medicine). Beijing: Tuanjie chubanshe, 1956.

Cheng Qianfan 程千帆. *Tangdai jinshi xingjuan yu wenxue* 唐代進士行卷與文學. Shanghai: Shanghai guji chubanshe, 1980.

Duan Yuming 段玉明. *Xiangguo si: zai Tang Song diguo de shensheng yu fansu zhijian* 相國寺：在唐宋帝國的神聖與凡俗之間. Chengdu: Bashu shushe, 2004.

Dudbridge, Glen. *Religious Experience and Lay Society in T'ang China: A Reading of Tai Fu's Kuang-i chi*. Cambridge University Press, 1995.

Ebrey, Patricia Buckley. *Emperor Huizong*. Cambridge, Mass.: Harvard University Press, 2014.

——. *The Inner Quarters: Marriage and the Lives of Chinese Women in the Sung Period*. Berkeley: University of California Press, 1993.

Ebrey, Patricia Buckley, and Peter N. Gregory, eds. *Religion and Society in T'ang and Sung China*. Honolulu: University of Hawaii Press, 1993.

Espenak, Fred. "Five Millennium Catalog of Solar Eclipses: 0601 to 0700 (601 CE to 700 CE)." Eclipse Predictions by Fred Espenak (NASA's GSFC). Accessed Dec. 26, 2018. <https://eclipse.gsfc.nasa.gov/SEcat5/SE0601-0700.html>.

Ess, Hans van. "Cheng Yi and His Ideas about Women as Revealed in His Commentary to the *Yijing*," *Oriens extremus*, 49(2010): 63–77.

Fu Xuanzong 傅璇琮. *Tangdai keju yu wenxue* 唐代科舉與文學. Xi'an: Shanxi renmin chubanshe, 2003.

Hanan, Patrick. *The Chinese Vernacular Story*. Cambridge, Mass.: Harvard University Press, 1981.

Holzman, Donald. "The Cold Food Festival in Early Medieval China." *HJAS* 46 (1986): 51–79.

Hucker, Charles. *A Dictionary of Official Titles in Imperial China*. Taipei: Southern Materials Center, Inc., 1985; Beijing: Peking University Press, 2007.

Idema, Wilt, and Beata Grant. *The Red Brush: Writing Women of Imperial China*. Cambridge, Mass.: Harvard University Asia Center, 2004.

Kao, Karl S. Y. "Bao and Baoying: Narrative Causality and External Motivations," *CLEAR* 11(1989): 115–38.

Kroll, Paul W. *Dharma Bell and Dhāraṇī Pillar: Li Po's Buddhist Inscriptions* (Kyoto: Scuola Italiana di Studi sull'Asia Orientale, 2001), 39–75.

Levy, Howard Seymour. "Tang Courtesans, Ladies and Concubines," *Orient/West* 3 (1962): 49–64.

——. "The Career of Yang Kuei-fei 楊貴妃," *T'oung Pao*, 45, 4/5 (1957): 474–489.

Li Fuchang 李福長. *Tangdai xueshi yu wenren zhengzhi* 唐代學士與文人生活. Jinan: Qi Lu shushe, 2005.

Li Hongqi 李弘祺. *Songdai jiaoyu sanlun* 宋代教育散論. Taipei: Dongsheng chuban, 1980.

Lü Simian 呂思勉. *Sui Tang Wudai shi* 隋唐五代史. Rpt. Hong Kong: Taiping Shuju, 1985.

Mollier, Christine. *Buddhism and Taoism Face to Face: Scripture, Ritual, and Iconographic Exchange in Medieval China*. Honolulu: University of Hawaii Press, 2009.

Rotours, Robert des. *Courtisanes chinoises a la fin des T'ang*. Paris: Presses Universitaires de France, 1968.

Schafer, Edward H. *Pacing the Void: Tang Approaches to the Stars*. Berkeley: University of California Press, 1977.

Shiba, Yoshinobu. *Commerce and Society in Sung China*. Michigan Abstracts of Chinese and Japanese Works on Chinese History, No. 2. Mark Elvin, trans. Ann Arbor: The University of Michigan Center for Chinese Studies, 1970.

Spring, Madeleine. *Animal Allegories in T'ang China*. New Haven, Conn.: American Oriental Society, 1993.

Sun Changwu. *Daojiao yu Tang dai wenxue*. Beijing: Renmin wenxue chubanshe, 2001.

——. *Tangdai wenxue yu fojiao*. Xi'an: Shanxi renbin chubanshe, 1985.

Sun, Kang-I Chang, and Haun Saussy, eds. *Women Writers of Traditional China: An Anthology of Poetry and Criticism*. Stanford, Calif.: Stanford University Press, 1999.

Tao Muning 陶慕寧. *Qinglou wenxue yu Zhongguo wenhua* 青樓文學與中國文化. Beijing: Dongfang chubanshe, 1993.

Wang Fengxiang 王鳳翔. "Wudai shiguo shiqi de zhongmenshi" 五代十國時期的中門使, *Shixue yuekan* 12(2003): 120–121.

Wang Meihua 王美華. *Lizhi xiayi yu Tang Song shehui bianqian* 禮制下移與唐宋社會變遷. Beijing: Zhongguo shehui kexue chubanshe, 2015.

Xiong, Victor. *Sui-Tang chang'an: A Study in the Urban History of Medieval China*. Ann Arbor: Center for Chinese Studies, University of Michigan, 2000.

——. *Emperor Yang and the Sui Danasty: His Life, Time, and Legacy*. Albany: SUNY Press, 2006.

Xu Song 徐松. *Tang Liang jing chengfang kao* 唐兩京城坊考. Beijing: Zhonghua shuju, 1985.

Yang Bo 楊波. *Chang'an de chuntian: Tangdai keju yu jinshi shenghuo* 長安的春天：唐代科舉與進士生活. Beijing: Zhonghua shuju, 2007.

Yang Guo 楊果 and Liu Yuchun 劉雨春. "Songdai guojia dui guanyuan suchang de guanli" 宋代國家對官員宿娼的管理, *Wuhan daxue xuebao* 武漢大學學報, 1(2011): 98–104.

Yang Lien-Sheng. "The Concept of *Pao* as a Basis for Social Relations in China." In *Excursions in Sinology*, 3–23. Harvard-Yenching Institute Studies no. 24. Cambridge, Mass.: Harvard University Press, 1969.

Yao Ping. "The Status of Pleasure: Courtesan and Literati Connections in T'ang China (618–907)," *Journal of Women's History*, 14. 2 (summer 2002): 26–53.

Zhang Xingwu 張興武. *Liang Song wangzu yu wenxue* 兩宋望族與文學. Beijing: Renmin wenxue chubanshe, 2010.

Zheng Zhimin 鄭志敏. *Xi shuo Tang ji* 細説唐妓. Taipei: Wenjin chubanshe, 1997.

Zhu Ziyan 朱子彥. "Zhongguo fengjian shehui houfei zhidu chutan" 中國封建社會后妃制度初探, *Xueshu Yuekan* 學术月刊, 11 (1993): 69–75.

Notes on the Translators

Weiguo Cao received his Ph.D. from the University of Wisconsin-Madison. His research interests include early Chinese narrative and historical works, the development of Chinese fictional writing, and the translation of ancient Chinese texts. He has taught at Arizona State University and is now Clinical Associate Professor at Washington State University. His publications include annotated translations of several chapters of Sima Qian's *Shi ji, The Grand Scribe's Records*, vols. 2 and 5.1 (Indiana University Press, 2002 and 2006), as well as an annotated translation of "The Tale of Hongxian" in *Tang Dynasty Tales: A Guided Reader* (World Scientific, 2010).

Robert Joe Cutter is a professor at the University of Nevada at Reno. He specializes mainly in early medieval and medieval Chinese literature.

Kenneth DeWoskin is Professor Emeritus of Chinese Literature at the University of Michigan, Ann Arbor. He has published widely on early medieval Chinese fiction and culture, and he is co-translator of *In Search of the Supernatural: The Written Record* (Stanford University Press, 1996).

Glen Dudbridge (1938–2017) was Lecturer in Modern Chinese at Oxford University (1965–1985), Professor of Chinese at Cambridge (1985–1989), and finally Shaw Professor of Chinese at Oxford until retirement in 2005. He had held visiting posts at Yale and UC Berkeley, and at the Chinese University of Hong Kong. He authored *The Hsi-yu chi: A Study of Antecedents to the Sixteenth-*

century Chinese Novel (Cambridge, 1970), *The Legend of Miao-shan* (Oxford, 1978), *The Tale of Li Wa: Study and Critical Edition of a Chinese Story from the Ninth Century* (Oxford, 1983), *Religious Experience and Lay Society in T'ang China: A Reading of Tai Fu's "Kuang-i chi"* (Cambridge, 1995), *Books, Tales and Vernacular Culture: Papers on China by Glen Dudbridge* (Brill, 2006), and *A Portrait of Five Dynasties China: From the Memoirs of Wang Renyu (880–956)* (Oxford, 2013).

Scott Galer earned a Ph.D. under Professor William H. Nienhauser, Jr. at the University of Wisconsin-Madison in *Shiji* studies and spent the first ten years of his full-time academic career teaching a broad range of undergraduate courses in Chinese language, literature, and culture. Galer currently serves as an associate academic vice president at Brigham Young University-Idaho, where he has worked for 21 years.

Beata Grant is Professor of Chinese and Religious Studies at Washington University in St. Louis. Her primary area of scholarly interest is writing by and about women of imperial China. Her publications include *Eminent Nuns: Woman Chan Masters of Seventeenth-Century China* (University of Hawaii Press, 2008), *Daughters of Emptiness: Poems of Chinese Nuns, Zen Echoes: Classic Koans with Verse Commentaries by Three Female Zen Masters* (Wisdom Publications, 2017) and, with Wilt L. Idema, *The Red Brush: Writing Women of Imperial China* (Asia Center Harvard University, 2004) and *Escape From Blood Pond Hell: The Tales of Mulian and Woman Huang* (Washington University Press, 2011).

James R. Hightower (1915–2006), Professor of Chinese Language and Literature at Harvard University, was a graduate of The University of Colorado (1936), with M.A. (1940) and Ph.D. (1946) from Harvard. He was a Fellow of the American Academy of Arts and Science and had held visiting appointments at the universities of Oxford, Hamburg, and British Columbia. He is the author of *Topics in Chinese Literature* (Harvard University Press,

1950; rev. ed., 1953), *Han Shih Wai Chuan: Han Ying's Illustrations of the Didactic Application of the Classic of Songs* (Harvard University Press, 1952), *The Poetry of T'ao Ch'ien* (Oxford University Press, 1970), and a number of articles in the *Harvard Journal of Asiatic Studies* and other learned periodicals.

Daniel Hsieh received his PhD from the University of Washington, Seattle. He is Associate Professor of Chinese at the Department of East Asian Languages, Purdue University, and the author of *Love and Women in Early Chinese Fiction* (Hong Kong: The Chinese University Press, 2008).

Jing Hu received a Master's degree in Comparative Linguistics from Peking University and another Master's degree in Chinese Linguistics from the University of Wisconsin-Madison. She is currently teaching Chinese at the University of Pennsylvania. Before coming to UPenn, she had taught Chinese at Smith College and Yale-NUS College for over a decade. She has published articles in the *Journal of Chinese Teaching and Research in the U.S., Tradition and Modernization, Tradition and Transition: Teaching Chinese Culture Overseas*, etc.

Wilt L. Idema studied Chinese Language and Culture at Leiden University. Following further study in Sapporo, Kyoto, and Hong Kong, he taught at Leiden University from 1970 until 1999, and at Harvard University from 2000 until his retirement in 2013. He has published extensively, alone and in cooperation with others, on China's vernacular literary traditions, including fiction, drama, and prosimetric narrative, as well as on China's tradition of women's literature. His most recent publications include *Two Centuries of Manchu Women Poets: An Anthology* (Seattle: University of Washington Press, 2017); *Mouse vs. Cat in Chinese Literature: Tales and Commentary* (Seattle: University of Washington Press, 2019); and *Insects in Chinese Literature: A Study and Anthology* (Amherst, NY: Cambria Press, 2019).

Alister Inglis is Professor of Chinese Language and Literature at Simmons University, Boston. He is the author of books and scholarly articles on Song dynasty literature, notably *Hong Mai's* Record of the Listener *and Its Song Dynasty Context*. He has also published literary translations of Hong Mai's *Record* and other Song period works, including Luo Ye's *Drunken Man's Talk*. His translations of Emperor Qianlong's bereavement poems were displayed in the "Empresses of China's Forbidden City, 1644–1912" exhibition at the Peabody Essex Museum in Salem, MA and the Freer and Sackler galleries in Washington, D.C. He is currently undertaking a comparative study of the classical language short story from the Tang to Yuan dynasties.

Paul W. Kroll is Professor Emeritus of Chinese at the University of Colorado, Boulder. He has published widely on medieval Chinese literature and cultural history, and is also the author of *A Student's Dictionary of Classical and Medieval Chinese* (Brill, 2014; rev. ed. 2017).

Zhenzhen Lu received her Ph.D. from the Department of East Asian Languages and Civilizations at the University of Pennsylvania with a dissertation on the vernacular works attributed to Pu Songling (1640–1715). She is currently an affiliated member of the Centre for the Study of Manuscript Cultures at the University of Hamburg and a visiting scholar at New York University. Her research explores Chinese vernacular literature and manuscript culture at the intersection of literary studies and cultural history, with past and forthcoming publications in *Manuscript Cultures*, *Sino-Platonic Papers*, and *CHINOPERL: Journal of Chinese Oral & Performing Literature*.

Richard John Lynn holds an A. B. from Princeton University (magna cum laude) and a Ph.D. from Stanford University. He has held faculty positions in New Zealand, Australia, U.S.A. and Canada. He is now Professor Emeritus of Chinese Thought and Literature, University of Toronto. His publications include: *Kuan*

Yün-shih 1286–1324 (Twayne, 1980), *Chinese Literature Draft Bibliography in Western European Languages* (Australian National University Press, 1980), *Guide to Chinese Poetry and Drama* (G. K. Hall, 1984), *The Classic of Changes: A New Translation of the I Ching as Interpreted by Wang Bi* (Columbia University Press, 1994), and *The Classic of the Way and Virtue: A New Translation of the Tao-te ching of Laozi as Interpreted by Wang Bi* (Columbia University Press, 1999). He is also editor of James J. Y. Liu, *Language—Paradox—Poetics: A Chinese Perspective* (Princeton University Press, 1988); *Zhuangzi: A New Translation of the Sayings of Master Zhuang as Interpreted by Guo Xiang* (Columbia University Press, 2020), *Huang Zunxian: Chinese Literatus in Japan (1877–1882)* (in preparation).

Victor H. Mair, Professor of Chinese Language and Literature at the University of Pennsylvania, has been teaching there since 1979. He specializes in Buddhist popular literature as well as the vernacular tradition of Chinese fiction and the performing arts. Beginning in the early 1990s, Professor Mair has led an interdisciplinary research project on the Bronze Age and Iron Age mummies of Eastern Central Asia. Among other results of his efforts during this period are six documentaries for television (Scientific American, NOVA, BBC, Discovery Channel, History Channel, and German Television), a major international conference, numerous articles, and a book, *The Tarim Mummies: Ancient China and the Mystery of the Earliest Peoples from the West* (Thames and Hudson, 2000). He is also the author of numerous other publications (including several anthologies from Columbia University Press) and is the editor of Sino-Platonic Papers, the ABC Chinese Dictionary Series (University of Hawai'i Press), and the Cambria Sinophone World Series. He blogs frequently for Language Log.

Trever McKay is Assistant Professor of Chinese Language and Literature at Brigham Young University — Idaho. Trained in classical literature at National Taiwan University, he enjoys a broad range of interests. He specializes in *Shiji* studies and the *Analects* of Confucius; his current research project is a book entitled *A Guided Reader to the Analects*. His other research interests include Lu Xun's short stories and pronunciation and tone correction in second-language learners. He has published an app, Chinese Tones, that aids students in the mastery of tones, in addition to correct pronunciation. He also has translated professionally for more than ten years and has worked for the National Central Library in Taiwan in this capacity for the last eight years.

William H. Nienhauser, Jr. earned his Ph.D. (1972) under Professor Wu-chi Liu at Indiana University and also studied under Professor Peter Olbricht at Bonn. He has taught at the University of Wisconsin since 1973, as Halls-Bascom Professor of Classical Chinese Literature since 1995. His research explores early Chinese biographies, historical and fictional. Besides two monographs on Tang literati, *Pi Rixiu* and *Liu Zongyuan*, Nienhauser has co-translated and edited eight volumes of Sima Qian's *Shiji* (The Grand Scribe's Records) done by teams of scholars and published by Indiana and Nanjing universities. His essays in Chinese appeared in *Zhuanji yu xiaoshuo Tangdai wenxue bijiao lunji* 传记与小说：唐代文学比较论集 (Zhonghua 2007) and he also edited *Tang Dynasty Tales: A Guided Reader* (2v., Singapore, 2010 and 2016). In addition to many fellowships, he received the Alexander von Humboldt Foundation's *Forschungspreis* for lifetime achievement in 2002.

Graham Sanders (PhD, Harvard) is Associate Professor of Classical Chinese literature at the University of Toronto. His work focuses on narrative depictions of the composition, performance and reception of poetry in pre-modern China. His publications include a chapter in *Idle Talk: Gossip and Anecdote in Traditional China* (University of California Press, 2013), an annotated translation of Shen Fu's *Six Records of a Life Adrift* (Hackett, 2011), and a book on poetic performance, *Words Well Put: Visions of Poetic Competence in the Chinese Tradition* (Harvard University Asia Center, 2006). His annotated, bilingual translation of the two most important collections of Tang poetry anecdotes is forthcoming as a volume in De Gruyter's *Library of Chinese Humanities*.

Kelsey Seymour received her Ph.D. in East Asian Languages and Civilizations from the University of Pennsylvania in 2018. Her research focuses on the intersection of religious experience, music, linguistics, and memory in pre-modern Chinese Buddhist chanting. In particular, she is interested in what religious literature can reveal about sound perception and sensory experience. She has held research fellowships at Academia Sinica in Taipei, the Max Planck Institute for the History of Science in Berlin, and Yale University.

Josiah Stork received his B.A. in Chinese literature from Middlebury College in 2015, attained his first M.A. — focusing on teaching Chinese as a foreign language — through Middlebury College's Chinese Language School and the Middlebury Institute of International Studies in 2017, and is currently pursuing a Ph.D. in Chinese literature at the University of Wisconsin-Madison. His main academic interests include early to mid-Imperial tale literature, the *Taiping Guangji*, dragons, and critical theory.

Jing Wang received her Ph.D. in Chinese literature from the University of Wisconsin-Madison. She has taught at Carnegie Mellon University and the University of North Carolina-Charlotte and is now Senior Lecturer and Associate Director of the Chinese language program at Princeton University. Her research interests include tales in the Tang-Song period and Chinese language pedagogy. She has published *Song Dynasty Tales: A Guided Reader* (World Scientific, 2017; co-authored with Zhenjun Zhang) and *First Step: An Elementary Reader for Modern Chinese* (Princeton University Press, 2014; co-authored with C.P. Chou). She has also published articles on Tang tales, the teaching of classical Chinese, and teaching Chinese language through film.

Shengyu Wang received his Ph.D. in Comparative Literature from the University of Chicago in 2017, and is currently Assistant Professor of Comparative Literature at Soochow University, China. His research interests include the fantastic and supernatural, crime, print culture, chinoiserie, translation, and media studies. His current book project examines Wang Tao's nineteenth-century classical Chinese tales serialized in the illustrated *Dianshizhai* 點石齋 *Pictorial.*

Yuhua Wen received her M.A. in English from Inner Mongolia University and is now Lecturer at the Foerign Language College, Inner Mongolia Agricultural University. She was a Fulbright TA at St. Lawrence University during the academic year of 2018.

Zheng Wen holds a Ph.D. in Chinese literature from the University of Wisconsin-Madison. Her main areas of research are classical Chinese poetry and poetry criticism. She is particularly interested in the traditional images of pre-modern Chinese poets and has published journal articles on a late Tang poet, Du Mu. She has taught Chinese at UW-Madison, Santa Clara University, Normandale Community College, and Carleton College.

Chen Wu earned her B.A. in Chinese Language and Literature (2006) and M.A. in Classical Chinese Philology (2009) from Fudan University and her Ph.D. in Pre-modern Chinese Literature (2016) from the University of Wisconsin-Madison. Her Ph.D. dissertation is titled "How a City Speaks: Urban Space in Chang'an and the Construction of Tang Dynasty Narratives." Since 2013, she has been teaching modern and classical Chinese in the Department of East Asian Languages and Cultures at Columbia University. Her research interests include classical Chinese, medieval Chinese narrative writings, and the interrelation between city and literature.

Zhenjun Zhang received his M.A. from Peking University and Ph.D. from the University of Wisconsin-Madison. He is currently Associate Professor of Asian Studies and Modern Languages and Literatures at St. Lawrence University. His research interests focus on pre-modern Chinese literature, especially fiction and its interaction with history, religions, and culture. His English publications include *Hidden and Visible Realms: Early Medieval Chinese Tales of the Supernatural and the Fantastic* (Columbia University Press, 2018), *Song Dynasty Tales: A Guided Reader* (World Scientific, 2017, co-authored with Jing Wang), and *Buddhism and Tales of the Supernatural in Early Medieval China: A Study of Liu Yiqing's* Youming lu (Brill, 2014). He is also the author of *Chuantong xiaoshuo yu Zhongguo wenhua* 傳統小說與中國文化 (Guangxi Normal University Press, 1996) and *Jingu yu chaoyue: cong Sanyan Erpai kan Zhongguo shimin xintai* 禁錮與超越：從 "三言二拍" 看中國市民心態 (Guoji wenhua 1988, co-authored with Mao Defu) as well as editor of several series of Classical Chinese novels and Daoist texts.

Xin Zou received her B.A. (2008) from Peking University, and her M.A. (2010) and Ph.D. (2017) in Chinese Literature and M.S. (2018) in Curriculum and Instruction from the University of Wisconsin-Madison. She is currently Lecturer in East Asian Studies at Princeton University. Her research focuses on classical Chinese literature and cultural history, especially the interaction involving social-political changes, language, and literature. She has published several journal articles and annotated translations as well as a book chapter; she is currently working on a book manuscript tracing the literary production and transmission of anecdotes from the Tang to the Northern Song dynasty. Xin Zou is also interested in language reform in modern China and Chinese language pedagogy, and she has co-authored *Eyes on China: An Intermediate-Advanced Reader of Modern Chinese* (Princeton University Press, 2019).

Index

The following list includes only important names of figures (historical or fictional) and places, selected terms, and most relevant book titles, which appear in the footnotes. Personal names with little information, frequently mentioned place names, and general official titles are excluded.